THE HIDDEN PLACES OF
ENGLAND

By Kate Daniel

Published by:
Travel Publishing Ltd
Airport Business Centre, 10 Thornbury Road,
Estover, Plymouth PL6 7PP

ISBN13 9781904434931

First Published: 1998   Second Edition: 2000
Third Edition: 2002   Fourth Edition: 2004
Fifth Edition: 2006   Sixth Edition: 2008
Seventh Edition: 2010

Please Note:

All advertisements in this publication have been accepted in good faith by Travel Publishing.

All information is included by the publishers in good faith and is believed to be correct at the time of going to press. No responsibility can be accepted for errors.

Editor: Kate Daniel

Printing by: Latimer Trend, Plymouth

Location Maps: © Maps in Minutes ™ (2010)
                        © Collins Bartholomews 2010 All rights reserved.

Cover Photo: Old Lighthouse, Spurn Point, Yorkshire
                        © www.britainonview.co.uk

Text Photos: See page 625

Foreword

This is the 7th edition of the *Hidden Places of England* which has been given a brand new cover design and page layouts. The new look will be applied to all future *Hidden Places* editions. The changes significantly improve the usefulness, accessibility and appeal of all titles in the series. We do hope you like the new look.

Editorially, the new style will continue Travel Publishing's commitment to exploring the more interesting, unusual or unique places of interest in the United Kingdom. In this respect we would like to thank the Tourist Information Centres in England for helping us update the editorial content of this book. The guide is packed with information on many interesting places to visit within each county. You will find comprehensive details of places of interest as well as advertisers of places to stay, eat and drink included under each village, town or city which are cross referenced to more detailed information in a separate, easy-to-use section to the rear of the guide.

The *Hidden Places* series is a collection of easy to use local and national travel guides taking you on a relaxed but informative tour of Britain and Ireland. Our books contain a wealth of interesting information on the history, the countryside, the towns and villages and the more established places of interest. But they also promote the more secluded and little known visitor attractions and places to stay, eat and drink many of which are easy to miss unless you know exactly where you are going.

We include hotels, inns, restaurants, public houses, teashops, various types of accommodation, historic houses, museums, gardens, and many other attractions all of which are comprehensively indexed. Most places are accompanied by an attractive photograph and are easily located by using the map at the beginning of each chapter. We do not award merit marks or rankings but concentrate on describing the more interesting, unusual or unique features of each place with the aim of making the reader's stay in the local area an enjoyable and stimulating experience.

Whether you are visiting England for business or pleasure or are a local inhabitant, we do hope that you enjoy reading and using this book. We are always interested in what readers think of places covered (or not covered) in our guides so please do not hesitate to use the reader reaction form provided to give us your considered comments. We also welcome any general comments which will help us improve the guides themselves.

Finally, if you are planning to visit any other corner of the UK we would like to refer you to the order form for all *Hidden Places* titles which can be found at the rear of the book and to our website at www.travelpublishing.co.uk for all titles published by Travel Publishing. In addition please use our fully searchable database of places to stay, eat, drink, shop and places of interest on www.findsomewhere.co.uk.

Travel Publishing

Did you know that you can also search our website for details of thousands of places to see, stay, eat or drink throughout Britain and Ireland? Our site has become increasingly popular and now receives monthly hundreds of thousands of visits. Try it!

website: www.findsomewhere.co.uk

Location Map

Contents

GEOGRAPHICAL AREAS:

ADVERTISEMENTS:

INDEXES AND LISTS:

BEDFORDSHIRE

Quite the hidden place, the often overlooked county of Bedfordshire is one of charming typically English villages and small market towns surrounded by a rich rural landscape. It is said that the agriculture here is further advanced than in any other English county; the rich soil provides a perfect environment for farming, wheat and beans being the primary crops.

Despite their modern appearance, the towns of Luton and Dunstable, in the south of the county, have their roots firmly in the past and it was at Dunstable that Archbishop Cranmer held court in 1533 to dissolve the marriage of Henry VIII and Catherine of Aragon.

The county town of Bedford also has a long history and has strong associations with John Bunyan, who was born nearby.

The county is littered with stately homes and old country houses, including the splendid Houghton House, which is widely believed to be the inspiration for the House Beautiful in *Pilgrim's Progress*, and magnificent Woburn Abbey, the seat of the Dukes of Bedford, which is famous for its superb art collection and its Wild Animal Kingdom and Leisure Park. The Abbey is certainly one of the county's finest attractions, but Bedfordshire is also home to Whipsnade Wild Animal Park, the largest centre of conservation in Europe, and the

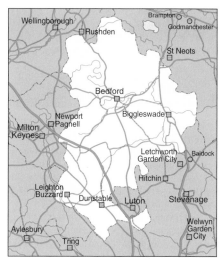

headquarters of the Royal Society for the Protection of Birds (RSPB).

There is a wealth of beautiful waymarked walks through the county of Bedfordshire; including 14 circular walks of varying length through the most interesting and peaceful places the county has to offer. As well as these, the 150 mile Ouse Valley Way, which starts in Northamptonshire and ends at the sea in Kings Lynn Norfolk, winds through Bedfordshire and makes a picturesque link between some of the counties rural villages and the town of Bedford.

BEDFORD

Bedford was already a thriving market place before the Norman Conquest but it is for its association with John Bunyan that the town is best known. The **Bunyan Museum**, on Mill Street in Bedford centre, is on the site where the Independent Congregation church and meeting house he was elected pastor for once

stood in 1707, and contains a wealth of information about this interesting and religious man – who wrote the famous *Pilgrim's Progress* during a two term imprisonment for unlicensed preaching at Bedfordshire County Gaol from 1660 to 1672.

For a greater insight into the history of the town and surrounding area the Bedford Museum is well worth a visit, which has fabulous changing exhibits as well as the

1

Bedford Suspension Bridge

forerunner of the modern tractor.

To the west of Biggleswade lies **Old Warden**, an enchanting village which was developed in the early 19th century by Sir Robert Ongley who also created the **Swiss Garden**, a romantic fantasy with a tiny thatched Swiss style cottage and arches of creepers. In the grounds of this Jacobean style mansion house, is the fantastic Shuttleworth Collection of historic aircraft.

permanent collections, as is the adjoining **Cecil Higgins Art Gallery** with its internationally renowned collection. These historical buildings are planned to be fully restored in the near future; the adjoining Bedford Gallery has already undergone a £2.5 million refurbishment completed in 2009.

Bedford provides much for visitors, including some lovely shops and a twice weekly market on Wednesdays and Saturdays on the banks of the River Ouse. The river offers some enchanting walks (particularly with a sunset), and itself is quite a feature of the town; a promenade runs along the riverside through the town centre, Embankment Gardens, Russell Park and Mill Meadows. The ornate Victorian Suspension Bridge across the river was opened on the same day as **Bedford Park** – another Victorian gem situated to the north of the town centre, which is a bustling place for socializing and relaxing during the summer months.

Old Warden Village

North of Biggleswade is the headquarters of the **Royal Society for the Protection of Birds**, called The Lodge. This nature reserve, which opened in 1961, has woodland, acid grassland and heath covering 180 hectares; the later is being restored to form the largest stretch of heathland in Bedfordshire (a vital habitat for native birds, and other British wildlife). There is also a shop here, open year-round.

AROUND BEDFORD

BIGGLESWADE

9½ miles SE of Bedford on the A6001

Biggleswade was the home of Dan Albone, the inventor of the modern bicycle and designer of the first practical tandem and a ladies cycle with a low crossbar and a skirt guard. He developed a racing cycle, which in 1888 set speed and endurance records with the doughty CP Mills in the saddle. He was also responsible for the Ivel Agricultural Tractor,

LUTON

18 miles S of Bedford on the A6

The largest town in Bedfordshire and perhaps best known for its Airport and Vauxhall cars, Luton first prospered in the 17th century on the strength of its straw plaiting and hat making industries. The **Stockwood Craft Museum and Gardens**, housed in a Georgian stable block, provides the opportunity to step back in time; also here is the **Mossman Collection** of over 60 horse-drawn vehicles. Close by is the magnificent house of **Luton Hoo**, which now houses a superb art collection. Its parkland was landscaped by Capability Brown.

Any visit to Luton should coincide with their spectacular International Carnival; every May Bank Holiday the streets are awash with colour, music and Rio-style dancers. A real must!

To the west of Luton, is nearby **Whipsnade** and their interesting **Tree Cathedral** (National Trust). Planted after World War I, the trees form the shape of a cathedral complete with nave, transepts and chancel – a tranquil day out. Also there is **Whipsnade Wild Animal Park**; the country home of the Zoological Society of London and one of Europe's largest wildlife conservation centres.

Tree Cathedral, Whipsnade

Woods, an area of mixed woodland and open meadows with muntjac deer and badgers, while, just to the north is the dramatic shell of **Houghton House** (English Heritage), reputed to have been the inspiration for the House Beautiful in *Pilgrim's Progress*.

A little further afield is the gorgeous **Silsoe and Wrest Park**, whose gardens present a living history of English gardening from 1700-1850, and include a fascinating collection of lead and stone statues.

WOBURN

12 miles SW of Bedford on the A4012

This originally Saxon hamlet is best known as the home of **Woburn Abbey**, the seat of the Dukes of Bedford. Along with the fantastic art collection and superb furniture in the house, Woburn has an antiques centre and a deer park that is also home to the **Wild Animal Kingdom and Leisure Park**.

Woburn Abbey

AMPTHILL

7½ miles SW of Bedford off the A507

A historic town that was a great favourite with Henry VIII but its castle was replaced by Ampthill Park in 1694 and the parkland, landscaped by Capability Brown, is now the **Ampthill Deer Park**. To the east lies **Maulden**

LEIGHTON BUZZARD

17½ miles SW of Bedford on the A4012

A prosperous market town where visitors can take a steam train journey on the **Leighton Buzzard Railway** on tracks laid in 1919 to carry sand from the local quarries. The town lies at one end of the Greensand Ridge Walk, which extends for some 40 miles across Bedfordshire to Gamlingay, Cambridgeshire.

BERKSHIRE

The county of Berkshire is one of the oldest in the UK, dating back to the 860's. The naturally formed northern border, created by the River Thames separates it from Oxfordshire. To the west, at the ancient town of Reading, the county's other principle river, the Kennet, joins the Thames, closely accompanied by the Avon Canal.

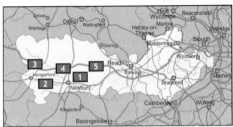

Often known as the Royal County of Berkshire, seeped in history and with some glorious countryside to explore, this county has much to offer visitors. The eastern region has been graced for over 900 years by the royal presence at Windsor; the Castle is a magnificent royal residence and Windsor Great Park is what remains of an ancient royal hunting ground.

Although it is the east which attracts the majority of visitors to the area; the west of Berkshire holds some glorious hidden treasures, and offers a more tranquil environment of rural towns and rolling countryside to explore. For those interested in everything equestrian; the prosperous old

wool town of Newbury (to the north of which are the Berkshire Downs) is a training ground for racehorses and holds regular races, also are the villages of West and East Ilsley where racehorses use the gallops on the downs as their training grounds.

Past famous residents of Berkshire include Jane Austin, who attended the Reading Ladies Boarding school, Kate Winslet and Elizabeth Taylor, who were both born in Berkshire and Oscar Wilde who was imprisoned in the county from 1895-1897. Every summer the town of Reading is flooded with thousands of people attending the Reading Festival - which is the second largest music festival in Britain.

Accommodation

Food & Drink

NEWBURY

A prosperous wool town in the Middle Ages, evidence of which can be seen in the splendid 'wool' Church of St Nicholas built in the 16th century. Two centuries later, Newbury became a busy coaching stop on the route between London and Bath and in 1810 came the

opening of the Kennet and Avon Canal. Newbury Lock, built in 1796, was the first lock to be built along the canal and is also the only lock to have lever-operated ground paddles.

Back in the town centre, beside Market Place, and housed in a 17th century cloth hall is Newbury Museum, which has over 100,000 objects and groups of pieces in its collections. Exhibits here include the story of

Kennet & Avon Canal, Newbury

the two battles fought nearby during the Civil War, the Kennet and Avon Canal, and a history of archeology in the area.

Near to the museum is Victoria Park, which is a lovely little park with a boating lake, bandstand, and an impressive statue of Queen Victoria with four lions dating from 1903 following the death of Victoria, which was originally located in Market Place.

To the north lies **Donnington**, home to 18th century **Grove House**, the childhood home of Beau Brummel, and to **Donnington Castle**, of which only the imposing twin-towered gatehouse survives.

AROUND NEWBURY

COMBE

7½ miles SW of Newbury off the A343

This isolated hamlet is overlooked by **Walbury Hill** which, at 974 feet, is the highest point in Berkshire. A popular place with walkers, it has an Iron Age hill fort on the summit, from where there are superb panoramic views. Close to the hill lies **Combe Gibbet**, one of the last public hanging places in the country, put to use once in 1676; tradition upholds that the

gibbet must stay since it's now part of the scenery, so it is replaced whenever an old one is damaged and needs to be taken down.

To the north of Combe is **Inkpen Common**, a Site of Special Scientific Interest where, along with the heath and woodland, a wet valley bog and pond have been created in an old clay pit.

HUNGERFORD

8½ miles W of Newbury on the A338

The town's heyday came in the 18th century, when the turnpike road from London to Bath was built, and the good times continued with the opening of the **Kennet and Avon Canal**. Several of the old coaching inns have survived and it was in 1688 at the Bear Hotel that a meeting took place between William of Orange and representatives of James II that culminated in the end of the House of Stuart and James's flight to France.

Today this is a lovely rural town, which has preserved traditions lost in much of England, including their very vocal town crier, and the 200 acre town common where some 175 cattle from both Commoners and Farmers graze during the summer; the rights to do so are bought from the Town & Manor of Hungerford, whose history goes back some 600 years. Adding to the rural charm of the

---

2 **THE DUNDAS ARMS**

Kintbury

18th century riverside inn offering imaginative food, draught beers and comfortable en suite accommodation.

See entry on page 309

---

1 **THE CASTLE INN**

Cold Ash, nr Thatcham

Well-kept ales and great home cooking brings the crowds to this delightful country inn.

See entry on page 309

---

3 **THE PHEASANT INN**

Shefford Woodlands

An inn of great charm and character and a magnet for racing folk, offering excellent food, cask ales and modern en suite rooms.

See entry on page 310

town is the surrounding countryside, which is glorious explored by foot or by narrow boat, trips on which run year round from the town down the Kennet and Avon canal.

LAMBOURN

11½ miles NW of Newbury on the B4000

Situated up on the Berkshire Downs, this village is best known as a centre for the training of racehorses. The Lambourn Trainer's Association organises guided tours of the village's famous stables and also trips up to the gallops to see the horses going through their paces.

To the north of the village are the **Lambourn Seven Barrows**, one of the most impressive Bronze Age burial sites in the country.

READING

The town grew up around its Abbey, which was founded in 1121 by Henry I and became one of the most important religious houses in the country. Reading is also one of only a handful of towns where kings of England have been laid to rest - Henry I was buried in the Abbey, and a plaque marks the approximate spot.

Adjacent to the ruins of **Reading Abbey** is **Reading Prison**, where Oscar Wilde was incarcerated and where he wrote *De Profundis*. His confinement inspired him to compose the epic poem *The Ballad of Reading Gaol* while in exile in Paris in 1898.

With the building of roads and the opening of the canal, Reading really began to boom and to become linked with great names such as Sutton Seeds, Huntley & Palmer biscuits and the brewing industry.

Abbey Gateway, Reading

Reading Museum tells the story of the town from its earliest beginnings. Situated on the banks of the River Kennet and housed in a range of canal buildings, **Blake's Lock Museum** concerns itself with the life of the town in the 19th and early 20th century. There is also the **Museum of English Rural Life**, part of the University of Reading, which provides some fascinating displays and historic pieces which follow the history of food, farming and countryside life up to the modern day.

AROUND READING

ALDERMASTON

9 miles SW of Reading on the A340

It was in this tranquil village that in 1840 the William Pear was first propagated by schoolmaster John Staid; it was first known as the Aldermaston pear, and a cutting of the plant is believed to have been taken to Australia, where it is now called the Bartlett pear. The lovely **Church of St Mary** provides the atmospheric setting for the York Mystery Cycle, 14th century nativity plays that are performed here each year.

Close to the village there is a delightful walk along the Kennet and Avon Canal to **Aldermaston Wharf**, a beautifully restored 18th century building that houses the **Kennet and Avon Canal Visitor Centre**.

Just outside of Aldermaston, along Church Rd, is **Aldermaston Manor**; a restored listed building with an impressive red brick facade, clock tower and 17th century chimney stacks

4	THE WINTERBOURNE ARMS

Winterbourne

An atmospheric village pub with award-winning traditional and contemporary meals and snacks.

See entry on page 311

towering over sweeping lawns and ancient parkland. It now offers bed & breakfast accommodation, and is a popular location for weddings.

PANGBOURNE

4½ miles NW of Reading on the A329

Situated at the confluence of the Rivers Pang and Thames, the town grew up in the late 19th and early 20th centuries as a fashionable place to reside, and the numerous attractive villas that have survived include a row of ornate Victorian houses known as the Seven Deadly Sins. It was to Pangbourne and **Church Cottage** that the author Kenneth Graham retired and wrote The Wind in the Willows, based on the original bedtime stories he invented for his son. An elegant iron bridge links the town with **Whitchurch**, on the opposite bank of the River Thames; it was at Whitchurch Lock that the characters in Jerome K Jerome's *Three Men in a Boat* abandoned their craft after a series of mishaps and returned to London.

SONNING

3½ miles NE of Reading off the A4

An attractive little village on the banks of the River Thames, this was once home to a palace belonging to the Bishops of Salisbury. Behind the wall of the old palace is Deanery Gardens, a well-hidden house built to the design of Lutyens. Since the early 1900's Sonning village held a **Regatta**, which was sadly ceased on the outbreak of the Second World War. To commemorate the millennium in 2000 the Regatta was again held in Sonning, and proved so popular as to once again become an annual event, with several

5 THE OLD BOOT INN

Standford Dingley

A cosy and very pretty listed building, serving an inspiring menu created by an award-winning chef.

See entry on page 311

hundred people coming to see everything from Dongalas to Canadian Canoes being raced through the water.

To the southeast, on the site of Woodley Airfield, is the **Museum of Berkshire Aviation**, which chronicles the history of this once thriving centre of the aircraft industry.

WARGRAVE

6½ miles NE of Reading on the A321

This peaceful and charming riverside village was affected by the revolutionary suffragettes movement in 1914 when a group of ladies burnt down the church in protest that the vicar refused to remove the word 'obey' from the marriage service. In the churchyard stands the **Hannen Mausoleum**, a splendid family monument designed by Lutyens in 1906.

The nearby **Druid's Temple** stands in the garden of **Temple Combe**, close to a house designed by the architect Frank Lloyd Wright. The only house of his in England, it was built in 1958 on an elaborate U-shaped design, and its many unusual features include suede-panelled interior walls.

COOKHAM

14 miles NE of Reading on the A4094

This small town on the River Thames was the birthplace of Sir Stanley Spencer, who used it as the setting for many of his paintings. The **Stanley Spencer Gallery**, housed in a converted Victorian chapel, has a permanent exhibition of his work. He was born here, spent most of his life here, and is buried in the churchyard of Holy Trinity.

Although a relatively recent development, Cookham Rise is actually where the earliest settlers in this area chose to live; there is evidence of some type of Roman settlement, which has implied it was a farming community, at the southern end of the village.

The Royal Manor of Cookham was held by the Crown until 1818 and today, although it has undergone many changes, monopolizing on its beautiful location has made it one of the most popular Thameside resorts; with many superb restaurants and inns, including Bel and the Dragon dating from 1417 and reputedly one of the oldest licensed houses in England.

BRACKNELL

10 miles SE of Reading on the A322

It was designated a New Town in 1948, but Bracknell dates back to the 10th century when the community stood at the junction of two major routes through Windsor Forest.

What now remains of the great royal hunting ground of Windsor Forest (also called Bracknell Forest) lies to the south and in this vast area of parks and nature reserves is the **Lookout Discovery Park**, an interactive science centre that brings to life the mysteries of both science and nature, as well as an outdoor adventure park, and picnic areas. Also here is a Go Ape! adventure park; what better way is there is see the forest than swinging and climbing through an exciting course up in the tree canopy?

WINDSOR

The largest castle in the country and a royal residence for over 900 years, **Windsor Castle** was built by William the Conqueror in the late 11th century as one of a chain of defences on the approaches into London. Down the centuries several monarchs have added to the Norman structure, most notably Henry VIII, Charles II and George IV. Various parts of the Castle are open to the public, including 16 state apartments that house a remarkable collection of furniture, porcelain and armour. Also here is the adorable **Queen Mary's Dolls' House**, which was designed by Lutyens in 1924 and has both electric lights and running water. In November 1992, a massive fire swept through the northeast corner of the castle but, after much restoration, the affected rooms, including **St George's Hall**, are now once again open to the public.

Frogmore House, a modest early 18th century manor house standing in Home Park, has acted as a second, more relaxed royal residence than the nearby castle. In the **Royal Mausoleum** Queen Victoria is buried beside her beloved husband Prince Albert. The Castle and

Windsor Castle

its environs are the final resting place of many other monarchs and royalty.

The charming town grew up beneath the walls of the castle and there is plenty here to interest the visitor. Windsor is the home of the Household Cavalry, at Combermere Barracks, and here there is the superb **Household Cavalry Museum**. A wonderful way to experience the sights of Windsor is by horse-drawn carriage, which runs year-round weather permitting. To the south of the town lies **Windsor Great Park**, the remains of the extensive royal hunting forest. Interestingly, Windsor is the home of Berkshire's only native cheese; named "Windsor red" it is a delicious cheddar veined with elderberry wine.

AROUND WINDSOR

ETON

1 mile N of Windsor on the A355

Situated just across the River Thames from Windsor, the town has grown up around **Eton College**, the famous public school that was founded in 1440 by Henry VI and was originally intended for the education of 70 poor and worthy scholars.

ASCOT

6 miles SW of Windsor on the A329

This was a small village until 1711 when Queen Anne moved the original Windsor race meeting here and founded the world famous **Ascot Racecourse**. The Royal Ascot Races, which are held in June, is a national treasure (although the hats worn by the royal guests get as much attention as the horses!).

BUCKINGHAMSHIRE

South Buckinghamshire, with the River Thames as its southern county boundary, lies almost entirely within the Chiltern Hills and is a charming and delightful area that has, over the years inspired many writers and artists, including Milton, Shakespeare and Roald Dahl. Though many of the towns and villages here have histories going back well before the Norman Conquest, the influence of London is never far away and several have been linked with the capital for many years by the Metropolitan Railway.

The links with London have also seen many famous and wealthy people make their homes here and, tucked away in the rolling countryside, can be found two fabulous former residences of the Rothschild family, Waddesdon Manor and Mentmore Towers. Buckinghamshire is also home to the country retreat of the Prime Minister, Chequers. The north of the county is dominated by the bustling New Town of Milton Keynes, overflowing with shops, although time away from the crowds can still be found in places

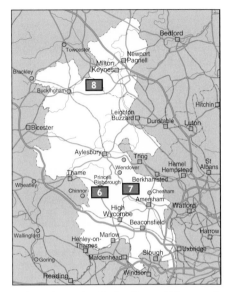

such as the quaint Market Town of Olney, and the nearby Emburton Country Park, in the far northern corner.

Food & Drink

6	The George & Dragon, Princes Risborough pg 10, 312
7	The Cock and Rabbit, The Lee, Great Missenden pg 10, 313
8	The Bell Inn & Restaurant, Beachampton, Stony Stratford pg 13, 312

HIGH WYCOMBE

The largest town in Buckinghamshire and originally an old Chilterns Gap market town, High Wycombe is traditionally known for its manufacture of chairs and, in particular, the Windsor design. Several old buildings survive today, including the Little Market House of 1761 built by Robert Adam and known affectionately as 'The Pepperpot'. Behind that is the Parish Church which was founded by the Normans and enlarged to almost its present day size in the 12th century; it remains the largest church in the county.

The centrally located **Wycombe Museum** has some interesting exhibits; not least the furniture portion which plots the history of High Wycombe's past in furniture making. Other attractions include **"The Rye"** - a park of over 22 hectares which has a man-made boating lake (seasonal) and a children's park; and the **Swan Theatre** that holds a year-round eclectic mix of productions.

Just to the north of the town lies **Hughenden Manor**, which was bought by

9

Hellfire Caves, West Wycombe

Prince, the eldest son of Edward III, this attractive place has a host of 17th and 18th century cottages. Above the village is the impressive enigma that is the Whiteleaf Cross; a huge carving into the chalk hills, which cannot be dated past 1742, but has been found depicted on a 14th century tile in a church in Monks Risborough near by. Also unusually the meaning or purpose of the cross has continued to elude archeologists.

Nearby is **Princes Risborough Manor House** (National Trust), which is an early example of a redbrick building – it dates from 1670.

One of the most famous residences in the country lies at nearby **Great Kimble**: the 16th century mansion, **Chequers**, has been the country house of the British Prime Minister since 1920.

GREAT MISSENDEN

5 miles N of High Wycombe on the A4128

This attractive village is home to the early 15th century **Old Court House**, one of only two court houses in the Chiltern Hundreds, and the home of Roald Dahl, the author of much loved children's books. It is now a brilliant **museum**, chronicling the life of this innovative writer and contains much for children to enjoy, and to expand their imaginations.

Benjamin Disraeli shortly after the publication of his novel *Tancred* and was his home until his death in 1881. Today, the remodelled 18th century house displays an interesting collection of memorabilia of Disraeli's life; the great Victorian Prime Minister lies buried in the estate church.

To the west of Wycombe lies the charming estate village of **West Wycombe** and **West Wycombe Park**, the home of the Dashwood family until the 1930s. The house dates from the early 18th century, and the grounds and parkland, landscaped by a pupil of Capability Brown, contain temples and an artificial lake shaped like a swan. Hewn out of the nearby hillside are **West Wycombe Caves**, which were created by Sir Francis Dashwood, Baron le Despencer, Chancellor of the Exchequer from 1762 to 1763, who employed his estate workers on the task after a series of failed harvests.

AROUND HIGH WYCOMBE

PRINCES RISBOROUGH

7½ miles NW of High Wycombe on the A4010

Once home to a palace belonging to the Black

---

6 THE GEORGE AND DRAGON

Princes Risborough

Friendly traditional pub, with a delicious and ever-changing menu with influences from around the world.

See entry on page 312

---

7 THE COCK & RABBIT INN

The Lee, nr Great Missenden

Wonderful authentic Italian cuisine, and a speciality in large groups and events, set within a picturesque countryside location.

See entry on page 313

WENDOVER

A delightful old market town situated in a gap in the Chiltern Hills, Wendover has several half-timbered, thatched houses and cottages, the best example of which are **Anne Boleyn's Cottages**. Once a month from April to July, Wendover's St Mary's church holds musical events from national and international acclaimed artists, which should not be missed.

Close by, on the edge of the Chiltern escarpment, lie **Wendover Woods**, 325 hectares created for recreational pursuits as well as for conservation and timber production by the Forestry Commission.

AMERSHAM

The town's main street has a good mix of fine old buildings, notably the 17th century Market Hall and **Amersham Museum**, housed in part of a medieval hall. On the hill above Amersham can be seen The Martyrs' Memorial to those who were burnt at the stake here for their religious beliefs during the reign of Queen Mary.

Amersham was a staging post for coaches and many of the old inns remain, including the **Crown Hotel** that many will recognise from the film *Four Weddings and a Funeral*.

To the east of Amersham is the picturesque village of **Chenies** and the fascinating 15th century **Chenies Manor House**. Originally the home of the Earls of Bedford (before they moved to Woburn), the

Chenies Manor House

house was built by the architect who enlarged Hampton Court for Henry VIII.

CHALFONT ST GILES

The most famous building in this typical English village is the idyllic 16th century **Milton's Cottage**, where the poet stayed in 1665 to escape the plague in London. Though he only lived here a short time, the blind poet wrote *Paradise Lost* and began *Paradise Regained* before moving back to London. The cottage and its garden are now a museum dedicated to the poet, and has been listed as a Grade I historical building. A fascinating place in the nearby **Newland Park** is the **Chiltern Open Air Museum**, dedicated to rescuing vernacular architecture.

Milton's Cottage, Chalfont St Giles

BEACONSFIELD

The old part of this town is known for its literary connections: the 17th century poet Edmund Waller was a resident (and is buried in the churchyard of St Mary and All Saints), and GK Chesterton, the poet Robert Frost and the children's author Enid Blyton all made Beaconsfield their home. Here, too, is **Bekonscot**, a rural model village which was created by Roland Callingham, a London accountant, in the 1920s and 30s. It was apparently the inspiration for Noddy's Toytown – Enid Blyton lived in a house called Green Hedges, a model of which can be seen in Bekonscot.

To the southeast lies **Stoke Poges**, whose

churchyard provided Thomas Gray with the inspiration to write his much-loved *Elegy Written in a Country Churchyard*. The poet is buried in the church; to the east stands the massive **Gray Monument**, built in 1799 by John Penn, grandson of William Penn, founder of Pennsylvania.

Just south of Beaconsfield lie **Burnham Beeches**, an area that has long been a place of leisure and relaxation for Londoners.

MARLOW

4 miles S of High Wycombe on the A4155

An attractive commuter town on the banks of the River Thames. It was at a riverside pub, the Two Brewers, that Jerome K Jerome wrote his masterpiece *Three Men in a Boat*. Today, Marlow is probably best known for its annual June Regatta.

River Thames, Marlow

To the west lies the much-filmed village of **Hambleden**, which was given to the National Trust by the family of the bookseller WH Smith (later Viscount Hambleden).

MILTON KEYNES

One of the town's most notable buildings is **Christ Church**, built in the style of Christopher Wren, which is the first purpose-built ecumenical church in Britain. The rural heritage of the villages that are now incorporated into its suburbs has not been forgotten and the **Museum of Industry and Rural Life** has a large collection of industrial, domestic and agricultural bygones; in the

Exhibition Gallery, displays of art, crafts and local history can be seen.

Milton Keynes, with its direct line to London, has become quite a contemporary and bustling place to be; the city centre alone has some 400 shops, ranging from large chains at the **thecentre:mk** and **Midsummer Place** shopping centre (one of the largest covered shopping areas in Europe), to smaller boutiques and special interest shops. As well as cafes, al fresco eateries and restaurants to cover all tastes.

AROUND MILTON KEYNES

OLNEY

8 miles N of Milton Keynes on the A509

This pretty town on the banks of the River Ouse is associated with William Cowper, reformed slave-trader, preacher and hymn-writer, who lived here between 1768 and 1786; his house is now the **Cowper and Newton Museum** (closed through winter). The museum not only concentrates on Cowper's life and work but also houses a nationally important Lace Collection from Olney's past in the heart of the bobbin lace making industry, which lasted 300 years before being snuffed out by cheaper machine-made lace in Nottingham.

BLETCHLEY

3 miles SE of Milton Keynes on the A5

Now virtually a suburb of Milton Keynes, Bletchley is famous as the home of **Bletchley Park**, the Victorian mansion that housed the country's wartime code breakers. It now houses a museum, which includes the different code breaking machines used here, and proves fascinating for young and old alike.

MENTMORE

12 miles SE of Milton Keynes off the B488

The village is home to the first of the Rothschild mansions, **Mentmore Towers**, which was built for Baron Meyer Amschel de Rothschild in the mid 19th century. A splendid building in the Elizabethan style and a superb example of grandiose Victorian extravagance, the house was sold in the 1970s and became the headquarters of the University of Natural Law, though now it is redeveloped as a hotel. To the southeast lies **Ivinghoe Beacon**, an Iron Age hill fort which provides a wonderful viewpoint on the edge of the Chiltern Hills. The Beacon is at one end of Britain's oldest road, the **Ridgeway National Trail** - the other end is at the World Heritage site of Avebury in Wiltshire.

AYLESBURY

16 miles S of Milton Keynes on the A418

The county town of Buckinghamshire since the 18th century, this ancient town sheltered by the Chiltern Hills is famous for its Aylesbury ducks. The old part of the town (now a conservation area) is centred on the market square and here, amongst the sleepy lanes, is the **King's Head Inn** where Henry VIII is said to have wooed Anne Boleyn.

Housed in a splendid Georgian building, the **County Museum** has an excellent section on Louis XVIII of France, who lived at Hartwell House during his years of exile. Also here is another treat for Roald Dahl enthusiasts, in the form of the Roald Dahl Children's Gallery which has some exciting hands-on exhibits for children to explore.

To the northwest, near the village of **Waddesdon**, is another of the county's magnificent country houses, **Waddesdon Manor**, built between 1874 and 1889 for Baron Ferdinand de Rothschild in the style of a French Renaissance château. The house contains one of the best collections of 18th century French decorative arts in the world. Close by, at **Quainton**, is the **Buckinghamshire Railway Centre**, a working museum with one of the largest collections of steam and diesel locomotives in the country.

MIDDLE CLAYDON

11 miles SW of Milton Keynes off the A413

Close to the village lies 17th century **Claydon House** (National Trust), best remembered for its associations with Florence Nightingale who

stayed here for long periods, especially during her old age (her sister had married into the Verney family, who owned the house). 'Florrie's Lorry', the carriage used by Florence in the Crimea, is one of the many fascinating exhibits on display.

BUCKINGHAM

10 miles W of Milton Keynes on the A413

Dating back to Saxon times, Buckingham was a prosperous place in the Middle Ages, though few old buildings survived a disastrous fire in 1725. As a consequence many of the buildings here are Georgian and the **Old Gaol Museum** is a fine example of mid 18th century architecture. One building that did survive the flames is **Buckingham Chantry Chapel**, built in 1475 on the site of a Norman building. A more recent addition to this delightful market town is the **University of Buckingham**, granted its charter in 1983.

To the north of Buckingham lies **Stowe School**, a leading public school that occupies an 18th century mansion that was once the home of the Dukes of Buckingham. The grounds of the house, **Stowe Landscape Gardens**, were created in the 18th century by Earl Temple and his nephew and they remain one of the most original and finest landscape gardens in Europe.

Stowe House, nr Buckingham

| 8 | THE BELL INN AND RESTAURANT |

Beachampton

A fantastic restaurant offering a cosy bar, an extensive  menu made up of traditional favourites and friendly service.

See entry on page 312

CAMBRIDGESHIRE

The southeast of the county is dominated by the county town, Cambridge, one of the leading academic centres of the world and a place that needs plenty of time to explore. The surrounding countryside is fairly flat and ideal for walking or cycling; it contains a surprising variety of habitats along with stately homes and windmills - a particular feature of East Anglia.

Extending over much of the county from The Wash are the flat fields of The Fens that contain some of the richest soil in England. Here, too, villages and small towns such as Ely were originally island settlements in the days when this was a misty landscape of marshes and bogs still rife with tales of ghosts and witches. The massive project of draining this land has spanned the centuries, starting with the Romans, who were the first to construct embankments and drains to lessen the frequency of flooding. Throughout the Middle Ages large areas of marsh and bog were reclaimed, and after the Civil War, the New Bedford River was cut to provide more drainage. First windmills and then steam and finally electric pumping engines have been used to remove the water from the fields. The Fens offer unlimited opportunities for exploration on foot, by car, by bicycle or by boat. Anglers and those with an interest in wildlife will be in their element here.

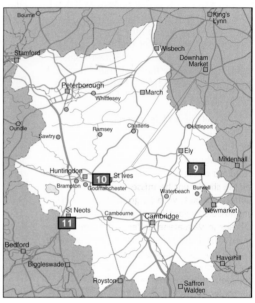

The old county of Huntingdonshire lies at the heartland of the rural heritage of Cambridgeshire and the former county town, Huntingdon, is famous as the birthplace and home of Oliver Cromwell. Places associated with the great Parliamentarian abound but there are also many ancient market towns and villages to discover along with numerous nature reserves and prehistoric sites. Cambridgeshire was the favourite shire of Rupert Brooke, and Grantchester his favourite place in the shire.

CAMBRIDGE

One of the world's leading university cities, Cambridge was an important market town centuries before the scholars arrived, as it stood at the point where the forest met the fenlands, at the lowest fording point of the River Cam. The oldest college is **Peterhouse**, founded by the Bishop of Ely in 1284, and in the next century Clare, Pembroke, Gonville and Caius, Trinity Hall and Corpus Christi followed.

The colleges reflect a variety of architectural styles but the grandest and most beautiful is undoubtedly King's College. Among the many university and college buildings to explore there are some that simply should not be missed, including **King's College Chapel**, with its glorious stained glass and Rubens' *Adoration of the Magi*; **Pepys Library** in Magdalene College; and Trinity's wonderful **Great Court**.

A trip by punt along the Backs of the River Cam gives a unique view to many of the colleges and the waterway also passes under six bridges including the **Bridge of Sighs** and

Mathematical Bridge, Cambridge

the extraordinary **Mathematical Bridge**.

A recent addition to the outside of Corpus Christi is the rather unusual, and deliberately terrifying, "**Grasshopper Clock**". The clock depicts the "eating" of time as the huge grasshopper rocks open jawed atop the golden dial, where LED lights, rather than hands, display the time. Although seemingly modern the mechanism running this clock is rooted in traditional clock making, and has

been predicted to run for two centuries.

Apart from the colleges, Cambridge has plenty of other grand buildings and some of the country's leading museums, including the **Fitzwilliam Museum**, renowned for its art collection and ancient world antiquities. One of the city's greatest treasures is the **University Library**, one of the world's greatest research libraries, with six million books, a million maps and 350,000 manuscripts. For many, the most interesting place to visit is the **Botanic Gardens**, not really a museum, but a wonderful collection of plants (over 8,000 plant species) that rivals the gardens at Kew and Edinburgh. The Gardens were opened in 1846 by Professor John Henslow, teacher and mentor of Charles Darwin. Other notable museums include the **Sedgwick Museum of Earth Sciences** which holds a fascinating display of fossils, **Museum of Zoology**, **Whipple Museum of the History of Science**, and the **Cambridge and County Folk Museum**, which is housed in a 15th century building that for 300 years was the White Horse Inn.

Among the city's many fine churches is the **Church of the Holy Sepulchre**, always known as the Round Church, one of only four surviving round churches in England.

The village of **Grantchester**, where Rupert Brooke lived for two happy years at The Orchard, can be reached by a pleasant walk from the city or a leisurely punt along the River Cam. The village was immortalised in Brooke's words:

> *"Stands the church clock at 3*
> *And is there honey still for tea?"*

The Orchard, Grantchester

The Orchard, first planted in 1868, became a tea garden by chance when a group of Cambridge students asked the owner if she could serve tea under the trees rather than on the front lawn. So started a tradition that continues to this day.

AROUND CAMBRIDGE

LODE

6 miles NE of Cambridge off the B1102

This attractive and peaceful village is home to **Anglesey Abbey**, an early 17th century mansion house that was built on the site of an Augustinian priory. It holds Lord Fairhaven's magnificent collection of paintings, furnishings, tapestries and clocks, and its 100 acres of gardens is a charming place for a peaceful stroll. To the south is the village of **Bottisham**, whose Holy Trinity Church was described by John Betjeman as 'perhaps the best in the county'.

Further afield, to the north, is **Denny Abbey** (English Heritage), which was founded in the 12th century by the Benedictine order but has also been the home of the Knights Templar, Franciscan nuns and the Countess of Pembroke. After the Dissolution of the Monasteries the abbey became a farmhouse and is now a listed Grade I building, and home to the **Farmland Museum**.

BURWELL

10 miles NE of Cambridge on the B1102

A sad sight in the churchyard of St Mary's is a gravestone that marks the burial place of some 78 people of Burwell who all died in a barn fire while watching a travelling Punch and Judy Show. The **Devil's Dyke**, thought to have been built to keep out Danish invaders, runs through Burwell on its route from Reach to Woodditton.

The **Burwell Museum** reflects many aspects of a village on the edge of the Fens up to the middle of the 20th century, and is beside the famous **Stephens Windmill**, built in 1820 and extensively restored, with more restorations expected to be undertaken through 2010.

To the southwest of Burwell lies **Swaffham Prior** where there are two churches in the same graveyard and two fine old windmills, one of which, an 1850 tower mill, has been restored and still produces flour.

DUXFORD

8 miles S of Cambridge off the A505

To the west of the village lies **Duxford Aviation Museum**, now part of the Imperial War Museum, with an outstanding collection of over 150 historic aircraft; major air shows are held here several times a year.

Between Duxford and Cambridge, close to Stapleford, there is some great walking, in parkland, where there are traces of an Iron Age hill fort, and on Magog Downs. To the west, near the village of **Shepreth**, is the **Shepreth L Moor Nature Reserve**, an important area of wet meadowland that is home to birds and many rare plants.

ARRINGTON

10 miles SW of Cambridge off the A1198

This village is home to the spectacular **Wimpole Hall**, one of the best examples of an 18th century country mansion in England. The lovely interiors contain fine collections of furniture and paintings, while the magnificent, formal gardens include a Victorian parterre and a rose garden.

Wimpole Hall, Arrington

MADINGLEY

2 miles W of Cambridge off the A1303

Madingley is home to one of the most peaceful and evocative places in the region, the **American Cemetery**. A place of

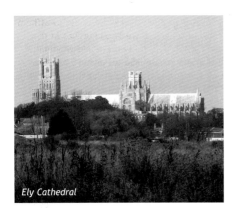

Ely Cathedral

fascinating and poignant.

Etheldreda was also known as St Awdrey, and an annual fair was held in her memory. The cheap jewellery and lace sold at the fair were known as St Awdrey's Lace, later corrupted to Tawdry, a word now applied to anything cheap and showy.

AROUND ELY

HADDENHAM

6 miles SW of Ely on the A1123

At 120 feet above sea level, Haddenham is the highest village in the Fens and, not surprisingly, it too has a windmill – **Haddenham Great Mill** which was built in 1803, has four sails and three sets of grinding stones. Last worked commercially in 1946, it was restored in the 1990s.

To the north, at Sutton, is a great family attraction, the **Mepal Outdoor Centre** on the shore of a 20 acre lake, includes a children's play park, an adventure play area, canoe and kayaking, boat hire, and a paintball course.

SOMERSHAM

11 miles W of Ely on the B1050

Once the site of a palace for the Bishops of

pilgrimage for the families of American service men who operated from the many wartime bases in the county, the cemetery commemorates 3,800 dead and 5,000 missing in action in World War Two.

ELY

The jewel in the crown of the Fens, the city owes its existence to St Etheldreda, Queen of Northumbria, who founded a monastery on the Isle of Ely in AD 673. However, it was not until 1081 that work on the present **Cathedral** began and it was completed more than a century later. The most outstanding feature is the Octagon, built to replace the original Norman tower that collapsed in 1322, but there are many other delights, including the 14th century Lady Chapel, the Prior's Door and St Ovin's Cross, the only piece of Saxon stonework in the building. It is worth taking the time to attend one of the different tours of the cathedral, exploring the multi-faceted history which has created such a beautiful building.

Even Ely's **Tourist Information Centre** is an attraction; housed in a pretty black and white timbered building that is the only known surviving house, apart from Hampton Court, where Cromwell and his family are known to have lived. The Old Gaol, in Market Street, houses **Ely Museum**, with nine galleries telling the Ely story from the Ice Age to modern times. The tableaux of the condemned and debtors' cells are particularly

Haddenham Great Mill

Ely, Somersham is now home to the **Raptor Foundation**; set in 20 acres of woodland, it is home to 300 birds of prey, mostly injured, orphaned or unwanted. This is a very popular attraction, with daily flying and falconry displays held year round.

MARCH

13 miles NW of Ely on the B1101

This settlement once occupied the second largest island in the great level of the Fens, and as the land was drained March grew as a trading and religious centre and, later, as a market town and hub of the railway. The **March and District Museum** tells the story of the people and history of the town and surrounding area. **St Wendreda's** uniquely dedicated church in March was described by John Betjeman as "worth cycling 40 miles into a headwind to see." Its roof, adorned with 120 carved angels, is certainly a stirring sight.

WISBECH

19 miles NW of Ely on the A1101

This town also lies at the centre of a thriving agricultural region and the 18th century saw many fine buildings constructed along the river. The finest of these is undoubtedly **Peckover House**, built in 1722 and bought at the end of the 18th century by Jonathan Peckover, a member of the Quaker banking family. Behind its elegant façade are charming panelled rooms and ornate plaster decorations.

The town was the birthplace in 1838 of Octavia Hill, co-founder of the National Trust, and the house in which she was born is now the **Octavia Hill Museum** where her work is commemorated. The tourist information centre is home to the fascinating **Lilian Ream Photographic Collection**; named after a daughter of Wisbech who at the time of her death in 1961 had amassed a collection of over 200,000 photographs of Wisbech people, places and events, making for a unique insight into the history and culture of the town.

The **Wisbech and Fenland Museum** is one of the oldest purpose-built museums in the country, and its numerous displays include the manuscript of Charles Dickens' *Great Expectations* and Napoleon's Sèvres breakfast set captured at Waterloo.

SOHAM

5½ miles SE of Ely off the A142

Downfield Windmill was built in 1726 as a smock mill and then rebuilt as a tower mill in 1890 after it had been destroyed by gales. Sadly another gale in recent years has again damaged this unique building, making its future an uncertain one unless the funds can be raised to repair it. To the southwest lies **Wicken Fen**, the oldest nature reserve in the country, famous for its rich variety of plant, insect and bird life. It is also home to Highland cattle and the wild Konik ponies. Wicken Windmill is an impressive smock mill restored to full working order.

HUNTINGDON

First settled by the Romans and the former county town of Huntingdonshire, Huntingdon was the birthplace, in 1599, of Oliver Cromwell. He attended Huntingdon Grammar School, where Samuel Pepys was also a pupil, before becoming the MP for Huntingdon in the Parliament of 1629. His school is now the **Cromwell Museum** and it houses the only public collection relating specifically to him. Opposite the museum stands **All Saints' Church**, which contains the Cromwell burial vault. On the Market Square, the 16th century Falcon Inn was Cromwell's headquarters during the Civil War.

Cowper House, with its impressive early 18th century frontage, was the home of the poet William Cowper from 1765 to 1767, and a former coaching inn, The George Hotel, is reputed to have been used by the highwayman Dick Turpin.

At nearby Hemingford Abbots stands

9 THE CHERRY TREE

Soham

Popular family orientated inn serving a range of real ales, a delicious traditional menu with a play area in its spacious beer garden.

See entry on page 314

Hemingford Grey, a manor that is one of the oldest continuously inhabited houses in England – it was built in around 1130.

A footpath leads from the famous Chinese Bridge (1827) to **Port Holme Meadow**, one of the largest meadows in England and the site of Roman remains as well as being home to a huge diversity of botanical and bird species.

AROUND HUNTINGDON

RAMSEY

7 miles N of Huntingdon on the B1040

It was in this pleasant market town in AD 969 that Earl Ailwyn founded **Ramsey Abbey**, which by the 12th century had become one of the most important in England. However, after the Dissolution the Abbey and its lands were sold to Sir Richard Williams, great-grandfather of Oliver Cromwell. Most of the buildings were demolished and, in 1938, the house was converted for use as a school – which it remains today. Nearby are the ruins of the once magnificent late 15th century stone gatehouse (National Trust) - only the porter's lodge remains, with an unusual large carved Purbeck marble effigy, dating to the 14th century, to represent Earl Ailwyn, founder of the Abbey.

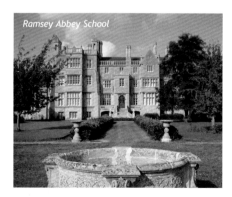
Ramsey Abbey School

Housed in an 18th century farm building and several barns is the **Ramsey Rural Museum**, where the exhibits include restored farm and traditional craftsmen's equipment.

WHITTLESEY

15 miles N of Huntingdon on the A605

This market town, where brick-making was a local industry, was the birthplace of the writer LP Hartley, author of The Go-Between, and of the soldier Sir Harry Smith, a hero of many 19th century Indian campaigns. The highlight of the year here is the ancient **Straw Bear Procession** when a man clad in a suit of straw dances through streets during a four-day January festival.

To the southeast lies **Flag Fen Bronze Age Excavation**, comprising massive 3,000-year-old timbers that were part of a major settlement and have been preserved in the peaty ground. A Roman road, re-creations of a Bronze Age settlement, a museum of artefacts and rare breed animals can also be seen here.

To the north is **Thorney Abbey**, though what stands today is only a small part of this once great Benedictine Abbey.

ST IVES

4 miles E of Huntingdon on the A1123

Oliver Cromwell lived in St Ives in the 1630s and a statue of him stands on Market Hill – the statue was erected here in 1901 after it was rejected by Huntingdon. Other notable townsfolk include Sir Clive Sinclair, who developed his pocket calculators in the town, and the Victorian rower John Goldie, whose name is remembered by the second Cambridge boat. The famous six-arched **River Bridge**, built in the 15th century, has a most unusual chapel in its middle: the two-storey Chapel of St Leger, one of only four surviving bridge chapels in the country. The **Norris Museum**, founded in 1933 by the St Ives historian Herbert Norris, has some interesting

10 NUTS BISTRO

St Ives

The aroma of good old fashioned home baking lures guests into this charming bistro where a range of homemade pies, pastries, cakes, quiches, soups, sandwiches and toasties are served daily.

See entry on page 314

displays plotting St Ives through the ages; though the real hidden wonder of this pretty riverside building is its gorgeous fragrant garden, made particularly lovely in May when the wisteria is in full bloom.

In early July the two day St Ives carnival and music festival fills the town with music, rides and colour; started by a vivid convoy of carnival floats, judged by the Mayor.

ST NEOTS

8½ miles SW of Huntingdon on the B1428

St Neots is a lovely town to explore on foot; with the many interesting sites and old buildings tucked away. The famous **Market Square** is one of the largest and most ancient in the country. A market has been held here every Thursday since the 12th century.

The first bridge over the River Great Ouse was built in 1180 in the town, which takes its name from the Cornish saint whose remains were interred in the priory before the Norman Conquest. The priory was demolished with the Dissolution of the Monasteries and in the early 17th century the old bridge was replaced by a stone one which became the scene of a battle during the Civil War.

St Neots Museum, housed in the former magistrates' court and police station (and still has the original cells!), opened in 1995, and tells the story of the town and the surrounding area through some eye-catching displays.

GRAFHAM

5 miles SW of Huntingdon off the B661

Created in the 1960s as a reservoir, **Grafham Water** offers a wide range of sports facilities in its 1,500 acres. The area is a Site of Special Scientific Interest, and a nature

Kimbolton Castle, Grafham

reserve at the western edge is run jointly by Anglian Water and the Wildlife Trust.

To the west lies Kimbolton, a place with plenty of history and several interesting buildings, including **Kimbolton Castle** where parts of the original Tudor building can still be seen.

The gatehouse at the Castle was added by Robert Adam in 1764. Henry VIII's first wife Catherine of Aragon spent the last 18 months of her life imprisoned here and died here in 1536. She is buried in Peterborough Cathedral.

PETERBOROUGH

Cambridgeshire's second city, Peterborough has a long and interesting history that dates back to the Bronze Age. In 1967 it was designated a New Town, and modern development and expansion have increased its facilities without, thankfully, destroying its historic heart. Henry VIII elevated the 12th century church to a **Cathedral** and his first wife Catherine of Aragon is buried here as, for a while, was Mary, Queen of Scots after her execution at Fotheringhay. Railway enthusiasts are in their element here with the twin attractions of **Railworld**, a hands-on exhibition dealing with modern rail travel, and the wonderful **Nene Valley Railway**, which operates between the city and its Museum at Wansford. Close by is the **Thorpe Meadows Sculpture Park**, one of several open spaces in and around the city.

Also on the outskirts of the city are **Longthorpe Tower**, part of a fortified manor house which is graced by some very fine 14th century domestic wall paintings, and **Peakirk Waterfowl Gardens**, home to hundreds of birds.

---

11 THE PLOUGH

Eynesbury

This recently refurbished village inn offers contemporary Gastro-pub cuisine and en suite accommodation in this historic part of Cambridgeshire.

See entry on page 315

CHESHIRE

There are many aspects to Cheshire: the rural landscape of the Cheshire Plains, the textile towns in the east, the ancient salt towns and the grand stately homes. Chester, the prosperous county town, was first established by the Romans, who built a fort here to protect against invasions from Wales. It is now a vibrant town, with such marvels as the Cathedral, the Zoo and the Amphitheatre left by the Romans, drawing many visitors here each year. Salt had been mined in Cheshire

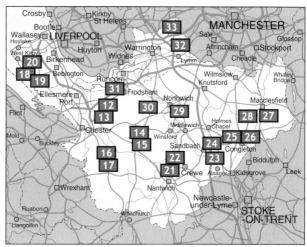

long before the Romans arrived but the particular need for brine for the fledgling chemical manufacturers along the River Mersey saw a great increase in activity.

Further east is the famous silk town of Macclesfield, while Styal was created as a model village for one of the first cotton mills in the area, Quarry Bank Mill. Throughout the county can be found relics and monuments to Cheshire's past industry, as well as many illuminating museums, and the Quarry Bank Mill is possibly the most imposing of them; still thick with the atmosphere of Industrial Revolution. The oddity of "White Nancy", at Bollington near Macclesfield, is worth the trek to reach, to see "Nancy" herself who has become the

areas mascot, and for the views of the county which are breathtaking.

Cheshire is also home to some of the country's grandest country houses, including Tatton Park, Arley Hall, Tabley Hall and Dunham Massey Hall. The ruins of Beeston Castle command as much respect as these; on the towering Beeston Hill 500 feet from the Cheshire Plain.

Though not as renowned for its literary connections as other counties, Cheshire has been home to both the English novelist Elizabeth Gaskell, who was married and spent most of her life in Knutsford, and a young Lewis Carol who is commemorated in a glorious stained glass window in Daresbury's All Saints Church.

Accommodation

Food & Drink

Continued

Food & Drink

Food & Drink

CHESTER

It was in AD 70 that the famous 20th Legion, the Valeria Victrix, established its headquarters and took full advantage of Chester's strategic position on the River Dee, close to the Welsh border. During this period the **City Walls** were first built; today they remain the most complete in the country and provide an excellent 2-mile walk as well as fine views of the River, Chester's glorious buildings and the Welsh mountains in the distance. At one point, the wall runs alongside St John Street, which was in Roman times the main thoroughfare between the fortress and the **Amphitheatre**, the largest such construction to be uncovered in Britain and one that was capable of seating 7,000 spectators. There are many varieties of walking tours available of Chester; the most unusual however has to be the one lead by a Roman Solider, evoking the exciting adventures of an Imperial warrior (runs on weekends in summer).

The Normans began the construction of what is now **Chester Cathedral**, a majestic building of weathered pink stone on a site that has been a place of worship for 1,000 years. It was originally an abbey – one of the very few to survive Henry VIII's closure of the monasteries in the 1540s – and the cloisters are regarded as the finest in England.

Chester has many museums telling the city's story from Roman times through the dark days of the Civil War to the present day. Visitors can also enjoy a unique shopping experience – two-tiered galleries of reconstructed medieval shops under covered walkways known as **The Rows**.

The very best way to appreciate the beauty and character of this ancient city is from the elegant showboats "The Lady Diana" and "Mark Twain", which run cruises year round.

The city has some ancient sporting links: **Chester Regatta** hosts the oldest rowing races in the world, and **Chester Races** are held on

The Rows, Chester

the oldest Racecourse in the country, the Roodeye. Finally, no visit to Chester is complete without a trip to **Chester Zoo**, at Upton-by-Chester on the city's northern outskirts, and where, surrounded by landscaped gardens, over 5,000 animals from 500 different species can be seen in near natural enclosures. A mile-long overhead railway provides a splendid bird's-eye view of the animals.

AROUND CHESTER

ASHTON

6½ miles E of Chester on the B5393

Maintained by the Forestry Commission since the early 1900s, **Delamere Forest**, once a hunting ground for royalty and the nobility, lies just a couple of miles northeast of Ashton and although it is an excellent place for walking and picnicking it remains a working forest of some 4,000 acres.

TARPORLEY

9 miles E of Chester off the A49

At the time when most of the surrounding area was part of Delamere Forest, Tarporley

was the headquarters of the forest wardens (the verderers) who meted out rough justice to offenders of the forest laws from their own courts. One such court was at Utkinton, just north of the town, and in an old farmhouse is the trunk of an ancient forest tree with its roots still in the ground. When the court was in session, the wardens placed the Hunting Horn of Delamere – their symbol of authority – on the tree.

Just east of Tarporley is the Cheshire Ice Cream Farm, where you can meet the animals, try the delicious ice cream in the Country Kitchen and buy some to take home for the freezer.

BEESTON

9½ miles SE of Chester off the A49

Rising some 500 feet from the Cheshire Plain, the craggy cliff of **Beeston Hill** is one of the most dramatic sights in the county and it is made all the more impressive by the ruins of **Beeston Castle** (the 'Castle of the Rock') on the summit. Although it was built in around 1220, the castle did not see military action until the Civil War when a Royalist captain and just eight musketeers captured the fortress and its garrison of 60 soldiers – without even firing a shot! Later, Cromwell ordered the castle to be partially destroyed

---

12 THE WHITE LION

Alvanley

Popular and historic village inn; offering the area's finest homemade cuisine, real ale and wine in a great family atmosphere.

See entry on page 316

---

13 THE BIRD IN HAND

Guilden Sutton

Spectacular village inn offering an inspired home cooked menu, with speciality desserts and quality real ales available.

See entry on page 317

---

14 MILL POOL

Little Budworth

The Mill Pool is a popular restaurant situated in an idyllic setting close to the famous Cheshire Motor Racing Circuit at Oulton Park

See entry on page 317

---

15 CABBAGE HALL

Little Budworth

A fine establishment offering the very best in cuisine and hospitality with full function facilities.

See entry on page 318

Beeston Castle Gateway

but it is still very imposing with walls 30 feet thick and a well 366 feet deep. An exhibition tells the 4,000-year story of the site.

Seen clearly from the top of Beeston Hill is another of Cheshire's fortifications, **Peckforton Castle**. Further south again from Beeston is another marvellous mock medieval construction, **Cholmondeley Castle**, built in the early 19th century and particularly noted for its gardens.

FARNDON

7 miles S of Chester off the B5130

During the Civil War, Farndon's strategic position, between Royalist North Wales and Parliamentarian Cheshire, along with its bridge, led to many skirmishes and these events are depicted in the stained glass windows of the parish church.

Farndon's most famous son, the cartographer John Speed, was born in the village in 1542. Speed followed his father's trade as a tailor, married, had 18 children and was nearly 50 before he began to devote his time to researching and producing his beautifully drawn maps.

NESTON

10 miles NW of Chester on the B5135

Right up until the early 19th century, Neston was the most significant town on **The Wirral**, the once desolate and wind swept peninsula that, following the rise of shipbuilding and other industries in the 19th century, has not only become a desirable place to live but has also been justifiably dubbed the 'Leisure Peninsula' by tourism officials.

After Neston became useless as a port, maritime traffic moved along the Dee estuary to **Parkgate** and, as the new gateway to Ireland, this still attractive village saw some notable visitors: John Wesley preached here while waiting for favourable winds to take him to Ireland, Handel landed here after

Salt Marshes, Parkgate

---

16 MITCHELLS

Tattenhall

Mitchells is a family run wine bar and restaurant with a big emphasis on local and seasonal produce with outside seating for brighter days.

See entry on page 319

---

17 FERNLEA COTTAGE

Tattenhall

Quality 4 star B&B set in 21 acres of stunning countryside, known for its filling home cooked breakfasts.

See entry on page 320

---

18 G.J'S COFFEE SHOP

Thurstaston

Charming coffee shop just 50 metres from the beach with unrivalled hospitality, offering the best in old fashioned, home cooking and cakes.

See entry on page 320

conducting his first performance of *The Messiah* in Dublin, and Turner came here to sketch the panoramic views across the estuary of the Flintshire hills.

To the east of Neston, centrally placed between the Dee and Mersey estuaries, is the village of **Willaston**, the home of **Hadlow Road Station**. Although a train has not run through here since 1962, the station, along with its signal box and ticket office, has been restored to appear as it would have done in the early 1950s. This is one of the more intriguing features of the Wirral Way, a nature reserve and walk that follows the track bed of the old railway between Hooton and West Kirkby. On the Mersey side of the Wirral peninsula lies **Eastham Woods Country Park**, an area of woodland that is home to all three species of native woodpecker.

Further up the Mersey lies **Ellesmere Port**, situated at the point where the Shropshire Union Canal meets the River Mersey. The canal basin is now home to the **National Waterways Museum**, housed in handsome Victorian buildings it contains fascinating displays and the original locks, docks and warehouses. Towards the top of The Wirral Peninsula, **Birkenhead** was a tiny, insignificant village until in 1824 William Laird set up a shipbuilding firm. It became Cammell Laird, one of the busiest and most

Port Sunlight

successful shipyards in the world. The **Wirrall Museum** tells the story of the shipyard.

The Birkenhead Heritage Trail takes in tram rides, an Edwardian street scene display, historic warships, a German U-Boat and a pumping station that was used to extract water from the Mersey railway tunnel.

Port Sunlight is a model village created in 1888 by William Hesketh Lever, later the 1st Viscount Leverhulme, for workers in his soap factory. It was named after his most famous product, Sunlight Soap. The **Lady Lever Art Gallery** is home to a marvellous collection of pre-Raphaelite paintings by Millais, Rossetti and Ford Madox Brown, portraits by Gainsborough and Reynolds and landscapes by Turner and Constable. Birkenhead is the birthplace of the actresses Glenda Jackson and Patricia Routledge.

NANTWICH

This attractive market town surrounded by the rich dairy farmlands of south Cheshire was once second only in importance in the county to Chester, its prosperity built on the mining of salt.

The most disastrous event in Nantwich's long history was its great fire in 1583 that saw some 600 thatched and timber-framed buildings destroyed. The most striking building to survive the fire, probably because it was surrounded by a moat, is the lovely black and white house in Hospital Street that is known as **Churches Mansion** after the merchant, Richard Churche, who built it in 1577. Another building spared from the fire is

---

19 FOX AND HOUNDS

Barnston Village

This traditional and homely country pub offers an impressive array of whiskeys, real ales and lagers alongside a popular value for money menu every lunchtime.

See entry on page 321

---

20 THE FARMERS ARMS

Frankby

Full of character and charm this historic inn offers truly delicious food, fine wine and ale at affordable prices in a pretty village setting.

See entry on page 322

St Mary's Church, Nantwich

the town's impressive 14th century church that is often called the **Cathedral of South Cheshire**.

During the Civil War Nantwich supported Cromwell's Parliamentarian army and, after several weeks of fighting, the Royalist forces were finally defeated on 25th January 1644 and the townspeople celebrated the victory by wearing sprigs of holly in their hair. There are records of the Civil War in the **Nantwich Museum**, which also contains exhibitions on the town's long history and its salt, dairy and cheese-making industries.

A few miles south of Nantwich, just off the A530 Whitchurch road, stands **Hack Green Secret Bunker**. Built as a centre of regional government in the case of a nuclear war, it was declassified in 1993 and has since become a major visitor attraction.

AROUND NANTWICH

CREWE

4 miles NE of Nantwich on the A534

Crewe is very much a product of the railway age and it was only when the Grand Junction Railway arrived here in 1837 and, five years later, moved all its construction and repair workshops to this site that the town was founded. The **Crewe Heritage Centre** offers a fascinating insight into Crewe's place in railway history.

CONGLETON

14½ miles NE of Nantwich on the A534

In the foothills of the Pennines, the land around Congleton has been inhabited since

---

21 ROYAL OAK

Worleston

Local produce and home made dishes are at the heart of its extensive and popular menu.

See entry on page 323

---

22 COACH & HORSES

Bradfield Green

A lovely and friendly family-run pub with beautiful grounds and play area that specialises in superb food.

See entry on page 323

---

23 THE BULL'S HEAD

Smallwood

A classic English country pub and restaurant in a stunning countryside location.

See entry on page 324

---

24 LOCK 57

Sandbach

On the banks of the canal this family run café/bistro offers flawless service and exquisite fine dining at affordable prices.

See entry on page 325

---

the Stone Age and the remains of a 5,000-year-old chambered tomb, known as **The Bridestones**, can be seen beside the road running eastwards from the town towards Leek. In Elizabethan times, the people of the town had such a passion for bear baiting that it became known locally as the Bear Town, and Congleton was the very last town in England to outlaw this cruel practice.

The town developed as an important textile centre during the 18th century with many of its mills involved in silk manufacturing, cotton spinning and ribbon weaving. In Mill Green, near the River Dane, part of the very first silk mill to operate here still stands.

Just a couple of miles south of Congleton lies the pretty village of **Astbury** set around a triangular village green. Black and white half-timbered houses have almost become a symbol for the county of Cheshire and one of the most stunning examples of all is **Little Moreton Hall**, a unique building which includes some remarkable wall-paintings and a pretty Knot garden.

Further south again lies the famous folly, **Mow Cop**, which was built by Randle Wilbraham in the 18th century on his Rode Hall estate to enhance the view from his house. This mock ruin stands on a rocky hill, some 1,100 feet above sea level and, from its summit, on a clear day, there are magnificent views across the Pennines to the northeast, Cheshire to the west, and northwards to Alderley Edge.

KNUTSFORD

The Knutsford of the 19th century that Elizabeth Gaskell wrote about so vividly has expanded a great deal, but its centre still evokes the intimacy of a small Victorian town with its narrow streets and cobbled alleyways. More recent is the **Gaskell Memorial Tower**, a tall blank-walled building that was erected in her memory by entrepreneur and glove manufacturer Richard Harding Watt in 1907. Her grave can be seen in the grounds of the Brook Street Unitarian Chapel in the town.

It was back in 1262 that Edward I granted the town a charter and the **Knutsford Heritage Centre**, housed in a timber-framed 17th century former smithy, is an ideal place to discover more of the town's long history.

Close by is an unusual exhibition, the **Penny Farthing Museum**. These curious machines were in fashion for just 20 years before the last model was manufactured in 1892, and the collection here includes a replica of the famous 'Starley Giant' with a front wheel that is seven feet in diameter!

Recently Knutsford's Regent Street has been developed into a burgeoning shopping area, with many quality local and chain retailers setting up shop – to much enthusiasm from Knutsford's residents.

Just north of Knutsford is **Tatton Park**, a historic country estate that is centred on a

25 YE OLDE WHITE LION

Congleton

At the heart of Congleton, this distinctive and traditional pub offers great homemade food and real ale from the Beartown Brewery.

See entry on page 326

26 CHURCH HOUSE INN

Congleton

A comfortable olde worlde pub serving the very best in traditional, home made food with a caravan park on site.

See entry on page 327

Tatton Park, nr Knutsford

magnificent Georgian mansion. A short walk from the grand house is **Home Farm**, the heart of the estate, where there are the old estate offices and many original farm animal breeds to be seen. Surrounding the mansion is a vast deer park that has a history stretching back to 8000 BC when the deer here were hunted for meat and clothing.

Another grand Georgian mansion, **Tabley House**, lies to the west of Knutsford. Designed by John Carr for the 1st Lord de Tabley in 1761, the house today is home to a wonderful collection of English paintings, including works by Turner, Reynolds and Opie, that were put together by Lord Tabley and his son, who were the founders of London's National Gallery.

To the south of Knutsford is the charming Cheshire village of **Lower Peover** and the delightful old coaching inn the **Bells of Peover**, which flies not only the Union Flag but also the American Stars and Stripes to commemorate the visit made here by General Patton and Eisenhower during World War II. For a time, in those dark days, General Patton lived at nearby Peover Hall.

AROUND KNUTSFORD

WILMSLOW

6 miles NE of Knutsford on the A538

Just to the north of the bustling commuter town of Wilmslow and surrounded by the 150-acre **Styal Country Park** is **Quarry Bank Mill** (National Trust), a grand old building dating from 1784 that was one of the first generation of cotton mills. Visitors can follow the history of the mill through a series of museum displays, see weaving and spinning demonstrations and discover what life was like for the children who lived at the Apprentice House. Also within the park is the delightful factory village of **Styal**, which was established by the mill's original owner, Samuel Greg, a philanthropist and pioneer of the factory system.

To the south of Wilmslow lies the long wooded escarpment, **Alderley Edge**, nearly two miles long, which rises to 600 feet and culminates in sandy crags overlooking the Cheshire Plain. Walkers can roam through the woods along the many footpaths, one of which leads to **Hare Hill Gardens**, whose Victorian grounds include fine woodland and a walled garden themed in blue, white and yellow flowers.

STALYBRIDGE

6 miles E of Manchester on the A57

Once called 'Little Venice' because the Huddersfield Narrow Canal and River Tame run directly through it; and with the North Pennine Moors stretching for miles to the east, Stalybridge was one of the earliest, and prettiest, cotton towns. One of the cotton workers' most prominent leaders was the Rev Joseph Rayner Stephens, and a granite obelisk in his memory stands in the town's Stamford Park.

BOLLINGTON

11 miles E of Knutsford on the B5091

A striking feature of this former cotton town is the splendid 20-arched viaduct that once carried the railway over the River Dean and which today is part of the **Middlewood Way**, a 10-mile country trail that follows a scenic, traffic-free route from Macclesfield to Marple. Just as remarkable as the viaduct is **White Nancy**, a bell-like stone structure built to commemorate the Battle of Waterloo, that stands on the 900 feet summit of **Kerridge Hill**, with possibly the most gorgeous view to be found in Cheshire. Originally White Nancy had a door shaped opening, with a stone table and bench inside; and although it has at some point been sealed up, the symbol which

White Nancy, Bollington

Bollington uses for its mascot still has the door. Recently Nancy underwent a drastic change, when some vandals painted her pink; however you'll be glad to know she is now back to brilliant white.

MACCLESFIELD

11 miles SE of Knutsford on the A523

The town nestles below the High Peak, and it was on this rock that Edward I and Queen Eleanor founded a church. Reached via a gruelling flight of 108 steps, the **Church of St Michael and All Angels** was extended in the 1890s, but its early core remains, including the Legh Chapel that was built in 1422 to receive the body of Piers Legh, who had fought at Agincourt and died at the Siege of Meaux.

It was in Macclesfield in 1743 that Charles Roe built the first silk mill beside the River Bollin. The industry flourished and, 150 years later, it had become known as the Silk Town. Several excellent museums tell the story of the town's connection with silk; The Silk Museum at Paradise Mill demonstrations can be seen on one of the 26 restored Jacquard handlooms, making the finest tie silk in Macclesfield. A few minutes walk away is the **West Park Museum**, whose exhibits include a collection of Egyptian antiquities and a gallery devoted to the work of Charles Tunnicliffe.

27 THE FOOLS NOOK INN

Sutton

A former coaching inn serving delicious food made from the finest local ingredients and produce

See entry on page 328

28 THE DAVENPORT ARMS

Marton

This former coaching inn is arguably one of the finest and most well known pubs in Cheshire

See entry on page 329

To the east of the town centre runs the **Macclesfield Canal**, one of the highest waterways in England, that was opened in 1831 and which links with the Trent and Mersey and the Peak Forest canals. Between Macclesfield and Congleton, the canal descends over 100 feet in a spectacular series of 12 locks before crossing the River Dane by Thomas Telford's handsome iron viaduct. Another unusual feature of this superbly engineered canal are the two 'roving bridges' south of Congleton that swing from one bank to the other, where the towpath changes sides, and enable horses to cross over without having to unhitch the towrope.

Close to the village of Warren, a couple of miles southwest of Macclesfield, is the black and white half-timbered **Gawsworth Hall** that was built in 1480 by the Fitton family. The celebrated beauty Mary Fitton is believed to be the 'Dark Lady' of Shakespeare's sonnets. Gawsworth's famous open-air theatre stages a summer programme that ranges from Shakespeare to Gilbert and Sullivan opera.

LOWER WITHINGTON

6½ miles SE of Knutsford on the B5392

To the northwest of this village, and visible from miles around, is the huge white dish of the world famous **Jodrell Bank** radio telescope that first came into service in 1957. Recent developments have added a new Observational Pathway, which stretches 180 degrees around the base of the Lovell Telescope, allowing people closer than ever before. Also there is a 3D theatre, superb 35-acre **Arboretum** which houses National Collections of Sorbus and Malus, and an award-winning Environmental Discovery Centre.

NORTHWICH

7 miles W of Knutsford on the A559

Although salt production in Cheshire began even before the Roman occupation, its extraction and processing at Northwich began on a major scale in 1670 when rock salt was discovered in nearby Marston. Its extraction from the Keuper marl of the Cheshire Plain has had some spectacular side effects – in Elizabethan times, John Leland recorded that a hill at Combermere suddenly disappeared into underground workings! Northwich later became notorious for the number of its buildings leaning at crazy angles due to the subsidence - the White Lion Inn lies a complete storey lower than its original height.

Cheshire's and Northwich's long involvement with salt is vividly recorded at the **Salt Museum** which is housed in what used to be the Northwich Workhouse, a handsome Georgian building designed by the architect of Arley Hall.

To the north of the town is one of the most impressive feats of engineering of the canal age and one of the country's most fascinating attractions – the **Anderton Boat Lift**, constructed in 1875 to transfer boats from the Trent and Mersey Canal to the Weaver Navigation 50 feet below. It was designed by Edward Leader Williams, the engineer behind the Manchester Ship Canal, and is now fully restored; two barges could enter the lift's upper tanks, two the lower, and, by pumping water out of the lower tank, the boats exchanged places and canals. A six-mile circular walk visits the Boat Lift, the Lion Salt Works and Great Budworth (Arley hall & Gardens), providing a fascinating insight into the area's industrial heritage and also its rural character.

About a mile north of Anderton, **Marbury**

Country Park was formerly part of a large country estate but the area is now managed by Cheshire County Council whose wardens have created a variety of habitats for plants, trees and animals.

In Victorian times, the **Old Salt Mine** at **Marston**, just northeast of Northwich, was a huge tourist attraction: in 1844, the Tsar of Russia sat down to dinner, along with eminent members of the Royal Society, in a huge cavern that was lit by 10,000 lamps. The village is home to the **Lion Salt Works Museum**, where volunteers keep alive the only surviving open-pan saltworks in the country.

GREAT BUDWORTH
6 miles W of Knutsford off the A559

To the north of this village of attractive old cottages lies another of Cheshire's great estates, **Arley Hall** and Gardens, where visitors can find one of its grandest houses in perfect harmony with one of the county's finest gardens. Along with the sumptuous stately home that had all the latest state-of-the-art innovations, the conservationist Squire Egerton-Warburton and his wife masterminded the magnificent gardens; he is credited with creating what is believed to be the first herbaceous border in England.

WARRINGTON

Warrington is North Cheshire's largest town – an important industrial centre since Georgian and Victorian times and with substantial buildings of those days to prove it. Its imposing **Town Hall** was built in 1750 in very grand style with windows framed in painfully expensive copper, and elaborately designed entrance gates. A major Victorian contribution to the town is its excellent **Museum and Art Gallery** in Bold Street, one of the earliest municipal museums. The exhibits are remarkably varied: among them are shrunken heads, a unique china teapot collection, a scold's bridle, Egyptian mummies, Roman artefacts and some very fine Victorian watercolours and oils.

---

29 FREEMASONS ARMS

Northwich

Small and well loved inn that prides itself on providing a variety of fine ales for its customers in its friendly environment.

See entry on page 330

---

30 THE TIGERS HEAD

Norley

A popular, family-run, traditional country inn serving traditional home made food with a delightful beer garden.

See entry on page 331

AROUND WARRINGTON

DARESBURY

5 miles SW of Warrington on the A558

All Saints Church in Daresbury has a unique stained glass window: there are panels depicting a Gryphon and a Cheshire Cat, others show a Mock Turtle, a March Hare and a Mad Hatter. This is of course the **Lewis Carroll Memorial Window**, commemorating the author of *Alice in Wonderland*. Carroll himself is shown at one side, dressed in clerical garb and kneeling. His father was Vicar of Daresbury when Carroll was born here in 1832 and baptised as Charles Lutwidge Dodgson. The boy enjoyed an apparently idyllic childhood at Daresbury until his father moved to another parish when Charles/Lewis was eleven years old.

RUNCORN

7 miles SW of Warrington on the A557

Runcorn is one of Britain's best known post-war new towns, developed around a much older town bearing the same name. Here, **Norton Priory** is always a delightful and intriguing place for a family outing, whatever the weather. The Augustinian priory was built in 1134 as a retreat for just 12 'black canons', so named because they wore a cape of black woollen cloth over a white linen surplice.

Work by the **Norton Priory Museum Trust** has uncovered the remains of the church, chapter house, cloisters and dormitory, and these finds are informatively explained in an audio-visual presentation.

LYMM

4 miles SE of Warrington on the A56

During the stage coach era, Eagle Brow was notorious, a dangerously steep road that dropped precipitously down the hillside into the village of Lymm. To bypass this hazard, a turnpike was built (now the A56), so preserving the heart of this ancient village with its half-timbered houses and well preserved village stocks. **Lymm Dam**, popular with anglers and bird-watchers, is part of a lovely woodland centre which is linked to the surrounding countryside and the canal towpath by a network of footpaths and bridleways.

DUNHAM MASSEY

4 miles E of Lymm on B5160

Dunham Massey Hall and Park (National Trust) has 250 acres of parkland where fallow deer roam freely and noble trees planted in the late 1700s still flourish. A restored water mill is usually in operation every Wednesday, and there are splendid walks in every direction. The Hall, once the home of the Earls of Stamford and Warrington, is a grand Georgian mansion of 1732 that boasts an outstanding collection of furniture, paintings and Huguenot silver.

---

32 THE BLACK SWAN

Rixton

A popular and charming community pub that has just undergone major refurbishment

See entry on page 333

---

31 THE OLD HALL HOTEL

Frodsham

Renowned family run hotel offering stylish and comfortable en suite accommodation, conferences and a mouth-watering selection of a la carte dishes.

See entry on page 332

---

33 COMFORTABLE GILL INN

Glazebury

Fantastically friendly local inn, serving up delicious home cooking, real cask ale and great entertainment throughout the week, with a party marquee available for hire.

See entry on page 334

CORNWALL

An isolated beauty that contains some of the most dramatic and spectacular scenery in the country. This is an apt description of Cornwall, a land of strong Celtic heritage and ancestry, a place dotted with monuments such as crosses, holy wells and prehistoric sights and where legends of old, particularly those surrounding King Arthur, still have a strong romantic appeal among the Cornish people and to visitors. Surrounded by rugged coastline, Cornwall has often been referred to as the English Riviera, encompassing pretty little fishing ports, secluded picturesque villages, narrow winding lanes and romantic seafaring traditions.

While the northern coastline is dramatic, the southern Cornish coast is one of sheltered coves. Here, too, is one of the country's largest natural harbours, at Falmouth, but many of the fishing villages expanded to manage the exportation of the vast quantities of mineral ore and china clay that were extracted from inland Cornwall. Finally, there is Land's End, the westernmost tip of England, where the granite of Cornwall meets the Atlantic Ocean in a dramatic series of steep cliffs.

There is no end to activities available to visitors in Cornwall; surfing is a popular past-time which has attracted many people to the

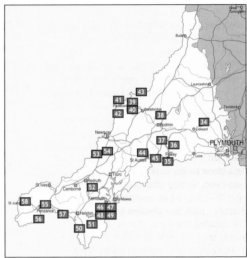

beautiful Cornish coast, and the gentle sandy beaches and many trained surfing schools offer the perfect opportunity to learn. For a calmer approach there is no better way to see the beauty of Cornwall than on foot, and the South-West Coast path provides nearly 300 miles of sign-posted footpaths of stunning variety. For cyclists, the Camel trail, which runs a level 14 miles along the Camel Estuary between Padstow, Wadebridge and Bodmin, can be a gentle and family-friendly day out.

Accommodation

Food & Drink

Continued

LAUNCESTON

Situated on the eastern edge of Bodmin Moor and close to the county border with Devon, it was here, shortly after the Norman Conquest, that William I's half-brother, Robert of Mortain, built the massive **Launceston Castle** overlooking the River Kensey. Although now in ruins, the 12-feet thick walls of the keep and tower can still be seen. Launceston also had a powerful Augustinian priory, founded beside the river in 1136; the main buildings have gone, but its chapel of ease remains.

Launceston is also the start of the **Tamar Valley Discovery Trail**, a 30-mile footpath from here to Plymouth that takes in many of the villages that litter the Cornwall-Devon border. At **St Ann's Chapel**, near Gunnislake, stands the **Tamar Valley Donkey Park**, Cornwall's only donkey sanctuary and home to more than two dozen donkeys (proudly claimed to be "Cornwall's happiest donkeys") and other rescued animals.

AROUND LAUNCESTON

CALSTOCK

12 miles SE of Launceston off the A390

Well known for its splendid views of the Tamar valley, this village was an important river port in the 19th century and its decline came with the construction of the huge Railway Viaduct which carries the picturesque Tamar Valley Line southwards to Plymouth.

Just to the southwest of Calstock is one of the best preserved medieval estates in the West Country – **Cotehele House** (National Trust), built between 1485 and 1624. Along with its Great Tudor Hall, fabulous tapestries and period furniture, the fortified granite house incorporates some charming features such as the secret spy-hole in the Great Hall and a tower clock with a bell but no face or hands. Surrounding the house are, firstly, the grounds, containing exotic and tender plants that thrive in the mild valley climate, and beyond that the estate with its ancient network of pathways that allow exploration of the valley.

The River Tamar runs through the estate and close to an old cider house and mill is **Cotehele Quay**, a busy river port in Victorian times and

Launceston Castle

now home to an outstation of the **National Maritime Museum**, an art and craft gallery and a licensed tea room. The restored Tamar sailing barge *Shamrock* is moored alongside the museum.

SALTASH

17 miles SE of Launceston on the A38

The 'Gateway to Cornwall', here the River Tamar is spanned by two mighty bridges. Designed by Isambard Kingdom Brunel in 1859, the iron-built **Royal Albert Bridge** carries the railway, while alongside is the much more slender **Tamar Bridge**, a suspension road bridge that was opened in 1961. To the south of Saltash lies **Mount Edgcumbe House**, to where the Earls of Edgcumbe moved when they left Cotehele House; it is surrounded by a country park that encompasses a stretch of heritage coast, numerous follies and one of Cornwall's greatest gardens including the national camelia collection with over 700

Mount Edgcumbe Country Park

varieties. The southernmost point of the country park takes in the stunning **Rame Head**, banked by 400 feet cliffs that guard the entrance into Plymouth Sound. Also on this peninsula is 18th century **Antony House**, home to a wonderful collection of paintings (many by Sir Joshua Reynolds), tapestries and furniture. Surrounding the house are the gardens and grounds landscaped by Humphry Repton. Recently this stunning location was chosen for the Tim Burton film adaptation of Alice in Wonderland; from which Anthony

House has adopted a Carol-esque air, with Mad Hatter tea parties and games of croquet available to visitors.

LISKEARD

13½ miles SW of Launceston on the B3254

Although it is a small town, Liskeard boasts some grand Victorian public buildings, including the Guildhall and the Public Hall, home to a local museum. In Well Street, lies one of Liskeard's most curious features – an arched grotto that marks the site of **Pipe Well**, a medieval spring reputed to have curative powers, especially for afflictions of the eye. It is said that the well has never run dry.

LOOE

20 miles SW of Launceston on the A387

The tidal harbour at Looe, created by the two rivers the East Looe and West Looe, made this an important fishing and seafaring port and it is still Cornwall's second most important port with fish auctions taking place at East Looe's famous **Banjo Pier**. East Looe is the older part, and housed in the 16th century **Old Guildhall** is the town's Museum.

The South East Cornwall Discovery Centre in West Looe introduces visitors to the wealth of wildlife, plant life and splendid scenery of the region. Nelson, a one-eyed seal who was a much loved regular visitor to Looe, is commemorated in a life-sized statue in the harbor. Looe beach is popular with tourists, and can become quite overrun on hot summer days; so for something a little different to escape the crowds catch a ferry over to Looe Island, previously owned by sisters Babs and Evelyn Atkins since 1965 when they achieved their unusual dream of

---

34 THE HAYLOFT RESTAURANT

Menheniot,
nr Liskeard

A restaurant filled with character serving freshly prepared food made with fine local ingredients

See entry on page 334

Looe River

having their own island, this area of Outstanding Natural Beauty is an isolated paradise and well worth the trip.

To the southwest of Looe is **Polperro**, many people's idea of a typical Cornish fishing village, its steep, narrow streets and alleyways filled with picturesque fisherman's cottages.

Two miles west of Looe, at Murrayton, is the famous **Monkey Sanctuary**, the world's first protected colony of Amazonian woolly monkeys.

FOWEY

24½ miles SW of Launceston on the A3082

A lovely old seafaring town, with steep, narrow streets, Fowey has one of the most

beautiful natural harbors along the south coast. The town's **Museum** is an excellent place to discover Fowey's colourful past and its literary connections: Daphne du Maurier (1907-1989) lived at Gribbin Head and Sir Arthur Quiller-Couch (1863-1944), son of a Cornish doctor, lived for over 50 years at The Haven, on the Esplanade.

To the south of Fowey lies **St Catherine's Castle**, part of a chain of fortifications that were built by Henry VIII to protect the harbours along the south coast.

Just up the River Fowey is **Golant** and the Iron Age lookout point of **Castle Dore Earthworks**, while further upstream is **Lostwithiel**, a small market town that was the capital of Cornwall in the 13th century. The strategic crossing point of the River Fowey here is protected by the surprisingly complete remains of 12th century **Restormel Castle**.

BODMIN

19½ miles SW of Launceston on the A389

Situated midway between Cornwall's two coasts and at the junction of two ancient trade routes, Bodmin has always been an important town, and Castle Canyke was built during the Iron Age to defend this important route. The foreboding building of **Bodmin**

---

35 **THE TOLL BAR**

Fowey

Stylish and contemporary, this popular bar and restaurant is best known for its glorious waterside terrace, serving delicious food throughout the day.

See entry on page 335

---

36 **THE SHIP INN**

Lerryn, nr Fowey

An olde worlde inn full of charm, friendly faces, and fresh homemade food

See entry on page 336

---

37 **THE ROYAL OAK**

Lostwithiel

Plenty of charm and character can be found at this pub which serves delicious home cooked food every day

See entry on page 337

---

38 **THE BLISLAND INN**

Blisland, nr Bodmin

A magnet for real ale connoisseurs (with an annual beer festival) and lovers of good home cooking.

see page 338

Jail, which was the last county jail in Cornwall, closing in 1927, is rich with ghost stories, and visitors continue to report strange sightings and figures appearing in photographs. A popular night ghost walk is run – though it is not recommended for the fainthearted!

To the south is **Lanhydrock House**, one of the most fascinating late 19th century houses in England, surrounded by wonderful formal gardens, woodland and parkland.

Lanhydrock House

BOLVENTOR

10½ miles SW of Launceston on the A30

Situated at the heart of **Bodmin Moor**, this scenic village is home to the former coaching inn that was immortalised by Daphne du Maurier in her famous novel, *Jamaica Inn*. Structurally little changed today, Jamaica Inn still welcomes visitors who come here not only seeking refreshment and accommodation but also to discover the secrets of the moors and the life and works of du Maurier.

Bodmin Moor is the smallest of the three great West Country moors; at 1,377 feet, **Brown Willy** is the highest point on the moor, while, just to the northwest, lies **Rough Tor**, the moor's second highest point. Throughout this wild and beautiful moorland there are remains of early occupiers, including Bronze Age hut circles and field enclosures and Iron Age hill forts.

To the south of Bolventor is the mysterious natural tarn, **Dozmary Pool**, a place that is strongly linked with the legend of King Arthur and said by some to be the place where the Lady of the Lake received the dying King's sword, Excalibur.

To the southeast lies the one-time mining village of **Minions**, and close by are the impressive **Bronze Age Hurlers Stone Circle** and **Trethevy Quoit**, an impressive enclosed chamber tomb that originally formed the core of a vast earthwork mound.

BUDE

15 miles NW of Launceston off the A39

A traditional seaside resort with sweeping expanses of sand, rock pools and Atlantic breakers, Bude has also developed into a popular surfing centre. Completed in 1820, the **Bude Canal** was an ambitious project that aimed to connect the Atlantic with the English Channel via the River Tamar. However, the only stretch to be finished was that between Bude and Launceston and it is now the Bude Canal Trail footpath.

Close to the canal's entrance stands **Bude Castle**, designed by the local 19th century physician and brilliant inventor, Sir Goldsworthy Gurney. What makes this building (now an office) particularly interesting is that it is thought to have been the first building in Britain to be constructed on sand. To celebrate the new millennium, Carole Vincent and Anthony Fanshawe designed the **Bude Light 2000**, the first large-scale public sculpture to combine coloured concrete with fibre optic lighting. To the south of Bude is one of the most dramatic places along this stretch of coastline, **Crackington Haven**, a tiny port overlooked by towering 400 feet cliffs.

Bude Haven

TINTAGEL

17 miles W of Launceston on the B3263

Tintagel Castle, set on a wild and windswept headland, is forever linked with the legend of King Arthur, and the village naturally owes much of its popularity to its Arthurian connections; one of its many interesting attractions on this theme is King Arthur's **Great Hall**. Also worth seeing here is the weather-beaten **Old Post Office**, a 14th century manor house that became a Post Office in the 19th century. Purchased by the National Trust in 1903 for £100, the building still has its original stone-paved medieval hall and ancient fireplace along with the ground floor office of the postmistress.

To the south lies the most famous slate quarry in Cornwall, **Delabole Slate Quarry**.

TRURO

The administrative and ecclesiastical centre of Cornwall, this elegant small city was once a fashionable place to rival Bath. The foundation stone of **Truro Cathedral** was laid in 1880 and this splendid Early English style building, with its celebrated Victorian stained glass window, was finally completed in 1910. The side streets of Truro offer some wonderful independent and specialist shops, brimming with unique clothes, home ware, antiques and bric-a-brac.

To the northeast lies **Probus**, a large village that is home to the 'really useful garden' – **Probus Gardens**. Here, too, is **Trewithen House and Gardens**, which were laid out in the early 20th century.

AROUND TRURO

NEWQUAY

10 miles N of Truro on the A392

A traditional English seaside resort, with all the usual trappings, Newquay also has a long history and for centuries was an important pilchard fishing village. On the Towan Headland stands a **Huer's Hut** from where the Huer would scan the sea looking for shoals of pilchards and, once spotted, he would cry 'hevva' to alert the awaiting fishing crews. Today, its beautiful rocky coastline and acres of golden sands have seen it develop into a popular seaside resort famous throughout the world for its surfing. At the end of May the whole town is flooded with people for the vibrant "Run to the Sun" festival; started in 1987 it celebrates VW and custom cars with a car show, though it has grown into an huge event which overruns Newquay.

Inland are the imposing engine house and chimney stack of **East Wheal Rose** mine, Cornwall's richest lead mine, and close by is the delightful small Elizabeth manor house, **Trerice**, which is also home to a Mower Museum.

PADSTOW

19½ miles NE of Truro on the A389

It was here that the Welsh missionary St Petroc landed in the 6th century and founded a Celtic Minster. Beginning at the door of the town's 13th century parish **Church of St Petroc**, the Saints Way is a middle-distance footpath that follows the route that was taken by travellers and pilgrims crossing

---

39 CAPTAINS COTTAGE

Padstow

Just like its owner, this small bed only is full of character, offering unbeatable hospitality and affordable en suite accommodation in Padstow's centre.

See entry on page 339

---

40 TREGEA HOTEL

Padstow

As one of the oldest buildings in Padstow, this period hotel holds both charm and convenience with all modern amenities and its very own contemporary restaurant within.

See entry on page 339

Padstow Harbour

Cornwall on their way from Brittany to Ireland.

Although the River Camel silted up in the 19th century, the Harbour remains the town's focal point and here are many of Padstow's older buildings, including **Raleigh Cottage**, where Sir Walter Raleigh lived while he was Warden of Cornwall, and the tiny Harbour Cottage. The harbour is also home to the **Shipwreck Museum**. Padstow has become a mecca for seafood chef Rick Stein enthusiasts, or indeed for anyone with a love of good seafood; he has an impressive four restaurants in the small town (The Seafood Restaurant, St Petroc's Bistro, a café and a fish & chip shop), as well as a cookery school, deli, patisserie and gift shop. When not overloading on Rick Stein, there are some pretty boutique shops and independent art galleries to explore, in addition to the usual tourist fare.

On the other side of the Camel Estuary are the small resorts of **Polzeath** and **New Polzeath** and a beautiful coastal path that takes in the cliffs and farmland of Pentire Point and Rumps Point.

The **Church of St Enodoc** is a Norman building that has, on several occasions, been virtually submerged by windblown sand. The beautiful churchyard contains the graves of many shipwrecked mariners and that of the poet Sir John Betjeman, who is buried here along with his parents. Betjeman spent many of his childhood holidays in the villages and coves around the Camel Estuary, and his affection for the local people and places was the inspiration for many of his works.

WADEBRIDGE

20 miles NE of Truro on the A39

Standing at the historic lowest bridging point on the River Camel, this ancient port and busy market town is now a popular holiday centre. The town is also home to the **Bridge on Wool**, which was constructed on bridge piers that were sunk on foundation of woolsacks; the bridge still carries the main road that links the town's two ancient parishes. The town's former railway station is now home to the **John Betjeman Centre**.

ST AUSTELL

12½ miles NE of Truro on the A390

When William Cookworthy discovered large deposits of kaolin, or china clay, in 1748, this old market town, a centre of tin and copper mining, was transformed. Over the years, the waste material from the clay pits to the north

---

41 WELL PARC HOTEL

Trevone

Warm and welcoming family run hotel that affords panoramic sea views from its popular restaurant, with fine en suite accommodation available.

See entry on page 340

---

42 TREDREA INN

Porthcothan

A cosy inn in a stunning location overlooking Porthcothan Bay with an extensive menu served either in the bar or restaurant.

See entry on page 341

---

43 LOCARNO

Port Isaac

Homely self catering accommodation nestled within the striking fishing village of Port Isaac, just five minutes' walk from the coast.

See entry on page 340

Charlestown Docks

In return for their hospitality, Wesley gave his hosts James and Mary Lelean his silver shoe buckles.

To the northwest of Mevagissey lie the famous **Lost Gardens of Heligan**, one of the country's most interesting gardens that was originally laid out in 1780 but lay undisturbed for 70 years before being rediscovered in 1990. Today, this beautiful and intriguing place is once again attracting visitors from all over the world.

and west of the town has been piled up into conical spoil heaps that have led to the area being nicknamed the Cornish Alps. More recently, action has been taken to soften the countryside and the heaps and disused pits have been landscaped with planting, undulating footpaths and nature trails.

In the heart of the Cornish Alps lies **Wheal Martyn**, an old clay works that is now home to the **Wheal Martyn China Clay Museum**. To the northeast, in the heart of the china clay area, lies the wonderful **Eden Project**, an ambitious undertaking that aims to "promote the understanding and responsible management of the vital relationship between plants, people and resources."

Rocks at Polstreath, nr Mevagissey

MEVAGISSEY

11½ miles E of Truro on the B3273

Mevagissey is the largest fishing village in St Austell Bay. Housed in a harbour building dating from 1745 are the **Mevagissey Folk Museum**, the World of Model Railway Exhibition and The Aquarium. In the 1750s, when John Wesley first came to Mevagissey to preach, he was greeted with a barrage of rotten eggs and old fish and had to be rescued from the crowd and taken to safety.

ST MAWES

7½ miles S of Truro on the A3078

This charming town in the shelter of Carrick Roads is dominated by its artillery fort, **St Mawes Castle**, which was built in the 1540s as part of Henry VIII's coastal defences.

FALMOUTH

8 miles SW of Truro on the A39

A spectacular deep-water anchorage that is the world's third largest natural harbour, Falmouth lies in Britain's Western Approaches and guards the entrance into **Carrick Roads**. Standing on a 200 feet promontory

---

44 THE SEVEN STARS

St Austell

At the centre of bustling St Austell, this lively inn is known for being the birthplace of the famous St Austell Brewery.

See entry on page 342

---

45 THE WELCOME INN

Par

A welcoming and traditional pub serving fresh homemade food with a smile

See entry on page 343

Pendennis Point

overlooking the entrance to Carrick Roads, Henry VIII's **Pendennis Castle** is one of Cornwall's great fortresses and, along with St Mawes Castle, it has protected Britain's shores from attack ever since its construction.

Falmouth's nautical and notorious past is revealed at the **National Maritime Museum Cornwall**. The town has become quite an active place for contemporary art, due in part to the renowned College of Art and Design here, and there are many interesting galleries to visit.

To the north lies **Feock**, one of the prettiest small villages in Cornwall and to the south lays **Restronguet Point**. It was from **Tolverne**, just north of Feock, that Allied troops left for the Normandy coast during the D-day landings and on the shingle beach the remains of the concrete honeycombed

mattresses can still be seen. Close by lies the estate of **Trelissick**, a privately owned 18th century house that is surrounded by marvellous gardens and parkland that offer wonderful views over Carrick Roads.

HELFORD

12½ miles SW of Truro off the B3293

A picture postcard village on the southern banks of the Helford estuary, Helford was once the haunt of smugglers, but today it is a popular sailing centre. From the village, the five-mile **Helford River Walk** takes in several isolated hamlets and a 200-year-old fig tree that grows in the churchyard at **Manaccan**.

On the northern banks of the River Helford are two glorious gardens: **Glendurgan Garden**, created in the 1820s, and **Trebah Garden** that has often been called the 'garden of dreams'.

LIZARD

22 miles SW of Truro on the A3038

The most southerly village in mainland Britain, Lizard is a place of craft shops, cafés and art galleries that lends its name to the **Lizard Peninsula**, an area that is physically separate from mainland Cornwall. The Lizard is known for its unique serpentine rock, a

---

46	BOSANNETH GUEST HOUSE

Falmouth

The aim at Bosanneth is simple – to ensure guests feel special and cared for.

See entry on page 344

47	ROSSLYN HOTEL

Falmouth

A lovely Victorian hotel that oozes charm and luxury close to Falmouth's town centre.

See entry on page 345

48	PRINCE OF WALES

Falmouth

A warm and welcoming pub in the heart of Falmouth that serves great food in cosy surroundings with live music and B&B accommodation

See entry on page 345

49	THE PIER CAFE

Falmouth

Set on the Prince of Wales pier, this is the perfect spot to indulge in a home-made Cornish cream tea.

See entry on page 346

green mineral that became fashionable in the 19th century after Queen Victoria visited Cornwall and ordered many items made from the stone for her house, Osborne, on the Isle of Wight.

To the south of the village lies **Lizard Point**, the tip of the peninsula, whose three sides are lashed by waves whatever the season.

To the northwest of Lizard, close to Mullion, is the popular sandy beach of **Poldhu Cove**, from where in 1901 Guglielmo Marconi transmitted the first wireless message from the clifftops and across the Atlantic. A granite column commemorates the event. A couple of miles inland, on **Goonhilly Downs**, is a monument to the latest in telecommunications – the **Earth Satellite Station**.

HELSTON

15 miles SW of Truro on the A394

Dating back to Roman times, this ancient stannary town also developed as a port but, today, it is best known for the famous **Festival of the Furry**, or Flora Dance, a colourful festival of music and dance with

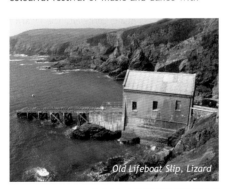
Old Lifeboat Slip, Lizard

ancient pagan connections. On the nearest Saturday to St Michael's Day (May 8th) the Flora Dance Festival is celebrated with dances led by the Helston Town Band; in the principal dances the participants wear top hat, tails and dress gowns.

Among the town's surprising number of Georgian, Regency and Victorian buildings are the **Helston Folk Museum** and 16th century Angel House, the former town house of the Godolphin family.

To the northwest lie **Trevarno Estate and Gardens**, and close by is the **Poldark Mine Heritage Complex**, with its underground tour of tunnels and the famous 18th century Poldark village.

To the east of the town is another interesting family attraction, **Flambards**, which is based around a faithful re-creation of a Victorian street. Nearby is the Royal Navy's land and sea rescue headquarters at **Culdrose**, one of the largest and busiest helicopter bases in Europe.

REDRUTH

8½ miles SW of Truro on the A393

This market town owes its past prosperity to its location – at the heart of Cornwall's mining industry – and some pockets of Victorian, Georgian and earlier buildings can still be found. In the 19th century the land around Camborne was the most intensely mined in the world with, in the 1850s, over 300 mines producing some two thirds of the world's copper! With such a history of mining it is not surprising that Camborne is home to the world famous **School of Mining** and its **Geological Museum**.

Immediately south of Redruth lies dramatic **Carn Brea**, a granite hill that rises

---

50 CAUNCE HEAD B & B

Mullion
Amazing cliff top bed and breakfast establishment with magnificent views, comfortable beds and a lovely country garden.

See entry on page 346

51 NEW YARD BISTRO

Trelowarren
A fabulous restaurant on the Trelowarren estate that prides itself on serving great food and drink with an informal setting.

See entry on page 347

some 738 feet above sea level and is crowned by a 90 feet monument to Francis Basset, a local benevolent mine and land owner. Nearby is the mysterious **Gwennap Pit**, a round, grass-covered amphitheatre that is thought to have been created by the collapse of a subterranean mine shaft.

To the north, along the coast, lie the two thriving holiday centres of **Porthtowan** and **Portreath**, which, although they developed as a copper mining village and ore exporting port respectively, are now the summer preserve of holidaymakers and surfers.

ST AGNES

8 miles NW of Truro on the B3285

Once known as the source of the finest tin in Cornwall, this old village still retains many of its original miners' cottages while, surrounding the village, are the ruins of old mine workings including the clifftop buildings of one of Cornwall's best known mines – **Wheal Coates**. The mine operated between 1860 and 1890 and the derelict Engine House is one of the more exceptional landmarks along this stretch of coast. The remains of **Wheal Kitty** provide panoramic views over this once industrial area. The tin production processes is explained on guided tours around **Blue Hills Tin Streams** at nearby **Trevellas**.

Wheal Coates, nr St Agnes

Just up the coast lies the holiday resort of **Perranporth** whose Celtic heritage is kept alive during the annual **Lowender Peran Festival** of music and dance.

In the dunes overlooking Penhale Sands, a mile from Perranporth, lies St Piran's Oratory, the oldest Christian church in the UK, burial place of the Saint who is said to have travelled from Ireland to Cornwall on a millstone. His landing place is marked by a Celtic cross.

PENZANCE

Cornwall's only promenade stretches from here to Newlyn, and other interesting buildings include the exotic **Egyptian House** created from two cottages in the 1830s, and the **Union Hotel**, where the first announcement in mainland England of the victory of Trafalgar and the death of Nelson was made. Penzance's links with the sea are remembered at the **Maritime Museum** and the **Trinity House National Lighthouse Centre**.

To the southwest lies **Newlyn**, the largest fish landing port in England. As well as being home to the **Pilchard Works Heritage**

---

52 THE LANNER INN

Lanner

A 200 year old inn steeped in history that offers great food, fine ales and en suite accommodation close to the Cornish coastline.

See entry on page 348

---

53 BOLINGEY INN

Bolingey

A very friendly and warm inn which serves excellent food and drink in a great location.

See entry on page 349

---

54 OAKRIDGE FARM

Goonhavern

Beautiful stone built Barn in peaceful countryside near the coast.

See entry on page 348

Museum, the town is known for its artistic associations: it was here in the late 19th century that the Newlyn School of art was founded.

AROUND PENZANCE

ZENNOR

5½ miles N of Penzance on the B3306

This delightful ancient village shows evidence of Bronze Age settlers and the **Wayside Folk Museum** has numerous exhibits that tell of this region's industrial past. DH Lawrence lived here with his wife Frieda during World War I and it was during his stay here, under police surveillance, that Lawrence wrote *Women in Love*. However, his pacifist tendencies and Frieda's German heritage (her cousin was the flying ace the Red Baron) caused them to be 'moved on' in October 1917.

By the porch in the church at Zennor is a memorial to John Davey, who died in 1891, stating that he was the last person to have any great knowledge of the native Cornish language Kernuack. It is said that he remained familiar with the language by speaking it to his cat. To the southeast of the village lies the Neolithic chamber tomb, **Zennor Quoit** while,

55 THE HONEY POT

Penzance

Known for its "incredible edibles," this homely café serves up the best selection of fresh homemade soups, lunches and cakes in the area.

See entry on page 350

56 THE OLD COASTGUARD HOTEL

Mousehole

A slice of luxury in this five star hotel with panoramic sea views, glorious sun terrace and a unique dining experience in the hotels own stylish restaurant.

See entry on page 352

close by, is **Chysauster Ancient Village**, a Romano-Cornish village that was built around 2,000 years ago and has one of the oldest identifiable streets in the country.

ST IVES

7 miles NE of Penzance on the A3074

Now one of the most-visited places in the county, this was once one of the most important fishing centres in Cornwall, and locally mined ores and minerals were exported from the harbour (St Ives Museum is housed in a former mine building). St Ives is home to **Tate St Ives**, dedicated to the work of 20th century painters and sculptures, and the **Barbara Hepworth Sculpture Garden and Museum**, housed in her former studio. Maritime art is a passion in St Ives; follow any of the winding streets and they will lead you to galleries showing some gorgeous contemporary art, much done by local artists.

Barbara Hepworth Sculpture Garden, St Ives

MARAZION

3 miles E of Penzance off the A394

For centuries the most important settlement around Mount's Bay, this harbour town of fine old inns and residential houses that overlook the sandy beach is now a windsurfing and sailing centre. To the northwest is **Marazion**

St Michaels Mount

be seen **Longships Lighthouse**, just off shore, and **Wolf Rock Lighthouse**, seven miles away. Just to the southeast, and protected by **Gwennap Head**, is **Porthcurno**, from where in 1870 the first telegraph cable was laid linking Britain with the rest of the world. Housed in a secret underground wartime communications centre is the **Porthcurno Wartime Telegraph Museum**. This interesting village is also home to the marvellous **Minack Theatre**, an open-air amphitheatre cut into the cliff that was founded by Rowena Cade in the 1930s.

Marsh, an RSPB reserve with breeding colonies of grey herons and visiting waders and wildfowl.

Situated a third of a mile offshore and connected to Marazion by a cobbled causeway that is exposed at high tide, **St Michael's Mount** rises dramatically out of the waters of Mount's Bay. In the 11th century, Edward the Confessor founded a priory on the mount and these remains are incorporated into the marvellous **St Michael's Mount Castle**.

LAND'S END

9 miles SW of Penzance on the A30

Mainland Britain's most westerly point and one of the country's most famous landmarks, it is here that the granite of Cornwall finally meets the Atlantic Ocean in a series of savage cliffs, reefs and sheer-sided islets. Land's End has been a tourist destination since the early 19th century, and down the years an ever-expanding complex of man-made attractions has been added to the majestic scenery that nature has provided. From this headland can

ST JUST

6½ miles NW of Penzance on the A3071

The westernmost town in mainland Britain, St Just was once a thriving mining centre, and the surrounding area is littered with industrial remains. A narrow road leads westwards to **Cape Cornwall**, the only cape in England and, along the way; the road passes the last remains of Cape Cornwall Mine – its tall chimney.

St Just marks the start of the **Tinners' Way**, an ancient trackway between the town and St Ives that follows ancient moorland paths.

To the northeast lies **Pendeen**, where tin has been mined since prehistoric times. The last of 20 or so mines in this area, **Geevor Tin Mine and Heritage Centre** not only preserves the mine but also offers visitors the chance to experience the conditions that miners had to endure underground. Also close by is the mighty **Levant Steam Engine**, housed in a tiny building perched high on the cliffs.

---

57 COVE CAFE

Praa Sands

A bright and airy cafe set on one of the most beautiful beaches in the south west offering locally sourced produce to eat in or take away.

See entry on page 351

---

58 THE QUEENS ARMS

St Just

A quality establishment with a strong focus on good food cooked to order.

See entry on page 353

CUMBRIA

The second largest county in England, Cumbria is much more than the Lake District National Park that lies within its boundaries. It was here that the British Celts managed to preserve their independence from the Saxons and the Norse influence can still be detected in the place names here. The county town, Carlisle, lies to the north, close to the Scottish border and was for centuries a base for English soldiers who planned their attacks on Scotland from here, as well as defending Carlisle from border raids. The Lake District National Park is not only home to England's largest lake, Windermere, but also to the country's highest peak, Scafell Pike; an area of magnificent crags, isolated fells and expanses of water. Of the county's coastline, the Furness Peninsula is probably the most attractive - a place of elegant and small seaside resorts and once an area of great ecclesiastical power.

Great monuments and buildings are plentiful throughout Cumbria. Be it the grandeur found in castles such as Carlisle Castle, Muncaster Castle, or the impressive shell of Lowther Castle; or the famous literary abodes, like adorable Hill Top where Beatrix Potter made her home, or Dove Cottage at Grassmere, the former home of poet William Wordsworth. Stately homes and mansions too are scattered through the county – Holker Hall being the most impressive among them. Long Meg and her Daughters, a Bronze Age

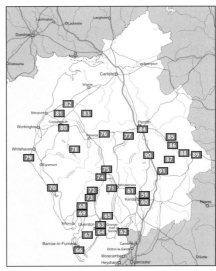

site seconded only by Stonehenge in size, is a magical place unique to the Lake District and a must see for visitors touring around Penrith. Naturally, the lakes (or 'waters' and 'meres' for the most part) are the main attraction for visitors, but Cumbria holds many other natural wonders from towering mountains and lush forests, to the scenic islands of Walney and Piel. This dramatic landscape has inspired Wordsworth and many other poets and artists; and provides some of the most beautiful and wild places to explore by foot in England.

KENDAL

The capital of south Lakeland, Kendal has royal connections: the Parr family lived at **Kendal Castle** until 1483, and it was Catherine Parr, a descendant, who became Henry VIII's last wife. Today, the castle's gaunt ruins stand high on a hill overlooking Kendal. The woollen industry, on which much of the town's prosperity was based, has long since disappeared, but there is one local product that all visitors should try: Kendal Mint Cake, a tasty, very sweet confection, sometimes covered in chocolate, that is cherished by climbers and walkers for its instant infusion of energy.

A number of interesting museums and galleries can be found in Kendal including the **Museum of Lakeland Life and Industry** and the **Abbot Hall Art Gallery** that includes the work of John Ruskin. The **Kendal Museum**, founded in 1796, is one of the oldest museums in the country and contains outstanding displays of archeology, and local history. At the town's Quaker Meeting House, the history of the Quaker Movement is told through a series of 77 panels that combine to form the **Quaker Tapestry Exhibition**.

59 SAWYERS ARMS

Kendal

An inn renowned for its warm hospitality, well kept ales and quality accommodation.

See entry on page 352

60 DICKIE DOODLES

Kendal

Open every evening from 8 till late, Dickie Doodles is a magnet for lovers of good music and well-kept ales.

See entry on page 354

AROUND KENDAL

RAVENSTONEDALE

14½ miles NE of Kendal off the A685

Known locally as Rissendale, this pretty village, clustered along the banks of Scandal Beck, lies on the edge of the Howgill Fells; its church, built in 1738, is one of the few Georgian churches in Cumbria.

SEDBERGH

9 miles E of Kendal on the A684

Although Sedbergh is in Cumbria it lies within the Yorkshire Dales National Park and the surrounding scenery is typical of the Dales. One spectacular local feature is **Cautley Crag**, a great cliff alongside which tumbles a beautiful narrow waterfall, **Cautley Spout**.

Firbank Knott, on nearby Firbank Fell, is considered to be the birthplace of Quakerism as it was here, in 1652, that George Fox gave his great sermon to inspire over a thousand 'seekers' from the whole of the north of England. The **Quaker Meeting House** is the oldest in the north of England.

Cautley Crag, Sedbergh

KIRKBY LONSDALE

11 miles SE of Kendal on the A65

There has been a bridge over the River Lune here for at least 700 years and, for centuries, it has drawn people who come here to experience what John Ruskin described as "one of the loveliest scenes in England." The subject of a painting by JMW Turner, the Devil's Bridge is said to have been built by Satan in just three days. The **Swine Market**, with its 600-year-old cross, has hosted a bustling market of traders displaying their wares every Thursday for more than 700 years.

LEVENS

4½ miles S of Kendal off the A590

To the south of the village and overlooking the Lyth valley is the superb Elizabethan mansion, **Levens Hall**, which was developed from a 14th century pele tower. Best known for its fine furniture and unique topiary gardens, it also houses a collection of working steam engines.

MILNTHORPE

7½ miles S of Kendal on the A6

Close to this market town on the A6 is the **Lakeland Wildlife Oasis** that, since opening in 1991, has established itself as one of the county's premier attractions.

GRANGE-OVER-SANDS

12 miles SW of Kendal on the B5278

This charming town on the north shore of Morecambe Bay is the starting point of the **Cistercian Way**, an interesting 33-mile long footpath through Furness to Barrow.

To the west of Grange lies **Cartmel**, one of

---

61 WILF'S CAFÉ

Staveley

Since 1997 **Wilf's Café** has been serving fresh, wholesome snacks and meals to an appreciative clientele of locals and visitors to the Lake District.

See entry on page 355

---

62 THE COMMODORE

Grange-over-Sands

Enjoying sweeping views over Morecambe Bay and offering good, wholesome food, real ales and en suite rooms.

See entry on page 356

the prettiest villages in Furness, that is dominated by the famous **Cartmel Priory** that was founded by Augustinian canons in 1188. It was dismantled in 1537, and all that is left are the substantial remains of the 12th century Gatehouse.

Just to the southwest of Grange lies Cumbria's premier stately home, **Holker Hall**, one of the homes of the Dukes of Devonshire. An intriguing blend of 16th century, Georgian and Victorian architecture, the Hall is surrounded by a large estate that includes a deer park, formal gardens and the **Lakeland Motor Museum.**

NEWBY BRIDGE

10 ½ miles SW of Kendal on the A592

The bridge here crosses the River Leven that runs from the southern tip of Windermere into Morecambe Bay, and visitors to this popular tourist destination can reach the famous lake by taking a steam train on the **Lakeside and Haverthwaite Railway.** Just to the north is Fell Foot Park, delightful landscaped gardens and woodlands that were laid out in the late 19th century.

ULVERSTON

17½ miles SW of Kendal on the A590

Ulverston boasts England's shortest, widest

and deepest canal, built by the engineer John Rennie in late 18th century. Crowning a hill to the north of the town centre is the **Barrow Monument**, a 100 feet-high replica of the Eddystone Lighthouse that was erected in 1850 to commemorate the explorer, diplomat and author Sir John Barrow. He served as a Lord of the Admiralty and it was his naval reforms that contributed to England's success in the Napoleonic Wars.

Even more famous was Stanley Jefferson, who was born in Argyle Street on 16 June 1890. Better known as Stan Laurel, he made more than 100 films in a 30-year career with his partner Oliver Hardy, and visitors can learn all about this celebrated duo in the town's **Laurel and Hardy Museum.**

BARROW-IN-FURNESS

24 miles SW of Kendal on the A590

Right up until the early 1800s, Barrow-in-

---

65 THE ANGLERS ARMS

Haverthwaite

In the heart of the beautiful Lake District National Park, food and drink are important contributors to the success of this thriving establishment.

See entry on page 359

---

63 THE STAN LAUREL INN

Ulverston

Comprises 3 rooms downstairs and 3 rooms upstairs for B&B guests with a superb dining area adorned with numerous Laurel & Hardy photographs and memorabilia.

See entry on page 357

---

66 THE BRIDGE CAFÉ

Barrow-in-Furness

Quality home cooking at café sited by Barrow's superb Dock Museum.

See entry on page 358

---

64 GILLAM'S TEA ROOM & GARDEN

Ulverston

Outstanding traditional tearoom in delightful 18th century building.

See entry on page 358

---

67 THE DERBY ARMS

Great Urswick

Ideally situated for exploring the scenic and historic delights of the Lake District with four quiet, comfortable en suite guest rooms.

See entry on page 360

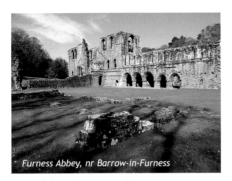
Furness Abbey, nr Barrow-in-Furness

black-backed gulls in Europe. Across the water from Walney can be seen the stark ruins of **Piel Castle**, on the small Piel Island. This house, fortified in the early part of the 14th century, was used as one of Furness Abbey's warehouses to offer protection from raiders; and was later found to also be protected from the King's Customs when it was utilized by the smuggling trade.

BROUGHTON-IN-FURNESS

19 miles W of Kendal on the A595

Some of the Lake District's finest scenery lies within easy reach of Broughton. A couple of miles west of the town is **Swinside Circle**, a fine prehistoric stone monument, 60 feet in diameter, while, to the north, in the peaceful hamlet of Broughton Mills, is the **Coleridge Trail**. During his 'circumcursion' of Lakeland in August 1802, the poet stopped to refresh himself at the Blacksmith's Arms here and the inn, built in 1748, has outwardly changed little since his visit.

RAVENGLASS

27 miles W of Kendal on the A595

The town's major attraction is the 15-inch narrow gauge **Ravenglass and Eskdale Railway** that runs for seven miles up the valleys of the Mite and Esk. One of the few

Furness was just a tiny hamlet but, in just 40 years, it became the largest iron and steel centre in the world and also a major shipbuilding centre. The impressive **Dock Museum** tells the story of the town through a series of audio-visual displays and an interactive film show brings to life the people who made Barrow so successful.

Furness Abbey, a magnificent ruin of red sandstone, is the focal point of south Cumbria's monastic heritage. Another historic building nearby is Dalton Castle, a 14th century pele tower that provided a refuge for the monks of the abbey against Scottish raiders.

To the south of Barrow lies the **Isle of Walney**, a 10-mile long island joined to the peninsula by a bridge from Barrow that is home to two important nature reserves: **North Walney National Nature Reserve**, with a great variety of habitats, including sand dunes, heath, salt marsh and shingle; and **South Walney Nature Reserve**, the largest nesting grounds of herring gulls and lesser

Piel Island & Castle, Barrow-in-Furness

68 THE BLACK COCK INN

Broughton-in-Furness

Inn with wonderful traditional ambiance offering excellent food, real ales and en suite rooms.

See entry on page 360

69 THE HIGH CROSS INN

Broughton-in-Furness

Traditional country inn offering excellent cuisine, real ales, beer terrace and beautiful en suite rooms.

See entry on page 361

Muncaster Castle, Ravenglass

WINDERMERE

8 miles NW of Kendal on the A591

The village was originally called Birthwaite, but when the railway arrived in 1847 the Kendal and Windermere Railway Company named the station after the nearby lake even though it was over a mile away. Within a few yards of Windermere Station (now serving a single-track branch line) is a footpath that leads through woodland to one of the finest viewpoints in Lakeland – Orrest Head.

Just to the north of Windermere is the village of **Troutbeck**, a designated conservation area with attractive old houses and cottages grouped around a number of wells and springs that, until recently, formed the only water supply. The best-known building here is **Townend**, an enchanting example of Cumbrian vernacular architecture.

Now all but merged with Windermere, **Bowness-on-Windermere** is an attractive town right on the edge of the lake; it is from

settlements on the route of the railway is Eskdale Green and close by are a group of buildings that make up Eskdale Mill where cereals have been ground since 1578 and which is in full working order.

Owned by the Pennington family since 1208, **Muncaster Castle**, just east of Ravenglass, is not only famous for its many treasures - including outstanding collections of tapestry, silver and porcelain - but also for its vast and beautiful grounds, which include an Owl Centre.

A focal point for fishing, beach casting, wind surfing and water skiing, **Seascale**, up the coast from Ravenglass, is one of the most popular seaside villages in Cumbria. Its Victorian wooden jetty was restored to mark the Millennium.

Lake Windermere

70 THE VICTORIA HOTEL

Drigg

A family run country hotel offering comfortable rooms at affordable prices, tasty home cooked food and a well stocked bar.

See entry on page 362

71 LAKES LODGE

Windermere

Two excellent offerings in one: a comfortable, well-appointed B&B hotel and tours by luxury mini-coach.

See entry on page 363

here that most of the lake cruises operate. Along with all the boating activity, the town is also home to the **Windermere Steamboat Museum** with its unique collection of Victorian and Edwardian steam launches, some of them still in working order. Just down the road from the museum is the **Old Laundry Visitor Centre**, the home of **The World of Beatrix Potter** where there are some fascinating re-creations of this much loved Lakeland author's books.

HAWKSHEAD

11 miles NW of Kendal on the B5285

It was in this charming little village at the head of Esthwaite Water that Beatrix Potter's solicitor husband, William Heelis, had his office; this is now **The Beatrix Potter Gallery**, which features an exhibition of her original drawings and illustrations along with details of her life. Using the royalties from her first book, *The Tale of Peter Rabbit*, Beatrix Potter purchased **Hill Top** in the village of Near Sawrey, having fallen in love with the place during a holiday. In accordance with her will, Hill Top has remained just as she would have known it and it is now full of Beatrix Potter memorabilia.

To the southwest of Hawkshead lies **Grizedale Forest**, acquired by the Forestry Commission in 1934 and famous for its 80 tree sculptures. The **Grizedale Forest Visitor Centre** contains some interesting displays and useful information for anyone navigating the forest, as well as a restaurant with a stunning picture window and terrace facing out into the deep green backdrop.

CONISTON

14 miles NW of Kendal on the A593

To the south of the once major copper mining

centre of Coniston is Coniston Hall, the village's oldest building. But it is the **Ruskin Museum** that draws most visitors to the village. Containing many of the famous man's studies, pictures, letters and photographs, as well as his collection of geological specimens, the museum is a fitting tribute to one of its most famous residents.

Coniston Water also has tragic associations with Sir Donald Campbell who, in 1955, had broken the world water speed record here. Some 12 years later, in an attempt to beat his own record, his boat, *Bluebird*, crashed while travelling at 320 miles per hour. In March 2001 his widow was present as the tailfin of the boat was hauled to the surface after 34 years. Campbell's body was recovered later and was buried in the village cemetery on September 12th 2001 - an event overshadowed by the tragic events in New York and Washington the day before.

Today, boats on Coniston Water are limited to 10 miles per hour, an ideal speed for the wonderful old steamship, the *Gondola*, which was built in 1859 and was restored by the National Trust in 1980.

AMBLESIDE

11½ miles NW of Kendal on the A591

The centre of the town is a conservation area and contains the town's most picturesque building. The **Bridge House**, a tiny cottage perched on a packhorse bridge, is now an information centre, but in the 1850s it was the home of Mr and Mrs Rigg and their six children. Close by, at **Adrian Sankey's Glass Works**, visitors can watch glass being made in the traditional way and admire the restored water mill that stands next to the studio. A short walk leads to the **Armitt Museum**,

72 THE SUN HOTEL

Coniston

Character and quality combine at a high level at this welcoming hotel with its own classic Lakeland pub next door.

See entry on page 364

73 THE CHURCH HOUSE INN

Torver

15th century inn with lots of charm offering outstanding food, real ales and en suite rooms.

See entry on page 363

74 THE OLD DUNGEON GHYLL HOTEL

Great Langdale, nr Ambleside

A perfect base for walkers, climbers and tourists in a dramatic setting at the head of Great Langdale Valley.

See entry on page 365

dedicated to the area's history since Roman times and to John Ruskin and Beatrix Potter. The **Homes of Football** is an exhibition of football memorabilia that covers the game from the very top level right down to amateur village football. Real sporting activity takes place in the summer in the famous Ambleside Sports, featuring traditional sports such as carriage driving, ferret and pigeon racing, Cumberland and Westmorland wrestling (a bit like sumo but thinner), fell racing and hound trailing. The main road leading northwards from the town climbs sharply up to the dramatic **Kirkstone Pass** that is so called because of the rock at the top (almost 1,500 feet above sea level) which looks like a church steeple.

GRASMERE

15 miles NW of Kendal on the A591

With one of the finest settings in all Lakeland, this compact rough-stone village is one of the most popular in the Lake District. Although it is the glorious scenery that draws many here, it is also its associations with Wordsworth, who lived at the tiny **Dove Cottage** from 1799 to 1808; in dire poverty he was obliged to line the walls with newspaper

Dove Cottage, Grasmere

for warmth. Today, this place of pilgrimage has been preserved intact, and next door is an award-winning museum dedicated to the poet's life and works.

Grief stricken after the death of their two young children, Mary and William Wordsworth moved from Grasmere to Rydal Mount in 1813, a handsome house overlooking tiny Rydal Water that lies just to the east of the village. The interior of the house has changed little since Wordsworth's day and it contains first editions of his works and personal possessions. The graves of Wordsworth and his sister Dorothy are in **St Oswald's Churchyard**, while a notable occupant of the town cemetery is William Archibald Spooner, sometime Warden of New College, Oxford. He gave his name to Spoonerisms and produced gems such as 'You have hissed all my mystery lessons' or 'Yes indeed: the Lord is a shoving leopard'.

KESWICK

The undisputed capital of the Lake District, Keswick has been a magnet for tourists since the mid 1700s and was given a huge lift by the Lakeland poets in the early 19th century. The grandeur of the setting is the biggest draw, but Keswick also offers man-made attractions; including the fascinating **Cumberland Pencil Museum** that draws boasts the largest pencil in the world; the **Cars of the Stars Museum** that contains (among many others) Bond's Aston Martin, the Batmobile and Chitty Chitty Bang Bang; and the popular **Theatre by the Lake** that hosts a year-round programme of plays, concerts, exhibitions, readings and talks. Another attraction lies east of the town: this is

---

75 DALE LODGE HOTEL

Grasmere

Family-owned and run hotel in idyllic village offering quality food, real ales and beautifully appointed en suite rooms.

See entry on page 366

---

76 THE WHITE HORSE

Keswick

Dating back to 1610, this charming inn offers a delightful array of homemade food, real ales, an unbeatable atmosphere and picturesque views.

See entry on page 367

Castlerigg Stone Circle, some of whose 38 standing stones are 8 feet high. Close by is the charming village of Threlkeld, the ideal starting point for a number of mountain walks, including an ascent of Blencathra.

Running south from Keswick is Borrowdale, home to the extraordinary Bowder Stone, a massive cube-shaped boulder weighing almost 2,000 tons that stands precariously on one corner apparently defying gravity.

AROUND KESWICK

POOLEY BRIDGE

12 miles E of Keswick on the B5320

This charming village stands at the northern tip of Ullswater and there are regular cruise departures from here during the season, stopping at Glenridding and Howton. Along the northern shore of the lake is a series of waterfalls that tumble down through a wooded gorge, known collectively by the name of the largest fall, **Aira Force**. The southern end of Ullswater is overshadowed by **Helvellyn** (3,115 feet) and an assault on its summit is best tackled from Glenridding.

---

77 PARK FOOT

Pooley Bridge

Offering the very best in caravan, camping and self-catering at site overlooking Ullswater.

See entry on page 366

---

78 DALEGARTH GUEST HOUSE AND CAMPSITE

Cockermouth

Offering 9 bedrooms, friendly hosts, hearty breakfasts and a 35 pitch campsite, Dalegarth is ideal for anyone wishing to visit this part of Cumbria.

See entry on page 368

It was while walking by Ullswater with his sister Dorothy that William Wordsworth came upon a mass of daffodils that inspired him to write the much-loved poem '*I wandered lonely as a cloud*'. In spring the banks of Ullswater still come alive with masses of daffodils.

BAMPTON

15 miles SE of Keswick off the A6

To the south of Bampton, lies **Haweswater**, the most easterly of the lakes - actually it's a reservoir, created in the late 1930s to supply the growing needs of industrial Manchester.

BUTTERMERE

8 miles SW of Keswick on the B5289

To many connoisseurs of the Lake District landscape, Buttermere is the most splendid of all the Lakes. The walk around Buttermere gives superb views of the eastern towers of **Fleetwith Pike** and the great fell wall made up of High Crag, High Stile, and Red Pike. Fed by both Buttermere and Loweswater, **Crummock Water** is by far the largest of the three lakes and its attractions can usually be enjoyed in solitude.

Buttermere with Fleetwith Pike

WHITEHAVEN

19 miles SW of Keswick on the A595

A handsome Georgian town which by the mid-1700s had become the third largest port in Britain, but the harbour's shallow draught halted further expansion. The harbour is now a conservation area and **The Beacon** tells the history of the town and its harbour. Also here are the **Harbour Gallery**, with an ongoing arts program; the **Met Office Gallery**, where visitors can monitor, forecast and broadcast the weather; and **The Rum Story**, which chronicles the town's connections with the Caribbean, housed in the original location of 1785.

To the south lies **St Bees Head**, a red sandstone bluff that forms one of the most dramatic natural features along the entire coast of northwest England. From here the 190-mile **Coast to Coast Walk** starts on its long journey across the Pennines to Robin Hood's Bay in North Yorkshire. **St Bees Head** is now an important nature reserve and the cliffs are crowded with guillemots, razorbills, kittiwakes, gulls, gannets and skuas.

Just inland from Whitehaven is the pretty town of **Egremont**, dominated by its 12th century Castle.

BRAITHWAITE

3 miles W of Keswick on the B5292

This small village lies at the foot of the **Whinlatter Pass**, another of Cumbria's dramatic routes, with a summit some 1,043 feet above sea level. The road also runs through **Whinlatter Forest Park**, the only Mountain Forest in England and one of the Forestry Commission's oldest woodlands.

MARYPORT

17 miles NW of Keswick on the A596

Dramatically located on the Solway Firth, Maryport is a charming Cumbrian coastal town rich in interest and maritime history. Some of the first visitors to Maryport were the Romans who built a clifftop fort here, **Alauna**, which is now part of the **Hadrian's Wall World**

Heritage Site. The award-winning **Senhouse Roman Museum** tells the story of life in this outpost of the empire.

COCKERMOUTH

10 miles NW of Keswick on the A66

A delightful market town since 1226, Cockermouth was the birthplace in the 1770s of both Fletcher Christian, who was to lead the mutiny on the *Bounty*, and William Wordsworth. The house in which the latter was born is now called **Wordsworth House** and contains a few of the poet's personal possessions.

Sadly, since the disastrous floods which hit the town in November 2009, Cockermouth is in the process of cleaning up and repairing the extensive damage, which could take some time. It is therefore advisable to phone the tourist information centre there (01900

---

80 THE BUSH

Cockermouth

With local brews, welcoming staff, exceptional food and a convivial atmosphere, a visit to The Bush will not disappoint!

See entry on page 368

---

81 THE BEECHES CARAVAN PARK

Gilcrux

Set in 2 acres of grounds, Beeches Caravan Park offers a perfect base for those wishing to explore the local area. Onsite facilities include a post office, shop, laundry service, restaurant and bar.

See entry on page 370

---

79 HARTLEY'S BEACH SHOP AND TEAROOM

St Bees

Friendly family-run business serving wholesome home-made food and selling walking and camping essentials.

See entry on page 369

---

82 BRANDRAW HOUSE

Aspatria

Stunning late Victorian bed and breakfast, perfect for short breaks or family holidays in Cumbria.

See entry on page 370

822634) before you visit, to avoid any disappointment.

Woolfest is still being held, just outside of Cockermouth at the Mitchells Lakeland Livestock Centre, at the end of June; celebrating all aspects of natural fibres - their sources, uses and products.

BASSENTHWAITE LAKE

4 miles NW of Keswick on the A66

Here's one for the Pub Quiz: Which is the only lake in the Lake District? Answer: Bassenthwaite, because all the others are either Waters or Meres. Only 70 feet deep and with borders rich in vegetation, Bassenthwaite provides an ideal habitat for birds - more than 70 species have been recorded around the lake.

At the northern end of the lake, at Coalbeck Farm, **Trotters World of Animals** is home to many hundreds of animals - rare breeds, traditional farm favourites, endangered species, birds of prey and reptiles.

On the eastern shore of Bassenthwaite Lake is the secluded **Church of St Bridget & St Bega** which Tennyson had in mind when, in his poem *Morte d'Arthur*, he describes Sir Bedivere carrying the dead King Arthur: "to a chapel in the fields, A broken chancel with a broken cross, That stood on a dark strait of barren land".

CALDBECK

13 miles N of Keswick on the B5299

Caldbeck is closely linked with John Peel, the famous huntsman who died in 1854 after falling from his horse and is buried in the churchyard here. His ornate tombstone is decorated with depictions of hunting horns and his favourite hound.

It was John Peel's great friend and drinking companion John Graves who wrote the words to the song that remembers the huntsman:

'D'ye ken John Peel with his coat so gray?
D'ye ken John Peel at the break of day?
D'ye ken John Peel when he's far away
With his hounds and his horn in the morning?'

Also buried here are John Peel's wife

Mary and their four children. Some 200 years ago Caldbeck was an industrial village, with corn mills, woollen mills, and a paper mill all powered by the fast-flowing 'cold stream' - the **Caldbeck Priest's Mill**, built in 1702 by the Rector of Caldbeck, next to his church, was a stone grinding corn mill, powered by a waterwheel which has now been restored to working order.

ULDALE

11 miles N of Keswick off the A591

To the northeast of Bassenthwaite Lake stretches the area known locally as the 'Land Back of Skidda', a crescent of fells and valleys constituting the most northerly part of the Lake District National Park.

PENRITH

The Saxon capital of the Kingdom of Cumbria, Penrith was sacked several times by the Scots and by the time of the Civil War **Penrith Castle** was in a ruined state. Cromwell's troops destroyed what was left but, today, the ruins remain impressive, standing high above a steep-sided moat. Other buildings in

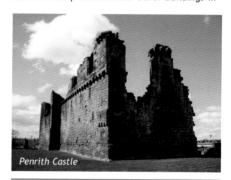

Penrith Castle

83 PONDEROSA GUEST HOUSE

Uldale

Located in a picturesque, peaceful location, Ponderosa guest house offers 2 comfortable en-suite bedrooms, as well as an adjacent self catering cottage.

See entry on page 371

the town include the Town Hall that is the result of a 1905 conversion of two former Adam-style houses, one of which was known as Wordsworth House as it was the home of the poet's cousin, Captain John Wordsworth.

Rheged Discovery Centre dedicates itself to 2,000 years of Cumbria's history, mystery and magic. A journey into the land of quaint at the **Lilliput Lane Visitors Centre** may not be for everyone, but a definite joy for some. Housed in the charming thatched Honeysuckle Cottage, it contains a huge collection of the miniature cottages, including a special model of Dove Cottage; Wordsworth's house at Grasmere.

The town of Penrith is dominated by **Beacon Hill Pike**, which stands amidst wooded slopes high above Penrith. The tower was built in 1719 and marks the place where, since 1296, beacons were lit to warn the townsfolk of an impending attack. To the

southeast of the town are the substantial remains of Brougham Castle standing on the foundations of a Roman fort.

AROUND PENRITH

LITTLE SALKELD

6 miles NE of Penrith off the A686

Close to the village are **Long Meg and her Daughters**, a most impressive Bronze Age site and second only to Stonehenge in size. There are more than 60 stones in the circle and the tallest, Long Meg, is 15 feet high.

Just to the south, in the village of **Edenhall**, is a Plague Cross that stands where there was once a basin filled with vinegar. This acted as a disinfectant into which plague victims put their money to pay for food from the people of Penrith.

APPLEBY-IN-WESTMORLAND

12 miles SE of Penrith on the B6260

The old county town of Westmorland, Appleby was originally built by the Norman, Ranulph de Meschines, who set it within a broad loop of the River Eden that protects it on three sides. The fourth side is guarded by Castle Hill: at its foot is 16th century Moot Hall and

---

84 **SCOTT'S FISH BAR AND STEAKHOUSE GRILL**

Penrith

This popular establishment offers an array of chip shop classics, wonderful steaks and other mouth-watering dishes.

See entry on page 371

---

85 **THE NEW INN COUNTRY PUB**

Appleby-in-Westmorland

A charming establishment serving real ales and exceptional food.

See entry on page 370

---

86 **CROWN AND CUSHION INN**

Appleby-in-Westmorland

Behind the typical Westmorland frontage, the inn offers superb accommodation, homemade traditional pub grub and real ales.

See entry on page 372

---

87 **THE THREE GREYHOUNDS INN**

Great Asby, nr Appleby-in-Westmorland

This is a picture postcard inn offering the very best in hospitality, real ales and traditional pub grub.

See entry on page 372

---

88 **SANDFORD ARMS**

Sandford, nr Appleby-in-Westmorland

A beautiful B&B, self-catering cottage and restaurant located in a charming village by the River Eden.

See entry on page 373

---

at its head rises the great Norman keep of Appleby Castle.

Appleby is best known for its **Gypsy Horse Fair**, when hundreds of gypsies flood into the little town with their caravans and horse-drawn carts. The trade, principally in horses, and the trotting races provide a picturesque and colourful spectacle.

KIRKBY STEPHEN

21 miles SE of Penrith on the A685

Surrounded by spectacular scenery, inside the church in this old market town, is the 10th century **Loki Stone**, one of only two such carvings in Europe to have survived. Loki was a Norse God and presumably Viking settlers brought their belief in Loki to Kirkby Stephen.

LOWTHER

4 miles S of Penrith off the A6

Lowther is the estate village to **Lowther Castle**, a once grand, fairytale-esque place that is now only an eerie shell. It was clearly once grand, as after one visit Queen Victoria is reputed to have said that she would not return as it was too grand for her. The grounds include the **Lakeland Bird of Prey Centre**, whose aim is to conserve birds of prey through education, breeding and caring for injured or orphaned birds before releasing them back into the wild. There have been talks of starting the restoration of this glorious building, and its extensive gardens, for some time, and finally in 2009 a £9 million project for the castle was approved.

SHAP

10 miles S of Penrith on the A6

In the stage coaching era Shap was an

important staging post for the coaches before they tackled the daunting climb up **Shap Fell** to its summit, some 850 feet above sea level. Much earlier, in medieval times, the village was even more significant because of nearby **Shap Abbey**, the last abbey to be consecrated in England (about 1199) and the last to be dissolved, in 1540. The nearby 16th century Keld Chapel was built by the monks of Shap Abbey.

GREYSTOKE

5 miles W of Penrith on the B5288

According to Edgar Rice Burroughs, **Greystoke Castle** was the ancestral home of Tarzan, Lord of the Apes, a fiction that was perpetuated in the dismal 1984 film Greystoke. Greystoke village itself is a gem, its attractive houses grouped around a trimly maintained village green. Nearby are the stables where Gordon Richards trained his two Grand National winners, Lucius and Hello Dandy.

CARLISLE

Carlisle was a major Roman centre that supported the military base that guarded the western end of Hadrian's Wall, and today the squat outline of 12th century **Carlisle Castle**

---

90 **THE GREYHOUND HOTEL**

Shap

Famous Westmorland hostelry offering excellent food, traditional hand-pulled ales, and en suite rooms.

See entry on page 374

---

89 **CHOFH'S TEAROOM & TAKEAWAY**

Brough

Well-established popular tearoom serving delicious locally sourced food.

See entry on page 373

---

91 **THE GEORGE HOTEL**

Orton

Traditional inn in picturesque village offering good home cooking, real ales and en suite rooms.

See entry on page 374

---

dominates the skyline of this fascinating city. After the Civil War, Cromwell's troops took the unusual step of rebuilding the Castle rather than demolishing it. Although one of the smallest in England, **Carlisle Cathedral** has many interesting features, including an exquisite east window that is considered to be one of the finest in Europe. It was here that Edward I excommunicated Robert the Bruce, and the bells were rung to welcome Bonnie Prince Charlie in 1745. The award-winning **Tullie House Museum & Art Gallery**, close to the cathedral, tells the fascinating story of the notorious Border Reivers, who occupied the lands from the 14th to the 17th century, with a law - or rather, a lack of it - unto themselves. Their treacherous deeds have also added such words as 'bereave' and 'blackmail' to the English language. The first railway to Carlisle opened as early as 1836 and today it is still an important centre of communications. It is also the northern terminus of the famous **Settle to Carlisle Railway** line, which takes in some of the most dramatic scenery that the north of England has to offer.

AROUND CARLISLE

BEWCASTLE

14 miles NE of Carlisle off the B6318

Now occupied by the ruins of a Norman Castle, a Roman fort once stood here, guarding the crossing over Kirk Beck. A more impressive reminder of the past stands in the village churchyard – **Bewcastle Cross**, erected around AD 670 and one of the oldest and finest stone crosses in Europe.

BRAMPTON

8½ miles NE of Carlisle on the A6071

To the east of this delightful little town, nestling in the heart of Irthing Valley, is **Lanercost Priory**, founded in 1166 by Robert de Vaux. An impressive red sandstone ruin set in secluded woodland, the priory suffered greatly in the border raids of the 13th and

14th centuries, one of them led by William Wallace. When the priory closed in 1536 much of its masonry was used for local houses.

South of Brampton are **Gelt Woods**, lying in a deep sandstone ravine carved by the fast-flowing River Gelt; most interesting is the **quarry** alongside the river, from which stone for Hadrian's Wall was quarried – herringbone pattern of chisel marks still visible along its face. Close by is **Talkin Tarn**, now the focus of a 120-acre country park, which has been a popular place for water sports for over 100 years.

GILSLAND

15 miles NE of Carlisle on the B6318

Located in one of the most picturesque settings along the whole length of Hadrian's Wall and overlooking the River Irthing, **Birdoswald Roman Fort** is one of the best preserved mile-castles along the wall. Set high on a plateau with magnificent views over the surrounding countryside, the early turf wall, built in AD 122, can be seen along with the fort, where all the components of the Roman frontier system can still be seen.

WIGTON

10½ miles SW of Carlisle off the A596

The pleasant market town of Wigton has, for centuries, been the centre of the business and social life of the Solway coast and plain, its prosperity being based on the weaving of cotton and linen. In the Market Place is the magnificent Memorial Fountain that was erected in 1872 by the philanthropist George Moore in memory of his wife.

SILLOTH

18½ miles W of Carlisle on the B5300

This charming old port and Victorian seaside resort has a two-mile-long promenade that provides wonderful views of the Solway Firth and the coast of Scotland. A popular attraction is the **Solway Coast Discovery Centre**, where Michael the Monk and Oyk the Oystercatcher guide visitors through 10,000 years of local history.

Derbyshire was at the forefront of modern thinking at the beginning of the Industrial Revolution, and the chief inheritor of this legacy is the county town of Derby, the home of Rolls-Royce and Royal Crown Derby porcelain; and now to many wonderful museums plotting this age of production. Derby attracts many paranormal enthusiasts due to its status as most haunted town in the UK, and the many eerie stories and haunted locations to be discovered are of interest to any visitor.

Ruins are abound through the county, remaining as mournful relics of the ages. Those such as the Norman ruins of Peveril Castle above Castleton, manage to remain and offer some gorgeous locations for visitors to enjoy; less fortunate however are ruins such as Riber Castle in Matlock, which become too dangerous and expensive to maintain and so are demolished or, in Riber Castle's case, are converted into apartments. An unusual case is that of Calke Abbey owned by the National Trust, which has been allowed to fall into gradual disrepair since 1924, preserved in the exact state the last occupant left it in; it must be seen to be believed!

Much of the county is dominated by the Peak District National Park, the first of the ten National Parks, whose landscape changes from deep limestone valleys to bleak, desolate moorland. Along with numerous attractive villages and small towns, ancient

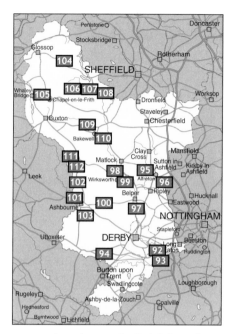

monuments and caves, the Park is home to two of the finest stately homes not just in Derbyshire but in the whole country – Haddon Hall and Chatsworth. There are two impressive Bronze Age stone circles in this area; Arbor Low and the Nine Ladies; the name of the latter comes from a story told of nine ladies who were turned to stone in punishment for dancing on a Sunday.

Accommodation

Accommodation

Continued

Food & Drink

Food & Drink

DERBY

As you would expect from a city officially voted the most haunted in the UK, Derby has a rich, and sometimes dark, history – which is gloriously illuminated for visitors through its many museums and heritage centres. For anyone coming to the city with an interest in its ghostly reputation, the first place to visit should be the **Derby Gaol**, which has been restored as close to the original Gaol as possible; with two cells which have the original doors, complete with the prisoners' original 'graffiti' - names, dates, and day markers etched into the wood, marking down

Derby Guildhall at Night

how many days the prisoner had until execution. The Gaol also runs very popular "ghost walks" around the city at night, which they do year round.

Beneath the **Guildhall**, now a theatre which attracts big names in music, comedy and drama, is a labyrinth of tunnels and catacombs. One of the tunnels used to link the old police lock-up to the Assize Courts (at that time in the Guildhall). Many prisoners would have trudged along those dark, dank tunnels, where they were sentenced, and then trudged back to be taken away and executed, transported, or imprisoned. It is no surprise then, that there have been many reports of ghostly apparitions and disembodied footsteps inside these tunnels.

Further trips into Derby's past, including a vibrant history of industry, can be found at a number of brilliant museums. The **Museum of Industry and History** is on the site of the world's oldest factories, the Silk Mills built by George Sorocold in 1702 and 1717. The foundations and parts of the tower from the 1717 mill are still visible. Rolls-Royce is of particular interest here; the city being famously linked to the name since the first of their motor-cars was built here (a Silver Ghost!). Among the exhibits are some great displays on the development of the Rolls-Royce aero engine.

Another famous name associated with Derby is Royal Crown Derby china; guided tours round the **Royal Crown Derby** factory, museum and shop offer an intriguing insight into the high level of skill required to create the delicate flower petals, hand-gilt plates and hand-painted porcelain, which is so instantly recognisable.

The city's **Cathedral of All Saints** possesses a fine 16th century tower, the second highest Perpendicular tower in England. Its treasures include a beautiful wrought iron screen by Robert Bakewell.

One of Derby's most interesting museums is **Pickford House**, situated on the city's finest Georgian street. Built in 1770 by the architect Joseph Pickford as a combined family home and place of work, the house offers an insight into the everyday lives of a middle-class family during the 1830s.

Melbourne Hall

AROUND DERBY

ILKESTON

8 miles NE of Derby on the A6007

The third largest town in Derbyshire, Ilkeston received its royal charter for a market and fair in 1252 and both have continued to the present day. Once a mining and lace-making centre, its history is told in the **Erewash Museum**, which is free to enter.

OCKBROOK

4 miles E of Derby off the A52

In this quiet village, a Moravian Settlement was founded in the mid-18th century when a congregation of the Moravian Church was formed. The Settlement has several fine buildings, including The Manse, built in 1822, and the Moravian Chapel.

To the north are the ruins of **Dale Abbey**, founded by Augustinian monks in the 13th century. The **Church of All Saints**, at Dale, is surely the only church in England that shares its roof with a farm.

MELBOURNE

6½ miles S of Derby off the B587

Melbourne's most famous son is Thomas Cook, who pioneered personally conducted tours and gave his name to the famous worldwide travel company. In 1841 Thomas Cook organised a trip from Leicester to

Loughborough for a temperance rally. 570 passengers each paid one shilling (5p).

The birthplace of the 19th century statesman Lord Melbourne, and also the home of Lady Caroline Lamb, **Melbourne Hall** is another fine building in this area of Derbyshire. The hall is surrounded by beautiful gardens, whose most notable feature is a wrought-iron birdcage pergola built in the early 1700s by Robert Bakewell.

To the south is the large Baroque mansion of **Calke Abbey** (National Trust) that has been dubbed the 'house that time forgot' as, since the death of the owner Sir Vauncy Harpur-Crewe in 1924, the house has been kept as he left it. In an exception to their usual policy, the Trust decided not to restore the house to its state of former grandeur; instead, they are simply preserving it in the exact state in

---

92 **THE SHAKESPEARE INN AND RESTAURANT**

Shardlow

Located by the marina in historic Shardlow, this inn offers up real ale and fine food in its own restaurant.

See entry on page 375

---

93 **THE OLD CROWN INN**

Cavendish Bridge, nr Shardlow

Beautiful olde worlde family run inn known for its large array of real ales, beer festivals and delicious food.

See entry on page 376

which they found it, as a sort of monument both to the eccentric family that lived there, and to all the other historic houses that were lost due to the massive cost of maintaining them. Sir Harpur-Crewe was an obsessive collector, and as so the rooms are brimming with stuffed birds and other taxidermy, preserved botanical specimens, child memorabilia, and paintings. The extensive gardens include a restored orangery.

REPTON

7 miles SW of Derby off the B5008

Repton, on the banks of the Trent, was established as the capital of the Saxon kingdom of Mercia in the 7th century, and a monastery founded. The parish **Church of St Wystan** is famous for its chancel and crypt, which claims to be one of the oldest intact Anglo-Saxon buildings in England.

Cromford Mill, Matlock

MATLOCK

Essentially a Victorian town, Matlock nestles in the lower valley of the River Derwent and is the administrative centre of Derbyshire as well as being a busy tourist centre bordering the Peak District National Park. Matlock once had the steepest gradient tramway in the world: the Depot can still be seen at the top of Bank Street. **Peak Rail** is a rebuilt, refurbished and now preserved steam railway running between Matlock Riverside station to its other terminus Rowsley South.

High up on the hill behind the town is the brooding ruin of **Riber Castle**, built in the 1860s by John Smedley, a local hosiery manufacturer who became interested in the hydropathic qualities of Matlock.

Unfortunately it is no longer possible to see inside the castle, as after years of debate and an uncertain future for the deteriorating building, it has been decided it will be converted into apartments; though it still makes for an affecting sight.

To the south of Matlock lies **Matlock Bath**, which developed into a spa town and by the early 19th century had become a popular summer resort. Many buildings connected with its heyday as a spa can still be visited. Down by the riverbank is the **Peak District Mining Museum** and **Temple Mine** that tells the story of lead mining in the surrounding area from as far back as Roman times.

High Tor Grounds, some 400 feet above Matlock, offer spectacular views along with nature trails, and on the opposite side of the valley are the **Heights of Abraham Country Park and Caverns**, featuring steep rocky gorges, vast caverns, fast-running rivers, woodland walks and refreshment areas. A cable car runs from Matlock railway station up to this unique attraction.

To the south of Matlock Bath is **Cromford**, the world famous 'model' village that was developed by Richard Arkwright into one of the first industrial towns. **Cromford Mill** and

the associated buildings and attractions are now an International World Heritage Site.

The **High Peak Trail**, which stretches some 17 miles up towards Buxton, starts at Cromford and follows the trackbed of the Cromford and High Peak Railway.

AROUND MATLOCK

CHESTERFIELD

9 miles NE of Matlock on the A61

A friendly, bustling town on the edge of the Peak District National Park, Chesterfield grew up around a market that was established over 800 years ago. The town centre has been conserved for future generations by a far-sighted council, and many buildings have been saved, including the Victorian Market Hall built in 1857. The town's most famous landmark is the **Crooked Spire of St Mary & All Saints' Church** – the magnificent spire rises to 228 feet and leans over 9 feet from its true centre point. The spire has eight sides, but the herringbone pattern of the lead slates tricks the eye into seeing 16 sides from the grounds. There are several tall tales as to

Crooked Spire, Chesterfield Church

how the spire became so twisted; one tells that a maiden getting married in the church was of such beauty and purity that the spire twisted itself trying to catch a glimpse of her, or another tells of a blacksmith persuaded to shoe the Devil, but was so nervous that he drove a nail into the Devil's foot causing him to shoot up in the air in pain, catching hold of and twisting the tower as he went.

Chesterfield owed much of its prosperity during the industrial age to the great railway engineer George Stephenson. His home, Tapton House, lies just outside the town; he retired here and carried out work and experiments in horticulture. His death was announced in one local newspaper under the headline 'Inventor of the straight cucumber dies.'

BOLSOVER

12½ miles NE of Matlock on the A632

Above the town on a limestone ridge stands **Bolsover Castle**, a fairytale folly built for Sir Charles Cavendish during the early 1600s on the site of a ruined 12th century castle.

AULT HUCKNALL

11 miles NE of Matlock off the A617

Situated on a ridge close to the Nottinghamshire border, this village is home to the magnificent Tudor house, **Hardwick**

---

95 **THREE HORSESHOES**

Wessington

Interesting 18th century pub, known best for its unbeatable hospitality and traditional Sunday roast.

See entry on page 378

---

96 **THE MOULDERS ARMS**

Riddings

Lively local thatched pub that prides itself on offering great pub food, real ale and local entertainment.

See entry on page 377

Hall. Set in rolling parkland, the house, with its glittering tiers of windows and crowned turrets, has the letters ES carved in stone: ES, or Elizabeth of Shrewsbury, is perhaps better known as Bess of Hardwick, who married and survived four husbands. Bess died at Hardwick and was buried in the Cavendish family vault in the Cathedral Church of All Saints in Derby. The formal gardens were laid out in the 19th century and the parkland, which overlooks the valley of the Doe Lea, is home to an impressive herd of Longhorn cattle and the ruins of Hardwick Old Hall.

CRICH

6 miles SE of Matlock off the A6

This large village, with its hilltop church and market cross, is the home of the **Crich Tramway Village**, which provides a wonderful opportunity to enjoy a tram ride through a lovingly restored period village. It also includes a wonderful museum. To the east stand the graceful ruins of the 15th century **Wingfield Manor** that held Mary Queen of Scots prisoner under the care of the Earl of Shrewsbury on two separate occasions.

RIPLEY

8½ miles SE of Matlock on the A610

Once a typical small market town, Ripley

expanded dramatically during the Industrial Revolution and the town's Butterley Ironworks created the roof for London's St Pancras station. Close to the town is the **Midland Railway Centre** at Butterfield, with steam trains running along a line from Butterley to Riddings.

HEANOR

12 miles SE of Matlock on the A6007

This busy town is centred on its market place where the annual fair is held as well as the twice-weekly market. Away from the bustle of the market are the Memorial Gardens, while to the south is Shipley Country Park, on the estate of the now demolished Shipley Hall.

BELPER

8 miles SE of Matlock on the A517

In 1776, Jedediah Strutt set up one of the earliest water-powered cotton mills here, harnessing the natural power of the River Derwent to run his mills. With the river providing the power and fuel coming from the nearby South Derbyshire coalfield, the valley has a good claim to be one of the cradles of the Industrial Revolution. Belper's industrial heritage is explained at the **Derwent Valley Visitor Centre**, located inside the historic North Mill, now one of the oldest surviving

---

97 **THE SPOTTED COW**

Holbrook

Known best for its delicious, modern English menu and luxury accommodation, this historic alehouse is must for weekends away in Derbyshire.

See entry on page 379

---

98 **THE RISING SUN**

Middleton, nr Matlock

Great food and live entertainment is the order of the day at this inn, which is located at the heart of Derbyshire

See entry on page 380

---

99 **THE MALT SHOVEL**

Wirksworth

A former coaching inn offering a high standard of cuisine, hospitality and accommodation, popular with walkers and cyclists.

See entry on page 381

---

100 **THE BLACK HORSE INN**

Hulland Ward

Traditional olde worlde country inn known for its fine hospitality and 45 choice strong menu that specialises in local game.

See entry on page 380

examples of industrialised water powered cotton mills in the world.

The Derwent Valley so closely resembled the topography of the Ruhr Valley that the reservoirs were the natural choice for the Lancaster bombers to practise dropping the Bounding Bombs prior to their attack on the Ruhr dams. The Valley was also used for the filming, in 1954, of *The Dam Busters*.

ASHBOURNE

11 miles SW of Matlock on the A515

Originally a small settlement lying on the northern bank of Henmore Brook, Ashbourne boasts many fine examples of 18th century architecture as well as some older buildings, notably the **Gingerbread Shop** that probably dates from the 15th century. Traditional Ashbourne gingerbread is said to be made from a recipe that was acquired from French prisoners of war who were kept in the town during the Napoleonic Wars. Also worthy of a second glance is the Green Man and Black's Head Royal Hotel; the inn sign stretches over the St John's Street and was put up when the Blackamoor Inn joined with the Green Man in 1825. Ashbourne was one of Dr Johnson's favourite places, and he visited the hotel so frequently that he even had his own seat – it's still there.

The area to the north of Ashbourne is dominated by the conical hill of **Thorpe Cloud**, which guards the entrance to **Dovedale**. The steep sides to its valley, the fast-flowing water and the magnificent white rock formations all give Dovedale a special charm. The **Stepping Stones**, a delight for children, are the first point of interest, and further up the dale is the limestone crag known as Dovedale Castle.

101 GALLERY CAFÉ

Ashbourne

Nestled within the regions premiere venue for contemp-orary arts and crafts, this award winning cafe opens daily with a focus on using fresh local produce to create simple, great tasting food.

See entry on page 382

102 THE BLUEBELL INN & RESTAURANT

Tissington

Located in Tissington is the glorious Bluebell Inn where guests can enjoy fine cuisine in the bar, restaurant or as part of one of the many function packages.

See entry on page 382

103 THE SARACENS HEAD

Shirley, nr Ashbourne

Fine country gastro pub, with a reputation for excellent English food in a stylish and relaxing atmosphere.

See entry on page 383

BUXTON

At the heart of the Peak District and England's highest market town, Buxton is also a spa town, whose waters are maintained at a constant temperature of 82 degrees F (28 degrees C). **St Anne's Well** still provides water and many people coming to the town make a point of trying the pure, tepid liquid. Among the notable architectural features of the town are The Colonnade, The Crescent, The Devonshire Royal Hospital and the attractive Edwardian **Opera House** that was

Buxton Opera House

restored in 1979. Gertrude Lawrence, Gracie Fields and Hermione Gingold all performed here, and on one famous occasion in the 1930s Douglas Fairbanks and Mary Pickford were in the audience to watch the great Russian ballerina Anna Pavlova. **Buxton Museum and Art Gallery** has a fine collection of Ashford Marble and Blue John ornaments, and visitors can explore the Wonders of the Peak through seven time zones. The ancient custom of **Well Dressing** has been a part of Buxton's cultural calendar since the Duke of Devonshire provided the townsfolk with their first public water supply at Market Place Fountain. From then on, High Buxton Well and St Anne's Well were decorated sporadically, and in 1923, the Town Council set about organising a well-dressing festival and carnival that continues to this day. Every year on the second Wednesday in July, this delightful tradition is enacted.

To the west of the town lies the 1,800 feet **Axe Edge**, from where the panoramic views of Derbyshire are overwhelming; just beyond, at 1,690 feet above sea level, the Cat and Fiddle Inn is the second highest pub in England.

AROUND BUXTON

LYME PARK
8 miles NW of Buxton off the A6

The ancient estate of Lyme Park was given to Sir Thomas Danyers in 1346 by a grateful King Edward III after a battle at Caen. Danyers then passed the estate to his son-in-law, Sir Piers Legh, and it remained in the family until 1946. Famous for its fantastic Palladian mansion, the work of Venetian architect Giacomo Leoni, the estate includes a late 19th century formal garden and a medieval deer park. The 1,400 acres of moorland, woodland and parkland at Lyme Park include an early-18th century hunting tower, Lyme Cage, so called because it was used to detain poachers. Lyme was Pemberley in the 1995 BBC film Pride and Prejudice.

HAYFIELD
8½ miles N of Buxton on the A624

This small town below the exposed moorland of **Kinder Scout**, the highest point in the Peak District, is a popular centre for

Kinder Scout, Hayfield

exploring the area and offers many amenities for hillwalkers. The town grew up around the textile industry, in this case wool weaving and calico printing, and many of the houses seen today were originally weavers' cottages. Hayfield was the birthplace, in 1914, of the actor Arthur Lowe, Captain Mainwaring in the much-loved TV series Dads Army.

GLOSSOP
13 miles N of Buxton on the A624

At the foot of the **Snake Pass**, Glossop displays an interesting mix of styles, the industrial town of the 19th century with its towering Victorian mills contrasting with the 17th

Snake Pass in Winter

104 THE SNAKE PASS INN

Bamford
Famous country inn offering the very best in accommodation, food and drink all day every day in an unrivalled location.

See entry on page 384

century village with its charming old cottages standing in the cobble streets. A little way north, at Hadfield, is the Longdendale Trail, which follows a former railway line and is part of the Trans-Pennine Trail.

PEAK FOREST

5 miles NE of Buxton off the A623

High on the White Peak plateau, Peak Forest takes its name from the fact that it once stood at the centre of the **Royal Forest of the Peak**. The Peak Forest Canal, completed in 1800, followed the valley of the River Goyt and had its terminal basin at Buxworth.

Within walking distance of Peak Forest is the renowned Eldon Hole, considered in legend to be the Devil's own entrance to Hell; thousands of pot-holers can testify to the inaccuracy of the legend that the pit is bottomless.

A few miles down the A623 and A6 roads from Peak Forest is the town of Chapel-en-le-Frith where you will find the stunning **Chestnut Centre Conservation and Wildlife Park**; home to Manoki - the UK's only giant otter. As you walk through the park's 50 peaceful acres of countryside and gentle woodland, you could see otters (one of the largest gatherings in Europe), 16 species of owls and other indigenous wildlife all in their

natural surroundings including, buzzards, pine martens, polecats, foxes, Scottish wildcats and deer – as well as wild flora.

EDALE

8½ miles NE of Buxton off the A625

Edale marks the start of the Pennine Way, the long-distance footpath inaugurated in 1965 that follows the line of the backbone of Britain for some 270 miles to Kirk Yetholm, just over the Scottish border. Not far from the village is the famous **Jacob's ladder**, overlooking the river, and nearby are the tumbledown remains of a hill farmer's cottage, the home of Jacob Marshall, who cut the steps into the hillside leading up to Edale Cross.

CASTLETON

8 miles NE of Buxton on the A6187

Situated at the head of the Hope Valley, Castleton is overlooked by the Norman ruins of **Peveril Castle**, the only Norman castle in Derbyshire, and by Mam Tor; to the west, the road runs through the Winnats Pass, a narrow limestone gorge. The hills to the west of Castleton are famous for their caves and the **Blue John Mine and Caverns** are one of Derbyshire's most popular attractions. The Blue John craft shop contains examples of jewelry and ornaments made from the pretty

---

105 THE NAVIGATION INN

Buxworth

Beautiful Village inn located on the Bugsworth Canal Basin offering truly traditional hostelry atmosphere and services.

See entry on page 385

---

107 ROUND MEADOW BARN

Hope

An outstanding bed & breakfast nestled in acres of countryside offering four guest rooms.

See entry on page 386

---

106 CAUSEWAY HOUSE

Castleton

Dating back to the 15th century this is a beautiful bed & breakfast at the heart of the Peak District

See entry on page 386

---

108 SCOTSMAN'S PACK COUNTRY INN

Hathersage

A traditional inn offering good quality food and comfortable en-suite rooms on the edge of Hathersage.

See entry on page 387

Peveril Castle, Castleton

Blue John stone – a prized ornamental variety of Fluor-Spar (Calcium Fluoride).

At the bottom of Winnats Pass lies **Speedwell Cavern**, a former lead mine that used boats on an underground canal to ferry the miners and iron ore to and from the rockface; they now ferry visitors. Peak Cavern, reached by a delightful riverside walk, has the widest opening of any cave in Europe.

EYAM

10 miles NE of Buxton off the B6521

This village, pronounced 'Eem', will forever be known as the Plague Village. In 1666, a tailor received a bundle of plague-infected clothing from London. The infection soon spread and the terrified villagers prepared to flee, but the local rector, William Mompesson, persuaded the villagers to stay, and as a result most of the neighbouring villages escaped the disease. Eyam was quarantined for over a year, relying on outside help for supplies of food that were left on the village boundary. Only 83 villagers survived out of 350.

The home of the Wright family for over 300 years, **Eyam Hall** is a wonderful, unspoilt 17th century manor house that is also home to Eyam Hall Crafts Centre and a licensed restaurant, both open year round.

ASHFORD IN THE WATER

9 miles SE of Buxton off the A6

Developed around a ford that spanned the River Wye, this was once an important crossing place on the ancient Portway; the medieval **Sheepwash Bridge** is one of three bridges in the village and is a favourite with artists. So-

called Black Marble, but actually a highly polished grey limestone, was mined nearby and, particularly during the Victorian era, it was fashionable to have decorative items and fire surrounds made from the stone. The founder of the marble works, Henry Watson, is remembered by a tablet in the great limestone **Church of the Holy Trinity**.

Ashford is perhaps most famous for its six beautifully executed well-dressings, which are held annually in early June. Rather than adhering strictly to the custom of depicting scenes from the Bible, the well-dressers of Ashford have pictured such unusual themes as a willow pattern to celebrate the Chinese Year of the Dog.

BAKEWELL

10½ miles SE of Buxton on the A6

The only true town in the Peak District National Park, Bakewell attracts many visitors, some to sample the confection that bears its name. One of the more famous guests at the Rutland Arms Hotel was Jane Austen, who stayed here in 1811; the town *and the hotel feature in* Pride and Prejudice.

Behind Bakewell's large parish church is the lovely aptly named **Old House Museum**, housed in what is thought to be the oldest house in Bakewell, dating back to 1534. The

---

109 THE WHITE LION

Great Longstone

A highly recommended establishment, well known for the high standard of food it serves and hospitality to match

See entry on page 388

---

110 BAKEWELL TART SHOP, COFFEE HOUSE AND BLOOMFIELD HOUSE

Bakewell

Renowned for making the traditional Bakewell tarts, this family run shop and café serves up a large selection of main meals, cakes and treats with luxury accommodation above.

See entry on page 389

late 17th century Bath House is one of the few other buildings remaining from the days when Bakewell was a minor spa town.

Bakewell is perhaps best known as the home of the Bakewell Tart (referred to locally as a pudding). A mile to the south of Bakewell stands romantic **Haddon Hall**, thought by many to have been the first fortified house in the country, though the turrets and battlements were put on purely for show. The home of the Dukes of Rutland for over 800 years, the hall has enjoyed a fairly peaceful existence, in part no doubt because it stood empty and neglected for nearly 300 years after 1640, when the family chose Belvoir Castle in Leicestershire as their main home. The 16th century terraced gardens are one of the chief delights and Haddon's splendour and charm have led it to be used as a backdrop to numerous television and film productions including *Jane Eyre, Moll Flanders* and *The Prince and the Pauper*.

The gritstone landscape of **Stanton Moor**, which rises to some 1,096 feet, lies to the south of Haddon and a Bronze Age stone circle on the moor is known as the Nine Ladies. Legend has it that one Sunday nine women and a fiddler came up onto the moor to dance and, for their act of sacrilege, they were turned to

Gardens, Chatsworth House

stone. Also in the area is the site of an Iron Age hillfort known as Castle Ring.

Northeast of Bakewell, near Edensor, lays the home of the Dukes of Devonshire, **Chatsworth House**, one of the finest of the great houses of Britain. The origins of the house as a great showpiece must be attributable to the redoubtable Bess of Hardwick, one of whose husbands, Sir William Cavendish, bought the estate in 1549. Over the years, the Cavendish fortunes have continued to pour into Chatsworth, making it an almost unparalleled showcase for art treasures. The gardens of Chatsworth, which used the talents of Capability Brown and Sir Joseph Paxton, also have some marvellous features, including the Emperor Fountain that dominates the Canal Pond. The gardens and house are closed through the winter, but the 1000 acre park, farm with petting areas and childrens adventure park, farm shop and restaurant are all open year round.

ARBOR LOW

9 miles SE of Buxton off the A515

This remote Bronze Age stone circle is often referred to as the Stonehenge of the Peaks, and although many of the stones now lie on the ground it is still an impressive sight. There are several stone circles in the Peak District but none offer the same atmosphere as Arbor Low, nor the same splendid views.

 BIGGIN HALL COUNTRY HOUSE HOTEL

Biggin-by Hartington

Elegant 17th century manor house hotel in the heart of the peak district with a reputation for fine English cuisine.

See entry on page 390

---

112 **BERESFORD TEA ROOMS**

Hartington

Cosy and full of charm, this village tea room offers a tempting array of homemade breakfasts, lunches and cakes throughout the day in the heart of Hartington.

See entry on page 391

DEVON

Known for its enchanting scenery, maritime history and bleak expanse of moorland, Devon, England's third largest county, has plenty to offer the visitor. To the southeast are the old textile towns, including Axminster that lent its name to the most luxurious of carpets, and Honiton, still famed for its lace. Here, too, lies the cathedral city of Exeter, the county capital, which has its roots firmly in Roman times. In recent times Exeter has become a popular shopping location for the region; with an eclectic mix of high street names and wonderful independent shops brimming with treasures.

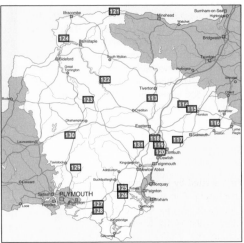

The south coast is littered with attractive and genteel seaside resorts that are particularly highly regarded for their mild climate. This area has been dubbed a "Jurassic Coastline" with World Heritage Status in recognition of the rocks and fossils found here; a unique geology which plots the Earth's story stretching back over 185 million years. Along this coast are the neighboring seaside towns of Paignton and Torquay; the latter was the birthplace of Agatha Cristie, and has many places of interest for lovers of her work. Between them lies the quaint thatched village of Cockington, one of the most photographed villages in England. To the west is Plymouth, where Sir Francis Drake famously insisted on finishing his game of bowls before leaving to intercept the Spanish Armada.

The middle of the county is dominated by Dartmoor National Park, home to the famous prison and a wealth of ancient monuments. The towering natural tors throughout Dartmoor make for lovely destinations for ramblers and walkers; the most unusual of which is Brent Tor with its small church teetering on top. Lastly, there is north Devon, with its spectacular coastline while, just inland, is Tarka country, the area of Devon that was made famous by Henry Williamson in his popular novel.

Accommodation

Accommodation

Continued

EXETER

First settled by the Romans, whose spectacular **Roman Bath House**, or Caldarium, was uncovered in the Cathedral Close in the 1970s, it was in the late 11th century that William the Conqueror took control of Exeter. After ordering the construction of **Rougemont Castle**, the gatehouse and tower of which can still be seen, work began on the construction of St

Rougemont Castle, Exeter

Peter's Cathedral, a massive building project that was not completed until 1206. Considered one of England's most beautiful medieval cathedrals, and one of the finest examples of decorated Gothic architecture in the country, it provides a picturesque centre to the city, with a green which is bustling with people during the summer months.

A new addition to Exeter's high street, already popular in the region for shopping, is the Princesshey Quarter which has over 60 new shops, restaurants, and cafes - many of which have alfresco seating giving it a continental flavor when the sun makes an appearance. The back streets and outskirts of the centre are overflowing with creative and independent shops, from vintage clothing and anything kitsch to secondhand books and antiques.

As well as being an ecclesiastical centre, Exeter was once also an important port and this is reflected in its dignified 17th century Custom House that now forms the centrepiece of the **Exeter Historic Quayside**. There are some excellent museums in Exeter, and other attractions include the **University Sculpture Walk**, which takes in works by Barbara Hepworth and Henry Moore, and guided tours through Exeter's dark Underground Passages; which were built to house the pipes that brought clean drinking water into medieval Exeter.

To the northeast of Exeter is the large estate of **Killerton**, which is centred on a grand 18th century mansion set in parkland that contains the Dolbury Iron Age hill fort and the 15th century Marker's Cottage.

AROUND EXETER

CADBURY

8 miles N of Exeter off the A3072

Cadbury Castle is an Iron Age hill fort that claims to have the most extensive views in Devon. To the northeast lies Bickleigh, a charming place of thatched cottages, which is home to Bickleigh Mill, now a craft centre, and, Bickleigh Castle, a moated and fortified late 14th century manor house.

TIVERTON

13 miles N of Exeter on the A396

A strategic point on the River Exe, in 1106, Henry I ordered the building of **Tiverton Castle**, around which the town began to develop. The castle was later destroyed on Cromwell's orders though the remains are

Knightshayes Court, Tiverton

substantial. A few miles north of Tiverton, up the Exe Valley, is **Knightshayes Court**, a striking house that was the home of the Heathcoat-Amory family.

OTTERY ST MARY

12 miles NE of Exeter on the B3177

This small town is justly proud of its magnificent 14th century **Church of St Mary**. The vicar here during the mid 18th century was John Coleridge, whose tenth child, Samuel Taylor, born in 1772, went on to become a celebrated poet.

A mile to the northwest of the town is **Cadhay**, a beautiful manor house that was built in 1550, while close by is **Escot Park and Gardens**, where visitors can see an arboretum and rose garden along with a collection of wildlife. Escot also has a huge variety of exciting and messy adventure play areas for children, which have proved very popular!

HONITON

16 miles NE of Exeter on the A30

Once a major stopping place on the great Roman road, Fosse Way, Honiton is best known for the lace that is still sought today. First introduced to east Devon by Flemish immigrants during the reign of Elizabeth I, the lace is still made here and can be bought from local shops and also seen in Allhallows Museum.

---

114 STAFFORD BARTON FARM

Broadhembury

In a beautifully picturesque location, this tranquil farmhouse bed and breakfast offers delicious breakfasts and a convenient base for exploring the local towns.

See entry on page 393

---

113 THE TROUT INN

Bickleigh

A family run inn located in the picturesque and unspoilt Exe Valley

See entry on page 392

---

115 AWLISCOMBE INN

Awliscombe, nr Honiton

This traditional and charming country inn located in a quiet farming community in the heart of Devon welcomes all for drinks all day every day.

See entry on page 393

AXMINSTER

24 miles NE of Exeter on the A358

This ancient town on the River Axe is famous for the carpets that bear the town's name. The creation of just one carpet took so much time that each one's completion was celebrated by a procession to St Mary's Church – which naturally has its own Axminster carpet. Carpets are still manufactured here and the factory welcomes visitors, while the **Axminster Museum** dedicates some of its exhibition space to the industry.

SEATON

20 miles E of Exeter on the B3174

Once a significant port, Seaton expanded during the Victorian era as wealthy families, looking for sea air, came here and built their villas. The railway line that brought many of the Victorians here has been replaced by the **Seaton Tramway**, which links the resort with the ancient town of **Colyton**, three miles inland. From Seaton, the **South West Coast Path** follows the coastline eastwards to Lyme Regis in Dorset. Considered by naturalists as the last and largest wilderness on the southern coast of England, this area of unstable cliffs, wood and scrub is a haven for wildlife.

To the west of Seaton is the picturesque old fishing village of **Beer**, best known for the superb white freestone that can be seen in churches all over Devon as well as in the Tower of London and Westminster Abbey.

SIDMOUTH

13 miles E of Exeter off the A3052

It was here that the future Queen Victoria saw the sea for the first time, brought here by her proud, penniless father, the Duke of

Kent. Some 50 years later, Queen Victoria presented a stained glass window to Sidmouth parish church in memory of her father.

Sidmouth Museum provides a very vivid presentation of the Victorian resort along with an interesting collection of local prints, a costume gallery and a display of lace. In 1912, Sir Joseph Lockyer founded the **Norman Lockyer Observatory** for astronomical and meteorological research.

The sleepy village of Sidmouth undergoes a transformation in the first week of August each year when it plays host to the vibrant International Folklore, Dance and Song Festival, and the streets are filled with music and joyous dancing.

BUDLEIGH SALTERTON

11½ miles SE of Exeter on the B3178

A famous Victorian visitor to Budleigh was the celebrated artist Sir John Everett Millais, who stayed here during the summer of 1870 in a curiously shaped house that is known as The Octagon. On the seafront is **Fairlynch Museum**, one of the very few thatched museums in the country.

Just to the north lies **Hayes Barton**, a wonderful E-shaped Tudor house that was the birthplace of Sir Walter Raleigh. On the banks of the River Otter stands **Otterton Mill**, a part medieval building, and **Bicton Park Botanical Gardens** that were laid out in the 18th century; the gardens now include a countryside museum and remarkable glasshouses, designed to recreate the natural environments of plants from different continents.

EXMOUTH

9 miles SE of Exeter on the A376

Situated at the mouth of the River Exe, this

---

116 THE KINGFISHER INN

Colyton

Truly the centre of its community, this vibrant inn offers a whole host of activities and events from themed food nights to pub quizzes for all, alongside a traditional locally sourced menu.

See entry on page 394

---

117 SIR WALTER RALEIGH

East Budleigh

A warm welcome will greet you at this thatched pub, which serves good quality food and real ales.

See entry on page 395

---

small fishing village was one of the first seaside resorts in Devon and was dubbed the 'Bath of the West'. On the northern outskirts of the town is one of the most unusual houses in Britain – **A La Ronde** – a unique 16-sided house described as having 'a magical strangeness that one might dream of only as a child'. It was built in the late 18th century on the instructions of two spinster cousins who were inspired by the basilica of the San Vitale at Ravenna. On the opposite bank of the river stands **Powderham Castle**, the home of the Earls of Devon, surrounded by one of the finest parks in the county.

BARNSTAPLE

One of the most attractive buildings here is **Queen Anne's Walk**, a colonnaded arcade that has a statue of Queen Anne on top of its central doorway. Opened in 1708, it was used by the Barnstaple wool merchants who accepted that any verbal bargain they made over the Tome Stone would be legally binding.

Barnstaple is also the northern terminus of the **Tarka Line**, a wonderfully scenic 39-mile route that follows the gentle valleys of the Rivers Yeo and Taw, where Tarka the Otter had his home. Walkers, too, can discover the countryside that inspired the novel by taking

---

118 THE ROYAL OAK

Exminster

A contemporary, but charm-filled, inn located in Exminster and close to the Exe Estuary nature reserve.

See entry on page 394

---

119 CHI RESTAURANT AND BAR

Kenton

Elegant restaurant serving outstanding authentic Chinese cuisine and also offering en-suite B&B accommodation.

See entry on page 396

---

the **Tarka Trail**, an unusual figure-of-eight long-distance footpath of some 180 miles that crosses over itself at Barnstaple.

AROUND BARNSTAPLE

MUDDIFORD

3½ miles N of Barnstaple on the B3230

Just to the southwest of this pretty village are **Marwood Hill Gardens** with their collections of rare and unusual trees and shrubs, while to the northeast lies **Arlington Court**, the family home of the Chichesters from 1534 until the last owner, Miss Rosalie Chichester, died in 1949.

COMBE MARTIN

9 miles N of Barnstaple on the A399

A popular seaside resort, with an exceptionally long main street. The village is home to a remarkable Grade II listed architectural curiosity, the 18th century **Pack o' Cards Inn**, which represents a pack of cards with four decks, or floors, 13 rooms and 52 windows.

LYNMOUTH

14 miles NE of Barnstaple on the A39

This pleasant village has benefited from two great enthusiasms, romantic scenery and sea bathing, and both Coleridge and Wordsworth came here on a walking tour in the 1790s, while Shelley visited in 1812. To aid the growing tourist trade the **Lynton-Lynmouth Cliff Railway** opened in 1890, linking the town with its neighbour Lynton, a place of chiefly Victorian architecture. To the west lies the **Valley of the Rock** that RD Blackmore

---

120 THE ANCHOR INN

Cockwood

This inn is famous for its delicious seafood  cuisine and picturesque harbour side location

See entry on page 397

---

transforms into the Devil's Cheesewring in his novel Lorna Doone. To the southwest is one of Exmoor's most spectacular wooded valleys, **Heddon Valley**.

CREDITON

26 miles SE of Barnstaple on the A377

This sleepy market town was, in AD 680, the birthplace of Wynfrith, who went on to become one of only a few Britons to become saints - he adopted the name Boniface. It was nearly 1,200 years before the people of Crediton gave their saint any form of recognition when in 1897 an east window was installed in the town's cathedral-like **Church of the Holy Cross** that depicts scenes from his life.

GREAT TORRINGTON

10 miles SW of Barnstaple on the A386

This hilltop town has several thriving industries, including **Dartington Crystal**, where visitors can see skilled craftsmen blowing and shaping the molten glass.

Just to the south of Great Torrington and occupying a breathtaking location in the Torridge Valley is the Royal Horticultural Society's **Rosemoor**, a wonderful place that includes mature planting in Lady Anne Palmer's magnificent garden and arboretum.

 121 LE BISTRO

Lynmouth

An outstanding bistro offering traditional home cooked classics, with an emphasis on English and French cuisine.

See entry on page 398

 122 SYDNEY HOUSE

Chulmleigh

A beautiful rural guest house serving fresh food, made from the finest local ingredients

See entry on page 399

BIDEFORD

8 miles SW of Barnstaple on the A386

This was once Britain's third busiest port, and evidence of this golden age can still be seen around the town in the various opulent merchants' houses that have survived. It was while staying here that Charles Kingsley wrote Westward Ho!, the swashbuckling Elizabethan story that is based around the town.

To the north, on the east bank of the River Torridge, are **Tapeley Park Gardens** – some 20 acres of gardens that have been divided into four distinctly different themed areas. Overlooking Bideford Bay is **Westward Ho!**, the only place ending with an exclamation mark, which developed into a resort following interest shown in Charles Kingsley's novel. Appledore, three miles north of Bideford, is a delightful old fishing village of narrow winding lanes and sturdy 18th and 19th century fishermen's cottages overlooking the Taw-Torridge estuary.

CLOVELLY

17 miles SW of Barnstaple on the B3237

This unbelievably quaint village, which tumbles down a steep hillside in terraced levels, is many people's idea of the typical Devonshire coastal village. Charles Kingsley lived and attended school here in the 1820s and the **Kingsley Exhibition** explores the novelist's links with the village, while the neighbouring Fisherman's Cottage provides an insight into what life was like in Clovelly at that time.

To the west lies **Hartland Point**, from where there are breathtaking views, **Hartland Abbey**, which houses a unique exhibition of documents that date back to 1160, and

123 HAM FARM

Dolton

Surrounded by five acres of landscaped gardens and grounds, Ham Farm offers a unique opportunity to experience natural Devon at its best with 7 luxurious cottages available for relaxing holidays any time of the year.

See entry on page 400

Hartland Point, Clovelly

Hartland Quay, where a museum records the many shipwrecks that have littered this jagged coastline.

HOLSWORTHY

26 miles SW of Barnstaple on the A388

This old market town lies just four miles from the Cornish border, serving a large area of rural Devon. Each Wednesday, it comes alive with its traditional street market, and in July the town plays host to the three-day long **St Peter's Fair**, an ancient event first held here in 1185. Holsworthy's most striking architectural features are the two Victorian viaducts that once carried the railway line through to Bude. Situated high above the southern outskirts of the town, they now form part of a footpath along the old track bed and it is possible to walk across them. Housed in an 18th century parsonage, the volunteer-run **Holsworthy Museum** gives visitors an insight into local history and traditions by various themed displays.

BRAUNTON

4 miles NW of Barnstaple on the A361

Claiming to be the largest village in Devon, Braunton is home to one of the few remaining examples of a Saxon open field strip system that is still actively farmed, while in the dunes is the **Braunton Burrows** nature reserve. Just to the northwest lies **Croyde**, renowned for its family-friendly beach, and close by, at Georgeham, is the house which Henry Williamson built and lived in after World War I, and where he wrote his famous novel, Tarka the Otter.

ILFRACOMBE

9½ miles NW of Barnstaple on the A361

Ilfracombe developed in direct response to the early 19th century craze for sea bathing and seawater therapies and the **Tunnel Baths** were opened in 1836, by which time a number of elegant residential terraces had been built on the hillside to the south of the old town.

TOTNES

Claiming to be the second oldest borough in England, Totnes, according to local legend, is said to have been founded by a Trojan named Brutus in around 1200 BC; the **Brutus Stone**, in the pavement of the town's main shopping street, commemorates this event. The first recorded evidence of the settlement was in the mid 10th century, when King Edgar established a mint here. There was already a

---

124 **WILLOWFIELD LAKE COTTAGES**

Braunton

A selection of beautiful self catering cottages nestled in the beautiful surrounds of Braunton Burrows Nature Reserve

See entry on page 401

---

125 **BAY HORSE INN**

Totnes

Good quality food, real ale, cider and a friendly welcome is the order of the day at this character-filled inn

See entry on page 402

Saxon castle here but the remains of **Totnes Castle** are of a once imposing Norman fortification. **Totnes Museum**, housed in an Elizabethan building, remembers the town's most famous son, Charles Babbage.

The real charm of modern Totnes is in its laid-back, creative community; which has cultivated a market with DIY flair, and many independent and small-business shops.

AROUND TOTNES

NEWTON ABBOT

7 miles NE of Totnes on the A381

It was here in 1688 that William, Prince of Orange, was proclaimed King William III and, while here, he stayed at the Jacobean manor house, Ford House, which had played host to Charles I in 1625. The whole character of this attractive town changed in the 1850s when the Great Western Railway made it their centre of locomotive and carriage repair works; it was also the junction for the Moretonhampstead and Torbay branch lines. Newton Abbot Racecourse is one of the most popular tracks in the southwest.

DAWLISH

14 miles NE of Totnes on the A379

From its earliest days as a seaside resort, Dawlish has attracted many distinguished visitors, including Jane Austen, John Keats and Charles Dickens, who in his novel of the same name had Nicholas Nickleby born near the town. To the northeast of the town is **Dawlish Warren**, a nature reserve that is home to many species of flowering plant, including the rare Jersey Lily.

TEIGNMOUTH

12 miles NE of Totnes on the A379

There are two distinct sides to this town – the popular holiday resort with its fine Regency residences and the working port on the northern bank of the River Teign.

Just north of the town lies the **Shaldon Wildlife Trust** breeding centre for rare small mammals, reptiles and exotic birds.

TORQUAY

6 miles E of Totnes on the A379

A genteel and elegant resort that has become known as 'The English Naples', Torquay, which grew up around Torre Abbey that was founded in 1195, was the birthplace, in 1890, of Agatha Christie. It was here that she began writing her crime novels while her second husband was away on active service during World War I. One of the town's most popular attractions is the **Agatha Christie Memorial Room** in the Abbot's Tower; while in **Torquay Museum** (the oldest in Devon) is a unique exhibition of the writer which includes never-before-seen photos loaned by the Christie family.

Just inland lies **Compton Castle**, a wonderful fortified manor house built between the 14th and 16th centuries. One mile up from the harbor will find at the prehistoric **Kents Cavern**, which provide informative tours, as well as activities for children (though, be warned, they can get very busy on wet days during high season!). A most recent attraction is **Living Coasts** on the harbour, a kind of zoo-by-the-sea and a natural habitat for seals, penguins and sea birds.

Castle Compton Gatehouse, Torquay

126 BISTRO 67

Totnes

A friendly and relaxed restaurant that serves magnificent food for the whole family.

See entry on page 402

PAIGNTON

5 miles E of Totnes on the A379

The development of Torquay saw neighbouring Paignton soon become a resort, complete with pier and promenade, which still appeals to families today. Near the centre of Paignton is the grand **Oldway Mansion**, modeled on the Palace of Versailles, it was once the home of Issac Merritt Singer the founder of the Singer Sewing Machine Company – though it is now utilized by the council.

Oldway Mansion, Paignton

Among the main attractions are **Paignton Zoo** and the **Paignton and Dartmouth Steam Railway** that follows the coastline along the bottom of Tor Bay before travelling through woodland to Kingswear. Here passengers alight and catch a ferry to Dartmouth. Just to the south, at Galmpton, lies **Greenway**, the house to which Dame Agatha Christie moved for the last 30 years of her life.

One mile north of Paignton, in Torbay, is the picturesque thatched village of **Cockington**. On the surface little appears to have changed of this village since its mention in the Domesday Book – and it obvious why it is one of the most photographed village in the country (even the public toilet is pretty and thatched!). A historic forge, tearooms, thatched pub, horse & carriage rides, and lakes & woodland perfect for walking are among the village's attractions.

BRIXHAM

7 miles E of Totnes on the A3022

Brixham was once the most profitable fishing

port in the UK and still supports a fishing fleet. The vicar at All Saints Church from 1823 to 1847 was the Rev Henry Lyte, who composed the hymn Abide With Me. The bells of the church play the tune every evening.

DARTMOUTH

7 miles SE of Totnes on the A379

One of England's principal ports for centuries, the town also has a long connection with the Royal Navy, the oldest of the British services (the Mayflower put in here for repairs before sailing on to Plymouth and on to America). Guarded by **Dartmouth Castle** (English Heritage), built by Edward IV after the War of the Roses and now containing some lovely exhibits on its history; Dartmouth's harbour is home to the handsome 18th century **Custom House**, while it's most famous building is the **Britannia Royal Naval College**. Dartmouth was the home of John (Jack) Russell, the 'sporting parson', a keen fox-hunting man who developed the breed of small terrier that bears his name.

The town's main street has many boutique-type shops and pleasant cafes; but no visit should miss a leisurely walk along the waterfront with its small pretty park with bandstand, gorgeous river views and hidden fort ruin at its end.

On the opposite bank of the Dart estuary are the impressive remains of **Kingswear Castle** that is a twin to Dartmouth's fortification. A huge chain was strung between the two castles when there was thought to be an added threat of invasion.

SALCOMBE

14 miles SW of Totnes on the A381

Standing at the mouth of the Kingsbridge estuary, this delightful town enjoys one of the most beautiful natural settings in the country. The harbour throngs with pleasure craft, and its old Customs House is home to the **Salcombe Maritime and Local History Museum**.

To the south of the town lies **Overbecks** (National Trust), a charming house that was built in 1913 and was the home of research chemist Otto Overbeck from 1918 to 1937.

The house holds Overbeck's wide-ranging collection, including late 19th century photographs of the area, local shipbuilding tools, model boats, toys and much more. The beautiful, sheltered garden, with views out over Salcombe estuary, is planted with many rare trees, shrubs and plants, giving it an exotic Mediterranean feel.

KINGSBRIDGE

11 miles SW of Totnes on the A381

At the head of the Kingsbridge estuary, this pretty town is a place of narrow alleys that has retained its Elizabethan market arcade, The Shambles, while its rather modest Victorian town hall has an unusual onion-shaped clock tower that adds a touch of glamour to the building.

For anyone looking to learn more about this area of Devon a visit to the **Cookworthy Museum of Rural Life** is a must.

Just offshore and reached by a causeway from **Bigbury on Sea** is **Burgh Island**, which is an island only at high tide. When the tide recedes, it can be reached by walking across the sandbank or by taking an exciting ride on the Sea Tractor. The whole of this 28-acre island, complete with its 14th century Pilchard Inn, was bought in 1929 by the eccentric millionaire Archibald Nettlefold, who built a hotel here in extravagant Art

Deco style. Notable guests at the hotel on Burgh Island included Noël Coward, The Duke of Windsor and Mrs Simpson, and Agatha Christie, who set two novels in this atmospheric location.

TAVISTOCK

This handsome old market town grew up around the 10th century **Abbey** and flourished following the discovery of tin on the nearby moors. The town seen today is essentially the creation of the Dukes of Bedford, who acquired the Abbey at the time of the Dissolution and remained there until 1911. While little remains of the Abbey, one of its legacies is the annual **Goose Fair**, a marvellous traditional street fair held in October. Tavistock was also permitted to hold a weekly market that, 900 years later, still takes place every Friday in the **Pannier Market**, one of the finest market buildings in the southwest.

Also, on the western side of Tavistock, can be found the **Tavistock-Morwellham Canal**, which was built in the early 19th century as the town and surrounding area were experiencing a copper boom. Today, **Morwellham Quay**, just south of the town, has been restored to re-create the busy atmosphere of the 1850s, when half the world's copper came through this tiny hamlet.

AROUND TAVISTOCK

LYDFORD

7½ miles NE of Tavistock off the A386

A royal borough in Saxon times, Lydford's

 EXETER INN

Modbury

A lovely country inn serving great food and drink and offering warm and comfortable accommodation.

See entry on page 403

---

128 **WEEKE VIEW**

Modbury

A bed & breakfast located on a working farm with beautiful views of rolling countryside and close to attractive beaches.

See entry on page 404

---

129 **SAMPFORD MANOR**

Sampford-Spiney

A beautiful manor, dating back to the 10th century offering lovely accommodation in magnificent surroundings.

See entry on page 404

---

former importance is reflected in its austere stone fortress **Lydford Castle**. To the southwest of the village, the valley of the River Lyd suddenly narrows to form the mile and a half long **Lydford Gorge**, one of Dartmoor's most spectacular natural features. A circular walk around the gorge begins high up before passing through the enchanting riverside scenes, including the thrilling Devil's Cauldron. Further south again is **Brent Tor**, a 1,100 feet volcanic plug that is one of the most striking sights in the whole of Dartmoor. The **Church of St Michael of the Rocks** stands on the top of it. The fourth smallest complete church in England, St Michael's is only 15 feet wide and 37 feet long and has walls only 10 feet high but three feet thick. There are stories as to how the small church came to be built on this precarious outcrop of volcanic rock; one tells of a wealthy merchant at sea during a massive storm, scared for his life he prayed to God that if He saved him that he would build a church on the first bit of land he saw – the merchant was saved and the first land he saw was the towering Brent Tor.

OKEHAMPTON

15 miles NE of Tavistock on the B3260

The town occupies a strategic position on the main route to Cornwall, and situated on the top of a wooded hill are the remains of **Okehampton Castle**, the largest medieval castle in Devon. Housed in an ancient mill is the **Museum of Dartmoor Life** while, in the surrounding courtyard, is the **Dartmoor National Park Visitor Centre**. To the south of Okehampton are Dartmoor's greatest peaks, **High Willhays** and **Yes Tor**, which rise to over 2,000 feet.

130 **WHITE HART INN**

Bridestowe

A rural village pub full of olde world charm providing traditional pub food with comfortable accommodation.

See entry on page 405

Outside of Okehampton, set amid beautiful Dartmoor countryside in the village of Sticklepath, is the **Finch Foundry**; the last remaining water-powered forge in England, which gives a unique insight into village life in the 19th century.

CHAGFORD

17 miles NE of Tavistock on the B3192

An ancient settlement that was one of Devon's four stannary towns, Chagford today is noted for the numerous ancient monuments that litter the surrounding countryside. Close by, near the pretty village of **Drewsteignton**, are two Iron Age hill forts along with the rather more modern **Castle Drogo**, designed by Sir Edwin Lutyens and built between 1910 and 1930.

PRINCETOWN

6½ miles E of Tavistock on the B3212

Situated at the heart of Dartmoor, some 1,400 feet above sea level, Princetown is the location of one of the country's best-known and most forbidding prisons – **Dartmoor Prison**, which first opened in 1809. Princetown is also home to the National Park's **Moorland Visitor Centre** that contains some excellent and informative displays about the moor. To the west lies **Widecombe in the Moor**, home to a grand old church that has been dubbed the **Cathedral of the Moors** and to a famous September fair. Sir Arthur Conan Doyle stayed in Princetown while gathering material for his most famous story The Hound of the Baskervilles. Fox Tor Mire became Grimpen Mire, where Sherlock Holmes lay low at **Grimspound**, the most impressive of all Dartmoor's Bronze Age relics.

BOVEY TRACEY

21 miles E of Tavistock on the B3344

To the north of this small town lies Parke, the former estate of the de Tracey family and now the headquarters of **Dartmoor National Park**; the present house dates from the 1820s and the grounds are home to a Rare Breeds Farm.

To the east of Bovey Tracey lies **Ugbrooke House and Park** that was built in the mid

18th century for the Clifford family and is still their home today. To the northwest is one of Dartmoor's most popular villages, **Lustleigh**, from where there are delightful walks, and Becky Falls Woodland Park.

BUCKFASTLEIGH

17 miles SE of Tavistock on the B3380

A former wool town on the banks of the River Mardle, Buckfastleigh is the western terminus and headquarters of the **South Devon Railway**, whose steam trains continue to make the seven-mile journey through the valley of the River Dart to Totnes. Another popular attraction close to the town is the **Buckfast Butterflies and Dartmoor Otters**, where the exotic butterflies can be seen in a specially designed tropical rain forest environment; the three species of otter include the native British otter.

BUCKLAND MONACHORUM

4 miles S of Tavistock off the A386

Tucked away in a secluded valley above the River Tavy, 13th century **Buckland Abbey** was the last home of Sir Francis Drake, who purchased it from his rival, Sir Richard Grenville.

PLYMOUTH

The most famous part of this historic city is undoubtedly **Plymouth Hoe**, the park and promenade overlooking Plymouth Sound where Sir Francis Drake was playing bowls when he was told of the approaching Spanish Armada. It is from the Hoe that hundreds of people flock every year to watch the stunning National Fireworks Competition in August. Also

131 THE VANILLA POD @ THE CRIDFORD INN

Trusham

An excellent restaurant and inn located in a truly idyllic setting.

See entry on page 406

Smeaton's Tower, Plymouth

here is **Smeaton's Tower**; a 72ft high lighthouse originally built out to sea on the Eddistone Reef in 1759. Just offshore, in the waters of the mouth of the River Tamar, lies **Drake's Island**, an English Alcatraz that was, in medieval times, known as St Nicholas' Island.

Plymouth's oldest quarter, the **Barbican**, is today a lively, open area of restaurants, pubs and an innovative small theatre, while close by is The Citadel, a massive fortress that was built by Charles II as a defence against a seaborne invasion. Near here is a reminder that Plymouth was the departure point for the Pilgrim Fathers; the **Mayflower Stone** stands at the point where they boarded their ship (they named their point of landing in America, Plymouth Rock). The names of the ship's company of *The Mayflower* are listed on a board on Island House, and their story is told in the **Plymouth Mayflower Visitor Centre**.

The Mayflower connection is everywhere in Plymouth. F H Jacka Bakery, which has claims to be the oldest commercial bakery in the UK, is reputed to have supplied the ship's biscuits for the vessel's voyage to America. **Plymouth Museum** in the town centre, has an informative permanent exhibition of the towns' maritime history, as well as exhibitions of art, natural history and chinaware. Down the road is the new development of **Drake Circus**, which has fast become the West Country's most popular shopping centre.

Five miles east of Plymouth, Plympton is home to **Saltram House and Park**, a prestigious 18th century mansion surrounded by a large estate near the tidal creek of the Plym estuary. The **Plym Valley Railway** runs from Marsh Mills, Plympton, to the local beauty spot of **Plym Bridge**.

DORSET

Although Dorset is not a large county, it provides an extraordinary variety of attractions. There are the dramatic cliffs of the western coastline and the more gentle harbours and bays to the east, while inland, chalk upland and heathland supports a wealth of bird and plant life. The most famous sight in Dorset is no doubt the Cerne Abbas Giant (or "Rude Giant" as it is otherwise known), a talisman for fertility carved into the chalk hillside above the delightful village Cerne Abbas. Nearby in Shaftesbury, visitors can find a familiar sight of a very different type; the quaint cobbled Gold Hill made famous by Hovis TV adverts.

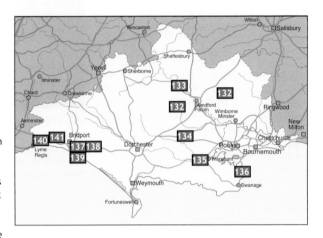

Over the years, many of the little ports have become seaside resorts of which the most famous is Lyme Regis, with its fossils and The Cobb, but the wonderful, natural harbour of Poole continues to be a commercial port – challenged in size only by the natural harbour in Sydney, Australia. The 7 miles of stunning sandy beaches along Bournemouth's seafront has recently had the exciting addition of Europe's first artificial surf reef, and this has fuelled a surge of other developments through the town which has attracted holiday makers and water sportsmen alike.

Inland are charming, ancient market towns, many of which have their roots in Roman times and, along with the Georgian elegance of Blandford Forum, there is historic Dorchester, one of the country's most appealing towns. It was close to the county town that Thomas Hardy was born and many of the towns and villages of the county have featured in the great writer's novels. The impressively eclectic mix of museums, including the fascinating Terracotta Warrior Museum, has something to interest every visitor.

BOURNEMOUTH

At the end of the 18th century, Bournemouth hardly existed, but once the virtues of its fresh sea air were advertised it began to expand as a resort. It continued to expand during the Victorian age; the splendid pier was built in 1855 and again in 1880 when a theatre was added. A unique monument to the booming Victorian age in Bournemouth's history is the building for the **Russell-Cotes Art Gallery and Museum**; a colourful and eccentric Victorian villa, which houses important collections of paintings, sculpture, furniture, and ceramics. It is reputed that poet Percy Bysshe Shelley's heart is buried in the churchyard of the **Church of St Peter** in Bournemouth, along with his wife Mary Wollstonecraft Shelley, author of *Frankenstein* – the rest of his ashes lie in a cemetery in Rome (he drowned off a beach in Italy).

The beautiful **Lower, Central and Upper Gardens** are located in the Bourne Valley, between the Borough Boundary and Bournemouth Pier. The Lower gardens are the most lively of the three, offering activity events for kids during the summer, and have many great facilities for visitors. Life in the Central and Upper gardens moves at a slower pace, and they are a most lovely place to bike ride, or peacefully watch the world go by.

Bournemouth has in recent years undergone something of a revival; the most remarkable transformation can be seen at **Boscombe**, located on the gorgeous seafront (and can be reached from Bournemouth by a pleasant sea-front walk or by small train in summer if you can't spare the time). Europe's first **artificial**

Russell-Cotes Museum, Bournemouth

surf reef (a football pitch-sized layer of sandbags along the seabed, which creates breaking waves from sea swell) in front of the golden sand beach was the first step in attracting people to this seafront. Following this the unusual mid-20th century modernist "Overstrand" building has been restored into contemporary beach "pods" – designed in vintage style by Hemingway couple of "Red or Dead" brand fame – and are available for daily hire or to buy. Since this there have been lively restaurants, cafes and shops popping up around the town, making it a desirable location to holiday, in or out of season.

AROUND BOURNEMOUTH

CHRISTCHURCH

5 miles E of Bournemouth on the A35

Situated at the junction of the Rivers Avon and Stour, Christchurch began life as a Saxon village and it was here that, in 1094, Ranulf Flambard began the construction of the magnificent **Christchurch Priory** that has ever since been used as a place of worship. Said to be the longest parish church in England, it is home to **St Michael's Loft Museum**. Christchurch is also home to the most modern of all the country's Scheduled Ancient Monuments – a World War II pillbox and anti-tank obstacles.

SANDBANKS

3½ miles SW of Bournemouth on the B3369

This spit of land, along with Studland to the southwest, almost cuts off Poole harbour from the sea, and it is these two headlands that provide the harbour with its shelter. At the top of the headland lies **Compton Acres**, a series of themed gardens that are separated by paths, steps, rock walls and terraces.

POOLE

4 miles W of Bournemouth on the A350

Once the largest settlement in Dorset, Poole has a huge natural harbour and a history that goes back to Roman times. The **Waterfront**

Museum, housed in an 18th century warehouse and the adjoining medieval town cellars, tells the 2,000-year story of the port. Poole Pottery made the famous red tiles for London Underground's stations and was the HQ of the US Navy during the Second World War. **Poole Harbour** is the second largest natural harbour in the world (Sydney Harbour is the largest).

Out in Poole harbour are several islands, the largest of which is **Brownsea Island**, where the heath and woodland are home to a wide variety of wildlife and where the Scout movement was born. In August 1907 20 boys came here under the auspices of Lieutenant-general Robert Baden Powell to learn about

Brownsea Island, Poole Harbour

scouting skills, fair play and good manners.

Just to the north of Poole lies **Upton Country Park**, a large estate of parkland, gardens and meadows that surround a handsome early 19th century manor house.

WIMBORNE MINSTER

7 miles NW of Bournemouth on the A31

A wonderful old market town, Wimborne Minster is dominated by its **Minster**, a glorious Norman building that is the best example of its kind in the county. Close by the Minster is the Priest's House, a 16th century town house that is now home to the **Museum of East Dorset Life**.

Around Wimborne there are several places of interest: to the east, at **Hampreston**, is **Knoll Garden**, a delightful, informal and typically English garden, which is also one the countries leading ornamental grass specialists, while further east again is **Stapehill**, a 19th

century Cistercian nunnery that is now a craft centre and countryside museum.

To the west of Wimborne lies **Kingston Lacy House**, a superb country house containing an outstanding collection of paintings that is set in attractive parkland. Elsewhere on the estate is the Iron Age hill fort of **Badbury Rings** and the 18th century White Mill.

BLANDFORD FORUM

An attractive market town in the Stour valley. The handsome Georgian buildings here were mostly designed by two talented architects, the brothers John and William Bastard, who were charged with rebuilding much of the town after a devastating fire in 1731. To mark the completion of the town's rebuilding in 1760, the **Fire Monument** was erected in front of the church and had a dual purpose – to provide water for fire fighting and for the public to drink.

To the northeast of the town lies **Blandford Camp** and the **Royal Signals Museum**, where there is a wealth of interactive displays on codes and code breakers, animals at war and the SAS.

AROUND BLANDFORD FORUM

SHERBORNE

16½ miles NW of Blandford Forum on the A352

In AD 705, St Aldhelm founded **Sherborne Abbey** as the Mother Cathedral for the whole of the southwest of England and the building that now occupies the site features some of

132 THE DROVERS	
Gussage All Saints	
THE CROWN	
Winterborne Stickland	
Two character filled pubs serving fresh food made from locally sourced ingredients.	
See entry on page 407	

84

the finest fan vaults in the whole country.

Sherborne's best-known resident was Sir Walter Raleigh, who, while enjoying the favouritism of Elizabeth I, was granted the estate of **Sherborne Old Castle** in 1592. This stark and comfortless residence was not to his taste, so he built a new castle, the splendid **Sherborne Castle**, which remains today one of the grandest of Dorset's country houses.

SHAFTESBURY

10½ miles N of Blandford Forum on the A350

This hilltop town, which stands over 700 feet above sea level, was founded in AD 880 by King Alfred who fortified the settlement here and established a Benedictine abbey for women installing his daughter as the first prioress. Just a hundred years later, King Edward, who was murdered at Corfe Castle, was buried at **Shaftesbury Abbey**, which soon became a place of pilgrimage. The nearby **Shaftesbury Abbey Museum** houses many of

Shaftesbury Abbey Ruins

the finds from the abbey's excavations, and state-of-the-art touch screen displays which bring the ancient religious house to life.

The town's most famous sight must be **Gold Hill**, a steep cobbled street, stepped in places and lined with delightful 18th century

cottages. Many people who have never visited the town will recognise this thoroughfare as it was made famous through the classic TV advertisement for Hovis bread. The cottage at the top of Gold Hill is home to the **Shaftesbury Museum**. Button-making was once an important cottage industry in the town and some of the products can be seen here including the decorative Dorset Knobs, which share their name with a famous, also locally-made, biscuit.

TOLPUDDLE

9 miles SW of Blandford Forum off the A35

Like so many villages beside the River Piddle, Tolpuddle's name was changed by the Victorians from the original – Tolpiddle. It was here in 1834 that the first trades union was formed when six villagers, in an attempt to escape from grinding poverty, banded together to form the Society of Agricultural Labourers, taking an oath of mutual support. The story of the martyrs is told in the **Tolpuddle Martyrs Museum**, housed in memorial cottages that were built in 1934 by the TUC.

To the west lies **Athelhampton House**, one of the finest stone-built manor houses in England, whose extensive gardens contain some unusual triangular topiary.

CERNE ABBAS

14½ miles SW of Blandford Forum on the A352

The most famous 'inhabitant' of this pretty village is the **Cerne Abbas Giant** (or, perhaps more aptly named, the "Rude Giant"), a colossal figure cut into the chalk hillside. The extraordinary club-brandishing full-frontal Cerne Abbas giant, 180 feet in height, is best

133 THE SAXON INN

Child Okeford

A picturesque country inn supplying comfortable beds and delicious food.

See entry on page 408

134 THE DRAX ARMS

Bere Regis

A traditional inn with low ceilings and a log burning stove in the inglenook fireplace with a great reputation for food and drink.

See entry on page 409

Hidden Places of England

Dorset

viewed from a lay-by on the A352, though according to legend a rather closer and more intimate encounter is required by women who wish to become pregnant. The village itself is endlessly quaint, with ancient pubs and quintessentially English tea rooms; a perfect place to stop for a relaxing afternoon or weekend break.

DORCHESTER

After capturing the Iron Age hill fort of Maiden Castle in around AD 50, the Romans went on to found Durnovaia. The hill fort is one of the biggest in England and nearby is another ancient monument utilised by the Romans, who converted the Neolithic henge monument of Maumbury Rings into an amphitheatre.

As with so many towns in Dorset, Dorchester played host to the infamous Judge Jeffreys and here he sentenced over 70 men to death. Later, in the 1830s, the town was once again the scene of a famous trial, when in the **Old Crown Court** the Tolpuddle Martyrs were sentenced. The Old Crown Court and its cells are now open to the public. The bloody history is soon forgotten however after a leisurely day is spent at the Borough gardens. Only a few minutes walk from the town centre, these gardens offer children's play area, bowling green, tennis courts and snack bar, and is brilliant for a relaxing picnic or to visit when one of the town's many exciting events are on.

The eclectic mix of museums in Dorchester includes the **Tutankhamun Museum, Terracotta Warrior Museum** (with a collection of amazing replica terracotta warriors), the **Teddy Bear Museum, The Keep Military Museum,** and the **Dorset County Museum.**

Just to the northeast of the town, lies **Max Gate**, the house that Hardy designed and lived in from 1885 until his death in 1928. Just to the east of Dorchester is the village of **Stinsford** that appeared as Melstock in Hardy's *Under the Greenwood Tree.* Hardy's heart is buried in the churchyard of the **Church of St Michael**, beside his first wife, and his parents are buried nearby. (Hardy's official funeral was at Westminster Abbey and

Wolfeton House, Dorchester

his ashes were placed in the south transept.)

Situated on the River Cerne, on the northern outskirts of Dorchester, is the attractive village of **Charminster**, the home of **Wolfeton House**, a splendid medieval and Elizabethan building surrounded by water meadows.

AROUND DORCHESTER

MORETON

7 miles E of Dorchester off the B3390

Moreton's Gothic **Church of St Nicholas** was wrecked by a Second World War bomb and its glass replaced with superb engraved glass by Laurence Whistler. In the cemetery is the grave of T E Lawrence - Lawrence of Arabia, Arabic scholar, traveller, soldier and man of action. To the northeast of this charming village is **Cloud's Hill**, a tiny redbrick cottage where Lawrence lived after retiring from the RAF in 1935. Lawrence had long been a devotee of Brough Superior motor cycles, calling his first (in 1922) Boanerges. It was in 1935, while riding a later version, which he named George VII, that he clipped the wheel of an errand boy's bicycle and sustained fatal injuries. The King of Iraq and Winston Churchill were among those who attended his burial in the graveyard at Moreton.

To the east of Moreton is **Bovington Camp**, where Lawrence served as a private in the Royal Tank Corps. The camp houses the **Tank Museum**, where the collection of 300 tanks and armoured vehicles starts with Britain's first tank, Little Willie, built in 1915.

CORFE CASTLE

18 miles SE of Dorchester on the A351

This greystone village is dominated by the majestic ruins of **Corfe Castle** high on a hill. An important stronghold that protected the gateway through the Purbeck Hills, the castle was constructed in the years immediately following the Norman Conquest. Now owned by the National Trust, the castle is part of an

Corfe Castle

extensive estate, with a network of footpaths taking in both the coastline and the inland heath, and encompassing important habitats for many rare species, including all six species of British reptile.

SWANAGE

20 miles SE of Dorchester on the A351

This seaside town, complete with its fully restored Victorian pier and its little exhibition, built its early fortune on Purbeck stone. The **King Alfred Column**, on the seafront, records that this was where the king fought and saw off the Danish fleet in AD 877. The column is topped by cannonballs that would, undoubtedly, have been a great help to King Alfred, had they been invented at the

time. These particular cannonballs date from the Crimean War.

An attraction not to be missed is the **Swanage Railway**, which uses old Southern Region and BR Standard locomotives to pull trains on a six-mile scenic journey to Norden, just north of Corfe Castle. The town holds a wonderful **Regatta and Carnival** for the first week of August, with over 100 different events including sandcastle competitions, fireworks displays and a carnival procession. Also, for music lovers, are the Jazz Festival (July) and Folk Festival (September).

To the north of Swanage lies **Studland**, whose fine sandy beach stretches from Handfast Point to South Haven Point and the entrance to Poole Harbour. The heathland behind the beach is a haven for rare birds and is a National Nature Reserve. A footpath leading along the coast takes in **Tilly Whim Caves**, named after the owner, Mr Tilly, who used a whim, or wooden derrick, to load stone into barges for transportation to Swanage.

EAST LULWORTH

12 miles SE of Dorchester on the B3070

This charming little village stands on a minor road that leads down to one of the country's best loved beauty spots, **Lulworth Cove**, an

Lulworth Cove

---

135 THE BRASSERIE

Wareham

A great little eatery that caters for breakfasts, lunches and dinner.

See entry on page 409

---

136 MANOR HOUSE HOTEL

Studland

A magnificent hotel aiming to offer a haven in which you can relax in comfort.

See entry on page 410

almost perfectly circular bay that is surrounded by towering cliffs. **Lulworth Castle** was built as a hunting lodge in the early 17th century and played host to seven monarchs before a devastating fire in 1929 reduced it to a virtual ruin. On the MoD's Lulworth Range is the deserted village of **Tyneham**, occupied in 1943 when the range had to be expanded for the testing of increasingly powerful weapons.

Portland Castle

WEYMOUTH
7 miles S of Dorchester on the A354

Weymouth owed its early prosperity to the woollen trade, but in the late 18th century it also began to develop as a resort.

One of the town's most popular tourist attractions is **Brewers Quay**, with specialist shops and a museum. Not far from Brewers Quay is **Nothe Fort**, which was built as part of the defences of the new naval base that was being established at nearby Portland. The fort is now the home of the **Museum of Coastal Defence**.

ISLE OF PORTLAND
11 miles S of Dorchester on the A354

The Isle of Portland is not, strictly speaking, an island but a peninsula that is joined to the mainland by the amazing **Chesil Beach**, a vast bank of pebbles worn smooth by the sea that stretches for 18 miles from the island westwards to Abbotsbury. The island's most famous building is **Portland Castle**, constructed by Henry VIII as part of his south coast defence. **Portland Museum** was founded by the birth control pioneer, Marie Stopes, and occupies a pair of thatched cottages.

At the tip of the island, **Portland Bill**, are

two lighthouses, the older of which (1788) is now a bird observatory and field centre.

ABBOTSBURY
8 miles SW of Dorchester on the B3157

This delightful village has three main attractions that draw holidaymakers here in their thousands each year – the **Swannery**, the **Sub Tropical Gardens** and the **Tithe Barn Children's Farm**. To the north lie several ancient monuments, among them Kingston Russell Stone Circle, a Bronze Age circle.

LYME REGIS
22 miles W of Dorchester on the A3052

During the 18th century, Lyme Regis developed into a fashionable seaside resort; the town's most famous landmark is undoubtedly **The Cobb**, which was built in

---

138 TRAVELLERS REST

Bridport

A group of self catered cottages that have been renovated to a very high standard of comfort.

See entry on page 411

---

137 THE GREEN YARD CAFE

Bridport

An award winning cafe that provides gorgeous food in lovely surroundings.

See entry on page 411

---

139 BEACH & BARNICOTT

Bridport

An historic restaurant and coffee bar serving high quality modern British cuisine with a Mediterranean twist

See entry on page 413

The Cobb, Lyme Regis

medieval times to protect the harbour. John Fowles set a part of The French Lieutenant's Woman on The Cobb, and the film of the book also used the location. Jane Austen stayed in the town writing a part of Persuasion, and Henry Fielding is said to have based the character of Sophie in Tom Jones on a local girl.

Lyme Regis is particularly famous for the fossils that were first discovered here in the early 19th century and there are fine specimens in **Lyme Regis Museum** and in the **Dinosaurland & Fossil Museum**. The fossil frenzy was fuelled by one Mary Anning, born in 1799, who with her family searched for fossils in the local cliffs and sold them to supplement the income of their carpenter father. The most famous discovery of Mary and her brother Joseph was the fossilised skeleton of an ichthyosaur; it took several years to free it from the cliff, and Mary sold it to the British Museum for £23. Visitors can go on their own thrilling **fossil-finding walks**, or longer **Jurassic Coast Tours**, or simply buy themselves a part of this Jurassic treasure trove to take home from a few shops in the town which specialize in fossils.

The restored Victorian **Town Mill**, offers a complex of craft studios and workshops, art gallery, peaceful garden, bakery and café/restaurant, in addition to the spectacle of the watermill itself.

The eight-mile stretch of coast to the east of Lyme Regis includes the highest cliff on the south coast, Golden Cap, and also the **Charmouth Heritage Coast Centre** that aims to further the public's understanding and appreciation of this area's scientific wealth.

BEAMINSTER

14 miles NW of Dorchester on the A3066

As a result of a series of fires, the centre of this ancient market town is largely a handsome collection of 18th and 19th century buildings. However, some older buildings did survive the fires, including the 15th century **Church of St Mary** with its splendid 100 feet tower from which, it is said, a number of citizens were hanged during the Bloody Assizes.

Just to the south of the town lies **Parnham House**, a beautiful Elizabethan mansion enlarged and refurbished by John Nash in the 19th century. Surrounded by glorious gardens, the house is certainly one of Dorset's finest Tudor residencies; between the 1970s up until recently it was owned by Beaminster's famous resident, the furniture maker John Makepeace and his wife Jennie – much of the house was dedicated to workshops where he created his marvelous contemporary furniture, and taught others his craft. It has recently been sold to a family from London, who wish to restore the house to its original grandeur – the Makepeaces' still live in the town.

To the southeast of Beaminster, **Mapperton Gardens** surround a fine Jacobean manor house with stable blocks, a dovecote and its own church.

 140 WESTWOOD GUEST HOUSE

Lyme Regis

A luxury bed and breakfast in a stunning location at the heart of the Jurassic Coast

See entry on page 412

 141 BEREHAYES FARM COTTAGES

Whitchurch Canonicorum

Seven delightful self-catering cottages within easy reach of Dorset's World Heritage Coastline

See entry on page 414

COUNTY DURHAM

County Durham is dominated by the marvellous city of Durham and, in particular, the magnificent cathedral that is now a World Heritage Site. Beyond Durham City are other towns which hold hidden treasures of their own; in particular is the grand Bowes Museum in Barnard Castle, which cannot help to take your breath away with its gorgeous façade

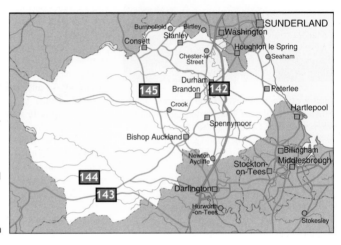

designed on a French château. In the aptly named town of Washington, can be seen the family home of the ancestors of George Washington – first President of America.

The county's prosperity was founded largely on coal mining, and now that the industry has all but disappeared the scars it created are being swept away. However, near the village of Ireshopeburn is a restored 19th century lead mine called Killhope, where you can get a taste for the life and work of a miner through the informative museum and

underground mine tours.

County Durham's countryside has always supported an important farming industry, and Central and South Durham still retain a gentle landscape of fields, woodland, streams and country lanes. Walkers are spoilt for choice with so much countryside to explore; the wild Durham Dales in the west are a very popular rambling location, as is the famous Pennine Way; a 250 mile trail from Derbyshire to Kirk Yetholm in Scotland, which passes through Upper Teesedale.

Accommodation

Food & Drink

DURHAM CITY

Arriving in Durham by train, the visitor is presented with what must be one of the most breathtaking urban views in Europe. Towering over the tumbling roofs of the city is the magnificent bulk of **Durham Cathedral**, third only to Canterbury and York in ecclesiastical significance but excelling them in architectural splendour. The cathedral owes its origin to the monks of Lindisfarne, who, in AD 875, fled from Viking attacks, taking with them the coffin of St Cuthbert. In AD 980 they finally settled at this easily defended site, where the River Wear makes a wide loop

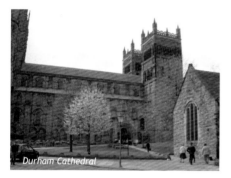
Durham Cathedral

around a rocky outcrop, and they built the White Church, where St Cuthbert's remains were finally laid to rest. The founder of the present cathedral was a Norman, William de St Carileph, Bishop of Durham from 1081 to 1096. He was determined to replace the little church with a building of the scale and style of the splendid new churches he had seen being built in France and in 1093 the foundation stones were laid. The result was the creation of the finest and grandest

example of Norman architecture in Europe. The Cathedral contains the tomb of the Venerable Bede, saint, scholar-monk and Britain's first true historian. Bede spent most of his life in Jarrow, where he died in AD735 and where he was initially buried. His body was later moved to its final resting place in the Cathedral in 1370.

Sharing the same rocky peninsula is **Durham Castle**, whose impregnability ensured that Durham was one of the few towns in Northumbria that was never captured by the Scots through force. The castle is now used as a hall of residence for the students of **Durham University**, which was founded in 1832, making it the third oldest English university, after Oxford and Cambridge.

The rest of Durham reflects the long history of the castle and cathedral it served. There are winding streets, the ancient Market Place, elegant Georgian houses and quiet courts and alleyways. It has a wonderful timeless quality with rowing on the Wear and relaxing riverside walks, and yet buzzes with a vibrant contemporary culture with superb cafés, artisan workshops, boutiques, galleries and museums; a real fusion of the new and the traditional.

The **Botanic Gardens**, run by the University, feature a large collection of North American trees, including junior-sized giant redwoods, a series of small 'gardens-within-gardens' and walks through mature woodland.

On the western outskirts of the city is the site of the Battle of Neville's Cross, fought between the English and the Scots in 1346. The Scots were heavily defeated and their king was taken prisoner.

AROUND DURHAM

HARTLEPOOL

15 miles SE of Durham on the A179

On 16 December, 1914 Hartlepool was the first town in Britain to suffer from enemy action, when it was shelled from German warships lying off the coast. Nowadays it is a thriving shopping centre, with some

142 **66 CLAYPATH**

Durham City
An ideal base for exploring the North East with comfortable rooms and a hearty breakfast prepared fresh to order.

See entry on page 413

outstanding tourist attractions, including the **Hartlepool Historic Quay and Museum**. Guided tours are available of *HMS Trincomalee*, Britain's oldest surviving warship, and the *PSS Wingfield Castle*, an old paddle steamer.

One of the more bizarre stories told in Hartlepool Museum concerns a monkey who was washed ashore on a piece of wreckage during the Napoleonic Wars. Not understanding its gibberish, the citizens decided that the monkey was a French spy and hanged the poor creature.

STOCKTON-ON-TEES

17 miles SE of Durham on the A177

Stockton-on-Tees is famous for being one end of the Stockton to Darlington railway, which opened in 1825 so that coal from the mines of South Durham could have access to the River Tees. Notable natives of Stockton include John Walker, the inventor of the humble friction match, born here in 1781; Thomas Sheraton, the furniture maker and designer, born here in 1751; and Ivy Close, who won Britain's first ever beauty contest in 1908.

DARLINGTON

17½ miles S of Durham on the A167

An ancient market town that was founded in Saxon times, Darlington's greatest claim to fame lies in the role it played, with its neighbour Stockton, in the creation of the world's first commercially successful public railway. The **Head of Steam** centre houses relics of the pioneering Stockton and Darlington Railway, including a replica of Stephenson's Locomotion No 1. Renovated and renamed from "Darlington Railway Centre and Museum" in 2008, it now contains innovative new exhibitions and interactive displays to thrill people of all ages.

STANHOPE

22 miles W of Durham on the A690

On the bank of the River Wear, in the heart of the Durham Dales which dominates the west of the county, the pretty Market Town of Stanhope is a hub for outdoor activities. A popular base for walkers, the glorious surrounding countryside offers such treasures as the nearby ford where you can cross the river using massive stepping-stones. It is also home to the counties only open-air heated swimming pool, and has an active arts and crafts scene.

CHESTER-LE-STREET

5½ miles N of Durham on the A167

A busy market town on the River Wear, the town's medieval **Church of St Mary and St Cuthbert** stands on the site of a 9th century cathedral that was established by the monks of Lindisfarne while they stayed here for 113 years before moving to Durham. **Waldridge Fell Country Park**, southwest of Chester-le-Street, is County Durham's last surviving area of lowland heathland.

To the northeast lies one of the regions most popular attractions, the award-winning **North of England Open Air Museum** at **Beamish**. Set in 200 acres of countryside, it illustrates life in the North of England in the late 19th and early 20th centuries by way of a cobbled street full of shops, banks and offices, a colliery village complete with drift mine, an old engine shed, a horse yard and terraced gardens. To the northwest of Beamish is **Causey Arch**, which claims to be the world's first single-arch railway bridge; it was built in 1726 by coalmine owners to take coal from Tanfield to the River Tyne.

In the old part of Washington, northeast of Chester-le-Street, is **Washington Old Hall**, the home of the Washington family, ancestors of

Beamish Open Air Museum

George Washington, the first American president. The present house was built in around 1623 and the interiors re-create a typical manor house of the 17th century. Also in Washington are the **Washington Wildfowl & Wetlands Centre**, a conservation area and bird watchers' paradise, and the **Glaxo Wellcome Wetland Discovery Centre**.

SUNDERLAND

11½ miles NE of Durham on the A690

Sunderland is one of Britain's newer cities: the **Church of St Michael and All Angels**, the first minster to be created in England since the Reformation, was proclaimed Sunderland Minster in January 1998. The **Sunderland Museum & Winter Gardens** has some stunning displays, not least the indoor gardens which hold some 2,000 flowers and plants, and gallery which boasts an extensive collection of paintings by LS Lowry, who considered Sunderland his 'second home'. Sunderland also claims the only theatre between Leeds and Edinburgh large enough to host West End shows; the **Sunderland Empire Theatre**. To the south of the city centre is the **Ryhope Engines Museum**, based on a pumping station that supplied the city and surrounding area with water.

On the north side of the Wear, in the suburb of **Monkwearmouth**, is an important site of early Christianity. Glass was first made in Sunderland in the 7th century at St Peter's Church and the **National Glass Centre** is close by.

PETERLEE

10½ miles E of Durham on the A1086

Peterlee was established as a New Town in 1948 to re-house the mining families that lived in the colliery villages around Easington and Shotton. It is named after an outstanding Durham miner and county councillor, Peter Lee, who fought all his life for the well-being of the local community. **Castle Eden Dene National Nature Reserve**, on the south side of the town, is one of the largest woodlands in the North East that has not been planted or extensively altered by man.

BARNARD CASTLE

This old market town derives its name from its Castle, founded in the 12th century by Bernard, son of Guy de Baliol, one of the knights who fought alongside William I. The town has an especially rich architectural heritage, with handsome houses, cottages, shops and inns dating from the 17th to the 19th centuries and an impressive octagonal Market Cross.

The town is home to the extraordinary **Bowes Museum**, a grand and beautiful building styled on a French château. The fabulous collections on show include paintings by Goya, El Greco, Turner, Boudin and Canaletto, tapestries, ceramics, a wonderful display of toys (the world's first toy train set) and the breathtaking life-size Silver Swan that is an automaton and music box.

AROUND BARNARD CASTLE

BISHOP AUCKLAND

12 miles NE of Barnard Castle on the A688

Auckland Castle, still the official palace of the Bishop of Durham, began as a small 12th century manor house and was added to by

---

143 THE ANCIENT UNICORN

Bowes, nr Barnard Castle

A real pub-lover's pub, with cask ales locally sourced food and en suite guest bedrooms

See entry on page 416

---

144 CLOVE LODGE

Baldersdale

Self-catering or Bed &Breakfast accommodation in farm cottage in area of outstanding natural beauty.

See entry on page 415

Bishop Auckland Castle

successive bishops. The palace grounds contain an ancient herd of red deer. At **Shildon**, three miles south of Bishop Auckland, is **Locomotion: The National Railway Museum**, whose exhibits include a full-size replica of Timothy Hackworth's *Sans Pareil* of 1829, built for the famous Rainhill Trials on the Liverpool to Manchester railways.

In the small village of **Escomb**, two miles northwest of Bishop Auckland, is one of the county's true hidden gems – the 7th century Church of St John the Evangelist, built using stone from the nearby Binchester Roman fort. It is one of only three complete Saxon churches in Britain.

PIERCEBRIDGE

10 miles E of Barnard Castle on the A67

The picturesque village green stands on the site of a once important Roman fort, one of a chain of forts on Dere Street. The remains of the fort, which are visible today, can be dated from coin evidence to around AD 270.

To the northwest lies **Gainford**, County Durham's most beautiful village. It sits just north of the River Tees and its core is a jostling collection of 18th and 19th century cottages and houses grouped around a green.

MIDDLETON-IN-TEESDALE

8 miles NW of Barnard Castle on the B6277

Middleton is the centre for some magnificent walks in Upper Teesdale; the most famous of these is the **Pennine Way** on its 250-mile route from Derbyshire to Kirk Yetholm in Scotland. It passes through Middleton-in-Teesdale from the south, then turns west along Teesdale, passing traditional, whitewashed farmsteads and spectacular, riverside scenery, including the thrilling waterfalls at **Low Force** and **High Force**.

IRESHOPEBURN

18 miles NW of Barnard Castle on the A689

This small village is home to the small independent **Weardale Museum** that includes a carefully re-created room in a typical Weardale lead miner's cottage, with furnishings and costumes in period. There is also a room dedicated to John Wesley, who visited the area on more than one occasion.

To the northwest lies **Killhope Mine**, the focal point of what is now the remarkable **North of England Lead Mining Museum**, which is dominated by the massive 34-feet high water wheel. There is also opportunity to go down into the darkness of the mine and experience for yourself the life of the miners who worked there.

145 THE BROWN HORSE

High Stoop, Tow Law

A conveniently placed hotel, offering a warm welcome, home cooked meals and comfortable ensuite bedrooms.

See entry on page 417

Killhope Mine

ESSEX

Bordering the north bank of the River Thames, southern Essex has long been a gateway to London, and while it contains much heavy industry, it also encompasses some very important marshland wildlife habitats. History, too, abounds in this part of the county - Henry VIII built the riverside Block Houses at East and West Tilbury, which later became Coalhouse and Tilbury Forts.

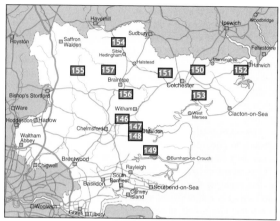

Southend-on-Sea is one of the country's best-loved venues for a family holiday or a day trip from London, and there are numerous nature reserves, the ancient royal hunting ground of Epping Forest and the yachting centre at Burnham-on-Crouch. Maldon remains famous for its traditionally produced sea salt.

Although Chelmsford is the county town, Colchester, which was first established in the 7th century BC, has the greater character. The country's oldest recorded town was the capital of Roman Britain until Queen Boudicca (Boadicea) burned the town to the ground. Other ancient towns abound in the county including Tiptree, home to the famous jam factory, Coggeshall, which is well known for

its lace, and Saffron Walden which takes its name from the Saffron crocus that was used to make dyestuffs.

Along the east coast, dubbed the 'Sunshine Holiday Coast', are the resorts of Clacton-on-Sea, Frinton-on-Sea and Walton-on-the-Naze that were all developed in the 19th century. Seafaring, fishing and shipbuilding were all once the mainstays of many of the settlements along this stretch of coast and Brightlingsea has the distinction of being the only limb of the Cinque Ports outside Kent and Sussex.

Accommodation

Food & Drink

Food & Drink

CHELMSFORD

Situated at the confluence of the Rivers Chelmer and Can, the town was first settled by Romans, who built a fort and brought Christianity to Essex. It was not until 1914 that the diocese of Chelmsford was created, though **Chelmsford Cathedral** (formerly the Parish Church of St Mary) dates from the 15th century and was built on the site of a much earlier church. The Marconi Company set up the world's first radio company in Chelmsford in 1899.

There are many beautiful parks and gardens in Chelmsford. They include; the manicured **Admirals Park and Tower Gardens** - 30 hectares of peaceful park and woodland on the banks of the River Can; the **Boleyn Gardens** - an established landscaped garden which includes ponds and wild flower areas, and an award winning Elements Garden crammed full of herbaceous plants; and the **Galleywood Common Local Nature Reserve** - a sprawling 47 hectares of heathland and woodland, popular with dog walkers, nature enthusiasts and local residents.

Other Chelmsford attractions include the **Riverside Ice and Leisure Centre**, which has several swimming pools for all abilities and an ice rink. There are also two theatres (the Civic and the Cramphorn), and a pedestrianised high street with many shops.

To the east, close to the village of **Danbury** (thought to take its name from the Danes who invaded this area in the Dark Ages), is **Danbury Country Park**, a pleasant stretch of open countryside with woodland and old pollarded trees, an 18th century ice house, a lake and ornamental gardens.

AROUND CHELMSFORD

MALDON

9 miles E of Chelmsford on the A414

Situated on the busy Blackwater estuary, Maldon's most distinctive feature is undoubtedly the 15th century **Moot Hall**. This building passed into the hands of the town corporation and was the seat of power in Maldon for over 400 years. The original brick spiral staircase (the best-preserved of its kind in England) and the 18th century courtroom are of particular interest.

Just outside the town, on **Northey Island** (which has large vital areas of undisturbed salt marsh owned by the National Trust), lies the site of one of the most decisive battles of England's early history when, in AD 991, the English leader, Byrthnoth, was killed by the invading Danes after a fierce three-day conflict. Maldon's **Millennium Gardens** were named in commemoration of the battle; also in commemoration is the ambitious 42ft embroidered tapestry, which marked the 1,000th anniversary of the Battle of Maldon - it can be found on display at the **Maeldune Heritage Centre** in the town (Maeldune being the Saxon name for Maldon).

Sea salt has been produced here for

147 WATERSIDE TEA ROOMS AND B&B

Maldon

Beautiful 16th century tea room specialising in delicious home cooking for all the family, with en suite accommodation also available.

See entry on page 418

146 THE WILLIAM BOOSEY

Hatfield Peverel

Long established inn offering excellent English and Thai cuisine, real ales and regular entertainment.

See entry on page 416

148 THE HOT PLATE CAFÉ

Maldon

Perfect for people watching, this light and airy modern café looks out onto Maldon's high street whilst serving a wholesome range of light bites, breakfasts, main meals and homemade cakes for all.

See entry on page 419

Maldon

generations, and the history of this industry is one of the topics explored in the **Maldon District Museum**. To the north, at **Langford**, is the **Museum of Power**, an ex-waterworks pumping station that houses engines, pumps and other interesting artefacts.

SOUTH WOODHAM FERRERS

9½ miles SE of Chelmsford on the B1012

Surrounded by the empty marshland of the Crouch estuary, South Woodham Ferrers is a successful 20th century new town that, surprisingly, boasts a traditional market square overlooked by buildings constructed in the old Essex style – with brick, tile and weatherboard. To the northwest of the town, at **Hyde Hall**, is the **Royal Horticultural Society Garden**, which includes a woodland garden, large rose garden, ornamental ponds,

herbaceous borders and the national collections of *malus* and *viburnum*.

BASILDON

12 miles S of Chelmsford on the A13

In **Wat Tyler Country Park**, 120 acres of meadows, woodland, marshland and ponds, is the **Motorboat Museum**, the only museum in the world devoted to the history of motor boats, concentrating on sports and leisure. Also in the park is the weird and wonderful sculpture trail – the product of a community-based project.

BURNHAM-ON-CROUCH

16½ miles SE of Chelmsford on the B1012

An attractive old village that is the county's main yachting centre. On the town's bustling quay is the **Burnham-on-Crouch and District Museum** featuring agricultural and maritime exhibits relating to this ancient area of Essex.

Mangapps Farm Railway Museum on the edge of town houses an extensive collection of railway relics, historic buildings and one of the largest collections of signalling equipment. Train rides are available when the museum is open.

To the northeast of Burnham, on the northern shore of the Dengie Peninsula, lies **Bradwell-on-Sea**, a village whose name is derived from the Saxon words 'brad pall' meaning 'broad wall'. Here is the site of **Bradwell Bay Secret Airfield**, which was used during World War II by aircraft that were unable to return to their original base. The village also has what could be the country's oldest church. **St Peter's-on-the-Wall**, built by St Cedd in the 7th century, was abandoned in the 14th century and forgotten for 600 years; it has been restored and reconsecrated.

SOUTHEND-ON-SEA

17 miles SE of Chelmsford on the A127

One of the country's best loved family resorts, Southend-on-Sea has seven miles of beaches, endless amusements and the longest pleasure pier in the world (1.33 miles), served by its own electric railway and with a

---

149 THE RED LION INN

Latchingdon

Popular inn to stay or dine, known for its unbeatable hospitality, warm atmosphere and delicious food.

See entry on page 418

97

little museum telling its story. The **Central Museum, Planetarium and Discovery Centre** features local history exhibits as well as astronomical displays. Several museums and galleries provide ample culture, and other attractions include the **Sealife Centre** and the renowned **Kursall** entertainment complex.

Canvey Island has two unusual museums, the **Dutch Cottage Museum** with many traditional Flemish features, built by one of Vermuyden's marshland drainage workmen, and the **Castle Point Transport Museum**, housed in a 1930s bus garage, with a fascinating collection of Eastern National buses and coaches and other commercial vehicles made between 1944 and 1981.

STANFORD-LE-HOPE

15 miles S of Chelmsford on the A1014

Lying between the town and the Thames estuary are **Stanford Marshes**, an ideal location for birdwatching and also the home to various species of wildlife. Close by is **Langdon Hills Country Park**, some 400 acres of ancient woodland and meadows that is home to many rare trees and from where there are spectacular views out over the Essex countryside.

TILBURY

19 miles SW of Chelmsford on the A1089

Chosen as the site for the Camp Royal in 1588 when the threat of invasion by Spain was imminent, **West Tilbury** (northeast of Tilbury) remains a quiet and hidden away backwater overlooking the Thames estuary. It was from here that Queen Elizabeth I made her famous speech;

'I know I have the body but of a weak and feeble woman: but I have the heart and stomach of a king, and a king of England too.'

The town of Tilbury itself is large and busy, industrial centre; though **Tilbury Fort**, an unusual 17th century building with a double moat, acts as a reminder of the past. Another fortification, **Coalhouse Fort**, was constructed as a primary defence against invasion of the Thames area.

Despite the industry that lines the Thames

Coalhouse Fort, Tilbury

estuary, the area around Tilbury is also rural, and the **Mardyke Valley**, which runs from Aveley to Orsett Fen, provides pleasant views and open spaces.

BRENTWOOD

10½ miles SW of Chelmsford on the A1016

Attractions in this town on the old pilgrim and coaching routes to and from London include a classically-styled modern cathedral, a picturesque cottage museum in a disused cemetery and a top entertainment venue. There have been breweries in Brentwood for 100 years, and although nothing now remains of the original brewers, the Brentwood Brewery Company is continuing the tradition of honest robust beers and ales which can be bought in many places throughout Essex.

Just southeast of the town centre is **Thorndon Country Park** and **Hartswood**, formerly a Royal deer park. To the northwest, at **South Weald**, is **Weald Country Park**, a former estate which was partially landscaped in the 18th century and features a lake, woodland and an ancient deer park. To the northeast of Brentwood and situated beside a Roman road is **Mountnessing Post Mill**, a traditional weatherboarded mill dating from 1807 that was restored to working order in the 1980s.

WALTHAM ABBEY

Originally a Roman settlement and home to a hunting lodge belonging to the early Saxon kings, the town grew up around this and an

Augustinian Abbey that was built in 1177 by Henry II. The Abbey's **Crypt Centre** explains the history of both the town and the Abbey, which was once one of the largest in the country and was the last to fall victim to the Dissolution in 1540.

Gunpowder production started here in the 17th century and by the 19th century the **Royal Gunpowder Mills** employed 500 workers. The once secret buildings and the surrounding parkland are now open to the public as part of the **Lee Valley Regional Park**, an important area of high biodiversity that sustains a large range of plant life and bird life. The park stretches 26 miles along the River Lea (sometimes also spelt *Lee*) from East India Dock Basin, on the north bank of the Thames in East London, to Hertfordshire. The **Lee Valley Park Farms** offer visitors a chance to interact with farmyard animals, and to see a working farm in action – a popular attraction with children.

Epping Forest, Harlow

AROUND WALTHAM ABBEY

HARLOW

10 miles NE of Waltham Abbey on the A414

Though much of it is modern, Harlow has several sites of historic interest. **Harlow Museum** occupies a Georgian manor house set in picturesque gardens, while **Harlow Study and Visitors Centre** is set in a medieval tithe barn and adjacent 13th century church. **Gibberd Gardens** on the eastern outskirts of Harlow, are the most unusual and wonderful creation of Sir Frederick Gibberd. This 7-acre garden was designed by Sir Frederick on the side of a small valley and includes some 80 sculptures among its many wonders.

At Chingford stands the **Queen Elizabeth Hunting Lodge**, a timber-framed building first used by Henry VIII. This unique Tudor survivor is situated in **Epping Forest**, the magnificent and expansive tract of ancient hornbeam coppice that offers miles of leafy walks and bridle paths along with some rough grazing and the occasional distant view. The Elizabethan Hunting Lodge was once the

destination for thousands of Londoners who came by bus to enjoy a day in the open air, and at the end of the day queued patiently and orderly for the journey home.

CHIPPING ONGAR

8 miles SE of Harlow on the A414

In 1155, Richard de Lucy built a castle here, of which only the mound and moat remain today. However, a contemporary building, the **Church of St Martin of Tours**, still stands. It was here that the explorer David Livingstone spent time as a pupil pastor before beginning his missionary work in Africa.

The town is surrounded by rural Essex and several ancient villages, including **Fyfield**, home to **Fyfield Hall**, the oldest inhabited timber-framed building in England; **Blackmore**, a village that was almost totally destroyed by the plague; and **Greensted**, which became the home of several of the Tolpuddle martyrs after their sentences had been commuted. Greensted's **Church of St Andrew** is the single surviving log church in England, the oldest wooden church in the world and the oldest wooden building in Europe.

To the west of the town lies **North Weald Airfield Museum**, which details the history of flying in this area from 1916 to 1964.

COLCHESTER

First established in the 7th century BC and

England's oldest recorded town, Colchester was an obvious target for the Romans, and the Emperor Claudius took the surrender of 11 British kings here. However, in AD 60 Queen Boudicca took revenge on the invaders and burned the town to the ground before going on to destroy London and St Albans. The walls, the oldest in the country, still surround the ancient part of the town and **Balkerne Gate** is the largest surviving Roman gateway in the country.

Colchester Castle

A thousand years later the Normans built Colchester Castle on the foundations of the Roman temple of Claudius and it boasts the largest Norman keep ever built in Europe. The **Castle Museum**, housed in the keep, is now one of the most exciting hands-on historical attractions in the country. Located in a fine Georgian building, the **Hollytrees Museum** displays a fine collection of toys, costumes, curios and antiquities from the last two centuries; the **Natural History Museum** concerns itself with the flora and fauna of Essex; and **Tymperleys Clock Museum** in Queen Street is home to a magnificent collection of 18th and 19th century Colchester-made clocks. Opened in late 2008 is **firstsite:newsite**, a new social space with a programme of exhibitions, workshops, lectures and films.

Colchester is famous for its **Zoo**, where the attractions include daily chances to help feed elephants and giraffes, a sea lion pool with viewing tunnel, and free-flying bird of prey displays. The town is even more famous for its oysters which are still cultivated on beds in the lower reaches of the River Colne – a visit to the **Oyster Fisheries** is a fascinating experience.

To the east of Colchester, at **Elmstead Market**, are the **Beth Chatto Gardens** that were designed and are still presided over by the famous gardener. Close by is the **Rolts Nursery Butterfly Farm**.

AROUND COLCHESTER

MANNINGTREE

7 miles NE of Colchester on the B1352

Situated on the River Stour, this ancient market town was a centre of the cloth trade in Tudor times before becoming a port serving the barges taking their wares to London. Manningtree is a centre for sailing, and from **The Walls** there are unrivalled views of the Stour estuary – a favourite subject of artists down the years.

DEDHAM

6 miles N of Colchester off the A14

This is true Constable country; the county's prettiest area. The village has several fine old

150 THE ARDLEIGH LION

Ardleigh

Now thriving, this village inn welcomes all to a vibrant atmosphere with delicious home cooked food, themed food evenings, karaoke, live music and Sky sports.

See entry on page 420

151 THE TREBLE TILE

West Bergholt

Welcoming old village hostelry noted for its excellent food, real ales and spacious garden.

See entry on page 421

buildings, especially the 15th century flint church familiar from so many Constable paintings. There are also good walks through the protected riverside meadows of Dedham Vale to **Flatford**, where Bridge Cottage, a restored thatched 16th century building, houses a display about Constable, who featured this cottage in several of his paintings (his father's mill is across the river lock in Dedham).

Here also is **Dedham Vale Family Farm** - a nicely undeveloped 16-acre farm boasting a comprehensive collection of British farm animals. Another artist associated with this area is Sir Alfred Munnings and, just outside the village, his former home, Castle House, now contains the **Sir Alfred Munnings Art Museum**.

HARWICH

16 miles NE of Colchester on the A120

This town has an important maritime history, the legacy of which continues through to the present day. The Elizabethan seafarers Hawkins, Frobisher and Drake sailed from here, Christopher Jones, master of *The Mayflower*, lived here and Samuel Pepys, the diarist, was an MP for the town in the 1660s.

When the town's two lighthouses, built in 1818, were aligned they indicated a safe shipping channel into Harwich harbour. **Harwich Maritime Museum** can be found in the **Low Lighthouse**, and another museum well worth a visit is the **Lifeboat Museum**, whose exhibits include Calcton's last off-shore 34 feet lifeboat. The **Ha'penny Pier Visitor Centre**, which contains a small informative Mayflower exhibition, is also on the Quay.

Harwich's importance as a port in the 19th century is confirmed by the **Redoubt**, a huge

grey fort similar in style to the Martello Towers, which has been opened as a museum.

WALTON-ON-THE-NAZE

16½ miles E of Colchester off the B1034

A traditional resort that is focused on its **Pier**, which was first built in wood in 1830, and the **Marine Parade**, which dates from the same period.

The wind-blown expanse of **The Naze**, to the north of Walton, is constantly changing shape as it is eroded by the wind and the tide but it remains a pleasant place for walking and for picnics. The **Naze Tower** was originally built as a beacon in 1720 to warn seamen off the West Rocks just offshore.

CLACTON-ON-SEA

13 miles SE of Colchester on the A133

First settled by hunters in the Stone Age, Clacton is another traditional family resort with a **Victorian Pier**, long sandy south-facing beach and lovely gardens, including the **Clifftop Public Gardens**. On the pier, apart from the traditional sideshows, big wheel, restaurants and fairground rides, there is the fascinating **Seaquarium and Reptile Safari**.

Close by are the ancient ruins of **St Osyth Priory** that was founded by Augustinian Canons and named after St Osytha, the martyred daughter of Frithenwald, the first Christian King of the East Angles, who was himself beheaded by the Danes in AD 653. In a **Martello Tower** at **Point Clear** is the **East Essex Aviation Museum** that contains interesting displays of wartime aviation, military and naval photographs, uniforms and other memorabilia with local and USAAF connections. To the north of Clacton is the

---

152 THE STINGRAY AND THE CROWN POST RESTAURANT

Harwich

An excellent bed and breakfast and pub, with a fantastic new restaurant next door offering the very best in traditional English cuisine

See entry on page 422

---

153 THE GREYHOUND

Wivenhoe

A popular pub and restaurant serving real ales and home cooked food made from locally sourced produce

See entry on page 424

Holland Haven Country Park that is an ideal place for watching the marine birds and other wildlife of this region.

BRIGHTLINGSEA

7½ miles SE of Colchester on the B1029

As well as a long tradition of shipbuilding and seafaring, Brightlingsea has the distinction of being the only limb of the Cinque Ports outside Kent and Sussex. It is also home to one of the oldest occupied buildings in Essex – the 13th century **Jacobes Hall** – that was used as a meeting hall during the reign of Henry III. There are numerous walks along Brightlingsea Creek and the River Colne which provide the opportunity to watch the birdlife on the saltings. Across the water from Brightlingsea, reached by a causeway, is **Mersea Island**, much of which is now a National Nature Reserve. The story of the Island, with special reference to its maritime heritage, is told in the **Mersea Island Museum** at West Mersea. A notable vicar of East Mersea (and father of 13 children) was Sabine Baring-Gould, who wrote the stirring hymn *Onward Christian Soldiers*.

TOLLESHUNT D'ARCY

9½ miles SW of Colchester on the B1026

The birthplace of Dodie Smith, the author of 101 Dalmatians, this modest village lies close to the **Maldon District Agricultural and Domestic Museum** at **Goldhanger**, featuring a large collection of vintage farm tools and machinery as well as printing machinery and domestic artefacts.

TIPTREE

8½ miles SW of Colchester on the B1022

Tiptree is famous as the home of the **Wilkin and Sons Jam Factory**, a Victorian establishment that now boasts a fascinating visitors' centre in the grounds of the original factory. Just to the east of Tiptree lies **Layer Marney** where a mansion to rival Hampton Court was planned but never completed. However, the massive eight-storey Tudor gatehouse was finished in 1525, and provides spectacular views out over the estate's formal gardens and across the surrounding countryside.

COGGESHALL

9½ miles W of Colchester on the A120

An ancient town whose prosperity was based on cloth and lace in the Middle Ages. Its attractions include the delightful half-timbered **Paycocke's House** that dates from around 1500 and features unusually rich panelling, wood carvings and a display of Coggeshall lace. The National Trust also owns the restored **Coggeshall Grange Barn**, which dates from around 1140 and is the oldest surviving timber-framed barn in Europe.

Paycocke's House, Coggeshall

To the south is the **Feering and Kelvedon Museum**, which is dedicated to manorial history and houses artefacts from the Roman settlement of Canonium; to the west are the **Cressing Temple Barns** which were commissioned in the 12th century by the Knights Templar and contain the timber of over 1,000 oak trees.

HALSTEAD

12 miles NW of Colchester on the A1124

Like Coggeshall and Braintree, Halstead was once an important weaving centre. The picturesque **Townsford Mill** is a reminder of the town's industrial heritage and this three-storey mill beside the River Colne, once a landmark site for the Courtauld empire. is now an antiques centre. Halstead's most famous product was once life-sized, mechanical elephants built by W Hunwicks; they could carry a load of eight adults and four children at speeds of up to 12 miles per hour!

To the east, at **Chappel**, is the **East Anglian Railway Museum**, where a comprehensive collection of period railway architecture, engineering and memorabilia can be seen. Railway enthusiasts should also visit the **Colne Valley Railway and Museum** at **Castle Hedingham**, where a mile of the Colne Valley and Halstead line has been restored to run steam trains. The village itself is dominated by its **Norman Castle** that was, in the 11th century, one of the country's strongest fortresses.

To the west of Halstead is the **Gosfield Lake Leisure Resort**, the county's largest freshwater lake, which lies in the grounds of **Gosfield Hall**, a Tudor mansion remodelled in the 19th century by its then owner, Samuel Courtauld.

SAFFRON WALDEN

This typical market town is named after the saffron crocus that was ground in the area to make dyestuffs and fulfil a variety of other uses in the Middle Ages. **Saffron Walden Museum** contains a wide range of exhibitions and displays, and among the many fascinating items are the gloves worn by Mary, Queen of Scots on the day that she died; here, too, are the ruins of historic Walden Castle. On the Common, once Castle Green, is the largest surviving **Turf Maze** in England, believed to be some 800 years old. Once the home of the 1st Earl of Suffolk and of Charles II, 17th century **Audley End House**, with its two large courtyards, was a rival in magnificence to Hampton Court. Though much of the house was demolished as it fell into disrepair, it

Audley End House, Saffron Walden

remains one of the country's most impressive Jacobean mansions and its distinguished stone façade is set off perfectly by Capability Brown's lake.

Just to the north of the town are the **Bridge End Gardens**, a wonderfully restored example of early Victorian gardens, complete with the wonderful **Hedge Maze**, which was planted in 1840 in the Italian Renaissance style and has 610 metres of paths.

Further North is the village of **Hadstock** whose parish **Church of St Botolph** claims to have the oldest church door in England – it is Saxon. The village of **Hempstead**, near Saffron Walden, was the birthplace in 1578 of William Harvey, the chief physician to Charles I and the discoverer of the circulation of the blood, and in 1705 of the highwayman Dick Turpin, whose parents kept the Bell Inn.

AROUND SAFFRON WALDEN

THAXTED

6 miles SE of Saffron Walden on the B184

Originally a Saxon settlement, this small and thriving country town has numerous

---

154 THE THREE BOTTLES

Great Yeldham

Fine old inn serving real ales and a famous Sunday lunch; also a well-kept beer garden.

See entry on page 423

---

155 THE MAYPOLE

Thaxted

With a good sense of humour, this down to earth village pub run by mother and daughter team offers delicious home cooked food, good real ale and live entertainment throughout the week.

See entry on page 425

attractively pargeted and timber-framed houses along with a magnificent **Guildhall** that dates from around 1390. Built as a meeting place for cutlers, it later became an administrative centre, then part of a school. It contains a small display of work by Thaxted artists. Built in 1804 by John Webb, the town's famous **Tower Windmill** remained in use until 1907 and now, fully restored, contains a rural life museum.

FINCHINGFIELD

10 miles SE of Saffron Walden on the B1053

A charming village of thatched cottages around a sloping village green; this is one of the most photographed villages in Essex. To the southwest lies the equally picturesque old market town of **Great Bardfield** whose most notable feature is its restored windmill that goes by the name of 'Gibraltar'. The **Great Bardfield Museum** occupies a 16th century charity cottage and 19th century village lockup, and has some informative displays with historical domestic and agricultural artifacts.

BRAINTREE

16½ miles SE of Saffron Walden on the A131

Situated at the crossing of two Roman roads, Braintree and its close neighbour Bocking

---

156 THE CROSS KEYS

White Notley

Quaint old village inn serving wholesome "pub grub", real ales and hosting international themed food evenings.

See entry on page 424

---

157 THE GEORGE

Shalford near Braintree

Beautiful 14th century country inn known for serving excellent English pub food and real ales in a charming period setting.

See entry on page 426

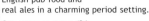

---

were brought together by the cloth industry when Flemish and then Huguenot weavers settled here. One Huguenot, Samuel Courtauld, established a silk mill here in 1816 and the **Braintree District Museum** has a number of associated displays. The town's magnificent former Town Hall is another legacy of the Courtauld family.

To the southwest of Braintree can be found the **Great Leighs Great Maze**, one of the most challenging in the world; this is also the take-off location for exhilarating hot-air balloon rides. To the northwest, at **Great Saling**, is the charming **Saling Hall Garden**.

GREAT DUNMOW

12 miles SE of Saffron Walden on the A120

This town is famous for the 'Flitch of Bacon', an ancient ceremony that dates back to the early 12th century when a flitch, or side, of bacon is awarded to the local man who "does not repent of his marriage nor quarrel, differ or dispute with his wife within a year and a day after marriage." In the parish church at **Broxted** a window commemorating the captivity and release of John McCarthy and the other Beirut hostages was dedicated in 1993.

STANSTED MOUNTFICHET

9 miles SW of Saffron Walden on the B1383

Though close to Stansted Airport, this village is worth a visit as it is home to a Norman Village, complete with domestic animals and the reconstructed **Mountfichet Castle**. The **House on the Hill Museum Adventure** incorporates a Norman Village, a **Toy Museum**, reputedly the largest in the world, with over 80,000 items on display, and Dinosaur Encounters.

To the north, at **Widdington**, lies **Mole Hall Wildlife Park** where visitors can see a range of wild and domestic animals along with butterflies, snakes and insects; the village is also home to Prior's Hall Barn (English Heritage), a fine medieval 'aisled' barn.

Between Stansted Mountfichet and Hatfield Broad Oak lies **Hatfield Forest**, a former Royal hunting forest where many features of a medieval forest can still be seen.

For many, Gloucestershire is the Cotswolds, the delightful limestone hills that sweep across the county from Tetbury in the south to Chipping Campden in the north. As well as providing some of the most glorious scenery and the prettiest villages in the country, the county is also home to the historic towns of Cirencester and Cheltenham. There are some grand and glorious buildings to be found in the areas around Cirencester, including the baroque mansion at Dyrham Park, Elizabethan mansion Chavenage House and Georgian Frampton Court which has been in the same family since its completion in the 1730s. The Spa town of Cheltenham, with its beautiful parks and lakes, holds the intriguing Pittville Pump Room (now a museum exploring the town's past) and some more modern interests in the Promenade; one of the most impressive boulevards in the country, which is an excellent shopping location.

However, Gloucestershire is not only about the Cotswolds. To the west, on the River Severn, is the ancient city of Gloucester – famous for its Cathedral, with the largest surviving medieval stained glass window in the country. Further downriver is the Vale of Berkeley, with the Norman Berkeley Castle. Near to Gloucester is Dymock, known for the "Dymock Poets" - a group which included Rupert Brooke, and later Robert Frost. Also,

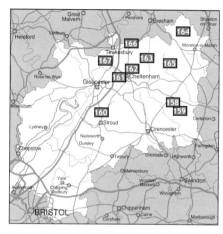

at nearby Newent, is the International Bird of Prey Centre that has one of the largest collections of birds of prey in the world.

On the opposite bank of the river lies the old royal hunting ground of the Forest of Dean, once an important mining and industrial area. Bounded by the Rivers Severn and Wye, the area has been effectively isolated from the rest of England and Wales and so has developed a character that is all its own. It holds several unique hidden treasures that now visitor should miss - not least the bizarre collection of oddities at the Littledean Jail.

Accommodation

Food & Drink

Food & Drink

CIRENCESTER

As **Corinium Dobonnorum**, this was the second largest Roman town in Britain and, although few signs remain of their occupation today, the award winning **Corinium Museum** features one of the finest collection of antiquities from Roman Britain as well as several room reconstructions. The site of a once grand Roman Amphitheatre, now little more than a dip in the park green, can be found signposted from the town centre.

Now dubbed the 'Capital of the Cotswolds', the Cirencester of today is a lively market town which has built upon the medieval wealth that was generated by its wool trade. One of the many legacies of this era is the magnificent **Church of St John**, perhaps the greatest of all the Cotswold 'wool churches', whose 120 feet tower dominates the town.

AROUND CIRENCESTER

BIBURY

7 miles NE of Cirencester on the B4425

Described by William Morris, founder of the Arts and Crafts Movement, as "the most beautiful village in England", Bibury remains

---

158 **THE RED LION INN**

Northleach

The bar serves four Cask marque accredited real ales and wholesome dishes using local produce, and when the weather is kind the courtyard and burgage garden really come into their own.

See entry on page 427

---

159 **THE SHERBORNE ARMS**

Aldsworth

The aim of the Jenvey family, since 1984, has been to provide a traditional English pub atmosphere along with honest, wholesome cooking.

See entry on page 428

---

a delightful place. The most photographed building here is **Arlington Row**, a superb terrace of medieval stone cottages built as a wool store in the 14th century and converted, 300 years later, into weavers' cottages and workshops.

FAIRFORD

9 miles E of Cirencester on the A417

Wealthy wool merchants financed the building of the splendid **Church of St Mary**, whose greatest glory is a set of 28 medieval stained-glass windows depicting the Christian faith in picture-book style.

TETBURY

9½ miles SW of Cirencester on the A433

In the heart of this charming old wool town is the superb 17th century **Market House** which is connected to the old trading centre by the ancient Chipping Stones. Among other places of interest is **Tetbury Police Museum** in the cells of the old police station.

Just to the northwest of the town stands **Chavenage House**, a beautiful Elizabethan mansion constructed in the characteristic E-shape of the period. Still occupied by descendants of the original owners, the house contains many relics from the Cromwellian period and Cromwell himself is known to have stayed here.

Chavenage House

To the southwest of Tetbury lies **Westonbirt Arboretum**, one of the finest collections of trees and shrubs in Europe that was founded by Robert Stayner Holford and added to by his son. Now managed by the Forestry Commission, it offers numerous delightful walks along some 17 miles of footpaths.

CHIPPING SODBURY

23 miles SW of Cirencester on the A432

A pleasant market town that still retains its ancient street pattern, Chipping Sodbury once enjoyed prosperity as a weaving centre, and it was during this period that the large parish church was built. A mile or so to the east lies **Old Sodbury**, whose church contains the tomb of David Harley, the Georgian diplomat who negotiated the treaty that ended the American War of Independence. Just beyond Old Sodbury is the **Badminton Park** estate, founded by Edward Somerset, the son of the Marquis of Worcester. The house is known for its important collection of Italian, English and Dutch paintings and the estate is the venue for **Badminton Horse Trials**, which were started by the 10th Duke of Beaufort in 1949.

To the south of Chipping Sodbury and standing on the slope of the Cotswold ridge is **Dyrham Park** (National Trust), a striking baroque mansion set in 110 hectares of garden and rolling parkland, with a fine collection of Delft porcelain and several Dutch paintings among its treasures.

NAILSWORTH

11 miles W of Cirencester on the A46

Another town that thrived on the local wool trade, Nailsworth still has several of its old mills and associated buildings.

Just to the east of the town, in Hampton Fields, is the extraordinary **Avening Long Stone**, a prehistoric standing stone pierced with holes that is said to move on Midsummer's Eve. Another ancient monument, **Nan Tow's Tump**, a huge round barrow tomb that is said to contain the remains of a local witch standing upright, can be found to the south near Ozleworth.

BERKELEY

21½ miles W of Cirencester on the B4066

This small town lends its name to the fertile strip of land known as the Vale of Berkeley. Its largely Georgian centre is dominated by the Norman **Berkeley Castle**, said to be the oldest inhabited castle in Britain. Built

Berkeley Castle

between 1117 and 1153 on the site of a Saxon fort, the castle has a rich and colourful history and as well as seeing the many treasures that the Berkeley family have collected over the centuries, visitors can explore the dungeons, the grounds and the medieval bowling alley.

Berkeley was also the home of Edward Jenner, the pioneering doctor and immunologist whose beautiful Georgian house, **The Chantry**, is now the **Jenner Museum**. At **Slimbridge** is the **Wildlife and Wetlands Centre** founded in 1946 by the great naturalist, artist, sailor and broad-caster Peter (later Sir Peter) Scott – the father of modern conservation.

STROUD

11 miles W of Cirencester on the A419

With the surrounding hill farms providing a constant supply of wool and the several Cotswold streams which join the River Frome here supplying water power, it is not surprising that Stroud became the capital of the Cotswold woollen industry. By the 1820s there were over 150 textile mills in and around the town though only six survive today – one of these specialises in green baize for snooker tables.

160 THE EDGEMOOR INN

Edge

Interesting locally-brewed real ales and a wide variety of home-cooked dishes at this family-friendly village pub.

See entry on page 429

To the east of Stroud lies the delightful village of **Bisley**, which stands some 780 feet above sea level and is known as 'Bisley-God-Help-Us' because of the bitter winter winds that sweep across the hillside. Below the village's impressive church are the **Seven Wells of Bisley** that are blessed and decorated with flowers each year on Ascension Day.

Just to the north of Stroud is the beautiful little wool town of **Painswick** which is known as the 'Queen of the Cotswolds'. Hidden away, to the north, amidst the magnificent Cotswold countryside is **Painswick Rococo Garden**, a unique 18th century garden (famous for its stunning naturalistic display of snowdrops) that features plants from around the world along with a maze, planted in 1999, which commemorates the gardens 250th anniversary.

Further north again is **Prinknash Abbey Park** (pronounced Prinnage) to where the Benedictine monks of Caldey Island moved in 1928. Part of the abbey gardens are given over to the **Prinknash Bird and Deer Park**.

FRAMPTON-ON-SEVERN

17½ miles W of Cirencester off the B4071

Frampton's large village green, which incorporates a cricket ground and three ponds, was formed when the marshy land outside the gates of **Frampton Court** was drained in the 18th century. The Court is an outstanding example of a Georgian country house and has been the seat of the Clifford family ever since it was completed in the 1730s. On the opposite side of the green is **Frampton Manor**, also owned by the Cliffords, a much-restored medieval manor whose lovely walled garden contains many rare plants.

To the west of Frampton, on a great bend in the river, is the **Arlingham Peninsula**, part of the **Severn Way Shepperdine-Tewkesbury Long Distance Footpath**.

The land on which the village of Arlingham stands once belonged to the monks of St Augustine's Abbey, Bristol, and is believed to be the point where St Augustine crossed the Severn on his way to convert the heathen Welsh tribes.

COLEFORD

A former mining town, Coleford developed into an important iron-processing centre due to the availability of local ore deposits and of the ready supply of timber for the smelting process. Still regarded as the capital of the **Royal Forest of Dean**, Coleford is also home to the **Great Western Railway Museum**, which is housed in an 1883 goods station and numbers several steam locomotives among its exhibits. Another treat for railway enthusiasts is the **Perrygrove Railway**, with its narrow-gauge steam train and treasure hunt through the woods.

To the southeast lies **Parkend**, which, like many communities in the area, was once based around the extraction of minerals. At the northern terminus of the Dean Forest Railway, just west of the village, is the RSPB's **Nagshead Nature Reserve**.

Just to the south of Coleford are **Clearwell Caves**, the only remaining working iron mine in the Forest of Dean, where ochres for use as paint pigments are produced. Visitors can tour the nine impressive caverns, and several marked walks explore surface mining remains.

AROUND COLEFORD

WESTBURY-ON-SEVERN

9 miles NE of Coleford on the A48

This village is best known as the home of **Westbury Court Garden**, a formal Dutch water garden laid out between 1696 and 1705 that is home to many historic varieties of apple, pear and plum. To the west lies **Littledean Hall**, reputedly the oldest inhabited house in England (and most haunted in the county), which has both Saxon and Celtic remains in its cellars and is thought to date from the 6th century. Westbury is an excellent place to view the famous **Severn Bore**, a tidal wave that several times a month makes its often dramatic way along the river.

Close by, at the village of Littledean, can be found one of the most eccentric and marvelous collections of oddities you are likely to find anywhere in the UK; **Littledean Jail** (or the "Alcatraz of the Forest" as the Grade II listed building has otherwise been called). The highly controversial collection amassed by owner Andy Jones and wife Nicola, contains (among the many, many various artifacts and displays) police memorabilia, correspondence and works from Britain's most dangerous prisoners, a five legged cat, celebrity scandal stories, a Dr Who Darlek, and a model of Littledean Jail created from 56,000 matches. Not to be missed! Though I would not recommend it for those of a sensitive nature.

LYDNEY

5½ miles SE of Coleford on the B4234

Lydney is the largest settlement between Chepstow and Gloucester, with a harbour and canal that served the iron and coal industries. The town is the southern terminus of the **Dean Forest Railway**, which operates a regular service of steam and diesel trains between here and Parkend. At Norchard Railway Centre, the line's headquarters, there is a railway museum, souvenir shop and details of restoration projects.

One of the key attractions in the area is **Lydney Park Gardens and Museum** on the western outskirts of the town. The gardens are not only a riot of colour, particularly in May and June, but they contain the site of an Iron Age hill fort and the remains of a Roman temple.

CHELTENHAM

This was a small, insignificant village until a mineral spring was accidentally discovered here in 1715 by a local man, William Mason, who built a pump room and began Cheltenham's transformation into one of Europe's leading Regency spa towns. In 1788, the spa received the royal seal of approval when George III spent five weeks here taking the waters with his family. As an entirely new town was planned and built on the best features of neo-classical Regency architecture

there are very few buildings of any real antiquity left, but one is the **Church of St Mary** that dates back in parts to the 12th century.

The tree-lined **Promenade** is one of the most beautiful boulevards in the country, and its crowning glory is the wonderful Neptune's Fountain modelled on the Fontana di Trevi in Rome. The Promenade is the premiere shopping street in Cheltenham, and has a wonderful mix of jewelry, arts & crafts and fancy boutique shops. At its top end is a lovely little park, with an outside bar, which is popular in the summer for relaxing with a picnic and watching the world go by.

For more extensive parkland you need only cross to the other side of the city centre where you'll find **Pittville Park**. Within the

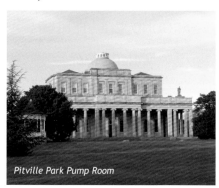

Pittville Park Pump Room

161 THE FOX & HOUNDS INN

Cheltenham

Behind the handsome Georgian frontage it's a comfortable, stylish place with two bars, a wood-panelled lounge and a restaurant at the rear.

See entry on page 430

162 THE PLOUGH

Prestbury

The Plough, which dates back to the middle of the 17th century, is full of character, with superb, picturesque gardens to match.

See entry on page 431

109

park is the magnificent Pump Room overlooking the broad gardens and lakes, which now houses the **Pittville Pump Room Museum** - using original period costumes to bring alive the story of Cheltenham from its Regency heyday to the 1960s.

Cheltenham Racecourse, two miles north of town at Prestbury Park, is the home of National Hunt Racing and stages numerous top-quality race meetings throughout the season, culminating in the prestigious March Festival when the Gold Cup and the Champion Hurdle find the year's best steeplechaser and hurdler. The town does get very busy during the festival, but it also has a great lively party atmosphere which makes it worth enduring the crowds and queues.

AROUND CHELTENHAM

WINCHCOMBE

5½ miles NE of Cheltenham on the B4632

The **Winchcombe Folk and Police Museum** tells the history of the town from prehistoric times, and the **Winchcombe Railway Museum and Garden** has one of the largest collections of railway equipment in the country: visitors can work signals and clip tickets and generally go misty-eyed about the age of steam. The Cotswold garden surrounding the building is full of old and rare plants. Set against the beautiful backdrop of the Cotswold Hills stands **Sudeley Castle**, a treasure house of Old Masters (Turner, Rubens, Van Dyck), tapestries, furniture, costumes and toys; the lovely grounds include a lake, formal gardens and a 15 feet double yew hedge.

Catherine Parr, the sixth and last wife of Henry VIII, was brought to Sudeley Castle after the King died. She married Sir Thomas Seymour, Baron Seymour of Sudeley and died at the Castle in 1548.

STANTON

10½ miles NE of Cheltenham off the B4632

One of the prettiest spots in the Cotswolds, the whole village was restored by the architect Sir Philip Scott in the years before World War I; his home from 1906 to 1937 was **Stanton Court**, an elegant Jacobean residence built by Queen Elizabeth I's Chamberlain. Beyond Stanton, on the road to Broadway, is **Snowshill Manor** (National Trust), an elegant mansion dating from Tudor times, which was once the home of Catherine Parr. It now contains a fascinating collection of crafts and artefacts assembled by the last private owner, Charles Paget Wade.

CHIPPING CAMPDEN

16 miles NE of Cheltenham on the B4081

The 'Jewel of the Cotswolds' and full of beautifully restored buildings, Chipping Campden was a regional capital of the wool trade from the 13th to the 16th century and much of the town dates from that era. The **Market Hall** was built in 1627 by the wool merchant, Sir Baptist Hicks; he also endowed a group of almshouses and **Old Campden House**, which was burnt down by Royalists to prevent it falling into the hands of the enemy.

STOW-ON-THE-WOLD

15½ miles E of Cheltenham on the A429

At 800 feet above sea level, this is the highest town in the Cotswolds and at one

---

163 THE OLD CORNER CUPBOARD

Winchcombe

One of Winchcombe's most interesting buildings - acquired its odd name after a customer pointed out that almost every angle had a cupboard!

See entry on page 430

---

164 THE BAKERS ARMS

Broad Campden

Traditional stone-built Cotswold hostelry serving wholesome and appetising food along with real ales.

See entry on page 432

---

time held a twice-yearly sheep fair on the market square where the town stocks still stand today. In Park Street is the **Toy and Collectors Museum**, housing a charming display of toys, trains, teddy bears and dolls, along with textiles and lace, porcelain and pottery.

BOURTON-ON-THE-WATER

13 miles E of Cheltenham on the A429

Probably the most popular of all the Cotswold villages, Bourton has the willow-lined River Windrush flowing through its centre, crossed by several delightful pedestrian bridges. Those with a keen nose will want to visit the unique **Perfumery Exhibition**, where the extraction and manufacture of perfume is explained and where there is also a perfume garden.

To the north, at **Lower Slaughter**, is the **Old Mill**, a restored 19th century flour mill with a giant water wheel. To the southwest is the traditional market town of **Northleach**, which is home to the fascinating **Keith Harding's World of Mechanical Music;** a fascinating museum of antique self-playing musical instruments housed in a 17th century merchant's house.

To the west of Northleach is **Chedworth Roman Villa**, a large, well-preserved villa that was discovered by chance in 1864. Excavations have revealed more than 30 rooms and buildings and some wonderful mosaics.

GLOUCESTER

In the 1st century AD, the Romans established a fort here to guard what was then the lowest crossing point of the River Severn; it was soon replaced by a much larger fortress and the settlement of Glevum quickly became one of the most important military bases in Roman Britain. It was at Gloucester that William the Conqueror held a Christmas parliament and also ordered the rebuilding of the abbey, an undertaking that included a magnificent church that was the forerunner of the superb Norman **Gloucester Cathedral**. The exquisite fan tracery in the cloisters of the Cathedral is the earliest and among the finest in existence and the great east window is the largest surviving medieval stained glass window in the country, measuring 72 feet by 38 feet. The young Henry III was crowned at the Cathedral, with a bracelet on his little head rather than a crown.

Gloucester Docks were once the gateway for waterborne traffic heading into the Midlands and the handsome Victorian warehouses are home to several award-winning museums. The **National Waterways Museum**, which is entered by a lock chamber with running water, tells the fascinating story of Britain's canals, and the **Robert Opie Collection** at the **Museum of Advertising and Packaging** takes a nostalgic look at the 1940s through to the 1970s with the aid of toys and food, fashions, packaging and a continuous screening of vintage TV commercials.

In the southwestern suburbs of Gloucester are the ruins of **Llanthony Abbey**, which was moved in the 12th century from its original site in the Black Mountains of Wales - bringing with it its Welsh name - because the monks were terrified of the Welsh.

AROUND GLOUCESTER

NEWENT

5 miles NW of Gloucester on the B4215

This is the capital of an area of northwest Gloucestershire that is known as the Ryelands, home of the renowned Ryelands sheep – an ancient breed famed for the quality of its wool. Naturally, therefore, this was one of the county's principal wool trading

165 THE HALFWAY HOUSE

Kineton

Behind the mellow Cotswold stone frontage the inn has been carefully modernised while retaining a traditional feel assisted by oak beams and cosy winter fires.

See entry on page 433

centres and there are a number of grand merchant's houses in the town. The most distinctive building, however, is the splendid timber-framed **Market House** which was built as a butter market in the 16th century with its upper floors supported on 16 oak pillars.

There are not a great many windmills in Gloucestershire but at **Castle Hill Farm** is a working wooden mill which provides great views from its balcony. A short distance south is the **International Bird of Prey Centre** that houses one of the largest collections of birds of prey in the world.

DYMOCK

10 miles NW of Gloucester on the B4215

In the years before World War I, this village became the base for a group of writers who became known as the **Dymock Poets**. The Dymock Poets included Rupert Brooke, Wilfred Gibson, Edward Thomas, John Drinkwater and Lascelles Abercrombie and was later joined by Robert Frost; they sent out its New Numbers poetry magazine from Dymock's tiny post office and it was also from here that Brooke published his War Sonnets, including *The Soldier*. Brooke and Thomas died in the Great War, which led to the dissolution of the group.

TEWKESBURY

A town of historic and strategic importance, the rivers restricted the town's lateral expansion, which accounts for the unusual number of tall buildings. Its early prosperity was based on the wool and mustard trades and the movement of corn by river also contributed to its wealth. Tewkesbury's main thoroughfares, High Street, Church Street and Barton Street, form a Y shape, and the area between is a marvellous maze of narrow alleyways and small courtyards hiding many grand old pubs and medieval cottages. At the centre of it all is **Tewkesbury Abbey**, one of the largest parish churches in the country, which was founded in the 8th century and completely rebuilt in the 11th. After the Dissolution, it was saved from destruction by

the townspeople, who raised £453 to buy it from the Crown.

The **Battle of Tewkesbury**, which took place in 1471 in a field south of town, was one of the fiercest in the War of the Roses and the battle site has been known as Bloody Meadow ever since. Following the Lancastrian defeat, those who had not been slaughtered in the battle fled to the Abbey, where the killing began again. The 17-year-old son of Henry VI, Edward Prince of Wales, was killed in the conflict and a plaque marking his final resting place can be seen in the abbey.

To the east of Tewkesbury the **Gloucestershire Warwickshire Railway** runs between **Toddington** and Cheltenham. The line commands wonderful views of the sleepy hamlets and villages, as the it runs though the beautiful Cotswold countryside.

Gloucestershire Warwickshire Railway

166 THE TEDDINGTON HANDS INN

Teddington

The spacious interior provides plenty of room to enjoy well-kept ales, excellent food and unbeatable hospitality.

See entry on page 432

167 THE RIVERSIDE INN

Tirley

A traditional inn serving home cooked food and real ales. Camping pitches are available as well as a self catering apartment.

See entry on page 434

HAMPSHIRE

Hampshire's coastal crescent, which stretches from Havant to New Milford in the west, is home to two of the country's most famous ports, Southampton and Portsmouth, and the maritime and naval traditions here remain strong. Both ports have a range of great maritime museums; Portsmouth even has the "Trafalgar Sail" - the largest single original artifact from the Battle of Trafalgar.

This contrasts greatly with the grand rolling scenery in the northern part of the county and the ancient landscape of the North Downs, home to the historic towns of Winchester and Andover. Near Winchester is the famous Roman site of Calleva Atrebatum; one of the most complete plans of any Roman town in Britain. Another impressive Roman sight can be found outside the town of Fordingbridge; the Rockbourne Roman Villa, which holds some glorious mosaics.

On the western bank of Southampton Water lies the New Forest, the largest wild area of lowland in Britain, which William the Conqueror set aside as his own private

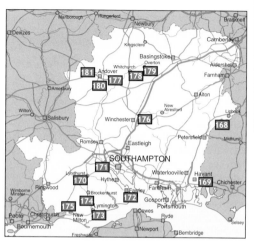

hunting ground over 900 years ago. The only large town of the New Forest, Lyndhurst, and the surrounding villages hold some interesting treasures, including many unique gardens, a 25 acre conservation park full of wildlife, the fortified castles Hurst and Calshot, and the Rufus Stone - marking the spot where the son of William the Conqueror was killed.

Accommodation

Food & Drink

Food & Drink

Places of Interest

SOUTHAMPTON

It was from this historic port that Henry V sailed for Agincourt in 1415 and the *Titanic* steamed out into the Solent on her tragic first and last voyage. The town was an obvious target for enemy bombing during World War II, but despite the numerous attacks several ancient buildings have survived including a section of the town's medieval walls and their most impressive feature – Bargate. Southampton's links with the sea are never far away and the story of the luxury liners that sailed from here, along with the port, is told at the **Maritime Museum** housed in the 14th century Wool House. Vibrant markets are held in the town centre on Fridays, with over 50 attractive continental-style stalls, and a smaller one on Saturdays. Other shopping can be found at WestQuay premiere shopping complex, the Mall Marlands, and at the very popular IKEA.

On the northern outskirts of Southampton lie **Itchen Valley Country Park** and **West End**, the village to which the Captain of the liner *Carpathia*, which rescued passengers from the *Titanic*, retired. His grave lies in an old burial ground near the village's **Local History Museum**.

AROUND SOUTHAMPTON

BISHOPS WALTHAM

8 miles NE of Southampton on the B3035

This charming small town was, for nearly 1,000 years, home of the country residence of

the Bishops of Winchester and at their sumptuous **Bishop's Palace** they played host to numerous monarchs. Built in 1136 by Henri de Blois, the palace was largely destroyed during the Civil War although the ruins remain an impressive sight.

PETERSFIELD

21 miles NE of Southampton on the B2070

The oldest building in this pleasant market town is the 12th century **Church of St Peter**. Also of interest are the town **museum** (which has a brilliant exhibition of the work of painter Flora Twort) and **The Heath** which is a 69 acre area of grass and heathland - the site of Bronze Age and Iron Age burial mounds - set around a 22 acre pond.

HORNDEAN

17 miles E of Southampton off the A3

This village has a long association with brewing and the company of George Gale, founded in 1847, offers guided tours that include the techniques of brewing. To the northwest lies **Queen Elizabeth Country Park**, an Area of Outstanding Natural Beauty which contains many Roman and Iron Age sites as well as the three hills of Butser, War Down and Holt Down. A new fun addition to the park is an all wooden play area for young children created by local sculptor Andy Frost. Nearby, **Butser Ancient Farm** is a living, working reconstruction of an Iron Age farm (though be warned, it is only open to the public from Oct to Easter on weekdays).

Further northwest lies **Hambledon**, the village where the rules of cricket were laid down in 1774 and where a monument stands on **Broadhalfpenny Down**, where the early games were played.

Bishop's Palace, Bishops Waltham

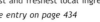

168 THE RISING SUN

Milland

This is one of the very best village inns in the region, a wonderful place to relax, have fun and enjoy a drink and a meal featuring the best and freshest local ingredients

See entry on page 434

HAVANT

18 miles SE of Southampton on the A27

Originally a Roman crossroads, the town developed into a leading manufacturing centre. The whole history of the town is explored and explained at **The Spring**; an integrated Arts & Heritage Centre with an exciting programme of events and activities and the first venue in the country to use performance and visual arts to illuminate local history, in addition to more traditional displays. To the north lies one of the south of England's most elegant stately homes, **Stansted Park**, which houses numerous treasures and stands in particularly attractive grounds. Great days out can be had at one of the park's other attractions; including a light railway, jewelry making workshop, and **Le Salon Du Chocolat** which offers visitors the chance to get creative with the delicious art of chocolate moulding. To the southeast is the picturesque village of **Emsworth**, for many years the home of the novelist PG Wodehouse.

To the south of Havant is **Hayling Island**, a traditional family seaside holiday resort with a five-mile sandy beach.

PORTSMOUTH

15 miles SE of Southampton on the A3

Portsmouth is the country's leading naval base, and **Portsmouth Historic Dockyard** is home to three of the greatest ships ever built. The most famous of all is HMS *Victory*, from which Nelson masterminded the decisive encounter with the French navy off Cape Trafalgar in 1805. Here, too, lies the *Mary Rose*, the second largest ship in Henry VIII's fleet, which foundered on her maiden voyage and was raised in 1983. HMS *Warrior*, the

Spinnaker Tower, Portsmouth

Navy's first ironclad warship, can also be seen. Within the Dockyard are several innovative museums and displays tracing the town's maritime history; including the **Dockyard Apprentice** and **Action Stations**, **Mary Rose Museum**, and the **Trafalgar Sail** – at 3,618 ft, the carefully preserved sail is recognised by experts as the largest single original artifact from the Battle of Trafalgar.

Dominating the Portsmouth skyline is the **Spinnaker Tower**, representing a billowing sail and extending some 550 feet into the sky. Southsea, the southern part of the city, also has much to offer: the D. Day Museum that commemorates the Allied invasion of France in 1944; the **Royal Marines Museum** housed in Eastney Barracks; and **Blue Reef Aquarium** where you can see marine life of all wonderful varieties, from local to tropical.

A plaque in Britain Street in Portsmouth marks the place where Isambard Kingdom Brunel was born in 1806, and the house in Old Commercial Road where Charles Dickens was born in 1812 is now a museum.

Southsea Castle, built in 1545 by Henry VIII, was altered in the early 19th century to accommodate more guns and men. Just offshore lies **Spitbank Fort**, a huge Victorian defence that is reached by ferry from Southsea pier.

169 THE BLUE BELL INN

Emsworth

Quayside inn serving appetising home-made food (with fresh fish as a speciality) and cask ales.

See entry on page 435

At the head of Portsmouth Harbour stands **Portchester Castle**, one of the grandest medieval castles in the country, built on the site of a Roman fort.

FAREHAM

10 miles SE of Southampton on the A27

Many aspects of this charming old town are exhibited in **Westbury Manor Museum**, housed in a 17th century farmhouse on the town's outskirts. Nearby are the **Royal Armouries** at **Fort Nelson** where the display of artillery, dating from the Middle Ages, is one of the finest in the world.

To the southeast lies Gosport, home to another of Lord Palmerston's forts, the circular **Fort Brockhurst**, and of the **Royal Naval Submarine Museum** located at HMS *Dolphin*, where visitors can look over several submarines. **Explosion! The Museum of Naval Firepower** is dedicated to the brave people who prepared Navy armaments from Trafalgar to the present day.

HAMBLE

5 miles SE of Southampton on the B3397

A major medieval trading port and once a centre of the shipbuilding industry on the River Hamble, this village is now famous throughout the world as a yachting centre, and some 3,000 boats have berths in the Estuary. To the south lies **Hamble Common**, an area of coastal heath with a wide range of habitats.

Just to the north of Hamble lies **Bursledon**, another village with a strong

Hamble Ferry

maritime heritage: it was here that King Alfred's men sank 20 Viking longships, and Nelson's flagship at the Battle of Copenhagen, *The Elephant*, was built here. Close by, on a hilltop setting, is **Bursledon Windmill**, fully restored to working order it is the only working windmill in the county. The village of Bursledon also has a relic of the county's industrial heritage – **Burlesdon Brickworks**, built in 1897 and after closing in 1974, restored and opened to the public.

ROMSEY

6½ miles NW of Southampton on the A3057

Romsey Abbey was founded in AD 907 by Edward the Elder, son of Alfred the Great, though most of what remains dates from the 12th and 13th centuries. Close to the Abbey stands the oldest secular building in the town, **King John's House**. Other places of interest here include **Romsey Signal Box**, home to numerous railway artefacts, and **Broadlands**, a gracious Palladian mansion set in grounds landscaped by Capability Brown which was the family home of Lord Palmerston, three times Prime Minister in the 1850s and 1860s. The house passed to the Mountbatten family, and it was Lord Louis who first opened it to the public, shortly before his death in 1979. The **Mountbatten Exhibition** commemorates his life.

To the northeast lies the **Sir Harold Hillier Garden and Arboretum**, which is based on the collection of this renowned gardener and now houses 11 National Plant Collections, as well as activity areas for children. Southeast of Romsey lies **East Wellow**, where Florence Nightingale was buried beneath the family monument on her death in 1910.

To the northwest is **Mottisfont Abbey**, which was originally an Augustinian priory but was adapted into a country mansion in the 16th century.

LYNDHURST

The only town of any size in the New Forest, Lyndhurst still remains its administrative centre. Next to the compact **Church of St**

Michael and All Angels in whose churchyard is the grave of Alice Liddell, the inspiration for Alice in Lewis Carroll's novels, stands **Queen's House**. Originally a medieval hunting lodge, the house is now the Headquarters of the Forestry Commission and also home to the **Verderers' Court**, an institution dating back to Norman times that still deals with matters concerning the Forest's ancient common rights. In the High Street, the **New Forest Museum and Visitor Centre** has numerous displays covering all aspects of the forest.

To the northeast, at Ashurst, is the **Otter, Owl and Wildlife Conservation Park** set in 25 acres of ancient woodland. And to the northwest, near the picturesque village of **Minstead**, are the **Furzey Gardens**, which were laid out in the 1920s and provide excellent views over the New Forest to the Isle of Wight.

Furzey Gardens, Minstead

Near Minstead stands the **Rufus Stone** that is said to mark the spot where William Rufus, King William II, son of William the Conqueror, was accidentally killed by an arrow from Sir Walter Tirel's bow while out hunting. Sir Walter made good his escape, and William's brother, who was also hunting in the Forest, lost no time in riding to Westminster to be crowned king Henry I.

AROUND LYNDHURST

BEAULIEU
7 miles SE of Lyndhurst on the B3056

Cistercian monks built an abbey by the River Beaulieu in the 13th century, and some of the abbey's buildings survive today, incorporated into a country estate now owned by Lord Montagu. The estate is most famous for its **National Motor Museum**, where over 300 historic vehicles are on display. Many Montagu family treasures can be seen in **Palace House**, the former Great Gatehouse of Beaulieu Abbey.

At the mouth of the River Beaulieu lies **Buckler's Hard**, a popular place for yachts and cruisers. Facing Buckler's Hard across the River Beaulieu stands **Exbury** where, in the 1920s, Lionel de Rothschild created **Exbury Gardens** with their world-renowned displays of rhododendrons, camellias and azaleas.

FAWLEY
10 miles SE of Lyndhurst on the A326

Despite the vast oil terminals and refineries of one of Europe's largest oil plants dominating the village, Fawley has retained some links with the past: the gardens of

170 STAG HOTEL

Lyndhurst

Providing ten comfortable ensuite bedrooms and an Italian restaurant this popular hotel is situated on the bustling Lyndhurst high street.

See entry on page 436

171 THE ANCHOR INN

Eling, nr Totton

When the sun shines the beer garden – with an enclosed area where children can play – is a delightful spot for enjoying a drink and something to eat.

See entry on page 436

172 THE JOLLY SAILOR

Ashlett Creek, nr Fawley

Sandwiched between the refinery at Fawley and the power station at Calshot, Ashlett Creek is an oasis of calm that's home to a variety of birdlife.

See entry on page 437

Cadland House, which were designed by Capability Brown, house the National Collection of *leptospermums*.

To the southeast lies Calshot, home to RAF bases during both World Wars; at the very end of a shingle spit stands Calshot Castle, built by Henry VIII, now restored as a pre-World War I garrison.

LYMINGTON
8 miles S of Lyndhurst on the A337

An ancient seaport and market town, Lymington was once a major manufacturer of salt and the St Barbe Museum & Art Gallery tells the story of this area, between the Solent and the New Forest, with special reference to the salt industry.

Just up the River Lymington is the pretty village of Boldre whose charming 13th century church has become a shrine to HMS *Hood* which was tragically sunk by the Bismarck in 1941. Charming as it is, this little village has its own ghost; the story tells of two smugglers in the 1600s that murdered a fancily adorned messenger passing their cottage on the edge of town, and buried him in the garden. In the 1920s a woman who had bought the cottage heard strange sounds like barrels being rolled and footsteps, and even discovered a gentleman in Cavalier attire in a

photo taken at the house. After she saw the same gentleman in a dream, telling her to dig in a certain place of her garden, she dug up a small chamber of 17th century bricks - but never found any remains.

NEW MILTON
9½ miles SW of Lyndhurst on the A332

The best-known landmark in this lively little town is its splendid Water Tower of 1900. A particularly striking octagonal building with a castellated parapet, it has the look of a castle rather than part of the town's water system. Just to the west of the town, the Sammy Miller Museum and Farm Trust holds the finest collection of fully restored motorbikes in Europe - though, unlike a static museum, these are all highly functioning machines which have been taken to demonstrations all over Europe.

To the southeast lies the unspoilt resort of Milford-on-Sea, from where a shingle spit extends out to sea; from its end it is less than a mile to the Isle of Wight. Here stands Hurst Castle, another in the chain of fortresses built by Henry VIII, while just inland are Braxton Gardens, with their beautiful roses and knot garden, farmers market brimming with local produce, and fully licensed café.

FORDINGBRIDGE
10 miles NW of Lyndhurst on the A338

The main feature here is the medieval Great Bridge which has seven elegant arches and is upstream from the original ford. The town was loved by painter Augustus John and he spend much of the last 30 years of his life at Fryern Court, an austere Georgian house.

To the north lies the unspoilt village of

---

173 LOUNGES OF LYMINGTON

Lymington

The friendliest of welcomes and a daytime selection of sweet and savoury delights.

See entry on page 437

---

174 THE RED LION, BOLDRE

Boldre

Quintessential New Forest pub serving outstanding food based on fresh, local ingredients.

See entry on page 438

---

175 THE POTTING SHED TEAROOM

Bashley

Delightful tearoom, within the Redcliffe Garden Centre, which serves their delicious homemade food 7 days a week, 364 days a year.

See entry on page 439

Breamore and 16th century **Breamore House** which overlooks the Avon Valley. The house has a fine collection of 17th and 18th century paintings of the Dutch School, and the grounds are home to the **Countryside Museum** and its reconstruction of a Tudor village. Close by, on Breamore Down, is a mizmaze, a circular maze cut into the turf – why, nobody knows.

To the northwest is **Rockbourne Roman Villa** where excavations have revealed the remains of a large villa, with some 40 rooms, superb mosaics and part of its underfloor heating system.

WINCHESTER

Winchester was the capital of King Alfred's Kingdom of Wessex in the 9th century, and two centuries later work began on the Cathedral. **Winchester Cathedral** is filled with priceless treasures, including copies of the Winchester Bible and Bede's Ecclesiastical History. The tombs of William II (William Rufus – see under Lyndhurst above), Jane Austen and Izaak Walton are among the many here, along with that of St Swithin, a 9th century bishop to whom the Cathedral is dedicated.

The area round the Cathedral holds a wealth of interest: the renowned **College**, with its beautiful chapel, founded in 1382; **Wolvesey Castle**, the chief residence of the medieval bishops, where, in 1554, Queen Mary first met Philip of Spain (the wedding banquet was held the very next day!). And of course there are the shops, which are a real marvel. Nearly every street through Winchester centre holds some interesting treasure trove of independent shops and delis, just waiting to be explored.

The only surviving part of **Winchester Castle** is its Great Hall, with a striking Authurian Round Table, and **Queen Eleanor's Garden**, a faithful representation of a medieval garden; the grounds are also the site of the **Peninsula Barracks**, which includes several military museums.

The story of the Red Cross in Hampshire is told at the **Balfour Museum**, and at the **Historic Resources Centre** there is a vast collection of historic records for this area. This centre is near the site of **Hyde Abbey**, which recent excavations have revealed as being the probable site of King Arthur's final burial place.

AROUND WINCHESTER

WHITCHURCH

11½ miles N of Winchester on the B3400

Once an important coaching stop between London and Exeter, Whitchurch has a unique attraction, **Whitchurch Silk Mill**, the last working silk mill in the south of England.

---

176 THE TROUT INN

Itchen Abbas

Picturesque and historic village pub, serving a tasty seasonal menu of locally sourced dishes.

See entry on page 439

---

177 THE HURSTBOURNE INN

Hurstbourne Priors

Pretty traditional English Inn with accommodation, serving fine cuisine and surrounded by rolling countryside.

See entry on page 440

BURGHCLERE

19 miles N of Winchester off the A34

This village is home to the **Sandham Memorial Chapel** where, in the 1920s, Stanley Spencer was commissioned to paint murals on the walls depicting scenes from World War I. The moving paintings are best seen on a bright day as the chapel has no lighting.

Southwest lies **Highclere Castle**, the largest mansion in the county, on the site of a former palace of the Bishops of Winchester.

BASINGSTOKE

17 miles NE of Winchester on the A30

Despite the extensive building work of the 1960s, there are still reminders of old Basingstoke to be seen including the evocative ruins of the 13th century **Chapel of the Holy Ghost** and the 19th century old Town Hall that is now home to the **Willis Museum** and **Sainsbury & Basingstoke Art Galleries**.

To the north lies **The Vyne**, a fine 16th century country house that is noted for its linenfold panelling, Gothic painted vaulting and a Tudor chapel with Renaissance stained glass.

To the east of Basingstoke is **Old Basing**, a place of narrow streets and old cottages and the ruins of **Basing House**. Built on a massive

 178 WATERSHIP DOWN

Freefolk

Traditional, family-friendly inn offering appetising home-cooked meals, real ales and a large beer garden.

See entry on page 441

179 THE OLD HOUSE AT HOME

Overton

Lively tradition pub, with a large beer garden, in the pretty village of Overton.

See entry on page 440

scale within the walls of a medieval castle, the house was once the largest private residence in the country.

SILCHESTER

22 miles NE of Winchester off the A340

This village is home to the famous Roman site of **Calleva Atrebatum** where on-going excavations have revealed one of the most complete plans of any Roman town in Britain. East of Silchester is the estate of **Stratfield Saye House**, which was presented to the Duke of Wellington as a reward for his defeat of Napoleon at Waterloo. It is full of Wellington artefacts, including books, flags and his ornate funeral carriage, and one whole room of the house is devoted to his beloved charger, Copenhagen. It is open to the public each year through July and August.

FARNBOROUGH

29 miles NE of Winchester on the A325

Famous for the Farnborough Air Show, the town is also home to **St Michael's Abbey**. St Michael's Abbey was built in a flamboyant French style by the Empress Eugénie in honour of her husband Napoleon III. Deposed at the end of the Franco-Prussian War, Napoleon III, nephew of the first Napoleon, was exiled to England in 1870 and died at Chislehurst in 1873. The grieving Eugénie founded the Abbey as a mausoleum for her husband, and later for their son Leopold, who died in the Zulu Wars in 1879. Eugénie herself was buried here when she died n 1920.

To the south lies **Aldershot**, a little-known village until the Army established the town as the most famous military centre in the country. The **Aldershot Military Museum**, housed in the only two surviving Victorian barrack blocks, tells the history of the military town and the adjoining civilian town.

ALTON

16 miles NE of Winchester on the A339

The town's impressive double-naved **St Lawrence's Church** was the scene of a dramatic episode during the Civil War when a large force of Roundheads drove 80 Royalists into the church, killing 60 of them. Elsewhere in the town, the **Allen Gallery** contains a fine collection of porcelain and pottery including the famous Elizabethan Tichborne spoons.

Just to the south is **Chawton House**, the home of Jane Austen from 1809 until shortly before her death in 1817, and now home to the **Jane Austen Museum**. A little further from Alton lays the attractive village of Selborne which was, in 1720, the birthplace of the naturalist Gilbert White. His house, **The Wakes**, is now the **Gilbert White Museum**. The Wakes also contains the **Oates Museum**, which is dedicated to Francis Oates, the Victorian explorer, and his nephew, Captain Lawrence Oates, who was a member of Captain Scott's ill-fated South Pole expedition.

NEW ALRESFORD

7 miles E of Winchester on the A31

Founded in about 1200, New Arlesford has long been a world centre of the watercress industry – so much so, that the railway line that carried the commodity to London was dubbed the **Watercress Line**. Now kept going by enthusiasts as a steam railway, it runs between here and Alton.

Close by is one of the finest stately homes in England, **Avington Park**, which stands on a site that was once used by the Romans. The **River Itchen**, renowned for its trout and watercress beds, rises close to the village of **Hinton Ampner** and here can be found **Hinton Ampner House and Gardens** (National Trust). The gardens here, designed by the 8th and last Lord of Sherborne Ralph Dutton, are widely acknowledged as a masterpiece of 20th century design.

STOCKBRIDGE

8 miles NW of Winchester on the A30

Situated on the trout-rich River Test, which flows through, under and alongside its broad main street, Stockbridge attracts visitors with its antique shops, art galleries and charming tearooms. To the south of the town lies **Houghton Lodge Gardens and Hydroponicum**, a charming 18th century cottage with glorious views over the Test Valley that also has a hydroponic greenhouse.

To the northwest is **Danbury Iron Age Hillfort** and nearby is the village of **Middle Wallop** which became famous during the Battle of Britain, when the nearby airfield was a base for squadrons of Spitfires and Hurricanes. The **Museum of Army Flying** houses an important collection that traces the development of Army flying from its beginnings during World War I.

ANDOVER

11 miles NW of Winchester on the A3057

A picturesque market town with a history going back to Saxon times, the market place is dominated by a handsome Guildhall; many of its coaching inns survive from the days when Andover was an important stopping place on the routes between London, Oxford and Southampton.

Just to the west of Andover, at **Weyhill**, is the **Hawk Conservancy and Country Park**, home to over 150 birds of prey from around the world. It was at the Weyhill October Fair that the future mayor in Thomas Hardy's novel *The Mayor of Casterbridge*, sold his wife and child.

---

180 THE CLATFORD ARMS

Goodworth Clatford

The Clatford Arms is gaining quite a reputation for its food, with local produce cooked to order with no compromise on quality and freshness.

See entry on page 442

---

181 HAWK CONSERVANCY TRUST

Weyhill, nr Andover

With flying displays, picnic areas, a cafe and sovenir shop, the Trust provides a fun filled day out for the whole family.

See entry on page 442

121

HEREFORDSHIRE

With its rolling landscape, pretty villages and charming market towns, Herefordshire is a delightful place to visit and, as it has few natural resources, there are few industrial scars to mar the countryside. Apples and hops are the traditional crops of the county and cider producing remains a thriving industry; there is a wonderful Cider Route around the county, which takes in all of the cider farms and producers – most beautiful (and kind to the environment) explored by bicycle. Sheep and cattle are a familiar sight; Hereford cattle still abound and their stock are now to be found in many parts of the world.

The River Wye, which enters England at Hay-on-Wye, winds its way through some of the most glorious countryside in all the land before finally joining with the River Severn

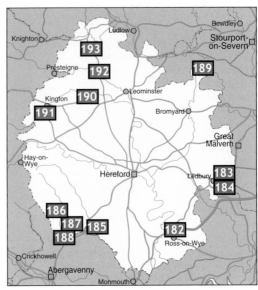

at its estuary. The whole length, which takes in many ancient villages and small towns, provides excellent walking, and the Wye Valley Walk follows the river for 112 miles, the majority in Herefordshire. The valley is a designated Area of Outstanding Natural Beauty, while the river itself was the first to be recognised as a Site of Special Scientific Interest.

Skirmishes with the Welsh were a common occurrence for many centuries and one of the county's best known landmarks, Offa's Dyke, was built in the 8th century as a defence against these marauders. A towering 1,400ft

above, on the Southern edge of the Hergest Ridge, is the haunted house of Hergest Court. Other interesting buildings throughout the county include the glorious ruins of Goodrich Castle near the picturesque village of Symonds Yat, 18th century Berrington Hall, and the market house in Ross-On-Wye which stands on pillars. The county town of Hereford has a beautiful Cathedral - often called the Cathedral of the Marches – which contains both the Chained Library, possibly one of the most important libraries of 17th century books in the country, and the medieval world map, Mappa Mundi.

Accommodation

Accommodation

ROSS-ON-WYE

This lovely old market town is signalled from some way out by the towering spire of **St Mary's Church**, which stands on a sandstone cliff surrounded by a cluster of attractive houses. Opposite the church is a row of rosy-red Tudor almshouses. In 1637, the town was visited by the Black Death and over 300 victims to the plague are buried in the churchyard, where their graves are marked by a simple cross. They were buried in the dead of night in an effort to avoid panicking the townspeople.

Market House, Ross on Wye

In the town's market square is the splendid 17th century **Market House**, with its open ground floor and pillars that support the upper floor, which is now the local Heritage Centre.

Opposite the Market House in Ross-on-Wye is a half-timbered house (now shops) that was the home of the town's greatest benefactor, John Kyrle. A wealthy barrister who had studied law at the Middle Temple, Kyrle settled in Ross in around 1660 and dedicated the rest of his life to philanthropic works: he donated the town's main public garden, The Prospect; he repaired St Mary's spire; he provided a constant supply of fresh water; and

he paid for food and education for the poor.

Another interesting building to look out for is **Thrushes Nest** that was once the home of Sir Frederick Burrows, a gentleman who began his working life as a railway porter and rose above his station to become the last Governor of Bengal.

Ross-on-Wye is well known for its International Festival of music, opera, theatre, comedy and film that takes place annually in August. Among the examples of modern public art littered around the town is a mural celebrating the life of the locally born playwright Dennis Potter.

To the south of Ross-on-Wye is **Hope Mansell Valley**, one of the loveliest and most fertile valleys in the region.

182 POTS AND PIECES TEASHOP & GALLERY

Ross-on-Wye

5-star rated teashop with a gallery of eye-catching gifts at affordable prices.

See entry on page 443

AROUND ROSS-ON-WYE

BROCKHAMPTON

4½ miles N of Ross-on-Wye off the B4224

This charming village is home to one of only two thatched churches in the country. The

Church of All Saints was designed by William Lethaby and built in 1902 by Alice Foster, a wealthy American lady, as a memorial to her parents. The Norfolk thatch is one of many lovely features of this beautifully situated church, which also has stained glass from Christopher Whall's studio and tapestries designed by Burne-Jones.

This is great walking country, and the once busy mining community of **Mordiford** is an excellent place from which to explore the Forestry Commission's **Haugh Wood**.

LEDBURY

11 miles NE of Ross-on-Wye on the A449

Mentioned in the Domesday Book as Ledeberge and granted its market status in the 12th century, this classic rural town is filled with timber-framed black and white buildings. Its most famous son was the Poet Laureate John Masefield, born in 1878 in a house called the Knapp, who wrote of his birthplace as 'A little town of ancient grace'. A much earlier poet born here was William Langland, born in 1332, the aouthor of *Piers Plowman*. In the centre is the **Barrett Browning Institute** that was erected in 1892 in memory of Elizabeth Barrett Browning whose family lived at nearby Colwall.

The town's symbol is the 17th century

183 MRS MUFFINS

Ledbury

Beautiful 16th century tea room offering tempting treats and tasty meals created with the very best in local produce.

See entry on page 443

184 THE PRINCE OF WALES

Ledbury

A delightful, traditional tavern serving lunchtime and evening food and an impressive selection of draught and bottled beers.

see page 444

Market House, which stands on wooden pillars and is attributed to the royal carpenter John Abel. Another notable landmark is the Norman parish church of **St Michael and All Angels**, with a soaring spire set on a separate tower, some magnificent medieval brasses, fine monuments - and bullet holes in the door, the scars of the Battle of Ledbury.

Overlooking the Malvern Hills, just to the east of Ledbury, lies **Eastnor Castle**, a fairytale castle that has the look of a medieval fortress but was actually built between 1881 and 1924. Wanting a magnificent baronial castle, the 1st Earl Somers engaged the young architect Robert Smirke, and the result is a fine example of the great Norman and Gothic architectural revival that was taking place at that time.

Eastnor Castle

SYMONDS YAT

5½ miles SW of Ross-on-Wye on the B4432

This inland resort and well-known beauty spot offers glorious views, walks, river cruises, wildlife, history and adventure including canoeing down the River Wye and rock climbing. The village is divided into east and west by the river and, with no vehicular bridge at this point, pedestrians cross by means of a punt ferry that is pulled across the river by a chain. Walking in the area is a delight, and among the many landmarks nearby are **Seven Sisters Rocks**, a collection of oolitic limestone crags; **Merlin's Cave; King Arthur's Cave**, where the bones of mammoths and other prehistoric creatures have been found; **Coldwell Rocks**, where peregrine parachuted into Nazi-occupied France to work with the Resistance. It is open on Wednesdays from April to October, or by prior arrangement out of season.

HEREFORD

Founded as a settlement near the unstable Welsh Marches after the Saxons had crossed the River Severn in the 7th century, Hereford grew to become an important centre of the wool trade. Fragments of the Saxon and medieval walls can still be seen today but Hereford's crowning glory is its **Cathedral**, often called the Cathedral of the Marches. Largely Norman, the Cathedral has, in its

River Wye from Symonds Yat

falcons nest; **The Biblins** with a swaying suspension bridge that provides a vertiginous crossing of the river; and **Yat Rock** itself, which rises to 500 feet above sea level at a point where the river performs a long, majestic loop.

The **Jubilee Maze** is an amazing hedge puzzle created to celebrate Queen Elizabeth II's Silver Jubilee (so popular the path inside is worn down 2 inches a year!) and, on the same site, there is a **Museum of Mazes** and a puzzle shop.

Upriver from Symonds Yat, at the little settlement of **Kerne Bridge**, where coracles are still made, walkers can hike up to the majestic ruins of **Goodrich Castle** in a commanding position overlooking the River Wye. Built of red sandstone in the 11th century by Godric Mapplestone, Goodrich Castle was the last bastion to fall in the Civil War when it finally gave way after a four and a half month siege. Brilliantly preserved, the ruins are now property of English Heritage, and include a visitor centre containing some fascinating artifacts from the site.

WORMELOW

10 miles NW of Ross-on-Wye on the A466

The **Violette Szabo GC Museum** celebrates the bravery of the young woman who

Hereford Cathedral

impressive New Library building, two of the country's most important historic treasures. The **Mappa Mundi** is a renowned medieval world map, drawn on vellum, it has Jerusalem as its centre and East at the top, indicating that East was the source of all things good and was religiously significant. Superimposed on to the continents are drawings of the history of humankind and the marvels of the natural world. These 500 or so drawings include cities and towns, Biblical events, plants, animals, birds and strange creatures, images of the peoples of the world and pictures from classical mythology. The other great treasure is the **Chained Library**, which houses 1,500 rare books that are all chained to their original 17th century book presses. At nearby All Saints Church is another impressive Chained Library of some 300 books donated by William Brewster in the 1730s.

The city's restored pumping station is now home to the **Waterworks Museum** where a wide range of Victorian technology is still very much alive in the shape of the collection of pumps along with Britain's largest triple expansion engine on display. The **Hereford Museum**, housed in a spectacular Victorian gothic building, tells the town's history through innovative interactive displays and has an art gallery with regularly changing exhibitions.

Hereford and cider are old friends and the Cider Museum tells the interesting story of cider production down the ages. Also on the outskirts of the city is the **Cider Mills of HP Bulmer**, the world's leading cider producer, where visitors can take guided tours with tastings.

AROUND HEREFORD

HOPE UNDER DINMORE

7½ miles N of Hereford on the A49

South of the village stretch the green spaces of **Queen's Wood Country Park**, a popular place for walking that also provides panoramic views over the surrounding countryside; its arboretum has a variety of over 650 rare and exotic tree specimens from all over the world.

Adjoining Queen's Wood Country Park is **Dinmore Manor**, where the Knights Hospitallers had their local headquarters, but today it is the manor's magnificent sheltered gardens that draw most people.

Just outside the village is **Hampton Court Castle & Gardens**, not to be mistaken with the London version. Founded in 1430 as a

reward for a knight's bravery at Agincourt, the castle and gardens have been remodelled several times during their long history, each generation adding new features according to the fashions of the day. The estate declined after World War Two until its sale in 1994 to the Van Kampen family, when a massive programme of building restoration was begun. Attention turned to the gardens in 1996 and designers Simon Dorrell and David Wheeler were chosen to provide an appropriately elaborate setting for the newly restored castle. Today, water canals, island pavilions, avenues and borders complement the established planting of earlier eras.

BROMYARD

13 miles NE of Hereford on the A44

This charming little market town on the banks of the River Frome is home to the **Teddy Bear Museum** housed in an old bakery. The **Bromyard Heritage Centre** tells the story of the local hop growing industry and illustrates life in the town down the centuries.

ABBEY DORE

10 miles SW of Hereford on the B4347

In the 12th century a **Cistercian Abbey** was founded here and the building, which was substantially restored in the 17th century, is

---

185 THE BRIDGE INN

Kentchurch

The Bridge Inn enjoys a picturesque setting in grounds running down to the River Monnow close to the Welsh border with a small caravan and camping park.

See entry on page 446

---

186 THE CROWN

Longtown

Fine old village hostelry offering excellent food, real ales, en suite rooms and bunkroom accommodation.

See entry on page 445

Hampton Court and Gardens

still used as the parish church. The gardens of **Abbey Dore Court**, through which the River Dore flows, are home to many unusual shrubs and perennials including a specialist collection of euphorbias, hellebores and peonies. The quaint Stables Tearoom here, run by the owner's Granddaughter, is a delight of home-cooking and local produce.

HAY-ON-WYE

17 miles W of Hereford on the B4348

Situated on the border with Wales, Hay-on-Wye is a must for bookworms as there are nearly 40 secondhand bookshops in this small town. Richard Booth, known as the King of Wye, opened the first bookshop here more than 40 years ago and he was also instrumental in setting up the annual **Hay Book Festival** that now draws thousands of people from all over the world. However, Hay is not just bookshops - there are plenty of antique shops here, too.

A few miles southeast of the town lie the ruins of **Craswall Priory**, which was founded in the 13th century by the rare Grandmontine order and abandoned just 200 years later.

EARDISLEY

13 miles NW of Hereford on the A4111

Inside the village's **Church of St Mary**

187 ALLT YR YNYS COUNTRY HOUSE

Walterstone

A beautifully preserved 16th century manor house lies at the heart of this outstanding hotel in the foothills of the Black Mountains.

See entry on page 447

188 THE CARPENTERS ARMS

Walterstone

Delightful traditional village inn serving delicious home-style cooking and real ales.

See entry on page 446

Magdalene is an early 12th century font that is decorated with figures that depict not only familiar religious themes but also two men engaged in an armed struggle. It is believed that these are a 12th century lord of the manor, Ralph de Baskerville, and his father-in-law, whom he killed in a dispute over land. As a penance, Ralph was ordered by the authorities to commission the extraordinary font. Outside the village, standing majestically by an old chapel, is a Great Oak that is thought to be some 800 years old.

Almeley Castle, just to the north east of Eardisley, was once the home of Sir John Oldcastle, who is believed to be the model for Shakespeare's Falstaff.

WEOBLEY

9½ miles NW of Hereford on the B4230

The steeple of this pretty town's parish **Church of St Peter and St Paul** is the second highest in Herefordshire and is a reminder that this was once a thriving market town.

As well as supporting the local farming communities, one of Weobley's more unusual sources of wealth was a successful glove making industry that flourished in the early 19th century when the traditional French source of gloves was cut off due to the Napoleonic Wars.

One of the town's many interesting buildings is the Throne Inn, where Charles I took refuge after the Battle of Naseby in 1645.

LEOMINSTER

The largest town in this part of Herefordshire, Leominster's unusual name is thought to be linked to the 7th century King of Mercia, Merewald, who was renowned for his bravery and so earned himself the nickname of 'the Lion'. The priory **Church of St Peter and St Paul**, which was originally King Merewald's convent, became a monastery in the 11th century and its three naves attest to its past importance. Close by, in Priory Park, is **Grange Court**, a fine timbered building that for many years stood in the Market Place. Built in 1633, the court is the work of the royal architect John Abel and displays his characteristic flamboyance in its elaborate carvings.

Other interesting attractions in the town are the **Leominster Folk Museum**, which has collections of many aretefacts that illustrate local life, and **Mousetrap Cheese Café**, where you can taste delicious local and continental hand-made cheeses including their own "Little Herefordshire", complimented with biscuits and relish. Two miles west of Leominster is **The Pleck Farm** where you can witness the cheese being made – you won't find much more local than that!

AROUND LEOMINSTER

ASHTON

3½ miles N of Leominster on the A49

This village is home to **Berrington Hall** (National Trust), an elegant 18th century mansion designed by Henry Holland, who later became architect to the Prince Regent.

Berrington Hall, Ashton

The house is noted for its fine furniture and paintings, a nursery, a Victorian laundry, a tiled Georgian dairy and above all its beautifully decorated ceilings: in the drawing room is the highlight, the central medallion of Jupiter, Cupid and Venus. The surrounding parkland was laid out by Holland's father-in-law, Lancelot 'Capability' Brown.

PEMBRIDGE

6½ miles W of Leominster on the A44

The influential Mortimer family were responsible for the medieval prosperity of historic Pembridge and the many handsome buildings bear witness to their patronage. The delightful 16th century **Market Hall** stands on eight oak pillars, the **Old Chapel Gallery** is housed in a converted Victorian chapel, and the 14th century church has a marvellous timber belfry.

SHOBDON

8 miles W of Leominster on the B4362

The **Church of St John the Evangelist** is one of the most flamboyant in the whole country, its 'wedding cake rococo' interior a jaw-dropping sight for first-time visitors.

Just north of the village of Shobdon is a

---

190 LOWE FARM

Pembridge

The Grade II listed farmhouse has five first-floor en suite bedrooms and guests have the use of a beautifully furnished lounge, a garden room and a lovely peaceful garden and hot tub.

See entry on page 449

---

189 HAYNALL VILLA

Little Hereford

Beautiful Georgian farmhouse bed and breakfast with award winning food and glorious country views.

See entry on page 448

---

191 THE CHOCOLATE BOX

Kington

A chocoholic's idea of heaven; also an attractive tea room and bistro serving excellent food.

See entry on page 448

collection of Norman sculptures known as the **Shobdon Arches** that, though greatly damaged by centuries of exposure to the elements, still demonstrate the superb skills of the 12th century sculptors.

KINGTON

12 miles W of Leominster on the A44

Close to the Welsh border, Kington, like other towns in Marches, was for centuries under threat of attack from the west. Its castle was destroyed many years ago, but outside the town, on Wapley Hill, are the earthworks of an ancient hill fort that is thought to be the site of King Caractacus' last stand. The most notable of all the defences in this border country is **Offa's Dyke**, the imposing ditch that extends for almost 180 miles from the Severn Estuary at Sedbury Cliffs to Prestatyn on the North Wales coast. Remnants of the wooden stakes unearthed down the years suggest that the dyke had a definite defensive role, rather than merely acting as a psychological barrier. This truly massive construction was in places almost 60 feet wide, and the stretch north of Kington is especially well preserved today and provides excellent and invigorating walking.

To the west of the town lies the impressive **Hergest Ridge**, which rises to around 1,400 feet, and on its southern edge is **Hergest Court**, once owned by the Vaughan family. Several of these feisty Vaughans are buried in the Vaughan Chapel in Kington's parish church. Hergest Court is rumoured to be haunted by a "Demon Black Dog"; said to have once been the pet of Black Vaughan,

Hergest Croft Gardens

who was beheaded, there are stories going back an age of a black dog being seen around the house carrying a severed head, and past residents of Hergest Court complained of constant nighttime howling and dog scratching at the doors.

Hergest Croft Gardens provide a dazzling display of colour from spring to autumn.

YARPOLE

3½ miles NW of Leominster off the B4361

Close to this delightful village with its jumble of cottages is **Croft Castle** (National Trust), whose parkland contains many ancient oak trees and an avenue of 350-year-old Spanish chestnut trees.

Behind the defensive exterior of Croft Castle, the elegant staterooms contain rare furniture, fine plasterwork and portraits of the Croft family, who have almost continuously occupied the castle since it was built in the 14th century.

Just a short walk from the castle is **Croft Ambrey**, an Iron Age fort from which there are stunning views.

HERTFORDSHIRE

Although Hertfordshire borders London, it remained essentially a rural county until the construction of the Grand Union Canal. There are still peaceful walks to be enjoyed along the canal's towpath, which flows through a gap in the Chiltern Hills on its journey to the Midlands.

It was in the Edwardian era that the first Garden Cities were conceived and built here following the plans of Ebenezer Howard. The two Garden Cities, Letchworth and Welwyn, both have fascinating museums which illuminate Howard's vision; the latter also having a delightful watermill.

After World War II, several old market towns were developed as New Towns to provide pleasant housing primarily for those made homeless during London's Blitz. Further north, the countryside remains chiefly rural and there are numerous villages of timber-framed cottages and quiet market towns to explore. There are two important Roman sites in the county; the Welwyn Roman Baths, which are thought to be either a villa or farm, is a stunning sight to see, as is Verulamium Park at St Albans with its Roman Amphitheatre.

There are also several grand stately homes, and various unique buildings, tucked away in the rolling countryside. In Ware is

the Scott Grotto, a network of shell-lined chambers made for the 18th century poet John Scott. The other side of Stevenage, in the village of Royston, is the mysterious Royston Cave – a man-made underground structure with religious wall carvings. Of the stately homes Knebworth House must be the most dynamic; now famous for the music concerts run here, there are a whole range events and activities held in the grounds year round.

ST ALBANS

As Verulamium, this was one of the most important major Roman cities in Britain. It was attacked and sacked by Boudicca in the 1st century and today, the remains of the rebuilt city, including the walls and the only Roman theatre in Britain, can be seen in **Verulamium Park**. An exciting new project uses hand held devices (available from **Verulamium Museum** free of charge) to give

visitors a multimedia tour of the Park, with information and recreated pictures creating the vivid image of what it would have been like here in Roman times. Close to the park, on the banks of the River Ver, is the restored 16th century **Kingsbury Watermill** which now contains a small museum on the upper levels, and The Waffle House downstairs.

The city's cathedral, **St Albans Abbey**, was built on the site where Alban, the first British martyr, was beheaded in the 4th century. The Abbey dates from the 11th

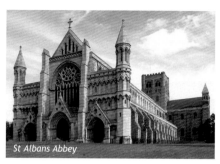

St Albans Abbey

century but was designated a **Cathedral** as recently as 1887. Among the many features inside are medieval paintings that are thought to be unique in England.

Another historic building lies in the market place – the **Clock Tower**, built between 1403 and 1412, is the only medieval town belfry in England and its original bell, Gabriel, is still in place. Also worthy of a visit are the city's two museums. The **Museum of St Albans** tells the history of the city from Roman times to the present day, and **St Albans Organ Museum** houses an amazing collection of working mechanical musical instruments, and holds regular organ concerts in its theatre.

AROUND ST ALBANS

HARPENDEN

4½ miles N of St Albans on the A1081

Harpenden's High Street is lined with many listed 17th and 18th century buildings, and the whole of the town centre is a conservation area. This charming agricultural community is the home of the **Experimental Station for Agricultural Research,** housed in Rothamsted Manor; which has a history in research into sustainable land management and its environmental impact that spans 160 years. The **Harpenden Railway Museum** has a small private collection of railway memorabilia.

HATFIELD

5 miles E of St Albans on the A1057

This historic town grew up around the gateway of the palace of the Bishops of Ely

but all that remains of the **Royal Palace of Hatfield**, where Elizabeth I spent her early life, is a single wing. This can be seen in the delightful gardens of the impressive Jacobean mansion, Hatfield House, which now stands on the site.

KING'S LANGLEY

5 miles SW of St Albans on the A4251

This historic village has a long and illustrious royal past: in the 13th century a palace was built from which Edward I governed England for a short period, while close by was a Dominican friary. Both sites are now occupied by the Rudolf Steiner School.

BERKHAMSTED

10 miles W of St Albans on the A4251

First settled by the Saxons, it was here, two months after the Battle of Hastings, that the Saxons finally submitted to William of Normandy; shortly afterwards, building work began on a castle. **Berkhamsted Castle** had a double moat, a very necessary precaution in this low-lying situation; an important fortification up until the 15th century, the castle is now in ruins. Of the few buildings that have survived from the past is **Dean John Incent's House**, an impressive black and white timbered jettied building – Dean Incent was the founder of the original Grammar School of 1554 that is now incorporated into Berkhamsted School.

Dean John Incent's House, Berkhamsted

131

TRING

13 miles NW of St Albans on the A4251

There was an Old Person of Tring,
Who embellished his nose with a ring
He gazed at the Moon,
every evening in June,
That ecstatic Old Person of Tring.

(Edward Lear)

This bustling market town on the edge of the Chiltern Hills has been greatly influenced by the Rothschild family. However, they are not the only people associated with Tring and in **St Mary's Church** lies the grave of the grandfather of the first US president, George Washington, while the 17th century Mansion House was reputedly used by Nell Gwynne. Another building of note is the **Market House**, which was built by public subscription in 1900 to commemorate Queen Victoria's Diamond Jubilee. It is now houses the council chamber and offices, and the pillared lower level (originally open) is a glass walled shop. The old Silk Mill first opened in 1824, and once employed over 600 people, but towards the end of the 19th century the silk trade fell into decline and Lord Rothschild ran the mill at a loss to protect his employees rather than see them destitute. From 1872 to the 1940s, the Rothschild family lived at Tring Park and their greatest lasting legacy is, perhaps, the **Walter Rothschild Zoological Museum**, first opened in 1892, which, on Walter's death in 1937, became part of the British Museum (Natural History).

Just north of Tring lies the Tring Reservoirs National Nature Reserve, four reservoirs built between 1802 and 1839 and declared a reserve in 1955.

MARKYATE

8 miles NW of St Albans off the A5

This quiet village of charming 18th and 19th century cottages and houses is home to a large mansion that stands on the site of Markyate Cell, a medieval nunnery. There is story of Kate Ferrers "The Wicked Lady of Markyate Cell"; a 17th century lady who disguised herself as a man and became a

highway robber, which inspired a novel and film in the 1940s. Sadly it has been found to be a romantic myth, probably a result of the popular trend in 18th century literature for stories of women getting up to mischief disguised as men.

STEVENAGE

Following World War II, Stevenage became the first of Britain's New Towns and it expanded into a pleasant residential town after the first houses were occupied in 1951. It was at Stevenage that the novelist EM Forster lived with his widowed mother from the age of 4 to 14 and **Howards End**, which featured in the book of the same name, is the house in which they lived; in the book, the village of Hilton is an adaptation of Stevenage. **Stevenage Museum** uses all the latest technology to tell the history of the town and surrounding area. Right in the heart of the town is Fairlands Valley Park; 120 acres of beautiful parkland, with watersports facilities, play park and café.

To the northeast lies one of Hertfordshire's last surviving post mills, **Cromer Windmill**, which dates from 1800 and ceased working in

Cromer Windmill

Knebworth House

the 1920s. To the south stands **Knebworth House**, the home of the Lytton family since 1490 – it was Edward Buler Lytton who wrote the enduring words "The pen is mightier than the sword". The present magnificent mansion was built during the 19th century and has played host to many famous visitors, including Charles Dickens, Benjamin Disraeli and Sir Winston Churchill. The unusual "Dinosaur Trail" around the grounds will take you past 72 life-sized dinosaurs grazing amongst the rhododendrons and the redwoods; the extensive adventure park is also a thrilling attraction for children.

AROUND STEVENAGE

LETCHWORTH

5 miles N of Stevenage on the A505

Letchworth is the first garden city where the ideals of Ebenezer Howard (to create a comfortable living environment with residential, industrial and commercial areas all within easy reach) were put into practice in the early 20th century. The offices of the town's architects are now home to the **First Garden City Heritage Museum**, a unique place that traces the history and development of Letchworth.

To the southeast lies **Hitchin**, an old market town which prospered from straw that was traded here for the local cottage industry of straw plaiting. Though the market declined, many of the town's older buildings have survived, including The Biggin, which was built in the early 17th century on the site of a Gilbertine Priory and became an

almshouse for the poor. **Hitchin Museum** is home to the largest collection of period costume in the county and it also includes the **Museum of Hertfordshire Imperial Yeomanry**, a Victorian chemist's shop, physic garden, and an art gallery.

ROYSTON

12 miles NE of Stevenage on the A10

Situated at the intersection of the Ickneild Way and Ermine Street, this was a favourite hunting base for royalty, and James I's Hunting Lodge still stands. Just below the intersection of the two ancient thoroughfares the man-made **Royston Cave** was discovered in 1742 but its purpose remains a mystery. Its most amazing feature is the extensive range of wall carvings, representing the Crucifixion, the Holy Family and several saints.

BISHOP'S STORTFORD

16 miles E of Stevenage on the A120

The completion of the **Stort Navigation** in 1769 aided the development of the town's two industries, malting and brewing, and during the age of the stagecoach this was a major stopping point on the route between London and Norwich. The excellent **Museum** brings the town's long history to life.

To the west is the unspoilt village of **Much Hadham** and the **Forge Museum and Victorian Cottage Garden**. Further west again is **Standon**, where, in a field, lies the Balloon Stone, a giant boulder that marks the spot where in 1784 Vincenzo Lunardi completed the first balloon flight in England.

WARE

10 miles SE of Stevenage on the A1170

Situated at the point where Ermine Street crosses the River Lea, Ware was the scene of a famous encounter between King Alfred and the Danes in AD 895. By the Middle Ages this was a market town to rival Hertford and several ancient buildings remain, including **Place House**, which is possibly one of Ware's two Domesday manor houses. The town's most interesting feature is **Scott's Grotto**, a series of passageways and artificial caves built by the poet John Scott in the late 18th century, the walls of which are covered in shells, and pieces of pottery & glass.

To the south lies **Hoddesdon**, a town that dates back to Saxon times and which was a thriving market place by the 13th century. Housed in a Georgian building, the **Lowewood Museum** concentrates its collections on the region's illustrious history.

In Lea Valley Park stands **Rye House Gatehouse**, one of the first brick built buildings in the country, where, in 1683, a plot to assassinate Charles II was formulated. The plot failed and the conspirators, including the tenant of Rye House, were executed.

Rye House Gatehouse

HERTFORD

8½ miles SE of Stevenage on the A119

Another Saxon town on the once important waterway of the River Lea that linked the town with London. The **Hertford Nature Walk** leads through the meadows between the Rivers Lea and Beane and takes in the canal basin that is known as The Folly. Hertford is very much a mix of old and new and among its interesting buildings is the Quaker Meeting House, said to be the oldest purpose-built meeting house in the world – it dates from 1669.

WELWYN GARDEN CITY

8 miles S of Stevenage on the A1000

One of the two garden cities in Hertfordshire that followed the ideas and plans of Ebenezer Howard (the other is Letchworth), the land for Welwyn Garden City was acquired in 1919 and building began a year later. Just to the south of the town lies **Mill Green Museum**, housed in the workers' cottages for the adjoining mill, which displays local artefacts from Roman times to the present day. Mill Green Mill is a delightful watermill that has been restored to working order and stands on the site of one of the four such mills that were listed in the *Domesday Book*. A famous son of Welwyn Garden City is the golfer Nick Faldo, born here in 1957.

Just to the north is the historic town of **Welwyn** that grew up along the route of the Great North Road. During excavations for the new A1(M) motorway, the famous **Welwyn Roman Baths** were discovered, part of a 3rd century villa or farm that was occupied for over 150 years.

AYOT ST LAWRENCE

5½ miles SW of Stevenage off the B651

A picturesque rural village whose most famous resident was Sir George Bernard Shaw, who lived here from 1906 until his death in 1950. His house, **Shaw's Corner** (National Trust), it is preserved as it was in his lifetime and contains many literary and personal mementoes.

ISLE OF MAN

The Isle of Man has an unusual status as a Crown Protectorate, with the Queen as Lord of Mann represented in the Island by the Lieutenant-Governor. The Manx Symbol is the Three Legs of Man, first officially used in the early 14th century on the Manx Sword of State. The legs, clad in armour and bearing spurs, run in a clockwise direction and bear the Latin motto 'Quocunque Jeceris Stabit' or 'Whichever way you throw it, it will stand'.

It is because of its own individual flare, and relaxed tranquil atmosphere, quite removed from that of England, which brings many people here each year on holidays and weekend breaks. A wonderful feature of the island is its vintage railways; be it the horse drawn trams at Douglas, the miniature railway at Curraghs Wildlife Park, the 100 year old trains which still scale the 2,036 feet of Sneafell Summit, or the railway line following the trail at the Great Laxey Mine, none of this exhilarating and unique rides are to be missed.

The most recognisable landmark on the

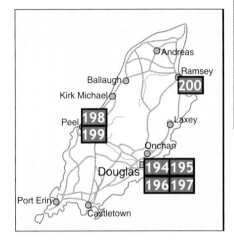

Isle of Man has got to be the Lady Isabella Wheel; with a diameter of 72ft it is the largest waterwheel in the world – and an impressive sight to be sure! Also renowned are the historic ruins of 11th century Peel Castle – once a Norse seat of power.

Accommodation

194	The Wyndham Hotel, Douglas	*pg 136, 451*
196	The Welbeck Hotel, Douglas	*pg 136, 451*

Food & Drink

195	Jak's Bar & Steakhouse, Douglas	*pg 136, 452*
196	The Welbeck Hotel, Douglas	*pg 136, 451*

Food & Drink

197	Chapters, Douglas	*pg 136, 453*
198	Marine Hotel, Peel	*pg 137, 454*

Places of Interest

199	Manx Sea Quest, Peel	*pg 137, 453*
200	Ballajora Artists, Ramsey	*pg 137, 453*

DOUGLAS

The island's capital, Douglas, is a lively resort where visitors can take a leisurely ride along the promenade aboard the **Douglas Bay Horse Tramway**, a remarkable and beautiful reminder of a bygone era. Another delightful means of travel is the **Victorian Steam Railway** that runs between Douglas and Port Erin. Following the line of the cliff tops, the

memorable journey also takes in bluebell woods and steep-sided rocky cuttings. The **Manx Electric Railway**, completed in 1899, operates the oldest working tramcars in the world and runs between Douglas and Ramsey.

No trip to the island is complete without a visit to the **Manx Museum**, where the Story of Man film gives a dramatic and vivid portrayal of the island's unique history.

On a headland overlooking Douglas Bay is a camera obscura known as the Great Union

Camera. Here, natural daylight is focused on to a white panel through a system of lenses to provide a 360° living image of the scene outside.

On the A1 road from Douglas towards Peel is the village of St John's, which is home to the the Manx-language primary school Bunscoill Ghaelgagh – part of an effort in recent years to revive the language following the death of the last native speaker Ned Mandrell in 1974.

AROUND DOUGLAS

CASTLETOWN

9 miles SW of Douglas on the A7

The original capital of the island, the town's harbour lies beneath the imposing battlements of the well-preserved 12th century **Castle Rushen**. Castletown is also home to the island's **Nautical Museum**, where the displays centre on the late 18th century armed yacht Peggy that sits in her contemporary boathouse.

Perched right on the southwestern tip of the island, **Cregneash Village Folk Museum** offers a unique experience of Manx traditional life within a 19th century crofting community. The centrepiece of Cregneash is Harry Kelly's Cottage. Kelly was a renowned

Cregneash crofter and a fluent speaker of the Manx language who died in 1934.

PORT ERIN

12 miles SW of Douglas on the A5

Situated between magnificent headlands, Port Erin has its own Arts Centre, which since 1975 has hosted the annual Mananan International Festival of Music and the Arts, now recognised as one of the island's most prestigious cultural events. Port Erin also has a small steam railway museum.

CALF OF MAN

15 miles W of Douglas

This small idyllic island, situated just off the southwestern tip of the island, is a National Trust bird sanctuary. In **Calf Sound**, the stretch of water between the island and the Isle of Man, the largest armada of Viking longships ever assembled in the British Isles congregated before setting off to invade Ireland.

PEEL

9 miles W of Douglas on the A1

On the western side on the island, Peel, which is renowned for its sunsets, typifies the unique character and atmosphere of the Isle of Man. It is traditionally the centre of the

---

194 THE WYNDHAM HOTEL

Douglas, Isle of Man

The **Wyndham Hotel** offers practical, comfortable accommodation just a few yards from the promenade and an easy walk from Douglas town centre.

See entry on page 451

---

196 THE WELBECK HOTEL

Douglas, Isle of Man

Up the hill just off the main promenade, the location is fairly quiet but at the same time convenient for all that Douglas has to offer.

See entry on page 451

---

195 JAK'S BAR & STEAKHOUSE

Douglas, Isle of Man

Jaks Bar & Steakhouse is one of the busiest pubs and restaurants on the Isle of Man and has just re-opened after extensive refurbishment.

See entry on page 452

---

197 CHAPTERS

Douglas, Isle of Man

Located in the heart of Douglas, Chapters offers not just one but a choice of 3 dining experiences.

See entry on page 453

Peel Castle

Manx fishing industry, including the delicious oak-smoked kippers and shellfish. Its narrow winding streets exude history and draw the visitor unfailingly down to the harbour, sandy beach, and magnificent castle of local red sandstone. The **Leece Museum** in Peel is well worth a visit. As is the **House of Manannan**, which uses state-of-the-art display techniques, to explore the Celtic, Viking and Maritime traditions of the Isle of Man. It is named after Manannan; the Island's great mythological sea god and protector who could shroud the place with a cloak of mist to protect it from its enemies.

Peel Castle, one of Isle of Man's principal historic monuments, occupies the important site of St Patrick's Isle. In the 11th century the castle became the ruling seat of the Norse Kingdom of Man and the Isles.

LAXEY

5 miles N of Douglas on the A2

Set in a deep, wooded valley, this village is home to one of the island's most famous sights, the **Great Laxey Wheel** that marks the site of a once thriving mining community. Known as the Lady Isabella Wheel, with a circumference of 228 feet, a diameter of 72 feet, and a top platform some 72 feet off the ground, it is the largest waterwheel in the

world. The wheel lies in Laxey Glen, one of the island's 17 National Glens. The Great Laxey Mine Railway, opened in 2004, carries passengers in tiny carriages along a stretch of the line where loaded wagons once rolled.

Situated above Laxey, in a beautiful glen, are the magnificent **Ballalheanagh Gardens**, while from Laxey station the **Snaefell Mountain Railway** carries visitors to the top of the island's only mountain. Built in 1895, the six original tram cars still climb the steep gradients to Snaefell's 2,036 feet summit from which there are outstanding views of the whole island and out over the sea to Ireland, Scotland and England.

RAMSEY

12 miles N of Douglas on the A18

This northernmost resort on the island is an attractive coastal town with a cosy harbour that is popular with visiting yachtsmen. Just to the north of the town stands the **Grove Rural Life Museum**, housed in a pleasantly proportioned Victorian house.

A short bus ride from Ramsey takes you to **Currahs Wildlife Park**, one of the most popular attractions on the island. It specialises in wetland species, nearly 100 altogether, many of them endangered in the wild, and also has a charming miniature railway line.

199 MANX SEA QUEST

Peel, Isle of Man

Operating out of Peel Harbour, the **Manx Sea Quest** is a powerful pleasure craft manned by a highly experienced crew, all of whom possess all the relevant safety qualifications.

See entry on page 453

198 THE MARINE HOTEL

Peel

Located on the Peel Promenade, this free house has an outstanding reputation for seving fresh homecooked food and a selection of real ales.

See entry on page 454

200 BALLAJORA ARTISTS

Ramsey, Isle of Man

Daphne MacOwan has a love for arts and crafts, and she has created an informal art gallery, **Ballajora Artists**, at her home in Ballajora.

See entry on page 453

ISLE OF WIGHT

Separated from the mainland by the Solent, is the Isle of Wight, where Queen Victoria sought solitude at Osborne House after the premature death of her husband. John Keats wrote his Endymion (first line: A thing of beauty is a joy for ever) while staying on the Island. Other notable visitors have described it as the Garden Isle and England's Madeira; about half of its 147 square miles have been designated Areas of Outstanding Natural Beauty.

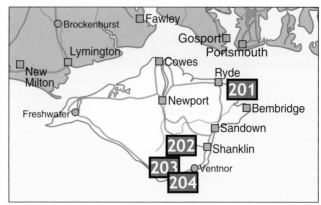

There are many well established museums and attractions throughout the island, as well as gorgeous historical buildings and sites. The excavated 3rd century Roman Villa at the capital city of Newport is an impressive sight; as is the famous Shanklin Chine, a ravine which drops down some 300 feet and offers an unrivaled beautiful location for walking. The maritime history is of great importance in the island's story, and it is told through many museums, such as the Cowes Maritime Museum, the Classic Boat Museum at Newport and the newly improved and expanded Shipwreck Centre and Maritime Museum just outside of the town.

Accommodation

Food & Drink

COWES

East and West Cowes are linked across the River Medina by a chain ferry. West Cowes is the home of the **Royal Yacht Squadron**, which organises Cowes Week, the famous regatta that is a firm fixture in the sailing and social calendar. The links with ships and shipbuilding go back centuries and Royal Navy craft, lifeboats, flying boats and seaplanes have all been built at Cowes. The narrow pedestrianised High Street is a delight, with some excellent shops, many catering for the yachting fraternity, as well as an array of fashionable clothing shops, gift shops, delicatessens, cafes, restaurants and lively pubs. High above the high street is the 1837 **Northwood House and Park**; a classical style mansion, which is sadly closed to the public at present, though the grounds have some excellent facilities including a tennis court and bowling green which are open.

The Isle of Wight's maritime history is charted at the **Cowes Maritime Museum**, which also houses a collection of racing yachts, while the **Sir Max Aitken Museum** has a collection of nautical paintings, instruments and artefacts.

On the eastern bank of the Medina lies 18th century Norris Castle, where the 12-year-old Princess Victoria stayed; she was so charmed by the island that she returned with her husband, Prince Albert, and built **Osborne House**, a mile to the south, in the style of an Italian villa. The **Isle of Wight Steam Railway** runs renovated steam trains along a preserved 5-mile track between Wootton and Smallbrook

Junction. Wootton is also home to **Butterfly World & Fountain World**, which includes an indoor sub-tropical garden with hundreds of exotic free-flying butterflies.

AROUND COWES

RYDE
6½ miles SE of Cowes on the A3054

For many visitors to the island, Ryde is their arrival point. The largest town on the Island has five miles of sandy beach and with all the usual seaside attractions and a marina, it remains a popular holiday spot. One of Ryde's Victorian churches, St Thomas, is now a Heritage Centre that features the transportation of convicts to Australia - many of the unfortunates left England in ships moored off Ryde. In the middle of Appley Park stands Appley Tower, which houses a collection of fossils, crystals and rune readings.

To the east lies **Seaview Wildlife Encounter Flamingo Park**, whose colonies of flamingos, penguins, macaws and waterfowl are among the largest in the country, while inland from Ryde is **Brickfields Horse Country**, a centre with more than 100 animals including magnificent Shire horses and miniature ponies.

BEMBRIDGE
10½ miles SE of Cowes on the B3330

Once a thriving fishing village, Bembridge is now a popular holiday and sailing centre. The village is home to the **Ruskin Gallery**, displaying an impressive collection of the 19th century artist's work. Here, too, is one of the island's best-known landmarks, the

---

201 THE ROADSIDE INN

Seaview, Isle of Wight

A beautifully presented inn on the coast, with spacious en-suit accommodation.

See entry on page 455

Northwood House & Park, Cowes

139

18th century Bembridge Windmill.

Further along the coast lies **Sandown**, the island's leading holiday resort, which has drawn such distinguished visitors as Lewis Carroll, Charles Darwin and George Eliot. The beaches and the museums are among the attractions, and to the north, near **Brading**, is a Roman Villa discovered in 1880. One of the island's oldest towns, Brading is also home to the **Lilliput Museum of Antique Dolls and Toys** while, close by, are two notable historic houses; **Nunwell House**, where Charles I spent his last night of freedom, is set within a glorious garden, and 13th century **Morton Manor** features an Elizabethan sunken garden surrounded by a 400-year-old box hedge.

Carisbrooke Castle, Newport

SHANKLIN

12 miles SE of Cowes on the A3055

To the south of Bembridge lies Sandown's more sedate neighbour Shanklin, which stands at the head of one of the island's most renowned landmarks, **Shanklin Chine**, a 300 feet deep wooded ravine. First opened in 1817 and a former refuge of smugglers, this ravine, mysterious and romantic, has long fascinated visitors with its waterfalls and rare flora. In the Heritage Centre at the top of the chine is an interesting exhibtion on the PLUTO (Pipe Line Under the Ocean) project for pumping fuel across the Channel to supply the troops involved in D-Day. The Chine also has a memorial to the Royal Marines of 40 Commando who used the Chine as an assault course before the disastrous assault on Dieppe in 1942.

NEWPORT

4 miles S of Cowes on the A3020

The island's capital and once a busy shipping centre on the River Medina, Newport still has many of its old riverside warehouses; one of them houses the **Classic Boat Museum**, and next door is the Isle of Wight Bus Museum with its impressive collection of passenger transport vehicles. In St Thomas' Church lies the tomb of Princess Elizabeth, Charles I's daughter, who died of a fever while the family were held prisoner at **Carisbrooke**

Castle. She was buried by the altar in the church at Newport. Queen Victoria restored the grave and dedicated a monument. Here, too, a 3rd century Roman Villa has been excavated, offering an insight into the sophistication of the late Romano-British designers and builders.

It was to the Isle of Wight that Charles I fled to get help to reach France. He was imprisoned in Carisbrooke Castle, from where, after a night at Nunwell House, he was taken for execution on Whitehall in January 1649.

An 8 minute drive east of Newport (along the A3056) will bring you to Arreton, which is the new larger location for the **Shipwreck Centre and Maritime Museum** (previously at Bembridge) that now also includes a Lifeboat Museum. It is part of a complex called Arreton Barns, which is a destination growing in popularity with tourists due to the many delightful craft shops and activities to enjoy.

VENTNOR

8 miles S of Cowes on the A3055

With much of its Victorian charm still intact, the town has much to offer today's visitors including the Ventnor Botanic Garden on the

site of the former Royal National Chest Hospital, the Smuggling Museum, and the Coastal Visitor Centre dedicated to the island's marine environment. Away from the town, St Boniface Down provides excellent walking country as well as spectacular views across the island. At nearby **Bonchurch**, the poet Algernon Swinburne is buried in the graveyard of the Church of St Boniface. Inland lies **Appuldurcombe House**, once the grandest mansion on the island, which is now home to the **Owl and Falconry Centre** where daily flying displays and courses in the age old art of falconry are held. The **Isle of Wight Donkey Sanctuary** lies close by, as does the village of **Godshill** with its magical **Model Village** and the **Nostalgia Toy Museum**.

Nestling in the heart of the Undercliff, to the southwest of Ventnor, is the ancient

St Catherine's Lighthouse

village of **St Lawrence** which is home to the **Rare Breeds Waterfowl Park**. From here the coast road continues round to **St Catherine's Point**, the wildest part of the island, where steps lead down to **St Catherine's Lighthouse**. On the most southerly tip of the island is **Blackgang Chine**, a Victorian scenic park that has been developed into a modern fantasy park.

CALBOURNE
9 miles SW of Cowes off the B3401

The most enchanting part of this picturesque village is Winkle Street, which has a row of charming old cottages opposite the village stream and an ancient sheepwash. Close by, in a lovely landscaped valley, is a superb 17th century **Water Mill** that incorporates a fascinating Rural Museum. Other activities to do here include relaxing trips down the stream via pedaloe or punt, and an air-drying clayplay area.

FRESHWATER
11 miles SW of Cowes on the A3054

This bustling town was the home of Alfred, Lord Tennyson, who was persuaded to move here by the pioneer photographer, Julia Cameron. Her home, **Dimbola Lodge**, houses a permanent exhibition of her work.

To the west lies the popular holiday spot of Totland and the famous multi-coloured sands of **Alum Bay**, and on the very western tip of the island are **The Needles**, three jagged slabs of rock with a lighthouse at the end of the most westerly.

North of Freshwater lies Yarmouth, a picturesque place with narrow streets, old stone quays and a castle built by Henry VIII after the town had been sacked by the French.

---

203 **THE WHITE HORSE**

Whitwell, Isle of Wight

One of the oldest and most beautiful buildings on the Isle of Wight, with a fresh award-winning menu.

See entry on page 456

---

204 **HERMITAGE COUNTRY HOUSE**

St Catherines Down, nr Ventor

Nestling within its own grounds of about 12 acres of garden and woods, Hermitage offers the perfect place to relax and unwind.

See entry on page 456

The Needles

KENT

'Kent, Sir – everybody knows Kent – apples, cherries, hops and women'. That's how Charles Dickens described Kent in *The Pickwick Papers*.

Kent is the first county that most cross-channel visitors encounter when visiting England (though for many the tunnel has removed the thrill of the sight of the White Cliffs of Dover), and few counties combine glorious open landscapes with such a rich

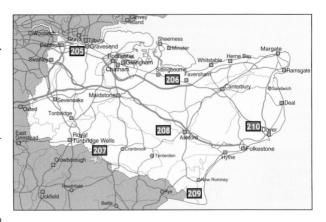

history. It was here that Julius Caesar landed in 55 BC; the Vikings followed 1,000 years later and the land was widely settled by the Normans following the defeat of King Harold in 1066. Throughout the centuries there has been a threat of invasion and, with the north Kent coast situated on the Thames estuary, it is not surprising that this area became the scene of great naval activity. On the south coast, the Cinque Ports were set up in the 11th century as a commercial alliance of significant ports – but the silting up of channels over the centuries has left some of them high and dry miles from the sea.

Visitors have flocked to the seaside resorts of Ramsgate, Herne Bay and Margate since Victorian times, but centuries ago Kent was a favourite place of pilgrimage as Christians made their way to Canterbury Cathedral.

The county's reputation as the 'Garden of England' is well earned, with green fields and orchards still abound. Rolling wooded countryside is dotted with windmills, and oast houses are still a common sight. Just outside of the village of Sheldwich can be found the National Fruit Collection, possibly the largest home to fruit trees and plants in the world, and Teynham is said to be the birthplace of the English Orchard. In contrast are the remote, flat lands of Romney Marsh,

sometime haunt of smugglers, and, of course, the White Cliffs of Dover, one of the most evocative sights in the land, a symbol of the country's strength that was immortalised in song by Vera (now Dame Vera) Lynn.

Throughout the county are the houses of many famous and prolific people; Sevenoaks holds Chartwell, the home of Sir Winston Churchill, and the nearby Down House, home of Charles Darwin for much of his life. Also there is The Red House which was the home of William Morris, and was designed and furnished by many influential artists including Rossetti, Burne-Jones and Madox Brown, and the grand Goodstone Park which was frequently visited by Jane Austen.

Accommodation

Food & Drink

ROCHESTER

The site was first settled by the Romans, but it was following the Norman invasion that William the Conqueror ordered his architect, Bishop Gundulph, to design a fortification to protect this strategic crossing point of the River Medway. Today, **Rochester Castle** remains one of the finest surviving examples of Norman architecture in the country. Bishop Gundulph was also ordered to build Rochester Cathedral on the site of a Saxon church that was founded in AD 604.

Rochester Castle

The city has close connections with the novelist Charles Dickens. An Elizabethan building houses the **Charles Dickens Centre**, The Royal Victoria and Bull Hotel featured in both *The Pickwick Papers* and *Great Expectations*, and **Restoration House** became Satis House in *Great Expectations*.

There is a wonderfully eclectic mix of shops to be found in Rochester; from fashion, to award-winning butchers and delis, all the way to antiques – there is something for everyone!

AROUND ROCHESTER

GRAVESEND
7 miles NW of Rochester on the A226

Gravesend marks the point at which ships entering the broad River Thames take on board a river pilot. On the A207, in Bexleyheath, is **The Red House** (National Trust), which was designed in 1859 by Philip

Webb for the newly married William and Janey Morris. The interior was decorated by Webb, Morris, Burne-Jones, Madox Brown and Rossetti; William Morris described the house as 'a joyful nook of heaven in an unheavenly world'. For Dante Gabriel Rossetti it was '.....more a poem than a house - but an admirable place to live in too'.

Nearby **Dartford** is best known nowadays for the Tunnel that runs under the Thames to emerge on the Essex side near West Thurrock. Robert Trevithick, the first man to carry passengers on a steam vehicle, spent the last years of his life working on inventions in a factory in Dartford and died in poverty in 1833 in the Bull public house (now the Royal Victoria and Bull). The factory workers paid for his funeral, and he is buried in Holy Trinity churchyard. Dartford is one of several places which claims to be the birthplace of Wat Tyler, leader of the Peasants Revolt (others include Deptford, Colchester and Maidstone).

An exciting new development to the town, **The Mick Jagger Centre** (named after the famous *Rolling Stones* front-man, who attended the centre's opening ceremony with his wife) is a brilliant music and arts venue which showcases a regular range of local and renowned musicians; an shining example of a community project, originally thought to be overly ambitious, really succeeding and bringing community and visitors together.

CHATHAM
1 mile SE of Rochester on the A229

Visitors to the historic **Chatham Dockyard** – now the **World Naval Base** – can appreciate the scale of modern fighting ships in the dry dock as well as the architecture of the most

---

205 **THE WHEATSHEAF**

Southfleet,
nr Gravesend

This traditional thatched pub dates back to the 15th century and offers home cooked food and plenty of refreshments.

See entry on page 457

complete Georgian dockyard in the world. Rope is still made in the traditional way in the long Ropery building, and the history of lifeboats is told at the **National Collection of the RNLI.** The **Museum of the Dockyard** tells the 400-year-old story of the site. A new development for 2010 is the **No1 Smithery**; a mixture of cultural venue, maritime exhibitions and art gallery, in the heart of the dockyard.

Close to the dockyard lies **Fort Amherst Heritage Park and Caverns**, the country's premier Napoleonic fortress that was home to a secret underground telephone exchange that co-ordinated air raid warnings during World War II.

To the east of Chatham lies **Gillingham**, the home of the fascinating **Royal Engineers Museum** where the diverse skills of this distinguished Corps are on display.

SITTINGBOURNE

10½ miles E of Rochester on the A2

Once a stopping point for pilgrims on their way to Canterbury, Sittingbourne has developed into a thriving market town. Visitors today can also take a nostalgic ride on a steam train along the Sittingbourne and Kemsley Light Railway. The vibrant market is held every Friday in the Forum Square.

In 1533, in nearby Teynham, Richard Harris, Henry VIII's fruiterer, planted England's first cherry tree along with apple trees and thus established the village as the birthplace of English orchards.

SHEERNESS

12 miles NE of Rochester on the A249

On the **Isle of Sheppey**, this town was once the site of a naval dockyard, the first to be surveyed by Samuel Pepys as Secretary to the Admiralty in the reign of Charles II, and it was here in 1805 that HMS *Victory* docked when it brought Nelson's body back to England following the Battle of Trafalgar. It is now a busy container and car ferry port, and the **Sheerness Heritage Centre** tells the history of the dockyard and its influence on the town's development. Sheppey is closely linked with the early years of British aviation: the Short brothers set up a factory here, and other notable pioneers who visited here include the future Lord Brabazon, the Hon Charles Rolls and the Wright Brothers.

To the southeast lies the seaside town of Minster where the 15th century abbey gatehouse is home to the **Minster Abbey Gatehouse Museum.**

On the southern tip of the island is the **Swale National Nature Reserve**, home to numerous wildfowl, while to the west lies **Elmley Marshes Nature Reserve**, an area of salt marsh.

LEEDS

11 miles SE of Rochester on the B2163

This village (not to be confused with the city in Yorkshire) is synonymous with the beautiful **Leeds Castle**, which stands in glorious landscaped gardens on two islands in the middle of the River Len. Built on a site once owned by Saxon kings, the castle was immaculately modernised by the last owner, Olive Paget, later Lady Baillie. The castle contains many superb antiques and tapestries, and in one of the medieval outbuildings is an idiosyncratic **Dog Collar Museum.** One of the gardens is named in

206 THE PLOUGH INN

Norton

This traditional village inn at the heart of the Kent country side offers home cooked food, fine ale and good conversation.

See entry on page 458

Leeds Castle

honour of Lady Baillie, who put so much back into the Castle until her death in 1974.

MAIDSTONE

8½ miles S of Rochester on the A229

Despite extensive development in modern times, Maidstone has retained many handsome historic buildings including **Chillington Manor**, a particularly fine Elizabethan residence that is now home to the **Maidstone Museum and Art Gallery**. Part of the museum's collection, The **Tyrwhitt-Drake Museum of Carriage** can be found in the stables that once belonged to the Archbishops of Canterbury. Opposite the stables is the 14th century **Archbishop's Palace**, where the clergy rested while travelling between London and Canterbury, and elsewhere in the town are the College of Priests, founded in 1395, and the 13th century Corpus Christi Fraternity Hall.

Just north of Maidstone town centre stands Allington Castle, the home of Sir Thomas Wyatt, the 16th century poet who takes some credit for introducing the sonnet into English poetry.

On the opposite bank of the River Medway is Tyland Barn, a beautifully restored 17th century building that houses the **Museum of Kent Life**. The surrounding 25 acres now hold fun and activities for all ages; including a hands-on farm, beautiful areas for walking, pottery workshops, and an adventure play area.

SEVENOAKS

The pride of this ancient market town is **Knole House**, one of the largest private homes in the country, with 365 rooms. In 1603, Elizabeth I granted the house to the Sackville family, and it was here, in 1892, that Vita Sackville-West was born.

To the east, close to the small village of **Ivy Hatch**, lies **Ightham Mote**, one of England's finest medieval houses. In the opposite direction, near the hamlet of French Street, stands **Chartwell**, Sir Winston Churchill's home from the 1920s until his

Chartwell House

death in 1965.

To the northwest of Sevenoaks is Biggin Hill RAF Station, whose entrance is flanked by a Spitfire and a Hurricane that act as silent reminders of the stalwart service these two aircraft, and their crews, gave during the dark days of World War II. Close to the station is **Down House** (English Heritage), where Charles Darwin lived for over 40 years until his death in 1882. The house is now a Museum dedicated to his life and work.

At nearby **Westerham**, a pleasant town near the Surrey border, are two statues of British heroes who had connections with the town. One is a tribute to Sir Winston Churchill, who made his home at nearby Chartwell, the other remembers General Wolfe, who defeated the French at Quebec in 1759. Wolfe was born in Westerham and his childhood home, renamed Quebec House, stands east of the town centre. Wolfe also has connections with nearby Squerryes Court, where one of the rooms has been set aside to display mementoes relating to the General.

ROYAL TUNBRIDGE WELLS

Surrounded by the unspoilt beauty of the Weald, Royal Tunbridge Wells is an attractive town that developed into a fashionable health resort in the 18th and 19th centuries after the discovery of chalybeate springs in 1606. One of the most famous features of the town is **The Pantiles**, a lovely shaded walk lined with elegant shops that were, in the days of the spa, the central focus of the hectic social life arranged by the Master of Ceremonies,

The Pantiles, Tunbridge Wells

Beau Nash.

To the east of Royal Tunbridge Wells, close to **Goudhurst**, is a charming Georgian manor house, **Finchcocks**, whose musical museum contains a magnificent collection of historic keyboard instruments. To the northwest of the town there are three wonderful places that are well worth exploring. **Penshurst Place** dates back to 1341 and is surrounded by glorious gardens that are a rare survivor of the Elizabethan age. A little further on is **Chiddingstone Castle**, a traditional squire's house with the appearance of a grand castle, while, close by, is one of the county's star attractions, **Hever Castle**, the childhood home of Anne Boleyn.

The Hever Castle Estate was bought in the early 20th century by the millionaire William Waldorf Astor; his extensive restoration work has created award winning gardens along with a castle filled with fine collections of paintings, furniture, tapestries and objets d'art.

AROUND TUNBRIDGE WELLS

LAMBERHURST

6 miles E of Tunbridge Wells on the A21

As this village lies on the main road between Royal Tunbridge Wells and Hastings, it once played an important role as a coaching stop but much of the village's prosperity is due to the iron industry of the Weald. The high street here is lined with attractive old houses and other buildings dating from those days.

Today, the village is associated with viticulture and the first vineyard was established here in 1972.

To the northwest of the village lies **Owl House Gardens,** a particularly pretty little cottage whose tenants, according to records dating from 1522, paid the monks at Bayham Abbey an annual rental of one white cockerel.

To the east of the Lamberhurst lies **Scotney Castle**, a massive, rust-stained tower that was built by Roger de Ashburnham in 1378 and that now incorporates the ruins of a Tudor house. However, what especially draws people to Scotney are the romantic gardens that are renowned for their autumn colours but are beautiful throughout all the seasons.

GROOMBRIDGE

4 miles SW of Tunbridge Wells on the B2110

Straddling the county border between Kent and Sussex, it is generally recognised that the Kent side of this village is the prettier and more interesting as this is where the triangular village green lies, overlooked by the tile hung cottages of the Groombridge estate. This charming village centre piece is also overlooked by **Groombridge Place**, a

Scotney Castle, Lamberhurst

207 CHEQUERS AT LAMBERHURST

Lamberhurst

Charming 12th century inn found in picturesque Lamberhurst of the castle district, serving a la carte and garden country cooking menus.

See entry on page 459

classical 17th century manor house that stands on the site of a medieval castle. The house is surrounded by superb parkland and **Gardens**, designed by the famous Jacobean diarist John Evelyn in a formal manner.

TENDERDEN

Often referred to as the 'Jewel of the Weald', despite being situated right on the border between the dense woodlands of the Weald and the flatter farmland that leads eastwards to Romney Marsh, Tenterden is a charming town of considerable age. Today's well-earned nickname is, however, a far cry from its earliest days when it was known as 'Tenet-ware-den' or 'pig pasture of Thanet'. Although pigs certainly did well here and in the surrounding area, sheep became more profitable.

For a real insight into the history of the town and the local area a visit to the **Tenterden and District Museum** is well worth while. The displays here cover over 1,000 years of history relating to hop-picking, farming, the area of the Weald, the Cinque Ports and Victorian domestic life.

Tenterden is also the home of the **Kent and East Sussex Railway** that runs for 10 miles between the town and Bodiam just over the county border in East Sussex.

AROUND TENTERDEN

WOODCHURCH

4 miles E of Tenterden off the B2067

In the heart of this large village lies the green

Woodchurch Windmill

around which are grouped several charming typically Kentish houses. One of the fine buildings to be found here is **Woodchurch Windmill**, an impressive white smock mill that was constructed in 1820. From the mill there are spectacular views over the marshes to the Channel coast. It is open to the public on a limited basis.

Also in Woodchurch is the **South of England Rare Breeds Centre** that, as its name suggests, is home to a large collection of rare British farm breeds, such as the Lincoln Longwool sheep that date back to Roman times and the Bagot goat that was brought to Britain by the Crusaders.

SMALL HYTHE

2 miles S of Tenterden on the B2082

Hard though it might be to imagine today, this little hamlet was once a flourishing port and shipbuilding centre. In the Middle Ages, the River Rother flowed past Small Hythe and was wide enough and deep enough to accommodate the ships of those days. One of Henry VIII's warships was built here.

Close to the village lies **Smallhythe Place**, a charming 16th century half-timbered house, best known for being the home of the famous Shakespearean actress Ellen Terry, who lived here between 1899 and 1928.

Small Hythe is also the home of **Chapel Down Vineyard**, where visitors can walk around the growing vines, tour the herb garden and take in the rural museum.

208 **THE DERING ARMS**

Pluckley

A fantastic award-winning seafood restaurant well known for its high quality fresh food and friendly atmosphere

See entry on page 460

NEW ROMNEY

13 miles SE of Tenterden on the A259

Known as the 'Capital of the Marsh', New Romney is an attractive old town with some fine Georgian houses, that was, at one time, the most important of the Cinque Ports. However, in 1287 a great storm choked the River Rother, on which the town stood, with shingle and caused the river's course to be diverted to Rye. The town lost its harbour and its status.

The town is best known as being home to the main station of the **Romney Hythe and Dymchurch Railway**, a charming 15inch gauge railway that was built in the 1920s primarily as an amusement for the dashing racing drivers, Captain Jack Howey and Count Zborowski. The railway is still a delightful way to explore this coastline. At the New Romney station can be found the **Romney Toy and Model Museum** housing a wonderful collection of old and not so old toys, dolls, models, posters and photographs.

DUNGENESS

15 miles SE of Tenterden off the A259

This southern-most corner of Kent, with its shingle beach, has been a treacherous headland, feared by sailors for centuries. Originally simple fires were lit on the beach to warn shipping of the dangers around this headland and, in 1615, the first proper lighthouse was erected. As the sea have retreated a succession of lighthouses has

been built and today there are two at Dungeness. As well as the makeshift fishermen's shacks and the lighthouses, the other key building on the headland is **Dungeness Power Station** where, at the Visitor Centre, there is an exhibition on electricity and the generation of nuclear energy. The headland is also home to the **Dungeness Nature Reserve** whose unique shingle flat lands have been described as 'the last natural undisturbed area in the South East and larger than any similar stretch of land in Europe'.

LYDD

13 miles SE of Tenterden off the A259

Like Old Romney, Lydd was once a busy port, linked to the Cinque Port of New Romney, but the changing of the course of the River Rother and the steady build up of land along the marsh put paid to this. Despite the loss of the port trade, and now lying some three miles from the sea, Lydd is an attractive place that has retained many mementoes of its more prosperous past.

Housed in the old fire station, **Lydd Town Museum** has a fascinating collection of memorabilia on the history of the town and local area, along with a Merryweather fire engine and an early 20th century horsebus. At Lydd Library, the **Romney Marsh Craft Gallery** has a permanent display of crafts for sale from both Romney Marsh and further afield.

CANTERBURY

It was here, in AD 597, that St Augustine founded an abbey which was to become the roots of Christianity in England. Lying just

Dungeness Beach

209 THE GEORGE HOTEL

Lydd

Established in 1620, this charming traditional hotel offers excellent dining, real ales and character.

See entry on page 461

Canterbury Cathedral

outside the city walls, **St Augustine's Abbey** is now in ruins, but a museum displays artefacts excavated from the site while, close by, is **St Martin's Church**, England's oldest parish church. However, both these buildings are overshadowed by the Mother Church of the Anglican Communion, **Canterbury Cathedral**, which was founded in AD 597 although the oldest part of the present building is the early 12th century crypt. Canterbury Cathedral is best known as the scene of the murder of Archbishop Thomas à Becket rather than for its ecclesiastical architecture. At the **Canterbury Tales Visitor Attraction** visitors are taken back to the 14th century and can meet the Knight, the Miller and other characters that tell their stories to keep the 'pilgrims' amused.

Canterbury predates its cathedral by many centuries and was the capital of the Iron Age kingdom, Cantii, as well as being settled by the Romans. The **Roman Museum** centres on the remains of a Roman town house, while the **Canterbury Heritage Museum** presents a full history of the city over the last 2,000 years – it also includes the adorable **Rupert Bear Museum**. In the **Kent Masonic Library and Museum** the history of freemasonry is explored.

AROUND CANTERBURY

HERNE BAY
7 miles NE of Canterbury on the A299

Originally a fishing village and a notorious

haunt for smugglers, this chiefly 19th century town has developed into one of the main resorts on the north Kent coast. Its story is told at the **Herne Bay Museum Centre**.

East of Herne Bay is Reculver. The Normans built two huge towers within the remains of the Roman fort, providing sailors with a landmark to guide them into the Thames estuary. Today, Reculver Towers and Roman Fort is in the care of English Heritage. During World War II, the Barnes Wallace 'bouncing bomb' was tested off the coast here. Several bombs were found here on the shore in 1997 – none of them containing explosives.

GOODNESTONE
6½ miles SE of Canterbury off the B2046

Close to the village lies Goodnestone (pronounced Gunston) Park, an estate that was frequently visited by Jane Austen and, today, **Goodnestone Park Gardens** are considered some of the finest in the southeast of England.

STELLING MINNIS
6½ miles S of Canterbury off the B2068

Close to this village on the edge of what remains of the once great Lyminge Forest is **Davison's Mill**, a mid-19th century smock mill that is now home to a Museum of milling implements and tools.

CHALLOCK
10 miles SW of Canterbury on the A252

Set in the dense woodlands known as Challock Forest, this pretty village is home to **Beech Court Gardens**, which are a riot of colour from spring through to autumn. To the north, close to the village of **Sheldwich**, lies the **National Fruit Collection** – home to what is probably the largest collection of fruit trees and plants in the world. Tucked away in the orchards and close to the village of **Throwley** is **Belmont**, a beautiful Georgian mansion house that is renowned for its impressive clock collection assembled by the 5th Lord Harris.

To the northeast, towards Canterbury, is one of the county's best-preserved villages,

Chilham, which is often used as a film location.

FAVERSHAM

9 miles NW of Canterbury on the A2

First settled by the Romans, the town grew steadily as a market town. For 400 years it was the centre of the country's explosives industry and **Chart Gunpowder Mills** is a lasting monument to the industry based here between 1560 and 1934. Faversham boasts over 400 listed buildings, among them the 16th century Guildhall and a 15th century former inn that is now the **Fleur de Lis Heritage Centre**.

WHITSTABLE

5½ miles NW of Canterbury on the A2990

Sometimes referred to as the 'Pearl of Kent', this town, centred on its busy commercial harbour, is as famous for its oysters today as it was in Roman times. On the harbour's East Quay, the **Oyster and Fishery Exhibition** tells the story of Whitstable's connections with fishing, and **Whitstable Museum and Gallery** explores the traditions and life of this ancient seafaring community. In Whitstable's Museum will be found references to some of the 'firsts' to which the town lays claim: the first scheduled passenger train ran between Whitstable and Canterbury; the first steamship to sail to Australia from Britain left here in 1837; the diving helmet was invented in the town; and the country's first council houses were built here.

Just inland from Whitstable is **Druidstone Wildlife Park**, home to a wide variety of animals and birds including otters, owls, rheas, wallabies and parrots; as well as a delightful bluebell woodland trail.

DOVER

This ancient town, which is often referred to as the 'Gateway to England', is Britain's major cross-Channel port. Many pass through but few stay for long, but with its long history going back to Roman times, it is well worth taking time to explore. It was the Romans who first developed Dover, basing their navy here, and right up to the present day, the town has relied on shipping and seafaring for its prosperity. It was a founder member of Edward I's Confederation of Cinque Ports, and as the old harbour silted up a new one was constructed in the 19th century. Much of the older part of Dover was destroyed by enemy bombs during the World Wars but, among the jumble of modern streets, some of the surviving ancient buildings can still be found.

Situated high on a hill above the cliff tops, and dominating the town from almost every angle, stands **Dover Castle**, dating back to 1180. However, one of the most spectacular sights and, one of World War II's best kept secrets, are the **Secret Wartime Tunnels** that were cut into Dover's famous **White Cliffs**, immortalised by Vera Lynn in a morale-boosting World War II song. It was from this labyrinth of tunnels that Winston Churchill masterminded the evacuation of nearly 350,000 troops from the beaches of Dunkirk.

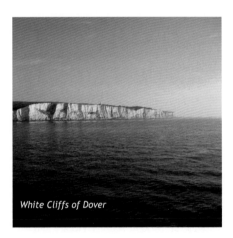

White Cliffs of Dover

210 **THE HOPE INN**

Lydden

Popular and convenient inn for guests using the Dover port located in a stunning location in the picturesque village of Lydden on the Kentish coastline.

See entry on page 462

For some, Lancashire is the brash seaside resort of Blackpool, for others a county dominated by cotton mills. However, there is much more to Lancashire than candyfloss and cotton. It is an ancient county, with many of its towns and villages dating back to Saxon times and beyond, and during the Civil War it remained fiercely loyal to the King and saw some of the bloodiest incidents of the whole bitter conflict.

Away from the brash resorts, which developed to provide attractions and amenities for the mill workers who made use of the new railway network to escape for a day or even a week's holiday, there are the more genteel towns of Lytham St Anne's and Southport with its elegant mile-long main boulevard. Inland lies beautiful countryside that includes the ancient hunting ground of the Forest of Bowland and, to the south, Pendle Hill, the scene of the notorious 17th century witch hunts. Morecambe Bay, beautiful but occasionally treacherous, offers glorious views and sunsets and is an important habitat for a variety of birdlife and other wildlife. On the towns promenade stands the statue of Comedian Eric Morecome; a popular sight for many visitors, it remains a testament to the fun and laughter he infused England with during his lifetime.

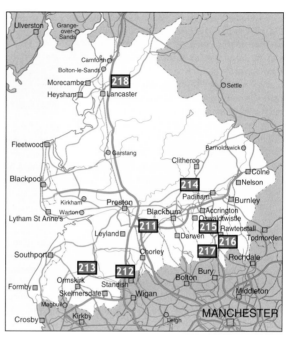

Accommodation

Food & Drink

Food & Drink

PRESTON

Preston is strategically positioned on the highest navigable point of the River Ribble, and although the port activity has declined, the docklands, now called Riversway, have become an area of regeneration with a marina. The complex is in the **Millennium Ribble Link**, itself part of a three-mile water park. The **Ribble Steam Railway** boasts the largest single collection of standard-gauge industrial locomotives in the country.

Dominating the Market Square is a magnificent neoclassical building, reminiscent of the British Museum, which houses the **Harris Museum and Art Gallery**. Fulwood Barracks is home to the Queen's Lancashire Regiment Museum.

On the northern outskirts of Preston is one of its most popular visitor attractions, the **National Football Museum**. In 1888, Preston North End was one of the 12 founder members of the Football League and its first champion. In 1887 the team recorded the biggest win in the FA Cup's history – 26-0 against Hyde United. Sporting stars hailing from Preston include Bill Beaumont and Andrew 'Freddie' Flintoff.

Other interesting museums of Preston include **The Museum of Lancashire** and **The Museum of the Queens Lancashire Regiment**.

AROUND PRESTON

GARSTANG

10½ miles N of Preston on the A6

This ancient market town dates back to the 6th century when a Saxon named Garri made his base here. At the excellent **Discovery Centre** displays deal with various aspects of the region, including the history of the nearby Forest of Bowland.

Just to the east of the town, on the top of a grassy knoll, are the remains of **Greenhalgh Castle**, built in 1490 by Thomas Stanley, the 1st Earl of Derby. Severely damaged in a siege against Cromwell in 1645-6, the Castle was

Greenhalgh Castle, Garstang

one of the last strongholds in Lancashire to hold out against Parliament. To the north, on the A6, are the remains of a 17th century tollhouse built when parts of the turnpike from Garstang to Lancaster were realigned.

CHORLEY

8 miles SE of Preston on the A6

A bustling and friendly market town, Chorley was the birthplace, in 1819, of Henry Tate, who founded the world famous sugar business of Tate and Lyle. A great benefactor, Henry gave vast sums of money to worthy causes, and endowed the art gallery that now bears his name.

The jewel in Chorley's crown is undoubtedly **Astley Hall**, built in the late 16th century and set within some beautiful parkland.

To the southeast is the charming village of Rivington, surrounded by moorland that forms the western border of the Forest of Rossendale.

Overlooking the village of Rivington, and with splendid views over west Lancashire, **Rivington Pike**, at 1,191 feet, is one of the area's high peaks. Just to the south of the

---

211 THE BOAT YARD

Riley Green, nr Preston

A quality establishment offering exceptional food and luxury accommodation.

See entry on page 462

village lies **Lever Park**, situated on the lower slopes of Rivington Moor, which was the home of William Hesketh Lever, who later became Lord Leverhulme.

LEYLAND

5 miles S of Preston on the B5253

The name is the clue: the town is best known for its associations with the manufacture of cars and lorries and the **British Commercial Vehicle Museum** is housed on the site of the former Leyland South Works, where commercial vehicles were produced for many years.

WIGAN

15 miles S of Preston on the A49

There is some fine countryside around Wigan, including the Douglas Valley Trail; Pennington Flash, a large lake formed by mining subsidence that is now a wildlife reserve and a country park; and Haigh Country Park, one of the first to be designated in England.

RUFFORD

10 miles SW of Preston on the A59

In this attractive village of pretty houses stands the ancestral home of the Hesketh family, the splendid 15th century Rufford Old

212 THE WHITE LION

Wrightinton

Unbeatable atmosphere in this historic family run village inn, known for its vast and exciting menu, and year round entertainment.

See entry on page 463

213 BRANDRETH BARN

Burscough

Picturesque bed and breakfast in a beautiful barn conversion located within a real working farm, with popular tea rooms attached.

See entry on page 464

Hall. In the outbuildings is the **Philip Ashcroft Museum of Rural Life**, with its unique collection of items that illustrate village life in pre-industrial Lancashire.

SOUTHPORT

15 miles SW of Preston on the A565

The rise of this popular seaside resort lies in the tradition of sea bathing that began at nearby Churchtown centuries ago. As the number of people celebrating Bathing Sunday grew, so did the need for a more accessible beach and a stretch of sand two miles south of Churchtown was deemed suitable. From the first simple hotel Southport has grown into an elegant and sophisticated resort that is centred on its main boulevard, Lord Street, a mile-long wide road built between the lands of the two neighbouring lords of the manor. Southport's Promenade is bordered by grand hotels on the land side and a series of formal gardens on the other. From the centre of the promenade extends Southport's Pier that, at 1,460 yards, was for a time the longest in the country.

Southport Pier

A unique Southport attraction is the **British Lawnmower Museum**, a tribute to the garden machine industry.

Along the coast to the southeast is the **Freshfield Nature Reserve**, with a pine forest that has one of the few colonies of red squirrels in England.

BLACKPOOL

15 miles NW of Preston on the A583

This classic British resort, with piers, funfairs, gardens, amusement arcades and a

Entrance to Pleasure Beach, Blackpool

promenade, was until the middle of the 19th century little more than a fishing village among the sand dunes of the Fylde coast. However, the fashion for taking day trips and holidays, assisted by the very expanding railway network, saw Blackpool develop rapidly. In 1889, the original Opera House was built in the Winter Gardens complex and two years later a start was made on the world famous Tower. Completed in 1894, **Blackpool Tower**, modelled on the Eiffel Tower in Paris, stands 518 feet high. The **North Pier**, designed by the peerless Eugenius Birch, was opened at the beginning of the 1863 season; it soon became the place to promenade and is now a listed building. The **Pleasure Beach**, which boasts its own railway station, is an attraction that continues to be extended and improved. The famous Blackpool Trams provide enjoyable trips along the front and out to these less busy sides of the town.

A couple of miles inland, **Marton Mere** is a Wildlife Trust bird reserve where more than 160 species have been recorded.

South of Blackpool lies **Lytham St Anne's**, a quiet place that was a small port before the expansion of Blackpool. As its neighbour grew, Lyham developed into a genteel, elegant resort famous for its Victorian and Edwardian architecture. Royal Lytham and St Anne's golf course is one of the finest links courses in the country and a regular host of the Open.

POULTON-LE-FYLDE
13 miles NW of Preston on the A586

The Romans were in the area and it was

probably their handiwork that constructed the Danes Pad, an ancient trackway. The town developed as a commercial centre for the surrounding agricultural communities and its Market Place remains its focal point.

Strolling around Poulton-le-Fylde now, it is hard to imagine that the town was once a seaport. But until relatively recently ships sailed up the River Wyre to **Skippool Creek**, now home to the Blackpool and Fleetwood Yacht Club.

Along the banks of the River Wyre is the Wyre Estuary Country Park, an excellent place for walking and discovering the area.

FLEETWOOD
17 miles NW of Preston on the A587

The town's **Museum**, overlooking the River Wyre, illustrates Fleetwood's links with the fishing industry that suffered greatly from the Icelandic cod wars. However, Fleetwood's real claim to fame is the Fisherman's Friend – a staggeringly successful lozenge made from liquorice, capsicum, eucalyptus and methanol that was used by fishermen to relieve sore throats and bronchial trouble caused by the freezing conditions found in the northern Atlantic waters.

BLACKBURN

The largest town in east Lancashire, Blackburn is notable for its shopping malls, celebrated three-day market, modern cathedral, and Thwaites Brewery, one of the biggest independent brewers of real ale in the north of England. Hard though it may be to imagine today, at the height of the textile industry, Blackburn was the biggest weaving town in the world. In 1931, it received arguably its most influential visitor when Mahatma Gandhi toured the area on a study trip of Lancashire's textile manufacture. Examples of the early machines, including James Hargreaves' Spinning Jenny and his carding machine, invented in 1760, can be seen at the **Lewis Textile Museum**.

In 1926 the Diocese of Blackburn was created and St Mary's Church, built in 1826, became the Cathedral of the Bishop of Blackburn.

Just to the northeast of Blackburn lies the charming village of Whalley, home of the well-preserved 13th century **Whalley Abbey**.

AROUND BLACKBURN

CLITHEROE

10 miles NE of Blackburn on the A671

This old stone town, just south of the Forest of Bowland, has always been considered the forest's capital and it is also Lancashire's second oldest borough, receiving its first market charter in 1147. Clitheroe is dominated by its 800-year-old **Castle**, standing on a limestone crag high above the town but now little more than a ruin. The **Castle Museum** – which has recently undergone a makeover - includes reconstructions of a clogger's workshop, a printer's shop, and a lead mine. Nearby **Pendle Hill** is a place rich in history and legend, famous for the tragic story of the Pendle Witches. In the early 17th century,

Clitheroe Castle

several women of the area were imprisoned in Lancaster Castle as a result of their seemingly evil practices and, having been found guilty, were publicly hanged.

To the west of Pendle Hill's summit is Apronfull Hill, a Bronze Age burial site. Also to the northeast lies Sawley Abbey, founded in the 13th century by the Cistercian monks of Fountains Abbey.

COLNE

14½ miles NE of Blackburn on the A6068

Before the Industrial Revolution turned this area into a valley devoted to the production of cotton cloth, Colne was a small market town that specialised in wool. In the centre of the town, next to the War Memorial, is the statue of Lawrence Hartley, the bandmaster on the ill-fated *Titanic* who heroically stayed at his post with his musicians and played *Nearer my God to Thee* as the liner sank beneath the waves of the icy Atlantic in 1912. Colne is also the unlikely home of the **British in India Museum**, where exhibits covering many aspects of the British rule over the subcontinent are housed.

To the northeast lies the **Earby Mines Museum** with a collection of lead mining tools and equipment used in the Yorkshire Dales.

ACCRINGTON

4½ miles E of Blackburn on the A680

This attractive Victorian market town is the home of the **Haworth Art Gallery**, which houses the largest collection of Tiffany glass in Europe. The collection was presented to the town by Joseph Briggs, an Accrington man, who worked with Louis Tiffany in New York for nearly 40 years.

Close by is another typical Lancashire

---

214 THE DOG INN

Whalley

A traditional inn offering a good selection of real ales and homemade food.

See entry on page 465

---

215 CORNER CAFE

Rossendale

This delightful cafe, surrounded by farm and moor land, has a strong focus on homemade food and good hospitality.

See entry on page 466

textile town, **Oswaldtwistle**, which could be considered to be the birthplace of the industry since it was while staying here that James Hargreaves invented his famous Spinning Jenny in 1764.

BURNLEY
10 miles E of Blackburn on the A646

A cotton town rich in history and the largest in this area of east Lancashire. With the Industrial Revolution and the building of the Leeds and Liverpool Canal, Burnley grew to become the world's leading producer of cotton cloth. A walk along the towpath of the canal leads through an area known as the Weavers' Triangle – an area of spinning mills and weaving sheds; foundries where steam engines and looms were made; canal-side warehouses and domestic buildings. On the outskirts of town is the **Towneley Hall Art Gallery and Museum**.

To the west of Burnley is **Gawthorpe Hall**, a splendid 17th century house that was restored with a flourish of Victorian elegance during the 1850s. Beautiful period furnishings are enhanced by the ornately decorated ceilings and the original wood-panelled walls, making the perfect setting for the nationally important Kay-Shuttleworth needlework and lace collection.

216 THE BUCK INN
Cowpe

Tucked away in a tiny hamlet, this inn wants mountain bikers and walkers to enjoy quality hospitality, food and drink.

See entry on page 467

217 FISHERMAN'S RETREAT
Shuttleworth

A delightful restaurant in an idyllic location and nestled in acres of beautiful countryside with over 500 whiskies available from the whisky bar.

See entry on page 468

DARWEN
4 miles S of Blackburn on the A666

The town is dominated by **Darwen Tower**, built to commemorate the Diamond Jubilee of Queen Victoria in 1897 and situated high on the moor. Another striking landmark is the chimney of the **India Mill**, constructed out of hand-made bricks and built to resemble the campanile (belltower) in St Mark's Square, Venice.

BOLTON
12 miles S of Blackburn on the A666

During the Civil War, the town saw one of the bloodiest episodes of the conflict when James Stanley, Earl of Derby, was brought back here by Cromwell's troops after the Royalists had been defeated. In a savage act of revenge for the massacre his army had brought on the town early in the troubles, Stanley was executed and his severed head and body, in separate caskets, were taken back to the family burial place at Ormskirk.

Impressive buildings here include 14th century **Smithills Hall** and the late 15th century **Hall-i'-th'-Wood**, a fine example of a wealthy merchant's house.

Six miles east of Bolton lies **Bury**, another typical Lancashire mill town that is more famous for its inhabitants that its buildings. Over the centuries the town has given the world the Pilkington family of glassworks fame, John Kay, the inventor of the flying shuttle, and Robert Peel, the politician who repealed the Corn Laws and founded the modern police force. On the outskirts of the

Hall-i'-th'-Wood, Bolton

town lies **Burrs Country Park** which, as well as offering a wide range of activities, also has an interesting industrial trail around the historic mill site.

Further east again is **Rochdale**, another cotton town, most famous as being the birthplace of the Co-operative Movement; in carefully restored Toad Lane, to the north of the town centre, is the world's first Co-op shop, the Rochdale Pioneers.

RIBCHESTER

5 miles NW of Blackburn on the B6245

Situated on the banks of the River Ribble, the village is famous for its **Roman Fort** on the northern riverbank, first established by Gnaeus Julius Agricola in AD 79. Although little of the fort's walls remain, the granary and its hypocaust have been excavated, revealing interesting finds that can be seen in the fort's **Roman Museum**.

LANCASTER

The capital town of Lancashire boasts a long and interesting history. It was in the 10th

Lancaster Castle & Priory

century that Athelstan, the grandson of Alfred the Great, had lands in the area, and during the reign of William the Conqueror large parts of what is now Lancashire were given by the grateful king to his cousin Roger of Pitou, who made his base at Lancaster. Queen Elizabeth II retains the title of Duke of Lancaster. Within yards of the railway station lies **Lancaster Castle**, a great medieval fortress founded by the Normans to keep out Scottish invaders and strengthened by John of Gaunt, Duke of Lancaster. In Church Street stands the 17th century Judge's Lodging, which now houses two separate museums, the **Museum of Childhood** and the **Gillow and Town House Museum**.

The town's rich maritime history is celebrated at St George's Quay, which, with its great stone warehouses and superb Custom House, is now an award-winning **Maritime Museum**.

One of the first sights visitors see of Lancaster is the great green copper dome of the impressive **Ashton Memorial**, built by the linoleum manufacturer Lord Ashton in memory of his wife and a landmark for miles around that stands on a hilltop in the centre of the splendid Edwardian Williamson Park. Pevsner described it as 'the grandest monument in England'.

AROUND LANCASTER

CARNFORTH

5 miles N of Lancaster on the A6

Not many towns are best known for their stations, but Carnforth is one of them: it was used as the setting for the 1940s film classic *Brief Encounter*. The old engine sheds and sidings are now occupied by Steamtown, one of the largest steam railway centres in the north of England.

Just to the north lies **Leighton Hall**, a fine early 19th century house that is now owned by a branch of the Gillow family; the fine furniture seen in the hall reflects the trade that made the family fortune.

Leighton Hall, Carnforth

FOREST OF BOWLAND

3 miles E of Lancaster

Designated an Area of Outstanding Natural Beauty in February 1964, this large and scenic area is a paradise for walkers and country lovers that is dotted with picturesque villages. Following the Norman Conquest, Bowland became part of the Honour of Clitheroe and the vast estates that belonged to the de Lacy family. In 1399, when the then Duke of Lancaster came to the throne as Henry IV, Bowland finally became one of nearly 100 royal hunting forests.

The remains of a Roman road can be clearly seen traversing the land and many of the villages in the area have names dating back to the Saxon period. Perhaps the most celebrated of the many routes across Bowland is the minor road from Lancaster to Clitheroe that crosses the Abbeydale Moor and the Trough of Bowland before descending into the lovely Hodder Valley around Dunsop Bridge.

At the heart of the Forest is **Slaidburn**, a pretty village of stone cottages and cobbled

Hark to the Bounty Inn, Slaidburn

pavements whose 13th century public house Hark to Bounty contains an old court room where, from around 1250, the Chief Court of Bowland, or Halmote, was held.

MORECAMBE

3 miles W of Lancaster on the A589

Featuring prominently on the Lancashire coastline, Morecambe has long been one of the most popular seaside resorts in the North, and it can truly be said to enjoy one of the finest views from its promenade of any resort in England – a magnificent sweep of coastline and bay, looking across to the Lakeland mountains. Many buildings date from Morecambe's heyday as a holiday destination, including the Midland Hotel, built in the early 1930s to designs by Oliver Hill.

Near the Stone jetty is the **Eric Morecambe Statue** with words from the song *Bring Me Sunshine* carved into the granite steps. The comedian was born John Eric Bartholomew in 1926. **Morecambe Bay**, a vast wide, flat tidal plain situated between Lancashire and Cumbria, is the home of many forms of marine life as well as being a very popular and important habitat for birds. It's also famous for a great delicacy – Morecambe Bay potted shrimps.

Morecambe Bay

The Bay is also very treacherous, and over the years many have fallen victim of the tides and the quicksands. In medieval times this perilous track formed part of the main west coast route from England to Scotland, and the monks of Furness would act as guides for travellers who wished to avoid the long overland route. Today, **Cross Bay Walks** are led by the Queen's Guide to the Sands.

LEICESTERSHIRE

Rolling fields, wooded gorges and meandering waterways make Leicestershire a perfect place for exploring – on foot, by bicycle or by boat. The county is divided into two almost equal parts by the River Soar, which flows northwards into the River Trent. The Grand Union Canal threads its way through South Leicestershire, while the Ashby Canal passes close to Bosworth Battlefield, in the west of the county.

Leicester, the capital, is one of the oldest towns in the country and retains outstanding monuments of almost every age of English history. Agriculture and industry go hand in hand here: the long-haired local sheep produced fine woollens, and by the end of the 17th century the now worldwide hosiery trade had been

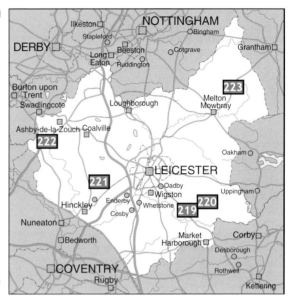

established. Loughborough has been famous for making bells for more than 100 years, while at Melton Mowbray pork pies have been made on a commercial scale since 1830. King Richard III spent his last days in the county before his death at the Battle of Bosworth in 1485, a battle that changed the course of British history.

The timelessly grand and elegant Belvoir Castle has what could be considered the most

stunning views in the county; over the Belvoir Valley and, on a clear day, miles and miles of rolling countryside. Also grand in their own right is Stanford Hall, and the serene ruins of Ashby Castle – a victim of the Civil War. There are many opportunities to escape the crowds and towns to places of tranquility; the parks at Hinckley and Market Bosworth are green havens, with activities available for days out, as well as the easily accessible National Forest – a must for any visitor.

Accommodation

Food & Drink

Food & Drink

LEICESTER

Designated Britain's first 'environment city' in recognition of its commitment to green issues, Leicester has numerous parks and open spaces but also a rich architectural heritage, with no fewer than 350 listed buildings. At the heart of Leicester's heritage is **Castle Park**, the old town, an area of gardens, churches, museums and other fine buildings. Here are concentrated many of the city's main attractions: **Castle Gardens** opened as a park in 1926; Castle Motte, a man-made mound built around 1070 by Leicester's first Norman lord; the **Church of St Mary de Castro**, founded in 1107 and still in use; the Great Hall of **Leicester Castle** built in the 12th century; and **Newarke Houses Museum**, a museum of social and domestic history contained in two 16th century houses.

Leicester's diverse cultural and religious heritage is represented by the **Jain Centre**, the **Guru Nanak Sikh Museum**; the **Jewry Wall and Museum**; and the **Church of St Martin**, which was in existence before 1086, was extended in the 14th and 15th centuries, restored in the 19th century and hallowed as the Cathedral of Leicester in 1927. One of the very finest buildings in the city is the **Guildhall**, built around 1390 for the Guild of Corpus Christi and used as the Town Hall from the late 15th century until 1876. Across the road from the Cathedral is **Wygston's House**, a part timber-framed building, one of the oldest in the city, which now houses displays of fashion, textiles and crafts.

Leicester is also home to the very popular **National Space Centre**, which has the UK's largest 360° planetarium, a futuristic Rocket

Tower, and hours of breathtaking discovery and interactive fun to be explored.

AROUND LEICESTER

HINCKLEY

11½ miles SW of Leicester on the A47

An old town whose Fair is mentioned in Shakespeare's Henry IV. In Lower Bond Street, a row of restored 17th century thatched framework knitters' cottages is home to **Hinckley and District Museum**. To the east lies **Burbage Common and Woods Country Park**, which contains one of the largest areas of grassland in the area.

MARKET BOSWORTH

11 miles W of Leicester off the A447

This market town is most famous as the battle site for the turning point in the Wars of the Roses, when in 1485 the forces of King Richard III were routed by those of Henry Tudor, who took the throne as Henry VII. The battle was immortalised in Shakespeare's play *Richard III*, where the King is heard to cry, *"My kingdom for a horse."* **Bosworth Battlefield** lies to the southwest of the town

220 THE OLD BARN INN

Glooston

A charming old inn, providing great food, comfortable ensuite bedrooms and a friendly atmosphere.

See entry on page 470

219 THE SWAN AT KIBWORTH

Kibworth

A charming country village pub with a top chef creating fabulous meals

See entry on page 468

221 THE WINDMILL INN AND BRASCOTE RESTAURANT

Brascot, nr Newbold Verdon

A warm and friendly award winning inn with a superb reputation for serving food and real ales.

See entry on page 470

and the Visitor Centre has details of the Battle and numerous artefacts and displays on the Tudor period.

Market Bosworth Country Park is one of many beautiful open spaces in the area whilst another is **Bosworth Water Trust's Leisure and Water Park** to the west of town. This is a 50-acre leisure park with 20 acres of lakes for sailing, boardsailing and fishing.

To the northwest of Market Bosworth lies **Twycross Zoo**, home to a wide variety of animals that include a famous primate collection, from tiny pygmy marmosets to huge Western lowland gorillas. To the north of Market Bosworth is a village with the wonderful name of Barton-in-the-Beans. The county was apparently once known as 'bean-belly' Leicestershire, on account of the heavy reliance on bean crops that formed part of the staple diet in needy times.

The composer George Frederick Handel regularly stayed at the nearby Gopsall Estate, where he composed the music for his glorious *Messiah*. The grandson of the estate's owner completed the job by writing the words.

MOUNTSORREL
6 miles N of Leicester off the A6

Situated on the banks of the River Soar, the village is home to **Stonehurst Family Farm and Motor Museum**, where the highlights range from baby rabbits and guinea pigs in cuddle corner to an impressive collection of vintage vehicles, including Leicestershire's first motor bus.

LOUGHBOROUGH
10 miles N of Leicester on the A6

There are two attractions at Loughborough that visitors certainly should not miss. In 1858, the bell foundry of John Taylor moved here from Oxford and the **John Taylor Bell Foundry Museum** covers all aspects of bell-founding from early times. The town is also the headquarters of the **Great Central Railway**, which runs steam trains every weekend and Bank Holiday, and daily in June, July, August and local school holidays.

COALVILLE
11 miles NW of Leicester on the A511

Originally called Long Lane, the town sprang up on a bleak common when Whitwick Colliery was opened in 1824. **Snibston Discovery Park**, built on the site of the former Snibston Colliery, provides the opportunity to explore a unique mixture of nature, history, art, science and technology with the help of the latest interactive technology.

To the northeast of Coalville, in a beautiful elevated position in Charnwood Forest, is **Mount St Bernard Abbey**, the first Catholic abbey to be founded in England after the Reformation.

ASHBY-DE-LA-ZOUCH
16 miles NW of Leicester on the A511

During the Civil War, **Ashby Castle** was besieged for over a year by the Parliamentarian Army until the Royalists surrendered in 1646. After the war the castle was partly destroyed to prevent its further use as a centre of resistance and almost wholly forgotten until Sir Walter Scott used the castle as the setting in Ivanhoe for the archery competition that Robin Hood won by

Ashby Castle

161

splitting the shaft of his opponent's arrow in the bull's eye.

To the east lies the **National Forest**, a truly accessible, multipurpose forest providing a full range of environmental, recreational and social benefits for current and future generations.

KEGWORTH

15½ miles NW of Leicester on the A6

A large village with many architectural reminders of its days as a framework-knitting centre. Topics covered at the **Kegworth Museum** include the knitting industry, saddlery, air transport and photography, and postcards of the 1920s. To the west lies **Donington Park**, home of the **Donington Grand Prix Collection** with over 130 exhibits in five halls covering 100 years of motor racing history.

MELTON MOWBRAY

This bustling market town is, of course, home to the pork pie, one of the most traditional of English delicacies. The Melton Hunt Cake is another local speciality and Stilton, the 'king of English cheeses', is also made here. The cheese has the longest history, dating back possibly as far as the 14th century, and the town became the market centre for Stilton.

In the town's oldest surviving bakery, **Ye Olde Pork Pie Shoppe**, visitors can watch the traditional hand-raising techniques and taste the pies and the Hunt cake. Another tasty attraction is the **Melton Carnegie Museum**, which has displays devoted to Stilton cheese, pork pies, as well as one plotting the history of fox hunting in the area. Visitors can also

222 THE ODD HOUSE COUNTRY INN

Snarestone

Freshly prepared quality food is what this inn, located at the heart of the national forest, prides itself on.

See entry on page 471

learn about 'Painting the Town Red', an occasion in 1837 when the Marquis of Waterford and his pals decided to decorate the town with red paint after a night's drinking, and even see a preserved two-headed calf, born in the town around 1900.

AROUND MELTON MOWBRAY

BELVOIR CASTLE

12 miles NE of Melton off the A607

The present **Belvoir Castle**, the Leicestershire home of the Duke of Rutland, was completed in the early 19th century after previous buildings had been destroyed during the Wars of the Roses, the Civil War and in the major fire of 1816. Over-looking the lovely Vale of Belvoir, the castle's stunning interior contains notable collections of furniture and porcelain, silks and tapestries, sculptures and paintings, along with the **Queen's Royal Lancers Museum**. The grounds are as splendid as the castle and are used for medieval jousting tournaments on certain days in the summer.

Belvoir Castle

WYMONDHAM

8 miles E of Melton off the B676

The six-sailed **Windmill**, dating from 1814, and partially restored, is one of only four of its kind in the country.

BURROUGH-ON-THE-HILL

5 miles S of Melton off the B6074

Burrough House, set in five acres of beautiful gardens, was a favourite meeting place of the

Prince of Wales and Mrs Wallis Simpson in the 1930s. To the northeast of the village is **Burrough Hill**, an Iron Age hill fort.

MARKET HARBOROUGH

In 1645 Charles I made Market Harborough his headquarters and held a council of war here before the **Battle of Naseby**. The development of turnpike roads led to prosperity and the establishment of coaching inns in the town, many of them still in business. The canals and the railways transformed communications and manufacturing industry became established, the most notable company being R W & H Symington, creators of the Liberty Bodice. The **Harborough Museum** incorporates the **Symington Collection of Corsetry**.

AROUND MARKET HARBOROUGH

FOXTON

2 miles NW of Market Harborough off the A6

The most famous site on the county's canals is the **Flight of Ten Locks** on the Grand Union Canal, one of the great engineer Thomas Telford's most impressive constructions. In the **Canal Museum**, halfway down the flight, the steam-powered boat lift of 1900 is undergoing restoration, and there are several other buildings and bridges of interest (including a swing-bridge) in this pretty village.

Foxton Locks

LUTTERWORTH

12 miles W of Market Harborough on the A4304

John Wycliffe was rector here under the tutelage of John of Gaunt. His instigation of an English translation of the Bible into English caused huge dissent. He died in 1384 and was buried in the church here, but when he was excommunicated in 1428 his body was exhumed and burned and his ashes scattered in the River Swift. Close to the church, **Lutterworth Museum** contains a wealth of local history from Roman times to World War II. Lutterworth is where Frank Whittle perfected the design of his jet engine.

About 3 miles southeast of Lutterworth and set in meadows beside the River Avon, **Stanford Hall** has been the home of the Cave family since 1430. The present house – pleasantly proportioned, dignified and serene, was built by the celebrated architect William Smith of Warwick in the 1690s. A superb staircase was added in around 1730, one of very few structural alterations to the house in its 300-year history: another was the Ballroom, which contains paintings that once belonged to Bonnie Prince Charlie's younger brother, Henry Stuart.

Stanford Hall

223 THE MARQUIS OF GRANBY

Waltham on the Wolds

A delightful old pub serving great food and well kept real ales.

See entry on page 471

163

LINCOLNSHIRE

Although it is the second largest county in England, Lincolnshire remains relatively unknown. It is largely rural and has some of the richest farmland in the country producing, particularly, potatoes, sugar beet and flowers. The annual Flower Parade in the market town of Spalding has some glorious sights and floats – and attracts an impressive 100,000 visitors a year. Another famous Lincolnshire fair takes place every year in Brigg; a charming traditional affair, the charter for which was granted in 1205.

The county has strong historical connections with Holland and Scandinavia and is blessed with many picturesque villages and towns

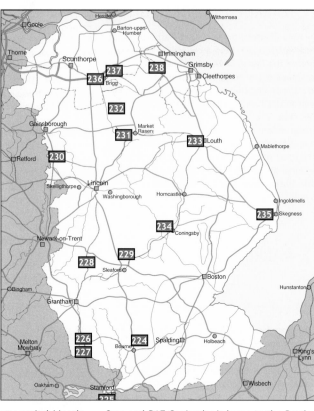

including the majestic county capital Lincoln with its marvelous cathedral, historic Stamford, acclaimed as the finest stone town in England, and Grantham, the birthplace of Margaret Thatcher. Woolsthorpe-by-Colsterworth saw Issac Newton's birth – descendants of the apple tree which inspired his findings on gravity are still growing here.

Along with its extensive coastline, which boasts a number of traditional seaside resorts, Lincolnshire has also played a part in history. It is home to the world's first military air academy, RAF Cranwell; the Dambusters – 617 Squadron – were stationed near Woodhall

Spa; and RAF Coningsby is home to the Battle of Britain Memorial Flight. The port of Grimsby is England's main fishing port.

There are some surprisingly grand houses hidden in the countryside here; Burghley House, which has some glorious gardens and a deer park, Normanby Hall built in 1825 holds many attractions, and the half 18th century palace/half Tudor dwelling of Grimsthorpe Castle which was visited by Henry VIII is quite unmissable. There are two unusual five-sailed windmills in the county – the Maud Foster Windmill and the Alford Windmill.

SPALDING

This small market town is known for its annual **Flower Parade**, which is held in early May, when marching bands lead a succession of colourful floats through the town (there is also the smaller Pumpkin Festival in autumn). Spalding is an interesting place to stroll around, and the jewel in its crown is undoubtedly **Ayscoughfee Hall Museum and Gardens**, a well-preserved medieval mansion standing in attractive riverside gardens that house, among other displays, a permanent exhibit honouring the explorer and oceanographer Captain Matthew Flinders.

A couple of miles south of Spalding, the **Gordon Boswell Romany Museum** has a colourful collection of Romany Vardos (caravans), carts and harnesses. To the north is the **Pinchbeck Engine and Land Drainage Museum**, which illustrates how the South Holland Fen was drained. Also here, at Pinchbeck, are the **Spalding Bulb Museum** and the **Spalding Tropical Forest**.

Pinchbeck Museum

Ayscoughfee Hall, Spalding

AROUND SPALDING

BOSTON

15 miles NE of Spalding on the A16

Boston's most famous landmark is the tower of the massive 14th century **St Botolph's Church**; it's popularly known as the **Boston Stump** – a real misnomer since it soars to 272 feet and is visible for 30 miles or more.

Maud Foster Windmill

Another striking building is the 15th century **Guildhall** that for 300 years served as the Town Hall and now houses the town Museum. It was here, in the Guildhall cells, that the Pilgrim Fathers were held in 1607 while they tried to escape to the religiously tolerant Netherlands. The town is home to the tallest working windmill in Britain, the **Maud Foster Windmill**, which is unusual in having five sails.

CROWLAND

8½ miles S of Spalding on the B1166

Founded by King Ethelbald of Mercia in the 8th century, the now ruined **Crowland Abbey** seen today dates from the 12th century and is the third to have been built on the site. The town is noted for its extraordinary 'Bridge without a River': when it was built in the

1300s, **Trinity Bridge** provided a dry crossing over the confluence of three small streams which have since dried up.

GRIMSTHORPE

12 miles W of Spalding on the A151

The village is home to **Grimsthorpe Castle**, which when viewed from the north is a stately 18th century palace; from the south, it is a homely Tudor dwelling. The Tudor part of the house was built at incredible speed in order to provide a convenient lodging place in Lincolnshire for Henry VIII on his way north to meet James V of Scotland in York. The royal visit took place in 1541 but the honour of the royal presence was tarnished by the adultery that allegedly took place here between Henry's fourth wife, Catherine Howard, and an attractive young courtier, Thomas Culpepper. A subsequently passed law declared it treason for an unchaste woman to marry the king, and both Catherine and her ardent courtier paid the ultimate price for their night of passion.

STAMFORD

An attractive market town with unspoilt Georgian streets and squares, Stamford is also noted for its rich cluster of outstanding

224 THE WISHING WELL INN

Dyke

Renowned village inn serving English cuisine and ale at its best, with en suite accommodation and adjacent campsite.

See entry on page 472

225 THE JOLLY BREWER

Stamford

Inviting 18th century pub offering great local food and a wide selection of real ales in a lively atmosphere.

See entry on page 472

churches. The most ancient ecclesiastical building is **St Leonard's Priory**, founded by the Benedictines in the 11th century, and a fine example of Norman architecture.

Secular buildings of note include the **Museum of Almshouse Life** and the **Stamford Museum**, which includes a display celebrating one of the town's most notable residents, Daniel Lambert, the keeper of Leicester Jail, who earned a solid living by exhibiting himself as the world's heaviest man; on his death in 1809 he weighed nearly 53 stone. Other famous residents include the flamboyant conductor and Promenaders' favourite Sir Malcolm Sargent ('Flash Harry'), who lies buried in the town cemetery, and William Cecil, 1st Lord Burghley, who was Elizabeth I's Chief Secretary of State. **Burghley House** is a wonderfully opulent Elizabethan mansion that houses a magnificent collection of treasures – as well as a beautiful dynamic garden, which includes a sculpture garden and deer park. The **Burghley Horse Trials** are held in these glorious grounds each year at the end of August.

AROUND STAMFORD

WOOLSTHORPE-BY-COLSTERWORTH

14 miles N of Stamford off the B6403

It was at Woolsthorpe Manor that Isaac Newton was born in 1642 and where the Father of Modern Science made some of his greatest discoveries. Descendants of the tree from which that famous apple dropped can still be seen in the garden. In a bedroom in the house is displayed Pope's famous epitaph

on Newton's birth: 'Nature and Nature's laws lay hid in night: God said, Let Newton be! And there was light'. A 17th century barn holds a **Science Discovery Centre** that helps to explain some of his achievements; which included research into colour and light, as well as a major role in reforming the corrupt system of the nation's coinage. From 1699 until his death in 1727 he held the post of Master of the Mint. Widely praised, he was more modest about his own achievements: 'If I have seen further than others, it is because I was standing on the shoulders of giants.'

GRANTHAM

This ancient market town on the banks of the River Witham has some pleasing old buildings including Grantham House, which dates back to around 1380, and the Angel and Royal Hotel, where King John held court and where Richard III signed the death warrant of the 2nd Duke of Buckingham in 1483. Grantham is perhaps best known as being the childhood home of Margaret Roberts, later Thatcher. **Grantham Museum** has special exhibits

Almshouses, Grantham

226 WHITE LION	**227** THE BLUE COW INN
Colsterworth	*South Witham*
Serving fine English cuisine and casque marque quality real ales throughout the week, the White Lion is fast becoming a destination pub.	Steeped in history, this lively (and haunted!) traditional inn offers its own ale, fine food and en suite guest accommodation 365 days a year.
See entry on page 474	*See entry on page 473*

167

devoted to both Lady Thatcher and Sir Isaac Newton.

AROUND GRANTHAM

SLEAFORD

10 miles E of Grantham on the B1517

Inhabited since the Iron Age and home to a massive Roman mint, Sleaford is a busy market town with one of the oldest stone church towers in the country. Other features of interest include the Money's Mill, a 70 feet high tower that was erected in 1796 to allow large quantities of corn to be brought here by barge and offloaded right outside the door.

To the northwest of Sleaford is the RAF College, **Cranwell**, which opened in 1920 as the first Military Air Academy in the world. The **Cranwell Aviation Heritage Centre** tells the Cranwell story and that of the many other RAF bases in the region.

LINCOLN

Lincoln Cathedral occupies a magnificent hilltop location, its towers soaring high above the Lincolnshire lowlands being visible

for miles around. Among its many superb features are the magnificent open nave, stained-glass windows incorporating the 14th century Bishop's Eye and Dean's Eye, and the glorious Angel Choir, whose carvings include the Lincoln Imp, the unofficial symbol of the city. The imposing ruins of the **Medieval Bishops' Palace**, in the shadow of the Cathedral, reveal the sumptuous lifestyle of the wealthy medieval bishops whose authority stretched from the Humber to the Thames.

Other notable buildings include **Lincoln**

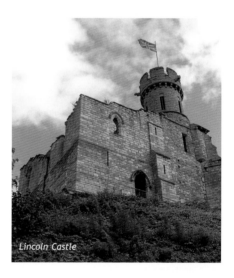

Lincoln Castle

Castle, which dates from 1068 and houses one of the four original versions of the Magna Carta; the **Jews House**, which dates from about 1170 and is thought to be the oldest domestic building in England to survive intact; and the most impressive surviving part of the old town walls, the **Stonebow**, which spans the High Street pedestrianised shopping mall. Lincolnshire's largest social history museum is the **Museum of Lincolnshire Life** that occupies an extensive barracks built for the Royal North Lincoln Militia in 1857. The newest museum in the county, opened in 2005, is **The Collection**, a major centre of art and archaeology running alongside the Usher Gallery.

---

228 THE RED LION

Caythorpe, nr Grantham

This classic quintessential English pub is known for offering restaurant style food in a wonderfully warm pub atmosphere.

See entry on page 475

---

229 THE COFFEE POT

Ruskington

Fantastic facilities and old fashioned values for home baking and local produce combine to make this popular high street café.

See entry on page 474

AROUND LINCOLN

GAINSBOROUGH

15 miles NW of Lincoln on A156

Britain's most inland port is located at the highest navigable point on the River Trent for seagoing vessels. During the 17th and 18th centuries in particular, the town prospered greatly, and although many of the lofty warehouses lining the river bank have been demolished, enough remain to give some idea of its flourishing past.

The town's most famous building is the enchanting **Gainsborough Old Hall**, a complete medieval and Tudor hall house, and one of the most striking architectural gems in the county. The hall was built in the 1470s by Sir Thomas Burgh, who entertained Richard III in the Great Hall. The hall is generally considered one of the best preserved medieval manor houses in the country.

Gainsborough Old Hall

Another notable building in Gainsborough is Marshall's **Britannia Works**, a proud Victorian reminder of Gainsborough's once thriving engineering industry.

MARKET RASEN

14 miles NE of Lincoln on the A631

Taking its name from the River Rase, Market Rasen was described by Charles Dickens as being "the sleepiest town in England." Much of the central part is a conservation area and includes two ecclesiastical buildings of some note: the **Centenary Wesleyan Chapel** of 1863 boasts an impressive frontage, while **St Thomas's Church** has a typical 15th century tower of local ironstone.

LOUTH

24 miles NE of Lincoln off the A16

One of the county's most appealing towns, Louth lies on the Greenwich Meridian beside the River Lud on the eastern edge of the Wolds. The town is best known for being the home of Alfred Lord Tennyson, who lodged here with his grandmother while attending the King Edward VI School. **Broadbank**, which now houses the **Louth Museum**, is an attractive little building with some interesting artefacts, including some amazing locally-woven carpets that were displayed at the Paris Exhibition in 1867. Louth's magnificent **Church of St James** has a wonderful Perpendicular Gothic steeple, the tallest steeple in Britain at almost 300 feet.

---

231 **THE NAGS HEAD**

Middle Rasen

Recently renovated this traditional village inn offers great food and entertainment throughout the week.

See entry on page 476

---

230 **THE BLACK SWAN GUEST HOUSE**

Marton, near Gainsborough

A very comfortable and characterful guest house in a Grade II listed former coaching inn. Super breakfasts.

See entry on page 476

---

232 **THE BULL INN**

South Kelsey

Olde worlde premises in idyllic country village offering award winning ales and a timeless tried and tested menu.

See entry on page 477

To the southwest of Louth lies Donignton-on-Bain, a peaceful Wolds village on the Viking Way that runs 147 miles from the Humber Bridge to Oakham in Rutland. The way is marked by Viking helmet symbols.

OLD BOLINGBROKE

22 miles E of Lincoln off the A155

Originally built in the reign of William I, **Bolingbroke Castle** later became the property of John of Gaunt whose son, later Henry IV, was born at the castle in 1367. During the Civil War, Bolingbroke Castle was besieged by Parliamentary forces in 1643 and fell into disuse soon after. The ruins still draw visitors from around the world every year.

Just to the south, at East Kirkby, is the **Lincolnshire Aviation Heritage Centre**, based in the old control tower. Exhibits include a Lancaster bomber, a Shackleton, military vehicles and a wartime blast shelter.

WOODHALL SPA

14 miles SE of Lincoln on the B1191

Woodhall became a spa town by accident when a shaft sunk in search of coal found mineral-rich water. In 1838 a pump room and baths were built, to be joined later by hydro hotels, and the arrival of the railway in 1855 accelerated Woodhall's popularity. By the early 1900s, the spa had fallen out of favour and the associated buildings disappeared one by one, but this beautifully maintained village has retained its decorous spa atmosphere.

Woodhall Spa had close connections with 617 Squadron, the **Dambusters**, during World War II. The Petwood House Hotel was used as the officers' mess and memorabilia of those days is displayed in the hotel's Squadron Bar. By the front door of the hotel lies one of Barnes Wallis' famous 'Bouncing Bombs' that were used in the attack on the Ruhr dams.

The highly unusual **"Kinema in the Woods"** building was originally built in the late 19th century, and now is the only cinema in the country to operate by projection from behind the screen.

SKEGNESS

In the early 1800s Skegness was still a tiny fishing village but it was already becoming famous for its firm sandy beaches and bracing sea air. As late as 1871, the resident population of Skegness was only 239 but two years later the railway arrived and three years after that the local landowner, the Earl of Scarborough, built a new town to the north of the railway station. A huge pier, 1,843 feet long, was built in 1880, chosen from 44 designs submitted.

The famous slogan 'Skegness is SO Bracing', was first used on posters by the Great Northern Railway in 1908 and appeared in many designs subsequently. In the best known of all the famous posters a jolly pipe-smoking fisherman is shown bouncing along the beach.

Natureland Seal Sanctuary on North Parade provides interest for all the family

---

233 MY FATHERS MOUSTACHE

Louth

Unusually named pub and restaurant known for its authentic Lincolnshire food and great entertainment.

See entry on page 477

---

234 THE CASTLE INN

Coningsby

Great family run inn serving wholesome homemade food and real ale with live entertainment on weekends.

See entry on page 478

---

235 POPPY'S RESTAURANT

Skegness

Exceedingly popular family restaurant and takeaway with a wide across the board menu packed with all your favourites.

See entry on page 478

with its seals and baby seal rescue centre and numerous other animal attractions.

Just outside Skegness **Gibraltar Point National Nature Reserve** is a field station among the salt marshes and dunes with hides, waymarked routes and guided tours. Yellowhammers and whitethroats nest here, and skylarks are more numerous than anywhere else in Britain.

AROUND SKEGNESS

MABLETHORPE

15 miles N of Skegness on the A52

The northernmost of the three popular Lincolnshire holiday resorts (Skegness and Sutton-on-Sea are the others) that almost form a chain along this stretch of fragile coast. Much of the original village of Mablethorpe has disappeared into the sea, including the medieval **Church of St Peter**. The Seal Sanctuary at North End is open every day from Easter to the end of September.

ALFORD

10 miles NW of Skegness on the A1104

Alford Manor House, built around 1660, claims the distinction of being the largest thatched manor house in England. Alford's **Five Sailed Windmill**, built of brick in 1813, stands a majestic six floors high and has five sails and four sets of grinding stones.

Alford Manor House

SCUNTHORPE

Much of Scunthorpe's industrial and social heritage is on display at the **North Lincolnshire Museum & Art Gallery** with exhibits that include an ironmonger's cottage.

Scunthorpe has also created a Heritage Trail which takes visitors through three of the parks created by Victorian benefactors - Scunthorpe is proud of its parks and gardens and has claimed the title of 'The Industrial Garden Town of rural North Lincolnshire'.

AROUND SCUNTHORPE

NORMANBY

4 miles N of Scunthorpe off the B1430

Normanby Hall was built in 1825 for the Sheffield family and extended in 1906. The 300-acre Park has plenty to see and enjoy, including a deer park, duck ponds, an ice house in the middle of the miniature railway circuit, a Victorian laundry and a walled garden. The **Normanby Hall Farming Museum** majors on rural life in the age of the heavy horse. Near the park gates, some picturesque estate cottages bear witness to the Sheffield family's reputation as good landlords.

Normanby Hall

BRIGG

7 miles E of Scunthorpe on the A10

King John was not universally admired but one of his more popular deeds was the granting of a charter (in 1205) which permitted this modest little town to hold an annual festivity on the 5th day of August. **Brigg Fair**, along with Widdecombe and Scarborough, has joined the trio of 'Best Known Fairs in England', celebrated in a traditional song and in a haunting tone poem based on Lincolnshire folk songs, composed by Frederick Delius in 1907.

800 years later, the fair still attracts horse traders from around the country, along with all the usual fun of the fair.

GRIMSBY

According to tradition it was a Dane called Grim who founded Grimsby. He had been ordered to drown the young Prince Havelock after the boy's father had been killed in battle. Grim could not bring himself to murder the child so he fled Denmark for England. After a tempestuous crossing of the North Sea, Grim and the boy arrived at the Humber estuary where he used the timbers of their boat to build a house on the shore. They lived by selling fish and salt, thus establishing the foundations of an industry for which Grimsby would become known the world over. A statue of Grim and the infant prince can be seen at the Humberside Polytechnic.

---

236 THE BLACK BULL

Brigg

Excellent family run inn known for serving up fresh and tasty home fresh produce and fine real ale throughout the year.

See entry on page 479

---

237 THE BLACK HORSE INN

Wrawby, nr Brigg

With a new licensee, there are big plans for this pub, which serves good quality pub grub made with locally sourced produce.

See entry on page 479

AROUND GRIMSBY

IMMINGHAM

7 miles NW of Grimsby off the A180

A small village until the early 1900s, Immingham's breakthrough came when a new port on the south bank of the Humber was proposed. Grimsby naturally thought that the honour should be hers, but consultants favoured Immingham because the deep water channel of the river runs close to the shore here. The **Immingham Museum** traces the links between the Docks and the railways and there is also an exhibit about the group of Puritans who, in 1607, set sail from Immingham to New England. A memorial to this event, the **Pilgrim Father Monument**, was erected by the Anglo-American Society in 1925. It originally stood near the point of embarkation, but is now located near the church.

CLEETHORPES

1 mile S of Grimsby on the A180

One of Cleethorpes' claims to fame is that it stands on zero longitude, ie on the Greenwich Meridian line. A signpost on the coastal path marks the Meridian line and points the way to London, the North Pole and other prominent places, an essential snap for the family album. Above the promenade is the sham ruin known as **Ross Castle**, named after the railway's general secretary, Edward Ross. Swathed in ivy, the folly marked the highest point of the cliffs, which the promenade now protects from erosion.

The town also boasts the last surviving seaside steam railway, the **Cleethorpes Coast Light Railway**.

---

238 THE KINGS HEAD

Keelby

A quality establishment preparing for a full refurbishment in October 2010

See entry on page 480

NORFOLK

The unique Norfolk Broads, to the east of the fine city of Norwich, contains beautiful stretches of shallow water, most of them linked by navigable rivers and canals. This is Britain's finest wetland area, a National Park in all but name; covering some 220 square miles to the northwest of Great Yarmouth. Three main rivers, the Ant, the

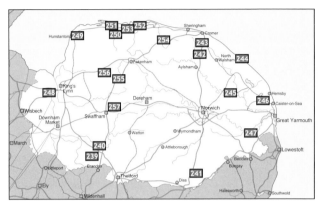

Thurne and the Bure, thread their way through the marshes, providing 120 miles of navigable waterways. This area is also a refuge for many species of endangered birds and plants, and during the summer and autumn the Broads are a favourite stopping off point for migrating birds.

The eastern coast, from Great Yarmouth to Sheringham, is almost one continuous strip of excellent sandy beaches, dotted with charming holiday resorts. Great Yarmouth, with its beautiful breezy promenade, two grand old traditional piers and all the fun of the fair, attracts a huge number of visitors every year; but the other elegant seaside resort towns such as Caister-on-Sea, Mundesley and Cromer have rewarding miles of quiet sandy beaches, spectacular sea views and the exhilarating, bracing sea air, away from the crowds.

Inland lies the county town, Norwich, which is famous for its Norman cathedral, its castle and a wealth of other historic buildings. Norwich is also the home of mustard and its best-known producer J & J Colman; whose work is remembered at The Mustard Shop, through many unique artifacts and memorabilia.

It is surprising to find one of England's most important medieval ports, King's Lynn, at the southern end of the underwater maze of sandbanks of the Wash but then, of course, keels were shallower. King's Lynn is still a busy port today; several ancient ports along the North Norfolk coast are now holiday resorts. A little way inland is the Royal family's country estate of Sandringham, and the grand mansion of Holkham Hall, which is home to superb collections of classical sculptures, paintings, and tapestries.

Accommodation

Accommodation

Continued

THETFORD

The town's strategic position, at the confluence of the Rivers Thet and Little Ouse, have made this an important settlement for centuries and excavations have revealed an Iron Age enclosure that is thought to have been the site of Boudicca's Palace.

Of **Thetford Castle**, only the 80-feet motte remains, but it's worth climbing to the top of this mighty mound for the views across the town. In the charming heart of the town is the striking **Ancient House**, a 15th century timber-framed house that is home to the **Museum of Thetford Life** containing replicas of the Thetford Treasure. The **King's House** is named after James I who was a frequent visitor here from 1608-18. The town's 12th century **Cluniac Priory** (English Heritage) is mostly in ruins, though the impressive 14th century gatehouse still stands. Thetford's industrial heritage is vividly displayed in the **Burrell Steam Museum**, which has full-size working steam engines, re-created workshops

and vintage agricultural machinery.

To the west of the town lies **Thetford Forest**, the most extensive lowland forest in Britain, planted by the Forestry Commission in 1922. In the heart of the forest are **Grimes Graves** (English Heritage), the earliest major industrial site discovered in Europe. At these Neolithic flint mines, Stone Age labourers extracted materials for their axes and knives from the chamber 30 feet below ground.

On the edge of Thetford Forest are the ruins of **Thetford Warren Lodge**, built in the early 15th century when the surrounding area was preserved for farming rabbits – a major element of the medieval diet.

AROUND THETFORD

WYMONDHAM

19 miles NE of Thetford on the B1172

The town is home to one of the oddest ecclesiastical buildings in the country – with

---

239 THE WEST END

Feltwell

An attractive building and a great spot to sit and enjoy a pint or celebrate those special occasions.

See entry on page 480

---

240 COLVESTON MANOR

Mundford

A charming and quaint place to get away from the hustle and bustle of everyday life.

See entry on page 481

the most glorious interior - **Wymondham Abbey**, which was founded in 1107 by William d'Albini, butler to King Henry I. Its two towers dominate the town's skyline, and can be seen from miles around.

Although many of the town's oldest houses were destroyed by fire in 1615, some older buildings escaped, including 12th century **Becket's Chapel**. Also of interest is **The Bridewell** which was built in 1785 as a model prison and reputedly served as a model for the penitentiaries established in the United States. It is now the **Wymondham Heritage Museum**. Displays include brushmaking and Kett's Rebellion.

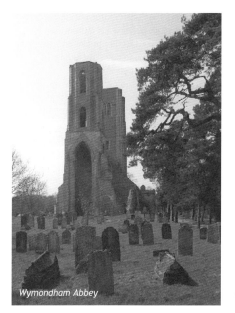
Wymondham Abbey

Wymondham's historic Railway Station was built in 1845 on the Great Eastern's Norwich to Ely line and, still in use; the buildings house a railway museum. Also is the volunteer-run **Mid-Norfolk Railway,** which runs some 11 miles (the longest heritage railway in East Anglia) through gorgeous countryside between Wymondham and Dereham; a favorite attraction for visitors to the town.

BANHAM

12 miles E of Thetford off the B1077

To the southwest of the village lies **Banham Zoo**, a 25 acre home to some of the world's most endangered animals including monkeys and apes – a particular concern here. It also has one of the largest birds of prey exhibits in the UK.

DISS

16 miles E of Thetford on the A1066

The past Poet Laureate, John Betjeman, voted Diss his favourite Norfolk town, and it's easy to understand his enthusiasm. Situated on the northern bank of the River Waveney, which forms the boundary between Suffolk and Norfolk, Diss is a pleasant old market town that developed on the hill overlooking The Mere and park. The **Diss Museum** in the market place is packed with information about the town's past, its trade, famous people and 'orrible murders.

Just northeast of Diss, is the **100th Bomb Group Memorial Museum**, a tribute to the US 8th Air Force that was stationed here at Dickleburgh Airfield during World War II. The museum has a fine collection of USAAF uniforms, decorations, combat records, equipment and wartime photographs. Two other interesting museums can be found at nearby Bressingham. The **Bressingham Steam Museum** boasts a fine collection of locomotives and traction engines, a Victorian steam roundabout and three narrow-gauge railway rides. On the same site are two delightful gardens – the Dell and Foggy Bottom – and the **National Dad's Army Collection**.

---

241 **THE CROWN INN**

Pullham Market

This 17th century inn is renowned for its fantastic hospitality, quality ale and fine food

See entry on page 482

NORWICH

By the time of the *Domesday Book*, Norwich was the third most populous city in England and the Normans built a Castle here that was replaced in the late 12th century by a mighty stone fortress. **Norwich Castle** never saw military action and, as early as the 13th century, it was already being used as the county gaol – a role it filled until 1889. The Castle is now a lively Museum with exhibitions ranging from Norfolk painters and Norwich silver to natural history, Lowestoft porcelain and a vast collection of ceramic teapots. Visitors can also tour the dungeons and battlements.

While the Castle's function has changed over the years, the **Cathedral**, consecrated in 1101, remains the focus of ecclesiastical life in Norfolk. The most completely Norman cathedral in England after Durham, this superb building has the largest Norman cloisters in the country and is noted for its 400 gilded bosses that depict scenes from medieval life. Among the cathedral's numerous treasures are the Saxon Bishop's Throne in the Presbytery, the 14th century altar painting in St Luke's Chapel and the richly carved canopies in the Choir. By the open market place is the Gothic masterpiece **St Peter Mancroft Church** with its massive embellished tower, 15th century windows depicting the New Testament, and a celebrated peal of bells. **City Hall**, which was modelled on Stockholm City Hall, was opened in 1938 by George VI. No mention of Norwich is complete without telling the story of Jeremiah Colman who, in the early 1800s, perfected his blend of mustard flours and spice to produce a condiment that was smooth in texture and tart in flavour. Together with his nephew James, he founded J & J Colman in 1823 and **The Mustard Shop** commemorates the company's history with a delightful shop, and many interesting artifacts from the company's history.

The Forum, a stunning contemporary development in the heart of the city, is an exciting combination of resources for the community and visitors alike. It includes

Norwich Castle

Europe's largest permanent digital screen gallery with free public access, places to meet and enjoy a meal and a drink at any time of day, the tourist information centre and the **Norfolk & Norwich Millennium Library** with over 120,000 books and the best in information technology – including 90 computers for free public use.

To the south of the city are the remains of **Venta Icenorum**, the Roman town that was established here after Boudicca's rebellion in AD 61. Three miles to the north, next to Norwich International Airport, is the City of Norwich Aviation Museum, whose exhibits include a Vulcan bomber.

Famous sons of Norwich include the recorder of Parliamentary proceedings Luke Hansard (1752), Rupert Everett (1959) and Matthew Parker (1509) sometime Archbishop of Canterbury, dubbed 'Nosey Parker' by Queen Elizabeth I.

AROUND NORWICH

AYLSHAM

12 miles N of Norwich off the A140

In the churchyard of **St Michael's Church** is the tomb of one of the greatest English 18th century landscape gardeners, Humphry Repton, who created some 200 parks and gardens around the country.

One of Repton's commissions was to landscape the grounds of **Blickling Hall**, which lies just to the north of the town. Built for Sir Henry Hobart in the 1620s, the Hall is perfectly symmetrical and its most spectacular feature is the Long Gallery that extends for 175 feet and has a glorious plaster ceiling.

Within a few miles of the Hall are two other stately homes, **Mannington Hall** and **Wolterton Park**. Repton also landscaped the grounds for the latter, an 18th century mansion that was built for the brother of Sir Robert Walpole, England's first Prime Minister.

Mannington Hall, Aylsham

SHERINGHAM
22 miles N of Norwich on the A149

A former fishing village which still has a fleet of fishing boats that are launched from the shore, Sheringham was transformed into a graceful seaside resort with the arrival of the railway.

Although Sheringham's railway line was closed in the 1960s, it was reopened in 1975 as the **North Norfolk Railway**; it is also known as the Poppy Line because these brilliant flowers can still be seen in the fields along the scenic five-mile route.

Just to the west of the town, footpaths lead to the lovely Repton-landscaped grounds of **Sheringham Park** (National Trust) from where there are grand views along the coast.

Yet more glorious scenery can be found at the aptly named Pretty Corner, a particularly beautiful area of woodland. Another delightful walk, and a real hidden gem, can be found just outside of Sheringham towards Cromer at the **Priory Maze and Gardens**; the natural beauty of these gardens, which have been so lovingly grown and include the ruins of Beeston Priory, have attracted numerous birds, insects and mammals which have made it their home.

A little further along the coast is the shingle beach known as Weybourne Hope (or Hoop) that slopes so steeply that an invading force could bring its ships right up to the shore. The garrison camp that defended this vulnerable stretch of beach during both World Wars now houses the **Muckleburgh Collection**, a fascinating museum of military equipment. East of Sheringham, at West Runton, is the highest point in Norfolk – **Beacon Hill**. Although only 330 feet high, it commands glorious views from the summit. Close by is the Roman Camp, which excavations have shown to have been an iron-working settlement in Saxon and Medieval times. The village, too, is home to the **Norfolk Shire Horse Sanctuary** where the heavy horses give demonstrations of the valuable work they once performed on farms.

CROMER
21 miles N of Norwich on the A149

A popular seaside resort since the late 18th century, Cromer is famous for its crabs, reckoned to be among the most succulent in England. **Cromer Pier** is the genuine article, complete with a Lifeboat Station and theatre, and on the promenade is a museum dedicated to the coxswain Henry Blogg and 200 years of Cromer lifeboats. **Cromer Museum** is housed

---

242 **SAFFRON TEA ROOMS**

Erpingham

A popular cafe with homemade cakes and light lunches waiting to be sampled.

See entry on page 481

---

243 **NEW INN AND SEREMBAN RESTAURANT**

Roughton

A great restaurant with an Oriental twist just three miles from the seaside town of Cromer

See entry on page 482

Cromer Pier

shipwrecks over the centuries and the victims lie buried in the graveyard of **St Mary's Church**. The large grassy mound on the north side of the church contains the bodies of the crew of the ill-fated HMS *Invincible* which was sunk on sandbanks here in 1801. On its way to join up with Nelson's fleet at Copenhagen, the ship sank with the loss of 110 sailors.

in a row of restored fishermens' cottages.

Just inland from Cromer is one of Norfolk's grandest houses, **Felbrigg Hall**, a wonderful Jacobean mansion dating from the 1620s.

NORTH WALSHAM

13½ miles NE of Norwich on the A149

A busy country town with an attractive market cross dating from 1600, North Walsham was the home of Horatio Nelson, who came to the town's Paston School at the age of 10. A dual place of interest is the unusual **Cat Pottery and Railway Junk Yard**, dealing in lifelike handmade pottery cats (and now dogs too) and transport memorabilia. To the west of North Walsham, near the village of Erpingham, is **Alby Crafts and Gardens** which promotes the excellence of mainly East Anglian and British craftsmanship.

To the northeast is the quiet seaside village of **Mundesley**, whose **Maritime Museum** in a former coastguard lookout is believed to be the smallest museum in the country.

HAPPISBURGH

17 miles NE of Norwich on the B1159

The coastal waters of Happisburgh (pronounced Hazeborough) have seen many

WROXHAM

7 miles NE of Norwich on the A1151

This riverside village, linked to Hoveton by a bridge over the River Bure, is the capital of the Norfolk Broads, and during the high season its boatyards are full of craft of all shapes and sizes. The village is also the southern terminus of the **Bure Valley Railway**, a nine-mile long steam railway that follows the course of the River Bure through glorious countryside to the market town of Aylsham.

Just to the north lies the **Wroxham Barns**, a delightful collection of beautifully restored 18th century barns that house a community of craftspeople, and to the east is **Hoveton Hall Gardens**, which offer visitors a splendid combination of lovely plants and both woodland and lakeside walks.

Further up the River Bure is the charming village of **Coltishall**, home to the **Ancient Lime Kiln**, a reminder of Norfolk's industrial heritage.

RANWORTH

9 miles E of Norwich off the B1140

A beautiful Broadland village, from where five Norfolk Broads, the sea at Great Yarmouth and the spire of Norwich Cathedral can be seen from the tower of **St Helen's Church**. Also to be seen is the National Trust's **Horsey**

---

244 THE HILL HOUSE INN

Happisburgh

Outstanding family run inn that prides itself on offering affordable and delicious food for all, with a large array of real ales and guest accommodation.

See entry on page 484

---

245 BURE RIVER COTTAGE RESTAURANT

Horning

Renowned seafood restaurant in the heart of Horning village, serving up a daily changing menu of fresh fish in a chilled out and contemporary setting.

See entry on page 485

Mill. Along with the views, the church houses one of the county's greatest ecclesiastical treasures - an early 15th century Gothic choir screen.

GREAT YARMOUTH

In Saxon times, Great Yarmouth was an island, but changes in the flow of the River Bure means that it is now a promontory. The seaward side has a five-mile stretch of sandy beach and numerous family amusements, as well as the **Maritime Museum of East Anglia** and the **Elizabethan House**, a merchant's house of 1596 which is now a museum of domestic life. Behind South Beach is the 144 feet Nelson's Monument crowned by a statue of Britannia.

Most of Yarmouth's older buildings are concentrated in the riverside part of the town, including the historic South Quay with an array of museums, including one celebrating the life and times of Horatio Nelson.

For centuries, incredible quantities of herring were landed at Yarmouth and the trade involved so many fishermen that there were more boats registered here than in London. It was a Yarmouth man, John Woodger, who developed the process to produce that great essential of a proper English breakfast – the kipper.

When the Romans established their fortress, Garionnonum, now known as **Burgh Castle** a few miles west of Great Yarmouth, the surrounding marshes were still under water and the fort stood on one bank of a vast estuary commanding a strategic position. Today's ruins are impressive, its walls of alternating layers of flint and brick rising to

Caister Castle, Great Yarmouth

some 15 feet in places.

To the north of Yarmouth lies **Caister-on-Sea**, a holiday resort that was an important fishing village for the Iceni tribe. The Romans built a castle here of which little remains; the **Caister Castle** seen today dates from 1432 and was built by Sir John Fastolf who distinguished himself leading the English bowmen at the Battle of Agincourt. The castle is home to a **Motor Museum** which houses an impressive collection of vintage and veteran cars, the oldest being a Panhard Levassor from 1893. About three miles west of Caister Castle, the pleasantly landscaped grounds surrounding an 1876 Victorian mansion have been transformed into the **Thrigby Hall Wildlife Gardens**, home for a renowned collection of Asian mammals, birds and reptiles.

---

246 THE KINGS HEAD
Filby

Delightful, traditional inn offering a warm welcome, fine home cooked food and real ales throughout the year.

See entry on page 485

---

247 THE LORD NELSON
Reedham

On the banks of the River Yare, this popular inn is the heart and soul of village life serving a traditional home cooked menu with a variety of live music evenings to suit all.

See entry on page 486

KING'S LYNN

An ancient town that is a harmonious mix of medieval, Tudor, Jacobean and Flemish architecture and with some of the finest old streets anywhere in England. One of the most striking sights in the town is the 15th century **Guildhall of the Holy Trinity** with its distinctive chequerboard design of black flint and white stone. Next to it, in the late-Victorian Town Hall, is the **Museum of Lynn Life**, whose greatest treasure is King John's Cup, a dazzling piece of medieval workmanship. Close by, standing proudly on the banks of the River Purfleet, is the handsome **Custom House** of 1683 that was designed by the local architect Henry Bell. Other buildings of note, and there are many, include the **Hanseatic Warehouse**, the South Gate, the Greenland Fishery Building and the Guildhall of St George, the oldest civic hall in England and now home to the **King's Lynn Arts Centre**. At the aptly named Saturday Market Place is the **Old Gaol House**, an experience complete with the sights and sounds of the ancient cells.

The pretty village of **Castle Rising**, just northeast of King's Lynn, is overshadowed by its massive Castle Keep, whose well-preserved

Castle Rising Castle

walls rise to some 50 feet. Built in 1150 to guard what was then the sea approach to the River Ouse, Castle Rising was much more a residential building than a defensive one and it was to here, in 1331, that Edward III banished his ferocious mother Isabella who had been instrumental in his father's murder.

AROUND KING'S LYNN

DERSINGHAM

8 miles NE of King's Lynn on the B1440

A large village close to some pleasant walks through Dersingham Wood and the adjoining Sandringham Country Park. The Royal family's country retreat, **Sandringham House** is a relatively recent addition to the family and was purchased by the Prince of Wales, later Edward VII, as a country refuge to match the retreats his parents enjoyed at Balmoral and Osborne.

To the north of Dersingham lies **Snettisham**, which is best known for its spacious, sandy beaches and the **RSPB Bird Sanctuary**.

HUNSTANTON

14½ miles N of King's Lynn on the A149

A busy seaside resort, Hunstanton boasts two unique features: its cliffs of colourful layers of red, white and brown strata and its west-facing position - unique for an east-coast resort! Developed in the 1860s with the arrival of the railways, the town was assured of its social standing after the Prince of Wales, later Edward VII, came here to recover from typhoid fever and it retains a distinct 19th century charm. The along the sandy

---

248 THE COACH AND HORSES INN

Tilney St Lawrence

Modest and friendly traditional village inn offering real ale and traditional pub food, with adjacent campsite.

See entry on page 487

---

249 FISHERS OF HUNSTANTON

Hunstanton

Popular restaurant, known for its traditional home made fish and chips style menu and

roof garden with stunning views across the bay.

See entry on page 488

beaches and beautiful waterfront can be found many attractions, including the **Sea Life Sanctuary** on the South Promenade.

To the north lies **Old Hunstanton**, a charming village at the beginning of the Norfolk Coastal Footpath which leads eastwards, around the coast, to Cromer. Just a little further up the coast is **Holme next the Sea**, which lies at the northern end of another long distance footpath, the 50-mile long Peddars Way which starts at Thetford. This village is the site of **Sea Henge**, a 4,500-year-old Bronze Age tree circle discovered on the beach.

To the south lies **Heacham**, the home of **Norfolk Lavender**, the largest lavender growing and distilling operation in the country. Visitors can take a guided tour around the working farm, which also contains the National Collection of Lavenders.

BURNHAM MARKET

19 miles NE of King's Lynn on the B1155

The largest of the seven Burnhams strung along the valley of the River Burn, Burnham Market has an outstanding collection of Georgian buildings surrounding its green. To the southeast lies **Burnham Thorpe**, the birthplace of Horatio Nelson, whose father was the rector here for 46 years. He was born

in 1758 at the now demolished Parsonage House, and both the local inn and the church contain memorabilia from his life.

WELLS-NEXT-THE-SEA

23½ miles NE of King's Lynn on the A149

Wells was a working port from the 13th century, and in 1859, to prevent the harbour silting up completely, an embankment, cutting off an area of marshland, was built; today, the harbour lies more than a mile from the sea. Running alongside the embankment, which provides a pleasant walk, is the **Harbour Railway** that runs from the quay to the lifeboat station by the beach. This narrow-gauge railway is operated by the same company as the Wells and Walsingham Railway which carries passengers on the delightful ride on the old Great Eastern route to Little Walsingham.

Just west of the town lies **Holkham Hall**, a glorious classical mansion built by Thomas Coke that was completed in 1762. The magnificent rooms are only overshadowed by the superb collections they contain, including classical sculptures, paintings by Rubens and Van Dyck, and tapestries. A museum at the Hall has exhibits of social, domestic and agricultural memorabilia.

Further along the coast, to the east, lies

250 WHITEHALL FARM

Burnham Thorpe

Lovely B & B and self catering accommodation on a working farm in stunning surroundings.

See entry on page 489

252 BOXWOOD GUEST HOUSE

Wells-next-the-Sea

Family run bed and breakfast offering luxurious contemporary accommodation; the perfect base for exploring the stunning Norfolk coastline.

See entry on page 489

251 THE HERO

Burnham Overy Staithe

Popular and friendly village pub, with a fine reputation for serving an exciting menu created with fresh local produce and extensive wine list.

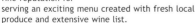

See entry on page 490

253 THE VICTORIA INN AT HOLKHAM

Holkham

A spectacular place to get away, glorious B & B rooms or magnificent self catering follies, topped off with a scrumptious restaurant.

See entry on page 491

181

the pretty village of **Stiffkey** (pronounced Stewkey) and the **Stiffkey Salt Marshes**, a National Trust nature reserve that turns a delicate shade of purple in July when the sea lavender is in bloom. The stately ruins of the great **Stiffkey Hall** have been transformed into a rose terrace and sunken garden and are open to the public.

Away from the coast can be seen the picturesque ruins of **Binham Priory**, founded in 1091 and once one of the most important religious houses in Norfolk.

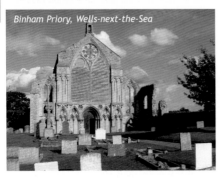
Binham Priory, Wells-next-the-Sea

CLEY-NEXT-THE-SEA
30 miles NE of King's Lynn on the A149

In early medieval times, Cley was a more important port than King's Lynn, a fact that is hard to believe today as the town lies a mile from the sea. The subject of thousands of paintings, **Cley Mill** was built in 1713, remained in use until 1921 and is now open to visitors during the season.

Another fine old mill can be found at the village of Glandford, which is also home to the **Glandford Shell Museum**, featuring seashells gathered from around the world, and the **Natural Surroundings Wild Flower**

Centre that is dedicated to gardening with a strong ecological emphasis.

To the west of Cley is one of the most enchanting of Norfolk's coastal villages, Blakeney, where the silting up of the estuary has created a fascinating landscape of serpentine creeks and channels twisting their way through mudbanks and sand hills. Down the B1156 from Blakeney is **Langham Glass & Rural Crafts**, where visitors can see regular demonstrations of glass-making and other traditional crafts.

THURSFORD GREEN
24 miles NE of King's Lynn off the A148

This village is home to one of the most unusual museums in Norfolk, the **Thursford Collection Sight & Sound Spectacular** – a fascinating collection of steam-powered traction engines, fairground organs and carousels. At the regular live music shows, the most astonishing exhibit, a 1931 Wurlitzer organ, displays its virtuosity.

To the northwest lies the village of **Little Walsingham** that still attracts pilgrims who come to worship at the **Shrine of Our Lady of Walsingham**. In 1061, the Lady of the Manor had a vision in which she was instructed to build a replica of the Holy House of Nazareth and her Holy House soon became a place of pilgrimage. In the mid 12th century, an Augustinian Priory was established to protect the shrine and, today, the largest surviving part, a stately gatehouse, can be seen on the east side of the High Street. Henry VIII went on to Slipper Chapel, a beautiful 14th century building at nearby Houghton St Giles.

Shrine of Our Lady of Walsingham

Other buildings of interest in the attractive village of Little Walsingham are the 16th century octagonal Clink in Common Place; the scant ruins of a 14th century Franciscan Friary; and the former Shire Hall that is now a museum.

FAKENHAM

20 miles NE of King's Lynn off the A148

A prosperous market town and home to a National Hunt Racecourse, Fakenham is a major agricultural centre for the region. An attractive town, it must be one of the few places in the country where the former gasworks have become an attraction and here they house the **Museum of Gas & Local History**. A mile from Fakenham on the A1067 Norwich road lies the **Pensthorpe Natural Centre of Norfolk**; a multi-award winning attraction for lovers of nature, wildlife, bird life and the great outdoors.

CASTLE ACRE

12 miles SE of King's Lynn on the A1065

William de Warenne, William the Conqueror's son-in-law, came here very soon after the Conquest and built a **Castle** that was one of the first, and largest, in the country to be built by the Normans. Of that vast fortress,

little remains apart from the gargantuan earthworks and a squat 13th century gateway.

Much more has survived of **Castle Acre Priory**, founded in 1090 and set in fields beside the River Nar. Its glorious West Front gives a powerful indication of how majestic a triumph of late Norman architecture the complete Priory must have been.

SWAFFHAM

14 miles SE of King's Lynn on the A47

A town with many handsome and interesting buildings, including the **Assembly Rooms** of 1817 and the elegant **Butter Cross**, a classical lead-covered dome standing on eight columns. Swaffham was the birthplace in 1874 of Howard Carter, who found and opened Tutankhamen's tomb.

Swaffham Museum is located in the Town Hall, and just to the southwest of the town, archaeologists have reconstructed a village from the time of Boudicca - Cockley Cley Iceni Village and Museums. A more recent addition to Swaffham's attractions is the **EcoTech Centre**, opened in 1998, which explores current innovations as well as technologies of the future. There's a

Ecotech Centre, Swaffham

255 MANOR HOUSE FARM
Wellingham, nr Fakenham

A conservation award winning farm bed and breakfast also sports luxurious self catering accommodation and unrivalled English gardens to enjoy.

See entry on page 492

256 THE DABBLING DUCK
Great Massingham

The light and friendly atmosphere at the Dabbling Duck accompanies a reputation for exquisite and creative cuisine, with en suite accommodation also available.

See entry on page 494

257 CORFIELD HOUSE
Sporle, nr Swaffham

A warm welcome awaits all guests at this period bed and breakfast in rural Norfolk.

See entry on page 493

St Withburga Well, Dereham

climbable wind turbine in the grounds.

Southwest of Swaffham lies Oxburgh Hall, a lovely moated house dating from the 15th century which was visited by Henry VII and his Queen in 1497.

DEREHAM

23 miles SE of King's Lynn off the A47

One of the most ancient towns in Norfolk, where in AD 654 St Withburga founded a nunnery. Her name lives on in **St Withburga's Well**, which marks the place where she was laid to rest. The poet William Cowper lived here for the last four years of his life, and in the nearby hamlet of **Dumpling Green**, one of the country's most celebrated travel writers, George Borrow, was born. A much less attractive character connected with the town is Bishop Bonner, the enthusiastic arsonist of Protestant heretics during the reign of Mary Tudor. Rector here before being appointed Bishop of London, he lived in the exquisite thatched terrace that is known as **Bishop Bonner's Cottages**, now the home of a small Museum.

To the north of the town, at Gressenhall, is the **Gressenhall Farm & Workhouse** housed in an imposing late-18th century former workhouse. The many exhibits here concentrate on the working and domestic life of Norfolk people over the last 150 years.

DOWNHAM MARKET

10 miles S of King's Lynn off the A10

A compact little market town on the very edge of the Fens, with the River Great Ouse and the New Bedford Drain running side by side at its western edge. Of particular note here in the market place is the elegant and highly decorated cast-iron **Clock Tower** that was erected in 1878.

Just to the south, at the village of **Denver**, is the **Denver Sluice** which was built in 1651 by the Dutch engineer, Cornelius Vermuyden, as part of a scheme to drain 20,000 acres of land owned by the Duke of Bedford.

Running parallel to this is the modern **Great Denver Sluice** that was opened in 1964. Also here is **Denver Windmill**, built in 1835 and reopened in 2000 after being carefully restored; the site includes a visitor centre, craft workshops, a bakery and a tea shop.

Denver Windmill

NORTHAMPTONSHIRE

Although a relatively small county, Northamptonshire has a lot to offer. The county town, Northampton, along with other local towns, is famed for its shoe industry; the county town's museum having the largest footwear collection in the world. Outside of the bustling towns, Northamptonshire remains essentially a farming county littered with ancient market towns and rural villages. Its history is as interesting as most – the decisive battle of Naseby was fought on its soil, and it was at Fotheringay Castle that Mary, Queen of Scots was executed.

There are many magnificent stately homes here but the most famous now is Althorp, the country estate of the Spencer family and the last resting place of Diana, Princess of Wales. The Tudor Sugrave Manor was built by the ancestors of George Washington, and has some great displays and tours for visitors. The grand sprawling Boughton House and the surviving shell of Kirkby Hall give brilliant insight into the history of Northamptonshire. There are also some more eccentric buildings to discover, including the creations of Sir Thomas Tresham – notably the unique Triangular Lodge at Rushton.

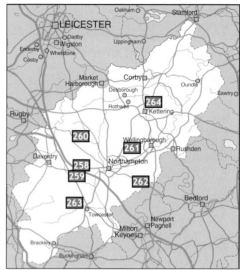

Two of the three remaining Eleanor Crosses, from an original twelve, are situated within the county; at Northampton and Geddington. They were built by a grief stricken King Edward to mark the stops his late wife's body would make on her journey back to London to be buried, and at the time would have been lavishly decorated. It is a tragic and romantic gesture which still resonates today. He also ordered that two wax candles were to burn for all time beside her tomb in Westminster Abbey. They burned for two and half centuries, and were extinguished only at the time of the Reformation.

For those wanting a slightly faster pace then a visit to Silverstone - the home of British motor racing and the British Grand Prix. Here you can take a Ferrari, Lotus, or Formula Silverstone one-seater, around the tracks at breakneck speed, and get a taste of professional racing for yourself.

NORTHAMPTON

By the 13th century Northampton was a major market town and its market square is reputed to have been the second largest in the country. The town is best known for its shoemaking and the first large order came in 1642 when 4,000 pairs of shoes and 600 pairs of boots were made for the army. The industry grew rapidly throughout the county and by the end of the 19th century 40% of the population was involved in the shoe trade. The **Central Museum and Art Gallery** has the world's largest and most fascinating collection of footwear, while the **Abington Museum**, set in a 15th century manor house, tells the county's military history.

There are many fine buildings here and, in particular, notably the wonderful 12th century **Church of the Holy Sepulchre**, one of only a handful of round churches in Britain. The Welsh House, one of the few buildings to survive a disastrous fire in 1675, recalls the time when Welsh drovers would bring their cattle to the market. The town's most prestigious building is the **Guildhall**, a gem of Victorian architecture built in 1864 by Edward Godwin.

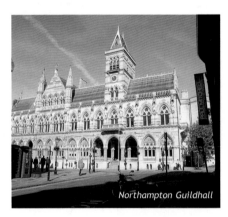

Northampton Guildhall

In the south part of Northampton town stands one of the three surviving Eleanor Crosses of the original 12 that marked the journey of King Edward with his wife's body from Nottinghamshire to London.

AROUND NORTHAMPTON

DAVENTRY

11½ miles W of Northampton on the A45

A historic town, which holds a colourful market along the High Street every Tuesday and Friday. In the Market Place stands the **Moot Hall**, built in 1769 as a private residence.

Just north of the town lies Daventry Country Park; close by is **Borough Hill**, the third largest Iron Age hill fort in Britain, and also the site of a Roman villa.

To the southeast of Daventry lies **Flore**, an ancient village whose wide green slopes down to the banks of the River Nene. Adams Cottage was the home of the ancestors of John Adams, President of the United States.

ALTHORP

5 miles NW of Northampton off the A428

The home of the Spencer family since 1508, **Althorp** remains exactly that - a classic family-owned English stately home. The present house was begun in 1573, and behind the stark tiling of the exterior is a wealth of fine paintings, sculpture, porcelain and furniture. Known widely by connoisseurs for

---

258 THE RED LION AND TRUCK STOP

M1, Junction 16, Weedon Road

An ideal place for truckers to rest with 24 hour security, shower facilities, and Great Pub Food.

See entry on page 495

---

259 THE OLDE SUN INN

Nether Heyford

A wonderful village pub filled with interesting bygones, serving cask ales and good simple food.

See entry on page 496

generations, Althorp is now known across the whole world since the death of Diana, Princess of Wales, in 1997; she lies at peace in the beautiful, tranquil setting of the Round Oval, an ornamental lake. The glorious **Literary Festival**, held here every year for a weekend in June, hosts some of the most influential and prolific writers working today; quite a treat, set within the grandeur of the house and grounds.

To the north is **Holdenby Hall**, which was built by Elizabeth I's Lord Chancellor, Sir Christopher Hatton, for the purpose of entertaining the Queen. At the time, it was the largest Elizabethan house in England but Elizabeth I only visited the house once. Later it became the palace and eventually the prison of Charles I, who was held here for five months after the Civil War.

Also north of Althorp is Cottesbrooke Hall, a magnificent Queen Anne house that is reputed to be the model for Jane Austen's *Mansfield Park*; close by is Coton Manor Garden, a traditional garden originally laid out in 1925 that embraces several delightful smaller gardens.

ASHBY ST LEDGERS

12½ miles NW of Northampton on the A361

From 1375 to 1605 the manor house at Ashby was the home of the Catesby family and it was in a room above the gatehouse that Guy Fawkes is said to have met Robert Catesby and hatched the Gunpowder Plot. Years of neglect left the gatehouse in a sorry state; it has now been completely conserved by Viscount Wimborne, but remains closed to the public. You can, however, see the fascinating wall paintings inside the Norman Church; St. Christopher, painted on the North wall, has

greeted visitors and wished the departing traveler well for over five hundred years.

KELMARSH

12 miles N of Northampton on the A508

This village is home to **Kelmarsh Hall**, an early 18th century house that was designed by James Gibb, best known as the architect of St Martin in the Fields, London, and is surrounded by beautiful gardens, woodland and farmland. To the southeast is another fine country house, 16th century **Lamport Hall**. Its grounds include the first Alpine garden and the first garden gnomes in England, along with the Hannington Vintage Tractor Club agriculture museum.

West of Kelmarsh is the site of the **Battle of Naseby**, where in 1645 Oliver Cromwell's Parliamentarian forces defeated Charles I and determined the outcome of the Civil War. **Naseby Battle and Farm Museum**, in Naseby village, contains a model layout of the battle, relics from the fight and a collection of bygone agricultural machinery.

Lamport Hall Gnome Rockery, Kelmarsh

WELLINGBOROUGH

10 miles NE of Northampton on the A509

An important market and industrial town, known for its iron mills, flourmills and tanneries, Wellingborough sits near the point where the River Ise joins the River Nene. There are many fine buildings through the town; of particular interest is the splendid stone-walled, thatch-roofed 15th century

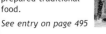 **THE CHEQUERS**

Ravensthorpe

This traditional country pub has a strong focus on freshly prepared traditional food.

See entry on page 495

Tithe Barn. An attraction in the centre of town is the **Millennium Rose Garden** at Swanspool Gardens while to the south is **Summer Leys Nature Reserve**, a year round haven for large numbers of birds.

Two miles south of Wellingborough lies Irchester Country Park, 200 acres of woodland walks and nature trails in a former ironstone quarry.

CASTLE ASHBY

6 miles E of Northampton off the A428

Dating from 1574, **Castle Ashby** is a fine Elizabethan mansion on the site of a demolished 13th century castle. The surrounding parkland was landscaped by Capability Brown. An 11 minute drive south down Denton Road will bring you to the village of Horton, and **The Menagerie**. It was built in 1756 as a zoo, dining pavilion and eye-catcher folly in the park of the former Horton House, and remains one of the few examples of architecture by Thomas Wright of Durham left in the world. The eclectic house and gardens, although now privately owned, can be visited by groups by previous appointment.

STOKE BRUERNE

6½ miles S of Northampton off the A508

This picturesque village lies on the Grand Union Canal, at the southern end of the famous **Blisworth Tunnel**. In addition to towpath walks and boat trips to the tunnel, the fascinating **Museum**, now part of National Waterways with many exciting new exhibits, housed in a converted corn mill, is a popular attraction.

Just south of the village is **Stoke Park**, a great house that was built by Inigo Jones in

the 1630s. The main house burnt down in 1886 and only the pavilions and a colonnade remain, but they are an impressive sight.

SULGRAVE

16 miles SW of Northampton off the B4525

Along with its old village stocks, the remains of a castle mound and its church, Sulgrave is home to **Sulgrave Manor**, a Tudor manor house built by the ancestors of George Washington, first President of the United States of America. The house is a treasure trove of George Washington memorabilia, including documents, a velvet coat and even a lock of his hair; and it is renowned for its informative and entertaining guided tours, which can be attended as individuals or part of a group.

Sulgrave Manor

CANONS ASHBY

12 miles SW of Northampton off the A361

A monastery belonging to the Black Canons once stood here, but after the Dissolution some of the ecclesiastical buildings were used to create **Canons Ashby House**, one of the finest stately homes in Northamptonshire,

---

261 OVERSTONE MANOR

Sywell

An impressive and charming manor serving quality food all day every day

See entry on page 497

262 THE RED LION

Hastings

This friendly, traditional country pub serves home cooked food with a friendly smile

See entry on page 497

Canons Ashby House

have their own taste of adrenaline rushing high speeds through many different driving experience days; what could be more thrilling than taking one of their Ferraris or Lotus' out on the track for a spin?

BRACKLEY

18 miles SW of Northampton on the A43

Dating back to Saxon times, the Castle built here in the early 12th century is said to have been the meeting place for the rebel barons who drew up the first version of Magna Carta in 1215.

To the southwest, on the boarder with Oxfordshire, lies the former manor house **Aynho Park**, a very grand 17th century country house that was originally the property of the Cartwright family, who, it is said, claimed the rents from their tenants in the form of apricots. It is now, for the first time in 400 years, available for private events.

now owned by the National Trust. Home of the Dryden family since the 1550s, it contains some marvellous Elizabethan wall paintings and sumptuous Jacobean plasterwork.

TOWCESTER

9 miles SW of Northampton off the A43

Called Lactodorum by the Romans and situated on their major route, Watling Street, this town became an important staging post on the route between London and Holyhead. Charles Dickens stayed here at the Saracen's Head, then called the Pomfret Hotel, and immortalised it in *The Pickwick Papers*. The parish **Church of St Lawrence**, on the site of a substantial Roman building, is one of the loveliest in the county, and close by is the Chantry House, formerly a school, founded by Archdeacon Sponne in 1447.

Towcester Racecourse is set in the beautiful parkland estate of Easton Neston, the family home of Lord Hesketh. There is racing of a different kind at nearby **Silverstone**, the home of British motor racing and the British Grand Prix, where visitors can

CORBY

True industry arrived at Corby only in the latter years of the 19th century with the building of the Kettering-Manton Railway. Corby was still essentially a small village until the 1930s, when Stewarts and Lloyds built a huge steel-making plant based on the area's known reserves of iron ore. That industry virtually stopped in 1980 but Corby remains a forward-looking modern town, with many cultural and leisure opportunities.

Just to the north lies **Rockingham Castle**, built by William the Conqueror on the slopes

263 THE BUTCHERS ARMS

Greens Norton

Revitalised inn at the heart of its community offering delicious Thai, Italian and French food alongside award winning real ales.

See entry on page 498

Rockingham Castle Gatehouse

of Rockingham Hill overlooking the Welland valley. The grand rooms are superbly furnished, and the armour in the Tudor Great Hall recalls the Civil War, when the castle was captured by the Roundheads. Owned and lived in since 1530 by the Watson family, it was here that Charles Dickens wrote much of *Bleak House*. East of Corby lays **East Carlton Countryside Park**, with its nature trails, craft workshops, and lovely country walks through extensive mature woodland.

AROUND CORBY

DEENE

4 miles NE of Corby off the A43

Originally a medieval manor, **Deene Park** was acquired in 1514 by Sir Robert Brudenell and has been occupied by the family ever since. It is surrounded by beautiful gardens filled with old-fashioned roses, and parkland containing rare trees. Close by is **Kirby Hall**, one of the loveliest Elizabethan ruins in England (although much of it still remains intact), which is best experienced using one of their brilliant audio guided tours. The hall has been a popular filming location, most notably it was used the film adaptations for Jane Austen's Mansfield Park (1999) and the infamous book *The life and opinions of Tristram Shandy* titled A Cock and Bull Story (2005).

Deene Park

FOTHERINGHAY

11½ miles NE of Corby off the A605

The first **Fotheringhay Castle** was built in around 1100 by the son-in-law of William the Conqueror, and the second, in the 14th century. The future Richard III was born here, but Fotheringhay is best known as being the prison and the place of execution of Mary, Queen of Scots, who was brought here in bands of steel and beheaded in the Banqueting Hall in 1587. The castle was pulled down in 1627.

Masonry from Fotheringhay Castle

At Nassington, just to the north, stands **Prebendal Manor House**, dating from the early part of the 13th century and the oldest house in Northamptonshire; it includes an award winning **Tithe Barn Museum**, which hosts many fun activities such as quill pen writing and dressing-up for children.

Oundle, which lies 10 miles east of Corby, on the A427, is a town rich in architectural interest, with many fine 17th and 18th century buildings. Oundle is best known for the Public School that was founded by Sir William Laxton in 1556; an inscription to his memory is written above the doorway in Greek, Latin and Hebrew.

BRIGSTOCK

5 miles SE of Corby on the A6116

On the banks of a tributary of the River Nene called Harpers Brook, this Saxon village has many delightful old cottages, a 16th century manor house, and a church with an unusual circular extension to its tower.

To the east lies **Lyveden New Bield**, a cross-shaped Elizabethan garden lodge erected to symbolise the Passion.

KETTERING

An important town standing above the River Ise, Kettering gained fame as a producer of both clothing and shoes and it was here that the missionary William Carey and the preacher Andrew Fuller founded the Baptist Missionary Society in 1792. Much of the old town has been swallowed up in modern development but there are still a few old houses in the narrow lanes. The **Heritage Quarter** around the church gives a fascinating, hands-on insight into the town's past, as does the **Manor House Museum**.

Just to the north lies **Geddington**, an attractive village that is home to the best preserved of the three surviving **Eleanor Crosses** that marked the funeral procession of Queen Eleanor, who had died at Harby in Nottinghamshire in 1290.

Just south of the village is one of the finest houses in the country, **Boughton House**, the Northamptonshire home of the Duke of Buccleuch. Originally a small monastic building, it has been transformed over the years into a magnificent mansion

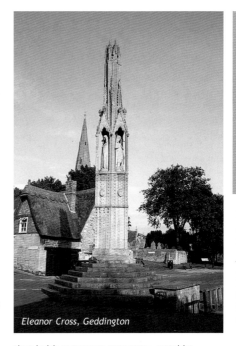

Eleanor Cross, Geddington

that holds numerous treasures, notably French and English furniture, paintings (El Greco, Murillo, 40 van Dycks) and collections of armoury and weaponry.

Hidden Places of England

Northamptonshire

AROUND KETTERING

RUSHTON

4 miles NW of Kettering off the A6

Rushton Triangular Lodge (English Heritage) is a unique folly built in 1597 and symbolising the Holy Trinity: three walls each with three windows, three gables and three storeys, topped by a three-sided chimney.

---

264 **THE STAR INN**

Geddington

A popular refreshment stop for locals and visitors, which serves top quality real ale and classic home cooked food

See entry on page 499

NORTHUMBERLAND

In the far north, beyond the city of Newcastle-upon-Tyne, Northumberland has one of the least populated and least well known of the country's 11 National Parks. An area of remote, wild and haunting landscapes; the most famous features of the Northumberland National Park are the Cheviot Hills and Kielder Forest. Within the National Park can be found the largest man-made lake in northern Europe, Kielder Water, and Kielder Castle – once a hunting lodge for the Duke of Northumberland, now the heart of activity in the National Park, including extensive Mountain Bike and orienteering trails.

Elsewhere in the county there are stretches of Hadrian's Wall; most rewarding to follow along the Hadrian's Wall Path, which runs the whole 84 mile length of the wall and passes some of the counties most dramatic scenery, as well as that over the boarder in Scotland. The little border towns along the wall were constantly under the threat of Scottish raids, and so you will find some fascinating fortifications, particularly strategically placed Roman encampments,

dotted along its length.

A wonderful feature of the county is the dramatic coastal castles - Dunstanburgh, Bamburgh, and Lindisfarne - each just as spectacular seen in winter as in the summer. The later is perched atop a rocky crag, cut off from the mainland of Lindisfarne Island (or the "Holy Island") at high tide. Another interesting building can be found near Warkworth Castle on the River Coquet; The Hermitage is a tiny chapel, nestled in peaceful riverside woodland, carved into the solid rock.

Accommodation

Food & Drink

HEXHAM

Founded in AD 674 by St Wilfrid, **Hexham Abbey** was once described as 'the largest and most magnificent church this side of the Alps'. Only the crypt of the original building survives, but the 13th century church that now occupies the site has many outstanding features, including marvellous carved stonework and a superb 16th century rood screen. The nearby early 14th century **Moot Hall**, built of Roman stone and once used as the courtroom of the Archbishop of York, now houses the Border History Library. The **Border History Museum**, housed in the 14th century gaol, tells the story of the border struggles between Scotland and England. Hexham is on the **Hadrian's Wall Path**, which runs the entire length of the Wall – all 84 miles of it!

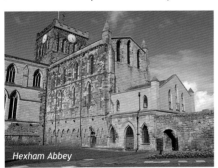
Hexham Abbey

AROUND HEXHAM

BARDON MILL

10 miles W of Hexham on the A69

This former mining village is a convenient starting point for walks along Hadrian's Wall, particularly to the two Roman forts of Vindolanda and Housesteads nearby. Both have extensive Roman remains and accompanying exhibitions.

HALTWHISTLE

15 miles W of Hexham on the A69

The origins of the name Haltwhistle are unknown but two suggestions are the watch 'wessel' on the high 'alt' mound, or the high 'haut' fork of two streams 'twysell'. It is difficult to imagine that this pleasant little town with its grey terraces was once a mining area, but evidence of the local industries

265 BOUCHON BISTROT

Hexham

Offering a touch of elegance, professionalism and relaxation in the French Bistrot style, Bouchon is not to be missed.

See entry on page 500

remain. An old pele tower is incorporated into the Centre of Britain Hotel in the town centre.

Three miles northwest of Haltwhistle, off the B6318, is **Walltown Quarry**, a recreation area on the site of an old quarry. Today, part of the Northumberland National Park, it contains laid out trails and it is possible to spot oystercatchers, curlews, sandpipers and lapwings.

KIELDER

20 miles NW of Hexham off the B6357

Kielder village was built in the 1950s to house workers in the man-made **Kielder Forest**, which covers 200 square miles of spectacularly beautiful scenery to the west of the Northumberland National Park. The forest

Kielder Water

is one of the few areas in Britain that contains more red squirrels than greys and is also home to deer and rare birds and plants. Within the forest is **Kielder Water**, the largest man-made lake in northern Europe. A pleasure cruise stops at several points of interest on the Lake, and an art and sculpture trail is laid out around its shores and in the trees. To the northwest is **Kielder Castle**, once a hunting lodge for the Duke of Northumberland and now a fascinating visitor centre. The castle has become a starting point for many mountain bike trails, with all levels of ability catered for, and bike hire available; there is also orienteering courses for those who prefer to keep their feet on the ground.

CHOLLERFORD

4 miles N of Hexham on the B6318

The remains of the Roman fort of **Chesters**, on Hadrian's Wall, include a well-preserved

---

268 THE SUN INN

Acomb

Located in an area that's rich in history and scenic splendour the inn has comfortable, well-priced guest accommodation for visitors touring this lovely part of Northumberland.

See entry on page 502

---

266 THE BLACK BULL

Haltwhistle

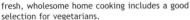

At the heart of Haltwhistle, down a cobbled street off the Market Square, stands the **Black Bull**, the town's only cask ale pub.

See entry on page 501

---

269 THE HADRIAN HOTEL

Wall, nr Hexham

Tourists, walkers and lovers of the countryside will fins excellent hospitality and comfortable accommodation close to Hadrian's Wall.

See entry on page 502

---

267 THE ANGLERS ARMS

Kielder Village

A choice of real ales is on tap, including the award-winning Anglers Ale, and in the separate restaurant area fresh, wholesome home cooking includes a good selection for vegetarians.

See entry on page 500

---

270 GREENCARTS

Neal, nr Hexham

A choice of B&B, bunkhouse and camping site on a farm next to Hadrian's Wall.

See entry on page 503

bathhouse and barracks and the museum houses a remarkable collection of Roman antiquities.

OTTERBURN

19 miles N of Hexham on the A696

Almost in the centre of what is now the **Northumberland National Park**, on a site marked by 18th century Percy Cross, the Battle of Otterburn took place in 1388 between the English and the Scots. This was a ferocious encounter, described by a contemporary as 'one of the sorest and best fought, without cowards or faint hearts'. **Otterburn Mill** dates from the 18th century, and on display are Europe's only original working 'tenterhooks', where newly woven cloth was stretched and dried. It is famous for its pram rugs, originally made for Queen Elizabeth on her birth in 1926 to line her royal pram, and it still made today.

North of the village are the remains of the Roman fort built by Julius Agricola in the 1st century.

PRUDHOE

10 miles E of Hexham on the A695

When **Prudhoe Castle** was built in the 12th century it was one of the finest in Northumberland, although now a ruin, a Georgian manor house in the courtyard tells its interesting story. To the west, at Mickley Square, is **Cherryburn**, the birthplace in 1753 of Thomas Bewick, the renowned illustrator and engraver.

WALLSEND

3 miles E of Newcastle on the A193

Wallsend, on the eastern edge of Newcastle

and actually in Tyne & Wear, is the site of mighty shipyards and of the reconstructed **Segedunum Roman Fort**, the last outpost on Hadrian's Wall. **Whitley Bay** is a resort at the mouth of the River Tyne, with safe beaches and spectacular views from the top of **St Mary's Lighthouse**.

St Mary's Lighthouse

SEATON SLUICE

8 miles NE of Newcastle on the A193

Inland from Seaton Sluice is **Seaton Delaval Hall**, a superb Vanbrugh mansion. The ancestral home of the Delavals was built in the early 18th century for Admiral George Delaval. It was recently saved from private sale, and an uncertain future, through one of the National Trusts biggest ever campaigns with the help of some 30,000 individuals, so that visitors can continue to enjoy this spectacular building and grounds for years to come.

MORPETH

28 miles NE of Hexham on the A192

Northumberland's county town has some distinguished buildings: its **Town Hall** was built to designs by Vanbrugh and the handsome bridge over the River Wansbeck was designed by Telford. The 13th century **Morpeth Chantry** has been over the centuries a cholera hospital, a mineral water factory and a school where the famous Tudor botanist William Turner was educated. The 14th century Church of St Mary in Morpeth has some of the finest stained glass in Northumberland, and in its cemetery is the grave of suffragette Emily Davison, who died under the hooves of the King's horse *Anmer* at the 1913 Epsom Derby meeting. Her funeral attracted thousands of mourners to Morpeth.

To the east is Ashington and the **Wansbeck Riverside Park**, which has been developed along the embankment and offers sailing and angling facilities, plus a four-mile walk along the mouth of the River Wansbeck. The famous footballing brothers Bobby and Jackie Charlton and the cricketer Steve Harmison are sons of Ashington.

ALNWICK

This impressive Northumberland town is dominated by the massive **Alnwick Castle**, which began as a Norman motte and bailey and was replaced in the 12th century by a stone castle. In the mid 19th century, the 4th Duke of Northumberland transformed the castle into a great country house which, still the home of the Dukes of Northumberland, contains many treasures, including paintings by Canaletto, Titian and Van Dyck. The **Museum of the Northumberland Fusiliers** is housed in the Abbot's Tower. The Castle is a favourite location for films, most famously doubling as Hogwart's School in the Harry Potter films. The **Gardens** have been redeveloped in the last few years and contain what is reputedly the largest treehouse in the country.

The only surviving part of the town's fortifications is 15th century **Hotspur Tower**, while all that is left of **Alnwick Abbey** is its 15th century gatehouse. **Hulne Park**, landscaped by Northumbria-born Capability Brown, encompasses the ruins of Hulne

Treehouse, Alnwick Gardens

Priory, the earliest Carmelite foundation in England (1242).

AROUND ALNWICK

WARKWORTH

6 miles S of Alnwick on the A1068

At the southern end of Alnmouth Bay, on the River Coquet, lies **Warkworth Castle**. The site has been fortified since the Iron Age, though what can be seen now is mainly late 12th and 13th century, including the great Carrickfergus Tower and the West Postern Towers. An unusual and interesting walk is signposted to **The Hermitage**, along the riverside footpath below the castle, where a ferry takes you across the river to visit the tiny chapel hewn out of solid rock. It dates from medieval times and was in use until late in the 16th century.

Warkworth Castle

AMBLE

7 miles SE of Alnwick on the A1068

Amble is a small port situated at the mouth of the River Coquet, once important for the export of coal, but now enjoying new

272 **TATE HOUSE**

Alnwick

A three-story late Victorian town house beautifully restored and opposite the Alnwick Gardens.

See entry on page 504

prosperity as a marina and sea-fishing centre. A mile offshore lies **Coquet Island**, where St Cuthbert landed in AD 684. The Island had a reputation in former times for causing shipwrecks, but is now a celebrated bird sanctuary, noted for colonies of terns, puffins and eider ducks. Managed by the Royal Society for the Protection of Birds, Coquet Island can be visited by boat trips departing from Amble quayside throughout the summer.

ROTHBURY

10½ miles SW of Alnwick on the B6341

This attractive town is a natural focal point from which to explore the valley of the River Coquet. The best-known of many delightful walks leads to the Rothbury Terraces, a series of parallel tracks along the hillside above the town. Just outside Rothbury is the house and estate of **Cragside**, whose owner, the industrialist, engineer and arms manufacturer Sir William Armstrong, devised a system with man-made lakes, streams and underground piping that made his home the first to be lit by hydroelectricity. The National Trust has sympathetically restored Cragside to show how upper middle class Victorians were beginning to combine comfort and opulence with the latest technological advances.

CRASTER

7 miles NE of Alnwick off the B1339

To the northeast of Alnwick is Craster, a small, unpretentious fishing village that is nationally known for its oak-smoked kippers. At one time, herring were caught in vast quantities around this coast, but a combination of over-fishing and pollution resulted in a dramatic decline in numbers, so the fish now mainly have to be imported.

273 **THE ELM TREE COFFEE SHOP**

Rothbury

A friendly, family-run coffee shop open every day for a selection of excellent, value-for-money snacks and meals.

See entry on page 505

During the curing season visitors can sniff around the sheds where the herring are hung over smoking piles of oak chips.

Craister Quarry was closed in 1939 and is now a small nature reserve called the Arnold memorial Site. It was this quarry that supplied London and other large cities with its kerbstones. This is the start point of a pleasant walk along the coastal footpath to Dunstanburgh Castle.

EMBLETON

7 miles NE of Alnwick on the B1339

The dramatic ruins of **Dunstanburgh Castle** stand on a cliff top east of the village, on a site that was originally an Iron Age fort. The castle, by far the largest in Northumberland, was built in 1313 by Thomas, Earl of Lancaster, and in the Wars of the Roses it withstood a siege from troops led by Margaret of Anjou, Henry VI's Queen.

BAMBURGH

13½ miles N of Alnwick on the B1340

Built on an epic scale and dominating the village, **Bamburgh Castle** dates back to the 6th century although the mighty fortress seen today was originally built in the 12th century. The tour of the Castle takes in the magnificent King's Hall, the Cross Hall, the Bakehouse, the Scullery, the Armoury and the Dungeons.

The village was the birthplace of Grace Darling, the Victorian heroine, who, in 1838, rowed out with her father from the Longstone Lighthouse in a ferocious storm to rescue five survivors from the wreck of the steam ship *Forfarshire* which had foundered on the Farne Islands rocks. The contemporary **Grace Darling Museum**, in Radcliffe Road remembers this iconic and heroic woman, and contains memorabilia of the famous rescue.

The Farne Islands are a group of 28 little islands that provide a sanctuary for many species of sea birds, including kittiwake, fulmar, puffin, and tern. They are also home to a large colony of Atlantic Grey seals which can often be seen from the beach of the mainland. Boat trips to the islands leave from

Guillemots on the Farne Islands

the harbour at Seahouses, down the coast from Bamburgh. It was on Inner Farne that St Cuthbert landed in AD 687, and a little chapel was built in his memory.

LINDISFARNE

18 miles NW of Alnwick off the A1

Northumberland's northern coastline is dominated by one outstanding feature – **Lindisfarne**, also known as **Holy Island**. Reached by a three-mile causeway, the island was settled in the 7th century by St Aidan and his small community of Irish monks from Iona. It was these monks who produced some of the finest surviving examples of Celtic art, the richly decorated Lindisfarne Gospels. St Cuthbert also came here, living on a tiny islet as a hermit before seeking further solitude on the Farne Islands.

Benedictine monks renamed Lindisfarne "Holy Island" when they came here in the 11th century and established **Lindisfarne Priory**.

Lindisfarne Castle, dramatically perched atop the outcrop of Beblowe Crag which is cut off from the mainland at high tide, is a beautiful and unusual sight; worth the visit for the views, as well as the intimate interior

and interesting history. It was established in Tudor times as a fortification to protect from invasion by the Scots, and in 1902 it was restored and converted into a summer home for Edward Hudson (founder of *Country Life*) by a young Sir Edward Lutyens. It is now in the care of the National Trust and is open to the public in the summer.

Lindisfarne is the finishing point of the 62-mile St Cuthbert's Way, a long-distance footpath opened in 1996; the trail begins at Melrose, across the Scottish border, and along the way passes through the Northumberland National Park and the Cheviot Hills.

CHILLINGHAM

11½ miles NW of Alnwick off the B6348

Chillingham is a pleasant estate village best known for the herd of wild, horned white cattle that roam the parkland of **Chillingham Castle**. They are perhaps the purest surviving specimens of the wild cattle that once roamed the hills and forests of Britain.

BERWICK-UPON-TWEED

For centuries, this former Royal burgh of Scotland was fought over by the Scots and the English, and changed hands no fewer than 14 times until it finally became part of England in 1482.

Berwick's original medieval walls, built in the 13th century by Edward I, are regarded as being the finest preserved fortifications of their age in Europe. The walk around the walls (about 1.5 miles) provides fine views of the town and the Northumberland coastline.

Housed in the clock tower of the Hawksmoor-designed barracks are the

---

274 THE BLACK BULL HOTEL

Wooler

This hotel is a former coaching inn with an Italian restaurant serving freshly prepared classic and modern dishes

See entry on page 504

---

275 SINNERS CAFE

Berwick Upon Tweed

A popular cafe specialising in home cooked food cooked to order and friendly service.

See entry on page 506

Berwick-upon-Tweed Borough Museum and Art Gallery, which explores the history of the town, and the King's Own Scottish Borderers Museum.

The Berwick skyline is dominated by the imposing Town Hall with its clock tower and steeple that rise to 150 feet, and which is often mistaken for a church. Guided tours in the summer enable visitors to explore the upper storeys, where there are civic rooms and the former town gaol as well as a small Cell Block Museum.

AROUND BERWICK-UPON-TWEED

HORNCLIFFE
4 miles W of Berwick off the A698

The village of Horncliffe, five miles upstream of Berwick, can only be reached by one road that leads into and out of the village, making it feel rather remote. Many visitors are unaware of the existence of the river, but there is nothing more pleasant than wandering down one of the paths leading to the banks to watch the salmon fishermen on a summer's evening.

Not far from the village the Tweed is spanned by the Union Suspension Bridge linking England and Scotland. It was built in 1820 by Sir Samuel Browne, who also invented the wrought-iron chain links used in its construction. This graceful structure, 480 feet long, was Britain's first major suspension bridge to carry vehicular traffic.

DUDDO
7 miles SW of Berwick on the B6354

Close to the village are the Duddo Stones, one of Northumberland's most important ancient monuments – sometimes known as "The Women" due to the narrowed bases, or waists. This ancient stone circle, which now consists of five upright stones over seven feet

high, dates back to around 2000 BC, and can only be reached from the village by foot.

FORD & ETAL
13 miles SW of Berwick off the B6354

The twin estate villages of Ford and Etal were built in the late 19th century. Etal is an attractive village, within which are the ruins of the 14th century castle, destroyed in 1497 by King James IV of Scotland on his way to Flodden.

Ford is a 'model' village with many beautiful stone buildings and well-tended gardens. Dating originally from the 14th century, but heavily restored in the 19th century, Ford Castle was the home of Louisa Ann, Marchioness of Waterford. In 1860 she built the village school and from 1862 until 1883 spent her time decorating it with murals depicting biblical scenes. As models she used local families and their children thus creating a pictorial gallery of life and work in the area at that time. Now known as Lady Waterford Hall, it is open to the public.

TILLMOUTH
9 miles SW of Berwick on the A698

The village of Tillmouth lies along the banks of the River Till, a tributary of the Tweed which is crossed by the imposing 15th-century Twizel Bridge, although a more modern structure now carries the A698 over the river. There are some lovely walks here and a well-signed footpath leads to the ruins of Twizel Castle and the remains of St Cuthbert's Chapel on the opposite bank.

276 THE RED LION
Milfield
A lovely country inn, providing comfortable accommodation and fine food. 
See entry on page 506

NOTTINGHAMSHIRE

Nottinghamshire is the home of the legendary Robin Hood and there are a variety of attractions in the town which tell the story of the man and the myth. Further north at Edwinstow can be found the Church of St Mary which, as legend puts it, the great romance of Robin Hood and Maid Marian were tied in holy matrimony. Sherwood Forest, part of a great mass of forest land that once covered much of Central England, is officially designated 'Robin Hood Country', and holds many hidden treasures.

The Industrial Revolution saw the mechanisation of the lace and hosiery industry of which Nottingham was a centre. Mills sprang up in the towns, taking the industry away from the homes, and the Nottinghamshire coalfields, which had been mined for centuries, saw their scale of operation expanded dramatically.

It was into this environment that DH Lawrence was born in the late 19th century and the family's terrace house is now a museum dedicated to the novelist, as well as the nearby Durban House which also has displays on the mining community who once lived there.

One of the gems of the county is Southwell Minster, a wonderfully graceful building that is probably the least well known of England's Cathedrals. The medieval town of Newark has many reminders of the Civil War, while the ancient village of Scrooby, in the far north of the county, is closely associated with the Pilgrim Fathers, who sailed to America on the Mayflower in 1620.

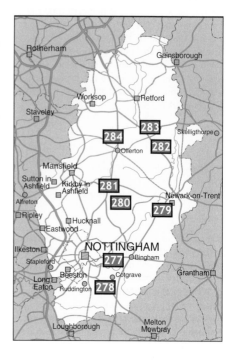

Of the many walks and trails to follow through the county, including an informative Mayflower trail in Worksop and, of course, Sherwood Forest, the most outstanding must be through the Cresswell Crags right on the boarder with Derbyshire. This dramatic gorge pitted with deep caves has been a goldmine for archeologists; finding the bones of prehistoric animals, twice the size of their modern counterparts!

Food & Drink

277 The Black Lion, Radcliffe-on-Trent   pg 201, 507
278 The Griffin at Plumtree, Plumtree   pg 201, 508
279 The Old Bakery, Newark   pg 203, 509
280 La Parisienne Cafe Bistro, Southwell   pg 203, 509
281 The Plough, Farnsfield   pg 204, 510

Food & Drink

282 The Crown Inn, Normanton-on-Trent   pg 204, 510
283 The Queens Hotel, East Markham   pg 204, 511
284 The Bay Tree Cafe Bar, Thoresby Park,
       Ollerton   pg 205, 512

NOTTINGHAM

At the heart of the city is its **Old Market Square**, believed to be the largest market square in the country. This was the setting for the famous Nottingham Goose Fair that began in medieval times and continues today; it is now held at Forest Fields on the edge of Nottingham. Not far from the square, **The Tales of Robin Hood** tells the story of the celebrated outlaw who is forever linked with the city.

On a rocky outcrop high above the city centre stands **Nottingham Castle**, home now to a museum and art gallery and to the **Sherwood Foresters Regimental Museum**. There are still the ancient maze of caves hidden beneath the walls of the castle. Naturally, it was used in the background for the film *Robin Hood* (2010).

Nottingham Castle

At the base of Castle Rock lies the famous **Trip to Jerusalem Inn**, where the crusaders are said to have stopped for a pint before setting off on their long journey to the Holy Land. Dating back to around 1189, it has claims to being the oldest pub in England; it was once the brewhouse for the castle.

Nottingham is built on sandstone, and one of the many caves tunnelled down the years to provide shelter or hiding places has been left as a memorial to the black days of the Second World War.

AROUND NOTTINGHAM

RAVENSHEAD
9 miles N of Nottingham on the A60

This village is home to **Longdale Lane Rural Craft Centre & Museum**, established in the 1970s and the oldest such centre in the country. It is situated in a re-created Victorian street which also houses the exhibition 'The history of Antiques and Collectables'.

Just to the southwest lies **Newstead Abbey**, a magnificent 13th century ruin attached to a Victorian reworking of a Tudor mansion that is one of the county's most historic houses. The abbey was founded by Henry II in the 12th century as part of his atonement for the murder of Thomas à Becket. It was once home to the infamous romantic poet Lord Byron, and his private quarters have been preserved, along with his person possessions.

RUDDINGTON
4 miles S of Nottingham on the B680

This historic village was once the home of many hosiery workers and several of their cottages still remain. There are two museums here: the **Ruddington Framework Knitters' Museum** and the **Ruddington Village Museum**, housed in the old village school building of 1852.

---

277 THE BLACK LION

Radcliffe-on-Trent

It is a thriving pub selling fine food and real ales. It hosts many events throughout the year.

See entry on page 507

---

278 THE GRIFFIN AT PLUMTREE

Plumtree

A stylish and relaxed venue serving traditional British and contemporary European cuisine in a comfortable, relaxed and customer friendly environment

See entry on page 508

BEESTON

4 miles SW of Nottingham on the A6005

Lying on the outskirts of Nottingham, Beeston is the home of Boots the Chemist, which was started by Jesse Boot in the late 19th century. Just to the north, in **Stapleford** churchyard, can be found the best preserved Saxon carving in the county in the form of a 10 feet cross shaft that dates from the late 11th century.

EASTWOOD

8 miles NW of Nottingham on the A610

This mining town was the birthplace of DH Lawrence and the Lawrence family home, a two up, two down, terrace house at 8a Victoria Street is now the **DH Lawrence Birthplace Museum**. Also there is the **Durban House Heritage Centre**, a gorgeous 'mansion-like building' where a young Lawrence would have come to collect his father's coal mining wages; it contains a fascinating display on the poet, as well as the town's mining history. As a young boy Lawrence was a sensitive, sickly child, who did not quite fit the mining mould and so spent much of his time wandering through the surrounding green countryside – a source of inspiration for his future works, which still provide lovely walking today. A place of pilgrimage for devotees of Lawrence,

Eastwood also attracts those with an interest in railway history.

It was at the Sun Inn in the Market Place that a group of 'Iron Masters and Coal Owners' gathered in 1832 to discuss the construction of a railway that would eventually become the mighty Midland Railway. A plaque on the wall of the inn commemorates the meeting.

The railway was formed to compete with the Erewash Canal, completed in 1779 and effectively put out of business by the 1870s. Almost a century later, following years of neglect, the canal was cleared and made suitable for use by pleasure craft.

HUCKNALL

7½ miles NW of Nottingham on the A611

Hucknall attracts a constant stream of visitors who come to **St Mary Magdalene Church** to gaze not so much at the 14th century font or the Kempe stained glass but at a simple marble slab set in the floor of the chancel that marks the last resting place of Lord Byron. He died in Greece in 1824 and his body was returned to England to be buried in the family vault. Also buried here is his daughter Ada, Countess of Lovelace, a noted mathematician and friend and colleague of Charles Babbage, inventor of the Analytical Engine, a predecessor of the computer. Guided tours of the church are available, and very informative.

Hucknall boasts another famous son, Eric Coates, who is best remembered as a composer of light music: his *Sleepy Lagoon* is immediately recognisable as the signature music of BBC Radio's long-running programme *Desert Island Discs*.

NEWARK-ON-TRENT

The cobbled market square of this elegant medieval town, where you will find a different vibrant market nearly every day of the week, is lined with handsome houses and inns. The most remarkable of these is the 14th century former **White Hart Inn**, whose magnificent frontage is adorned with 24

DH Lawrence Birthplace Museum

plaster figures of angels and saints. Dominating one side of the square is the noble Georgian **Town Hall**, which now houses the town's civic plate and regalia and an art gallery displaying works by Stanley Spencer, William Nicholson and notable local artists.

The imposing riverside 12th century castle, which has a history of battle during the English Civil War (at the end of which part of the castle was destroyed), has a charming garden, perfect for a peaceful summer afternoon. The grounds also contain the **Gilstrap Heritage Centre.**

Newark possesses several other reminders of the Civil War and of the two small forts that were built to guard this strategic crossing over the River Trent only the **Queen's Sconce** has survived. Nearby is the **Governor's House,** where the governors of Newark lived during the Civil War and also where Charles I quarrelled with Prince Rupert after the prince had lost Bristol to Parliament.

With such a wealth of history inside its boundaries, Newark naturally has its fair share of museums and, along with those in the town, to the east is the **Newark Air Museum**, one of the largest privately managed collections in the country.

AROUND NEWARK-ON-TRENT

SIBTHORPE
6 miles S of Newark off the A46

All that remains above ground of a priests' college, founded here in the 14th century, is the parish church and a Dovecote that stands in the middle of a field. Of the three Archbishops of Canterbury born in Nottinghamshire, Thomas Cranmer is by far

the best known, but Sibthorpe was the childhood home of Thomas Secker, Archbishop from 1758 to 1768.

SOUTHWELL
6 miles W of Newark on the A612

Undoubtedly one of England's most beguiling towns, Southwell is dominated by its **Minster**, whose twin towers, with their pyramidal Rhenish Caps, are unique in this country. The present building was erected in three phases between 1150 and 1290. Octagonal in design, the Chapter House has been hailed as the pinnacle of the decorated period of architecture. The Cathedral stands in a delightful precinct surrounded by attractive buildings, while to the south stand the ruins of the palace of the archbishops of York built

Southwell Minster

279 THE OLD BAKERY

Newark

Sample the olde worlde charms of this listed tearoom whilst enjoying a deliciously cooked lunch or homemade scone.

See entry on page 509

280 LA PARISIENNE CAFÉ BISTRO,

Southwell

Popular café bistro offering delicious homemade French and Moroccan themed food all day.

See entry on page 509

in the 14th and 15th centuries. Just outside town is the **Workhouse**; an authentic 19th Century institution restored by the National Trust, where visitors can find out what life was really like for Victorian paupers.

Southwell can claim to be the birthplace of the Bramley apple. The story goes that in the early 19th century, two ladies planted some apple pips in their cottage garden in the nearby village of Easthorpe. Nature took its course and one of the seedlings grew into a tree. By this time, Matthew Bramley owned the cottage and the quality of the tree's fruit began to excite public interest. Henry Merryweather, a local nurseryman, persuaded Bramley to let him take a cutting, which he subsequently propagated with enormous success.

MANSFIELD

16 miles W of Newark on the A617

The second largest town in the county, Mansfield stands at the heart of what were once the great North Nottinghamshire coalfields. That industry has now vanished but Mansfield still has the atmosphere of an industrial town. The most distinctive structure in Mansfield is undoubtedly the great railway viaduct, built in 1875, which sweeps through and above the town, carried by 15 huge arches of rough-hewn stone.

LAXTON

9 miles NW of Newark off the A616

Laxton is one of the few places in the country that has managed to retain its open field farming system. Devised in the Middle Ages, this system was generally abandoned in the 18th and 19th centuries when the enclosure of agricultural land took place. The site has a

Visitor Centre and Museum. Another unique feature of this interesting village is the magnificent **Dovecote Inn** that is owned by the Queen.

Nearby is the **Beth Shalom Holocaust Centre**, the first of its kind in England when it was established in 1995, it sensitively explores the history and implications of the Holocaust. It is set in two acres of peaceful landscaped gardens.

Just north of the village, along a lane close to the church, is the Norman motte, known as **Castle Mound**, which lies almost hidden beneath the trees. At the beginning of the 12th century, the stewardship of Sherwood Forest moved to Laxton and the village became the administrative centre for the forest. As a consequence, the motte and bailey castle was one of the biggest in this part of the country.

OLLERTON

12½ miles NW of Newark on the A6075

Ollerton is a delightfully preserved cluster of old houses, a charming Georgian coaching inn, a church set beside the River Maun and the ancient **Ollerton Water Mill** – the only working watermill in Nottinghamshire.

To the south lies the pretty conservation village of **Wellow**, whose village green has the

282 THE CROWN INN

Normanton-on-Trent

Recently refurbished village inn noted for its excellent cuisine and choice of real ales.

See entry on page 510

281 THE PLOUGH

Farnsfield

A popular and charming village pub serving traditional home cooked food

See entry on page 510

283 THE QUEENS HOTEL

East Markham

Picture postcard English pub known for its excellent brand of hospitality, award winning real ales and colossal across the board menu.

See entry on page 511

tallest permanent Maypole in England, 60 feet high and colourfully striped like a barber's pole, with a cockerel perched on the top. The colourful Maypole celebration on the 31st of May every year is an important event for the whole village community, and is a delight to see if you have the opportunity.

Close by lies **Rufford Country Park**, in the grounds of Rufford Abbey, which contain nine formal gardens near the house along with a display on Nottinghamshire's history.

EDWINSTOWE

13½ miles NW of Newark on the A6075

Lying at the heart of **Sherwood Forest**, the life of this village is still dominated by the forest, as it has been since the 7th century when Edwin, King of Northumbria died in the Battle of Hatfield in AD 632; the village developed around the church built on the spot where he was slain. The **Church of St Mary** was the first stone building in Edwinstowe and, according to legend it was here that the marriage took place between Robin Hood and Maid Marian. Today the village high street is brimming with character, and has a host of bustling individual and unique shops.

Two minutes walk away is the **Sherwood Forest Visitor Centre** and the start of many

Sherwood Forest, Edwinstowe

284 THE BAY TREE CAFE BAR

Thoresby Park,
nr Ollerton

This delightful cafe has a fine reputation for high quality home cooked food and good hospitality

See entry on page 512

peaceful walking and cycling trails through the forest.

CRESSWELL

21 miles NW of Newark on the A616

Cresswell village is actually in Derbyshire but its most famous feature lies just inside the Nottinghamshire border. **Cresswell Crags** form a dramatic limestone gorge pitted with deep, dark and mysterious caves and here the bones of prehistoric bison, bears, wolves, woolly rhinos and lions twice the size of their modern descendants have been found. The Visitors' Centre contains some fascinating archaeological finds and there are some pleasant walks past the lakes to the crags.

RETFORD

Retford is actually two communities, East and West Retford, set either side of the River Idle. **Cannon Square** takes its name from a Russian cannon dating from 1855 and weighing over two tons, still standing proud in the centre of town. Also in the centre is the landscaped Kings Park, beside the river bank, which provides a lovely location to stroll and relax during your visit.

One of Retford's most infamous visitors was the highwayman Dick Turpin, and several historic inns still stand as a reminder of the days of stage coach travel. Another man who stood and delivered here, though in a more respectable fashion, was John Wesley, who conducted many open air meetings in East Retford. The **Bassetlaw Museum** is housed in Amcott House, an imposing late 18th century town house, and is full of collections covering a variety of subjects including local history, archaeology, and fine art.

AROUND RETFORD

MATTERSEY

5 miles N of Retford off the B6045

To the east of the village lie the ruins of **Mattersey Priory**, founded in 1185 for the

205

Gilbertine Order, the only monastic order to be established by an Englishman, Roger de Mattersey. The original priory buildings at Mattersey were destroyed by fire in 1279 so the remains seen today are of the 14th century dormitory, refectory, and the walls of the Chapel of St Helen.

NORTH WHEATLEY

4 miles NE of Retford off the A620

Famous for its strawberries that are sought after for their delicious taste and excellent quality; beside the village is Goacher's Farm, where you are able to pick your own strawberries (as well as a whole variety of other fruit and vegetables) when they are in season.

North Wheatley is also home to a peculiar 17th century brick house, known as the **Old Hall**, where all the external features, including the vase-like decorations, are made from bricks. Just to the south is the splendid **North Leverton Windmill**, which was built in 1813 and still grinds corn today.

WORKSOP

7 miles W of Retford on the A60

One of the major attractions of Worksop is the 14th century **Priory Gatehouse** that was originally the portal to a large Augustinian monastery; the gatehouse and the **Church of**

Mr Straw's House, Worksop

St Mary and St Cuthbert are all that remain today. There is also a wayside shrine, which makes it a unique ecclesiastical attraction.

Mr Straw's House, along with an endowment of one million pounds, was bequeathed to the National Trust by William Straw in 1990. It was found that nothing in this seemingly ordinary Edwardian semi-detached house had been altered or added to since 1932, though it had been occupied by Straws until the death of the last Straw in 1990. **Worksop Museum** has a Pilgrim Fathers exhibition and is the start of the **Mayflower Trail** that guides visitor around the local sites connected with the Fathers.

SCROOBY

7 miles NW of Retford on the A638

This ancient village is best known for its links with the Pilgrim Fathers and, particularly, with William Brewster. Having formed his radical ideas on religion at Cambridge and in the Netherlands, Brewster returned to England, settling in Scrooby. For these beliefs he was imprisoned for a short time, before going back to Amsterdam, and after some years he returned to England and became an Elder of the Separatist Church; it was a group of some 40 members of this church who, in 1620, boarded the Mayflower for that famous voyage.

Worksop Priory

OXFORDSHIRE

A county of ancient towns and villages, whose capital, Oxford, 'that sweet city of dreaming spires', has dominated the surrounding area for centuries. The first scholars arrived at this walled Saxon town in the 12th century and, since then, this great seat of learning has influenced thinking and scientific research around the world.

To the southeast of Oxford can be found the opulent Garsington Manor; until 1927 it was the home of a wealthy socialite, who entertained a whole generation of writers, artists and intellectuals, and it now holds an exciting annual open-air opera festival showcasing new talent.

The southeastern part of the county is dominated by the River Thames and among the charming riverside towns and villages is Henley-on-Thames, the country's home of rowing and known worldwide for its annual Regatta. Along the banks of the river can be found some lovely hidden treasures; in particular is the village of Mapledurham, which is home to the only flour mill still working on the Thames, and the grand Mapledurham House - imortalised as Toad Hall in *The Wind and the Willows*.

To the west lie the Vale of the White Horse and an area of downland which is littered with ancient monuments; not least the eponymous "White Horse" carved into the hillside above Uffington, now thought to be

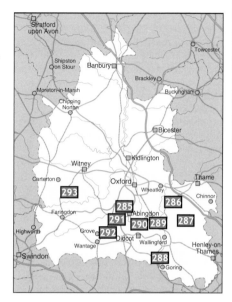

dated at around 3000 years old. Here, too, is Wantage, the birthplace of Alfred the Great.

Oxfordshire's most famous feature, however, is undoubtedly Blenheim Palace, the magnificent 18th century mansion that was the gift of a grateful queen to her loyal subject the Duke of Marlborough. A World Heritage Site, the palace is grand and opulent - it was also the birthplace of Sir Winston Churchill, whose modest room can be seen.

Accommodation

Food & Drink

ABINGDON

One of England's oldest towns, Abingdon grew up around a 7th century Benedictine **Abbey**. Twice sacked by the Danes, it was all but derelict by the 10th century, but under the guidance of Abbot Ethwold it again prospered and in its heyday was larger than Westminster Abbey. Little remains today except the late 15th century Gatehouse. The gorgeous Grade I listed Town Hall in the centre is now an excellent museum, and it is possible to climb right up to its roof to gain spectacular panoramic views of the town.

AROUND ABINGDON

THAME

14½ miles NE of Abingdon on the A418

Founded in AD 635 as an administrative centre for the Bishop of Dorchester, Thame became a market town in the 13th century and its main street is lined with old inns and houses. The imposing **Church of St Mary** and the **Prebendal House** both date from the 13th century, while the town's famous school was founded in 1558.

STONOR

16 miles SE of Abingdon on the B480

The village is the home of Lord and Lady Camoys and their house, **Stonor**, which has been in the family for over 800 years. Set in a wooded valley and surrounded by a deer park, the house contains many rare items, paintings and a medieval Catholic Chapel. The peaceful park surrounding the house has become a haven for many varieties of bird, including Britain's most rare and regal bird the Red Kite, which has been successfully reintroduced here; you are almost guaranteed to see them circling the skies above on a visit.

HENLEY-ON-THAMES

19 miles SE of Abingdon on the A4155

In 1829, the first University boat race between Oxford and Cambridge took place here and, within a decade, the event was enjoying royal patronage. Today, **Henley Regatta** is a stylish as well as a sporting occasion that remains a popular annual event. There is opportunity for visitors to take to the water themselves, in one of the many boats available for hire.

River Thames, Henley

---

285 THE CROWN & THISTLE

Abingdon

A lovely traditional coaching inn with great accommodation and a fine restaurant.

See entry on page 513

---

286 THE PLOUGH

Great Haseley

A very pretty pub in a very pretty village, excellent food and drink at good prices.

See entry on page 513

---

287 THE GOOSE

Britwell Salome

Part-18th century village inn offering tasty home-cooked food based on seasonal locally sourced ingredients.

See entry on page 514

Beside the town's famous 18th century bridge is the **Leander Club**, the headquarters of the world famous rowing club and here, too, is the **River and Rowing Museum**, which traces the rowing heritage of Henley.

MAPLEDURHAM

17 miles SE of Abingdon off the A4074

Hidden down a little lane that leads to the River Thames, this tiny unassuming village is home to the Elizabethan **Mapledurham House**, which has several notable literary connections. Alexander Pope was a frequent visitor in the 18th century; the final chapters of John Galsworthy's *The Forsythe Saga* were set here; and it became the fictional Toad Hall in *The Wind in the Willows*. A hidden gem in the village is the beautiful **Mapledurham Watermill**, which appeared in the Domesday Book, and still grounds flour today; the last of its kind on the River Thames.

GORING-ON-THAMES

12 ½ miles SE of Abingdon on the B4526

Situated on a particularly peaceful stretch of the River Thames, this ancient town began to develop in the 19th century after Brunel had laid the tracks for the Great Western Railway through Goring Gap.

DIDCOT

5 miles S of Abingdon on the A4130

Although this town is overshadowed by the giant cooling towers of Didcot power station, it has a saving grace in the form of the **Didcot Railway Centre**, which is a shrine to the days of the steam locomotive and the Great Western Railway.

Didcot Railway Centre

To the north lies the pretty village of **Sutton Courtenay** where, in the churchyard of the Norman church, are the graves of Herbert Asquith, the last Liberal Prime Minister, and Eric Blair, who is better known as novelist George Orwell.

---

288 THE BEETLE & WEDGE

Moulsford-on-Thames

Buzzy informal riverside restaurant with rooms, famous for dishes from its open charcoal grill.

See entry on page 515

---

289 THE FLEUR DE LYS

Dorchester-on-Thames

A lovely country pub that boasts excellent accommodation.

See entry on page 515

---

290 THE RAILWAY INN

Culham

Lively hostelry offering delicious food, real ales, en suite rooms and a beautiful garden.

See entry on page 516

---

291 THE CROWN

Marcham

A traditional country pub with a penchant for fine ales. A fine menu is also on offer, created using fresh, local produce.

See entry on page 516

WANTAGE

The birthplace of Alfred the Great in AD 849, Wantage remained a royal manor until the end of the 12th century and in the central market place is a huge statue of the King of all the West Saxons. Only the **Church of St Peter and St Paul** has survived from medieval times. Opposite the church is the **Vale and Downland Museum Centre** which is housed in a 16th century building and a reconstructed barn.

AROUND WANTAGE

UFFINGTON

6 miles W of Wantage off the B4507

This large village was the birthplace, in 1822, of Thomas Hughes, the author of *Tom Brown's Schooldays*, and he incorporated many local landmarks in his well-known work. The **Tom Brown's School Museum** tells the story of Hughes's life and works, as well as mementoes of the late poet laureate, Sir John Betjeman, who spent many happy years living in Uffington. The village is best known for the **Uffington White Horse**, a mysteriously abstract figure of a horse, some 400 feet long, which was created by removing the turf on the hillside to expose the gleaming white chalk beneath; it has been dated at around 3000 years old. Close by lies the **Blowing Stone** (or Sarsen Stone), a piece of glacial debris that is perforated with holes and, when blown, emits a sound like a foghorn.

BUSCOT

12 miles NW of Wantage on the A417

This small village is home to two National Trust properties: **Buscot Old Parsonage**, a William and Mary house with a small garden beside the River Thames, and **Buscot Park**, a grand late Georgian house that houses the Faringdon Art Collection, which includes paintings by Rembrandt, Rubens, Reynolds and Burne-Jones.

Just downriver from the village lies 16th

century **Kelmscott Manor House**, which was the home of William Morris between 1871 and his death in 1896. The grounds include a lovely orchard.

Further along the river again is the tiny hamlet of **Radcot**, which boasts the oldest bridge across the Thames – Radcot Bridge dates from 1154.

OXFORD

This elegant town is synonymous with its leading University; often considered the academic centre of England. The colleges all have their own distinctive features, and one of the most beautiful is **Christ Church** (known as 'The House'), which was founded in 1525 as Cardinal College by Thomas Wolsey. The main gateway leads through the bottom of **Tom Tower** (designed by Christopher Wren) and into Tom Quad, the largest of the city's quadrangles, and the college's chapel is the official seat of the Bishop of Oxford; **Christ Church Cathedral** is also England's smallest.

As well as the college buildings, Oxford has many interesting places for the visitor to explore. The 18th century **Radcliffe Camera** is England's earliest example of a round reading room and this splendid building still serves this purpose for the **Bodleian Library**.

292 THE BLACK HORSE

East Hanney

A great country pub which serves great food and hosts several excellent events throughout the year.

See entry on page 517

293 THE TALBOT HOTEL

Bampton

A comfortable night's sleep and a hearty breakfast awaits you at this pleasant hotel dating back to the 16th century.

See entry on page 517

Sheldonian Theatre, Oxford

One of Oxford's most famous buildings is the magnificent **Sheldonian Theatre**, which was designed and built in the Roman style by Christopher Wren between 1664 and 1668 while he was Professor of Astronomy at the University. The ceiling has 32 canvas panels, depicting Truth descending on the Arts, and the theatre is used for such events as matriculation and degree ceremonies, though is also available to the public throughout the year.

The **Ashmolean Museum**, which first opened in 1683, was originally established to house the collection of John Tredescant and his son; this internationally renowned museum is home to many treasures, including archaeological collections from Europe, Egypt and the Middle East. The Ashmolean's original building is now home to the **Museum of the History of Science** where among a remarkable collection are Einstein's blackboard and a large silver microscope made for George III.

The **Botanic Gardens** are a peaceful place, founded in 1621, a teaching garden where the plants grown were studied for their medicinal and scientific uses. The rose garden commemorates the work of Oxford's scientists in the discovery and use of penicillin. The University is also responsible for the lovely **Harcourt Arboretum** at **Nuneham Courtenay**, 4 miles south of Oxford.

To the southeast of the city lies the 16th century **Garsington Manor**, the home of the socialite Lady Ottoline Morrell between 1915 and 1927. With her husband Philip she played host to a whole generation of writers, artists and intellectuals including Katherine Mansfield, Siegfried Sassoon, TS Eliot, Rupert Brooke and Bertrand Russell. In the spirit of Lady Morrell is the open-air Garsington Opera festival, held here annually during the summer it showcases the best of young British singers.

AROUND OXFORD

EYNSHAM

6½ miles W of Oxford on the A40

To the south of this ancient market town lies **Stanton Harcourt Manor**, which dates back to the 14th century and is noted for its well-preserved medieval kitchen. It was while staying here that Alexander Pope translated Homer's *Iliad*, working in a 15th century tower that is now called Pope's Tower.

WOODSTOCK

8 miles NW of Oxford off the A44

Woodstock is known the world over and attracts visitors by the million to the magnificent **Blenheim Palace**, one of the very few sites in the country on the World Heritage List. The estate was a gift from Queen Anne to John Churchill, 1st Duke of Marlborough, for his victory at the Battle of Blenheim during the Spanish War of Succession, but the Queen's gratitude ran out before the building work was finished and the Duke had to meet the remainder of the costs himself. Designed by Sir John Vanbrugh and built between 1705 and 1722, the house is also famously associated with Sir Winston Churchill, who was born here in 1874, and among the grand collections, there are intimate mementoes from the great

Blenheim Palace

statesman's life. The surrounding parkland was landscaped by Capability Brown. The graves of Sir Winston and his parents lie in the churchyard of St Martin, which was formerly the parish church of Woodstock.

LOWER HEYFORD

12 miles NW of Oxford on the B4030

To the south of the village, which stands on the banks of the River Cherwell, is **Rousham**, a fine 17th century house built for the Dormer family, with magnificent gardens laid out by William Kent in 1738; they represent the first phase of English landscape gardening and remain the only complete William Kent garden to have survived.

CHIPPING NORTON

At 650 feet above sea level, this is Oxfordshire's highest town and was once an important centre of the wool trade. This medieval prosperity can be seen in the grandeur of the spacious **Church of St Mary**, which, like many other buildings in the town, endured substantial remodelling in the 19th century. To the west of the town centre is the extraordinary 19th century **Bliss Tweed Mill**, which was designed by George Woodhouse, a Lancashire architect, in the style of Versailles. It has now been converted into luxury apartments, though the dramatic exterior can still be enjoyed (including the tall Tuscan factory chimney and domed front roof, which has been unfortunately described to resemble a toilet plunger; I am sure not the architect's intension!).

To the north, beyond **Over Norton**, are the **Rollright Stones** – one of the most

Rollright Stones

fascinating Bronze Age monuments in the country. These great slabs of stone stand on a ridge which affords fine panoramic views.

AROUND CHIPPING NORTON

BANBURY

12½ miles NE of Chipping Norton on the A361

This historic market town has managed to preserve many of its old buildings and to retain its status as a leading livestock market. The famous **Banbury Cross** in Horsefair dates only from 1859 as the previous cross was destroyed by the Puritans during the Civil War.

To the southwest of Banbury, in an old courthouse, is the **Bloxham Village Museum**, where the displays concentrate on the lives of Oxfordshire's rural inhabitants. Close by is the 14th century moated mansion, **Broughton Castle**, which was remodelled into a fine Tudor home in the 16th century. The castle

Broughton Castle, Banbury

figured prominently in the Civil War, when its secret room was used by leaders of the Parliamentary forces to lay their plans. The interior is lushly furnished with original artifacts, giving a true picture of how inhabitants of the castle lived, and the gardens are extensive and beautifully maintained; a gentle stroll along the water and through the landscaped grounds is the perfect end to a day spent here.

CHARLBURY

5½ miles SE of Chipping Norton on the B4022

Charlbury was once famous for its glove-making as well as being a centre of the Quaker Movement – the simple **Friends Meeting House** here dates from 1779 and there is also a Friends cemetery. Close to the Meeting House is **Charlbury Museum**, where the town's charters can be seen.

On the opposite bank of the River Evenlode from the main town lies **Cornbury Park**, a large estate that Elizabeth I gave to Robert Dudley. Although most of the house now dates from the 17th century, this was originally a hunting lodge in Wychwood Forest and it had been used since the days of Henry I.

Just to the west is **Ditchley Park**, a restrained, classical, early 18th century house with superb interiors; it was used as a weekend headquarters by Sir Winston Churchill during World War II when Chequers was thought to be unsafe.

WITNEY

10½ miles S of Chipping Norton on the A4095

Situated at the bottom of the valley of the River Windrush, Witney developed as a planned town in the early Middle Ages. Wool was the economic base of life here and Witney developed weaving and, in particular, the making of blankets. The **Blanket Hall**, which sports the arms of the Witney Company of Weavers, was built for the weighing and measuring of blankets in an age before rigid standardisation.

Just outside the town is the **Cogges Manor Farm Museum**, which tells the stories of the lives of those who have worked the surrounding land for centuries. To ensure the future of this beautiful building and its vital contents, the museum is now under the care of a charitable trust that will be closing it to the public and conserving it throughout 2010.

Just to the west of Witney lies **Minster Lovell**, one of the prettiest villages along the River Windrush and home to the once impressive 15th century manor house, **Minster**

Lovell Hall. Built between 1431 and 1442, this was one of the aristocratic houses of Oxfordshire and home of the influential Lovell family. Although the hall was dismantled in the 18th century, the remains in this serene setting are extremely picturesque.

SHIPTON-UNDER-WYCHWOOD

6 miles SW of Chipping Norton off the A361

The suffix 'under-Wychwood' is derived from the ancient royal hunting forest, **Wychwood Forest**, the remains of which lie to the east of this village. Though cleared during the Middle Ages, it was still used as a royal hunting ground until well into the 17th century; 150 years later there was little good wood left and the forest was rapidly cleared to provide arable land. A recent project has secured 22 acres of this farmland with the intention of replanting and restoring the forest.

BURFORD

11 miles SW of Chipping Norton on the A361

This quaint country town, traditionally the "Gateway to the Cotswolds", was once an important centre of the wool trade. Many old inns from its popular revival with the stage coaching era still remain. The present high street appears to have changed little in hundreds of years; lined with rustic charming buildings containing some lovely individual shops.

With the atmosphere of a small cathedral, the wonderful **Church of St John** was built on the wealth of the wool trade and has several interesting features, including a memorial to Edmund Harman, Henry VIII's barber and courtier, that contains what could be the first representation of a native American Indian in this country. The town's 16th century courthouse, with its open ground floor, is now home to the **Tolsey Museum**.

Two miles out of the town is the **Cotswold Wildlife Park and Gardens**; its 160 acres of parkland, surrounding a stunning Victorian Manor House, is brimming with local and exotic wildlife, many now endangered.

RUTLAND

The motto of England's smallest county is, appropriately, 'multum in parvo' ('much in little'). It has two delightful market towns, Oakham and Uppingham, and 52 small, unspoilt villages of thatch and ironstone cottages clustered round their churches.

The county's central feature is Rutland Water, which extends over 3,300 acres and is the largest man-made reservoir in Europe. Started in 1971 to supply water to East Midlands towns, it was created by damming the valley near Empingham. There's good walking around its 26-mile shoreline, some great bird-watching (including wild ospreys), excellent trout and pike fishing, and a wide variety of water sports. The Anglian Bird Watching Centre at Egleton has excellent facilities and is the base from which the famous annual British Bird Watching festival is run.

Curiously for such a pastoral, peaceful county, it was Rutland men who were prime movers in two of the most dangerous conspiracies in England's history. In a room over the porch of Stoke Dry Church, the Gunpowder Plot was hatched with the local lord of the manor, Sir Everard Digby, as one of the ringleaders. Some 75 years later, Titus Oates and his fellow conspirators hatched the anti-Catholic 'Popish Plot' at his home in Oakham.

Barnsdale Woods

OAKHAM

The heart of this lively county town can be found at its market, a vibrant affair held here every Wednesday and Saturday.

Just off the Market Place is **Oakham Castle**, a romantic, evocative fortified manor house built between 1180 and 1190, with the earliest surviving example of an aisled stone hall in the country. Only the Great hall survives. One of the most unusual attractions is a collection of horseshoes presented by royalty and nobility to the Lord of the Manor.

The Great Hall, Oakham Castle

Notable natives of Oakham include the infamous conspirator Titus Oates, born here the son of a Baptist minister in 1649. The famed midget Jeffrey Hudson was born in 1619 in a cottage that still stands today.

One of Rutland's best-known landmarks, **Normanton Church**, stands on the very edge of **Rutland Water**, which was formerly part of the Normanton Estate and now houses a display dedicated to the construction of the reservoir by Anglian Water and a history of the area.

Rutland Water

The water is a haven for a huge variety of birds and wildlife, and its nature reserve has been designated a European Special Protection Area. There are 22 hides and many nature trails, giving visitors a great opportunity to observe the life flourishing within it; of particular interest and beauty are the Ospreys, which can be seen here between May and September. The famous British Bird Watching Fair takes place every year in August from the **Anglian Water Birdwatching Centre**, which has a viewing gallery, knowledgeable staff and interesting exhibits available all year round.

Around the water are 25 miles of scenic pathways, which can be used for walking and cycling (bicycle hire facilities are available). The huge variety of other activities popular here include fishing, sailing, windsurfing and canoeing; self hire and qualified tuition allow all levels of ability to be catered for.

To the northeast of Oakham is **Cottesmore**, the home of the **Rutland Railway Museum**, an open-air working steam and diesel museum open some weekends.

In the tiny village of **Tickencote**, off the A1 west of Stamford, stands the **Church of St Peter**, famed for its glorious sexpartite vaulting over the chancel. Equally breathtaking is the chancel arch, and other treasures include a fine 13th century font and a life-size wooden effigy of a 14th century knight.

UPPINGHAM

This picturesque stone-built town is the major community in the south part of the county. The town is known for its bookshops and art galleries, but whereas other places are dominated by castles or cathedrals, in Uppingham it's the impressive **Uppingham School** that gives the town its special character. The school was founded in 1584 by Robert Johnson, Archdeacon of Leicester, who also founded Rutland's other celebrated public school at Oakham. For more than 250 years, Uppingham was just one of many such small grammar schools, giving rigorous instruction in classical languages to a couple of dozen sons of the local gentry. Then, in 1853, the Reverend Edward Thring was appointed

Uppingham School

LYDDINGTON

3 miles SE of Uppingham off the A6003

A quiet village where English Heritage oversees the **Bede House**, one of the finest examples of Tudor domestic architecture in the country. This house of prayer was once

headmaster. During his 43-year tenure the sleepy little school was transformed.

The Old School Building still stands in the churchyard, with trilingual inscriptions around the walls in Latin, Greek and Hebrew. In its place rose a magnificent complex of neo-gothic buildings: not just the traditional classrooms and a (splendid) chapel, but also a laboratory, workshops, museum, gymnasium and the most extensive school playing fields in the country.

The old school, the 18th century studies, the Victorian chapel and schoolrooms, and the 20th century great hall, all Grade I or Grade II listed, can be visited on a guided tour on Saturday afternoons in summer.

Bede House, Lyddington

part of a retreat for the Bishops of Lincoln and was later converted to almshouses, a role it fulfilled until 1930.

SHROPSHIRE

The glorious border county of Shropshire hides a turbulent past, when the Marcher Lords divided their time between fighting the Welsh and each other. The remains of their fortresses can be seen in various places, and one of the finest Roman sites in the country is at Wroxeter - Viroconium was the first Roman site to be developed in this part of the country.

There are ancient market towns that serve the rich farmland and some magnificent stately homes; and Shropshire saw the birthplace of the Industrial Revolution that began at Ironbridge Gorge. This stretch of the Severn Valley is now a World Heritage Centre, which ranks it alongside the Pyramids, the Grand Canyon and the Taj Mahal, and several interesting museums can be found here. The Gorge was once full of the underground tunnels, pits and shafts of industry; the only remaining one of these open to public is the atmospheric Tar Tunnel, where natural bitumen was once mined for a variety of uses – including medicinal.

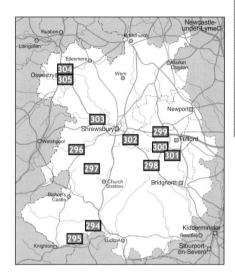

Shrewsbury, the "town of flowers", was the birthplace of Charles Darwin and the home of Robert Clive (Clive of India), and there are fascinating exhibits and memorials for both of these great men. The town's position on a calm horse-shoe bend in the River Severn offers some lovely scenery and pathways to enjoy; the views from its stunning Norman Castle are particularly breathtaking. Another beautiful castle can be found at Ludlow; although now a ruin it continues to be a lively location for many of the town's events. Outside of the village of Tong is Boscobel House, where Charles II hid after his defeat at the Battle of Worcester in 1651; the secret room can still be seen today.

Along with man-made places of interest, visitors will find spectacular scenery around Wenlock Edge, Long Mynd and Clun Forest.

LUDLOW

Often referred to as 'the perfect historic town', Ludlow has more than 500 listed buildings along with a medieval street pattern that remains virtually intact. **Ludlow Castle** was built on a rocky promontory above a curve of the River Teme by the Normans in the 11th century as one of a string of castles along the Marches. It has been home to many distinguished families and to royalty, including Edward V and Prince Arthur; it was also the headquarters of the Council of the Marches, which governed Wales and the border counties until 1689. The grand ruins of the castle still stand, and offer a fascination insight into the town's history for visitors, particularly with one of their guided tours. Many events are hosted in and around it, including archery, falconry, and the delightful Medieval Fayre at Christmas.

Ludlow Castle

Ever since 1960, the town has played host to the annual Ludlow Festival, one of the country's major arts festivals that lasts for a fortnight in June and July and the centrepiece of the event is an open-air performance of a Shakespeare play in the castle's inner bailey.

The parish **Church of St Laurence** is one of the largest in the county; the ashes of AE Housman, author of *A Shropshire Lad*, lie beneath the north door, and he is commemorated by a tablet on the outer wall. Other places to see are **Castle Lodge**, which was once a prison and later the home of the officials of the Council of the Marches, the Georgian **Dinham House**, the Feathers Hotel and the **Museum**.

Just northwest of the town lies Ludlow Racecourse, a charming, rural National Hunt course, while a few miles to the southeast lies the village of **Burford**. On the banks of the River Teme stands **Burford House**, whose four acre garden is filled with well over 2,000 varieties of plants. The garden is also the home of the National Collection of Clematis.

AROUND LUDLOW

BISHOP'S CASTLE

12 miles NW of Ludlow on the B4385

Surrounded by the great natural beauty of the border country, little remains of the castle that was built here in the 12th century for the bishops of Hereford. The **House on Crutches Museum** is situated in one of the oldest and most picturesque of the town's buildings – its gable end is supported on wooden posts that explain the unusual name. North of Bishop's Castle lie the **Stiperstones**, a rock-strewn quartzite outcrop rising to a height of 1,700 feet at the Devil's Chair. A bleak, lonely place, the ridge is part of a 1,000-acre National Nature Reserve.

ROCKE COTTAGE TEA ROOMS

Clungunford

A delightful olde-world tea room serving the very best in home cooking and refreshments

See entry on page 518

THE BARON AT BUCKNELL

Bucknell, nr Knighton

A fine country inn full of charm and character. Excite your taste buds with traditional honest food inspired by the countryside and cooked from the heart.

See entry on page 519

CHURCH STRETTON

12 miles N of Ludlow on the A49

Just behind the High Street is the **Church of St Laurence** that has Saxon foundations and, over the aisle, is a memorial to three boys who were tragically killed in a fire in 1968.

A mile from the town centre are Carding Mill Valley and the **Long Mynd**. The valley and the moorland into which it runs are very popular for walking and picnicking.

Just to the southwest lies the pretty village of **Little Stretton** that nestles in the Stretton Gap. The most interesting building here is the black and white timber-framed **All Saints Church**, with its thatched roof and general cottage-like appearance.

BRIDGNORTH

16½ miles NE of Ludlow on the A458

Straddling the River Severn, this ancient market town comprises Low Town and, some 100 feet up on sandstone cliffs, High Town. In 1101, Robert de Belesme built a Castle here but all that remains now is part of the keep tower. The **Northgate Museum** is a good place to start a tour of this interesting town; brimming with local treasures, it presents an intimate history of life here through the ages.

Bridgnorth is the northern terminus of the wonderful **Severn Valley Railway** but the town has another irresistible attraction in the **Castle Hill Cliff Railway**, a funicular railway built in 1892 that links the two parts of the town. Sir John Betjeman likened a ride on this lovely little railway to a journey up to heaven. The alternative to the railway is seven sets of steps or the meandering, historic Cartway.

MUCH WENLOCK

16½ miles NE of Ludlow on the A4169

Among the mellow buildings of this delightful small town are some places of real beauty, including the timber-framed **Raynald's Mansion**, the magnificent 16th century **Guildhall**, and the **Corn Exchange**, built in 1851 and which contains the local public library.

The most interesting building is the **Priory of St Milburga** that was originally founded as a nunnery in the 7th century by King Merewald, who installed his daughter Milburga as head of the house. Among the remains, the Prior's Lodge, dating from around 1500, is particularly impressive, while away from the main site is St Milburga's Well, whose waters are reputed to cure eye diseases.

---

296 BARLEY MOW HOUSE

Aston Rogers, nr Shrewsbury

Charming 18th century farmhouse bed and breakfast with a choice of three individually styled rooms, located within beautiful grounds.

See entry on page 518

---

297 THE BOTTLE AND GLASS INN

Picklescott

Historic and friendly village inn in picturesque Pickelscott, where fine home cooking, real ales and comfy guest accommodation are in plenty.

See entry on page 520

---

298 THE GEORGE AND DRAGON INN

Much Wenlock

At the heart of its local community, this friendly village pub offers good real ale and wholesome home cooked food every day.

See entry on page 521

---

299 THE RED LION

Wellington

Local ales and wholesome home cooked food served in this pleasant inn, opposite the Wrekin.

See entry on page 521

TELFORD

Telford is a sprawling modern town that absorbed several existing towns in the Shropshire coalfield. The name chosen in the 1960s commemorates Thomas Telford, whose influence can be seen all over the county.

AROUND TELFORD

IRONBRIDGE

3 miles S of Telford off the B4373

This town, at the centre of **Ironbridge Gorge**, is part of an area of the Severn Gorge where the world's first cast-iron bridge was constructed and where, over 250 years ago, the Industrial Revolution first began in earnest. In this locality, now designated a World Heritage Centre, the first iron wheels, the first iron rails and the first steam railway locomotive were made. There are a large amount of walking and cycling routes to explore through the gorge, where nature has reclaimed the former industrial sites and become a glorious wooded valley; a perfect way to introduce you this area.

The **Ironbridge Visitor Centre** offers the ideal introduction to the series of museums here, including the **Museum of Iron** at **Coalbrookdale**, and the neighbbouring furnace that was used by Abraham Darby when he first smelted iron with coke; the **Jackfield Tile Museum**, which houses a fine collection of wall and floor files from Victorian times through to the 1950s (and a chance to make some of your own through the fun tile decorating workshops); and the **Coalport China Museum** with its marvellous displays of porcelain that span over two centuries.

Nearby is the extraordinary **Tar Tunnel**, which was a popular tourist attraction in the 18th century as well as being one of the most interesting geological phenomena in Britain; an eerie experience to walk through, with the walls still oozing bitumen (just don't forget your hard-hat!). It would be hard to believe that banquets would be held down in this cold damp atmosphere; but they indeed were during the 1970s, further down in the wider section of tunnel.

Further upstream from Ironbridge is one of the finest ruined abbeys in England, **Buildwas Abbey**, virtually complete, though roofless after 850 years.

Buildwas Abbey, Ironbridge

---

300 THE COALBROOKDALE INN AND FOUNDRY MASTERS HOUSE

Coalbrookdale

This handsome and historic old hostelry offers luxurious period accommodation, with an unrivalled friendly atmosphere in its award winning bar and restaurant.

See entry on page 522

---

301 MAWS CAFÉ & CHOCOLATE SHACK

Jackfield, nr Ironbridge

Popular café serving a range breakfasts, snacks and main meals made with fresh local produce, along with delicious array of homemade chocolates for dessert.

See entry on page 523

SHIFNAL

4 miles E of Telford on the A464

On the A41 at **Cosford**, near Shifnal, the **RAF Museum** houses an important collection of aircraft, aero engines and weapons of war from all over the world.

TONG

6 miles E of Telford on the A41

Charles Dickens set the closing chapters of The Old Curiosity Shop in Tong and Little Nell's home was right by the church.

To the east of the village lie the ruins of White Ladies Priory, a 12th century nunnery dedicated to St Leonard. Nearby is **Boscobel House** (English Heritage), a timber-framed building where Charles II hid after his defeat at the Battle of Worcester in 1651. The secret room where he hid can be seen, as can the Royal Oak, which was grown from an acorn taken from the original tree in which the King escaped a house search by Cromwell's men.

SHREWSBURY

Often referred to as the "Town of Flowers", the beautiful displays of flora throughout the town have, over the years, won it an array of awards.

Situated in a horseshoe bend in the River Severn, this lovely county town occupies, almost, an island site and it was on the two well-protected hills here that the Saxon town developed. Later, the Normans built a **Castle**, which last saw action in the Civil War, and a great Benedictine Abbey on the site of a Saxon wooden church. The **Abbey Church** remains a place of worship to this day, and the Castle is now home to the **Shropshire Regimental Museum**. Close to the abbey is the **Shrewsbury Quest**, which presents the sights and sounds of medieval Shrewsbury as it grew and prospered on the wealth generated by the woolen trade.

It was at Shrewsbury that Charles Darwin was born and educated and, earlier, Robert

302 THE BELL INN

Cross Houses

Friendly family run pub serving fine ale and food, with en suite guest accommodation and campsite.

See entry on page 523

Clive, Clive of India, lived in the town and was Mayor in 1762. His home, **Clive House**, contains mementoes from his life along with a display dedicated to Charles Darwin, whose statue can be seen opposite the castle.

Just outside Shrewsbury, at **Longden Coleham**, is a museum with a difference – the **Coleham Pumping Station** – which houses the splendid Renshaw pumping engines that powered Shrewsbury's sewerage system until 1970.

One of the many guided tours and

Shrewsbury Castle

suggested walks in this marvellous town leads north to a place known as the **Battlefield**. It was here, in 1403, that the armies of Henry IV and the insurgent Harry Hotspur met; in the brief but bloody battle there were many casualties, including Hotspur.

To the southeast of the town lies the village of **Atcham**, and close by is one of the finest houses in Shropshire, the splendid neo-classical **Attingham Park** with grand Regency interiors and delightful grounds that were landscaped by Humphry Repton.

A little further from Shrewsbury lies **Wroxeter**, home to one of the most important Roman sites to have been excavated. Known as **Viroconium**, it was the first town to be established by the Romans in this part of the country. Six miles north of Shrewsbury on the A49 stands the village of **Grinshill**. This is a neat, quaint little place and the area is a walker's paradise; the hill rises to 630 feet above sea level, and its greatest asset is the substance from which it is made – sandstone. The Romans quarried it for the construction of Wroxeter, and in more recent times it was

Hidden Places of England

Shropshire

221

used for the door surrounds of No 10 Downing Street. The quarry has revealed many rare fossils and has accordingly been designated a Site of Special Scientific Interest.

AROUND SHREWSBURY

WEM

10½ miles N of Shrewsbury on the B5476

Although this is a peaceful place today Wem was virtually destroyed during the War of the Roses and, later, it was again attacked during the Civil War.

Fortunately some notable buildings survived the great fire that devastated much of the town in the 17th century and these include **Astley House**, the home of the painter John Astley. Another famous person associated with the town is Judge Jeffreys, of the Bloody Assizes, whose official residence was at Lowe Hall.

Wem is the home of the modern sweet pea, which was developed by the 19th century nurseryman, Henry Eckford, and the Sweet Pea Show and carnival take place here annually.

WHITCHURCH

19 miles N of Shrewsbury on the A49

First developed by the Romans and known as Mediolanum, Whitchurch has been the most important town in the northern part of the county for centuries. The main street is dominated by the tall sandstone tower of **St Alkmund's Church**, while hidden away in the heart of the town are the Old Town Hall Vaults, where the composer Edward German was born in 1862. Whitchurch is also the home of **Joyce Clocks**, the oldest tower clockmakers in the world, and many of their clocks can be seen around the town.

The long-distance footpath, the Shropshire Way, passes near Whitchurch, as does the Llangollen Canal, and nature lovers can explore the local wetland habitats at Brown Moss, which lies just to the south of the town.

MARKET DRAYTON

17 miles NE of Shrewsbury on the A529

Mentioned in the *Domesday Book* as Magna Draitune, Market Drayton changed its name when Abbot Simon Combermere obtained a Royal Market charter in 1245; a market continues to be held here every Wednesday. To the east of town is the village of **Moreton Say**, where locally born Robert Clive, Clive of India, is buried in St Margaret's Church.

A few miles southwest of Market Drayton lays a beautiful Georgian mansion, **Hawkestone Hall**, which was the ancestral home of the Hill family from 1556 until 1906. Hawkestone Park is a woodland fantasy of caves, follies, grottoes and secret tunnel and pathways. Although now a spiritual retreat, it is open to the public from 14th to the 31st of August every year.

Hawkestone Hall, Market Drayton

NESSCLIFFE

9 miles NW of Shrewsbury on the A5

Close to the village is **Nesscliffe Hill Country Park** where paths lead up through woodland to the hill, a sandstone escarpment, from which there are glorious views out across

303 THE WINGFIELD ARMS

Montford Bridge

A popular pub with a growing reputation for the quality homemade dishes it serves

See entry on page 524

Shropshire and to Wales.

A short distance north of Nesscliffe is the village of **Ruyton-XI-Towns**, which acquired its curious name in medieval times when 11 communities were united into the one borough of Ruyton.

OSWESTRY

17 miles NW of Shrewsbury off the A5

This important market town takes its name from Oswald, a Saxon king who was killed in a battle in AD 642 and whose dismembered body was hung on the branches of a tree. Local legend then tells an eagle swooped down and carried off one of his arms and, where the limb fell to the ground, a spring bubbled up to mark the spot and it was around St Oswald's Well that the town developed while the well became a place of pilgrimage.

Due to several fires that ravaged the town's old timber-framed buildings, Oswestry's architecture is chiefly Georgian and Victorian but various fine old buildings do still remain including **St Oswald's Church**. Standing in the grounds of the church is the 15th century **Holbache House** that was once a grammar school and now houses a Heritage Centre.

In 1559, a plague killed almost a third of the town's inhabitants and the Croeswylan

Stone commemorates this disaster as well as marking the spot to which the market was moved during the days of the infection.

Oswestry was the headquarters of the Cambrian Railway Company until it amalgamated with the Great Western Railway in 1922 and as recently as the 1960s there were over 1,000 railwaymen in the area. One of the old engine sheds now houses the **Cambrian Museum of Transport**, where a collection of railway memorabilia, along with some old bicycles and motorbikes, is on display.

About five miles south of Oswestry lies the village of **Llanymynech** that was once a town of some standing, with a major canal and a thriving industry based on limestone. The quarried limestone was taken, after processing, to the nearby canalside wharf on the Montgomery Canal that was built at the end of the 18th century chiefly for this purpose.

ELLESMERE

15½ miles NW of Shrewsbury on the A495

The most impressive building here is undoubtedly the parish **Church of St Mary the Virgin**; built by the Knights of St John, it has an exceptional 15th century carved roof in the chapel. This church overlooks **The Mere**, the largest of several local lakes, which is home to herons, Canada geese and swans, and an ideal place for boating enthusiasts and anglers.

304 COURTYARD CAFÉ

Oswestry

Cosy courtyard café in the centre of Oswestry where home cooking is a premium.

See entry on page 523

305 THE WALLS

Oswestry

A fine dining experience awaits you at The Walls, which offers homemade quality food made from the freshest local ingredients

See entry on page 525

The Mere, Ellesmere

223

Somerset has more than its fair share of natural beauty. The wilds of Exmoor and the ranges of spectacular hills such as the Quantocks and the Mendips add to this county's allure. In the far northwest is Exmoor, once wild hunting country: its abundance of prehistoric sites, ancient packhorse bridges and wild deer and ponies easily make it one of the more romantic and mysterious spots.

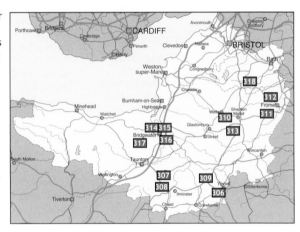

As the Mendips are limestone, the hills are full of holes, and, in particular, this area is known for its caves at Wookey Hole and the spectacular Cheddar Gorge, which carves a path right through the hills as well as lending its name to the cheese. Below the hills is the charming and ancient city of Wells, from where the county's plain stretches out to Glastonbury, a place shrouded in mystery and steeped in early Christian and Arthurian legends.

Somerset is home to the West Countries largest city, Bristol, which is steeped in maritime history (with an intriguing floating harbour) as well as much vitality and contemporary culture. Outside of Bristol are the popular seaside resorts of Weston-Super-Mare and Clevedon, both with many attractions and their own piers. Clevedon Pier is a particularly graceful sight, built in the 1860s and fully restored, it is the only intact Grade I listed pier in the country.

YEOVIL

Situated in Wyndham House, the **Museum of South Somerset** documents the social and industrial history of the town and surrounding area. From glove-making, to flax and hemp production, to engineering, and newspaper printing, the enthralling exhibits contain collections of artifacts which reveal an accurate picture of life in the town through the ages. It even has, on its upper floor, a recreated Roman kitchen and dining room, complete with mosaic floor.

To the south lies **Barwick Park**, an estate that is littered with bizarre follies, while to the west is the magnificent Elizabethan mansion, **Montacute House** (National Trust), which has one of the grandest long galleries in the country and extensive gardens which include the famous wibbly wobbly hedges. Montacute village is also the home of the **TV and Radio Memorabilia Museum**. In the lanes to the southeast of Montacute and close to the village of **West Coker** is the magnificent **Brympton d'Evercy Manor House** dating from Norman times but with significant 16th and 17th century additions.

Montacute House, nr Yeovil

306 THE PEN MILL HOTEL

Yeovil

A popular hotel serving the very best in local seasonal produce.

See entry on page 526

AROUND YEOVIL

SPARKFORD

7 miles NE of Yeovil off the A303

Home to the **Haynes Motor Museum**, which holds one of the largest collections of veteran, vintage and classic cars and motorbikes in the country. Just to the east of Sparkford is **Cadbury Castle**, a massive Iron Age hill fort that is also believed by some to be the location of King Arthur's legendary Camelot.

CASTLE CARY

11½ miles NE of Yeovil on the B3152

Once the site of an impressive Norman castle, this little rural town has some interesting old buildings, including a handsome 18th century post office, a tiny 18th century lock-up called the Round House, and a splendid Market House that is now home to the **Castle Cary District Museum**.

CREWKERNE

8 miles SW of Yeovil on the A356

A thriving agricultural centre during Saxon times, Crewkerne even had its own mint in the decades that led up to the Norman invasion. The town lies close to the source of the River Parrett, from where the 50-mile long River **Parrett Trail** follows the river through some of the country's most ecologically sensitive and fragile areas. Just a couple of miles southwest of Crewkerne, close to the village of **Clapton**, are the interesting **Clapton Court Gardens**.

CHARD

15 miles SW of Yeovil on the A30

Although Chard has expanded rapidly since World War II, it still retains a pleasant village-like atmosphere; its museum is located in the attractive thatched **Godworth House** and is open each year from May until October. Chard claims to be the birthplace of aviation, as it was here in 1848 that the Victorian aeronautical pioneer John Stringfellow (1799-1883) first demonstrated that engine-powered flight was possible.

To the northwest of the town is a 200-year old corn mill, **Hornsbury Mill**, now a hotel and beautiful wedding venue; to the northeast lies **Chard Reservoir Nature Reserve**, a conservation area that is an important habitat for wildlife.

Close to the county border lies **Forde Abbey**, which was founded in the 12th century by Cistercian monks. The remains of the Abbey were incorporated into the grand private house of the Prideaux family, and among the many treasures are the renowned Mortlake Tapestries brought from Brussels by Charles I. The 30 acres of award-winning garden surrounding it are equally superb.

Forde Abbey, nr Chard

ILMINSTER

13 miles W of Yeovil on the A358

On the outskirts of the ancient agricultural and ecclesiastical centre of Ilminster is the handsome part-Tudor mansion, **Dillington House**, the former home of the influential Speke family. It is now a leading venue for learning and events.

MARTOCK

6 miles NW of Yeovil on the B3165

The old part of Martock is blessed with an unusually large number of fine buildings, including the **Treasurer's House** (National Trust), a small two-storey house dating from the late 13th century, and a 17th century Manor House, the home of Edward Parker, the man who exposed the Gunpowder Plot.

To the east of Martock are the enchanting **Tintinhull House Gardens**, with woodland, orchards, and small pools set within landscaped garden.

YEOVILTON

5 miles NW of Yeovil off the A37

Here is one of the world's leading aviation museums, the **Fleet Air Arm Museum**, which contains a unique collection of aircraft, many on permanent display.

MUCHELNEY

9½ miles NW of Yeovil off the A372

Muchelney is the location of an impressive part-ruined Benedictine monastery, **Muchelney Abbey**, thought to have been founded by King Ine in the 8th century. Opposite the parish church stands the Priest's

---

307 FROG STREET FARMHOUSE

Hatch Beauchamp

A delightful farmhouse providing a haven of tranquility for those wanting to escape the noise and stress of the modern world.

See entry on page 527

---

308 THE SQUARE AND COMPASS INN

Ashill

Fine old traditional inn with large gardens offering very good food, drink and 8 large double ensuite bedrooms; also purpose built venue for conferences and weddings.

See entry on page 526

---

309 ASH HOUSE HOTEL

Martock

This elegant Hotel provides top quality accommodation set in 1.5 acres of beautiful gardens

See entry on page 528

House, a late medieval hall house that was built by the abbey.

WELLS

The first church here is believed to have been founded by King Ine in around AD 700 but the present **Cathedral of St Andrew** was begun in the 12th century. Taking over three centuries to complete, the treasures of this wonderful place include the 14th century **Astronomical Clock**, one of the oldest working timepieces in the world. Set in the pavement outside the Cathedral walls is a length of brass that extends over the prodigious distance leapt by local girl Mary (Bignall) Rand when she set a world record for the long jump. To the south of the cathedral's cloisters is the **Bishop's Palace**, a remarkable fortified medieval building that is surrounded by a moat fed by the springs that give the city its name. On the northern side of the cathedral green is 14th century **Vicar's Close**, one of the oldest planned streets in Europe.

To the north of the city lies **Wookey Hole**, where the carboniferous limestone has been eroded away over the centuries to create over 25 caverns. During prehistoric times, lions, bears and woolly mammoths lived in the area.

Wookey Hole, Wells

The **Great Cave** at Wookey contains a rock formation known as the Witch of Wookey that casts a ghostly shadow and is associated with the gruesome legends of child-eating. Nearby lies the dramatic **Ebbor Gorge**, now a National Nature Reserve managed by English Nature.

CHEW MAGNA
11½ miles N of Wells on the B3130

The nucleus of this former wool village is its three-sided green at the top of which is the striking early 16th century **Church House** while, behind a high wall adjacent to the churchyard, lies **Chew Court**, a former summer palace of the Bishops of Bath and Wells.

To the south of Chew Magna are the two reservoirs constructed to supply Bristol with fresh water but that also provide a first class recreational amenity.

NORTON ST PHILIP
15½ miles NE of Wells on the A366

The monks who founded the now-ruined Priory were also responsible for building the village's most famous landmark – the splendid **George Inn** – that was originally established as a house of hospitality for those visiting the priory.

To the west is one of the finest Neolithic monuments in the west of England, **Stoney Littleton Long Barrow** that was built over 4,000 years ago.

SHEPTON MALLET
5 miles E of Wells on the A371

From before the Norman Conquest and through the Middle Ages Shepton Mallet was at first a centre of woollen production and then a weaving town. Several fine buildings date back to those prosperous days including the 50 feet **Market Cross**, which dates from around 1500, and The Shambles, a 15th

310 MANOR FARM BED & BREAKFAST

Dulcote

17th century farmhouse in idyllic setting offering quality bed & breakfast accommodation.

See entry on page 529

century wooden shed where meat was traded. Each year, Shepton Mallet plays host to two agricultural shows: the **Mid-Somerset Show** in August and, in May, the **Royal Bath and Wells Show**.

FROME
14½ miles E of Wells on the A362

Frome's old quarter is an attractive conservation area where can be found the **Blue House** that was built in 1726 as an almshouse and a boy's school and is one of the town's numerous listed buildings.

GLASTONBURY
5½ miles SW of Wells on the A39

The name Glastonbury has become synonymous with its festival of contemporary performing arts; held here since 1970. More than this though, this ancient town of myths, legends and tales of King Arthur and the early Christians is an attractive market town dominated by the dramatic ruins of its abbey. If the legend of Joseph of Arimathea is to be believed, **Glastonbury Abbey** is the site of the earliest Christian foundation in the British Isles. However, it is the Abbey's connection with King Arthur and his wife Queen Guinevere that draws most visitors to Glastonbury, as this is thought by some to be

their last resting place. Even the **Somerset Rural Life Museum** cannot escape from the influence of the Abbey as the impressive 14th century barn here once belonged to the Abbey.

To the east of the town lies **Glastonbury Tor**, a dramatic hill that rises above the surrounding Somerset Levels. The 520 feet Tor has been inhabited since prehistoric times and excavations have revealed evidence of Celtic, Roman and pre-Saxon occupation. It has long been associated with myth and legend (Joseph of Arimathea is said to have built a church here) and has been identified as the Land of the Dead, the Celtic Otherworld, a Druid temple, an Arthurian hill fort, home to Gwyn ap Nudd (King of the Fairies) and a rendezvous point for passing UFOs.

In the nearby village of **Street**, the Clark family began to produce sheepskin slippers in the 1820s; the oldest part of the Clark's factory is now a fascinating **Shoe Museum**.

BURNHAM-ON-SEA
15 miles W of Wells on the B3140

A large and popular seaside resort whose most distinctive landmark is the **Low Lighthouse**, a curious square structure that is raised above the beach on tall stilts. To the northeast lies Brent Knoll, whose 445 feet summit is crowned with the remains of an Iron Age hill fort.

CHEDDAR
7½ miles NW of Wells on the A371

This sprawling village is best known for its dramatic limestone gorge, **Cheddar Gorge**, which is characterised by its high vertical cliffs, from which there are outstanding views.

311 THE GEORGE AT NUNNEY

Nunney

Well respected and popular 13th century inn in beautiful Nunney, known for its dog friendly environment and succulent game dishes.

See entry on page 529

312 THE BELL INN

Buckland Dinham

A fine historic village inn serving homemade traditional British food

See entry on page 530

313 LOWER WITHIAL FARM COTTAGES

East Pennard

In the picturesque village of East Pennard with glorious views across Avalon Vale and Glastonbury Tor these four luxury farm cottages offer a tranquil rural retreat throughout the year.

See entry on page 530

Cheddar Gorge

This village is also renowned for its caves and, of course, its cheese. The term 'Cheddar cheese' refers to a recipe that was developed in the mid 19th century by Joseph Harding, a farmer and pioneer food scientist from near Bath who made the first scientific investigation into cheese making.

From the nearby remote village of **Charterhouse** a footpath leads up onto **Black Down**, which at 1,067 feet is the highest point in the Mendips; from here, to the northwest, the land descends down into Burrington Combe, a deep cleft that is said to have inspired the Reverend Augustus Toplady to write *Rock of Ages*.

The Mendip Hills were once a royal hunting ground and, to the northwest of Cheddar, lies **King John's Hunting Lodge** (National Trust), home to an excellent **Local History Museum**.

TAUNTON

Founded by the Saxon King Ine in the 8th century, Taunton, the county town of Somerset, had by Norman times grown to have its own Augustinian monastery, a Minster and a Castle – an extensive structure whose purpose had always been more as an administrative

centre than as a military post. The **Castle** is now the home of the **Somerset County Museum**; due to be reopened to the public, newly renovated, in 2011. Somerset's famous County Cricket Ground occupies part of the priory grounds and a section of the old monastic gatehouse now houses the fascinating **Somerset County Cricket Museum**.

Taunton's attractive **National Hunt Racecourse** is one of the best country courses in Britain.

In the lanes to the north of Taunton lie the beautiful Hestercombe Gardens on the south-facing foothills of the Quantocks just north of the village of Cheddon Fitzpaine.

AROUND TAUNTON

WELLINGTON

6 miles SW of Taunton on the A38

It was from this pleasant old market town that the Duke took his title and, to the south, stands the **Wellington Monument**, a 175 feet obelisk erected to commemorate his great victory at Waterloo.

Wellington Monument

BISHOP'S LYDEARD

4½ miles NW of Taunton off the A358

This large village is the southern terminus of the **West Somerset Railway**, the privately operated steam railway that runs to Minehead on the Bristol Channel coast.

NETHER STOWEY

9½ miles N of Taunton on the A39

It was while staying in a friend's cottage here that Samuel Taylor Coleridge wrote most of his famous works, including *The Rime of the Ancient Mariner*. When not writing, he would go on long walks with his friend and near neighbour William Wordsworth. The Coleridges stayed here for three years and **Coleridge Cottage** now displays mementoes of the poet.

HINKLEY POINT

13½ miles N of Taunton off the A39

Hinkley Point is perhaps best known for its great power stations and, at the **Hinkley Point Visitor Centre**, visitors can find out just how the adjacent power station creates electricity while, the **Hinkley Point Nature Trail** leads walkers through a wide diversity of habitats.

BRIDGWATER

9 miles NE of Taunton on the A38

Situated at the lowest bridging point of the River Parrett, Bridgwater is an ancient inland port and industrial town. As the river began to silt up, Bridgwater underwent something of an industrial renaissance, as the river mud that closed the port also proved to be an excellent scourer when baked.

To the southwest, near Enmore, is the small redbrick country mansion of **Barford Park**, a delightfully proportioned Queen Anne house that is set in extensive grounds which incorporate a large area of woodland. Further southwest again is **Fyne Court**, which is the headquarters of the **Somerset Wildlife Trust** and whose grounds have been designated a nature reserve.

BURROW BRIDGE

9 miles NE of Taunton on the A361

This village on the River Parrett is home to one of several pumping stations that were built in Victorian times to drain the Somerset Levels - the **Pumping Station** is open to the public occasionally throughout the year; here, too, is the **Somerset Levels Basket and Craft Centre**.

---

314 COBBLESTONES

Bridgewater

In an idyllic location on the banks of the river Parrett this homely and traditional inn welcomes all.

See entry on page 531

316 THE BOAT AND ANCHOR

Huntworth, nr Bridgewater

A traditional hostelry and B&B nestled alongside the pretty Taunton-Bridgewater canal.

See entry on page 532

315 ADMIRAL BLAKE LTD

Bridgewater

Family owned for fifty years this fish and chip shop restaurant and takeaway serves all your favourites in a warm and homely environment.

See entry on page 531

317 TYNTE ARMS

Enmore

Thriving traditional inn offering tasty home-cooked food, real ales and comfortable en suite rooms.

See entry on page 533

Just west of Burrow Bridge, the **Bridgwater and Taunton Canal** winds its way through some of the most attractive countryside in the Somerset Levels and the restored locks, swing bridges and engine houses add further interest to this picturesque walk.

Just northwest of the village of **Westonzoyland** is the site of the last battle to be fought on English soil when, in July 1685, the forces of James II heavily defeated the followers of the Duke of Monmouth in the bloody Battle of Sedgemoor.

EXMOOR & QUANTOCK HILLS

The characteristic heartland of the **Exmoor National Park** is a high, treeless plateau of Devonian shale carved into a series of steep-sided valleys by the prolonged action of the moor's many fast-flowing streams.

Exmoor is crisscrossed by a network of paths and bridleways, which provide superb opportunities for walking and pony-trekking. Many follow the routes of the ancient ridgeways across the high moor and pass close to the numerous hut circles, standing stones, barrows and other Bronze and Iron Age remains which litter the landscape. The remarkable medieval packhorse bridge known as **Tarr Steps** lies to the north of the village of **Hawkridge**, near Dulverton.

MONKSILVER

13 miles NW of Taunton on the B3188

To the southwest of this pretty village of charming old houses and thatched cottages are the **Brendon Hills**, the upland area within the Exmoor National Park from where, in the mid 19th century, iron ore was mined in significant quantities and then carried down a steep mineral railway to the coast for shipment to the furnaces of South Wales.

WATCHET

15 miles NW of Taunton on the B3191

It was at Watchet that, in the 6th century, St Decuman is said to have landed from Wales

with the cow that he brought along to provide sustenance. It was also from Watchet that Coleridge's imaginary crew set sail in *The Rime of the Ancient Mariner*.

To the south of Watchet, in the village of **Williton**, are the diesel locomotive workshops of the **West Somerset Railway** and the **Bakelite Museum**, a fascinating place providing a nostalgic look at the 'pioneer of plastics'. Just to the west lies **Cleeve Abbey**, the only monastery in Somerset that belonged to the austere Cistercian order.

MINEHEAD

21½ miles NW of Taunton off the A39

A popular seaside town at the foot of the wooded promontory of North Hill, now a nature reserve, Minehead is one of the county's oldest settlements. As the port declined, the town began to expand as a seaside resort and in 1962 a popular holiday camp was opened.

To the west of Minehead lies the village of **Selworthy**. This picturesque and much photographed village is situated on the side of a wooded hill. Just to the northwest lies **Selworthy Beacon**, one of the highest points on the vast Holnicote Estate. Covering some 12,500 acres of Exmoor National Park, it includes a four-mile stretch of coastline between Minehead and Porlock Weir. **Dunkery Beacon**, the highest point on Exmoor, rises to 1,700 feet.

To the southeast lies **Dunster**, dominated by **Dunster Castle**, a medieval fortification that was remodelled in 1617 and was one of the last Royalist strongholds in the West

Dunster Castle, Minehead

Country to fall during the Civil War. In the castle's parkland is 18th century **Dunster Working Watermill**; little remains of Dunster Priory apart from its priory church and an unusual 12th century dovecote.

PORLOCK WEIR

26½ miles NW of Taunton off the A39

Once an important seaport, Porlock Weir is a picturesque place where a Submerged Forest, a relic of the Ice Age, can be seen at low tide. From Porlock Weir a pretty mile-long walk leads up through walnut and oak woodland to **Culbone Church**, the smallest church in regular use in England, and certainly one of the most picturesque. A true hidden treasure, measuring only 33 feet by 14 feet, this superb part-Norman building is set in a wooded combe that once supported a small charcoal-burning community and was at other times home to French prisoners and lepers. The **South West Coast Path** passes this lovely secluded church.

To the west lies **Doone Valley**, a long enclosed sweep of green pasture and mature woodland that was immortalised by RD Blackmore in his classic romantic novel *Lorna Doone*.

DULVERTON

19 miles W of Taunton on the B3222

Situated in the wooded Barle Valley on the edge of Exmoor, Dulverton is a pretty little town where the headquarters of the Exmoor National Park can be found in an old converted workhouse.

BRISTOL

Situated at a strategically important bridging point at the head of the Avon gorge, the West Country's largest city and sometime administrative centre of the county of Avon, Bristol was founded in Saxon times and soon became a major port and market centre. In the early 19th century, the harbour was expanded when a semi-artificial waterway, the Floating Harbour, was created by diverting the course of the River Avon to the south.

SS *Great Britain, Bristol*

Today, the main docks have moved down stream to Avonmouth and the **Floating Harbour** has become home to a wide assortment of pleasure and small working craft. Much of Bristol's waterfront has now been redeveloped for recreation, and several museums tell of the city's connections with the sea. The **Maritime Heritage Centre** is dedicated to the history of shipbuilding in Bristol and has a number of historic ships moored at the quayside, including Brunel's mighty SS *Great Britain*, the world's first iron-hulled passenger liner, launched in 1843.

At the heart of the harbourside is the **Arnolfini** gallery of art, film, literature and music; one of Europe's leading centres for the contemporary arts.

Five miles northeast of Bristol, along the B4054, you will find the fascinating **Kings Western Roman Villa**. Discovered during the construction of a housing estate here in 1947, the extensive remains include a bath suite and living quarters with beautiful mosaic floors. Open days for visitors are conducted throughout the year.

AROUND BRISTOL

WESTON-SUPER-MARE

17 miles NW of Wells on the A370

A popular seaside resort with all the trappings, including the Edwardian **Grand Pier** (one of the last traditional iron-piled piers), the Winter Gardens and an Aquarium,

Donkeys on Weston-Super-Mare Beach

as well as the fascinating **North Somerset Museum**. Close by is the start of the Mendip Way, a 50-mile long footpath that takes in the whole length of the Mendip Hills and ends at Frome.

CLEVEDON

18½ miles NW of Wells on the B3133

Clevedon Pier is a remarkably slim and graceful structure that was built in the 1860s from iron rails intended for Brunel's ill-considered South Wales Railway. When part of the pier collapsed in the 1970s, its long-term future looked bleak but, following an

Clevedon Pier

extensive restoration programme, the pier is now the landing stage in the summer for large pleasure steamers, and provides a lovely stroll (particularly at sunset – said to be the most beautiful in the west country) with views stretching over the Estuary.

BATH

The ancient Celts were the first to become aware of the healing powers of the mysterious steaming spring here but it was the Romans who were the first to enclose the spring. The restored Roman remains centre on the Great Bath, a rectangular lead-lined pool that stands at the centre of the complex system of buildings. In the 8th century the Saxons founded a nunnery here but the present-day **Bath Abbey** dates from the 15th century and is considered to be the ultimate example of English Perpendicular church architecture.

Bath developed into a magnificent Georgian spa resort under the influence of three gentlemen: Beau Nash, who became the Master of Ceremonies; the architect father and son, both called John Wood; and the entrepreneur Ralph Allen, who made his first fortune developing an efficient postal system for the provinces and his second as the owner of the local quarries that supplied most of the honey-coloured stone for the city's wonderful Georgian buildings.

Among the many fine buildings here are **Queens Square**; the **Royal Crescent**, the first terrace in Britain to be built to an elliptical design; the **Pump Room** completed in 1796; and the **Assembly Rooms**. Spanning the River Avon is the magnificent **Pulteney Bridge** that was inspired by Florence's Ponte Vecchio. Among the most interesting of Bath's several museums are the **Bath Postal Museum**, with its reconstruction of a Victorian sorting office, and the **Jane Austen Centre** – the novelist spent a good deal of time here.

Just to the east of the city lies the 16th century country mansion, Claverton Manor, now the **American Museum and Gardens**.

318 PITFOUR HOUSE

Timsbury

A luxury award winning bed and breakfast offering comfortable accommodation and home cooked food.

See entry on page 534

233

STAFFORDSHIRE

Southern Staffordshire encompasses many changing landscapes; from busy industrial towns to areas of breathtaking natural beauty. The towns of Stafford and Burton upon Trent both have a rich industrial history. Burton upon Trent's past brewing trade is still alive and well, and the Marston's Brewery tours are an exciting and informative peek into how it continues to run today. As well as its industrial heritage, the ancient town county town of Stafford is not to be missed for its noble castle ruins – which still provide a dynamic setting for many events throughout the year. For a more peaceful side of the county look no further than the tranquillity of Cannock Chase. Along with the Hednesford Hills, the Chase provides a wonderful open area of woodland and moorland that is one of the county's great recreational areas.

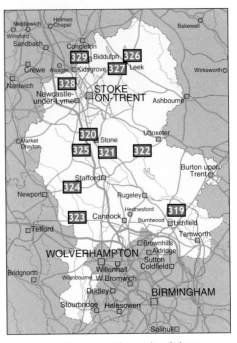

One legacy of the Industrial Revolution and a feature throughout the whole of Staffordshire is the canal network. The motorways of their day, the network linked not only the industrial centres of the county with each other but also with the rest of the country.

The northeast of the county, some of which lies in the Peak District National Park, is an area of undulating moorland that makes ideal walking and cycling country. However, the Industrial Revolution has left its mark here in the form of two great reservoirs – Rudyard and Tittesworth.

Staffordshire is, of course, home to the Potteries, the area around Stoke-on-Trent that is world famous for its pottery industry. The natural resources of coal and clay found here and the foresight of such men as Wedgwood and Minton saw what began as a cottage industry explode into one of the great factory systems of the 18th century. Today the town of Stoke-on-Trent is bustling with this age-old tradition, with many opportunities to see the works of these masters, and to create pottery masterpieces of your own.

Also in the north of the county is a fascinating collection of gardens, each with their own story and character; the fragrant, characteristically English Dorothy Clive Garden is a garden of commemoration created by a grieving Colonel Harry Clive; Trentham Gardens, once the grounds of a great hall, have all the style of Capability Brown and Sir Charles Barry, who both had a hand in its design; and Consall Nature Park is a RSPB reserve of great beauty and importance. Most unusual, however, is the Biddulph Grange, which is exotic to the extreme – taking visitors around the world from Egypt, to the Himalayas, and China, through its imaginative gardens.

Hidden Places of England

Staffordshire

LICHFIELD

Lichfield Cathedral is particularly renowned for the three magnificent spires that dominate the city's skyline. Inside there are many treasures, including the beautiful 8th century illuminated manuscript The Lichfield Gospels and Sir Francis Chantrey's famous sculpture *The Sleeping Children*. The surrounding Cathedral Close is regarded by many as the most original and unspoilt in the country, and, being separated from the rest of the city by Stowe and Minster Pools, it is also a peaceful haven of calm.

Lichfield's most famous son is Dr Samuel Johnson, the poet, novelist and author of the first comprehensive English dictionary. The son of a bookseller, Johnson was born in 1709 in Breadmarket Street, and the house is now the **Samuel Johnson Birthplace Museum**. Another famous son is Erasmus Darwin, the doctor, philosopher, inventor, botanist and poet, and the grandfather of Charles Darwin. **Erasmus Darwin's House** has touch-screen computers to access Darwin's writings and inventions, and a garden with herbs and shrubs that would have been familiar to the good doctor.

The Wall Roman Site, **Letocetum**, has the remains of a bath house and mansion, the most substantial in the country.

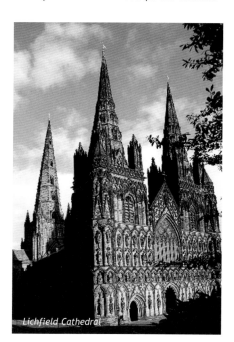

Lichfield Cathedral

AROUND LICHFIELD

ALREWAS

5 miles NE of Lichfield off the A38

The **National Memorial Arboretum**, to the

235

east of this pretty village, is the first large arboretum and wildlife reserve to be created in Britain for 200 years. A substantial grant from the Millennium Commission has transformed this 150-acre former gravel quarry into a sylvan temple whose themes are remembrance and reconciliation. The central feature is the Millennium Avenue, created from cuttings from a 2,000-year-old lime tree.

BURTON UPON TRENT
11 miles NE of Lichfield on the A38

Burton has long been famous for its brewing industry that began many centuries ago - even the monks of the Benedictine Abbey, founded here in 1100, were not the first to realise that Burton well water was specially

Marston's Brewery, Burton upon Trent

319 THE SWAN AT FRADLEY
Fradley Junction, nr Alrewas

This charming canal side inn prides itself on offering all of its guests great traditional home cooked food, real ale and fine wine.

See entry on page 535

suited to brewing. **Marston's Brewery** still exists in the town, and the visitor centre runs informative tours, which end with a pint or two over some food in their traditional style pub.

TUTBURY
13 miles NE of Lichfield on the A511

This historic small town is dominated by the imposing remains of **Tutbury Castle**, where Mary, Queen of Scots, was imprisoned for a while. During the Civil War, Tutbury Castle remained loyal to the Crown while the town was under the control of Parliament. After a three-week siege, the castle surrendered and in the following year, 1647, Parliament ordered its destruction. The substantial ruins make for an eerie sight at night and, for the brave among you, the castle runs brilliantly atmospheric ghost hunting tours through the building and grounds.

TAMWORTH
7 miles SE of Lichfield on the A51

Dominating Tamworth is the fine Norman motte and bailey **Castle** that originally dates from the 1180s. The Town Hall, built in 1701, was paid for by Thomas Guy, the local Member of Parliament, who was the founder of the London hospital that bears his name.

To the south of Tamworth lies **Drayton Manor Family Theme Park**, and further on stands **Middleton Hall**, the former home of Francis Willoughby, a 17th century naturalist and a founder member of the Royal Society.

To the northwest of Tamworth is the village of Whittington that is home to the **Museum of the Staffordshire Regiment** (The Prince of Wales's) at the Victorian Whittington Barracks.

BURNTWOOD
4 miles W of Lichfield on the A5190

The 700 acres of land and water known as **Chasewater Heaths** are an unexpected find in this otherwise urban setting. Criss-crossed by paths and bridleways, it supports many and varied plants and animals, some so rare that a large area has been designated a Site of

Special Scientific Interest. The volunteer-run **Chasewater Railway**, a former colliery railway, operates passenger services behind tank engines between Brownhills West and Norton Lakeside stations.

STAFFORD

The county town of Staffordshire is Saxon in origin, though little of its early history is visible except for the extensive earthworks close to the castle and the foundations of a tiny Saxon chapel in the grounds of **St Mary's Church**. The grounds of the impressive remains of the Norman fortress, **Stafford Castle**, are used for historical re-enactments and also include a medieval herb garden. There is an illuminating visitor centre, with audio-visual displays exploring the castles history. Open air performances of Stafford Festival Shakespeare are run in the summer, with the stunning backdrop of the castle.

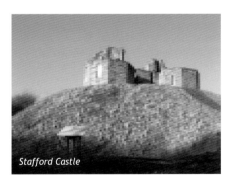
Stafford Castle

One of the most interesting of the many old buildings in Stafford is the **Ancient High House**, a beautiful Elizabethan house built in 1595 that is the largest timber-framed town house in England. It now houses the **Museum of the Staffordshire Yeomanry**, and a heritage shop.

Close to the High House is the **Collegiate Church of St Mary**, an unusual building that dates in part from the late 12th century and was added to in the early English, Gothic and Victorian styles. Sir Izaak Walton was baptised here on 21st September 1593 and his bust can be seen on the north wall of the nave. Each

year, at a civic service, a wreath is placed around the bust to commemorate his probable birthday (9th August).

To the north of Stafford lies the ancestral home of the Earl of Harrowby, **Sandon Hall**, which was rebuilt in 1850 after the earlier house had been damaged by fire.

AROUND STAFFORD

STONE
7 miles N of Stafford on the A51

The Trent and Mersey Canal played a large part in Stone's early economic development and, today, it still brings work to the town through the building of holiday canal cruisers and a growing tourist trade. The beautiful riverside location of the town has produced a thriving continental-style café culture, complimented by the bustling markets.

UTTOXETER
12 miles NE of Stafford on the A518

Today, the town is perhaps best known for its Racecourse, a popular National Hunt track with around 20 days of racing including the stamina-sapping Midlands Grand National held in the spring. Uttoxeter is a traditional, rural

320 LAKESIDE TAVERN
Meaford

Vibrant family run inn serving delicious pub food, fine wine and real ale throughout the day, with a convenient caravan site to the rear.
See entry on page 534

321 THE GREYHOUND INN
Burston

A family run pub serving good quality traditional food and three real ales
See entry on page 536

market town, with a busy livestock and street market on Wednesdays.

GREAT HAYWOOD

5 miles E of Stafford on the A51

This ancient village has the longest packhorse bridge in England. Built in the 16th century, the **Essex Bridge** still has 14 of its original 40 arches spanning the River Trent.

To the southwest lies one of the most impressive attractions in the county, **Shugborough Hall**, the 17th century seat of the Earls of Lichfield. The wonderful staterooms and former servants' quarters have been beautifully restored, and the magnificent 900-acre estate includes **Shugborough Park Farm**, home to rare breed animals and host to demonstrations of traditional farming, as well as a huge range of exciting events run throughout the year.

ABBOTS BROMLEY

10 miles E of Stafford on the B5234

This delightful 13th century village in the Vale of Trent is best known for its annual **Horn Dance**, the origins of which are lost in the mists of time. It is thought that the Horn Dance was first performed at the three-day Bartelmy Fair, granted to the Abbots of Burton by Henry III in 1226 to celebrate St Bartholomew's Day. In early September each year six male dancers carry the ancient reindeer horns around the village with six others and a fool, a hobby horse, a bowman and Maid Marian, the last being a man in drag.

RUGELEY

7½ miles SE of Stafford on the A51

To the west of Rugeley lies **Cannock Chase**, a surprisingly wild 20,000 acres of heath and woodland that has been designated an Area of Outstanding Natural Beauty.

In the unique military cemeteries near **Broadhurst Green**, some 5,000 German soldiers from World War I lie buried. The **Museum of Cannock Chase** at the Valley Heritage Centre illustrates the social and industrial heritage of the area, and there are special exhibits in the Toys Gallery and the Coal Face Gallery.

CANNOCK

9 miles S of Stafford on the A34

To the southwest of Cannock is the Elizabethan **Moseley Old Hall**, which retains much of the original panelling and timber framing. The Hall sheltered King Charles II for a short time following his defeat at the Battle of Worcester in 1651.

WESTON-UNDER-LIZARD

10 miles SW of Stafford on the A5

Situated on the site of a medieval manor house, **Weston Park** has been the home of the Earls of Bradford for 300 years. Disraeli

Shugborough Hall

---

322 **THE GRANGE**

Lower Loxley, nr Uttoxeter

A converted 17th century barn offering the very best in traditional farm house food, hospitality and accommodation

See entry on page 537

---

323 **THE HARTLEY ARMS**

Wheaton Aston

This friendly inn sits in an idyllic location on the banks of the Shropshire Union canal and is known for the excellent quality of traditional food that it serves daily.

See entry on page 538

was a frequent visitor here and on one visit presented the house with a grotesque stuffed parrot, which still enjoys the hospitality of Weston Park.

In the very south of the county, west of Wolverhampton, lies the village of **Perton**, scene of the Tough Guy Challenge. Started in 1987 and held twice a year, it is an eight-mile cross-country run followed by a series of obstacles such as flame pits, barbed wire and underwater tunnels; casualties are not unusual.

Izaak Walton's Cottage, Shallowford

ECCLESHALL

6½ miles NW of Stafford on the A5013

For over 1,000 years **Eccleshall Castle** was the palace of the bishops of Lichfield before becoming a family home when the Carter family moved from Yorkshire. The present simple sandstone house is typical of the best architecture of the William and Mary period and incorporates part of the 14th century castle.

A little way north of Eccleshall is **Mill Meece Pumping Station**, where two magnificent steam engines are kept in pristine condition. An exhibition tells the story of water and the history of the station.

Set in beautiful grounds in the tiny hamlet of **Shallowford**, to the northeast of

Eccleshall, is **Izaak Walton's Cottage**, a pretty 17th century half-timbered cottage that was once owned by the famous biographer and author of *The Compleat Angler* and is now a museum.

LEEK

William Morris, founder of the Arts and Crafts movement, lived and worked in Leek for many months between 1875 and 1878 and much of his time here was spent investigating new techniques of dyeing while also reviving the use of traditional dyes. **Leek Art Gallery** has displays on the intricate work of the famous Leek School of Embroidery that was founded by Lady Wardle in the 1870s.

Leek was the home of James Brindley, the 18th century engineer who built much of the early canal network. A water-powered corn mill built by him in 1752 in Mill Street has been restored and now houses the **Brindley Water Museum**, which is devoted to his life and work.

To the northwest of Leek is the village of **Rudyard**, the name chosen for their son by Mr and Mrs Kipling in fond memory of the place

---

324 THE HORNS INN

Gnosall

A friendly village pub and restaurant serving good quality traditional food.

See entry on page 539

---

325 LABOUR IN VAIN

Yarnfield, nr Stone

A traditional English village pub set in the heart of the community and offering good value, locally sourced food.

See entry on page 539

---

326 THE BUTTERCROSS CAFÉ

Leek

Renowned for serving the best homemade cakes in town this charming café is centrally located and also serves up a good range of breakfasts and light lunches.

See entry on page 540

---

where they first met in 1863. The west shore of the reservoir is a section of the Staffordshire Way, the long distance footpath that runs from Mow Cop to Kinver Edge, near Stourbridge.

AROUND LEEK

LONGNOR

8½ miles NE of Leek on the B5053

Found on a gentle slope between the River Manifold and the River Dove, Longnor was the meeting point of several packhorse routes. The **Market Square** is one of the oldest in England, dating back to medieval times. The village also has some fascinating narrow flagged passages that seem to go nowhere but suddenly emerge into the most beautiful scenery.

FROGHALL

6½ miles SE of Leek on the A52

To the southeast of this once-busy port for transporting limestone, lies **Hawksmoor Nature Reserve** and bird sanctuary that covers some 300 acres of the Churnet Valley and includes glorious landscapes, abundant natural history and industrial architecture.

CROXDEN

12 miles SE of Leek off the B5032

Tucked away in this secluded hamlet are the romantic ruins of **Croxden Abbey**, founded by the Cistercians in 1176. Although only the west front, south transept wall and a few of the eastern cloisters remain, the Abbey is well worth a visit.

CHEDDLETON

3 miles S of Leek on the A520

As well as being home to the **Churnet Valley Railway and Museum**, this village is also home to the restored Cheddleton Flint Mill, which lies in the rural surroundings of the Churnet valley. The small museum includes a rare 18th century 'haystack' boiler and a Robey steam engine, and there are also exhibits that relate to the preparation of raw materials for the pottery industry

To the south, **Consall Nature Park** is an RSPB reserve, a quiet and peaceful haven with much to delight the avid birdwatcher.

STOKE-ON-TRENT

It was the presence of the essential raw materials for the manufacture and decoration of ceramics, in particular marl clay, coal and water, which led to the concentration of pottery manufacturers in this area. Though production started in the 17th century, it was the entrepreneurial skills of Josiah Wedgwood and Thomas Minton, who brought the individual potters together in factory-style workplaces, that caused the massive leap forward in production in the 18th century. There were also hundreds of small establishments producing a whole range of more utilitarian chinaware; production in The Potteries reached its height towards the end of the 19th century.

Among the many centres and museums telling the story of Stoke and pottery are the **Royal Doulton Visitor Centre**, the **Gladston**

327 THE HOLLYBUSH INN

Denford, nr Leek

A charming inn serving traditional homemade food and up to six real ales with a picturesque canal-side location.

See entry on page 542

Etruria, Stoke-on-Trent

Pottery Museum and the **Wedgwood Visitor Centre and Museum**. The **Potteries Museum and Art Gallery** houses the world's finest collection of Staffordshire ceramics; and, of course, there is much opportunity to get messy and create your own pottery masterpieces throughout the town.

Etruria, to the west of the city centre, was created by Josiah Wedgwood in 1769 as a village for the workers at the pottery factory. Though the factory has gone (it moved to Barlaston in the 1940s), **Etruria Hall**, Wedgwood's home, is still standing in what is now the National Garden Festival site.

To the south of Stoke-on-Trent are **Trentham Gardens** that were landscaped by Capability Brown and given a more formal style by Sir Charles Barry, whose work can be seen in the lovely Italian gardens. Although the Hall was demolished in 1911, this style can still be recognised in such buildings as the orangery and sculpture gallery.

AROUND STOKE-ON-TRENT

NEWCASTLE-UNDER-LYME
2 miles W of Stoke-on-Trent on the A53

One of Newcastle-under-Lyme's oldest buildings is the **Guildhall**, built in 1713 to replace an earlier timber building, which stands beside the base of a medieval cross. The **Borough Museum and Art Gallery**, set in eight acres of parkland, houses a wonderful collection of assorted items from clocks to teapots and paintings to clay pipes. A mile from the town centre, the **New Victoria Theatre** was Europe's first purpose-built 'theatre-in-the-round'.

To the southwest, on an ancient packhorse route from Newcastle-under-Lyme, is the village of **Madeley**, much of which has been designated a conservation area. Its charming focal point is The Pool, formed by damming the River Lea to provide waterpower for the corn mill, and now a haven for birds. Further southwest again is the quintessentially English **Dorothy Clive Garden** that was designed in the 1930s by Colonel Harry Clive in memory of his wife.

BIDDULPH
5 miles N of Stoke-on-Trent on the A527

The gardens at **Biddulph Grange** (National Trust) are among the most unusual and remarkable in the whole country. The numerous high points include the Egyptian garden with a pyramid and clipped yew obelisks, and the Chinese garden features a joss house, a dragon parterre, a temple and a watch tower. The parterres and the Shelter House and Dahlia Walk have been restored to the way they were in the middle of the 19th century.

Biddulph Grange

---

328 PLOUGH INN

Bignall End

A superb village inn with a strong focus on traditional homemade food with up to seven real ales available at any one time.

See entry on page 541

---

329 CHESHIRE VIEW

Mow Cop

With unrivalled views across the Cheshire Plains, this charming 300 hundred year old pub offers friendly service, great food and accommodation.

See entry on page 543

SUFFOLK

For much of its length the River Stour forms the county boundary between Suffolk and Essex, and here lies some of the county's most attractive and peaceful countryside. The beauty is largely unspoilt and those travelling through the area will come upon a succession of picturesque, ancient wool towns and villages, historic churches, stately homes and nature reserves.

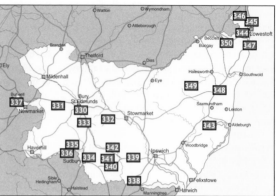

There is the wonderful preserved medieval town of Lavenham, the atmospheric old wool town of Long Melford and, of course, East Bergholt. This was the birthplace, in 1776, of John Constable, and two of his most famous subjects – Flatford Mill and Willy Lot's Cottage – can still be seen today looking much as they would have done in the great artist's day.

Much of inland Suffolk remains rich farmland, with ancient towns and villages along with some of the finest windmills and watermills in the country. The little market towns of Stowmarket and Needham Market are full of interest, and in this part of the county some of the best-preserved windmills and watermills are to be found.

While Suffolk has few equals in terms of picturesque countryside and settlements, it is also very much a maritime county, with more than 50 miles of coastline. The whole stretch is a conservation area, with miles of waymarked walks and cycle trails and an abundance of bird and wildlife. This coast has also been a constant source of inspiration for distinguished writers, artists and musicians. Between the major port of Ipswich in the south and the fishing port of Lowestoft in the north are some charming and popular seaside resorts, such as Southwold and Aldeburgh, which have tried their hardest to escape any brash commercialism and retain the charming and genteel atmosphere of a bygone age. The whole of this coastal stretch is known as the "Sunrise Coast", due to its easterly direction (those eager enough can rise early to witness some of the most beautiful sunrises to be seen in England).

The southeast of the coast is dotted with Martello Towers, built due to the treat of Napoleonic invasion. Today Aldeburgh's at Slaughden is the most northerly (and the largest) left standing, while the tower at Shoreham in Sussex the southernmost.

BURY ST EDMUNDS

This glorious Suffolk town takes its name from St Edmund, who was born in AD 841 and came here as a young man to become the last king of East Anglia and the patron saint of England before St George. A staunch Christian, he was tortured and killed by the Danes in AD 870 and, after he was canonised in AD 910, his remains were moved to the abbey at Beodricsworth (later St Edmundsbury) where his shrine became incorporated into the Norman Abbey Church. The town grew up around the Abbey and soon became an important place of pilgrimage.

The **Abbey** was dismantled after the Dissolution but the imposing remains can be seen in the colourful **Abbey Gardens** beyond the splendid **Abbey Gate** and Norman Tower. Originally the Church of St James, **St**

Abbey Gardens, Bury St Edmunds

Edmundsbury Cathedral was accorded cathedral status in 1914 and the 15th century building has been added to over the years. The latest work was a Millennium project to crown the Cathedral with a 140 feet Gothic-style lantern tower. Also in the complex is **St Mary's Church**, whose detached tower stands just as it did when erected in the 12th century. The **Abbey Visitor Centre**, situated in Samson's Tower, has displays concerning the abbey's history.

There are many fine buildings throughout the town; among the most interesting are the Victorian **Corn Exchange** with its imposing colonnade; the **Athenaeum**, hub of social life since Regency times and scene of Charles Dickens's public readings; **Cupola House**, where Daniel Defoe once stayed; the **Angel Hotel**, where Dickens and his marvellous

330 THE CABIN

Bury St Edmunds

A warm welcome and homemade dishes await visitors to this hidden gem

See entry on page 542

creation Mr Pickwick stayed. Along with its beautiful buildings, there are many other places of interest in Bury, including museums, galleries and the **Theatre Royal**. Built in 1819 by William Wilkins, who was responsible for the National Gallery, and recently magnificently restored, it is still very much a working theatre.

To the southwest, near **Horringer**, stands the extraordinary **Ickworth House**. Built in 1795 by the eccentric 4th Earl of Bristol, the massive structure comprises a central rotunda and curved corridors; it was designed to house his various collections that include paintings by Titian, Gainsborough, Hogarth and Reynolds and a magnificent collection of Georgian silver. The house is surrounded by an Italian garden and a park landscaped by Capability Brown.

Ickworth House, Horringer

AROUND BURY ST EDMUNDS

IXWORTH

6 miles NE of Bury St Edmunds on the A143

This is superb walking country and **Knettishall**

Parish Church, Walsham-le-Willows

Heath Country Park, close to the border village of **Barningham**, is the official starting point of the **Peddars Way National Trail**. Nearby is the pretty village of **Walsham-le-Willows** with its weatherboarded and timber-framed cottages and its ancient parish church.

WOOLPIT

7½ miles E of Bury St Edmunds off the A14

Famous for its bricks, the majority of the old buildings here are faced with 'Woolpit Whites', the yellowish-white brick that looked very much like more expensive stone. Some of the brick was used in the building of the senate wing of the Capitol in Washington DC. Red bricks were also produced and the village's **Bygones Museum**, open in summer, includes a brick-making display.

A charming Woolpit legend concerns the Green Children, a brother and sister with green complexions who appeared one day in a field, apparently attracted by the church bells. Though obviously hungry, they would eat nothing until some green beans were produced. The boy survived for only a short

331 THE WEEPING WILLOW	**332** THE FIVE BELLS
Barrow	*Rattlesden*
This grade II listed inn is home to live music, delicious home cooked food and a range of quality real ales. 	This pub dates back to the 1700s and serves three real ales, which are popular with locals and visitors. 
See entry on page 542	*See entry on page 544*

Hidden Places of England · *Suffolk*

time, but the girl thrived, lost her green colour and was baptised and married a man from King's Lynn – no doubt leaving many a Suffolk man green with envy!

To the southeast is the group of villages collectively known as **The Bradfields** – St George, St Clare and Combust – that lie in a particularly delightful part of the countryside. Here, too, are **Bradfield Woods**, which have been managed by coppicing for hundreds of years.

LAVENHAM

10½ miles SE of Bury St Edmunds on the A1141

Lavenham is the most complete of all the original medieval wool towns. The medieval street pattern still exists, along with the market place and cross, and the finest of its many listed buildings is the superb 16th century timbered **Guildhall** (National Trust) which was originally the meeting place of the Guild of Corpus Christi, an organisation that regulated the production of wool. **Little Hall** is hardly less remarkable, a 15th century hall house with a superb crown post roof.

Originally a 13th century home for

Lavenham Guildhall

Benedictine monks, **The Priory** is now a beautiful half-timbered house dating from around 1600 and, in the original hall, is an important collection of paintings and stained glass whilst the extensive grounds include a kitchen garden, herb garden and a pond.

John Constable went to school in Lavenham and one of his school friends was Jane Taylor, who wrote the words to *Twinkle, Twinkle Little Star*.

SUDBURY

The largest of the wool towns and once a busy port on the River Stour. Along with its three medieval churches, Sudbury is famous as being the birthplace, in 1727, of the painter Thomas Gainsborough; **Gainsborough's House** has more of the artist's work on display than any other gallery. Other buildings of interest are the Victorian **Corn Exchange**, now a library; **Salter's Hall**, a 15th century timbered house; and the **Quay Theatre**, a thriving centre for the arts.

Northwest of Sudbury lies the attractive village of **Cavendish** where, housed in a 16th century rectory, the **Sue Ryder Foundation Museum** was opened by the Queen in 1979. Further upriver lies the medieval wool town

334 WAGGON AND HORSES

Sudbury

This handsome and historic inn in the centre of Sudbury offers accommodation, home cooking and a selection of quality real ales.

See entry on page 545

333 THE METCALFE ARMS

Hawstead

Traditional village inn that prides itself on serving up restaurant quality food at pub prices.

See entry on page 544

335 THE BLACK LION

Glemsford

Newly opened family orientated inn at the heart of its community, dedicated to serving top quality food at affordable prices.

See entry on page 545

of **Clare**, 'a little town with a lot of history' that is renowned for its **Ancient House**, a timber-framed building dating from 1473 noted for its remarkable pargeting. Another place of historical significance is **Nethergate House**, once the workplace of dyers, weaver and spinners. **Clare Castle Country Park** contains the remains of the castle and moat and has a visitors' centre in the goods shed of a disused railway line.

AROUND SUDBURY

LONG MELFORD

2 miles N of Sudbury off the A134

The heart of this atmospheric old wool town is its long and, in places, fairly broad main street filled with antique shops, bookshops and art galleries. Some of the town's houses are washed in the characteristic Suffolk pink that was originally created by mixing ox blood or sloe juice into the plaster. At the northern end of the street lies a 14-acre green and also **Holy Trinity Church**, an exuberant manifestation of the prosperity of the town in ages past.

Edmund Blunden lived in Long Melford from 1965 to 1974 and is buried in the churchyard – his grave reading the fitfully poetic lines *'I live still to love still things quiet and unconcerned.'*

To the east of the town lies 16th century **Melford Hall**, whose attractions include the panelled banqueting hall where Elizabeth I was entertained and a Beatrix Potter room where some of her watercolours and first editions of her books are on display. She was a frequent visitor to the house as her cousins,

the Hyde Parkers, were the then owners. Further north is **Kentwell Hall**, a beautiful moated Tudor mansion.

HAVERHILL

15 miles W of Sudbury on the A1307

Although fire destroyed much of the town in 1665, **Anne of Cleves House**, (where the fourth wife of Henry VIII spent the remainder of her days), has been restored. **Haverhill Local History Centre**, in the Town Hall, has an interesting collection of memorabilia, including over 6,000 photographs, dating from 1860. To the northeast lies **Kedington**, home to the 'Cathedral of West Suffolk', the **Church of St Peter and St Paul**.

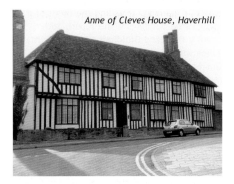
Anne of Cleves House, Haverhill

NEWMARKET

The historic centre of British horse racing, Newmarket is home to some 60 training establishments, 50 stud farms, the world famous thoroughbred sales and two racecourses. The majority of the population is involved in racing in one way or another and,

---

336 **THE PINKUAH ARMS**

Pinkuah

Bustling and popular local inn known for its range of fine wines, real ales and delicious food which stems from its owners' Italian roots.

See entry on page 546

---

337 **THE WHEATSHEAF INN**

Exning

Charming 17th century coaching inn offering excellent home-cooked food, real ales and quality en suite accommodation.

See entry on page 547

among the racing art and artefact shops and galleries, there are the saddlers – one even has a preserved horse on display - Robert the Devil, the runner-up in the 1880 Derby. The **National Horseracing Museum** chronicles the history of the sport from its royal beginnings through to the top trainers and jockeys of today. Close by is **Palace House**, which contains the remains of Charles II's palace, while in the same street is **Nell Gwynn's House** that some say was connected to the palace by an underground tunnel.

To the southeast of Newmarket is the pretty village of **Dalham**, where the vast majority of the buildings are still thatched. The village is also the home of **Dalham Hall** which was built in the early 18th century on the orders of the Bishop of Ely, and was the home of the Duke of Wellington for several years.

AROUND NEWMARKET

MILDENHALL

9 miles NE of Newmarket on the A11

For an insight into the town's heritage, the excellent **Mildenhall and District Museum** contains a wealth of local history exhibits, including the artefacts from the nearby RAF and USAAF base and the story of the **Mildenhall Treasure**, a cache of 4th century Roman silverware found by a ploughman in 1946 and now in the British Museum. This parish is the largest in Suffolk and it is fitting that it also boasts the magnificent **Church of St Mary**, which dominates the heart of the town.

WEST STOW

9 miles NE of Newmarket off the A1101

In 1849, a Saxon cemetery was discovered here and further excavations have revealed traces of a Roman settlement and the Saxon layout of this village. Several buildings have been constructed using 5th century tools and methods and this fascinating village is now part of the **West Stow Country Park**.

IPSWICH

A Roman port and the largest in Anglo Saxon Britain, Ipswich prospered on the exportation of wool, textiles and agricultural products. Of the great Victorian buildings here the most memorable are the **Old Custom House**, the **Town Hall** and the splendid **Tolly Cobbold Brewery**, rebuilt at the end of the 19th century. **Christchurch Mansion** survives from an older age, a beautiful Tudor home in glorious parkland, with a major collection of works by, most notably, Constable and Gainsborough. The town's **Museum** displays a wealth of exhibits from natural history through to a reconstructed Roman villa, while the **Ipswich Transport Museum** concerns itself with vehicles both mechanical and self-propelled.

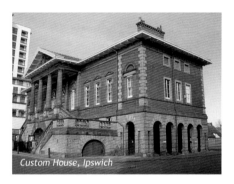

Custom House, Ipswich

The town's most famous son is undoubtedly Thomas Wolsey, who was born here in 1475 and who went on to become Lord Chancellor under Henry VIII.

On the outskirts of the town lies **Orwell Country Park**, an area of wood, heath and reed beds by the Orwell estuary. (George Orwell, born Eric Blair, took his name from the river; he often stayed with his parents in Southwold.)

Three miles south of Ipswich stands a tall, slender redbrick tower. Perhaps it is just a folly, perhaps a look-out tower, but the favourite story is that **Freston's Tower** was built by Lord de Freston as a place of study for his daughter Ellen, with a different one-room storey for each subject that filled her day: charity, tapestry, music, literature and astronomy.

AROUND IPSWICH

HELMINGHAM

8 miles N of Ipswich on the B1077

This village is home to the grand **Helmingham Hall**, a moated Tudor house, and there's another moated hall in the nearby village of **Otley**, the home of Bartholomew Gosnold, who sailed to the New World, discovered Cape Cod and founded the settlement of Jamestown, Virginia.

WOODBRIDGE

7 miles NE of Ipswich on the A12

A market town for over 1,000 years, Woodbridge stands at the head of the Deben estuary and is a place of considerable charm, character and history. Shipbuilding flourished here and it was in a Woodbridge ship that Sir Francis Drake sailed in the 16th century.

The town's splendid Shire Hall now houses the **Suffolk Horse Museum** which is devoted to the Suffolk Punch breed of heavy working horse – the oldest such breed in the world. Other buildings of note are the town's two marvellous mills, both still in working order – **Tide Mill** dates from the late 18th century and uses the power of the sea to turn its wheels and **Buttrum's Mill**, named after the last miller, is a tower mill standing just west of the town centre.

Burial Chamber Reconstruction, Sutton Hoo

On the opposite bank of the River Deben, lies **Sutton Hoo**, a group of a dozen grassy barrows that hit the headlines in 1939 when excavations unearthed the outline of an 80 feet long Saxon ship filled with a great hoard of treasure. It is believed that the ship was the burial place of Raedwald, a King of East Anglia who died in about AD 625. This is one of the most important archaeological sites in the country, and the National Trust provides impressive facilities for visitors.

ORFORD

16½ miles NE of Ipswich on the B1084

Although the keep is all that remains of Henry II's **Castle**, it remains an impressive sight and the climb up the spiral staircase provides some splendid views. The Castle and the grand 14th century **St Bartholomew's Church** are a reminder that Orford was once an important town and a thriving port until the steadily growing shingle bank of Orford Ness gradually cut it off from the sea.

Though the sea has gone the river remains and, in the summer, the quayside is alive with yachts and pleasure craft. Across the other side of the river lies **Orford Ness**, the largest vegetated shingle spit in England and home to a variety of rare flora and fauna as well as a lighthouse. Now owned by the National Trust, the Ness can be reached by ferry, and there are also boat trips to the RSPB reserve of **Havergate Island**, the haunt of avocet and tern.

FELIXSTOWE

10 miles SE of Ipswich on the A14

The original fishing hamlet from which the Victorian town was developed is now called **Felixstowe Ferry** – a cluster of holiday homes, fishing sheds and a Martello Tower.

The southernmost tip of this peninsula is **Landguard Point** where a nature reserve supports rare plants and migrating birds. Close by is **Landguard Fort**, which was built in 1718 to protect Harwich Harbour, and is now home to the **Felixstowe Museum** with its displays of local history, model aircraft and model paddle steamers.

Willy Lott's Cottage, Flatford

EAST BERGHOLT

9 miles SW of Ipswich on the B1070

It was in this picturesque village that John Constable was born and, although his actual house is no longer standing, the site is marked by a plaque. Close by is Moss Cottage, which he once used as his studio, and the parish **Church of St Mary**, which contains memorials to Constable, his family and his friends.

A leafy lane leads south from the village to the River Stour and two of Constable's favourite subjects, **Flatford Mill** and **Willy Lot's Cottage**. At nearby **Flatford**, **Bridge Cottage** houses a Constable display. The Constable Trail starts in the village, and carries on all the way to Dedham in Essex.

The villages of Capel St Mary, Brantham and Stratford St Mary all have links with Constable, and it was in Stratford that Henry Williamson, author of *Tarka the Otter*, saw his first otter.

NAYLAND

14 miles SW of Ipswich on the B1087

A charming village found on a particularly beautiful stretch of the River Stour, Nayland

has two fine 15th century buildings – **Alston Court** and the **Guildhall** – while its original 15th century wooden Abels Bridge was replaced a century later by a humped-back bridge that allowed barges to pass underneath.

HADLEIGH

8½ miles W of Ipswich on the B1070

This once prosperous wool town has a harmonious variety of architectural styles – from timber-framed buildings to elegant Regency and Victorian houses – but the gem here is the 15th century **Guildhall** with its two overhanging storeys.

There are two good walks from Hadleigh: over the medieval Toppesfield Bridge and along the River Brett; and along the disused railway track between the town and Raydon to the south.

339 THE ORANGERIE

Hadleigh

Home cooked food and warm hospitality awaits visitors to The Orangerie, which is well known for its delicious food and cakes.

See entry on page 548

340 THE FOX AND HOUNDS

Groton

Vibrant family run inn perched on a scenic village location. Known for its traditional menu of fine English cuisine, the inn is popular throughout the year.

See entry on page 548

338 FOUNTAIN HOUSE TEA ROOM

East Bergholt

A popular tea room serving the very best in homemade cakes, pastries, sandwiches and traditional meals.

See entry on page 547

341 EDWARDSTONE WHITE HORSE

Edwardstone

In the midst of the idyllic Suffolk countryside is this popular inn offering delicious homemade organic food, fine ale from its onsite brewery and self catering accommodation.

See entry on page 549

To the northwest is the photogenic postcard village of **Kersey**, whose main street has a Water Splash; this and the 700-year-old Bell Inn have featured in many films. Nearby, every year in the unspoilt village of Chelsworth, the garden-proud community opens up their delightful gardens to the public.

STOWMARKET
11 miles NW of Ipswich on the A14

In the heart of Suffolk, Stowmarket enjoyed a period of rapid growth when the River Gipping was still navigable to Ipswich, and again when the railway arrived. Much of the town's history is brought to life at the **Museum of East Anglian Life** which is surrounded by meadowland on the old Abbot's Hall estate, where the aisled barn dates from the 13th century. Serious scenic walkers should make for the **Gipping Valley River Park Walk**, which follows the former towpath all the way to Ipswich.

At **Stonham Barns**, to the east of Stowmarket, is the **Suffolk Owl Sanctuary**, as well as a golf course, fishing lake and local arts and crafts shops.

ALDEBURGH
24 miles NE of Ipswich on the A1094

This is yet another town that had flourishing fishing and shipbuilding industries – Drake's *Greyhound* and *Pelican* were built at Slaughden, which was long ago taken by the sea. This village was also the birthplace, in 1754, of the poet George Crabbe, who created the character Peter Grimes, a solitary fisherman, who later became the subject of an opera by another Aldeburgh resident, Benjamin Britten. It was Britten who, in 1948, started the **Aldeburgh Festival**, a world-

Snape Maltings Concert Hall

renowned arts festival based mainly at **The Maltings** at nearby **Snape**.

The most interesting of Aldeburgh's older buildings is the **Moot Hall**, a 16th century timber-framed hall which has a little museum of the town's history. Aldeburgh also has a Martello Tower, built in 1814; it never saw action, though its guns were manned until the middle of the 19th century.

Benjamin Britten's grave, along with those of his friend Peter Pears and Imogen Holst, is in the churchyard of **St Peter and St Paul**; the latest tribute to Britten is a huge metal clam shell designed by Maggie Hambling. The words on its rim – 'I hear those voices that will not be drowned' – are taken from Britten's opera *Peter Grimes*. It stands on the beach between Aldeburgh and the unique holiday village of **Thorpeness** with its mock-Tudor houses and the general look of an eccentric film set. Inland, the busy town of **Leiston** is home to the fascinating **Long Shop Museum**, once the works of the renowned Garrett engineering works. Back along the coast is what remains of the one-time capital of East Anglia, **Dunwich**, which over the centuries was claimed by the sea. **Dunwich Heath** is one of Suffolk's most important conservation areas, while nearby **Minsmere**, best reached through the village of Westleton, is a marvellous RSPB sanctuary.

---

342 THE RED LION

Bildeston

A lively village pub serving reasonably priced home cooked food and three real ales

See entry on page 550

---

343 THE SHIP INN AT BLAXHALL

Blaxhall

A true taste of the country is offered at this village inn, serving traditional homemade food and seafood, with separate luxury chalet accommodation available.

See entry on page 551

LOWESTOFT

The most easterly town in Britain, Lowestoft's heyday as a major fishing port came during the late 19th and early 20th centuries. Now a popular holiday resort, its main attractions are its lovely golden sands, safe swimming and two piers - one of these, **Claremont Pier**, built in 1902, was a landing place for daytrippers arriving on the famous Belle steamers.

The history of the town and its links with the sea are detailed in the **Lowestoft and East Suffolk Maritime Museum** and, nearby, the **Royal Naval Patrol Museum** remembers the minesweeping service.

Just north of the town is the largest theme park in East Anglia, **Pleasurewood Hills**. A little further afield lies **Somerleyton Hall**, one of the country's grandest and most distinctive stately homes, built in the Italian style by Samuel Morton Peto. Along with magnificent wood carvings and notable paintings, the grounds include a renowned yew-hedge maze created in 1846, a little miniature railway and, still part of the estate, **Fritton Lake Countryworld**.

Close by is **Herringfleet Windmill**, a beautiful black-tarred smock mill which is the last survivor of the Broadland wind pumps whose job it was to assist in draining the marshes. A little way south of Lowestoft, at

Carlton Colville, is the **East Anglia Transport Museum** where visitors can enjoy rides on buses, trams and trolleybuses. Further south again is the small resort of **Kessingland**, the home of the **Africa Alive! Wildlife Park**; 100 acres of coastal parkland, thriving with a huge variety of the protected exotic animals of Africa.

AROUND LOWESTOFT

SOUTHWOLD

10 miles S of Lowestoft on the A1095

The most interesting building at this civilised seaside resort is **Buckenham House** which, despite its classic Georgian exterior, actually dates from the mid 16th century and was built for a wealthy Tudor merchant. Many features from that age survive, including the brickwork and heavy timbered ceilings.

The town's maritime heritage is recorded in the **Museum**, which is housed in a Dutch-style cottage, and in the **Sailors Reading Room**. The resort also has traditional bathing huts, and a brilliant white **Lighthouse** that's over 100 years old. It stands 100 feet tall and its light can be seen 17 miles out to sea.

On the other side of the River Blyth is **Walberswick** which was also once a

---

344 THE RED HERRING BAR AND RESTAURANT

Lowestoft

A popular restaurant, renowned far and wide for its fine cuisine.

See entry on page 552

---

346 THE VILLAGE MAID

Lound

A picturesque village pub serving good quality traditional cuisine

See entry on page 554

---

345 THE WHITE HORSE

Corton

A popular pub and restaurant serving an excellent blend of freshly prepared family favourites, pub classics and elegant restaurant style dishes

See entry on page 553

---

347 THE WATERFRONT

Kessingland

A popular seaside restaurant with an extensive menu of continental and modern English cuisine.

See entry on page 555

---

flourishing fishing port. Today, it is best known for its bird sanctuary, Walberswick and Westleton Heaths. Inland lies one of the wonders of Suffolk, the **Church of the Holy Trinity** at **Blythburgh** that rises from the reed beds and is visible for miles around. Dubbed the 'Cathedral of the Marshes', its grandeur reflects the days when Blythburgh was a prosperous port until the river silted up.

HALESWORTH

14 miles SW of Lowestoft on the A144

An ancient market town, Halesworth reached its peak as a trading place when the River Blyth was made navigable as far as here in 1756. Along with some fine architecture the chief attraction here is the **Halesworth and District Museum**, housed in the town's station buildings.

FRAMLINGHAM

25 miles SW of Lowestoft on the B1119

This old market town is dominated by the **Castle** that was built by Roger Bigod, 2nd Earl of Norfolk, in the 12th century. Still in remarkably good condition, nine of the castle's 13 towers are accessible and, on one side, the view is of a noted bird sanctuary. In the north wing is the **Lanman Museum**, devoted to agricultural, craftsman's tools and

Framlingham Castle

domestic memorabilia.

On the village green at **Saxtead Green** is a particularly attractive white 18th century **Post Mill** which dates back to 1796 and is, arguably, the best example of such a mill in the world.

BECCLES

8 miles W of Lowestoft on the A145

One of the few buildings to survive the fires that ravaged Beccles in the 16th and 17th centuries is **Roos Hall**, a gabled Dutch-style building dating from 1583. Another Dutch-style building houses the **Beccles and District Museum**.

Nearby is the **Moo Play Farm** – an attraction which proves endlessly delightful for children up to 12 years old.

BUNGAY

13½ miles W of Lowestoft on the A144

An ancient town on the River Waveney, Bungay is best known for its **Castle**, which was built by Hugh Bigod, 1st Earl of Norfolk, as a rival to Henry II's castle at Orford. It was another Bigod, Roger, who came to Bungay in 1294 and built the round tower and mighty outer walls that still stand today. At **Flixton** is the **Norfolk and Suffolk Aviation Museum** which stands on the site of the USAAF Liberator base of World War II.

---

348 **THE HALF WAY CAFÉ**

Darsham

Homely café in Darsham popular near and far for its range of homemade breakfasts and meals created using locally sourced produce and meats.

See entry on page 556

---

349 **THE KINGS HEAD (THE LOW HOUSE)**

Laxfield

True olde worlde thatched pub that really understands the meaning of atmosphere, serving great English food and real ale year round.

See entry on page 557

---

350 **THE RINGSFIELD HORSESHOES**

Ringsfield

A picturesque village inn, surrounded by the Suffolk countryside, serving fine food and real ales

See entry on page 556

SURREY

Although the northern part of Surrey, which once ran all the way up to the south bank of the River Thames through the capital, has seemingly been engulfed by Greater London, this is an area rich in stately homes, notably the most magnificent royal palace of all – Hampton Court.

In among this prosperous commuter land there are also several excellent racecourses, including Epsom, home of The Derby and The Oaks. The influence of London is soon lost as the countryside to the south and west gives way to leafy lanes, green fields and two famous natural features – the Hog's Back and the Devil's Punch Bowl.

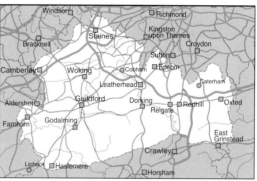

Guildford, the county town of Surrey, is home to one of only two Anglican cathedrals built in England since the Reformation – the other is in Liverpool. While many travel through the county on their way to the south coast, it is well worth pausing here and taking in the quintessentially English villages, such as Chiddingfold, the old Georgian market towns of Godalming and Farnham, and the genteel Victorian towns such as Haslemere that developed with the arrival of the railway.

For those who require convincing of Surrey's natural beauty, you need look no further than the impressive range of stunning gardens and parks throughout the county. The 2,400 acres of open land at Richmond Park is roamed by noble deer; Claremont Landscape Garden has been created over the years by the greatest names in gardens, each infusing it with their own style and passion; the RHS's Wisley Garden in internationally admired; and there is the dramatic vision of Leith Hill, rising 965 feet above sea level, and whose southern face is covered with a glorious Rhododendron wood planted by the famous potter Wedgwood's grandson, Josiah.

WEYBRIDGE

A surprisingly old settlement on the River Wey, this town once possessed a palace, Oatlands Park, where, in 1540, Henry VIII married his fifth wife, Catherine Howard. In 1907, the world's first purpose-built motor racing track was constructed on the nearby **Brooklands** estate and, although racing on this world-famous banked circuit came to an end with the outbreak of World War I, the old Edwardian clubhouse still stands, home to the **Brooklands Museum**.

AROUND WEYBRIDGE

RICHMOND

9 miles NE of Weybridge on the A316

Situated on a sweeping bend on the River Thames, the older part of this charming town is centred on **Richmond Green**, a genuine village green. Handsome 17th and 18th century houses flank the southern edges of the green, while the southwestern side was the site of 12th century Richmond Palace, where Elizabeth I died in 1603.

Richmond Hill leads upwards from the town centre and commands breathtaking views that both Turner and Reynolds have captured. A little further up the hill is an entrance to **Richmond Park**, some 2,400 acres of open land on which deer roam.

KINGSTON UPON THAMES

7 miles NE of Weybridge on the A308

Kingston was a thriving medieval market town and ancient and modern buildings can be found side by side; close to the functional 1930s Guildhall is the **Coronation Stone**, which is said to have been used in the crowning of at least six Saxon kings.

A couple of miles southwest of Kingston lies one of the most magnificent royal residences, **Hampton Court**, which was built in 1516 by Cardinal Wolsey, Henry VIII's Lord Chancellor. After Wolsey's fall from power, the palace came into royal possession and the buildings and magnificent gardens seen today are the work of Henry VIII, Charles II and William III. The most famous feature in the 60 acres of grounds is undoubtedly the Maze, first planted in 1713.

Hampton Court, Kingston Upon Thames

ESHER

4½ miles E of Weybridge off the A3

The town has an excellent racecourse, **Sandown Park**, and is also home to the beautiful **Claremont Landscape Garden** (National Trust), begun in 1715 and believed to be one of the earliest surviving examples of an English landscape garden. Over the years, some of the greatest names in garden history were involved in its creation, including Capability Brown, John Vanbrugh and Charles Bridgeman.

COBHAM

4 miles SE of Weybridge on the A245

A busy residential town, Cobham has a **Bus Museum** with the largest collection anywhere of London buses. To the north lies 19th century **Foxwarren Park**, a bizarre house with eerie gables and multi-coloured bricks, while to the west is **Painshill Park**, a white 18th century house with particularly fine grounds. Just beyond Painshill, on Chatley Heath, is a unique Semaphore Tower that was once part of the Royal Navy's signalling system for relaying messages between Portsmouth and the Admiralty in London.

WOKING

6 miles SW of Weybridge on the A320

Amidst the largely Victorian buildings in this commuter town is the **Shah Jehan Mosque**, the first purpose built mosque in Britain.

To the east of Woking is the Royal Horticultural Society's internationally renowned **Wisley Garden**; one of the finest of its kind in the world.

LIGHTWATER

9½ miles SW of Weybridge on the A322

For many Londoners, Lightwater represents the first taste of countryside from the metropolis. The visitor centre at **Lightwater Country Park** has a fascinating collection of exhibits about the history and natural history of this area of heath and woodland.

VIRGINIA WATER

6 miles NW of Weybridge on the B389

The water referred to here is a large artificial lake that is set within the mature woodland at the southern end of Windsor Great Park. The picturesque ruins on the lakeside are the genuine remains of a Roman temple that once stood at Leptis Magna in Libya and the Valley Gardens contain an unusual 100 feet totem pole that was erected here in 1958 to mark the centenary of British Columbia.

Just to the west of this selected residential community is the famous **Royal Wentworth Golf Course**, while to the north are the historic fields of Runnymede where King John sealed the Magna Carta in 1215.

GUILDFORD

The ancient county town of Surrey, where Henry II built a Castle on high ground, is the home of one of only two new Anglican cathedrals to have been built since the Reformation (the other is Liverpool); the impressive **Guildford Cathedral** was consecrated in 1961. A few years later, in 1968, the **University of Surrey** was relocated from London to Guildford and on its pleasant, leafy hillside site, the campus contains a number of striking buildings.

Back in the city centre, **Guildford Museum** has an exhibition devoted to Lewis Carroll, who died here in 1898, and at the foot of the castle is the famous **Yvonne Arnaud Theatre**.

The culturally vibrant town is the hub of shopping and arts for the area, and holds an award winning summer festival **GuilFest** every July; hosting big name and local bands, street performers, theatre, and much more.

Just east of Guildford lies **Clandon Park**, a magnificent 18th century country mansion renowned for its superb marble hall, sumptuous decorations and fine plasterwork. Further on lies the distinctive brick house of **Hatchlands Park**, which was designed in the mid-18th century for Admiral Boscawen after his famous victory at the Battle of Louisburg.

To the west of Guildford lies a ridge, known as the **Hog's Back**, which dominates the surrounding landscape; the main road following the ridge offers fantastic views.

AROUND GUILDFORD

GODALMING
4 miles SW of Guildford on the A3100

A market town since the early 14th century, Godalming later became a centre for the local textile industry before becoming an important staging post between London and Portsmouth in the 18th century. The town's most interesting building is arguably the **Pepperpot**, the former early-19th century town hall that

used to house an interesting **Museum of Local History**, which has since found new premises in **Wealden House** opposite. However, the town is best known for **Charterhouse**, the famous public school that moved from London to a hillside site north of the town in 1872. Among its most striking features are the 150 feet Founder's Tower and the chapel designed by Giles Gilbert Scott as a memorial to the First World War dead.

HASLEMERE
12 miles SW of Guildford on the A286

This genteel town owes much of its development to the arrival of the railway in 1859 that saw it become a comfortable residential place for well-to-do commuters. However, some notable pre-Victorian buildings still exist, among them the Town Hall of 1814 and the Tolle House Almshouses. The **Haslemere Educational Museum** was founded in 1888 by local surgeon and Quaker, Sir James Hutchinson.

ELSTEAD
6½ miles SW of Guildford on the B3001

An attractive village on the River Wey, Elstead is home to an 18th century watermill – **Elstead Mill**, standing four storeys high and topped with a Palladian cupola.

FARNHAM
10 miles W of Guildford on the A31

After the Norman Conquest, the Bishop of Winchester built himself a castle on a rise above the town centre. An impressive building, **Farnham Castle** remained in the hands of the Bishops of Winchester until 1927.

Other historic buildings here include a row of 17th century gabled almshouses and Willmer House, a handsome Georgian building that is now home to the **Farnham Museum**.

Just to the southeast are the atmospheric ruins of 12th century **Waverley Abbey**, the first Cistercian abbey to be built in England. Close by, near the attractive village of Tilford, is the **Rural Life Centre and Old Kiln Museum**, a museum of rural life covering the years from 1750 to 1960.

REIGATE

Once an important outpost for the de Warenne family, the assertive Norman rulers whose sphere of influence stretched from the south coast to the North Downs, Reigate retains an attractive mix of Victorian, Georgian and older buildings, despite its rapid postwar expansion. Just off the high street is the brilliant **Harlequin Theatre and Cinema**, showing an eclectic mix of theatre and film year round.

Just to the northwest lies Reigate Heath, a narrow area of open heathland that is home to the unique **Windmill Church**, the only church in the world to be situated in a windmill.

Reigate Windmill

AROUND REIGATE

LIMPSFIELD
9 miles E of Reigate off the A25

In the churchyard here lies the grave of the composer Frederick Delius, who died in France in 1934 but had wished to be buried in an English country graveyard. Sir Thomas Beecham, a great admirer of Delius, read the funeral oration and conducted an orchestra playing works by Delius. Sir Thomas died in 1961 and was originally buried at Brookwood Cemetery near Woking. In 1991 his body was transferred to Limpsfield, where he was buried close to Delius. Also lying here are the conductor Norman del Mar and the pianist Eileen Joyce. **Detillens**, a rare 15th century hall house, contains collections of period furniture, china and militaria.

LINGFIELD
9½ miles SE of Reigate on the B2028

'Leafy' Lingfield's **Church of St Peter and St Paul** has been enlarged down the years to create what has become known as the 'Westminster Abbey of Surrey'. Features include a rare double nave and an exceptional collection of monumental brasses. Near the village of **Outwood**, the **Post Mill**, built in 1665, is recognised as the country's oldest working windmill.

Lingfield racecourse stages a year-round programme of all-weather racing and still retains its turf circuit.

DORKING
5½ miles W of Reigate on the A25

An ancient settlement that stands at the intersection of Stane Street and the Pilgrims' Way, Dorking owes much of its character to the Victorians. Just to the north of the town lies **Box Hill**, whose 563 feet summit rises sharply from the valley floor.

To the northwest of Dorking is **Polesden Lacey** (National Trust), a Regency villa that was extensively modified by the Edwardian hostess Mrs Ronald Greville. Four miles southwest of Dorking, **Leith Hill** is the highest point in the southeast of England, at 965 feet above sea level. On the southern slopes of the hill is a lovely rhododendron wood planted by Josiah Wedgwood, grandson of the illustrious potter.

EPSOM
7 miles NW of Reigate on the A24

The old market town of Epsom is known throughout the world as the home of the world's premier classic race, **The Derby**. Racing was formalised in 1779 when a party of aristocratic sportsmen, led by Lord Derby, established a race for three-year-old fillies that was named after the family home at Banstead – The Oaks. This was followed a year later by a race for all three-year-olds, The Derby, which was named after the founder himself.

Sussex saw one of the most momentous events in England's history when, in 1066, William, Duke of Normandy landed with his army at Pevensey and went on to defeat the Saxon King Harold at Battle on the

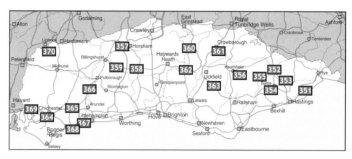

14th of October. Battle Abbey was built on the spot where Harold fell, and both here and in nearby Hastings there are museums and exhibitions detailing this historic victory; most notable is the 1066 Story at Hastings Castle, a popular attraction within the castle ruins bringing the epic battle to life.

The south coast has been no stranger to invasion and, in the days before the establishment of the Royal Navy, the confederation of Cinque Ports provided fleets of ships to defend the coast. Today, the Sussex coast is best known for the elegant and genteel resorts of Eastbourne, Bexhill, Rottingdean, Worthing and, of course, vibrant Brighton. The most dramatic and stunning feature of the coastline are the Seven Sisters; a series of undulating chalk cliffs.

Inland the rolling landscape of the South Downs provides glorious walking country and the South Downs Way long distance footpath follows the crest of the hills from Winchester to Beachy Head near Eastbourne. Here there

are numerous ancient market towns and a wealth of fine stately homes but Sussex is also renowned for its glorious gardens such as Wakehurst Place, Herstmonceux and Leonardslee.

Through the ages the county has been home to some of the most prolific and influential writers in England, and their preserved houses and other landmarks serve as a tribute to their works. At various times Lamb House in Rye was the home of Henry James and EF Benson; Rudyard Kipling made Bateman's, a stunning Jacobean dwelling, his home for some years, describing it as "untouched and unfaked"; AA Milne, the creator of *Winnie the Pooh*, is remembered in Hartfield's 500 year old sweet shop Pooh Corner; the controversial Virginia Woolf lived in her home in Rodmell with her husband until her death in 1941; and a plaque has been placed in Worthing at the place where Oscar Wilde's house stood, where he wrote *The importance of being Earnest*.

Accommodation

Accommodation

Food & Drink

Food & Drink

Places of Interest

HASTINGS

This was the principal town of a small Saxon province long before William the Conqueror landed nearby but it was to Hastings that the victorious William returned after the battle that took place six miles away. The **Castle** he built is now in ruins, but a medieval siege tent contains a permanent display – the **1066 Story at Hastings Castle**. After the Conquest, Hastings became a leading Cinque Port, a role it played until the harbour began to silt up in Elizabethan times. However, the fishing industry has managed to survive and the tall wooden huts used for drying nets remain a familiar feature. The Church of St Nicholas is home to the **Fishermen's Museum**, where the centerpiece is the old sailing lugger *The Enterprise*. The town also has its own version of the Bayeux Tapestry, the Hastings Embroidery.

351 TWO SAWYERS

Pett Village

Beautiful 16th century village inn, known for its fine selection of real ales, wines and traditional pub dishes.

See entry on page 558

AROUND HASTINGS

RYE

9 miles NE of Hastings on the A259

A picturesque town and Cinque Port; its harbour gradually silted up and it now lies further down the Rother estuary. **Rye Harbour Nature Reserve**, at the river mouth, is a large area of sea, saltmarsh, sand and shingle that supports a wide range of plant, animal and bird life.

One of Rye's many interesting buildings is the handsome Georgian residence, **Lamb House** (National Trust), which was the home of the novelist Henry James from 1898 to his death in 1916. A later occupant was the

Camber Castle, Rye

prolific writer EF Benson, best remembered for his Mapp and Lucia novels and various volumes of reminiscences.

To the south lies **Camber Castle** (English Heritage), a fine example of the coastal defences built by Henry VIII.

NORTHIAM

9 miles N of Hastings on the A28

The picturesque village of Northiam is the southern terminal for the **Kent and East Sussex Railway** that runs steam trains to Tenterden during the summer. Just to the northwest lies **Great Dixter House**, one of the finest late medieval hall houses in the country, with superb gardens designed by Lutyens.

To the west lies **Bodiam Castle**, begun in 1385 and one of the last great medieval fortresses to be built in England. Bodiam was once the centre of a thriving hop-growing region, served by 'The Hoppers' Line' of the Kent & East Sussex Railway.

BATTLE

6 miles NW of Hastings on the A2100

This historic settlement is renowned as being the site of the momentous battle, on 14 October 1066, between the armies of Harold, King of England, and William, Duke of Normandy. Battle Abbey was built on the spot

where Harold fell. Battle was once home to one of the country's largest and most successful Gunpowder Works which kept British ships loaded throughout the Napoleonic wars and most likely supplied the powder used in the Guy Fawkes' plot.

HERSTMONCEUX

11½ miles NW of Hastings on the A271

This village is famous as being the home of

Herstmonceux Castle

354 THE BULL INN

Battle

Handsome and historic inn in the centre of Battle, known for its collection of fine wine and real ale, and traditional homemade food.

See entry on page 561

352 THE SEVEN STARS INN

Robertsbridge

Prosperous 14th century inn serving a good selection of wines, beers and local Sussex ale, not to mention the home cooked food and famous Sunday carvery.

See entry on page 559

353 THE QUEENS HEAD

Hastings

A popular pub offering a friendly welcome, homecooked food and tranquil surroundings.

See entry on page 560

355 THE NETHERFIELD ARMS

Netherfield

A lovely traditional pub with beautiful, award winning grounds and panoramic views of the English Channel.

See entry on page 562

356 STAR INN

Old Heathfield

A 15th century inn that is packed to the rafters with character and charm offering excellent food, drink and hospitality.

See entry on page 563

15th century **Herstmonceux Castle** - to where, in 1948, the Royal Observatory at Greenwich moved. Although the Observatory has since moved on again, the castle is now home to the **Herstmonceux Science Centre**.

BURWASH

13 miles NW of Hastings on the A265

An exceptionally pretty village and one time centre of the Wealden iron industry, Burwash is home to **Rampyndene**, a handsome 17th century timber-framed house. Just outside the village stands **Bateman's**, a Jacobean house that was the home of Rudyard Kipling from 1902 until his death in 1936. It is now under the care of the National Trust, and remains much as it was when Kipling lived here – including his atmospheric book-lined study.

To the south of Burwash is **Brightling**, the home of the Georgian eccentric, 'Mad' Jack Fuller. One of the first people to recognise the talents of the great painter Turner, Fuller also built several imaginative follies including Brightling Needle, a 40 feet stone obelisk.

BEXHILL

5 miles W of Hastings on the A259

This small seaside resort was founded in the 1880s by the influential De La Warr family and among the many late-Victorian buildings is the striking **De La Warr Pavilion**, built in the 1930s and now a beautifully maintained, renowned centre for arts and culture.

A seemingly conservative resort, Bexhill played host to the birth of British motor racing in 1902, an event that is remembered annually with the **Bexhill Festival of Motoring** held in May. Bexhill was also the first seaside town to allow mixed bathing on its beaches - a very daring move back in 1900!

HAYWARDS HEATH

The oldest part of this town is centred on the conservation area around Muster Green, an open space where the 16th century Sergison Arms can be found. Modern Haywards Heath grew up around its station on the Brighton line.

AROUND HAYWARDS HEATH

HORSHAM

10½ miles NW of Haywards Heath on the A281

An ancient town that dates back to Saxon times, Horsham's architectural gem is **The Causeway**, a tree-lined street that runs from the town hall to the Church of St Mary and the gabled 16th century Causeway House that is now home to the **Horsham Museum**.

To the southeast is the village of **Lower Beeding**, home to the beautiful **Leonardslee Gardens** that were laid out in this natural valley in the late 19th century.

CRAWLEY

8½ miles NW of Haywards Heath on the A23

One of the original new towns created after

357 SPRINGFIELDS

Horsham

Award-winning, stylish, modern and well appointed hotel offering quality en suite accommodation and excellent breakfasts.

See entry on page 564

358 CAMELIA BOTNAR HOMES & GARDENS

Cowfold

This large nursery in Cowfold, West Sussex has a great selection of plants, bedding, shrubs and trees. Showrooms of our handcrafted woodwork, ironwork and pottery and a Bistro for freshly cooked, home made food.

See entry on page 565

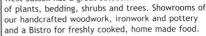

359 THE SELSEY ARMS

Coolham

Appealing old hostelry offering good home-cooked food, real ales and two pleasant beer gardens.

See entry on page 566

the New Towns Act of 1946, Crawley has swallowed up several ancient villages. Just to the north lies **Gatwick Airport**, which first opened to commercial air traffic in 1936.

To the south of Crawley, near Handcross, are the superb gardens of **Nymans** created by William Robinson and Gertrude Jekyll. Close by are the smaller but equally delightful **High Beeches Gardens**.

WEST HOATHLY

5 miles N of Haywards Heath off the B2028

A historic settlement whose most impressive building is the **Priest House**, a 15th century house that was the estate office for the monks of Lewes Priory and is now a museum.

To the southwest lies **Ardingly**, home of Ardingly College public school, the showground for the South of England Agricultural Society and, at the top of Ardingly Reservoir, **Wakehurst Place**, the Tudor home of the Culpeper family. Today, the magnificent gardens are administered by the Royal Botanic Gardens at Kew; Wakehurst is also home to the **Millennium Seed Bank**, a project that aims to ensure the survival of over 24,000 plant species worldwide – much like a horticultural Noah's Ark.

EAST GRINSTEAD

9 miles N of Haywards Heath on the A22

East Grinstead was an important centre for the Wealden iron industry and a busy market town, and several buildings remaining from those prosperous days. The **Town Museum** in East Court is a fine building that was originally constructed in 1769 as a private residence; the Greenwich Meridian passes through the town at this point.

Bluebell Line, nr Standen

To the south lies **Standen** (National Trust), a remarkable late Victorian country mansion that is a showpiece of the Arts and Crafts Movement. From near Standen, the famous **Bluebell Railway** offers a pleasant steam-powered journey through the Sussex Weald.

To the east of East Grinstead is the old hunting settlement of Hartfield, which was the home of AA Milne, the creator of *Winnie the Pooh*. The village's 300-year-old sweet shop, **Pooh Corner**, is now full of Winnie the Pooh memorabilia; Poohsticks Bridge spans a small tributary of the River Medway.

BUXTED

10½ miles E of Haywards Heath on the A272

The village has long been dominated by the

361 THE BRICKLAYERS ARMS

Crowborough

Friendly and relaxed local pub known for putting on great live entertainment and serving up fantastic homemade, traditional food.

See entry on page 567

360 HOLLY HOUSE B&B

Chelwood Gate

Comfortable family home offering en suite rooms and memorable breakfasts.

See entry on page 565

362 THE BULL ON THE GREEN

Newick

Fine old traditional inn with an excellent restaurant and comfortable en suite rooms

See entry on page 568

great house of **Buxted Park**, built along classical lines in 1725, restored after a fire by Basil Ionides and now a hotel.

To the southwest, on the other side of Uckfield in the village of **Piltdown**, an ancient skull was discovered in 1912 by an amateur archaeologist that was, for a time, believed to have been the 'missing link' until exposed as a hoax in 1953.

To the west lies Sheffield Green, home to the splendid 18th century mansion **Sheffield Park** (National Trust) whose superb Capability Brown gardens are open to the public.

BRIGHTON

It was Dr Richard Russell's enthusiasm for sea bathing, taking the sea air and even drinking seawater that saw Brighton grow from an insignificant little fishing village called Brighthelmston into a popular seaside resort. But it was the patronage of the Prince Regent, who first came here in 1783, which saw the village completely transformed. Wishing to have a permanent base here, the Prince built his famous **Royal Pavilion**, and the magnificent, exotic building seen today was the creation of the architect John Nash. The gardens surrounding this early 19th century pleasure palace based on a maharajah's palace are also Nash's work.

As the Prince took up almost permanent residence in the resort a period of rapid expansion took place of which the Royal Crescent is probably the greatest feature. However, **The Lanes**, the tiny alleyways of the old village, are equally interesting with

their antique shops, restaurants and smart boutiques.

The best-known features on the seafront are the **Palace Pier** which has for more than a century been one of Brighton's greatest attractions, the **Volk's Electric Railway**, the first public electric railway in Britain, and the **Sea Life Centre**, home to the longest underwater tunnel in Europe.

Just to the west lies **Hove**, a genteel place that developed alongside its neighbour. At the **Hove Museum and Art Gallery** stands a wooden pavilion, the **Jaipur Gateway**, which was transported here from Rajashtan in 1886.

AROUND BRIGHTON

HURSTPIERPOINT
7 miles N of Brighton on the B2116

This ancient village is dominated by **Hurstpierpoint College** and its chapel while, to the south of the village lies **Danny**, the ancestral home of the Norman Pierpoint family. It was in this impressive E-shaped Elizabethan mansion that Lloyd George drew up the terms of the armistice that ended World War I. Closer to Brighton, at Poynings, is one of the greatest natural features of the South Downs. The **Devil's Dyke** is a huge steep-sided ravine that attracts tourists, walkers and hang-gliders.

LEWES
7 miles NE of Brighton on the A27

It was in this historic settlement, the county town of East Sussex, that William the Conqueror's powerful friend, William de Warenne, constructed a **Castle** and founded the great Priory of St Pancras. A substantial part of the castle remains today.

HAILSHAM
18 miles NE of Brighton on the A295

A pleasant market town that was once the centre of a thriving rope and string industry. To the southwest lies **Michelham Priory**,

Palace Pier, Brighton

which was founded in 1229. Many of the priory's buildings are now incorporated into a grand Tudor farmhouse, whose rooms contain many treasures, and the gardens cover an attractive range of planting styles.

NEWHAVEN

10 miles E of Brighton on the A26

Two early visitors on the packet boat from Dieppe were the fleeing King and Queen of France, Louis Philippe and Marie Amelie. They spent a night in 1848 at the Bridge Inn (registering as Mr & Mrs Smith!) before taking a train to London, where they were met by Queen Victoria's coach and taken to Buckingham Palace.

Along the coast to the east lies **Seaford**, a once thriving port that is home to **Martello Tower No 74**, the most westerly of these defensive structures, which now houses the **Seaford Museum of Local History**. Seaford Head, a nature reserve, is an excellent place from which to view the **Seven Sisters** - a spectacular series of clifftop undulations.

Seven Sisters, nr Seaford

363 **BLACKBERRY FARM**

Whitesmith

Blackberry farm offers the perfect family day out with acres of animals for petting, impressive indoor and outdoor play areas and a licensed café for the grownups.

See entry on page 570

To the west of Newhaven, in a gap in the cliffs, lies **Rottingdean** and **North End House**, the home of the artist Sir Edward Burne-Jones. Inland is the village of **Rodmell**, where **Monk's House** was the home of Virginia and Leonard Woolf from 1919 until her death in 1941. The house, now in the care of the National Trust, is filled with books and paintings and is surrounded by a lush garden.

SELMESTON

13 miles E of Brighton off the A27

Selmeston is best known as the home of the artist Vanessa Bell, who shared **Charleston Farmhouse** with her husband Clive and her lover, Duncan Grant.

To the south, beyond Alciston with its medieval dovecote, is the beautiful village of **Alfriston**, whose splendid 14th century church is often referred to as the **Cathedral of the Downs**. Beside the church is the **Clergy House**, the first building acquired by the National Trust (for £10 in 1896) and a marvellous example of a 14th century Wealden hall house. To the north lies **Drusillas Park**, a child friendly zoo set in attractive gardens.

To the west of Selmeston lies **Firle Beacon** which, at 718 feet, dominates the surrounding countryside and **Firle Place**, a wonderful Tudor manor that houses superb collections of European and English Old Masters, French and English furniture and Sèvres porcelain.

EASTBOURNE

20 miles E of Brighton on the A259

A stylish and genteel seaside resort, Eastbourne's rapid growth from two small villages was instigated by the 7th Duke of Devonshire from the 1850s. Several buildings predate this expansion, including the Redoubt Fortress that is now the **Military Museum of Sussex**. The sea has always played an important part in the life of Eastbourne and there is an **RNLI Lifeboat Museum** close to the lifeboat station.

To the southwest of Eastbourne lies **Beachy Head**, one of the most spectacular

Beachy Head, Eastbourne

chalk precipices in England, almost 600 feet high. This is also the end of the South Downs Way, a long distance bridleway established in 1972.

To the northeast lies **Pevensey**, landing place for invading Roman legions and in 1066 for William the Conqueror and his troops; it was William's half-brother, Robert de Mortain, who built **Pevensey Castle**.

SHOREHAM-BY-SEA
6 miles W of Brighton on the A259

An ancient port that has suffered from the silting up of its river; its earlier importance is reflected in the construction of Shoreham Fort, which was part of Palmerston's coastal defence system. The history of Shoreham, particularly its maritime past, is explored at **Marlipins Museum**, part of which is located in the oldest lay building in the county, while at Shoreham Airport, which first opened in 1934, is the **Museum of D-Day Aviation**.

WORTHING
10 miles W of Brighton on the A259

An ancient fishing community, Worthing developed into a fashionable seaside resort in the late 18th century and boasts one of the oldest piers in the country. The **Worthing Museum and Art Gallery** has a nationally important costume and toy collection along with displays on smuggling and the town riots of the 19th century. A plaque on the

esplanade marks the site of the house where Oscar Wilde wrote *The Importance of Being Earnest*.

A bustling centre for shopping and socializing in one of the many cafes and restaurants; Worthing has something to cater for everyone's taste, with over 400 shops ranging from high street names to individual boutiques along wonderful pedestrianised streets.

CHICHESTER

Founded by the Romans in the 1st century, Chichester has also been an ecclesiastical centre for over 900 years and its **Cathedral** is unique on two counts: it is the only medieval English cathedral which can be seen from the sea, and it has a detached belfry.

One of its most distinctive modern buildings is the **Chichester Festival Theatre**, opened in 1962 and the focal point of the annual Chichester Festival.

Just east of the city are the splendid remains of **Fishbourne Roman Palace** that was built in around AD 75 for the Celtic King Cogidubnus.

Further west again is the pleasant village of Bosham, where legend has it that King Canute ordered back the waves.

AROUND CHICHESTER

GOODWOOD
2 miles N of Chichester off the A286

The spectacular country home of the Dukes of Richmond, **Goodwood House** was built in the

364 THE DINING ROOM
Chichester
Offers an outstanding dining experience either in the elegant restaurant, patrons, conservatory or the enchanting courtyard garden.
See entry on page 569

late 18th century by the architect James Wyatt and, along with a fine collection of paintings, gruesome relics from the Napoleonic Wars are on display. The house is the focal point of the vast Goodwood Estate that incorporates the world famous **Goodwood Racecourse**, the venue of the fashionable 'Glorious Goodwood' meeting first held in 1814.

Nearby **Singleton** is the location of the famous **Weald and Downland Open Air Museum**, an exemplary museum with over 40 reconstructed historic rural buildings. At West Dean lies **Charleston Manor**, an ancient house that was originally built in 1080 for William the Conqueror's cupbearer and is now the centrepiece of a remarkable garden created by members of the Bloomsbury Group.

Just to the southwest, and overlooked by Bow Hill, is **Kingley Vale National Nature Reserve**, home to the finest yew groves in Europe – several trees here are more than 500 years old.

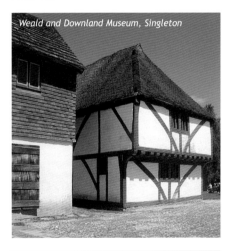
Weald and Downland Museum, Singleton

PETWORTH

13 miles NE of Chichester on the A285

What brings most people here is the grand estate of 17th century **Petworth House**, which has the look of a French château and is home to the National Trust's finest collection of art from the 15th to 19th centuries, and some superb ancient and neo-classical sculpture.

To the south of the Petworth Estate is the Coultershaw Water Wheel and Beam Pump, one of the earliest pumped water systems; it was installed in 1790 to pump water two miles to the house.

PULBOROUGH

14½ miles NE of Chichester on the A29

Situated on Roman Stane Street, Pulborough was an important staging post along the old coaching route between London and Chichester. To the southeast lies the **RSPB's Pulborough Brooks Nature Reserve**, where a nature trail leads to views overlooking the wet meadows of the Arun Valley.

To the southwest of Pulborough, near **Bignor**, is one of the largest Roman sites in Britain – some 70 buildings surround a central courtyard and many of the fine mosaics uncovered can be seen in the Museum.

TANGMERE

2½ miles E of Chichester off the A27

This village is associated with the nearby former Battle of Britain base, RAF Tangmere, which is now home to the **Tangmere Military Aviation Museum**. The heroic deeds of the pilots are also remembered in the local pub, the Bader Arms.

---

365 MOUNT PLEASANT HOUSE

Eastergate

Gracious Georgian house of character in tranquil grounds offering quality bed & breakfast accommodation.

See entry on page 571

---

366 AMBERLEY MUSEUM

Amberley

This fabulous 36 acre open air site is dedicated to the industrial heritage of the South East with some truly remarkable static and live exhibits.

See entry on page 570

ARUNDEL

9½ miles E of Chichester on the A27

A settlement since before the Roman invasion, this peaceful town lies beneath the battlements of the impressive 11th century **Arundel Castle**. Another historic site is the **Maison Dieu**, a medieval hospital that was founded in 1345.

To the north lies the attractive village of **Amberley** and **Amberley Castle**, originally a fortified summer palace for the bishops of Chichester.

BOGNOR REGIS

5½ miles SE of Chichester on the A259

A quiet fishing village with some elegant Georgian features. King George V came here in 1929 to convalesce and granted the town the title Regis. The town is best known nowadays for its annual international **Birdman Rally**, when competitors hurl themselves off the pier in an attempt to make the longest unpowered flight.

SELSEY

7½ miles S of Chichester on the B2145

A modest yet popular resort, whose town's most impressive building is **Selsey Windmill**, built in 1820. A Lifeboat Station was established here in 1860 and there is now an interesting **Lifeboat Museum** along with a more recent station.

The town's East Beach was the scene for smuggling in the 18th century and during World War II sections of the famous Mulberry Harbour were gathered here before D-Day.

WEST WITTERING

6½ miles SW of Chichester on the B2179

Situated close to the beautiful inlet that is Chichester's natural harbour, this charming seaside village is home to **Cakeham Manor House**, once a summer palace of the bishops of Chichester.

SOUTH HARTING

10 miles NW of Chichester on the B2146

One of the most attractive villages on the South Downs, South Harting stands at the foot of Harting Down where the South Downs Way footpath skirts around Beacon Hill, one of the highest points on the Downs. The magnificent house **Uppark** (National Trust) lies on the crest of a hill to the south, with grounds and gardens laid out by Humphry Repton.

---

367 ELMER HOTEL

Middleton on Sea

Friendly traditional pub with good food, real ales and light, comfortable en suite rooms.

See entry on page 572

---

369 THE BARLEY CORN

Nutbourne

A popular pub serving home cooked food and real ale. Locals and visitors frequent this olde worlde establishment.

See entry on page 574

---

368 MALTHOUSE RESTAURANT

Felpham

A popular restaurant serving the very best in traditional a la carte dishes, succulent roasts and fresh seafood specialities.

See entry on page 573

---

370 THE RISING SUN

Milland

This is one of the very best village inns in the region, a wonderful place to relax, have fun and enjoy a drink and a meal featuring the best and freshest local ingredients

See entry on page 573

WARWICKSHIRE

A rich vein of medieval and Tudor history runs through Warwickshire, and the romantic ruins of Kenilworth Castle, the grandeur of Warwick Castle and the elegance of Royal Leamington Spa set the tone for this most delightful of counties. But Stratford-upon-Avon is most visitors' focal point, a town dominated by William Shakespeare and all things Shakespearian.

Another town that has found fame through one of its citizens is Rugby, as it was the young scholar William Webb Ellis who, in the early 19th century, broke the rules of football and picked up the ball and in so doing founded the game that bears the name of the town. Close by is the ancient village of Dunchurch that is often dubbed the 'Gunpowder Plot Village' as it was here that the conspirators waited to hear if their mission had been accomplished.

Throughout the county are some truly grand and impressive houses; overlooking the River Avon is Charlecote Park with beautiful grounds designed by Capability Brown; the 17th century Upton House recreates the life of a 1930s millionaire; Ilmington House stands proudly at the foot of the Downs, part of the Coltwolds hills; Ragley Hall was once the home of the Marquess of Hertford; and neighbouring grand residences Packwood House and Baddesley Clinton both offer a beautiful day out, courtesy of the National Trust. For something slightly more ancient look no further than the Rollright Stones, on the boarder with Oxfordshire. These three

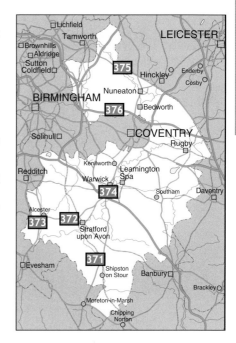

Neolithic stone structures give insight into the ceremony of ancient man in this region.

In its modern history Warwickshire has a deep connection with British motoring, and this story is told through the extensive exhibits at Gaydon's Heritage Motor Centre and the National Motorcycle Museum outside Meriden – a village which is also the traditional Centre of England.

Accommodation

Food & Drink

STRATFORD-UPON-AVON

It was here, in 1564, that William Shakespeare was born and having found fame in London, retired to his birthplace and lived here until his death in 1616. Few towns are so completely dominated by one man. The half-timbered house that is **Shakespeare's Birthplace** has been returned to the way it must have looked in his day and a room thought to have been his father's workshop has been re-created with the help of the Worshipful Company of Glovers. Further along, on Chapel Street, stands **Nash's House**, another half-timbered building that belonged to Shakespeare's granddaughter, Elizabeth Hall; it now contains an exceptional collection of Elizabethan furniture and tapestries, as well as displays on the history of Stratford. Its spectacular Elizabethan-style knot garden is an added attraction.

Shakespeare's Birthplace - Stratford

In Old Town is one of the best examples of a half-timbered gabled house in Stratford, **Hall's Croft**, which was named after Dr John Hall, who married Shakespeare's daughter Susanna in 1607. This impressive house, along with outstanding 16th and 17th century furniture and paintings, has a reconstruction of Dr Hall's consulting room, accompanied by an exhibition detailing medicinal practices during Shakespeare's time. Outside, the beautiful walled garden features a large herb bed. In a beautiful setting by the River Avon, is 13th century **Holy Trinity Church** where Shakespeare is buried by the north wall of the chancel. The grave of his wife Anne Hathaway is close by.

The town is also home to three theatres, as well as the internationally renowned Royal Shakespeare Company, and the most famous is, of course, the **Royal Shakespeare Theatre** that opened in 1879 with a performance of *Much Ado About Nothing* starring Ellen Terry and Beerbohm Tree. The Royal Shakespeare Theatre Summer House in Avonbank Gardens is home to the **Stratford Brass Rubbing Centre**, which contains a large collection of exact replicas of brasses of knights and ladies, scholars, merchants and priests.

To the west of the town is an Elizabethan farmhouse that is now known as **Anne Hathaway's Cottage**, as it was here that Shakespeare's wife was born. Another notable house connected with the Bard is that of his mother, situated in the village of Wilmcote: **Mary Arden's House** is a striking Tudor farmhouse that contains the Shakespeare Countryside Museum of farming and rural life.

AROUND STRATFORD-UPON-AVON

WELLESBOURNE

5 miles E of Stratford off the A429

Wellesbourne Airfield, located just outside of this pretty local village, is home to a fascinating museum, and runs its own flying club which proves very popular. Every Saturday (and Holiday Monday) the airfield is transformed into the **Wellesbourne Market**; one of the UK's largest outdoor market, it is a vibrant affair brimming with over 500 stalls and many events and activities to make it a great day out.

To the southeast lies **Compton Verney Manor House**, a magnificent manor that is home to a fine art collection that includes British portraiture, European Old Masters and modern works, along with a unique collection of British Folk Art. On the other side of Wellesbourne lies 16th century **Charlecote Park** (National Trust), a magnificent stately home occupying landscaped grounds overlooking the River Avon that were laid out by Capability Brown; graceful fallow deer have roamed the park since Tudor times.

KINETON

10½ miles E of Stratford off the B4086

The palatial 17th century **Upton House** (National Trust), 10 minutes along the A422 from Kineton, offers visitors the chance to experience a weekend house party for a 1930s millionaire which is, as you can imagine, quite an indulgent affair. The house is also home to a fine collection of art,

Charlecote Park, Wellesbourne

including pieces by El Greco, Stubbs and Bosch, and sweeping grounds incorporating a kitchen garden, terraces and a tranquil water garden. More lush greenery can be found at nearby **Burton Dassett Country Park**, a hilly expanse of untouched countryside perfect for walking. The views from the top of the hills are particularly breathtaking, and atop one of these stands an interesting stone beacon.

Also near to Kineton is the village of Gaydon, and the **Heritage Motor Centre** which has fascinating exhibits exploring the rich history of the British car industry, as well as hosting a great variety of events throughout the year – including Gaydon's Mini festival, celebrating the life of the small iconic car.

ILMINGTON

7 miles S of Stratford off the B4632

This pretty village lies at the foot of the **Ilmington Downs**; the highest point in the county at 850 ft and the northern end of the

Cotswold Hills, it provides an almost uninterrupted 360° view which is breathtaking. A majority of the dwelling here are built in the local warm honey coloured sandstone, a beautiful feature of villages throughout the Cotswolds, and there is also **Ilmington Manor**, a fine Elizabethan house once owned by the de Montfort family, whose picturesque gardens are opened to the public on open days throughout the year.

SHIPSTON-ON-STOUR

10½ miles S of Stratford off the A3400

This attractive town, once an important sheep market centre for the area (the name deriving from the ancient name "Sheep-wash-Town"), is the counties Gateway to the Cotswolds. The family-run **Whichford Pottery** nearby is a must-visit attraction, and gives brilliant insight into local crafts. See and speak to the talented craftsmen while they are working on their terracotta creations, or visit their gallery The Octagon which showcases a fine range of pottery, as well as other British art and crafts.

Seven miles south of the town, on the boarder with Oxfordshire, is the atmospheric and fascinating Neolithic site of the **Rollright Stones**. There are three parts to the stones; the ceremonial stone circle 'The King's Men', the 'King Stone', and the 5000 year old burial chamber 'The Whispering Knights', which is believed to be part of a Neolithic long barrow.

ALCESTER

7 miles W of Stratford off the A435

An ancient Roman market town built on the Icknield Street Encampment, Alcester boasts several very pretty cottages on Maltmill Lane and a handsome Norman church.

371 **THE FOX & GOOSE COUNTRY INN**

Armscote

Traditional features and contemporary styling create an attractive atmosphere at this country inn known for its restaurant styled food at great value prices.

See entry on page 575

Just to the south lies the village of **Arrow** and the 17th century home of the Marquess of Hertford, **Ragley Hall**. One of England's great Palladian country houses, it was inherited by the 8th Marquess in 1940. Completely renovated in a style befitting its age, the Hall boasts a wonderful collection of treasures, and out in the landscaped park there are formal gardens, an impressive collection of carriages and a country trail. **Roman Alcester Heritage Centre** explores everyday life in and around Roman Alcester. At nearby Kinwarton stands the National Trust's **Kinwarton Dovecote**, a 14th century circular dovecote that still houses doves and retains its 'potence', a pivoted ladder giving human access to the nesting boxes.

A little way north along the A435 from Alcester is the village of Coughton; the crowning glory of which is **Coughton Court**, grand home of the Throckmorton family for almost 600 years. They were very prominent in Tudor times and were instigators of Catholic emancipation, playing a part in the Gunpowder Plot - the wives of some of the Gunpowder Plotters awaited the outcome of the Plot in the imposing central gatehouse. Three days every September the Throckmorton family holds an illuminating literary festival at the court.

WARWICK

Standing by the River Avon, Warwick is in a good defensive position and became part of Crown lands just after the Norman Conquest. Dominating the town, much of **Warwick Castle** was destroyed during the Barons' revolt in 1264, led by Simon de Montfort, and the majority of the present castle dates from the 14th century. The towers at each end are very impressive - one is known as Caesar's Tower and is shaped rather like a cloverleaf.

Warwick Castle

The castle's exterior is best viewed from Castle Bridge, where the 14th century walls can be seen reflected in the waters of the River Avon. There is much to explore along the ramparts and in the 60 acres of grounds, which include a re-created Victorian formal rose garden, the Peacock Gardens and an expanse of open parkland designed by Capability Brown. Events throughout the year include Medieval Tournaments, open-air fireworks concerts and special entertainment days.

The centre of Warwick is dominated by elegant Queen Anne architecture and there is

---

372 LARKRISE COTTAGE

Upper Billesley,
nr Stratford Upon Avon

A stunning bed &
breakfast nestled in
acres of countryside
offering two guest
bedrooms.

See entry on page 575

---

373 THE LORD NELSON

Alcester

200 year old traditional
family-run pub in the
heart of historic Roman
Market town of
Alcester.

See entry on page 576

374 ROBBIE'S OF WARWICK

Warwick

Housed within a beautiful
listed Tudor building in the
centre of Warwick, Robbie's
is a contemporary restaurant
specialising in international
cuisine.

See entry on page 576

also a wealth of museums including several honouring the county's regiments. One of the most important buildings in Warwick is St John's House, dating from 1666, which contains the **Museum of the Royal Warwickshire Regiment**. Two of Warwick's medieval town gateways have survived, complete with chapels and one of these, Westgate Chapel, forms part of **Lord Leycester's Hospital**, a spectacularly tottering and beautiful collection of 15th century half-timbered buildings enclosing a pretty galleried courtyard.

To the west of Warwick lies **Hatton Country World**, a uniquely charming blend of family fun and country shopping that is situated on a farm built by the descendants of Sir Richard Arkwright, the inventor of the Spinning Jenny. Along with the extensive craft village, the farm is home to the largest collection of rare breed farm animals in Britain.

AROUND WARWICK

KENILWORTH

4 miles N of Warwick on the A452

Although the town was here before the *Domesday Book* was compiled, Kenilworth's name is invariably linked with its castle and, today, the remains of **Kenilworth Castle** (National Heritage) stand as England's finest and most extensive castle ruins. The tales of this great fortress, immortalised in Sir Walter Scott's novel Kenilworth, are many and varied. The marvellous Norman keep, the oldest part of the ruins, was built between 1150 and 1175 and John of Gaunt's Great Hall once rivalled London's Westminster Hall in

palatial grandeur. A glorious recreated **Elizabethan Garden** in the castle grounds was opened in 2009, and has made a beautiful addition to this already grand and historical site.

ROYAL LEAMINGTON SPA

2 miles E of Warwick on the A452

This attractive town boasts a handsome mixture of smart shops and Regency buildings and **The Parade** is undoubtedly one of the finest streets in Warwickshire. Rapidly taking advantage of the fashion for taking the waters, Leamington Spa developed in the first few decades of the 19th century and was given the title 'Royal' by the grace of the new Queen, Victoria. The **Pump Rooms** were opened in 1814 by Henry Jephson, a local doctor who was largely responsible for promoting the spa's medicinal properties and therefore the popularisation of this elegant spa resort by the rich. Immediately opposite the spa itself are Jephson's Gardens containing a Corinthian temple that houses his statue.

SOUTHAM

8½ miles SE of Warwick on the A423

It was in this attractive town by the River Itchen that Charles I spent the night before the battle of Edge Hill. The Roundheads also came into the town, and Cromwell himself arrived with 7,000 troops in 1645. In the main street is the surprisingly named Old Mint Inn, a 14th century stone building that takes its name from an occurrence following the battle of Edge Hill. Charles I commanded his local noblemen to bring him their silver treasure, which was then melted down and minted into coins with which he paid his army.

HENLEY-IN-ARDEN

9 miles W of Warwick on the A3400

Henley's mile-long High Street has examples of almost every kind of English architecture from the 15th century onwards, including many old timber-framed houses built from Arden oak. Little remains today of the **Forest of Arden**, the setting adopted by William

Kenilworth Castle

Packwood House, Henley-In-Arden

Shakespeare for *As You Like It*, as its stocks were diminished in the 18th century by the navy's demand for timber. The town emerged initially under the protection of Thurston de Montfort, Lord of the Manor in 1140, and Beaudesert Castle, home to the de Montfort family, lies behind the **Churches of St John and St Nicholas**, where remains of the castle mound can still be seen.

There are two beautiful houses under the care of the National Trust just to the north of Henley-in-Arden; **Packwood House** near Lapworth is a grand 16th Century building, which contains a fine collection of 16th-century textiles and furniture, and whose extensive gardens include a famous collection of Yew trees; and **Baddesley Clinton**, a 3 minute drive from Packwood, is an elegant 15th century house which, during the Elizabethan era, was used as a refuge for persecuted Catholics – the priest's holes can still be seen. The grounds of Baddesley Clinton are just as illuminating, with a romantic lake and stewponds, it provides a lovely walk.

RUGBY

Rugby's Market Place is surrounded by handsome buildings that act as reminders of the town's origins during the reign of Henry III. **Rugby Town Trail**, a two-hour walk that brings to life the town's history from its Saxon beginnings to the present day, begins at the Clock Tower in Market Place. The tower was intended to commemorate the Golden Jubilee of Queen Victoria in 1887, yet it was not completed until 1889 because over-indulgent citizens had dipped too deep into the Tower funds to feast and drink at the Jubilee. Also along the trail is the house where Rupert Brooke was born (his statue stands in Regent Place), and **Caldecott Park** with its beautiful floral displays, trees and herb garden.

Rugby is bounded by two of the greatest Roman roads, Fosse Way and Watling Street, which meet just northwest of Rugby, at High Cross, one of the landmarks of the area.

The town is best known for **Rugby School**, founded in 1567 and moved to its present site in 1750. It was here that the game of Rugby originated when, in 1823, the story goes that William Webb Ellis broke the rules during a football match by picking up the ball and running with it.

The **James Gilbert Rugby Museum** is housed in the original building where, since 1842, the Gilberts have been making their world-famous rugby footballs. The most famous headmaster of Rugby school was Dr Thomas Arnold, Head from 1828 to 1842. He is buried in the school chapel. One of his pupils was Thomas Hughes, who wrote *Tom Brown's Schooldays* based on his experiences at the school. Another old boy was Rupert Brooke, whose father was a housemaster.

AROUND RUGBY

DUNCHURCH
2 miles SW of Rugby on the A426

On the 5th of November 1605, the Gunpowder Plot conspirators met at the **Red Lion Inn**, Dunchurch, to await the news of Guy Fawkes' attempt to blow up the Houses of Parliament. The Red Lion still exists today but as a private residence known as Guy Fawkes House.

RYTON-ON-DUNSMORE
6 miles W of Rugby off the A45

This village is home to the **Henry Doubleday Research Association** at Ryton Gardens, an organic farming and gardening organisation that leads the way in research and advances in horticulture. The grounds are landscaped with thousands of plants and trees, all organically grown. Ryton Pools Country Park, which opened in 1996, has a 10-acre lake that is home to great crested grebes, swans, moorhens and Canada geese. Pagets Pool, near the northeastern end of the park, is one of the most important sites in Warwickshire for dragonflies.

To the north is **Brandon Marsh Nature Centre**, 200 acres of lakes, marshes, woodland and grassland that provide a home and haven for many species of wildlife.

NUNEATON
13½ miles NW of Rugby on the A444

Originally a Saxon town known as Etone, the 'Nun' was added when a wealthy Benedictine priory was founded here in 1290. The Priory ruins are adjacent to the **Church of St Nicholas**, a Victorian building occupying a Norman site that has a beautiful carved ceiling dating back to 1485. **Nuneaton Museum and Art Gallery** features displays of archaeological interest ranging from prehistoric to medieval times.

Nuneaton Museum also has a permanent exhibition of the town's most illustrious daughter, the novelist George Eliot. Born at Arbury Hall in 1819, Eliot, whose real name was Mary Ann Evans, was an intellectual giant and free thinker. Her father was a land agent on the estate; she portrays this, her first home, as Cheverel Manor in her novel *Mr Gifgil's Love Story.*

NEWTON REGIS
20 miles NW of Rugby

One of the most unspoilt villages in Warwickshire, Newton Regis has been voted Best Kept Small Village on numerous occasions. Near the Staffordshire border and between the M42 and B5453, this lovely village is built around an attractive duck pond which was once a quarry pit. The village's name is thought to derive from its former royal ownership, having once been the property of King Henry II.

MERIDEN
18 miles NW of Rugby off the A45

A 500 year old monument in the centre of the beautiful village of Meriden recognises its status as the traditional **Centre of England** (with the development of modern mapping technology the actual centre has been found to be 11 miles away on a Leicestershire farm), and as such it has become a place of interest for many visitors. Its location is also convenient, being close to two large cities; 5 miles from Coventry and 12 miles from Birmingham. Another monument in the village remembers the brave cyclists who lost their lives in WW1 and WW2. The village was a favourite meeting place for cyclists on the A45 and it was once the location for the Triumph Motorcycle factory; now located at nearby Hinckley in Leicestershire, where the famous brand has been revived.

Two miles from the village is the **National Motorcycle Museum**, recognised as the finest and largest of its kind in the world. The extensive collection of motorbikes is both impressive and nostalgic, serving as a fitting tribute to and a living record of the once great British industry that dominated for some sixty years.

375 THE BULL AT WITHERLEY

Witherley

Handsomely converted, this 18th century coaching inn now offers a large and exciting snack and a la carte menu, with guest accommodation alongside the River Amber.

See entry on page 577

376 THE RED LION

Corley Moor

Popular with families, this 16th century inn is known for its excellent hospitality and fine food.

See entry on page 577

WILTSHIRE

A county rich in prehistoric remains, Wiltshire also has one of the highest concentrations of historic houses and gardens in the country as well as some fine downland and woodland that provide excellent walking or cycling.

The industrial heritage of the county takes many forms – Brunel's Great Western Railway centred on Swindon, brewing at Devizes, carpet making at Wilton and the Kennet and Avon Canal. The jewel in Wiltshire's crown is the fine city of Salisbury with its magnificent cathedral; a grand affair in Early English style with the tallest spire in England (a later addition to the building) – reaching up an awe-inspiring 404 feet to the heavens.

But it is for its ancient monuments, white horses and the intriguing crop circles that the county is best known; and which lends it a uniquely mystical ambience. Along with the Stone Circles at Avebury, Silbury Hill, West Kennet Long Barrow and the White Horse at Westbury, Wiltshire is, of course, home to Stonehenge. A World Heritage Site, these massive stone blocks are one of the greatest mysteries of the prehistoric world. Close by is an even more ancient monument that is often overlooked – Woodhenge.

The stunning historic houses are popular with visitors to the county, the most renowned being Longleat House; famous for its surrounding Safari Park, the walls of the house provide just as exotic an experience,

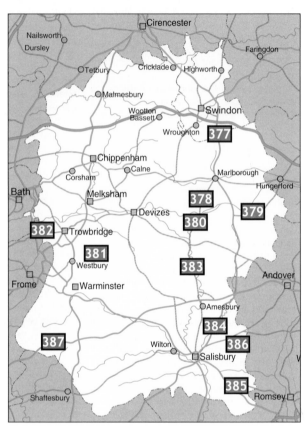

many of the rooms having been painted by eccentric Lord Bath in his characteristically vibrant style. Many of the other houses in Wiltshire hold their own treasures, Bodwood House, quite literally, as it is the home of the Shelborne family heirlooms. There is also Mompesson House, a fine example of Queen Anne architecture; Wilton House which was remodelled by James Wyatt following a fire in 1647, and has an amazing Double Cube room; Philipps House which is surrounded by the green expanse of Dinton Park; and Stourton House which is the perfect example of classical English style, dating from 1720s.

Accommodation

Food & Drink

Food & Drink

Places of Interest

SWINDON

The largest town in Wiltshire, lying in the northeast corner between the Cotswolds and the Marlborough Downs, Swindon was an insignificant agricultural community before the railway line between London and Bristol was completed in 1835. In 1843, Isambard Kingdom Brunel, the Great Western Railway's principal engineer, decided that Swindon was the place to build his locomotive works.

Within a few years it had grown to be one of the largest in the world, with as many as 12,000 workers on a 320-acre site that incorporated the Railway Village: this was a model development of 300 workmens' houses built of limestone extracted from the construction of Box Tunnel. This unique example of early Victorian town planning is open to the public at the **Railway Village Museum**. The Great Western Railway Museum, now called **Steam**, houses a collection of locomotives, nameplates and signalling equipment along with exhibitions on the life of Brunel and of the men and women who built and repaired the rolling stock for God's Wonderful Railway. The site also contains the **National Monuments Record Centre** - the public archive of the Royal Commission on the Historical Monuments of England, with 7 million photographs, documents and texts.

On the western outskirts of Swindon is

STEAM Museum, Swindon

Lydiard Park, one of Wiltshire's smaller stately homes, which is the ancestral home of the Viscounts Bolingbroke.

Just south of the town lies Wroughton Airfield, a historic World War II airbase which is home to the National Museum of Science and Industry's collection of large aircraft.

---

377 PATRIOTS ARMS

Chiseldon

Fine old hostelry offering good food, real ales, regular live entertainment and a spacious beer garden.

See entry on page 578

AROUND SWINDON

MARLBOROUGH

10 miles S of Swindon on the A346

Marlborough College was founded in 1843 primarily for sons of the clergy. Built on the site of a Norman castle, the first mansion here was replaced in the early 18th century by a building that became the Castle Inn and is now C House, the oldest part of the college.

To the southeast of the town lies the ancient woodland of **Savernake Forest** where Henry VIII hunted wild deer.

Situated in a beautiful valley that bears its name, **Pewsey** is a charming village that was once the property of Alfred the Great. The **Heritage Centre**, housed in an 1870 foundry building, is well worth a visit, but the

378 MAGGIE VIGAR-SMITH

Marlborough

Bed & breakfast with a difference in relaxed and artistic environment.

See entry on page 578

379 THE SWAN INN

Wilton

Friendly hostelry in picturesque village serving fantastic home-cooked food.

See entry on page 579

380 THE FRENCH HORN

Pewsey

The Australian chef offers extensive menu ranging from traditional favourites to dishes based on kangaroo and wild boar meat.

See entry on page 579

most interesting feature here lies just south of the village on Pewsey Down. The original **Pewsey White Horse** was cut in 1785 and apparently included a rider, but it was redesigned by George Marples and cut by the local fire brigade to celebrate the coronation of George VI.

AVEBURY

10 miles SW of Swindon on the A4361

This village is home to the **Avebury Stone Circles**, the most remarkable ritual megalithic monuments in Europe and now a World Heritage Site, under the care of the National Trust. Many of the archaeological finds from the site are displayed in the **Alexander Keiller Museum**, which also describes the reconstruction of the site by Keiller in the 1930s.

Avebury also has a gem from more recent times: **Avebury Manor** dates from the Elizabethan era and is surrounded by a walled garden that features a wishing well, topiary and an Italian walk.

Avebury Manor

This area abounds with ancient monuments. To the south lies **West Kennet Long Barrow**, one of the country's largest Neolithic burial tombs; on nearby Overton Hill is The Sanctuary, an early Bronze Age monument of giant standing stones.

To the west of West Kennet, by the A4, lies the largest man-made prehistoric mound in Europe, **Silbury Hill**, which dates from around 2800 BC and rises some 300 feet. No bones or any other clues as to the purpose of the mound has been found, but it might have some connection with the nearby Avebury Stone Circles.

CRICKLADE

6½ miles NW of Swindon on the B4040

The only Wiltshire town on the River Thames, Cricklade has many buildings of interest, including the famous school founded by the London goldsmith Robert Jenner in 1651, and the elaborate Victorian clock tower. Nearby, North Meadow is a National Nature Reserve where the rare snakeshead fritillary grows.

CHIPPENHAM

An important administrative centre in King Alfred's time, Chippenham later gained prominence from the wool trade and was a major stop on the London to Bristol coaching route. In the flood plain to the east of Chippenham lies the footpath known as **Maud Heath's Causeway**, a remarkable and ingenious walkway consisting of 64 brick and stone arches that was built in the 15th century at the bequest of Maud Heath. She had spent most of her life as a poor pedlar trudging her way between the village of Bremhill and Chippenham but she died a relatively wealthy woman and her will provided sufficient funds for the construction and upkeep of the causeway.

To the south lies **Lacock Abbey**, which was founded in 1232 by Ela, Countess of Salisbury, in memory of her husband William Longsword, stepbrother to Richard the Lionheart. The

estate later passed into the hands of the Talbot family, whose most distinguished member was the pioneering photographer, William Henry Fox Talbot, who carried out his experiments here in the 1830s.

Today, the National Trust's estate village of **Lacock** is one of the county's real treasures, with its delightful assortment of mellow stone buildings seemingly remaining unaltered over the centuries. The **Fox Talbot Museum** commemorates the life and achievements of a man who was not just a photographer but a mathematician, physicist, classicist and transcriber of Syrian and Chaldean cuneiform. The cloisters of Fox Talbot's house were used as a classroom at Hogwart's School in the Harry Potter films.

AROUND CHIPPENHAM

MALMESBURY

9 miles N of Chippenham on the B4040

England's oldest borough is dominated by the impressive remains of the Benedictine **Malmesbury Abbey**, founded in the 7th century by St Aldhelm. In the 10th century, King Athelstan, granted 500 acres of land to the townsfolk in gratitude for resisting a Norse invasion. This land is still known as King's Heath and is now owned by 200 residents who are descended from those far-off heroes.

In the **Athelstan Museum** are numerous displays, including one of lace making and another of early bicycles, while a more recent piece of local history concerns the Tamworth Two – the pigs who made the headlines with their dash for freedom.

To the east lies **Easton Grey**, whose elegant 18th century manor house was used as a summer retreat by Herbert Asquith, Prime Minister between 1908 and 1916.

CALNE

5 miles E of Chippenham on the A4

Calne is a former weaving centre in the valley of the River Marden and the prominent **Wool**

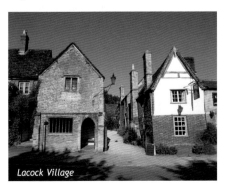
Lacock Village

Church reflects the town's early prosperity; inside, is a memorial to Dr Ingenhousz, who is widely credited with creating a smallpox vaccination before Edward Jenner.

A short distance from Calne, to the west, stands **Bowood House**, which was built in 1625 and is now a treasury of Shelborne family heirlooms, paintings, books and furniture. It was in the Bowood Laboratory at Bowood House that Dr Joseph Priestley, tutor to the 1st Marquis of Lansdowne's son, conducted experiments that resulted in the identification of oxygen.

The **Atwell-Wilson Motor Museum**, to the east of Calne, has a collection of over 70 vintage and classic cars and motorcycles from the years 1924 to 1983.

DEVIZES

9 miles SE of Chippenham on the A342

Devizes was founded in 1080 by Bishop Osmund, nephew of William the Conqueror, who built a timber castle here between the lands of two powerful manors. After the wooden structure burnt down, the Bishop of Sarum built a stone castle in 1138 that survived until the end of the Civil War, when it was demolished.

Devizes Wharf

Devizes **Visitor Centre** is based on a 12th century castle and takes visitors back to medieval times, when Devizes was home not just to its fine castle but also to anarchy and unrest during the struggle between Empress Matilda and King Stephen.

Many of the town's finest buildings are situated in and around the old market place, including the Town Hall and the Corn Exchange. Devizes stands at a key point on the Kennet and Avon Canal and the **Kennet and Avon Canal Museum** tells the complete story of the waterway in fascinating detail. Many visitors combine a trip to the museum with a walk along the towpath; the town really buzzes in July when the Canalfest is held at the Wharf.

TROWBRIDGE

11 miles S of Chippenham on the A361

Trowbridge is the county town of Wiltshire, chosen due to its location near the geographical centre of the county. It still has a number of old industrial buildings from its past as a major weaving centre, and an interesting waymarked walk takes in many of them. The parish **Church of St James** contains the tomb of the poet and former rector George Crabbe, who wrote the work on which Benjamin Britten based his opera *Peter Grimes*. Trowbridge's most famous son was Isaac Pitman, the shorthand man, who was born in Nash Yard in 1813.

BRADFORD-ON-AVON

10 miles SW of Chippenham on the A363

A historic market town at a bridging point on the River Avon, which is spanned by a superb nine-arched bridge with a lock-up at one end. The town's oldest building is the **Church of St**

---

381 **THE DUKE AT BRATTON**

Bratton

A traditional country pub serving traditional homemade food.

See entry on page 580

---

382 **THE NEW INN**

Lower Westwood, nr Bradford on Avon

Gorgeous traditional village inn, serving a delicious fresh menu including fish and game caught by the owners.

See entry on page 580

Lawrence that is believed to have been founded by St Aldhelm in around AD 700. It 'disappeared' for over 1,000 years, during which time it was used variously as a school, a charnel house for storing the bones of the dead and a residential dwelling; it was re-discovered by a keen-eyed clergyman who looked down from a hill and noticed its cruciform shape.

Another of the town's outstanding buildings is the mighty **Tithe Barn**, which was once used to store the grain from local farms for Shaftesbury Abbey.

On the edge of the town, **Barton Farm Country Park** offers delightful walks in lovely countryside beside the River Avon and the Kennet and Avon Canal. **Barton Bridge** is the original packhorse bridge that was built to assist the transportation of grain from the farm to the tithe barn.

Half a mile south of the town, by the River Frome, is the Italian-style **Peto Garden** at Iford Manor, laid out between 1899 and 1933 by the architect and landscape gardener Harold Ainsworth Peto.

To the west, in the middle of the village of Holt, stands **The Courts**, an English country garden of mystery with unusual topiary, water gardens and an arboretum.

CASTLE COMBE

5½ miles NW of Chippenham on the B4039

The loveliest village in the region, and for some the loveliest in the country, Castle Combe was once a centre of the prosperous wool trade, famed for its red and white cloth. Many of the present buildings date from the 15th and 16th centuries, including the covered **Market Cross** and the **Manor House**, which was built with stones from the Norman castle that gave the village its name.

SALISBURY

The glorious medieval city of Salisbury stands at the confluence of four rivers, the Avon, the Wylye, the Bourne and the Nadder. Originally called New Sarum, it grew around the present Cathedral.

Surely one of the most beautiful buildings in the world, **Salisbury Cathedral** is the only medieval cathedral in England to be built all in the same Early English style – apart from its spire, the tallest in England, which was added some years later and rises to an awesome 404 feet. The Chapter House opens out of the cloisters and contains, among other treasures, one of the four surviving originals of the Magna Carta. The oldest working clock in Britain, and possibly in the world, is situated in the fan-vaulted north transept; it was built in 1386 to strike the hour and has no clock face.

The Close, the precinct of the ecclesiastical community serving the Cathedral, is the largest in England and contains a number of museums and houses open to the public, including, in the 17th century King's House, **Salisbury Museum**, home of the Stonehenge Gallery and The **Royal Gloucestershire, Berkshire and Wiltshire Museum**, housed in a 13th century building called **The Wardrobe**, which was originally used to store the bishop's clothes and documents. **Mompesson House** is a perfect example of Queen Anne architecture that is noted for its plasterwork, an elegant carved oak staircase, fine period furniture and the important Turnbull collection of 18th century drinking glasses.

Mompesson House, Salisbury

There are many other areas of Salisbury to explore, and on a huge mound to the north are the ruins of **Old Sarum**, abandoned when the bishopric moved into the city. Old Sarum became the most notorious of the 'rotten boroughs', returning two Members of

Parliament, despite having no voters, until the 1832 Reform Act stopped the cheating. A plaque on the site commemorates Old Sarum's most illustrious Member of Parliament, William Pitt the Elder. In the town centre is a bustling selection of individual shops, and a vibrant charter market which has been held in the town every Tuesday and Saturday for almost 800 years.

AROUND SALISBURY

AMESBURY

7 miles N of Salisbury on the A345

It was here that Queen Elfrida founded an abbey in AD 979, in atonement for her part in the murder of her son-in-law, Edward the Martyr, at Corfe Castle. Henry II rebuilt the

abbey's great **Church of St Mary and St Melor**, whose tall central tower is the only structure to survive from the pre-Norman monastery.

Two miles west of Amesbury stands **Stonehenge**, perhaps the greatest mystery of the prehistoric world, one of the wonders of the world and a monument of unique importance. Stonehenge's orientation on the rising and setting sun has always been one of its most remarkable features, leading to theories that the builders were from a sun-worshipping culture or that the whole structure is part of a huge astronomical calendar.

WILTON

3 miles W of Salisbury on the A30

The third oldest borough in England, and once the capital of Saxon Wessex, Wilton is best known for its carpets and the **Wilton Carpet Factory**, on the River Wylye, continues to produce top-quality Wilton and Axminster carpets.

To the south of the town stands **Wilton House**, the home of the Earls of Pembroke that was designed by Inigo Jones in the 17th century after the original house had been destroyed by fire in 1647. Later remodelled by James Wyatt, Wilton House features the amazing Double Cube Room and a fine art collection.

To the west lies **Dinton**, a lovely hillside village that is home to **Little Clarendon House**, a near perfect Tudor manor house, and **Philipps House**, a handsome early 19th century mansion that stands in the beautiful grounds of Dinton Park. Further west again are the ruins of **Old Wardour Castle**, a unique six-sided castle that dates from the 14th century.

---

383 ENFORD HOUSE

Enford, nr Pewsey

Delightful Grade 2 listed house in the heart of the Salisbury Plain, available for B&B or holiday lettings.

See entry on page 581

---

384 THE PORTON HOTEL

Porton

Elegant hotel, dating from 1900, which serves up a wonderful locally-sourced menu and cosy en-suite rooms.

See entry on page 581

---

385 THE KINGS HEAD

Whiteparish

Unique traditional pub brimming with character, in an unspoilt village near Salisbury.

See entry on page 582

---

386 THE LORD NELSON

Middle Winterslow

Historic traditional pub just east of Salisbury with a fresh and vibrant menu.

See entry on page 582

Old Wardour Castle

STOURTON

23 miles W of Salisbury off the B3092

The main attraction of this beautiful village is **Stourhead**, one of the most famous examples of an early 18th century English landscape garden, and a place renowned for its striking vistas and woodland walks. **Stourton House** is a classical masterpiece dating from the 1720s and on the edge of the estate is the imposing King Alfred's Tower, a redbrick folly erected in 1772 that commemorates the king who reputedly raised his standard here against the Danes in AD 878.

WARMINSTER

19 miles NW of Salisbury off the A36

This historic town on the western edge of Salisbury Plain has a number of distinguished

Stourhead House

old buildings and some interesting monuments of varying age. **The Obelisk**, with its feeding troughs and pineapple top, was erected in 1783 to mark the enclosure of the parish; the Morgan Memorial Fountain stands in the Lake Pleasure Grounds; and Beyond Harvest is a statue in bronze by Colin Lambert of a girl sitting on sacks of corn.

To the west of town, **Cley Hill** is an Iron Age hill fort with two Bronze Age barrows; it is renowned as a place for sighting UFOs. The region is also noted for the appearance of crop circles, and some have linked the two phenomena.

Just to the west of Warminster is **Longleat House**, the magnificent home of the Marquis of Bath that dates from the 1570s and is filled with a superb collection of old masters, beautiful furniture, rare books and murals by the eccentric Lord Bath. The glorious grounds, landscaped by Capability Brown, are famous as the home of the Safari Park established in the 1960s.

North of Warminster is **Westbury**, a major centre of the wool and cloth trades in the Middle Ages and with many fine buildings still standing as a legacy of those prosperous days.

To the east of Westbury is the town's best known feature, the famous Westbury **White Horse** that dates from 1778 and replaces an earlier horse carved to celebrate King Alfred's victory over the Danes in AD 878. Above the horse's head are the ruins of Bratton Castle, an Iron Age hill fort covering 25 acres.

---

387 **ANGEL CORNER TEA ROOMS**

Mere

Lovely traditional tea-rooms, with an exotic twist, brimming with home-made cakes and art.

See entry on page 583

WORCESTERSHIRE

The southern part of Worcestershire is dominated by the spectacular ridge of the Malvern Hills in the west, which provides excellent walking country along with breathtaking views, and the Vale of Evesham in the east, an attractive area with charming towns and villages built of the warm Cotswold stone.

Most of the county's industry is centred in the northern part, where there are numerous examples of industrial archaeology to interest the historian. Canals here were once as important as roads and the area around Kidderminster and Redditch is dominated

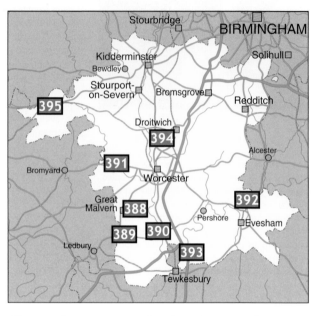

by three such waterways: the Worcester & Birmingham Canal, the Staffordshire & Worcester Canal and the Droitwich Canal. The arrival of the railways saw a rapid decline in water transport and, although this network is now much smaller than it was, the Severn Valley Railway, from Kidderminster to Bridgnorth, has survived and flourishes today as people flock here to relive the days of steam travel.

Between these two very different sections of Worcestershire lies the county town of Worcester, an ancient place that is well known for its glorious cathedral and as being the home of Royal Worcester porcelain. The city also contains the wonderful medieval Greyfriars, with its picturesque walled garden.

It was near here, at Lower Broadheath, that one of Britain's greatest composers, Sir Edward Elgar, was born, and a museum in the village tells the story of his amazing life. There is an eclectic mix of wonderful

museums throughout the county; the most dramatically located would be the Worcester County Museum which is housed in the beautiful Hartlebury Castle.

The charming historical buildings in Worcestershire are all worthy of visiting, there are a particular few however which are unique in design, style or location, and are a most interesting feature of this area. There is, for example, Hagley Hall with its stunning rococo interior, Hanbury Hall where you can see beautiful murals painted by Sir James Thornhill (best known for his frescoes in the dome of St Paul's Cathedral), Chateau Impney which was built in the most extravagant style of a French chateau, and the equally extravagant Witley Court which, although now a ruin, has now been lovingly preserved along with its fountains inspired by the works of Bernini in Rome. Less excessive, but just as breathtaking, is Broadway Tower, from which you can get some of the best views in the county.

Accommodation

Food & Drink

WORCESTER

Situated on the River Severn, Worcester is a bustling county capital that is dominated by its **Cathedral**. Built by St Wulstan, the only English bishop not replaced by a Norman following the Conquest, the Cathedral, with its 200 feet tower and 11th century crypt, is a magnificent example of classic medieval architecture. One of the many tombs here is that of King John, adorned with a fine sculpture showing the King flanked by Bishops Oswald and Wulstan; outside is a statue of Sir Edward Elgar, who was born at nearby Lower Broadheath.

Right in the centre of the city stands a wonderful survivor from the past - **Greyfriars** (National Trust), a medieval house with a pretty walled garden. By contrast, the imposing Guildhall is a marvellous example of Queen Anne architecture that was designed by a local man, Thomas White. At the **City Museum and Art Gallery** there are dynamic displays of contemporary art and archaeology, fascinating for people of all ages. The nearby **Tudor House** is a beautifully atmospheric building, previously a museum, but now owned and run by a team of dedicated volunteers (Open Sat and Wed 10am-4pm).

During the Civil War the **Battle of Worcester** was fought in 1651 and the **Commandery**, a stunning complex of buildings behind a small timber-framed entrance, was used as the Royalist headquarters. Now the **Commandery Civil War Centre** is home to a series of period rooms that offer a fascinating glimpse of the architecture and style of Tudor and Stuart times while also acting as the country's only museum devoted to the story of the Civil War.

With charming old buildings, a splendid cathedral, interesting museums and a compact **National Hunt Racecourse**, Worcester certainly has much to offer visitors, but no trip to the city would be complete without a visit to the **Royal Worcester Porcelain Visitor Centre**. Royal Worcester is Britain's oldest continuous producer of porcelain and the factory was founded in 1751 by Dr John Wall, who

Powick Bridge, nr Worcester

283

intended to create "a ware of a form so precise as to be easily distinguished from other English porcelain." Just to the southeast is Worcester Woods Country Park, a glorious place with ancient oak woodland, wildflower meadows and waymarked trails.

To the south of Worcester lies **Powick Bridge**, the scene of the first and last battles in the Civil War – the last, in 1651, ending with Charles II hiding in the Boscobel Oak before journeying south to nine year's exile in France.

It was at **Lower Broadheath**, just to the west of Worcester, that Edward Elgar was born in 1857, and, although he spent long periods away from the village, it remained his spiritual home. There are various **Elgar Trails** to follow, and the **Elgar Birthplace Museum** is housed in a redbrick cottage.

AROUND WORCESTER

MALVERN

7½ miles S of Worcester on the A449

Best known for its porcelain, annual music and drama festivals, Malvern water and Morgan cars, Malvern, beneath the northeastern slopes of the Malvern Hills, was a quiet and little known place with a priory at its centre before the discovery of its spring waters started its growth. The hotels, baths and pump room were built in the early 19th century and the arrival of the railway provided easier access. The station is one of the many charming Victorian buildings, and a Regency cottage houses one source of the spring waters, **St Anne's Well**, where visitors can still sample the waters.

The centre of the town is dominated by a much older building, the priory **Church of St**

Mary and St Michael, whose east and west windows (gifts from Henry VII and Richard III respectively) contain a wonderful collection of stained glass. The 14th century Abbey Gateway still remains, now the home of the **Malvern Museum**. The town's heritage as an agricultural and market centre has not been lost, as close by is the permanent site of the **Three Counties Show**, one of the country's premier agricultural shows.

Great Malvern is the largest of the six settlements that make up the Malverns. To the south lies **Little Malvern**, where a simple headstone in the churchyard marks the grave of Sir Edward Elgar and his wife Caroline. In the churchyard at West Malvern is the grave of Peter Mark Roget of Thesaurus fame.

UPTON-ON-SEVERN

9 miles S of Worcester on the A4104

As one of the few bridging points on the River Severn, this unspoilt town was a Roman station and an important medieval port. It also played a role in the Civil War when in 1651 Charles sent a force to Upton to destroy the bridge; but after a long and bloody struggle the King's troops were defeated and Cromwell's men regained the town.

The **Tudor House** contains a museum of Upton past and present, and the 16th

---

389 THE DELL HOUSE

Worcestershire

Self catering holiday homes and an award winning B&B nestled in two acres of woodland on The Malvern Hills.

See entry on page 584

---

388 BLUEBIRD TEAROOMS

Great Malvern

A popular cafe offering a wide selection of home cooked cakes, scones, sandwiches and lunchtime meals.

See entry on page 583

---

390 THE THREE KINGS

Hanley Castle

A traditional country inn with a lively little bar serving a fine selection of real ales.

See entry on page 584

---

century White Lion Hotel was the setting for some of the scenes in Henry Fielding's novel *Tom Jones*.

Northeast of Upton, close to Earls Croome, lies **Croome Landscape Park**, which was Capability Brown's first complete landscape commission.

ALFRICK

6½ miles W of Worcester off the A44

The village church's claim to fame is that Charles Dodgson (better known as Lewis Carroll) once preached here but, today, it is nature lovers who are drawn to this charming village. To the northwest lies **Ravenshill Woodland Nature Reserve** where waymarked trails lead through woodland that is home to many breeding birds while, to the south, is Knapp and Papermill Nature Reserve, whose woodland and meadow are rich in flora and fauna.

To the east is the spectacular valley of **Leigh Brook**, a tributary of the River Teme, which winds its way through glorious countryside, and in the village of **Leigh**, in the grounds of **Leigh Court**, stands a massive 14th century Tithe Barn with great cruck beams and wagon doors.

EVESHAM

' *Who travels Worcester county takes any road that comes, when April tosses bounty to the cherries and the plums'*. Thus did the poet John Drinkwater describe his favourite county.

This bustling market town lies at the centre of the Vale of Evesham, an area that has long been known as the Garden of England as it produces a prolific harvest of soft fruits, apples, plums and salad vegetables. The **Blossom Trail**, which starts in the town, is a popular outing, particularly when the fruit trees are in blossom, and the waymarked trail follows a route from the town's High Street to Greenhill, where the **Battle of Evesham** took place.

At this point, the River Avon meanders in a loop around the town and Abbey Park is an excellent place for a riverside stroll although all that remains of the **Abbey**, which was built in around AD 700 by Egwin, Bishop of Worcester, is the magnificent bell tower and the home of the Abbey Almoner that dates from around 1400. At the **Almonry Heritage Centre**, visitors can view a unique collection of artefacts that include displays showing the history of the Abbey and the defeat of Simon de Montford at the Battle of Evesham in 1265. He was buried by the high altar, and a stone marking the site was unveiled by the Speaker of the House of Commons in 1965, the 700th anniversary of his death.

AROUND EVESHAM

PERSHORE

6 miles NW of Evesham on the A44

This glorious market town, with its fine Georgian architecture, occupies an attractive location on the banks of the River Avon. Its crowning glory is undoubtedly its 7th century **Abbey**, which combines outstanding examples of both Norman and Early English architecture. Although only the choir remains of the original church, it is still a considerable architectural treasure, and the vaulting in the chancel roof is magnificent.

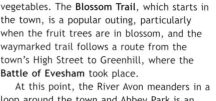

---

391 THE ROYAL OAK

Broadwas-on-Teme

Food is the star of the show at this popular village pub, classic pub grub at lunchtime and a huge choice from display cabinets in the evening.

See entry on page 585

---

392 EVESHAM COUNTRY PARK

Evesham

Enjoy shopping in a relaxed atmosphere and find a bargain in the courtyard shops, extensive garden centre and Millets Farm Shop.

See entry on page 586

Pershore Bridge, which is now a favourite picnic spot, still bears the scars of damage it sustained during the Civil War.

INKBERROW

9 miles N of Evesham on the A422

William Shakespeare stayed at the village inn, **The Old Bull**, in 1582, and it later won fame as the original of The Bull at Ambridge, the home of The Archers. Another handsome building in the village, the 18th century Old Vicarage, played host, in an earlier guise, to Charles I, while he was on his way to Naseby. Some maps that he left behind are now kept in the church.

MIDDLE LITTLETON

4 miles NE of Evesham off the B4085

Situated close to the River Avon along with the other Littletons – North and South – this village is home to a huge **Tithe Barn** that dates from the 13th century and that was once the property of the Abbots of Evesham; it is still in use as a farm building. Just to the north, in an area of fertile limestone, is **Windmill Hill Nature Reserve** while, to the southeast, near Honeybourne, is the **Domestic Fowl Trust and Honeybourne Rare Breeds Centre** where pure breeds of poultry, along with rare farm animal breeds, are conserved.

BROADWAY

5 miles SE of Evesham on the B4632

One of the most beautiful villages in England, this quintessential Cotswold village has a broad main street that is lined with houses and cottages built of golden Cotswold stone.

On top of Broadway Beacon stands **Broadway Tower**, a folly that was built by the

6th Earl of Coventry at the end of the 18th century. Designed by James Wyatt, the tower now contains various displays and exhibitions, while the surrounding area is a delightful country park.

BREDON

8 miles SW of Evesham on the B4079

The most outstanding building here is undoubtedly **Bredon Barn**. This huge 14th century Cotswold stone barn has a dramatic aisled interior, marvellous beams and two porches at the wagon entrances.

KIDDERMINSTER

Standing on the banks of the River Stour, Kidderminster is known chiefly as a centre of the carpet-making industry that began here as a cottage industry in the early 18th century. The introduction of the power loom instigated the move to a more industrialised method and carpet mills were built – the enormous chimneys still dominate the skyline. The industry also brought wealth to the town and surrounding area and this is reflected in the size of **St Mary's Church**, the largest parish church in the county, which stands on a hill overlooking the town. Outside the Town Hall is a statue to Kidderminster's best known son, Rowland Hill, a teacher, educationalist and inventor who founded the modern postal system and introduced the penny post.

The **Severn Valley Railway** runs from Kidderminster to Bridgnorth, in Shropshire, and at the town's station is the **Kidderminster Railway Museum**, where a splendid collection of railway memorabilia can be seen in an old

393 **THE FOX & HOUNDS INN**

Bredon

Fine food and drink brings both a loyal local clientele and visitors from further afield to this wonderful 16th century thatched and timbered country hostelry.

See entry on page 585

St. Mary's Church, Kidderminster

Great Western Railway grain store.

AROUND KIDDERMINSTER

HAGLEY

6 miles NE of Kidderminster on the A456

In 1756, George, 1st Lord Lyttleton, commissioned the creation of what was to be the last great Palladian mansion in Britain, **Hagley Hall**, an imposing building with a restored rococo interior. In the surrounding parkland, there are temples, cascading pools and a ruined castle along with a large herd of deer.

BROMSGROVE

8½ miles SE of Kidderminster on the A448

Along with some very handsome timber-framed buildings in the High Street, there stands a statue of AE Housman, Bromsgrove's most famous son.

Close to the town centre is the **Bromsgrove Museum** where there are displays of local crafts and industry, including the Bromsgrove Guild, an organisation of craftsmen that was founded in 1894. The skilled craftsmen of this guild designed and made the gates and railings of Buckingham Palace.

Two popular annual events are held here: the Music Festival, which hosts a wide range of musical entertainment from orchestral concerts to jazz, and the Court Leet, the ancient form of local administration whose annual colourful procession has been revived.

Just northeast of Bromsgrove near the village of **Burcot** is the notorious **Lickey Incline**. This stretch of railway is, at 1 in 37.7, the steepest gradient in the whole of Britain's rail network. One especially powerful locomotive, No. 58100, '*Big Bertha*', the Lickey Banker, spent its days up until the late 1950s helping trains up the bank, a task that was later performed by massive double-boilered locomotives that were the most powerful in the whole BR fleet. The steepness of the climb is due to the same geographical feature that necessitated the construction of the unique flight of locks at Tardebigge (to the southeast of Bromsgrove), where in the

space of 2½ miles the canal is lifted by no fewer than 30 locks.

In the churchyard of St John the Baptist in Bromsgrove are the graves of Thomas Scaife and Joseph Rutherford, who were killed in 1840 when the boiler of their locomotive blew up as they were climbing Lickey Incline.

To the south of Bromsgrove is the **Avoncroft Museum of Historic Buildings** that takes visitors on a walk through seven centuries of English history and where each building provides a snapshot of life in its particular period. Behind the museum's shop is another unique attraction, the **BT National Telephone Kiosk Collection**.

REDDITCH

14½ miles SE of Kidderminster on the A448

It was along the banks of the River Arrow that the town's famous needle-making industry was founded. Housed in one of the historic buildings in the beautiful valley is the **Forge Mill Needle Museum** and Bordesley Abbey Visitor Centre that offers a unique glimpse into a past way of life.

DROITWICH

8½ miles SE of Kidderminster on the A38

Salt deposits, a legacy from the time when this area was on the seabed, were mined here for 2,000 years, and the Romans named it Salinae, the place of salt. The natural Droitwich brine, which is pumped up from an underground lake 200 feet below the town, contains about 2½ pounds of salt per gallon – ten times that of sea water – and it is often likened to the waters of the Dead Sea. The first brine baths were built here in the 1830s and by 1876, under the influence of the 'Salt King' John Corbett, Droitwich had developed into a fashionable spa.

394 HADLEY BOWLING GREEN INN

Hadley Heath

Bar and restaurant menus offer 'fine dining without the formality' and guest accommodation numbers 9 well-equipped en suite rooms.

See entry on page 587

Many of the buildings in present day Droitwich were owned by Corbett, including the Raven Hotel, but his most remarkable and lasting monument is undoubtedly **Chateau Impney** on the eastern side of the town at Dodderhill. Designed in the style of an ornate French château by a Frenchman, Auguste Tronquois, the house has soaring turrets, a mansard roof and classical French gardens.

To the east of Droitwich lies **Hanbury Hall** (National Trust), a fine redbrick mansion in William & Mary style. Along with a splendid collection of porcelain, the interior of the house is famous for its murals by Sir James Thornhill, who is perhaps best known for his frescoes in the dome of St Paul's Cathedral. The surrounding grounds include a formal garden, an orangery and an 18th century icehouse.

STOURPORT-ON-SEVERN
3½ miles S of Kidderminster on the A451

Situated at the centre of the Worcestershire waterways, Stourport-on-Severn is a canal town of glorious Georgian buildings with an intricate network of canal basins. Prosperity and growth came quickly once the Staffordshire and Worcestershire Canal had been dug, and although the commercial trade has now gone the town still prospers, as the barges laden with coal, timber, iron and grain have given way to pleasure craft.

Just to the east of the town lies **Hartlebury Castle**, a historic sandstone castle that was once owned by the Bishops of Worcester and was used as a prison for captured Royalist troops during the Civil War. It now houses the **Worcester County Museum**.

GREAT WITLEY
8½ miles SW of Kidderminster on the A443

This village is home to two remarkable buildings. Once one of the largest houses in Europe, **Witley Court** was a palatial mansion that was funded by the riches of the Dudley family but, following a devastating fire in 1937, the shell stood neglected for many years. The ruins have been made safe and accessible and along with the massive Poseidon and Flora fountains inspired by

Bernini's fountains in Rome, they are a sight not to be missed. Adjacent to these haunting ruins is **St Michael's Church**, whose rather nondescript exterior does nothing to prepare visitors for the spectacularly flamboyant Baroque interior: stained glass by Joshua Price, plasterwork by Bagutti, canvas ceiling paintings by Bellucci.

BEWDLEY
3 miles W of Kidderminster on the B4190

Situated on the western bank of the River Severn and linked to its suburb, Wribbenhall, by a fine Thomas Telford bridge, Bewdley was once a flourishing port but it lost some of its importance when the Staffordshire and Worcestershire Canal was opened. It has now won fame with another form of transport, the **Severn Valley Railway**, which operates a full service of trains hauled by a variety of steam locomotives. Running from Kidderminster to Bridgnorth, the home of the railway since 1965, the route takes in several scenic attractions including the Wyre Forest and the Severn Valley Country Park and Nature Reserve. There are six stations along the track, each of them an architectural delight.

The **Bewdley Museum** contains exhibitions that are themed around the River Severn and the Wyre Forest and depicts local crafts such as charcoal burning, coopering and brass making. The town was the birthplace of Stanley Baldwin, Earl Baldwin of Bewdley, who was Prime Minister in 1923-1924, 1924-1929 and 1935-1937. He died at his home, **Astley Hall** (5 miles south of Kidderminster), opposite which is a memorial stone inscribed 'Thrice Prime Minister'. His ashes lie with those of his wife in the nave of Worcester Cathedral.

395 **THE FOUNTAIN INN**

Tenbury Wells

The inn enjoys a delightful setting above the Teme Valley and is a great favourite with both locals and visitors to the area.

See entry on page 587

YORKSHIRE

The largest county in England, Yorkshire has a rich industrial and ecclesiastical heritage along with a wide diversity of countryside that helps to make it one of the most intriguing regions of England. This diversity is reflected in the huge range of museums throughout the county; ranging from mining and industry, railways, police and horse-drawn carriages, to Captain Cook, Roman settlements, and even cheese (delicious Wendsley Dale).

The Yorkshire Dales National Park is an area of rich farmland, high moorland and deep valleys.

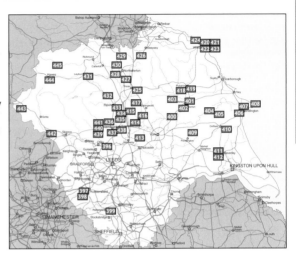

The predominant limestone has given rise to a host of interesting natural features, none more so than Malham Cove, Malham Tarn and Aysgarth Falls. Most unusual is Mother Shipton's Cave, which contains a petrifying well, with water so rich in lime it seemingly turns objects into stone.

South of the Dales is Brontë country, an area forever associated with the tragic family, but one that also has strong links with the textile industry. Here also is the volunteer run Keighley and Worth Valley Railway, made famous in the 1970s film *The Railway Children*.

The northeast of the county is dominated by the North York Moors National Park that incorporates not only the Cleveland Hills but also some spectacular coastline, including the old port of Whitby. Here, too, are elegant market towns such as Richmond and Ripon, and the famous spa town of Harrogate. The castle at Richmond is a particularly wonderful sight – from its tactical vantage point atop a 100 ft rocky promontory.

Above all, there is York, a fabulous city centred on its magnificent cathedral that has a long and colourful history going back over 2,000 years. The glorious 'Shambles', a network of winding ancient streets, here is a wonder for visitors with unique shops and points of interest in every turn. Not far north of York can be found one of the prettiest villages in the country, Coxwold, and Shandy Hall; once the home of Laurence Stern, the author of the infamously odd novel *Tristram Shandy*.

Accommodation

Food & Drink

Food & Drink

Places of Interest

HALIFAX

Halifax boasts one of Yorkshire's most impressive examples of municipal architecture, the glorious 18th century **Piece Hall**, a large quadrangle surrounded by colonnades and balconies behind which are some 40 specialist shops. Adjacent to the hall is the **Calderdale Industrial Museum**, which provides an insight into Halifax's textile heritage as well as celebrating the town's greatest contribution to modern motoring, the cats-eye. Halifax also has one of the largest parish churches in England.

On the outskirts of the town is the **Bankfield Museum**, the home between 1837 and 1886 of Edward Akroyd, the largest wool manufacturer in Britain, which now houses an internationally important collection of textiles and costumes from around the world.

To the east of Halifax lies **Shibden Hall and Park**, a distinctive timber-framed house dating from 1420, situated in 90 acres of parkland.

AROUND HALIFAX

KEIGHLEY

10 miles N of Halifax on the A650

Lying at the junction of the Rivers Worth and Aire, Keighley still retains a strangely nostalgic air of the Victorian Industrial Revolution; several of the old mill buildings survive.

Just northeast of the town lies 17th century **East Riddlesden Hall**, which has one of the largest and most impressive timber-framed barns in the North of England that now houses a collection of farm wagons and agricultural equipment.

ILKLEY

14 miles NE of Halifax on the A65

One of the most famous West Yorkshire attractions has to be **Ilkley Moor**, immortalised in the well-known song; like any of the Yorkshire moors, Ilkley Moor can look inviting and attractive on a sunny day but ominous and forbidding when the weather is bad – best to wear a hat.

BRADFORD

10 miles NE of Halifax on the A650

The **Bradford Industrial Museum** and Horses at Work, housed in an original worsted spinning mill complex built in 1875, re-creates life in Bradford in late Victorian times as well as offering horse-bus and tram rides. Of related interest is Britain's only **Museum of Colour**, where the fascinating story of dyeing and textile printing from Ancient Egypt to the present day is explained. The **National Media Museum**

houses an IMAX, one of the largest cinema screens in the world.

HOLMFIRTH

11 miles SE of Halifax on the A635

As the location for the television comedy, *The Last of the Summer Wine*, Holmfirth is familiar to millions who have never visited this little Pennine town. The town is home to the **Holmfirth Postcard Museum**, which has a comprehensive collection of the traditional saucy seaside postcard produced by Bamfords of Holmfirth in the first half of the 20th century.

HAWORTH

8 miles NW of Halifax off the A6033

Haworth is the home of the Brontë family and in its time was also a thriving industrial town. **The Parsonage**, built in 1777, is the focus of most Brontë pilgrimages and is now given over to the **Brontë Parsonage Museum**.

The **Brontë Way**, a 40-mile footpath with a series of four guided walks, links the places that provided inspiration to the sisters. All the siblings were buried in the family vault except Anne, who was buried at Sacrborough. The town is the headquarters of the **Keighley and Worth Valley Railway**, a thriving

---

397 GOLCAR LILY

Golcar

Historic and beautiful country inn renowned for serving up fine English food, with stunning views across the Colne Valley.

See entry on page 589

---

396 THE WHARFEDALE INN & RESTAURANT

Arthington

The inn offers a place for locals to meet over a glass of real ale, a restaurant and comfortable accommodation.

See entry on page 588

---

398 MOONRAKER FLOATING TEAROOM

Slaithwaite

This quirky tea room is set on a narrow boat on the Huddersfield canal, with a fine reputation for wholesome, home cooking.

See entry on page 588

volunteer-run railway that serves six stations (most of them gas-lit) in the course of its length; it is most famous for being used in the 1970s film *The Railway Children*.

SHEFFIELD

In recent years Sheffield has re-invented itself. England's fourth largest city, it is still busy with its steel, cutlery, engineering and toolmaking industries but is also a vibrant, international, multi-cultural city whose image was given a fillip by the worldwide success of *The Full Monty* which was filmed in and around Sheffield.

The city's premier museum is the **Kelham Island Museum** which tells the story of Sheffield in a living museum. Sheffield's industrial heritage is celebrated in a number of museums, the most picturesque of which is undoubtedly the **Bishop's House Museum** which dates from around 1500 and is the earliest timber-framed house still standing in the city. A museum of a very different nature is the Sheffield Bus Museum, which has recently been renamed the **South Yorkshire Transport Museum** and has relocated to Aldwarke, just north of Rotherham. Sheffield also has three outstanding galleries devoted to the visual arts: the **Millennium Galleries** that not only showcase Sheffield's impressive metalware collection but also provides space to show the city's wonderful collection of paintings, drawings and natural history exhibits; the **Graves Art Gallery** with a wide-ranging collection of British art from the 16th century to the present along with European paintings and a fine collection of watercolours, drawings and prints; and the **Site Gallery**, devoted to photographic and new media exhibitions and events.

AROUND SHEFFIELD

RENISHAW
9 miles SE of Sheffield on the A616

This sizeable village gives its name to

Renishaw Hall, home of Sir Reresby and Lady Sitwell and located about a mile or so to the northwest. The beautiful formal Italian gardens and 300 acres of wooded park are open to visitors, along with a nature trail and a Sitwell family museum, an art gallery, a display of Fiori de Henriques sculptures in the Georgian stables, and a café.

ROTHERHAM
7 miles NE of Sheffield on the A630/A631

The town's most striking building is undoubtedly the **Church of All Saints**. With its soaring tower, pinnacled buttresses and battlements, and imposing porch, it is one of the finest examples of perpendicular architecture in Yorkshire. It dates mainly from the 15th century although there is evidence of an earlier Saxon church on the site.

Dramatically set within the former Templeborough steelworks, **Magna** was the UK's first science adventure park.

BARNSLEY
10 miles N of Sheffield on the A61

The county town of South Yorkshire, Barnsley stands on the River Dearne and derived its Victorian prosperity from the rich seams of coal hereabouts. It has an appropriately imposing Town Hall although the building is comparatively recent, completed in 1933. The town's most impressive museum is actually located a few miles to the west, in the village of **Cawthorne**. **Cannon Hall** is a magnificent 18th century country house set in formal gardens and historic parkland. It offers unique collections of pottery, furniture, glassware and paintings, along with the 'Charge Gallery' which documents the story of the 13th/18th Royal Hussars.

About a mile to the south of Barnsley is the **Worsbrough Mill and Country Park**. The Grade II listed mill dates from around 1625. A steam mill was added in the 19th century and both have been restored to full working order to form the centrepiece of an industrial museum. Another three miles to the southeast, situated in attractive South Yorkshire countryside just off the M1 (J36), the **Elsecar Heritage Centre** is an imaginative science and history centre which is fun and educational for all the family.

DONCASTER

Originally a Roman settlement, Doncaster later had one of the country's most important railway works, where steam locomotives were turned out in their thousands, including the A4 Pacifics, among which was the record-breaking *Mallard*. Doncaster is also a renowned centre of horse-racing, and the venue for the final classic of the racing year, the St Leger.

On the northwestern outskirts of Doncaster lies **Cusworth Hall**, home to the Museum of South Yorkshire Life while, a little further on, is **Brodsworth Hall**, a remarkable example of a Victorian mansion that has survived with most of its original furnishings and decorations intact.

AROUND DONCASTER

SELBY

18 miles N of Doncaster on the A63

Selby Abbey was completed in the 13th century and has suffered more than most down the centuries. It was severely damaged by Cromwell's troops during the Civil War and in 1690 the central tower collapsed. Major restoration work was carried out during the 19th century, but in 1906 a disastrous fire swept through the Abbey. Despite all this, the building is still a beautiful edifice, and the famous Washington Window that depicts the coat of arms of John de Washington, a 15th century Prior of the Abbey and a direct ancestor of George Washington, remains intact.

CONISBROUGH

5 miles SW of Doncaster on the A630

The town is best known for its 11th century **Conisbrough Castle**, which features prominently in one of the most dramatic

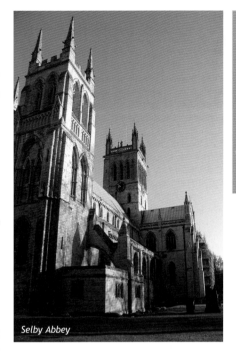

Selby Abbey

scenes in Sir Walter Scott's novel *Ivanhoe*. The most impressive medieval building in South Yorkshire, Conisbrough Castle boasts the oldest circular keep in England.

PONTEFRACT

15 miles NW of Doncaster on the A639

When it was built in the 11th century, **Pontefract Castle** was one of the most formidable fortresses in Norman England. In medieval times it passed to the House of Lancaster and became a Royal Castle – Richard II was imprisoned here and murdered in its dungeons on the orders of Henry Bolingbroke, who then assumed the crown as Henry IV. The castle was a major Royalist stronghold during the Civil War, after which it was destroyed by Cromwell's troops. Today it is a gaunt ruin with only sections of the inner bailey and the lower part of the keep surviving intact.

The town is most famous for its Pontefract Cakes. Liquorice root has been grown here since monastic times and there is even a small planting of liquorice in the local park.

YORK

At the centre of this glorious city is **York Minster**, which stands on the site of an even older building, the headquarters of the Roman legions. Its stained glass windows – there are more than a hundred of them – cast a celestial light over the many treasures within. A guided tour of the Great Tower gives spectacular views across the city, while a visit to the crypt reveals some of the relics from the Roman fortress that stood here nearly 2,000 years ago.

The network of medieval streets around the Minster is one of the city's major delights. Probably most famous of these ancient streets is **The Shambles** – its name comes from 'Fleshammels', the street of butchers and slaughterhouses. Above several shops along Stonegate, one of the attractive and architecturally interesting streets in the city, can be seen the signs of the various tradesmen who had their shops here. Above No.33 is a small red devil, the traditional sign of a printer, and legend has it this mischievous imp had a habit of stealing the bible, which is chained to the shop beside him.

Continuing to prosper into the 19th century, York became the hub of the railway system in the north at the instigation of the entrepreneur George Hudson, founder of what became the Great Northern Railway. Close to the magnificent railway station is the **National Railway Museum**, the largest of its kind in the world.

One of York's most unusual attractions is the **Jorvik Centre**, an innovative exhibition of Viking York complete with authentic sounds and even smells.

Railway Museum, York

AROUND YORK

MALTON

17 miles NE of York on the B1248

Malton has been the historic centre of Ryedale ever since the Romans came and built a large fort beside the River Derwent. Many relics from the site can be seen in the **Malton Museum**, along with items from the Iron Age settlement that preceded the Roman garrison.

The River Derwent has always been vitally important to Malton as it provides an essential element for what was once a major industry in Malton - brewing. In the 19th century there were nine breweries here, but now only the Malton Brewery Company survives.

Old Malton is located just to the north of the Roman Fort, an interesting and historic area on the edge of open countryside. To the

399 THE WHITE SWAN INN

Thornton le Clay

An outstanding pub which offers a friendly welcome and serves good food, made from locally sourced produce, and real ale.

See entry on page 590

400 THE NEW GLOBE INN

Malton

Traditional inn found in vibrant Malton, offering en suite guest accommodation, fine ale and authentic food year round.

See entry on page 590

401 HYDE PARK

Norton

Run by a large, fun and friendly family this popular village inn offers great entertainment, fresh home cooked bar food and award winning ales.

See entry on page 591

north is **Eden Camp**, a themed museum dedicated to re-creating the dramatic experiences of ordinary people living through World War II, and next door is **Eden Farm Insight**, a working farm with a fascinating collection that includes old farm machinery and lots of animals.

To the southwest, lying in the folds of the Howardian Hills, stands one of the most glorious stately homes in Britain, **Castle Howard**. Well known to television viewers as the Brideshead of *Brideshead Revisited*, Castle Howard has impressed visitors ever since it was completed in the early 1700s.

Sledmere House

SLEDMERE

22 miles NE of York on the B1253

The village is home to **Sledmere House**, a noble Georgian mansion built by the Sykes family in the 1750s. Inside, there is fine furniture by Chippendale and Sheraton; outside, gardens and parkland landscaped by Capability Brown.

Across the road from Sledmere House are two remarkable, elaborately detailed, monuments: an Eleanor Cross, modelled on those set up by Edward I in memory of his queen, and the **Waggoners Memorial**, which commemorates the 1,000-strong company of men the Sykes family raised from the Wolds

during World War I.

BRIDLINGTON

38 miles NE of York on the A165

The old town lies a mile inland from the bustling seaside resort, with its amusements and ten-mile stretch of sandy beach. Bridlington Priory was once one of the wealthiest in England but it was ruthlessly pillaged during the Reformation.

On the northern outskirts of Bridlington is **Sewerby Hall**, a monumental mansion built between 1714 and 1720. Set in 50 acres of garden and parkland, the house was first opened to the public in 1936 by Amy Johnson, the dashing, Yorkshire-born pilot who captured the public imagination with her

---

402 THE GRAPES INN

Slingsby

Popular village inn known for its great family food bursting with local produce, real ales and fine art work displayed on its walls created by the inn's owner!

See entry on page 592

---

403 THE THREE TUNS INN

West Lutton

A taste of idyllic country life is readily available in this charming village inn serving real ale and light bites daily.

See entry on page 593

---

404 THE SHIP INN

Langtoft

An historic inn serving good quality home cooked food at the heart of the Yorkshire Wolds.

See entry on page 592

---

405 NORTHCOTE HOTEL

Bridlington

Family-run hotel close to the seafront offering quality accommodation in comfortable suites.

See entry on page 594

daring solo flights to South Africa and Australia. The Museum here houses some fascinating memorabilia of Amy's pioneering feats. Close by is **Bondville Miniature Village**, one of the finest model villages in the country.

A few miles north of Bridlington is the picturesque and dramatic scenery of **Flamborough Head**. The Head's first, and England's oldest surviving Lighthouse, was built in 1674 and its original beacon was a basket of burning coal.

STAMFORD BRIDGE

6 miles E of York on the A166

Just a few days before the Battle of Hastings, King Harold II, the last Anglo-Saxon king of England, had clashed at **Stamford Bridge** with his half-brother Tostig and Hardrada, King of Norway, who between them had mustered some 60,000 men. Harold's troops were triumphant but immediately after this victory they marched hurriedly southwards to the south coast, where William the Conqueror had landed, and to defeat at the Battle of Hastings.

DRIFFIELD

26 miles E of York on the A166

Located on the edge of the Wolds, Driffield

was once the capital of the Saxon Kingdom of Dear, a vast domain extending over the whole of Northumbria and Yorkshire.

To the northeast lies **Burton Agnes Hall**, an outstanding Elizabethan house with fabulous gardens.

HORNSEA

37 miles E of York on the B1242

This small coastal town can boast not only the most popular visitor attraction in Humberside, **Hornsea Pottery**, but also Yorkshire's largest freshwater lake, **Hornsea Mere**, a refuge for over 170 species of birds. Also here, housed in a converted 18th century farmhouse, is the North Holderness **Museum of Village Life**.

BEVERLEY

27 miles SE of York on the A1035

In medieval times, Beverley was one of

---

408 THE GAIT INN

Millington

Traditional village inn serving appetising food and real ales; superb beer garden.

See entry on page 597

---

406 THE SHIP INN

Sewerby

The Ship Inn is a terrific find located in the tiny village of Sewerby, 500 yards from the coastline. Two beer festivals are held over the May day weekend the August bank holiday.

See entry on page 595

---

407 THE NORTH STAR HOTEL

Flamborough

An elegant hotel and restaurant located on the beautiful and dramatic cliffs of East Yorkshire.

See entry on page 596

---

409 THE OLD STAR INN

Kilham

Behind the whitewashed exterior, with tiled roof and shuttered windows, the public areas are immaculate, with beams, open fires, half-panelling and paintings by a local artist.

See entry on page 598

---

410 THE TROUT INN

Wansford, nr Driffield

There is an excellent choice of good wholesome home cooking, which is all freshly prepared and cooked to order.

See entry on page 599

TADCASTER

9 miles SW of York off the A64

Situated on the River Wharfe, since the 14th century Tadcaster's major industry has been brewing and three major breweries are still based here: John Smiths, Samuel Smiths and the Tower Brewery, owned by Bass Charrington. The distinctive brewery buildings dominate the town's skyline and provide the basis of its prosperity.

The oldest building in Tadcaster is **The Ark**, dating back to the 1490s. During its long history, The Ark has served as many things and it now houses the Town Council offices.

WETHERBY

10 miles W of York on the A1

Situated on the Great North Road, at a point midway between Edinburgh and London, Wetherby was renowned for its coaching inns, of which the two most famous were The Angel and The Swan & Talbot. It is rumoured that serving positions at these inns were considered so lucrative that employees had to pay for the privilege of employment in them!

To the northeast, in 1644, one of the most

Beverley Minster

England's most prosperous towns and it remains one of the most gracious, with its great **Minster**, built between 1220 and 1450, dominating the landscape. An unusual feature of the **Guildhall** is a figure of Justice with her scales but without her blindfold. When an 18th century Town Clerk was asked the reason for this, he replied, "In Beverley, Justice is not blind."

Exhibits at Beverley's **Museum of Army Transport** include a wagon in which Lord Roberts travelled during the Boer War and the Rolls-Royce used by Field Marshal Montgomery as a staff car in France.

---

411 THE POPPY SEED

Beverley

Outstanding delicatessen and coffee shop serving quality home-cooked food prepared to the highest standards.

See entry on page 599

---

412 THE WOOLPACK INN

Beverley

Fine old traditional hostelry offering excellent food, half a dozen real ales and a welcoming atmosphere.

See entry on page 600

---

413 THE CHEQUERS INN

Bilton-in-Ainsty

The **Chequers** is a 19th century coaching inn of real character in a pretty village, the picturesque setting enhanced by lovely gardens.

See entry on page 601

---

414 THE CROWN INN

Great Ouseburn

Impressive 18th century inn with a real sense of character known; for its restaurant quality food and community spirit.

See entry on page 602

important encounters of the Civil War took place on **Marston Moor**. The forces of Thomas Fairfax and Oliver Cromwell inflicted a heavy defeat on Prince Rupert's army. Wetherby has a popular National Hunt racecourse.

BOROUGHBRIDGE

16 miles NW of York on the B6265

This attractive and historic town dates from the reign of William the Conqueror and the bridge over the River Ure, from which the village takes its name, was built in 1562, forming part of an important road link between Edinburgh and London. To the west are the great **Devil's Arrows**, three massive Bronze Age monoliths, which are the most famous ancient monument in Yorkshire. Further on is one of the area's finest stately homes, 18th century **Newby Hall**, standing in magnificent gardens.

Newby Hall, Boroughbridge

To the east of Boroughbridge is **Aldborough Roman Museum** (English Heritage) housing relics from this once thriving Roman city.

EASINGWOLD

12 miles NW of York off the A19

Easingwold's prosperity dates back to the 18th century when it flourished as a major stage coach post. Later, it enjoyed the distinction of having its own private railway.

A little to the southeast of Easingwold is **Sutton Park**, a noble early 18th century mansion that contains some fine examples of Sheraton and Chippendale furniture.

HULL

Extensively battered by the Luftwaffe during World War II, this ancient port has risen from those ashes to be once again one of the country's busiest ports. Its most famous son is William Wilberforce, born here in 1759. After becoming the town's Member of Parliament, Wilberforce began a campaign to outlaw the slave trade, which was successful after a 30-year struggle; the **Wilberforce House Museum** presents a history of the trade and Wilberforce's efforts to eradicate it forever. Many other museums and trails tell the story of Hull's connection with the sea and fishing.

The other great point of interest here is the **Humber Bridge**, one of the world's

---

416 THE BLACK HORSE

Tollerton

18th century village hostelry offering quality food, real ales, beer garden and children's playground.

See entry on page 604

---

415 THE BLACK BULL INN

Boroughbridge

Former coaching inn noted for its excellent food, real ales and quality en suite rooms.

See entry on page 603

---

417 THE GOLDEN LION

Helperby

Traditional village hostelry serving appetising home-cooked food and real ales; regular live entertainment.

See entry on page 604

Humber Bridge, Hull

longest single-span bridges with an overall length of 2,428 yards that was opened in 1981.

PICKERING

The largest of the four market towns in Ryedale and possibly the oldest, claiming to date from 270 BC, Pickering lies at the heart of the fertile Vale of Pickering. Housed in a gracious Regency mansion, the **Beck Isle Museum** has intriguing re-creations of typical Victorian domestic rooms, shops, workshops and even a pub. The town is the southern terminus of the **North York Moors Railway**, whose steam trains run to Grosmont.

To the south lies Flamingo Land, a zoo and fun park in the wooded parkland of Kirby Misperton Hall.

AROUND PICKERING

WHITBY

17½ miles NE of Pickering on the A171

Whitby was one of the earliest and most important centres of Christianity in England, and high on the cliff that towers above the old town stand the imposing and romantic ruins of **Whitby Abbey**. It was here in the 7th century the Synod of Whitby met and settled, once and for all, the precise date on which Easter should be celebrated. As an apprentice, James Cook, later the renowned Captain Cook, lived in Whitby, and the handsome house in Grape Lane where he lodged is now the **Captain Cook Memorial Museum**. According to Bram Stoker, Whitby was the place where Count Dracula, in the form of a wolf or large dog, came ashore from a crewless ship that had drifted into harbour.

A popular souvenir of Whitby is jet, a lustrous black stone that enjoyed enormous popularity in Victorian times when, after the death of Prince Albert, jewellery in jet was

---

418 THE ASHFIELD COUNTRY MANOR HOTEL

Kirby Misperton

The hotel is under new ownership and offers comfortable en-suite rooms as well as good quality food.

See entry on page 605

---

419 THE BLACK BULL INN

Pickering

First class hospitality in a relaxed country inn atmosphere greets guests as this handsome inn, known for fine cuisine and its great en suite accommodation.

See entry on page 605

---

420 THE GROVE

Whitby

Handsome Edwardian building offering stylish 4-star en suite accommodation.

See entry on page 607

---

421 THE MIDDLE EARTH TAVERN

Whitby

Harbourside inn offering good food, real ales, en suite rooms and regular entertainment.

See entry on page 606

the only ornament the Queen would allow herself to wear.

The **Esk Valley Line** from Whitby to Middlesbrough runs across the North York Moors on a 90-minute journey that rivals the Settle-Carlisle line in scenic splendour.

To the south of the town lies **Robin Hood's Bay**, where once smuggling was as important as fishing.

SCARBOROUGH

15½ miles E of Pickering on the A170

With its two splendid bays and dramatic clifftop castle, Scarborough was targeted by the early railway tycoons as the natural candidate for Yorkshire's first seaside resort. Even before the advent of the railway, Scarborough had been well-known to a select few who travelled to what was then a remote little town to sample the spring water.

422 TIFFIN CAFÉ

Whitby

Popular town centre café serving homemade dishes based on fresh, locally sourced ingredients.

See entry on page 607

423 JAVA

Whitby

Popular town centre café offering an appetising selection of wholesome food.

See entry on page 607

424 ESTBEK HOUSE

Sandsend

Stunning Georgian property comprising luxury accommodation and the area's most prestigious restaurant known for its mouth-watering menu and 200 strong wine list.

See entry on page 608

Anne Brontë came to Scarborough in the hope that the spa town's invigorating air would improve her health, a hope that was not fulfilled. She died at the age of 29 and her grave lies in **St Mary's** churchyard at the foot of the castle.

Built between 1158 and 1168, **Scarborough Castle** occupies the site of a Roman fort and signal station and its gaunt remains stand high on Castle Rock Headland, dominating the resort's two sweeping bays.

Down the coast from Scarborough lies **Filey**, one of the first Yorkshire resorts to benefit from the early 19th century craze for sea bathing.

COXWOLD

16½ miles SW of Pickering off the A170

At the western end of the village stands the 500-year-old **Shandy Hall**, home of Laurence Sterne, vicar of Coxwold in the 1760s. Sterne was the author of *Tristram Shandy*, a wonderfully bizarre novel, which does not even get to the protagonists birth until volume III! It opened a vein of English surreal comedy inherited by the likes of the Goons and Monty Python. In 2005 a film adaptation of the book, titled *A Cock and Bull Story*, took full comic license with this most eccentrically written piece of literature.

Just to the south of Coxwold is **Newburgh Priory**, founded in 1145 as an Augustinian monastery and now a mostly Georgian country house with fine interiors and a beautiful water garden. To the north are the lovely, cream-coloured ruins of **Byland Abbey** that was built by the Cistercians in 1177.

Byland Abbey, Coxwold

HELMSLEY

11 miles W of Pickering on the A170

One of North Yorkshire's most popular and attractive towns, Helmsley lies on the banks of the River Rye at the edge of the North York Moors National Park. Founded in the early 1100s, **Helmsley Castle** was badly damaged during the Civil War and is today a romantic and picturesque ruin. Just to the west of Helmsley are the hauntingly beautiful remains of **Rievaulx Abbey**, standing among wooded hills beside the River Rye. Founded in 1131, this was the first Cistercian abbey in Yorkshire and, with some 700 people eventually living within its walls, became one of the largest.

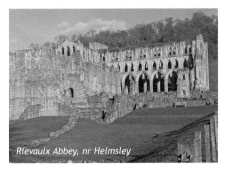

Rievaulx Abbey, nr Helmsley

To the southeast lies **Nunnington Hall**, a late 17th century manor house set beside the River Rye with a picturesque packhorse bridge within its grounds.

THIRSK

23 miles W of Pickering on the A61

Thirsk has become famous as the home of veterinary surgeon Alf Wight, better known as James Herriot, author of *All Creatures Great and Small*, who died in 1995. **The World of**

James Herriot is housed in his original surgery in Kirkgate and offers visitors a trip back in time to the 1940s, exploring the life and times of the world's most famous country vet.

On the edge of town, the **Trees to Treske Visitor Centre** is an imaginative exhibition exploring how trees grow, the character of different woods and examples of the cabinetmaker's craft. Nearby is **Thirsk Racecourse**, known to devotees of the turf as the 'Country Racecourse'.

To the northwest of Thirsk is **Sion Hill Hall**, one of the last great country houses. Completed in 1913, the rooms have not altered since they were built and they are home to one of the best collections of Georgian, Victorian and Edwardian artefacts in the north of England.

HUTTON-LE-HOLE

6½ miles NW of Pickering off the A170

Long regarded as one of Yorkshire's prettiest villages, Hutton-le-Hole has a character all its own. Facing the green is the **Ryedale Folk Museum**, an imaginative celebration of 4,000 years of life in North Yorkshire; among the historic buildings is a complete Elizabethan Manor House rescued from nearby Harome.

GREAT AYTON

22 miles NW of Pickering on the A173

This appealing village set around the River Leven is an essential stopping point for anyone following the **Captain Cook Country Tour**, a 70-mile circular trip taking in all the major locations associated with the great sailor. Cook's family moved to Great Ayton when he was 8 years old and he attended the little school that is now the **Captain Cook Schoolroom Museum**.

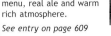 **425 BAGBY INN**

Thirsk

Modest but fantastic village inn known for its excellent home cooked menu, real ale and warm rich atmosphere.

See entry on page 609

 **426 THE BLACKWELL OX INN**

Carlton-in-Cleveland

Thai chefs prepare a mouthwatering variety of authentic Thai dishes in the kitchens of the **Blackwell Ox Inn**.

See entry on page 609

NORTHALLERTON

27½ miles NW of Pickering on the A168

The county town of North Yorkshire, and once an important stop on the coaching route from Newcastle to London.

To the northeast is **Mount Grace Priory**, a 14th century building where a well-appointed two-storey monks' cell has been restored to give a vivid impression of what life was like in what was clearly one of the more comfortable 14th century monastic houses.

GOATHLAND

11 miles N of Pickering off the A169

A major attraction in this pleasant moorland village is **Mallyan Spout**, a 60 ft waterfall locked into a crescent of rocks and trees. Just to the north is Beck Hole, a little village that plays host to the World Quoits Championship. The game, which appears to have originated in Eskdale, involves throwing a small iron hoop over an iron pin set about 25 feet away.

Mallyan Spout, Goathland

PATELEY BRIDGE

Considered to be one of the prettiest towns in the Dales, Pateley Bridge is perfectly situated as a base from which to explore Upper Nidderdale. Much of the town seen today was built in the prosperous years when it was a flourishing textile town with a local mining industry.

The **Nidderdale Museum** is housed in one

---

427 WOODY'S AT THE BLACK SWAN

Thornton-Le-Moor

A popular public house incorporating a superb destination restaurant and four superb guest bedrooms.

See entry on page 610

---

428 THE OLD ROYAL GEORGE

Morton-upon-Swale

Fine old traditional village inn serving appetising home-made food and real ales.

See entry on page 611

---

429 THE BLACK BULL INN

Great Smeaton

Traditional 18th century coaching inn that now operates as a cosy bar, restaurant and convenient bed and breakfast for exploring the Yorkshire countryside.

See entry on page 612

---

430 THE WHITE SWAN

Danby Wiske

Nearby one of the county's finest coastal walks this traditional village inn serves fine food, real ales and offers bed and breakfast or camping accommodation throughout the year.

See entry on page 612

of the town's original Victorian workhouses and presents a fascinating record of local folk history. To the east are **Brimham Rocks**, an extraordinary natural sculpture park where the millstone grit boulders have been formed into fantastic shapes by years of erosion.

AROUND PATELEY BRIDGE

LEYBURN

16 miles N of Pateley Bridge on the A684

The main market town and trading centre of mid Wensleydale, Leyburn is an attractive town with a broad market place lined by handsome late Georgian and Victorian stone buildings.

To the east, and surrounded by walled and wooded parkland, is **Constable Burton Hall**, famous for its gardens. To the south, on the banks of the River Ure, is **Jervaulx Abbey**, one of the great Cistercian sister houses to Fountains Abbey, set in beautiful gardens.

RICHMOND

22 miles N of Pateley Bridge on the A6108

Alan Rufus, 1st Earl of Richmond, built the original **Richmond Castle** in 1071 and the site, 100 feet up on a rocky promontory overlooking the River Swale, is both imposing and well chosen. The first completely Norman stone castle in the country, it is now a ruin, though much of the original stonework remains intact. One of the grandest buildings in the town is the **Culloden Tower**, which was erected in 1747 by the Yorke family, one of whose members had fought at the Battle of Culloden the previous year. Richmond is also home to England's oldest theatre, the Georgian

Richmond Castle

Theatre Royal, which opened in the 1780s and originally formed part of a circuit that included Northallerton, Ripon, and Harrogate. The **Georgian Theatre Royal Museum** contains a unique collection of original playbills as well as the oldest and largest complete set of painted scenery in Britain.

Just outside the town lies **Easby Abbey**, founded in 1155 and now a delightful monastic ruin which looks down to the River Swale.

MASHAM

10½ miles NE of Pateley Bridge on the A6108

Set beside the River Ure, picturesque Masham is best known for its beer. **Theakston's Brewery** was founded in 1827 by two brothers, Thomas and Robert Theakston, and its modern visitor centre illustrates the process of brewing and the art of cooperage. The **Black Sheep Brewery** is also well worth a visit. It too offers a guided tour and visitors get the chance to sample the traditionally made ale.

---

431 THE SANDPIPER INN

Leyburn

This ivy clad traditional inn serves fresh homemade modern and traditional British cuisine.

See entry on page 613

432 THE BULL INN

West Tanfield

17th century inn built on the ruins of a ferryman's cottage offering good food, drink and accommodation with a genuine welcome.

See entry on page 614

RIPON

10 miles NE of Pateley Bridge on the A61

This attractive city, on the banks of the Rivers Ure, Skell, and Laver, dates from the 7th century, when Alfrich, King of Northumbria, granted an area of land to the church. Later that century, St Wilfrid built a church on the high ground between the three rivers but the crypt is all that remains of his church; the magnificent 12th century **Cathedral of St Peter and St Wilfrid** now stands on the site.

The **Spa Baths**, opened in 1905 by the Princess of Battenberg, are a reminder of Ripon's attempt to become a fashionable spa resort. Not far from the Cathedral is the 17th century House of Correction, which now houses the **Ripon Prison and Police Museum**.

To the southwest of the city are the magnificent **Studley Royal Gardens**, created

Fountains Abbey, nr Ripon

in the early 18th century. Adjoining the gardens is the glorious **Fountains Abbey**, the pride of all the ecclesiastical ruins in Yorkshire and a World Heritage Site. The abbey, which was founded in 1132, was one of the wealthiest of the Cistercian houses and its remains are the most complete of any Cistercian abbey in Britain.

A few miles east of Ripon, by the River Swale, is the village of Cundall, one of the few villages in the country named **Thankful Village** by Arthur Mee. The term refers to villages whose serving soldiers all came home safely from the Great War.

RIPLEY

7½ miles SE of Pateley Bridge off the A61

Ripley Castle has been home to the Ingilby family for over 600 years, granted to them when Thomas Ingilby killed a wild boar that was charging at King Edward III. The castle stands in an outstanding Capability Brown landscape, and the walled garden contains the National Hyacinth Collection.

---

433 MASONS ARMS

Bishop Monkton

A French themed restaurant with French decor and new French chef. All of the food served is homemade and freshly prepared to order.

See entry on page 615

---

434 THE CROWN INN

Roecliffe

A lovely old coaching inn in a picturesque conservation village, one of the most highly regarded eating places in the region.

See entry on page 616

---

435 THE ROYAL OAK

Bilton-in-Ainsty

The oak that gave the pub its name is a huge old tree standing proudly at the front, while beer gardens to the front and rear add to the appeal

See entry on page 617

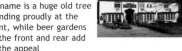

---

436 BLEIKERS AT THE MALT SHOVEL

Brearton

A destination restaurant renowned throughout Yorkshire and far beyond retaining many original features, including exposed beams and a splendid oak partition wall.

See entry on page 618

HARROGATE

12 miles SE of Pateley Bridge on the A61

One of England's most attractive towns, Harrogate retains many of its original spa buildings including the **Royal Pump Room** and the **Royal Baths Assembly Rooms**, which in their heyday were full of rich visitors sampling the waters.

To the east lies the town of **Knaresborough** and **Mother Shipton's Cave**, the home of a Petrifying Well where the lime-rich water has seemingly turned to stone an array of objects from old boots to bunches of grapes.

SKIPTON

14 miles SW of Pateley Bridge on the A59

Skipton's origins can be traced to the 7th century, when the farmers christened it

Sheeptown. The Normans decided to build a castle to guard the entrance to Airedale and Skipton became a garrison town. **Skipton Castle**, home of the Cliffords, is one of the most complete and well-preserved medieval castles in England, and its most striking feature is the impressive 14th century gateway.

For many years Skipton remained just a market town, until, with the development of the factory system in the 19th century, textile mills were built and cottages and terraced houses constructed for the influx of mill workers. The **Leeds and Liverpool Canal**, which flows through the town, provided a cheap form of transport as well as linking Skipton with the major industrial centres of Yorkshire and Lancashire.

To the east, in a village that is part of the Duke of Devonshire's estate, are the

---

437 REGENT COTTAGE

High Harrogate

A lovely 19th century town house that sleeps six in stylish comfort ideally situated in the heart of High Harrogate.

See entry on page 619

---

438 YE OLDE CHYMIST SHOPPE AND THE LAVENDER ROOMS

Knaresborough

Downstairs, Ye Olde Chymist Shoppe draws in locals and visitors with a sweet tooth while upstairs, the quality, busy and bustling Lavender Rooms seats 38 diners.

See entry on page 619

---

439 THE SUN INN

Norwood

Situated within the picturesque Washburn Valley this family friendly country inn offers a range of real ales and large traditional country menu throughout the day.

See entry on page 620

---

440 THE BLACK BULL

Kettlesing

Traditional country inn, family run and family friendly, offering appetising food and real ales.

See entry on page 621

---

441 COLD COTES GUEST ACCOMMODATION

nr Harrogate

This Victorian farmhouse and renovated barn has six luxurious en-suite rooms of the highest of standards.

See entry on page 620

---

442 NEWTON GRANGE B&B AND SELF-CATERING

Gargrave

Charming Grade II listed Georgian house on working sheep farm in secluded rural location.

See entry on page 622

substantial ruins of **Bolton Priory**, an Augustinian house that was founded in 1155 by monks. Upstream from the ruins is one of the most visited natural features in Wharfedale, a point where the wide river suddenly narrows into a confined channel of black rock through which the water thunders. This spectacular gorge is known as **The Strid** because, over the centuries, many heroic (or foolhardy) types have attempted to leap across it as a test of bravery.

GRASSINGTON

11 miles W of Pateley Bridge on the B6265

One of the best loved villages within the Yorkshire Dales National Park, Grassington in many ways typifies the Dales' settlement with its characteristic market square. Known as the capital of Upper Wharfedale, the historically important valley roads meet here and the ancient monastic route from Malham to Fountains Abbey passes through the village. The **Upper Wharfedale Folk Museum** is housed in two converted 18th century lead-miners' cottages.

To the east is the wonderful 500,000-year-old-cave at **Stump Cross Caverns**, a large show cave with a fantastic array of stalactites and stalagmites.

MALHAM

17 miles W of Pateley Bridge off the A65

Malham village was originally two settlements, Malham East and Malham West, which came under the influence of a different religious house: Bolton Priory and Fountains Abbey respectively.

To the north is **Malham Cove**, a limestone amphitheatre that is the most spectacular section of the mid-Craven fault; as recently as the 1700s, a massive waterfall that was higher than Niagara Falls cascaded over its edge! These days the water disappears through potholes at the top, called water-sinks, and re-appears through the cavern mouth at **Aire Head** near the village. Not far away is the equally inspiring **Gordale Scar**, a huge gorge carved by glacial melt water with an impressive waterfall leaping, in two

Malham Cove

stages, from a fissure in its face. Further north of the scar is **Malham Tarn**, a glacial lake that, by way of an underground stream, is the source of the River Aire.

SETTLE

22½ miles W of Pateley Bridge on the B6480

This small market town is best known today as the home of the scenically unrivalled **Settle-Carlisle Railway**, a proudly preserved memento of the glorious age of steam. The line took six years to build, being completed in 1876, and incorporated 21 major viaducts and 14 tunnels. The workmen on the line endured the harshest of conditions, and many lost their lives; over 100 lie buried in the graveyard at Chapel-le-Dale. Settle is dominated by one of the huge viaducts and by the towering limestone cliffs of Castleberg Crag.

INGLETON

30 miles W of Pateley Bridge off the A65

Ingleton Waterfalls have been delighting visitors since 1885, and along the four miles of scenic walks, the stretch of waterfalls includes interesting names such as Pecca Twin Falls, Holly Bush Spout, Thornton Force, and Baxengill Gorge. The second principal network of caves in the area is **White Scar Caves**. Discovered in 1923, this network has been under exploration ever since. At Ingleborough, the peak has been used as a beacon and a fortress for 2,000 years.

RIBBLEHEAD

28½ miles NW of Pateley Bridge on the B6255

Lying close to the source of the River Ribble is an impressive structure, the 24-arched **Ribblehead Viaduct**, which was built to carry the Settle-Carlisle Railway. It took five years to build (the work was completed in 1876) and claimed the lives of more than 200 workers.

HAWES

25½ miles NW of Pateley Bridge on the A684

One of the local industries was rope-making and at the **Hawes Ropeworkers**, next to the **Dales Countryside Museum**, visitors can see experienced ropers twisting cotton and man-made fibres to make halters, hawsers, picture cords, dog leads and clothes lines. Wensleydale's most famous product (after its sheep) is its soft, mild cheese, and at the **Wensleydale Cheese Experience** its history is told through a series of interesting displays.

Just to the north and located in a natural amphitheatre of limestone crags, is **Hardraw Force**, the highest unbroken waterfall in England above ground. Because of an

undercut in the cliff, walkers can view the water from behind, just as Turner and Wordsworth famously did.

AYSGARTH

18 miles NW of Pateley Bridge on the A684

The village is famous for the spectacular **Aysgarth Falls** where the River Ure thunders through a rocky gorge and drops some 200 feet over three huge slabs of limestone which divide this wonderful natural feature into the Upper, Middle and Lower Falls. The **Dales National Park** has a Visitor Information Centre here and, just a short walk away, is the **Yorkshire Museum of Horse-Drawn Carriages**, where a collection of nearly 60 Victorian coaches is housed in a 200-year-old mill overlooking the Falls.

To the northwest lies the once important market town of **Askrigg**, which became **Darrowby** in the popular television series *All Creatures Great and Small*. The village has been popular with tourists since the days of Turner and Wordsworth, many of them coming to see the impressive waterfalls at **Whitfield Fill Force** and **Mill Gill Force**.

REETH

23 miles NW of Pateley Bridge on the B6270

At the junction of the River Swale and its main tributary Arkle Beck, Reeth is home to the **Swaledale Folk Museum**, housed in what was once the old Methodist Sunday School. The Museum tells how local mining, farming and craft industries have shaped the lives of those living in this beautiful dale. Other aspects of Swaledale life, including the impact of Wesleyan Methodism are also revealed.

---

443 NEW BUTTS FARM

High Bentham

An attractive farmhouse B&B on the edge of the Yorkshire Dales National Park offering dinner if required.

See entry on page 622

---

444 BECKINDALES LICENSED CAFÉ

Hawes

Excellent family-run eating place serving quality home-cooked food.

See entry on page 623

---

445 SWALEDALE WOOLLENS

Muker

Quality hand-crafted woollen garments and accessories from Swaledale, Wensleydale and Welsh wools.

See entry on page 624

Accommodation, Food & Drink and Places to Visit

The establishments featured in this section includes hotels, inns, guest houses, bed & breakfasts, restaurants, cafés, tea and coffee shops, tourist attractions and places to visit. Each establishment has an entry number which can be used to identify its location at the beginning of the relevant county chapter. This section is ordered by county and the page number in the column to the right indicates the first establishment in each county.

In addition full details of all these establishments and many others can be found on the Travel Publishing website - www.findsomewhere.co.uk. This website has a comprehensive database covering the whole of the United Kingdom.

1 THE CASTLE INN

Cold Ash Hill, Cold Ash,
nr Thatcham, Berkshire RG18 9PS
Tel: 01635 863232
website: www.thecastleatcoldash.co.uk

Nick and Maggie Hex have held the lease at **The Castle Inn** since 994, and they continue to win new friends at their delightful mid-Victorian hostelry. Voted Community pub of the year by the local CAMRA branch. Included in the Good Beer Guide 2009, and has been Cask Marque accredited since 2002. Four real ales on tap all the time, including one from the excellent local brewer, West Berkshire Brewery. An open log fire banishes winter chills in the bar, and in summer the sunny

south-facing terrace is a popular spot, enhanced by colourful window boxes and hanging baskets.

Maggie's cooking ensures that everyone who eats here leaves well filled and happy. Her homemade pies, curries, chilli, lasagne and Sunday roasts are great favourites, and there's plenty of choice on the printed menus and blackboard specials. There is a senior citizens lunch menu Mon - Fri and a roast on Sundays. Booking is recommended at the weekend. Food is served every session except Monday night, when players stay mean and hungry for the weekly quiz which starts at 8.30pm. The Inn is family and dog friendly and there is even scooby snacks for well behaved dogs! Follow The Castle Inn on Facebook - The Castle Inn Cold Ash.

2 THE DUNDAS ARMS

Station Road, Kintbury, Berkshire RG17 9UT
Tel: 01488 658263
e-mail: info@dundasarms.co.uk
website: www.dundasarms.co.uk

Set in an area of outstanding natural beauty on the banks of the River Kennet and The Kennet and Avon canal, **The Dundas Arms** has been providing sustenance for hungry and thirsty travellers since the end of the 18th century. The inn has been in the same family for more than thirty years and the proprietor, David Dalzell-Piper, has worked and cooked in the business throughout that time.

The convivial bar offers draught beers from Adnams Brewery, Southwold, West Berkshire Brewery, Ramsbury Brewery and one guest beer. On warmer days, there is the option to sit outside, overlooking the river. A choice of imaginative bar food is available from the blackboard selection.

The restful and simple elegance of the restaurant evokes the ambiance of a French auberge. With views over the canal, it provides a comfortable setting in which to enjoy local produce imaginatively cooked. To complement your meal, there's an extensive and varied wine list.

The Dundas Arms also offers comfortable accommodation in five rooms situated on the ground floor of the old stable block. These peaceful rooms, all with telephones and en suite bathrooms, have patio doors leading to a terrace which overlooks the River Kennet.

3 THE PHEASANT INN

Shefford Woodlands, nr Hungerford,
Berkshire RG17 7AA
Tel: 01488 648284
Fax: 01488 648971
e-mail:
enquiries@thepheasant-inn.co.uk
website: www.thepheasant-inn.co.uk

Behind its white clapboard frontage, **The Pheasant** is an inn of great charm and character, and a popular spot to meet for a drink, a chat or a meal. It's also an ideal place to spend a night or two in one of the eleven new contemporary hotel rooms when exploring the surrounding countryside or enjoying the top class racing at nearby Newbury. The interior is very traditional with beams, flagstone floors and country furniture - some tables for four are separated booth-style by wooden partitions. This is horse racing territory so much of the décor (as well as the conversation) has a racing theme with photos, cartoons and sketches of jockeys, trainers and owners. These include the exploits of Charlie Brooks, jockey, trainer and one-time part owner of the pub.

Much of the pub's success is due to the energy and personality of mine host Johnny Ferrand who also part owns a fish company in Cornwall. In the bar (which is open from 11am to midnight, noon until 10.30pm on Sundays) an excellent selection of drinks includes cask ales from local breweries such as Loddon, an extensive wine list including 6 house wines, spirits, liqueurs and non-alcoholic choices.

A very talented kitchen team led by Head Chef Clive Jory is kept busy preparing traditional British dishes, many with a modern twist. Perennial favourites such as their famous fish and chips, a range of fresh fish, venison, steaks, risottos along with interesting dishes sourced locally (pheasant, duck and wild boar terrine) and exotic options such as coconut-spiced tempura of red mullet fillets. Lunchtime brings bar snacks and baguettes although a full menu is always available. For guests staying awhile, The Pheasant has 11 top-of-the-range bedrooms in a modern extension. With Newbury racecourse and the training centre of Lambourn nearby, the pub is naturally the first choice for many racing folk, but it also offers a convenient

refreshment stop for motorists on the busy M4 - leave at junction 14, take the A338 Wantage road and immediately turn left on to the B4000 Lambourn road.

4 THE WINTERBOURNE ARMS

Winterbourne, nr Newbury, Berkshire RG20 8BB
Tel: 01635 248200
e-mail: winterbournearms@tiscali.co.uk
website: www.winterbournearms.tablesir.com

Overlooking the green in the village from which it takes its name, **The Winterbourne Arms** has a reputation for friendly hospitality that brings patrons from many miles around. The premises date back some 300 years and part was once a bakery - the old ovens can still be seen in the pub's restaurant. The intimate restaurant and bar extends into fine gardens for summer dining, and in winter the roaring log fire and candlelight create a warm atmosphere. The food is big and gutsy traditional British and European fare with an occasional oriental twist using the best local produce. The friendly staff here know their stuff and add humour to their daily work - and all this just 5 minutes from junction 13 on the M4.

5 THE OLD BOOT INN

Standford Dingley, Berkshire RG7 6LT
Tel: 01189 744292
e-mail: johnintheboot@live.co.uk
website: www.oldbootinn.co.uk

Widely regarded as the 'jewel in the crown of Berkshire,' the tiny village of Stanford Dingley is home to **The Old Boot Inn**, an extraordinarily pretty little pub in a breathtakingly beautiful part of the country.

Take full advantage of the idyllic location and enjoy a countryside stroll before making your way to the inn – you'll be met by owner John Haley, who has been serving real ales, fine wines and fresh food for the last 15 years. Two traditional fireplaces warm the restaurant, creating a cosy home-away-from-home where you can sit back and enjoy some really fabulous food.

The restaurant has recently seen the appointment of award-winning chef Rody Warot (see chef profile: *www.chef-consultant-expert.com*); with his culinary expertise and flair, the menus burst with creative, inspirational dishes. Rody likes to describe his style of cooking as 'bistronomie' – gastronomy without the fuss. Challenging the common misconception that simple dishes require less skill and attention to detail, Rody prepares perfectly executed dishes with expertly balanced flavours. Choose from tempting appetisers like beautifully fresh oysters from Guernsey served on ice with shallot red wine vinegar, terrine of duck foie gras with date chutney, smoked salmon blinis with tangy citrus horseradish and chive creme fraiche, and delicate grilled sardines served with warm new potatoes and black olive salad. If you want to begin your culinary adventure with something really special, try Rody's special paté...

6 THE GEORGE AND DRAGON

High Street, Princes Risborough, Buckinghamshire HP27 0AX
Tel: 01844 343087
website: www.georgeanddragonpr.co.uk

The George and Dragon is a friendly traditional pub situated in the heart on the High Street of Princes Risborough. The building started as a traditional coaching inn in this historic Chilterns market town. Well placed for the local Ridgeway national trail, it provides a welcoming atmosphere for those wanting to relax in a warm and pleasant environment.

Within the pub is an excellent restaurant called 'Richards' which provides a varied and regularly changing menu, offering a range of styles - from traditional English pub food to exotic dishes from around the world. This is the influence of the head chef Richard Burns, who has travelled extensively, cooking in many parts of the world including the Middle East and Asia – and has even cooked for the Thai Royal Family! There is a comprehensive bar snack menu also available for those searching for a lighter meal.

There is a large car park at the rear of the pub off the main road, and a decked area for fair weather drinking and eating at the rear of the building - where you can walk down the cobbled path which many a historian would love to travel.

8 THE BELL INN AND RESTAURANT

Beachampton, near Stony Stratford,
Buckinghamshire MK19 6DX
Tel: 01908 563861
e-mail: info@thebellrestaurant.co.uk
website: www.thebellrestaurant.co.uk

Set in the picturesque village of Beachampton, **The Bell Inn** offers the very best in village restaurant cuisine. The restaurant has recently been refurbished to an extremely high standard and is popular with locals and visitors. The dining area is full of charm and can seat up to 60 diners and away from the restaurant is a cosy bar area with a good range of beers, wine and ales, for sale. The extensive menu combines traditional hearty food with a contemporary twist and among the most popular dishes is Woburn venison steak smothered in a redcurrant jus served with dauphinoise potatoes & roasted vegetables. A la carte menu has something for everyone and there is a separate children's menu to

suit the taste of younger diners. All of the dishes are freshly prepared and cooked using the finest local ingredients. There is a large outside play area to keep children occupied and on brighter days many diners and punters like to enjoy refreshments in the large garden area, which leads on to several fields. Food is served Monday – Thursday between 12pm-9.30pm, Friday – Saturday between 12pm – 10pm and from 12pm – 9pm on Sundays. There is plenty of off road parking.

7 THE COCK & RABBIT INN

The Lee, Great Missenden, Buckinghamshire HP16 9LZ
Tel: 01494 837540 Fax: 01494 837512
e-mail: Victoria.parola@btconnect.com
website: www.graziemille.co.uk

The Cock & Rabbit's location in the pretty village of The Lee, within the Chiltern Hills Area of Outstanding Natural Beauty, may seem an unlikely place to find delicious authentic Italian cuisine, but that is exactly what owner Gianfranco Parola is passionate about.

There are two aspects to the Cock & Rabbit, which both perfectly compliment the fine Italian Cuisine; social and romantic. The first is a bar and pub area (which will be recognised by many from its appearances on *Midsummer Murders*!) The relaxed, cosy atmosphere has made it very popular with the locals, and it is a perfect place to unwind with a drink and a bite to eat after a busy day. Quite different is the restaurant and dinning area, which has intimate candle-lit tables perfect for a romantic meal for two. There is also, in the summer months, a delightful outside terrace dining area overlooking the restaurant's pretty garden and to the fields beyond.

The Inn specializes, and is very experienced, in hosting large groups and events, such as wedding parties and business functions, and there is a larger dining area which is often used for this purpose. This large dining suite is able to sit sixty people, with the garden terrace able to seat a further forty people. It is easy to see how this spectacular location would perfectly suit your event (particularly a beautiful summer wedding reception); the backdrop of rolling countryside, organised and friendly staff there to ensure the day is as relaxing for you as it is for your guests, and the delicious food, which is both satisfyingly fresh and perfect for social occasions.

The menu is a tempting combination of fresh natural ingredients and inspired recipes, adding a contemporary twist to the traditional Italian fayre. Dishes include *Tournedo Rossini* (Fillet steak on toast with pate and Madeira sauce), *Gnocci Verdi al Barolo e Funghi* (Delightful little potato dumplings combined with spinach, mushroom and rich red wine) and the deliciously indulgent signature dish *Salmone Graziemille* (Fresh Scottish salmon in dill, cream and Champagne sauce). To start, or go along side your main dish, is a variety of wonderfully fresh salads, including a refreshing *Avocado Tre Colore* (Avocado with Mozzarello & Tomato). For desert there is a range of fresh cakes and fruit, including a rich and light *Tiramisu* which is the perfect way to end your meal, along with a coffee.

9 THE CHERRY TREE

Fordham Road, Soham, Cambridgeshire CB7 5AH
Tel: 01353 720405

Open all day every day, **The Cherry Tree** is known for its warm, family orientated atmosphere and delicious food. Martin and his children Sam and Steve have been here for the past five years and offer a wide range of soft and alcoholic beverages alongside a small but well kept selection of real ales. Guests can drink or dine within the main inn or take a seat in the spacious beer garden in the summer which is filled with swings, slides and adventure playgrounds for the kids to enjoy. The menu is created using the best in locally sourced produce, ranging from traditional mains and pub favourites to lighter bites and snacks. Owing to popularity, booking is recommended on Sundays and summer weekends.

www.findSOMEWHERE.co.uk
For people who want to explore the United Kingdom

Places to Eat and Drink

10 NUTS BISTRO

1 Station Road, St Ives, Cambridgeshire PE27 5BH
Tel: 01480 463759

Vivien and Duncan Costello are your hosts at **Nuts Bistro**, located on the main Station Road in St Ives. The couple have been running the bistro for the past five years and have established a popular name for themselves, owing to the high quality of homemade food they serve day in day out.

Open from 8:30am-4pm Monday to Saturday and from 11am-3pm on Sundays throughout the year, guests are guaranteed to find a warm welcome waiting. The contemporary interior of the cafe is given warmth by its hosts and its attractive red brick counter. The pleasant aroma of home baking fills the cafe at all hours, laden with the promise of your order. The menu includes homemade soup, quiche, pies, pastries, toasties and Paninis. Popular dishes include chicken and stilton toastie, steak and kidney pie, and homemade leek and potato soup. All dishes are created using local produce where possible, and are made fresh to order on a first come first served basis. Also popular at the Bistro are the range of mouth watering desserts and cakes, including the classic cream tea. Vivien and Duncan are proud to say that 95% of their cakes are homemade; so satisfaction is guaranteed. Children welcome, cash and cheque only.

11 THE PLOUGH

Montagu Street, Eynesbury, St Neots, Huntingdon, Cambridgeshire PE19 2TD
Tel: 01480 473361

Nestled within the heart of Eynesbury just off the main A428 is the Plough. The Plough has been central to life in Eynesbury for many years and plays an interesting part in its history. Eynesbury makes up part of the present day St Neots, but historically stood as its own separate village. Though now joined, Eynesbury still enjoys a rich yet simple way of life to which the Plough belongs.

It has been privately owned for the past sixteen years and run by a manager, however the owners have now decided to take the reins and run the place themselves. This has begun with a complete refurbishment of the inn from top to bottom, trading in its outdated and cold interior with dark wooden furniture for fresh and contemporary styling that highlights the inn's beautiful original features through clean lines and light colours.

Open from 4pm on Monday to Thursday and all day on Fridays, weekends and bank holidays, the inn sees a dedicated following from its locals, and a steady thoroughfare from visitors from further afield. Popular with ale lovers, the inn endeavours to offer up to four real ales at any one time; rotating frequently to ensure that there is always a new ale to sample.

Food is served daily from opening time until 10pm each day, from a menu serving a fantastic range of gastro-pub styled food. All the classic pub favourites are served fresh with a gourmet twist, including generous roast dinners, homemade pies and garden salads. Each dish is prepared fresh on the premises each day, using locally sourced produce. Children are welcome and can dine from their own menu.

Guests are also welcomed to stay at the Plough, in one of nine beautifully appointed rooms. The refurbishment extended to these rooms, four of which have full en suite facilities. The rooms range from singles to doubles and twins with some scope for family rooms. Light and airy, these rooms provide a welcome retreat for guests exploring this tranquil part of Cambridgeshire. Rooms come on a room only basis, but large cooked breakfasts can be arranged on request.

12 THE WHITE LION

Manley Road, Alvanley nr Frodsham,
Cheshire WA6 9DD
Tel: 01928 722949
e-mail: broadoakpub@btconnect.com

The historic **White Lion** is situated in the
picturesque village of Alvanley on the B593, a
short drive off the main A56. The inn itself dates
back to the early 19th century when it once
stood as one of the area's finest coaching inns.
Today the inn still welcomes locals and visitors
to the area alike, who come to enjoy the fine cuisine
and warm atmosphere within.

Licensee Darren Sayle has been running the White
Lion since February 2007, but has over 17 years of
previous experience in the trade. Locals say it's that
experience which has put the White Lion back on the
map and achieved its status as one of the most popular
village inns around. Darren works with a dedicated
team who open the inn all day every day for drinks.
Three real ales are on offer from the Robinson's
brewery range, with Old Stockport making regular
appearances. A fine wine list accompanies this to
include a choice selection of reds, whites, roses and
champagnes.

The White Lion's speciality however, is its food;
which is served up 12-9pm Sundays to Thursdays and
from 12-9:30pm on Fridays and Saturdays. The menu is
created using the very best local produce; which
includes potatoes grown in a nearby field; perfect for
homemade chunky chips. To start, you can choose
from dishes such as chicken tikka skewers, Wexford
mushrooms and a fresh prawn and smoked salmon
salad. Or if you fancy sharing why not order a platter
of antipasti, nachos, or the combo platter which
includes breaded prawns, wedges, garlic bread and
beer battered chicken goujons. For mains, there is
something for everyone with a selection of hearty
grills and steaks; classic pub dishes like traditional fish
and chips, homemade beef and ale pie, and minted
lamb shank; or a fine choice of other tempting
creations which include a homemade chicken kiev, pan
fried calves liver with bacon and red onion gravy,
salmon and smoked haddock fishcakes and a delicious
fish crumble. Vegetarians are also well catered for
with dishes like goat's cheese and ricotta cheesecake
and vegetable stovie to choose from. Those with a

lighter appetite also have plenty of choice with a fine array of filled baguettes, sandwiches and
jackets of offer. Children have their own menu and are most welcome, especially on Sundays
when a popular family Sunday roast is served.

Why not stop off on a Tuesday night for a truly delectable meal and follow it up with the
weekly quiz at 9pm, where all the family can get involved. All credit cards except Diners taken.

13 THE BIRD IN HAND

Church Lane, Guilden Sutton,
Chester, Chesire CH3 7EW
Tel: 01244 300341 Fax: 01244 301677
e-mail: llydpalmer@aol.com
website: www.thebirdinhandchester.co.uk

Hidden in the village of Guilden Sutton, just two miles east of Chester is **The Bird in Hand**; a historic coaching inn that dates back over 200 years. When experienced tenant LLoyd Palmer took over the inn in 2009 he employed head chef Emma Woodhouse and subsequently breathed a new lease of life into the pub and it now stands as the heart of its community. Both Lloyd and Emma pride themselves on offering guests a great range of real ales with up to four rotating brews on offer at any one time.

Alongside this, Emma serves up an inspired home cooked menu from 6-9pm Monday to Thursday, 6-9:30pm on Fridays, 12-9:30pm on Saturdays and from 12-7pm on Sundays. Her dishes include pan seared duck breast with mash and blackberry jus, smoked haddock and pea risotto, pheasant casserole, Mediterranean veg and stilton bake and home cooked pies. Most popular however is Emma's delicious dessert menu which includes poached pears in mulled wine syrup, Eton mess and a very indulgent chocolate fudge cake.

Guests can dine throughout the inn or take a seat outdoors in the spacious rear beer garden. On Mondays a popular quiz is held from 9pm, with the occasional live band stopping in to perform too, see website for details. All major credit cards taken.

14 MILL POOL

Oulton Mill Lane, Little Budworth,
nr Tarporley, Cheshire CW6 9BE
Tel: 01829 760444
website: www.millpoolrestaurant.co.uk

Described as Cheshire's hidden lakeside gem, the **Mill Pool** is a popular restaurant situated in an idyllic setting. Close to the famous Cheshire Motor Racing Circuit at Oulton Park, the child friendly restaurant (smaller portions available) is an impressive establishment with a good reputation. Business partners, Paul and Tony, have owned the Mill Pool for more than 20 years and are well known in the North West, having introduced the famous steak and kebab shops to Manchester in the 70s and 80s.

The Mill Pool, which was established in 1989, is marginally off the beaten track (the A49) and boasts fantastic views across its picturesque lakeside location. The extensive evening menu has plenty of mouth watering traditional dishes to choose from. All are prepared, cooked and served to a high standard. Homemade steak & kidney pie, slow roasted lamb shoulder on creamy mashed potato and roast gravy, and goat's cheese tart, are among the exquisite and reasonably prices dishes on offer. The restaurant, which can seat more than 100 people, is open every lunch time (except Saturdays) between 12pm-2pm and every evening from 6pm. Credit cards taken except American Express and Diners. Disabled access is not a problem.

15 CABBAGE HALL

Forest Road, Little Budworth, nr Tarporley, Cheshire CW6 9ES
Tel: 01829 760292
e-mail: information@cabbagehallrestaurant.com
website: www.cabbagehallrestaurant.com

Cabbage Hall offers the ultimate dining experience. Set in rural Cheshire, it offers a warm welcome, comfortable surroundings, and the highest standard of friendly service and quality cuisine. Chef Patron, Robert Kisby, took over Cabbage Hall in March 2009 and it is one of the most popular places to eat out for quality dining. Robert, an award winning chef, is a well known chef in the UK and has 36 years experience. His head chef Michael Brooks has also 30 years experience. Together they combine quality ingredients and attention to detail to create some extremely fine dishes.

The food served is built on classic cuisine and presented in a modern style - Robert's take on traditional dishes, will have you returning for more. Cabbage Hall has a refreshing style of menu, offering an unique style of sharing platter food, the simple "one dish" menu, great value for money set menu, wonderful a la carte selection, the exceptional grill menu, both meat & fish, and Sunday lunch. Robert's signature dishes are the hors d'oeuvres, Yehudi Menuhin soup, the saffron, leek and lobster risotto, rib eye Bourguignonne, the "Retro" Platter and the chocolate marquise. Robert also has a passion for great wines and offers a selection to meet all tastes and for those wishing to really indulge.

Having established itself as a favourite venue for lunch and dinner, Cabbage Hall is ideal for private hire and events for all manner of special occasions or business requirements.

Dating back to 1876, Cabbage Hall is an impressive establishment, both inside and out. The décor is undeniably glamorous; from the luxury of the baroque lounge, where you can relax with a pre or post dinner drink, to the intimacy and splendour of the restaurant settings. Robert's expertise in hospitality and attention to detail allows him to play the perfect host to very special parties, celebrations or corporate events all offering a bespoke service to suit all your personal needs.

Located just a couple of miles from Delamere Forest, a touch further from the historic city of Chester and only 45 minutes from the hustle of Manchester, on brighter days diners can enjoy the privacy of the garden and rural surroundings.

Food is served Monday – Saturday 12pm-10pm and Sunday from 12pm-3pm. Disabled access is not a problem.

16 MITCHELLS

Lynedale House, High Street, Tattenhall, Chester, Cheshire CH3 9PX
Tel: 01829 771477
e-mail: information@mitchellswinebar.co.uk
website: www.mitchellswinebar.co.uk

With a big emphasis on local and seasonal produce, **Mitchells** is a family run wine bar and restaurant located in the delightful village of Tattenhall. If it is a wonderful dining experience you are after then Mitchells could provide your ideal night out. Even from the outside, this impressive establishment, with its wide, panelled windows is inviting to passersby. Inside, it offers a relaxing environment, where visitors can enjoy food, wine and service of the highest standard.

Mediterranean cuisine is the focus of the menu and all of the food is fresh and homemade. Main dishes on the extensive menu include king prawns Aribiatta, baked breast of pheasant and braised shank of lamb with red wine & rosemary. Owners, Martin and Peterene Cocking, have built up a good reputation in the area and have many returning diners. Food can be enjoyed in the modern dining area, which has a real fire for colder days. On brighter days diners can choose to sit on outside dining tables overlooking the lawn. For those with lighter appetites there is a wide range of delicious lite bites to choose from including spicy lamb in pitta bread and

Thai sweet chilli chicken open sandwich. All of the dishes are freshly prepared and reasonably priced, and this is perhaps why Mitchells is so popular. The menu is changed every month and offers a great balance between fresh fish, steaks, vegetarian options and lite bites. Mitchells' popular range of delicious homemade sweets may be just too tempting to miss out on. All of them are homemade and among the most favoured is tangy orange and chocolate sponge pudding. There is a wide selection of coffee and teas, and cheese (local and regional) and biscuits, to round off the evening.

Mitchells offers a great selection of wines, local cask ales from the Weetwood Brewery in Oscroft, and continental lagers. Its themed evenings throughout the year are popular with locals and visitors. Mitchells is closed on a Monday and Saturday lunchtimes and open from 12pm – 3pm Tuesday – Thursday (food served until 2.15pm) and 12pm – 5pm on a Sunday (food served until 4pm). For evening service Mitchells is closed on a Monday and Sunday. It is open from 6.30pm – 10.45pm Tuesday – Wednesday food served until 9pm), until 12am on a Friday (food served until 9.30pm) and from 6pm – 12am on a Saturday (food served until 9.30am). Disabled access is not a problem.

17 FERNLEA COTTAGE

Chester Road, Tattenhall,
Chester, Cheshire CH3 9AQ
Tel: 01829 770807
e-mail: stevegb@talktalk.net
website: www.fernleacottage.co.uk

Steve and Sally Brown welcome you to their quality 4 star bed and breakfast, found just off the main A41 on the Chester – Whitchurch Road. The couple have lived here for the past 30 years and opened their doors for guests four years ago. Sally grew up in the farm house to the rear of the property, and knows the area very well so is perfectly placed to give advice on what to see and do.

The B&B itself was formerly a set of farm cottages and were converted to the highest standard a few years ago; now offering two tastefully decorated and spacious rooms. Each room comes fully equipped with a TV, refreshment tray and a fresh, home cooked breakfast each morning from 7:30-9am prepared by Sally herself. Guests say that it is enough to fill you up for the whole day, perfect for exploring the scenic area or indeed the 21 acres of countryside in which the cottage is set. In the evenings guests are free to take advantage of the cosy guest lounge which comes with comfortable leather sofas and stunning views across the gardens.

18 G.J'S COFFEE SHOP

Station Road, Thurstaston,
Wirral CH61 OHN
Tel: 01516 484959
Mobile: 07746311537
e-mail: sheryl.baguley@btconnect.com

Found just 50 metres from the beach off the A540 in Thurstaston is the popular **G.J's Coffee Shop**. Its proprietors, Sheryl and Andy have been here for the past 3 years and have established quite the following amongst walkers, bikers and tourists to the area.

Open all year round between 10am-5:30pm and much later on hot summer evenings, Sheryl serves up a tried and tested menu of old fashioned homemade cooking. There is a daily choice of homemade soups, hot waffles, breakfast and filled Paninis alongside popular main meals such as homemade fishcakes, steak and kidney pie with cheesy mash and rich onion gravy and Sheryl's famous Welsh Rarebit recipe with ale on doorstep toast. Those with a sweet tooth will not be disappointed with a choice selection of cakes and desserts also available.

Sheryl also caters for parties and special occasions and takes booking for groups of 10 or more; please ring ahead. With plenty of gifts and crafts also on offer in the shop, and a warm welcome for all including children and dogs, why not stop by?

19 FOX AND HOUNDS

Barnston Village, Wirral CH61 1BW
Tel: 01516 487685
e-mail: ralphleech@hotmail.com
website: www.the-fox-hounds.co.uk

The Fox and Hounds is located on the A551 Barnston Road, just a short drive from Chester in the village of Barnston. This country pub boasts a nostalgic feel, with an array of antique and period items adorning the walls which include hats, plates, clocks and other memorabilia. The fine wooden furniture, decked with plush green leathered cushions creates a traditional appeal that extends to the way the inn is run. Owner Ralph Leech has run the Fox and Hound for many years and prides himself on offering his guests good value food and drink in a homely atmosphere.

The inn is open all day every day for drinks, with the bars well stocked at all times. Ralph ensures that there is an impressive choice of six real ales for his guests with a further five lagers for the rest. Whiskey lovers will also be happy, with over 60 malts to choose from at any one time.

Most popular however, is the food. Guests come from miles around to enjoy the traditional fayre on offer each lunchtime from 12-2pm every day apart from Sundays. All dishes are freshly prepared on the premises and include something for everyone with a range of light bites, starters, platters, mains and vegetarian dishes. Those with a smaller appetite can chose from dishes like potted shrimps, southern fried chicken goujons, homemade soup and lemon pepper chicken ciabattas. Main dishes include Olde English fish pie, special recipe lasagne, meat pie, king prawn salad and the chefs own curry of the day. If guests can't find something they fancy on the menu, the kitchen are more than happy to cook up something else as long as they have the ingredients – who could ask for more? On Sundays a traditional roast is available for all the family from 12-2:30pm, with a choice of beef, lamb, pork or half a chicken. Booking is strongly advised at all times to avoid disappointment. The dessert menu here is also popular and changes regularly with the specialties of Cheshire Farm dairy icy cream sundaes.

Ralph also offers facilities that can be hired out for a range of events such as for corporate lunches, birthday parties, anniversaries and funerals. Please ring for details.

20 THE FARMERS ARMS

Hillbark Road, Frankby, Wirral CH48 INU
Tel: 01516 410159

Not many British inns have had a book written about them, but **The Farmers Arms** in Frankby certainly has. The book records the building of the inn in 1866 and how the cellar, which could contain 9 barrels, was cut out of solid rock. It originally had just two rooms, one on each side off the porch which were known respectively as the Front Parlour and the Spit and Sawdust.

Today the inn remains the heart and soul of Frankby, and is run by local mother and son team Dawn and Elliott Snowden. They are ably assisted by manageress Katherine Campbell and Head Chef Jackie who come together to ensure that guests are guaranteed first class, friendly service and truly delicious food.

Guests can dine throughout the inn, where old wooden beams and vintage memorabilia are in plenty. The cosy bars are full of character and offer lots of comfortable and cosy nooks for guests to relax in. On sunny days the spacious beer garden also provides a pleasant respite with pretty views across the inn's gardens. Open all day every day, guests can chose from up to four real ales which include Deuchers IPA and Bombadier. A good range of soft drinks and spirits are also available, with a handsome wine list to accompany your meal.

Food is available daily between 12-9pm from Jackie's great value menu which includes only homemade dishes cooked fresh to order from local produce. To start choose from homemade soup of the day, Farmhouse pate and melba toast, or deep fried breaded mushrooms. For mains there is an impressive range of meat, poultry, fish and vegetarian dishes with some good old pub classics on offer too. Popular dishes include Cumberland sausage ring, minted lamb steaks, smoked fisherman's crumble and lemon chicken tagliatelle. Jackie also cooks up a tasty selection of curries all served with rice or chips. The team also offer a fantastic "two dine for £9.99" deal where a couple can chose their favourite meal and drink each for under ten pounds. A separate sandwich menu is also available for those who fancy a lighter bite.

Children and families are very welcome. All major credit cards accepted apart from American Express and Diners.

21 ROYAL OAK

Main Road, Worleston, nr Nantwich, Cheshire CW5 6DN
Tel: 01270 624138
e-mail: hollinsheadbars@gmail.com
website: www.hollinsheadbars.com

Robert and Rachel Hollinshead have owned the **Royal Oak** for 21 years, which has a good reputation among locals and visitors. Inside, the traditional pub has dark wood paneling and beautifully exposed stone walls. Open every day, the Royal Oak serves four real ales and serves food from 11.30am-3pm and 6pm-9pm seven days a week. Local produce is at the heart of the menu, which has a wide selection of home made dishes, and there is a separate dining area for those not wanting to sit in the bar to eat. Such is its popularity bookings needs to be made for Saturdays and Sundays.

22 THE COACH & HORSES

Middlewich Road, Bradfield Green, Crewe,
Cheshire CW1 4QZ
Tel: 01270 522626

The Coach and Horses is a family run business located in the hamlet of Bradfield Green. The beautiful grounds and play area surrounding the property make it fabulous for families and the atmosphere is also a terrific reason to visit. Trevor and Sarah Moss are the landlords here and together with their two children Christopher and Helen, the family have treated their visitors to great food and great company. Although having only taken over the Coach and Horses recently, Trevor has over 25 years experience in the trade and his expertise has enabled him to entice new customers daily.

The large and homely dining room features a magnificent fireplace and a lovely wooden floor. The scrumptious menu is redrawn daily on chalk boards around the room and dishes that can be found on offer include meat, chicken, fish veggie options and daily specials. Sourcing the best of local produce, the chefs create stunning meals that won't break the bank; examples include lamb chop trio, classic bangers & mash, smoked chicken salad and braised lamb's liver. There are always 2 or 3 real ales served, Tetley's bitter and mild are the regulars and a rotating guest ale, which during the summer can be enjoyed in the beer garden. Food is served Tuesday-Friday 12-2pm and 5-9pm and Saturday and Sunday 12-9pm.

23 THE BULL'S HEAD

Newcastle Road, Smallwood, Cheshire CW11 2TY
Tel: 01477 500247
website: www.thebullsheadatsmallwood.co.uk

The Bull's Head is a classic English country pub and restaurant, in a stunning countryside location. Dating back 300 years, it was once a blacksmiths and coaching inn, and still retains its original open oak beams and Cheshire brick fireplaces.

The Bull's Head is one of the most popular places to eat out in the area and its traditional menu is popular with locals and visitors. Having previously owned the lease since May 2001, Ian and Sharon Evans have owned the pub since October 09 and in addition to the extensive menu have a daily changing specials board offering additional mouth watering options (gluten free selections on the menu). Steak & ale pie, garlic beef, honey & mustard salmon and mushroom stroganoff are among the quality dishes served.

The beautiful main dining room seats 80 and the two conservatories each seat up to 24. With award winning gardens, the views from the conservatories are magnificent and on brighter days children and adults can enjoy the large lawn area and rural views.

The pub has three popular rotating guest ales and provides a good meeting place for special occasions and business meetings. Food is served Sunday to Friday 12pm to 9pm and Saturday 12pm to 9.30pm.

findSOMEWHERE.co.uk
For people who want to explore Britain and Ireland

Places to Stay

Our easy-to use website contains details and locations of places to stay, places to eat and drink, specialist shops and places of interest throughout England, Wales, Scotland and Ireland.

Places to Stay:	**Places to Eat and Drink:**	**Places of Interest:**	**Specialist Shops:**	**Gardens:**
Hotels, guest accommodation, bed & breakfast, inns, self-catering accommodation	Restaurants, pubs, inns, cafes, tea rooms	Historic buildings, gardens, art galleries, museums, nature parks, wildlife parks, indoor and outdoor activities	Fashion shops, art and craft shops, gift shops, food and drink shops, antique shops, jewellery shops	Garden centres and retail nurseries

24 LOCK 57

The Canal Centre, Hassall Green, Sandbach,
Cheshire CW11 4YB
Tel: 01270 762266 Fax: 01270 762270
e-mail: enquiries@lock57.co.uk
website: www.lock57.co.uk

Located just a short drive from the centre of
Sandbach, **Lock 57** is renowned in the area for its
exquisite menu and faultless service. It is owned and
run by the Hark family, headed by son and
spectacular chef Edward, and his parents Barry and
Gail. The family have been here for the past six
years and have created quite a following, with guests
coming from all over Cheshire to sample their fayre.
They have a focus on delivering high quality food;
that consistently pleases with a range of subtle and
complementary flavours to tantalise the palette.

All the food here is made fresh to order, from
locally sourced ingredients. There are a variety of
extensive, yet innovative menus so guests are
guaranteed to find something they like; regardless of
whether they are coming for breakfast, a light lunch
or a full three course evening meal.

The breakfast menu encompasses a delightful
range of toasts with various toppings to include
simply baked beans or more exotic; smoked salmon
and scrambled eggs, or perhaps a full breakfast
platter with the best bacon and organic sausages
from the local farm.

The lunch menu offers up Cajun chicken salad,
ham hock terrine and bruschetta for starters along
with a selection of mains that include seared salmon
with risotto, homemade steak and kidney pie and a
puff pastry tart topped with sundried tomato
chutney, roasted peppers and goats cheese. A lighter
lunch menu is also available for those with a smaller
appetite, with a choice of deliciously healthy options
such as crab bruschetta, or a selection of filled
sandwiches, baguettes and ciabattas with fillings
from Arctic Prawns to hot lamb shoulder. All of the
above menus are served daily from 9:30am-4:30pm in
the summer months, and from 9:30am-3:30pm in the
winter months.

The restaurant menu is served up every
Wednesday to Saturday evening and continues to
show off Edward's culinary flare with a selection that includes seared sea bass, duck breast with
vanilla parsnip puree, char-grilled fillet of beef and roasted chicken. Guests here not only rate
the food, but commend the service for being subtle and attentive, without hovering.

Lock 57 isn't just popular for its food though, it's pretty location on the banks of the canal
make it a popular drinking hole for not only canal goers and walkers, but also for others from the
towns who come to enjoy the respite of the quite country surroundings, not to mention the
impressive wine, spirit and champagne collection that graces the bar.

25 YE OLDE WHITE LION

22 High Street, Congleton, Cheshire CW12 1BD
Tel: 01260 272702

Ye Olde White Lion lies in the heart of the Congleton community, in South East Cheshire. Once known as 'Beartown' for supposedly using the town's bible money to purchase a bear for bear baiting in Elizabethan times, the town is steeped in history and has a wealth of interesting English architecture to go with it.

Ye Olde White Lion continues this theme, dating back to when it was once an old coaching inn. Its distinctive white and black beamed exterior clearly marks its presence on the high street, offering a warm welcome to residents and visitors to Congleton alike. Within, new owner Joe Manning retains its olde worlde feel with original brick walls, traditional furnishings and a roaring log fire. Joe only took over in December 2009, but after working at the inn for a period, fell in love and bought it himself.

Joe and the team offer an array of wholesome home cooked food, most of which is freshly prepared on the day of purchase. This is available over the lunch period from 12-3 Tuesday-Saturday. For the Sunday speciality they serve a hearty roast dinner with a selection of different means and for the vegetarians nut roast is offered. The Sunday roasts are nearly always a sell out, booking is advised. Children are welcome and catered for. Fresh soup and specials are served together with the usual pub classics. The specials range from vegetarian lasagne to beef bourginon and the soups from chicken broth to leek and potato all of which are a real treat and extremely popular. As an alternative to bar crisps and peanuts, hearty portions of home cooked pie are available all day.

The bar here is also well stocked and always has at least three real ales to choose from which include Abbot Ale and a rotating ale from the local Beartown Brewery. A good selection of other alcoholic and soft drinks are available each day from 11am until close. Although most of the White Lion's guests vie for a cosy seat before the fire, in the summer months; the hidden decked patio to the rear of the inn also provides a popular spot to while away the afternoon. Cash only please.

26 CHURCH HOUSE INN

Buxton Road, Congleton, Cheshire CW12 2DY
Tel: 01260 272466
website: www.churchhousecongleton.co.uk

Located a mile from the centre of the beautiful market town of Congleton, the comfortable olde worlde **Church House Inn** is a family run, traditional pub. It has been run by tenants, Barbara and Graham Withers, for the past ten years.

There is a strong focus on home-made food and the extensive menu offers plenty of traditional dishes including lamb hot pot, gammon egg & chips, and fish pie & peas, among others. There is a good selection of filled jacket potatoes and baguettes and sandwiches for those with a lighter appetite. All dishes are prepared to order and staff members are happy to advise those who have any special dietary requirements (vegetarian and dairy free meals are marked on the menu). The menu changes each week and there is a separate menu for gluten-free meals. Pensioners can have a two course lunch Monday to Friday lunchtimes which, at £4.95, is great value for a main course, dessert and tea or coffee. Food is served Monday – Thursday 12-12.30pm and 6-8pm (longer in the summer months). On Friday-Sunday food is served 12-8pm. It is advisable to book for Sunday lunch and for parties over six.

Owned by Robinson's Brewery of Stockport the Church House Inn serves some fantastic real ales and has a really warm atmosphere. Unicorn Bitter, Double Hop and Old Stockport bitter are among the most popular of the real ales served. Large beer gardens can be found at the front and rear of the impressive establishment. It has some exceptional flower displays, which have won awards for the last five years. There is a putting green and a play area for the younger children, safely away from the large car park.

The pub, which is within walking distance of the Macclesfield canal, doubles up as an ideal venue for those wanting to hold a function for a special occasion. Marquees can be erected in the summer months and BBQs can be had outside. The Church House Inn's games room has pool, darts, TV (for sporting events) and cards and dominoes are available from the bar. For smokers there is an area at the rear of the pub, which has comfortable seating, tables, plants and even a grapevine.

An all year round touring caravan park has just opened. Offering five pitches, it stands in ¼ acre and has electric hook ups, waste disposal and running water on site.

27 THE FOOLS NOOK INN

Leek Road, Sutton, Macclesfield,
Cheshire SK11 0JF
Tel: 01260 253662
e-mail: info@foolsnook.com
website: www.foolsnook.com

The Fools Nook Inn is a traditional country pub, historically a coaching inn, serving great home-cooked classics just a short drive from Macclesfield. Experienced licensees Stuart and Zoe took over the running of the pub at the end of November 2009 and make lovely hosts. Not only does this family-run pub serve some of Britain's favorites, the Chef, Stuart, also manages to cultivate popular dishes from around the world into an ever-changing seasonal menu, using as much local produce as is possible. Great in any season, The Fools Nook is the place to combine fantastic food with beautiful surroundings whatever the weather; from open fires in the winter to summer BBQs on the large patio.

This traditional country pub is also great for visiting the true Cheshire countryside and is centrally placed for many walks and waterways including the Macclesfield Canal running adjacent to the Fools Nook and is on the intersection of 3 national cycle routes (55, 70 and 71).

The establishment is growing a great reputation for its fine cuisine and friendly atmosphere. With Thursday quiz nights and Friday evening barbeques in summer (May – September), free Wi-Fi and unique offers The Fools Nook is a venue that is great for any occasion! Whether you're looking for a mid-afternoon snack, light bite or a 3 course sit down meal there is something for everyone. All dishes are reasonably priced and there are various vegetarian meals to choose from. Booking is advised to avoid disappointment, but not a necessity.

The wine list gives a good selection of whites, rose, reds and sparkling from around the world. The bar is well stocked and as a member of Cask Marque a good pint of real ale is always available from an ever changing selection. The Fools Nook is child friendly with half portions available and dogs are welcome in the patio area.

The Pub can be found alongside the A523, a short drive out of Macclesfield, opposite bridge 49 on the canal. Local attractions include Gawsworth Hall and Macclesfield Forest.

The Fools Nook has disabled access and all reasonable catering requirements can be catered for. Food is served daily from 12:00pm – 9:00pm and the bar serves from 12:00 – 11:00pm.

Ring Stuart and Zoe for any further details with regards to special requirements. Seasonal accommodation may be available of which Stuart or Zoe can inform you of availability, prices and any other details you may require.

28 THE DAVENPORT ARMS

Congleton Road, Marton, A34 between Alderley and Congleton,
Cheshire SK11 9HF
Tel: 01260 224269
e-mail: enquiries@thedavenportarms.co.uk
website: www.thedavenportarms.co.uk

The Davenport Arms is arguably one of the finest and most well known pubs in Cheshire. With a focus on real ales and fine wines as well as a menu created using only fresh ingredients, it is extremely popular with locals and visitors. Inside, the log fire adds to the relaxed and cosy atmosphere. Owners Ron and Sara have been at the Davenport Arms since November 2003. The establishment has a strong reputation for its fine cuisine, well-kept ales and high standard of hospitality. Dating back to the 18th century, The Davenport Arms, started off as a farmhouse and was once part of the Capesthorne Estate. The picturesque church of St James & St Paul just opposite was built in 1343 and is said to be the oldest half timber church still in use in Europe.

The extensive menus (the printed menus change every three months) offer traditional and contemporary dishes cooked to a high standard. The Davenport Arms has been featured in the AA Best Pubs in Britain Guide and The CAMRA Good beer guides since 2008. The evening menu has a wide variety of dishes for diners to choose from. All of the dishes are reasonably priced with main meals including pan fried Lamb's liver on a  bed of creamy mash with a caramelised red onion & bacon jus; breast of duck with a honey & soy dressing, sautéed greens & boiled baby potatoes; as well as some traditional favourites. There is also an extensive lunch menu with main dishes including pork & leek sausages on a bed of creamy mash with real gravy; and Mediterranean vegetable crepe, creamy cheese sauce & dressed garden salad. Lighter bites include a selection of salads, filled baguettes and wraps. Following a meal there are plenty of tempting homemade desserts that can be chosen from the dessert board, as well as the option to have a British cheese board, and liqueur coffee.

The pub is child friendly and has an excellent children's adventure playground. The Davenport Arms is closed on Monday lunchtimes (excluding Bank Holidays), but is open every other session and all day on Friday, Saturday and Sunday. Food is served Tuesday – Friday between 12pm – 2.30pm, 12pm - 9pm on Saturday and 12pm - 8pm on Sunday. The pub is extra busy on the first Saturday of August each year because of the annual Gooseberry Show – one of the oldest in Cheshire. No problems with disabled access.

29 FREEMASONS ARMS

43 Castle Street, Northwich,
Cheshire CW8 1EY
Tel: 01606 79310

Known to Northwich's inhabitants as the area's
best drinking establishment, is the **Freemasons
Arms,** located just a few minutes' walk from the
town centre in Castle Street. Well known and
loved owners Les and Cal Little are the longest
serving licensees in the area, having run the inn
for the past 18 years. They have created a
brilliantly hospitable environment where locals and visitors to
Northwich mix freely after enjoying a wander around
Northwich's pretty streets.

Les and Cal pride themselves on running a traditional inn
that specialises in the art of good old fashioned conversation
and fine drink. They serve a good variety of wines, spirits and
soft drinks alongside Les's very own selection of real cask
ales, with two always available. The regular brew is Websters
Bitter, with another rotating guest ale on offer. A good choice
of keg ales is now also on offer so there is something to suit
every one.

What the inn lacks in size, it more than makes up for with
character and is certainly worth a visit if you prefer the simpler things in life.

30 THE TIGERS HEAD

Pytchley's Hollow, Norley, Frodsham,
Cheshire WA6 8NT
Tel: 01928 788309

The Tigers Head is a popular, family-run, traditional country inn. The beamed ceilings add to the character of the olde worlde pub. Leaseholder, Tracey Whitlow, runs the pub, which can be found off the B5152 or the main A49, with her son, John. The Tigers Head is an impressive establishment with a delightful beer garden that can be enjoyed on brighter days. Inside, it has a warm and friendly atmosphere and the dark wood paneling and furniture add to the old fashioned nature of the place.

The menu is very traditional, with favourites including fish pie (cod, salmon and prawns cooked in a home made mornay sauce topped with mashed potatoes), meat chilli (home-made with minced beef, red kidney beans, tomatoes, onion, garlic, chilli & tomato puree, served with rice) and lasagne (home made with minced beef, tomatoes, herbs, onions, garlic and a bechamel sauce topped with cheese and served with two slices of garlic bread). Among the vegetarian options are sweet potato & spinach lasagne, red Thai vegetable curry and mixed bean chilli). All of the dishes are reasonably priced, which is just one reason why customers return time and again to sample the food on offer. Starters include black pudding in a wholegrain mustard sauce, garlic mushrooms and breaded camembert. If you still have room for pudding, the tempting desserts include jam sponge pudding and traditional home made bread and butter pudding. Locally sourced produce is used where possible and booking need to be made Thursday, Fridays and Saturdays to avoid disappointment.

The pub is child friendly and there is a special Tiger Cub Corner menu, offering youngsters' favourites. For those with a lighter appetite filled jacket potatoes and sandwiches are available. Food is served 12-2pm and 5.45pm-8.45pm on week days and all day on Saturday and Sundays. During the winter the pub is closed on Monday lunch times. A choice of roast dinners is the only option available on Sunday lunchtime. Five real ales are served at the Tigers Head. Cumberland Ale is the regular and perhaps the most popular of those served.

On a Tuesday evening from 9pm there is a quiz, which is popular among locals and visitors to the area. There is sometimes other entertainment (ask for details). Off road parking is available. For accommodation ring for details. Disabled access is not a problem.

31 THE OLD HALL HOTEL

Main Street, Frodsham, Cheshire WA6 7AB
Tel: 01928 732052
Fax: 01928 739046
e-mail: info@oldhallhotelfrodsham.co.uk
website: www.oldhallhotelfrodsham.co.uk

The Old Hall Hotel is located conveniently on the Main Street in the plesant town of Frodsham. The hotel is popular with both business travellers and holiday makers alike who can enjoy the close proximity of commercial business centres of Runcorn, Widnes and South Liverpool and the historic city of Chester nearby. Families visiting the hotel often comment on the range of activities available in the area which include the beautiful Delamere Forest, Chester Zoo, Chesire Oaks Outlet Shopping Village and the mountains and coastline of North Wales which are just a short drive away. Whatever kind of holiday you're after, shopping or scenic – the hotel is ideally placed to offer it.

The hotel itself has been owned and run by the charming Winfield family for many years. They have worked hard to ensure that their guests enjoy a comfortable and stylish stay, furnishing the hotel in a cosy, yet contemporary way that is sure to please the eye. Guests can choose from 26 spacious en suite rooms which come in a variety of sizes from singles to doubles with an added option of a luxurious bath, all of which come with wifi access. Guests can take advantage of the hotel's cosy lounge area with a variety of squashy arm chairs to relax in, before a crackling open fire.

The hotel's restaurant also provides a pleasant haven in which to relax with clean, elegant lines and first class service. It is renowned for its selection of mouth-watering dishes which come on either the A la Carte menu or the Table d'Hote menu. Starters include game terrine with apricot and date chutney, oak smoked Scottish salmon and oven baked onion soup. Main courses are equally as tempting with a fine array of dishes to include pan fried halibut with king prawn ragout and crayfish broth for seafood lovers, slow roasted Aylesbury duck and pan fried medallions of venison in a rich Madeira sauce. Vegetarians are also well catered for with dishes like butternut squash and sweet potato glazed

cannelloni, or filo tarlet of wild mushrooms and leeks on chive butter sauce.

The hotel is also open for morning coffees, luncheon and afternoon teas, with a conference suite available to hire.

32 THE BLACK SWAN

550 Machester Road, Rixton,
Warrington, Cheshire WA3 6LA
Tel: 0161 7779673
e-mail: info@theblackswan-pub.co.uk

Once an important stop on the Liverpool –
Manchester coaching route, **The Black Swan** has
a history that dates back to 1667. It was
originally called the Old Swan and acquired its
present name when black swans, which were
native to Australia, first appeared in the area on
the nearby Mersey and Glaze rivers. The first
recorded landlord was one Robert Clare, who
was licensed to serve ale and food and to stable
horses for 2/= (10p) a year.

Since 1999 the tradition of hospitality
(without the horses) has been carried on in fine
style by Liz and Mike Morrison, who attract
patrons from near and far with outstanding food,
fine ales, wine and high-class service. The
establishment has just undergone a major
refurbishment, but the Morrison's have
maintained the bar's period charm and
character, with beams, burnished brass and
memorabilia. Two of three real ales are always
available, with Deuchars IPA the resident ales,
and the bar also stocks a full range of other
draught and bottled beers, lagers, cider,

spirits, liqueurs and non alcoholic drinks.
The hosts aim to provide an excellent and
enjoyable dining experience, and the
talented chefs in the kitchen certainly
make it happen, for all tastes and
appetites. The extensive menus offer lite
bites, including filled sandwiches and
burgers to starters (including garlic
mussels and mushrooms stuffed with
stilton and bacon) and main courses.
Among the most popular of dishes are
chilli con carne, battered cod,
Cumberland sausage ring, daily pie and
toad in the hole. Curries cooked to

traditional, authentic recipes are always a favourite, and apple pie is just one of several tempting
desserts. Sunday lunch is a favourite family occasion, with roasts the centrepiece; an interesting
alternative way of serving this is as a 'Grandma Batty', with everything presented in a Yorkshire
pudding.

The pub is a popular venue for all occasions, including weddings, christenings, birthdays and
business meetings and an extensive buffet is available. As well as being a fine destination
restaurant, The Black Swan is also very much at the social heart of the community; Tuesday is
Bingo, Wednesday and Thursday are quiz nights, Friday is live entertainment and Saturday brings
the bold and the brave to the mic for the karaoke session. The pub can be found at Hollins Green
on the A57 road from Warrington towards Salford and Manchester.

33 COMFORTABLE GILL INN

458 Warrington Road, Glazebury,
Chesire WA3 5NX
Tel: 01742 677742
website: www.comfortablegill.com

Situated between Leigh and Warrington, opposite the award winning Bents Garden Centre in the pleasant town of Glazebury is the **Comfortable Gill Inn**. It is run by a true gentleman, landlord Victor Roberts, who insists that there are no strangers at his inn; just friends you haven't met yet. No request is too small for Victor, and satisfaction is guaranteed with a choice of 3 comfortable upstairs bed and breakfast rooms, with separate shower and bathroom opposite.

Guests and non-residents can also enjoy the benefits of all well stocked bar in the pub below which offers a good selection of real cask ales, wines, beers and spirits all day every day. The inn also serves a fine range of delicious home cooking each day from 12-7pm which can be enjoyed in the inn's warm and friendly restaurant area or outdoors in the spacious beer garden; which sports plenty of benches and a children's play area. A large marquee is erected in the summer months and can also be hired out for various functions and parties, complete with bar, dance floor and disco lighting.

The inn is great for a quiet drink or a livelier night out with the family with live entertainment on Thursday and Friday nights, pool table, darts board and duke box with all the classics on!

34 THE HAYLOFT RESTAURANT

Lower Clicker Road, Menheniot, Liskeard,
Cornwall PL14 3PU
Tel: 01503 240241
e-mail: linda@hayloftrestaurant.co.uk

Occupying the former hayloft of Lower Clicker Farm, the popular **Hayloft Restaurant**, has plenty of charm. It maintains plenty of character features and its beamed ceilings add to the comforting atmosphere of the establishment. Owned by Lynda Dell'Anno and her husband, head chef, Vito, since February 2006, the restaurant is an ideal venue for those wanting to dine comfortably. The extensive a la carte menu is full of delicious dishes of traditional Italian and English cuisine. The dishes are all freshly prepared and are made with locally sourced ingredients, including meat, fish dairy produce, fruit and vegetables.

The restaurant can be found just off the main A38 and has plenty of rural views to be enjoyed. For those visiting the area it is close to the fishing town of Looe as well as the town of Liskeard, and is close to Bodmin Moor. For those wanting to head further afield the city of Plymouth is a 40 minute drive away. The Hayloft is happy to cater for people's needs and it can be booked for private functions, whether it is a family party or corporate meeting (it has WiFi internet access available as well as presentation facilities). Ring for details.

35 THE TOLL BAR

Lostwithiel Street, Fowey,
Cornwall PL23 1BD
Tel: 01726 833001
e-mail: jodiemorcom@btconnect.com
website: www.thetollbarfowey.co.uk

Jodie Morcom welcomes all to her vibrant establishment in the heart of Fowey; **The Toll Bar**. Jodie has been running the bar since August 2009 and has created an impressive business that combines contemporary design and sumptuous food with a truly stunning location. The Toll Bar sports a glorious water side terrace which looks out across the river Fowey across to Polruan, giving guests' unrivalled views throughout the year, and the perfect sun terrace in the summer months.

Inside the walls of the Toll Bar, the atmosphere is equally pleasant with a spacious, modern restaurant leading onto the terrace, complete with rows of stylish brown leather dining chairs and wooden tables. In the day time the light from the terrace spills through creating an airy, fresh feel; whilst at night time diners soak up the cosy, candlelit atmosphere created by the team. Customers can unwind with a wide selection of fine wines, spirits and beers throughout the day, with a good choice of soft drinks also available.

Throughout the day, guests can choose from a wide selection of light bites to include a range of filled sandwiches and Paninis to traditional meals which include lasagne, chilli, steak and ale pie, fish and chips and a small . In the evenings, the menu continues to use only the best in local produce. All dishes are cooked fresh to order by a professional chef, guaranteeing satisfaction. Dishes include Moules marineres; pizzas; chicken, asparagus and sundried tomato terrine; Thai fish cakes; lamb rack; succulent steaks; and a variety of vegetarian dishes like leek and stilton risotto with lemon oil; and spinach, ricotta and pine nut pancake cannelloni. The menu also includes their own grass reared beef.

It will come as no surprise that the Toll Bar is a popular venue for both locals and visitors to Fowey alike, who flock to the picturesque town to enjoy not only the views and idyllic way of life, but the collection of quirky shops and boutiques that are scattered throughout the winding streets.

36 THE SHIP INN LERRYN

Fore Street, Lerryn, nr Lostwithiel, Cornwall PL22 0PT
Tel: 01208 872374 or 01208 808012
website: www.theshipinnlerryn.co.uk

The Ship Inn Lerryn: a "well-kept secret"

The Ship Inn Lerryn, voted in the 'Top 50 Best Pubs of Britain', is a traditional Cornish coaching inn. In colloquial Cornish it dates from 'backalong' – i.e. from the sixteenth century. It is steeped in history and is located on the tidal estuary of the River Lerryn and confluence of the River Fowey, in an area of outstanding natural beauty.

The Bar

The owners and staff love to make you welcome from the moment you step in the door. On offer is an extensive range of reasonably priced real Cornish ales, cider and wine by the glass or bottle. There are extensive spirits and single malt whiskys plus local apple juice, elderflower pressé and other soft drinks. Dogs and children are extremely welcome and often make instant companions.

The Restaurant

Our carefully prepared and locally produced food is served anywhere within the inn: either in the very well presented restaurant, the more rustic bar area, the front of the pub or the beer garden. We hope to offer something for everyone: including freshly prepared beer battered cod, local Fowey mussels, vegetarian lasagne or Greek feta salad, crab salad, homemade burgers and child/lighter bite sized portions. One of our customers commented that our fat chips were 'dangerously good!'

The Accommodation

We offer you restful, well maintained and thoughtful accommodation. We have a choice of five rooms at The Ship Inn, or two nearby cottages on a self-catering or b&b basis: either Tides Reach, a two bedroom riverside cottage very close to the inn; or Manely, a four bedroom Georgian farmhouse property located in a small hamlet a mile away.

Customers get a 10 per cent discount for mentioning Hidden Places or findsomewhere.co.uk

37 THE ROYAL OAK

Duke Street, Lostwithiel, Cornwall PL22 0AG
Tel: 01208 872552

Dating back to the 13th century, The Royal Oak, has plenty of charm and character. Local rumours suggest there was once a tunnel leading up to Restormal Castle and that this could have been a possible gateway for the Black Prince. It is currently undergoing a major refurbishment to bring the establishment up-to-date with modern ways while keeping all the charm and character of the pub.

Elaine and Keith Burton took over the running of this child friendly pub at the end of November 2009 and they are hoping the makeover will create a warm and contemporary feel. There are six comfortable rooms, all of which have en-suite facilities and are being refurbished as part of the major changes taking place. From the outside The Royal Oak is a lovely old stone building painted white with a fantastic original arch stained-glass window. Inside, the solid wood flooring and original wooden beams add to the character of the place and the open log fires create a warm and cosy atmosphere on a cold winter's day. There is seating for up to 60 diners and another 40 can be seated outside in warmer weather. Traditional roast dinners are perhaps the favourite dish at The Royal Oak and the carvery area serves roasts every day of the week. Fresh home cooked food is

the focus of the extensive menu and the hand cut chips are a must. Juicy steaks as well as fish and seafood dishes are among the most popular dishes and the pub's beef and guiness pie is Keith and his team's speciality. Bread arrives fresh from local bakers daily and all the icecream served is sourced from local farms.

There are plenty of popular attractions in the area, which is why Lostwithiel is an ideal place for visitors to South East Cornwall to stay. The pub is close to the beautiful Fowey river and the nearest beach is just six miles away. The nationally acclaimed Eden Project, near St Austell, is within 15 minutes reach and the Lost Gardens of Heligan are a 20 minute drive away. The Royal Oak is open all day (most of the year) and food is served between 12pm and 9pm Monday Saturday (in the summer) and 12pm to 6pm on a Sunday. Disabled access is not a problem. Outside there is a covered, heated smoking area with seating. Dogs are welcome.

38 THE BLISLAND INN

Blisland, nr Bodmin, Cornwall PL30 4JF
Tel: 01208 850739

The **Blisland Inn**, one of the most popular pubs in the whole county, stands in the heart of a village signposted off the main A30 and the B3266. The handsome stone building with white-shuttered windows stands opposite Blisland's large village green on the site of the previous Victorian inn and since arriving here in 1993 hosts Margaret and Gary Marshall have made it a magnet for those who appreciate the qualities of the traditional English country inn. Every inch of the beams and ceilings are covered in beer badges and mugs, and beer-related posters and memorabilia fill the walls, along with a fascinating collection of clocks and barometers.

Up to seven real ales are on tap in the bar and lounge, including Blisland Bulldog and Blisland Special brewed for the pub by a local micro-brewery. That number increases considerably during the annual beer festival, and in their time here Margaret and Gary have offered up to 2,500 different real ales from breweries large and small all across the United Kingdom. They also stock local farm cider, apple juice and fruit wines, as well as a full range of other drinks both alcoholic and non-alcoholic.

The outstanding choice for real ale connoisseurs is matched by an excellent variety of home cooking that caters for a range of palates and appetites. Sandwiches, salads and basket meals are among the lighter snacks and meals, and favourite main courses include the fresh fish specials, lasagne, rib-eye and fillet steaks with all the trimmings and hearty home-made pies cooked in a rich beer gravy. Other choices – the menu changes daily – could include a spicy cauliflower soup, a platter of smoked salmon & prawns, moussaka, beef & tomato Madras curry and, for vegetarians, a tasty leek & mushroom bake. Seasonal game is another speciality. The food is served at lunchtime between 12 and 2 and in the evening from 6.30 to 9. It's best to book to be sure of a table in the evening and for Sunday lunch, when traditional roasts are the centrepiece. Families with children are very welcome (and their dogs) and the pub has a separate family room. All the major cards are accepted.

Blisland, reached down a maze of pretty country lanes, is a pleasant village with some fine Georgian and Victorian houses. It also has a church which no less a figure than Sir John Betjeman described as 'dazzling and amazing'. This is excellent walking country, with the Camel Trail and Blisland Manor Common nearby, and Margaret and Gary are always pleased to deal with fresh-air thirsts and appetites.

39 CAPTAINS COTTAGE

2 Church Lane, Padstow, Cornwall PL28 8AY
Telephone: 01841 533419
website: www.padstowparadise.com

A warm welcome awaits any guest of the **Captain's Cottage** bed only, you will surely be greeted by its bubbly owner Lynette. She has been running the cottage for over 20 years, receiving guests from all walks of life from sight seers, walkers and sun worshippers. The cottage itself is over 200 years old and offers just two rooms, both of which have en suite bathroom facilities. The rooms are spacious and fresh, with sunlight simply pouring through the large sash windows. Guests have the benefit of tea and coffee making facilities and the calming effect of Lynette's tasteful and contemporary decoration. Double from £23 pp and Single £30.

www.fiNdSOMEWHERE.co.uk
For people who want to explore the United Kingdom

Specialist Shops

40 TREGEA HOTEL

16-18 High Street, Padstow, Cornwall PL28 8BB
Tel: 01841 532455
e-mail: enquiries@tregea.co.uk
website: www.tregea.co.uk

Located in the vibrant Cornish hotspot of Padstow, is **Tregea Hotel**. It is one of Padstow's oldest buildings, dating back to 1645, and is well known for retaining that period charm. It's found tucked away in one of Padstow's charming side streets and is just minutes from the harbour side that holds galleries, craft and clothes chops in galore, not to mention the extensive selection of fine eateries created by the well known TV chef Rick Stein.

The hotel itself holds eight en suite rooms, all of which are finely appointed with plasma TVs, DVD players, and wifi access, which are cleverly fitted so as not to detract from the period feel of the rooms which have luxurious cotton bed linens, bespoke furniture and their own eye-catching works of art. Guests also have the option of relaxing in the hotels comfortable sitting room, warmed each evening with a roaring log fire. By contrast the dining room, known as the Estuary Restaurant has contemporary design with a light and airy feel, serving up equally contemporary food for breakfast lunch and dinner. The menu comprises a delicious selection of locally sourced dishes including fresh seafood from the harbour. Open all year round to residents and non-residents, but closed on Tuesdays.

41 WELL PARC HOTEL

Dobbin Lane, Trevone, nr Padstow,
Cornwall PL28 8QP
Tel: 01841 520318
e-mail: wellparc_1@hotmail.com
website: www.wellparc.co.uk

Well Parc Hotel is just a stone's throw away from many of North Cornwall's popular surfing beaches, glorious coastal paths and the charming fishing village of Padstow. The hotel is owned and run by Sally and Ray Mills with the help of their daughters Lee and Jodie, Storm the dog, and Splodge and Sparky the cats.

The family serve up a delightful range of freshly prepared meals each day, all of which are created with locally sourced produce. Guests can choose from a range of light bites and main meals to include juicy local steaks, fresh homemade soup, and slow roasted lamb shank in red wine and rosemary sauce. Food is served all day from Easter to the end of September, and then daily from 12-2pm and 7-9:30pm throughout the rest of the year in the restaurant which commands panoramic views across the sea.

There are 10 rooms to choose from, all of which are spacious, stylish and comfortable with tea and coffee facilities. Six rooms have en suite bathrooms, whilst the others share. The inn is popular with visitors to Cornwall and locals alike, who enjoy the range of charity events the family arranges such the Tuesday night quiz, and summer BBQs and fetes which can be enjoyed in the inn's pretty courtyard terrace which also afford its own gazebo which is licensed for weddings. Please ring for details.

43 LOCARNO

71 New Road, Port Isaac, Cornwall PL29 3SD
Tel: 01208 880268

Nestled away in the tiny fishing village of Port Isaac on the rugged North coast of Cornwall is **Locarno**. Guests are offered a warm welcome by Rachael Hicks, who has been running this superb collection of self catering accommodation since 1953. She offers a wealth of local knowledge alongside the warm and homely environment she has created for visitors to Port Isaac, complete with plenty of outdoor space for summer BBQs and lazy afternoon drinks. There are two self catering flats available, each sleeping five and ten guests respectively, with a separate bungalow also available, sleeping up to six guests. Many guests will find Port Isaac strangely familiar, as its golden beach provides the back drop for the television series Doc Martin, starring Martin Clunes.

42 TREDREA INN

Porthcothan Bay, nr Padstow,
Cornwall PL28 8LN
Tel: 01841 520450
e-mail: tredreapub@live.co.uk

The stunning bay of Porthcothan attracts thousands of visitors every year, the long sandy beach and protected cove make for a family friendly place to spend summer days, and for sustenance and victuals, guests need look no further than the **Tredrea Inn**. Ably managed by Lucie and Nathan, who moved down from London in the summer of 2009 to enjoy the relaxed lifestyle, the Tredrea Inn has enjoyed an upswing in its already admirable reputation. Joined by their dog Ollie, Lucie and Nathan create a warm and welcoming ambience in this cosy inn that boasts several original features.

The recent refurbishment of the sixty cover restaurant has skilfully matched contemporary decor with the wooden floors, beamed ceilings and open fireplace that remain from the original build. Panoramic views over the bay create a wonderful backdrop to every visit, be it for a full meal or just a pint or a glass of wine. Outside there is a large decking area for al fresco dining, the decking providing superb views over the bay and faces west for some truly spectacular sunsets during the summer.

An extensive menu offers great pub food, all cooked fresh to order using locally sourced produce and in a home cooked style, as well as tapas style dishes and daily changing specials. Sumptuous examples of the fine menu include steak & ale pie, beer battered cod and home made chips and sharing platters including calamari and chorizo.

Exceedingly well stocked, the bar offers a large selection of ales, lagers, ciders, wines and spirits. The Tredrea Inn also has a good reputation for its Sunday roast dinners, extremely popular with locals and visitors alike, followed by live entertainment. The inn is a favourite with those enjoying live music, regular shows are put on and always draw a sizeable crowd. Small and quaint, Porthcothan is a great spot to stop off after a day sightseeing, Padstow is merely 10 minutes away and the beaches and nightlife of Newquay are less than 10 miles away. Always keen to promote community spirit, Lucie and Nathan have encouraged darts and pool teams to compete at the pub, and put on regular quiz nights. There is also an entire games room to keep children occupied. The Tredrea Inn is open from midday till late during the winter and from 10 am till late in the summer, although the hours are flexible during busy periods.

44 THE SEVEN STARS

East Hill, St Austell PL25 4TW
Tel: 01726 72648
e-mail: admin@7starsinn.co.uk
website: www.7starsinn.co.uk

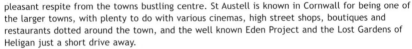

The **Seven Stars** is located centrally in St Austell, just a few minutes' walk down from the train station and shops (Near to Lloyds Bank & Natwest).

It is a popular watering hole for both St Austell's inhabitants and visitors to the area, who find a pleasant respite from the towns bustling centre. St Austell is known in Cornwall for being one of the larger towns, with plenty to do with various cinemas, high street shops, boutiques and restaurants dotted around the town, and the well known Eden Project and the Lost Gardens of Heligan just a short drive away.

The Seven Stars is run by the bubbly personalities of Stuart and Darren, who took over the pub in early 2010. They have created a vibrant and fun environment to be in, with all the traditional pub values still in tow. Since their arrival they have re-decorated entirely with classy neutral colours, yet still retaining some beautiful features such as an ornate Victorian fireplace. They provide all essential modern facilities, with a flat screen TV fitted with Sky for all the big sporting events, Stuart & Darren will be happy to screen any event they are not currently showing – just ask at the bar. Guests can enjoy a good range of entertainment which includes karaoke – EVERY Sunday from 7.30pm, live music and regular events each week, with a quiz machine and fruit machine on site also.

The building originally dates back to the mid 19th century, when it proudly stood as the birthplace of the famous St Austell Brewery. Stuart and Darren maintain its history and stock a good range of "St Austell" real ales. An Ideal resting place for anyone who has just finished the tour at the nearby St Austell Brewery, which is an only minute up the road. They have received the "Cask Marque" Award for the quality of their real ales. They also stock a good range of wines, beers and spirits; all served daily until Midnight. Opening times vary depending on the season, but they are guaranteed to be open at lunch time! As they serve up a fine selection of traditional pub grub every day. They focus on serving up wholesome homemade food created with the best locally sourced produce. Popular dishes include local beer battered fish and home-made chips, home-made melt in the mouth pies and a selection of light bites, Panini's and baguettes – don't see anything you like on the menu? Just ask and the guys will do all they can to accommodate!

The pub has a smoking area and court yard out the back for those who want a quiet drink out of the way of the hustle and bustle of the main town. Whether you're simply stopping for a bite to eat after a long day's shopping, or a friendly drink en route to one of the nearby seaside towns of Mevagissey or Fowey, the Seven Stars welcomes everyone, young, old, children and dogs included! (Ask at the bar for a treat for your furry friend).

45 THE WELCOME INN

39 Par Green, Par, Cornwall PL24 2AF
Tel: 01726 816894
e-mail: welcomeinn.htm
website: www.entertainmentfinder.biz

Inside, **The Welcome Inn** has beautiful low-beamed ceilings and an open log fire creates a nice and cosy atmosphere in the colder months. It really is a traditional cottage style pub and there is a magnificent slate floor adding to the charm oozing from the establishment. Owned by Sarah and Mike Ceasar, The Welcome Inn does what it says. Staff welcome locals, visitors and families with a warm and friendly manner. The bar and dining area can seat around 30 people and in warmer weather up to 100 people can be seated on the traditional wooden benches in the delightful outside area. The garden is enormous and has a gazebo, barbecue area and children's play area to keep younger customers occupied.

All of the food is prepared freshly by Sarah and her kitchen team. Traditional homemade food is the order of the day with steak & ale pie, beef stew, and Sarah's famous dumplings among the most popular choices from the menu. Specialty local sausages are made by Sarah's brother Andrew at the local Tywardreath Butchers. Sarah makes chutneys and desserts from her own apple tree in the garden.

The pub is just ten minutes away from the Charleston Shripwreck and Heritage Centre, which is popular with visitors to this part of Cornwall. The nearest beach is less than a five minute walk away and in the summer many beachgoers will stop at the pub for cool refreshment or something to eat. A little further afield is the spectacular Carlyon Bay, The Lost Gardens of Heligan and the world famous Eden Project. Sarah and Mike are very involved with raising money for charities in the area and staff and customers at the pub recently took part in a nude charity calendar to raise up to £5,000 for Mount Edgcumbe Hospice – a charity in nearby Torpoint. The team is planning to raise more cash for the Hospice Association by holding a garden party (everyone welcome) on August Bank Holiday Sunday 2010. Sarah has already raised £300 for the Hospice Association by donating money she received for her 40th birthday. Her son Ashley is cycling to Lands End to raise money for the children's hospice.

The toilet facilities have recently undergone a major refurbishment and disabled access is not a problem. The pub has darts and pool teams and has live music and barbecues in the summer. It is open Monday-Saturday 11am-12am and Sunday 12pm-11pm.

46 BOSANNETH GUEST HOUSE

Gyllyngvase Hill, Falmouth, Cornwall TR11 4DW
Tel: 01326 314649 Fax: 01326 314649
e-mail: stay@bosanneth.co.uk
website: www.bosanneth.co.uk

The aim at Bosanneth is simple – to ensure guests feel special and cared for.

Originally selected by local gentry for its closeness to the Cornish coast **Bosanneth** boasts far reaching views across Falmouth Bay and is less than two minutes from Gyllyngvase Beach and the Cornish Coastal Path.

Original features within the house have been respected and preserved while the owners have dared to add modern amenities and contemporary finishes. Beautifully designed rooms have touchy-feely fabrics, luxurious furnishings and today's essential features such as wi-fi and flat screen TVs.

Bosanneth's portfolio of rooms include deluxe, executive and standard doubles and a delightful single room. Deluxe rooms have stunning sea views and oversize beds. All beds are of the highest quality with deep mattresses, mattress-toppers, and sumptuous white linen. Without exception guests recognise attention to detail throughout the premises.

Set within a small but imaginative garden Bosanneth has been the winner of the Falmouth in Bloom's small hotel's gold award since 2002. Sub-tropical specimens, architectural shapes and carefully selected colours grace this little oasis against the backdrop of the ocean.

Bosanneth is now famous for its lovingly prepared home cooked meals. No guest ever goes hungry but at the same time every dietary need is respected and accommodated wherever possible.

Breakfast at Bosanneth is a relaxed affair. The buffet offers freshly prepared fruit salad, a range of cereals, yogurts and porridge. A Full Cornish Breakfast pleases the heartiest of eaters offering locally sourced meats, free-range Cornish farm eggs and all the trimmings. Alternatives include smoked salmon, kippers and a Full Vegetarian Breakfast. Homemade jam and a range of regular and speciality teas compliment it all.

The AA has recently presented Bosanneth with a Dinner Award recognising good, honest home cooked meals that satisfy and delight. Dinner is available from Easter to October. Three-course home-cooked meals are traditional and hearty including soups, pies, stews, fresh veg and fiendish desserts. Locally sourced ingredients include meats and the freshest fruit and vegetables.

The AA has also awarded Bosanneth with a top ten placement within the UK for customer service and friendliness. The award recognises the blend of high quality hotel standards with the warmth, care and personal attention of a smaller, homely establishment.

Bosanneth's setting is both hidden and exposed – hidden from the regular tourist trap but exposed to all that is Cornish. Cornwall is 98 miles long and Falmouth is central to the county within easy reach of all major attractions including Eden, The Lizard Penninsular, Lands End, the northern reaches of Tintagel and Padstow, the great gardens of Cornwall, the shopping centre of Truro, and a range of beaches, coves and special hiding places along the coastline.

47 ROSSLYN HOTEL

110 Kimberley Park Road,
Falmouth, Cornwall TR11 2JJ
Tel: 01326 312699
e-mail: mail@rosslynhotel.co.uk
website: www.rosslynhotel.co.uk

Just a ten minute walk from the hustle and bustle of Falmouth's town centre and 15 minutes to the award winning sandy beaches, **The Rosslyn Hotel** is a Victorian built hotel which has been tastefully renovated and refurbished to a very high standard. The hotel still retains many of its original features; such as the classic large rooms with high ceilings and a spectacular panoramic bay window at the front which floods the dining room with light all day long. Owners Angela and Roy have been here for eight years now and have imposed their warm and friendly personality on the place; all 26 rooms are welcoming and cosy. All of the rooms have en suite bathrooms and are stocked with all of the amenities one would expect, including a couple of extras, such as a CD player.

Incorporated into the hotel is the pinewood restaurant, whose chefs work tirelessly to produce dishes that are made fresh to order using locally sourced ingredients, needless to say, the fish is always popular. The most delightful aspect of the Rosslyn Hotel are the wonderful gardens, open to the public as well as guests during the summer, with a patio area for pre and post dinner drinks.

48 PRINCE OF WALES

4 Market Strand, Falmouth, Cornwall TR11 3DB
Tel: 01326 311114
e-mail: jaynegrigg@btinternet.com
website: www.princeofwalesfalmouth.co.uk

Ideally situated across the road from the pier where passenger ferries dock, **The Prince Of Wales** does a roaring trade with tourists and locals alike. David and Jayne have run the pub now for four years and the bustling town of Falmouth is well suited to these convivial hosts. Having been born locally david is well known in the area and as a direct consequence the welcome you receive on entering the pub is a warm and friendly one.

The traditional stone building boasts large picture windows that set the scene for your visit, inside the brightly lit bar area has a pool table and darts. Keen to be as hospitable as possible there is a fine menu on offer, which boasts hearty pub classic meals, all created using locally sourced ingredients. Changing with the seasons, the menu ranges from warming curries and casseroles in the winter, to salads and seafood during the summer.

Also a popular entertainment venue, the Prince of Wales hosts jam sessions, live bands and karaoke evenings that are always well attended. Upstairs are two rooms available for hire for bed & breakfast at very reasonable rates.

49 THE PIER CAFÉ

Prince of Wales Pier, Falmouth,
Cornwall TR11 3DF
Tel: 01326 313278

Stunning panoramic views of Falmouth harbour whilst enjoying fresh crab sandwiches is just a normal day at **The Pier Café**, set as it is on Prince of Wales pier and this is just one of the reasons it is one of Falmouth's busiest cafes. Owned and run for five years by Lyn, who has many more years experience in the hospitality trade, the Pier Cafe offers a warm welcome to all custom, regular or new.

Obviously the main draw is the excellent food, the excellent menu typified by home-made cakes, doorstep sandwiches, ice cream and scones for the Cornish cream teas. For those seeking a more hearty feed, the Pier Cafe all day breakfast utilises the local award winning sausages, free range eggs and thick cut bacon to create a truly special full English.

The interior has been decorated in a gentle nautical theme, with great local artwork and photographs being displayed on the walls. The atmosphere and ambience is very chilled out and relaxed; Lyn and her friendly staff encourage you to visit and just sit awhile to escape the hustle and bustle of the busy port.

50 CAUNCE HEAD B&B

Predannack, Mullion, Helston,
Cornwall TR12 7HA
Tel: 01326 240128
e-mail: sarahaneville@googlemail.com
website: www.cauncehead.com

Caunce Head B & B certainly has a long and varied history; originally a mine captain's house, this 300 year old property has been built out of the serpentine stone that Lizard peninsula is famous for. Through the years, it has been owned by a member of the Bloomsbury set, an artist (providing the inspiration for the studio room) and been the set of the Sherlock Holmes short story; 'The Devils Foot'. Nowadays though, it is in the capable hands of Sarah and David who pride themselves on owning the ideal spot for those seeking peace and tranquillity in the beautiful Cornish countryside.

Standing high on the cliffs above the pretty village of Mullion, Caunce Head offers a truly unique place to spend a long weekend whilst exploring the lovely area.

The three en-suite rooms are all exquisitely decorated and furnished with items as antique as the house, all reasonably priced, and each with a view more magnificent than the previous; the Mounts Bay room offers St Michaels Mount as the focus point. In the morning, after a great night's sleep, chef David prepares scrumptious English breakfasts on the Aga, these are not to be missed.

51 NEW YARD BISTRO

Trelowarren, Mawgan, Helston, Cornwall TR12 6AF
Tel: 01325 221595
e-mail: kirsty.newyardrestaurant@trelowarren.com
website: www.trelowarren.com

Recently described as one of the finest restaurants in Cornwall by a large national newspaper, the **New Yard Restaurant** has no intention of resting on its laurels. The staff are always striving towards the restaurant's motto; 'we try to have the kind of restaurant where we like to eat in ourselves with informal service, good food and good wine'. Managed by Kirsty for the last two years and ably supported by head chef Olly, they ensure that the ingredients used are as fresh as possible. Clams are found in the nearby Helford River, fish and shellfish are caught by local day boats, game, fruit and herbs are gathered from the Trelowarren estate on which the restaurant stands and meat, poultry and seasonal vegetables come from local suppliers.

A contemporary and neutral style is utilised inside, with lovely wooden floors and a large wood burning open fire the main attractions inside this smart eatery. The walls are adorned with local art that changes frequently and fits in well with the original features from its former coach-house status, such as stained glass windows and granite lintels. Inside there is space for 50+ covers, but outside there is also space for another 20 when the weather permits, with wooden tables and chairs fitting in nicely with the herb garden. Formally the courtyard, it is surrounded by haylofts and stables that date back to the late 17th century and that have been sympathetically renovated.

The fresh ingredients all come together to create sumptuous dishes, and the menu is truly excellent, catering for all tastes and preferences, head chef Olly creating new and imaginative dishes on a regular basis. A typical dinner could be Falmouth bay potted crab to start, to rabbit loin with black pudding to follow and rosewater & cardamom rice pudding to finish. There is also a great light lunch menu, which serves as a good way to quieten hungry urges as you explore the wonderful Trelowarren estate.

The restaurant serves food between 10.30 and 2 pm and 7 to 9 pm all year round, with the hours increasing during the summer months. Trelowarren estate, where the restaurant is located, offers a huge amount for guest and visitors to do; there is a swimming pool that can be used all year round, a gym, a sauna and tennis courts. Not to mention the 1000 acres of grounds to explore, be it on foot or by bicycle.

52 THE LANNER INN

The Square, Lanner, Redruth, Cornwall TR16 6EH
Tel: 01209 215611 Fax: 01209 214065
e-mail: info@lannerinn.co.uk website: www.lannerinn.co.uk

A short fifteen minute drive away from the picturesque South Cornwall coastline, Lanner is a traditional Cornish village just minutes away from Gwennap Pit and the main town of Redruth with the famous port of Falmouth about 7 miles away. At the heart of this village is the cosy **Lanner Inn**, attracting walkers and cyclists and visitors looking for a good feed and a warm bed. The six rooms available are all en suite and have been individually decorated in a modern and contemporary style, complete with flat screen televisions.

Downstairs, the characterful bar and dining room have two splendid wood burning stoves to keep the place warm in the cold winter months and the 200 year old oak beams add to the traditional atmosphere. The pub enjoys a well earned reputation for keeping fine ales, utilising both national and local breweries to change the choice around at regular intervals. In its 200 year history the inn has been a coaching inn and at one stage a "tally" when owned by the local tine mines.

A varied Bar Food Menu is on offer and served in the comfortable dining room or you may like to eat out in our Beer Garden when the weather permits.

54 OAKRIDGE FARM

Bodmin Road, Goonhavern, Truro,
Cornwall TR4 9QG
Tel: 01872 540596
e-mail: oakridgefarm@hotmail.com
website: www.oakridgefarm.co.uk

Oakridge Farm is Cornish through and through, with the original farm and stone granary barn built around 1815 using stone quarried from the farm site itself and roofed with Cornish slate that lasted almost 150 years. Although the farm has been added to several times over the years, it still has that traditional feel and look today. Oakridge Farm today consists of eight beautiful cottages that bear appropriately rustic names; such as Treamble Barn and Holly cottage, which vary from two to seven berths in a variety of combinations. Four of the cottages have been converted from the old stone granary in a sympathetic manner and are decorated and furnished to a high standard, there is also a flat in the middle of St. Agnes village.

An especially nice touch is the guest welcome pack, which contains for example, a bottle of wine, home baked cakes, fair trade tea and coffee, fresh flowers and free range eggs! Set in ten acres of land, facilities include large gardens, outdoor play areas, pool tables, table football, badminton, 24 hr laundry room, barbeques and a lot more besides. There are also a friendly farm animal area, meet Petal the pig, Snoopy the Shetland pony and Cuthbert the cockerel as you explore this wonderful site.

Penwartha Road, Bolingey, nr Perranporth, Cornwall TR6 0DH
Tel: 01872 571626
e-mail: carolneathey@bolingey.co.uk

The quaint and quiet hamlet of Bolingey is home to the 17th century **Bolingey Inn** and is the perfect secluded location for this lovely public house. Originally a counting house for the local mine, the inn has undergone minimal renovations over the years and so has managed to retain most of the traditional features. Carol and Mike provide a warm and friendly welcome as you enter the cosy bar, warmed by a lovely open fire and typified by the gaggle of gossiping locals stood at the bar. Owners for four years now, Mike and Carol enjoy a superb reputation for great food, courtesy of the head chef, Chris Kemp who has ensured that all the food is fresh, and cooked to order.

Extremely popular, the extensive menu is packed full of home cooked dishes with vegetables sourced from Carol and Mike's allotment, home made chips and deserts to finish. Specialities include steak & ale pie, beef wellington and a treacle sponge oozing with syrup. The proximity to the coast means that fresh seafood is extremely easy to come by and daily specials take full advantage of this, for example salmon with crab and parmesan crust and monkfish in a tarragon cream sauce. The inn has a certificate of excellence from Cask Marque and the bar is always stocked with four real ales, two of which are Cornish.

Happy to accommodate all sorts, the Bolingey Inn plays host to walkers, ramblers, locals, cyclists and sports people from all over, even four legged friends are welcome, dogs are allowed into the bar area and onto the stunning patio. Located out the front, the patio is a sheltered sun trap that enables the Bolingey Inn to serve food outside all year round, there is also a covered, heated smoking area. Very into their sports, Mike and Carol have established a veterans rugby team, called the Barbarians, who play games for various charities and events. Also a popular entertainment venue, there is live music on every last Thursday of the month and a monthly quiz night, complete with a curry themed menu.

The hamlet of Bolingey is situated just one mile from the bustling town of Perranporth and its famous beach, the location is excellent with several sites to see, including Healey's cider farm and all of Newquay's attractions.

55 THE HONEY POT

5 Parade Street, Penzance,
Cornwall TR18 4BU
Tel: 01736 368686
e-mail : kath.e.hawkins@fsmail.net

Open: Monday – Saturday 10am-6pm

The Honey Pot is tucked away in the centre of Penzance, opposite the Acorn Theatre, and is hugely popular with locals and visitors alike. It is widely known as one of the best cafés in the area, and is home to Kathy Hawkins' "Incredible Edibles". Kathy has been running the café for just over four years, having re-opened it in the building which housed the original "Honey Pot", opened c. 1925. Hard work, passion, and delicious, good quality and fairly-priced food have built it up to being the thriving place it is today.

Visitors to The Honey Pot comment on the homely atmosphere, with comfy cushions, stripped pine floors, antique furniture, local art and fresh flowers which grace every table. Adding to the appeal is the mouth-watering aroma which drifts from the kitchen (almost everything you eat here is cooked or baked on the premises) where Kathy does most of the cooking herself.

The Specials board changes daily to reflect the best in local and seasonal produce, but usually offers at least two of our famed soups, such as 'Butternut squash, leek and saffron', 'Sweet potato, coconut and red chilli' or 'Lebanese lentil spinach and lemon'. Soups are served either alone, with ciabatta, dressed herby salad, or both. Gluten-free bread is also available, and special diets are more than adequately catered for. Specials might include our Homity Pie, Beef Lasagne, Feta and Roast Mediterranean Vegetable Tart, or Felafels with Minted Yoghurt and salad, for example. The salad dressing- (a closely-guarded secret recipe), has proven so popular, it is now available to buy.

To accompany morning coffee, for dessert, or with afternoon tea, there is a jaw-dropping variety of cakes, slices and fancies, which are in constant production on the premises. During the Summer months, the local Strawberry and vanilla Pavlova is outshone only by the Peach and Raspberry one. The Honey Pot has become a regular haunt for many locals who describe the cakes as decadent, frivolous, and utterly delicious. A wide selection of teas, excellent coffee, and cold drinks is available, and whilst not licensed, guests are welcome to 'Bring their own.'

The Honey Pot is open Monday to Saturday, 10am-6pm, and is an ideal spot to take morning coffee, lunch or even a cream tea in the afternoon. The highlight of a trip to Penzance; a seaside town offering an eclectic mix of galleries shops and activities, which includes daily boat and helicopter links to the nearby Isles of Scilly.

57 THE COVE CAFE

Westcliffe, Praa Sands, Penzance,
Cornwall TR20 9TQ
Tel: 01736 763751
e-mail: jacqueline@aol.com
website: www.cafecove.co.uk

Touted as one of the most amazing beaches in the south of Cornwall, Praa Sands beach is perfect for swimming, sunbathing and all manners of beach related sports. Overlooking the beach and offering food and drinks to weary revellers is **The Cove Cafe**, a friendly and welcoming establishment that caters for everybody's needs. On entering this bright and airy cafe, Jacqueline the owner, is on hand to provide a bubbly welcome and ensure that every visit is a special one. Inside, the modern decor is colourful and attractive, enhanced by the large picture windows that let the light flood in from the magnificent views across the sands.

Located just 15 minutes from the historic town of Penzance and its links with the majestic Isles of Scilly, the Cove Cafe is the perfect place to stop off to quell the hunger and quench the thirst of a hard days sightseeing. Fully licensed, during the summer, the cafe serves food from 11 am to late (around 9 ish) all week long and fine food it is too. Jacqueline ensures that the dishes are created using locally sourced produce, a highlight being the fresh cod with home-made batter, chips and mushy peas. With the option of eating in the 40 cover restaurant, outside in the sunshine or as a takeaway, the menu is packed full of classic favourites, for example home-made lasagne, fish pie, scampi and chips and 100% beef burger with onion chutney.

The popular lunch menu is perfect for those just seeking a snack, with Panini, jacket potatoes and sandwiches all featured with a variety of fillings and toppings, including the south west favourite, crab! The cakes have to be seen to be believed, created by Jacqueline using her grandmother's recipes, the sheer size alone is magnificent, not to mention the quality, one slice is never enough.

Popular during the warm summer, the outside seating features new decking and wooden furniture, situated in a sun trap, it is the perfect place to hold a private party. Happy to cater for dogs, the cafe also has provision for disabled visitors.

56 THE OLD COASTGUARD HOTEL

Mousehole, Penzance, Cornwall TR19 6PR
Tel: 01736 731222 Fax: 01736 731720
e-mail: bookings@oldcoastguardhotel.co.uk
website: www.oldcoastguardhotel.co.uk

Nestled within the ancient village of Mousehole, just south of Penzance is the **Old Coastguard Hotel**. This modern establishment sits in stark contrast with the quaint selection of traditional seaside cottages that line the streets of the village; providing a luxurious haven for visitors from both near and far. Whether on a weekend break away, or on a longer tour of the Cornish coast, the hotel makes an ideal base, as it is just minutes from a fine array of art and crafts shops, pubs, restaurants and a short drive from the spectacular Lands End.

Its owner, Tamsin Bond has been at the hotel for the last six months, renovating the hotel to the finest 5 star standard across all areas. She offers 15 en suite guest bedrooms throughout the year, 14 of which have glorious panoramic views across the sea, some with their own balconies. The understated contemporary design extends from the bedrooms, right through to the stylish bar and restaurant area that offers a unique and delicious dining experience for all guests.

Refreshments are available on the spacious sun terrace throughout the day, which ends at the shore, but guests can enjoy a full meal each night choosing from a mouth-watering selection like fresh Newlyn crab linguine with garlic and coriander, pigeon breast with port and juniper sauce with parsnip puree, Cornish bouillabaisse or a St Just juicy rib eye steak.

59 SAWYERS ARMS

Stricklandgate, Kendal, Cumbria LA9 4RF
Tel: 01539 729737
e-mail: gillianwalber@btinternet.com

Located at the heart of the popular town of Stricklandgate in Kendal, Sawyers Arms is renowned locally and further afield for its hospitality, well kept ales and quality accommodation. This historic building dates back to the late 18th century, when it used to be a former coaching inn. To this day the inn provides a restful night's sleep for weary travellers in one of eight en-suite bedrooms. Open all day everyday it prides itself on offering a good selection for its drinkers all year round.

www.findSOMEWHERE.co.uk
For people who want to explore the United Kingdom

Places to Visit

58 THE QUEENS ARMS

Botallack, St Just, Cornwall TR19 7QG
Tel: 01736 788318
e-mail: info@queensarms-botallack.co.uk
website: www.queensarms-botallack.co.uk

With a strong focus on good food cooked to order, The Queens Arms is a quality establishment. All of the food it serves is freshly cooked using local produce and is definitely worth the wait. There is an extensive menu to choose from and a daily specials menu. All of the beef, pork and lamb are from local farms within a three mile radius and most of the pub's fish comes from Newlyn and St Ives. During the season fresh lobster will be available on a 24 hour order basis (weather permitting). Around 50 guests can be seated in the dining area. Among the most popular dishes is trio of Cornish fish and Doombar battered fish and chips.

As well as good quality food, up to fourreal ales and Cornish cider are served along with a good selection of wines, spirits and lagers. In the summer, the outside beer garden is well used and is also the venue for the pub's annual beer festival. On colder days and during the winter, the fire provides a warm and cosy atmosphere.

Dating back to the early 1600s the original building used to be a private residence, before becoming a pub called the New House in 1856. The Queens Arms is "Taste of the West" accredited and mentioned in many Good Food & Good Pub guides.

Located in the grounds of the pub is The Queens Lodge – a comfortable and well finished lodge designed to sleep one or two people. It is an ideal place to stay for visitors to the area. It has a bedroom that can either be a double or twin bed, a bathroom with a shower, a lounge/dining area with a colour TV and a fully equipped kitchen, including fridge, oven and hob, microwave and all utensils. The grade two listed building is surrounded by greenery and is within walking distance of the cliffs.

For visitors to the area there is plenty to see and do. As well as beautiful countryside and magnificent coastline to explore there are other spots popular with holiday makers. Cornwall is home to the largest preserved mining site in the UK, Geevor Mine. Other popular attractions include St Michael's Mount, Lands End, the open air Minack Theatre and Paradise Park – home to plenty of tropical birds.

The Queens Arms caters for functions – ring for details. If you have any special dietary requirements please let your waiter/waitress know when ordering your meals.

60 DICKIE DOODLES

Yard 2, Stricklandgate, Kendal, Cumbria LA9 4ND
Tel: 01539 738480
e-mail: dickie-doodles@hotmail.com
website: www.dickiedoodles.com

Open every evening from 8 till late, **Dickie Doodles** is a magnet for lovers of good music and well-kept ales. For years, Shaun Bainbridge dreamed of opening a live venue, open seven days a week. Then in 1999 he came across these premises which were closed and empty at the time. He transformed them into what has become an unqualified success with wide appeal. It is home to a multitude of musical talents covering many areas of the modern music spectrum and with performers ranging from talented amateurs to well-known professionals. It's music all the way and the whitewashed walls are hung with musical instruments as well as modern artwork The week unfolds as follows:

Monday: Acoustic jamming

Tuesday: Electric jamming (there's a super in-house sound system)

Wednesday: Traditional folk music

Thursday: New and up-and-coming bands

Friday and Saturday: Professional rock bans

Sunday: Some or all of the above.

Entrance is free (over 18s only) and drinks (cash only) include a good choice of draught and bottled beers and lagers. Dickie Doodles also hosts arts and crafts exhibitions showcasing the work of talented local artists and makers. Shaun is a blacksmith by trade and some of his forgework is also on display.

Stricklandgate is one of the busy narrow streets at the heart of old Kendal and the yards (alleyways) are a distinctive feature of the town. They were designed as a defence against the constant threat posed by marauding Scots and could be sealed off by closing the single small entrance, keeping families and livestock safe inside. The Scottish have long since settled down and it's now tourists from around world who come in peace to Kendal throughout the year. And for those who love their music, Dickie Doodles is definitely the place to head for.

61 WILF'S CAFÉ

Mill Yard, Back Lane, Staveley, nr Kendal,
Cumbria LA8 9LR
Tel: 01539 822329 Fax: 01539 822969
e-mail: food@wilfs-cafe.co.uk
website: www.wilfs-cafe.co.uk

'Much More Than Just a Café'

Since 1997 **Wilf's Café** has been serving fresh,
wholesome snacks and meals to an appreciative
clientele of locals and visitors to the Lake District.
Wilf Williamson, Charlotte and chef Martin Lovett
make a winning team who with their regular and
seasonal staff create a wonderfully relaxing ambience
in which to enjoy home cooking at its best. Success
has brought steady expansion, and there are seats for
up to 120 inside, where smart modern furnishings
combine with well-chosen artwork on the walls. When
the weather is kind the seats outside on decking
overlooking the River Kent are always in demand.

The café is open all week from 9am to 5pm,
starting half an hour earlier on summertime
weekends. Breakfast, served until 11.30, caters for all
appetites. Wilf's Big Meaty Breakfast will satisfy the
biggest morning appetite and there's an equally
hearty vegetarian alternative. Diners can also build
their own platefuls or choose just a snack – perhaps a
BLT, veggie burger, bacon butty, crumpet or croissant.
The Hot Stuff section of the menu proposes Wilf's
famous veggie chilli, jacket potatoes and the
immensely popular rarebits – toasted granary bread
with melted cheese, salads and a variety of tasty
toppings. The selection of salads, sandwiches and
cakes is equally wide, and to round off a meal there's
always a hot pudding or English Lakes delicious ice
cream. Wilf's relies on the best local produce,
including free-range eggs, organic milk from Low
Sizergh and meat from Lakes Speciality Foods. Hot
drinks include Fairtrade teas and coffees, and high
among the cold drink favourites are milk shakes made
with English Lakes ice cream.

Those wanting something a little stronger can walk
through a connecting door to the Hawkshead Brewery
Hall to take a tour, sample a beer or two and come
back with a glass to enjoy with their meal. Wilf's is
primarily a daytime place but it also holds speciality
themed-cuisine evenings with set menus and Bring Your Own wine.

The mill that once stood here was at the centre of the once thriving boobin industry, and after
the demise of that industry the yard has become home to several enterprises. James, the baker,
supplies almost all of the bread used by the cafe.

Staveley lies about a mile off the A591 between Kendal and Windermere.

62 THE COMMODORE

Main Street, Grange-over-Sands, Cumbria LA11 6DY
Tel: 015395 32381

Occupying a prime picturesque location in the attractive resort of Grange-over-Sands, **The Commodore** is an impressive black and white building that enjoys sweeping views over Morecambe Bay. The hotel is run by John and Joanne Errington, an enthusiastic couple who took over here in December 2009, although John had worked here on and off for 13 years, most of that time as manager.

Good wholesome food is a priority here. Amongst the starters are a home-made soup of the day and mushrooms in a rich creamy garlic sauce. Main course choices include steaks, chicken and fish dishes with Whitby scampi a popular choice. The regular menu is supplemented by daily specials. For lighter appetites there's a snack menu offering a good selection of sandwiches, ciabattas, baked potatoes, ploughman's and burgers. Children have their own menu. Food can be enjoyed throughout the bars or, in good weather, on the patio which enjoys glorious views over the bay. And by the time you read this, the Upperdeck Restaurant will be open and able to accommodate up to 50 diners. Food is served from noon until 2.30pm (3pm on Saturday and Sunday); and from 5.30pm to 8.30pm every day. On Sundays, a roast lunch with all the trimmings is added to the menu. To accompany your meal, the bar offers a wide range of beverages including up to 4 real ales, with Theakston's Best as the regular brew and the others sourced from local breweries.

If you are planning to stay in this lovely part of the county, The Commodore has 4 attractively furnished and decorated guest bedrooms, four of which have en suite facilities. The room tariff includes a superb full English breakfast.

The hotel accepts all major credit cards apart from American Express and Diners; there's good wheelchair access to the ground floor and patio; and there is parking adjacent.

63 THE STAN LAUREL INN

31 The Ellers, Ulverston, Cumbria LA12 0AB
Tel: 01229 582814
e-mail: thestanlaurel@aol.com
website: www.thestanlaurel.co.uk

The **Stan Laurel Inn** started life as
The Britannia, later changing its
name to celebrate the memory of
Ulverston's best-loved son. Stan
Laurel, born Arthur Stanley
Jefferson, lived only a few yards
from the pub in Argyle Street
before achieving worldwide fame as
the smaller half of Laurel & Hardy,
perhaps the finest comedy duo in
the history of the cinema. In its
new role the pub expanded into
next-door cottages and into a rear
extension; it now comprises three
distinct rooms on the ground floor
and three rooms upstairs for Bed &
Breakfast guests. The hosts since
2007 have been Trudi and Paul
Dewar, who created a superb dining area adorned with
numerous Laurel & Hardy photographs and memorabilia.

Paul is a top-notch chef whose cooking attracts not
just locals but visitors from throughout the region and
beyond. Many of the local B&Bs recommend it and it's the
venue of choice for many chefs in the area. Paul's food
can be enjoyed in the restaurant, in the pool room or in
the darkwood-furnished bar, where up to six real ales are
on tap, always including one from the Ulverston Brewery
with a Laurel & Hardy-themed name. His menus really do
offer something for everyone, from starters/snacks like
seafood pancake, Stilton-sauced mushrooms and pork,
chicken & apricot terrine to fish & chips, super salads,
lasagne, grills, curries and pies. There's always a good
choice for vegetarians and Paul offers special 2-for-1
deals at various times of the week. Sunday lunch brings a
choice of at least two roasts, always including traditional
roast beef & Yorkshire pudding, with the full menu also
available. Super sweets round off a meal in fine style.

The three guest rooms at the inn also pay homage to
the comic geniuses. Laughing Gravy, an en suite double,
is named after the couple's pet dog in the 1931 film of
the same name. Another Fine Mess (actually very neat and tidy!) is an en suite triple that takes its
name from Hardy's best-known catch phrase. The Lonesome Pine is a single with a separate
shower and toilet. It remembers a song from the 1937 film *Way Out West* that became a surprise
hit single in 1975.

No visit to Ulverston is complete without spending a fascinating hour or two at the Laurel &
Hardy Museum, which remembers the pair with letters, photographs, personal items large and
small, films and documentaries.

64 GILLAM'S TEA ROOM & GARDEN

64 Market Street, Ulverston,
Cumbria LA12 7LT
Tel: 01229 587564
website: www.gillams-tearoom.co.uk

Voted one of the top ten tearooms in the UK by *The Times*, **Gillam's Tea Room & Garden** really is something special. The Gillam family have been providing fine food and excellent service in Ulverston since 1892. Doug Gillam has created a tearoom of real charm and character, housed in a delightful 18th century building. Exposed beams in the first floor room are believed to be salvaged ship's timbers, and the sashed windows, Regency style, were re-created by a local craftsman. Log fires add to the welcoming atmosphere.

The menu here is very much influenced by the high class tearooms of yesteryear, offering a tempting selection of cakes and tearoom fayre made using only the finest organic ingredients. Tea-time treats include Cumberland Fruit Teabread, fruit scones, and a range of alluring home-made cakes. The menu also offers an appetising selection of light meals, salads, oven-baked jacket potatoes, and hot and cold sandwiches. All the drinks served here are certified organic and include a fine selection of loose leaf teas, speciality coffees, award-winning traditional English soft drinks, beers, ciders and wines. And if you are lucky with the weather, you can enjoy all this in the sunny garden.

66 THE BRIDGE CAFÉ

The Dock Museum, North Road,
Barrow-in-Furness, Cumbria LA14 2PW
Tel: 01229 876331
e-mail: Val.morley@sadexo.uk.com
website: www.dockmuseum.org.uk

The Dock Museum in Barrow-in-Furness is one of the leading attractions in the North of England, and after exploring this superb modern museum visitors can take a break in **The Bridge Café**. Val Morley, who has managed the coffee shop since 2003, provides a tempting variety of tempting made-to-order hot and cold meals and snacks, daily specials, homemade cakes and speciality teas and coffees. There are light bites such as freshly made soup of the day with a crusty roll and croutons, or home-made fruit scones. Other options include jacket potatoes, toasties and paninis, sandwiches and baguettes. Kiddies have there own menu and vegetarian options include tuna and cheese melt or sausage served with chipped potatoes and garden peas. The café has seating for 46 inside, and many more at picnic tables outside on the terrace.

The museum and the cafe are open from 10am to 4.30pm in season (closed Monday) and from 10.30am to 3.30pm out of season (closed Monday and Tuesday). All major credit cards are accepted at the café; admission to the museum is free.

65 THE ANGLERS ARMS

Haverthwaite, nr Ulverston, Cumbria LA12 8AJ
Tel: 01539 531216
e-mail: g.wayman@yahoo.co.uk

Trina, Graham and Sheena welcome visitors to the **Anglers Arms**, a substantial whitewashed building standing just 200 yards from the main A590 and a short drive from Ulverston. They have created a warm, informal ambience that's a perfect setting for enjoying good home-cooked food and expertly kept cask ales,

and they welcome young and old alike (and their dogs!) into their excellent hostelry in the heart of the beautiful Lake District National Park.

Food and drink are equally important contributors to the success of this thriving establishment. The news has spread that head chef Graham is a master of his trade, so it's often 'full house' here and booking is recommended – and essential at peak times in the season. Favourite starters include the day's homemade soup, breaded Brie with rocket leaves and onion compote, grilled black pudding and Paul's famous flavour-packed Stilton and Guinness-infused chicken liver pâté. Mains run from sirloin and gammon steaks to tuna with garlic & parsley butter, beer-battered cod, lasagne, burgers, steak & ale pie, liver & onions, slow-cooked lamb Henry with rosemary, thyme, garlic and a rich red-wine gravy, mushroom stroganoff and vegetable balti. This already impressive choice is supplemented by daily specials, and meals end with a choice of hard-to-resist desserts. Children have their own menu or can

have smaller portions of some items from the main menu. Food is available from 12 to 2 and 5.30 to 9 Monday to Friday and from 12 to 9 Saturday and Sunday.

The menu acknowledges top suppliers: McKays Meats of Ulverston, Woodbine Dairy of Newton-in-Furness, Grange Bakery for handmade bread, JD Fisheries of Carnforth and McClures of Windermere for dry goods. The Anglers Arms is also a magnet for lovers of real ale with up to 10 mainly local brews always available and as many as 30 during the August Beer Festival.

Just across the road is the southern terminus of the steam-hauled Lakeside & Haverthwaite Railway, built to take passengers and goods to the steamers on Lake Windermere. It closed in 1965, but enthusiasts rescued this scenic stretch which re-opened in 1973 amid much local celebration. Travellers on this preserved line can take the train to Lakeside – perhaps followed by a boat trip on the Lake

67 THE DERBY ARMS

Horse Close Lane, Great Urswick,
nr Ulverston, Cumbria LA12 0SP
Tel: 01229 586348
e-mail: kaydudley@hotmail.com
website: www.derbyarmsurswick.co.uk

The **Derby Arms** is the social hub of the village of
Great Urswick, which lies just off the A590 about
three miles south of Ulverston. Hosts Kay and Tony
Dudley are really putting the inn back on the map.
The locals love it and visitors from outside the area also
enjoy the warm welcome and the homely, friendly
atmosphere. The bar is open all day, every day for drinks.
There is always a good choice of real ales, which include
Hartleys XB, Dizzy Blonde and regular guest ales. Bar snacks
and meals ,including homemade pies, curries, and
baguettes are served informally in the evenings at
weekends.

Across the road, in the converted stables, are four quiet,
comfortable guest rooms with en suite facilities, central
heating, TV, radio, hospitality tray and hairdryer. It's an ideal retreat for a break from the rush of
daily life and a great base for walking cycling and fishing – daily and weekly permits are available
at the Inn for fishing on the village Tarn.. The Derby Arms is also ideally situated for exploring the
almost endless scenic and historic delights of the Lake District and the Furness Peninsula.

68 THE BLACK COCK INN

Princes Street, Broughton-in-Furness,
Cumbria LA20 6HQ
Tel: 01229 716529
e-mail: black.cock@live.co.uk
website: www.blackcockinncumbria.com

The **Black Cock Inn** stands at the heart of the
attractive little town of Broughton-in-Furness. As
befits a building that dates back as far as the 15th
century, the interior is rich in old world charm, and
the lounge bar with its low-beamed ceiling and roaring winter log
fires give it a wonderful traditional ambiance. There's always a
selection of real ales and lagers on offer in the bar which is open
from morning 'til night, every day during the summer months.

The inn has long had a fine reputation for the variety and
quality of the food it serves. All the dishes are specially prepared
by the team of chefs using the best ingredients, locally sourced
where possible. There are always vegetarian dishes on the menu
and a good choice of desserts. Food is served every day at
lunchtimes and in the evenings. Your meal can be savoured in the bar area, in the separate dining
rooms or, in good weather, in the courtyard garden which in summer is a riot of colour and scent
from a mass of flowers.

And if you are planning to stay in this scenic part of the county, the inn has five comfortable
and very well-appointed en suite guest bedrooms.

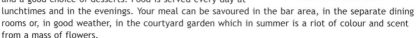

69 THE HIGH CROSS INN

Broughton-in-Furness, Cumbria LA20 6ES
Tel: 01229 716272
e-mail: welcome@highcrossinn.com
website: www.highcrossinn.com

The High Cross Inn is situated high on the hills surrounding the delightful village of Broughton-In-Furness, just off the A595. It offers spectacular panoramic views of the surrounding snow-capped mountains in winter months. Parts of the inn date back to its status as an 18th century farmhouse, which later became a favoured ale house. Today, the inn has a very traditional feeling with log fires and farmhouse furniture. Its spacious dining room opens up onto a large circular bay window filling the room with natural light. From here you can enjoy the scenic views of the valley below or if you prefer, from the terrace complete with picnic tables where you can soak up the summer sun.

Leaseholders Angela and Michael took over here in May 2009 and have already received excellent reviews from all those that visit. The quality of the food on offer here is a major attraction. "Traditional... Homemade... Local... Seasonal... Fresh..." These five words most accurately describe Angela and Michael's recipe for the dining experience at their inn. The menu has something for everyone. Amongst the starters you'll find a spicy Thai beef salad; main courses range from a hearty Lancashire hot pot, through steaks to a creamy mushroom Stroganoff. A specials board is also available offering seasonal dishes. Most dishes can be cooked to half portion as a children's menu. You can enjoy your meal either in the cosy bar, the traditional stone-walled restaurant (recently refurbished), or in the conservatory restaurant overlooking the Duddon Valley. Food is served all day: 11am to 8.45pm, Monday to Saturday; noon until 8pm on Sunday.

To complement the diverse menu, there's an extensive list of wines and a developing list of real ales, lagers and (coming soon) continental beers. Of the 4 real ales, 3 rotate from local breweries with Ennerdale as the regular brew. Accommodation is also available all

year round, with seven beautiful rooms to let, all of them with en suite facilities. Angela and Michael also offer a scrumptious breakfast in their tariff, making the High Cross Inn the perfect place to take a break in the unbeatable beauty of Cumbria. They also put on live music every fortnight, with excellent disabled access for both the bar and restaurant. All major credit cards accepted.

70 VICTORIA HOTEL

Station Road, Drigg, Cumbria CA19 1XQ
Tel: 01946 724231
e-mail: enquiries@thevicardrigg.co.uk
website: www.thevicardrigg.co.uk

Situated in the village of Drigg on the west Cumbria coast, **The Victoria Hotel** is a family run country hotel with a warm and welcoming atmosphere from the moment you enter. The Vic, as it is known locally, was built in about 1885 to service the Furness railway which still runs along the coast from Barrow-in-Furness to Carlisle. Drigg is known for its sand dunes which form, what is believed to be, the largest nesting sites in Europe for black headed Gulls and is also a sanctuary for rare Natterjack toads. Tenants Sandra and Peter are Cumbrian born and bred and took over at the Victoria in 2008. While this is their first venture into licensing, they have been in the catering industry for nearly 20 years.

The Victoria was extensively renovated in 2006 and features six quality en suite rooms, all with digital colour televisions and tea & coffee making facilities. The hotel is named for Queen Victoria and in keeping with this tradition, the rooms are all named after her children: Leopold, Louise, Alice, Beatrice, Edward and Alfred. The room rates are very reasonable and the tariff includes a hearty English breakfast, a great way to start the day.

Another popular feature of the hotel is the comfortable restaurant, which offers a delicious array of home cooked treats. Sandra cooks alongside an employed chef using food sourced from local suppliers. For example, the meat is sourced from Wilson's Butchers of Egremont and the delicious ice cream is supplied from Hartley's of Egremont. There is something for everyone and guests can expect to see dishes such as sumptuous steaks from Victoria's Grill, homemade lasagna, toasted sandwiches, and the local Cumberland sausage; the home made pies are extremely popular also, and with steak & kidney, meat & potato, steak & ale and chicken & mushroom to choose from, you'll be spoilt for choice. The menu also features a variety of all day breakfasts, fish dishes, a vegetarian selection and a range of sandwiches. The restaurant is open for service from 12 pm to 2 pm and 6 pm to 9 pm Tuesday – Sunday and there is a sample menu available on the excellent website. With such a tempting menu, it is advisable to book on Friday and Saturday evenings.

The bar is open every afternoon and evening session and all day Friday, Saturday and Sunday. The bar is very well stocked and features 2 real ales, Jennings Bitter and a rotating guest ale. Once a fortnight there is a quiz on Friday night from 9 pm and all are welcome to participate.

71 LAKES LODGE

1 High Street, Windermere, Cumbria LA23 1AF
Tel: 015394 42751 / 88133 Fax: 015394 46026
e-mail: admin@lakes-hotel.com
website: www.lakes-hotel.com

Located in the heart of Windermere, about 150 yards from the
railway and coach stations, **Lakes Lodge** is a handsome mid-
Victorian traditional stone building that was originally a bank.
The ambience throughout Andrew and Marie Dobson's hotel is warm
and inviting, and the bed rooms - doubles, twins and family rooms -
offer space and comfort in abundance. They all have en suite
facilities, central heating, television, beverage tray, fridge and
hairdryer; three of the rooms are located on the ground floor. The
tariff includes a full English breakfast. The owners and staff are
always ready with advice for walkers, golfers and pursuers of other
outdoor activities.

Windermere and the surrounding area are rich in scenic, cultural
and historic interest, and the best way to enjoy it all is through
Andrew's other excellent enterprise, Lakes Supertours. Luxury high-topped mini-coaches, with
ample leg room and fine visibility, offer a number of half-and full-day tours around Lakeland. They
are driven by friendly, well-informed driver-guides, and participants have ample opportunity to take
a stroll and photograph the sites. The itineraries include the Complete Beatrix Potter's Lakeland and
Wordsworth Tour, and by coach and boat on Borrowdale, Buttermere and Ullswater. And for extra
convenience for guests at the Lakes Lodge, all the tours start from the hotel forecourt.

73 THE CHURCH HOUSE INN

Torver, Coniston, Cumbria LA21 8AZ
Tel: 01539 441282
e-mail: churchhouseinn@hotmail.co.uk
website: www.churchhouseinntorver.com

Located in the quiet village of Torver, in the shadow of
Coniston Old Man, **The Church House Inn** dates back to the
15th century and still retains many of its original
features. It is full of charm and character with low
ceilings, wooden panelling, beams, slate floors, and
log burning fires.

Mine hosts at the Church House are Michael and
Mandy who took over here in 2006. Michael is
regarded as one of Cumbria's most renowned chefs,
having worked in some of the most prestigious
restaurants both in the UK and in France. He
naturally chooses to only cook from the freshest, top
quality ingredients, 80% of which are sourced within
Cumbria to create his extensive menu. The menu
changes four or six times a year but typical dishes include warm potted Morecambe Bay brown
shrimps amongst the appetisers; Cumberland tattie hot pot and daube of beef Bourguignonne,
both made with beef from a Coniston farm, amongst the main dishes. To accompany your meal,
there's a choice of up to 5 real ales from Cumbrian breweries.

The inn also offers comfortable en suite accommodation in 5 rooms, all with lots of character.

72 THE SUN HOTEL

Coniston, Cumbria LA21 8HQ
Tel: 01539 441248
Fax: 01539 441219
e-mail: stay@thesunconiston.com
website: www.thesunconiston.com

The Sun Hotel is one of the favourite destinations in Cumbria, whether it's just for a drink, a meal or a holiday in one of the most delightful surroundings. It was built in 1902 by the local brewery on the Walna Scar Road leading up to the Old Man of Coniston, on the old packhorse trail to the west. The brewery already owned a 16th century pub on the site so it made sense to build the hotel next to it.

The premises are warm, comfortable and very friendly, a tribute to the interest and effort invested by the family owners. Families with children (and pets) are very welcome at The Sun, and the 8 guest bedrooms, all with en suite facilities or a private bathroom, include 3 family rooms. Five cooked breakfast options get the day off to the best of starts, preparing guests for a day's walking or exploring the many and varied attractions within easy reach of the hotel. Alternative accommodation is available in a holiday flat at the back of the hotel, with 2 bedrooms, 2 bathrooms, a lounge and a mini-kitchen.

The owners are always making improvements, one of the most striking being the revealing of handsome wood panelling in the drawing room. The chefs expect their guests to work up good appetites on their excursions, and they make excellent use of locally-sourced produce, including fell-bred traditional English and Scottish beef cattle, on menus that take their inspiration from both traditional English and foreign cuisines. A lovely conservatory was added in 2001, and this and the lounge look out over the terrace to the garden that runs down the hill towards the lake and the village.

The superbly restored pub is a real gem, with exposed stone walls, flagstones, beams and a splendid old range in the fireplace. It's the perfect setting for meeting or making friends over a drink - there are 5 real ales and 35 wines available - or enjoying something from the bar menu.

74 THE OLD DUNGEON GHYLL HOTEL

Great Langdale, Ambleside,
Cumbria LA22 9JY
Tel: 01539 437272
e-mail: olddungeonghyll@btconnect.com
website: www.odg.co.uk

Visitors approaching the **Old Dungeon Ghyll Hotel** are treated to some magnificent views over the rugged scenery of the Great Langdale Valley and the stunning location is just the beginning of a truly memorable stay. This marvellous hotel was originally an inn with a farmhouse, which is the way it was run until 1949, and the oldest part is the middle section. Another part was added at a later date and the stables at the north end were converted into a dining room. The shippon at the other end became the Climbers Bar, where the old cow stalls still stand intact. In the Hikers Bar, real ales, of which there are at least six during the season, with Yates, Theakstons and a Jennings brew as the regulars.

The Old Dungeon Ghyll hotel has been attracting walkers, climbers, tourists and lovers of the great outdoors for 300 years and the latest owners Neil and Jane have been the proprietors for more than 25 years now. Neil, a keen fell runner, and Jane have continued to improve and develop this popular family hotel whilst keeping the rustic features and charm. The hotel's reputation has grown under their care and guests come from all over the world to the hotel which takes its name from one of the most dramatic of the Lake District waterfalls, tumbling 60 feet down a nearby fell. Neil and Jane both cook and the hearty home made dishes on the bar and restaurant menus cater perfectly for appetites sharpened by the bracing surroundings.

Guest accommodation at the Old Dungeon Ghyll comprises 13 warm, comfortable bedrooms, most with en suite facilities and some boasting four poster beds. The resident's lounge is a great place to relax, meet the other guests to swap stories and plan the next day's activities. The hotel is amply equipped; there is even a drying room to

dry those wet clothes. In the days when charabancs brought visitors from Little Langdale over Blea Tarn Pass, they would stop at the top and blow the horn, one toot for every passenger needing a meal! Over the years, the hotel has become very popular with climbing clubs and a favourite venue for club dinners, attracting many of the big names in climbing, including Sir John Hunt, Joe Brown and Don Whillans. Clubs are still very welcome and the hotel is the start point of several walks and climbs, including the famous peaks of Crinkle Crags, Bowfell and the Langdale Pikes.

75 DALE LODGE HOTEL

Grasmere, Cumbria LA22 9SW
Tel: 01539 435200 Fax: 01539 435570
e-mail: enquiries@dalelodgehotel.co.uk
website: www.dalelodgehotel.co.uk

Set in the heart of the idyllic Lake District village of Grasmere, **Dale Lodge Hotel** is a wonderful place to relax and unwind. It has recently been refurbished but great care was taken to retain its charming Georgian character. The hotel is owned and run by the Roberts family - Brian and Gillian and their son Alex. For all of them good food is a top priority and the hotel's Lodge Restaurant offers a menu of classic dishes with a modern twist prepared by head chef James Goodall.

Not many hotels can boast their own 'local'. Stepping into Tweedies Bar after a long day on the fells is like stepping into a little piece of heaven. Here you can unwind in front of the log burning fire and sample a pint of the award-winning guest ales - in all, there are 7 hand pumps and a scrumpy tap. Tweedies also serves what is probably the best pub food around and features local and seasonal produce prepared in an innovative and tempting style.

The accommodation at Dale Lodge comprises 12 beautifully appointed en suite rooms plus 4 luxury mews set in their own terraced area with an outdoor hot tub.

77 PARK FOOT

Howtown Road, Pooley Bridge,
Penrith, Cumbria CA10 2NA
Tel: 017684 86309 Fax: 017654 86041
e-mail: holidays@parkfootullswater.co.uk
website: www.parkfootullswater.co.uk

One of Cumbria's premier holiday parks, **Park Foot** offers the very best in caravan, camping and self-catering accommodation. Set in 40 acres of picturesque grounds looking down on Ullswater, the park was created in 1949 and is still owned and run by the same family. The caravan and camping area is superbly equipped with a full range of amenities, including a shop and licensed bar. Some caravans are available for sale.

If you prefer self-catering, Park Foot has a total of 15 different properties to choose from. Blanton House is a handsome stone building recently converted to a high standard into 2 separate holiday cottages, each of which can sleep up to 6 people. Then there's Parklands, a lovely detached bungalow which can accommodate up to 10. Woodside Cottages is a small row of 5 cottages, each of which sleeps between 4-6 people. Also available are 2 lodges, 4 log cabins and 'Beckside', a stone-built cottage with disabled access which can accommodate up to 6 people. It is located next to the shop and tennis court, and opposite the clubhouse and reception. Out of season, short breaks are available in the self-catering properties.

76 WHITE HORSE

Scales, Keswick, Cumbria CA12 4SY
Tel: 01768 779883
e-mail: katyure@hotmail.co.uk
website: www.thewhitehorseinnscales.co.uk

Situated just off the A66 amidst beautiful surroundings, **The White Horse Inn** is located at Scales and is well worth a visit. Dating back to 1610, the building has character, style, and is equally traditional and historical with a hint of modernism, thanks to proud tenants Barry and Katy. Starting off life as a farmhouse and then alehouse, eventually becoming an inn in the early 18th century, the property was once a meeting place for highway men and smugglers; today times have changed, but the social hub of the inn remains the same, with locals and tourists gathering to enjoy a real ale in a pleasant and warm environment.

Barry and Katy McGeachy took over the premises in March 2009 and made their mark by undergoing a refurbishment of the bar and lounge areas. The recommendations for quality hospitality and service continue flood in by word of mouth and by the number of customers returning time and time again.

Open every session and all day Saturday and Sunday there are 3 real ales to enjoy, Sharp's Edge Bitter being the regular, with two rotating guest ales on offer. Food is available every day from 12, until 8 Monday til Thursday, and until 9 Friday, Saturday and Sunday, with bar snacks being served all day Saturday and Sunday as an extra. The chefs produce quality cuisine, using local produce and local suppliers wherever possible; however prime Aberdeen Angus beef is always used.

The food here is exceptional and offers great value for money. Diners can expect to sample dishes such as Cumberland sausage & mash, braised lamb shank, horseshoe gammon steak, ploughmans lunch and venison haunch steak to name but a few. The Sunday roast is a firm favourite therefore it is advisable to book. Food can be eaten throughout the inn, creating a warm and sociable atmosphere and children are more than welcome, meaning that the White Horse Inn is great for families. The inn holds regular events such as live music nights, race nights and games leagues, please ring for more details.

78 DALEGARTH GUESTHOUSE AND CAMPSITE

Hassness Estate, Buttermere, Cockermouth, Cumbria CA13 9XA
Tel: 01768 770233
e-mail: dalegarthhouse@hotmail.co.uk
website: www.dalegarthguesthouse.co.uk

Surrounded by picturesque countryside and only 200 yards from
Buttermere lake, is the popular **Dalegarth Guest House and Campsite**.
The main house has 9 bedrooms, and owners James and Kelly are always
on hand to make sure your stay is a memorable one. There is a spacious
living room complete with a real log fire and a selection of books, games and music. A hearty full
English breakfast is included in the tariff. Dalegarth also sports a large 35 pitch campsite.

www.findSOMEWHERE.co.uk
For people who want to explore the United Kingdom

Places to Eat and Drink

80 THE BUSH

Main Street, Cockermouth, Cumbria CA13 9JS
Tel: 01900 822064
e-mail: joesf@btinternet.com

For those looking for a real treat, why not pause awhile at **The
Bush Hotel** and sample the local brews, experience the local
atmosphere and enjoy exceptional food. Leaseholder Joe Fagan
and bar manager Jim Weldon, all with considerable local
experience, offer a warm welcome to all who visit this former
coaching inn. The food here is second to none, and the
monthly changing menu is created using locally sourced
produce. Available at lunchtimes only, diners can expect to see
dishes such as; homemade steak pie, beer battered cod and
chips, wholetail Whitby scampi, gammon steak and baked
potatoes. The desserts are equally as tempting, with chocolate
fudge cake and sticky toffee pudding the firm favourites.

The inn is open all day, everyday, offering a large selection
of drinks from the local Jennings Brewery, including Jennings
Bitter, Cocker Hoop, Cumberland Ale and Snecklifter; add to
these a monthly Jennings guest ale and a rotating nationally brewed ale and visitors will be spoilt
for choice. There's also a good range of other draught and bottle beers and lagers, stout and
cider. This is definitely one of the best places in Cockermouth to socialize over a drink, with a
convivial atmosphere created by the management, the staff and locals and visitors of all ages.
Children and dogs are made welcome and all major credit cards are accepted. When the weather
is kind, the beer garden is a popular spot for alfresco sipping. The Bush also hosts occasional
music nights; please ring for more details.

79 HARTLEY'S BEACH SHOP AND TEAROOM

Beach Road, St Bees, Cumbria CA27 0ES
Tel: 01946 820175 Fax: 01946 820456
website: www.hartleys-ice-cream.co.uk

Occupying a superb position overlooking the foreshore at St Bees, **Hartleys Beach Shop & Tea Room** is one of the most popular places in the region for enjoying a snack. It's a long, single-storey building which has been around for 20 odd years and its reputation ensures locals, tourists, walkers and holidaymakers alike all swarm like bees to a honeypot. As the tearoom is situated more or less at the beginning of the famous Coast to Coast walk across the Pennines, it is much visited by those at the end of the walk. The sunny yellow colour scheme brightens up even the most overcast of days and the warm welcome extended by the Richardson family who have owned and run the premises for many years, adds to the atmosphere.

The tea room is open daily from 9am to 8pm (5pm out of season), with hot food served until 4 o'clock. The food choice runs from made-to-order sandwiches with generous fillings like tuna savoury, corned beef & onions and chicken mayo, to soup, beans on toast and home-made cakes, teacakes and scones. Very few summer visitors leave without trying one or more of the delicious ice creams, which are made by the firm established by the Hartley family in 1931 in Egremont, where they are still made. The ice creams come in more than 60 flavours, with some diabetic varieties and also eight flavours of sorbets. They are sold to the public and to the retail and catering trades in tubs from 125ml to 10 litres, and freezer packs are a speciality. They are made fresh every day in the Church Street creamery in Egremont, and new lines include semi-freddo desserts - a perfect way to end a meal. The actual ice-cream store is situated on Church Street in Egremont and is open between 11 am and 5 pm from January to March and until 7 pm in the busier summer months. To drink, guests can choose from cold soft drinks, milkshakes, tea and a variety of coffees.

The business was taken over in 1981 by the Richardson family, who run the beach shop with friendly, hardworking staff. The tea room has seats for 48 inside, and when the weather is kind, tables and chairs are set outside. Hartleys at St Bees also has a gift shop and mini-mart selling walking and camping essentials.

81 THE BEECHES CARAVAN PARK

Gilcrux, Wigton, Cumbria CA7 2QX
Tel: 01697 321555
website: www.thebeechescaravanpark.com

Renowned for its idyllic location, with views toward Scotland and excellent amenities, **Beeches Caravan Park** is a must for those looking to explore this picturesque part of Cumbria. Situated just 5 miles north of Cockermouth and just over 3 miles from the Solway Coast at Allonby, the park offers 12 luxury caravans set within two acres of picturesque grounds. The park is owned and maintained by Henry Airey who has been providing a quality service to all who visit since 2002. The site is open all year round and there is a minimum of two nights stays onwards.

The on site facilities include a post office, shop, laundry service and even the parks own restaurant and bar complete with log fire and takeaway service which opens every evening and weekend lunchtimes (also open to non-residents). Caravans are equipped with WC, shower, full kitchen, colour TV and gas fire, sleeping 6 with a wonderful children's playground on site also on their doorsteps making this a hassle free holiday for any family.

82 BRANDRAW HOUSE

2 West Street, Aspatria, Cumbria CA7 3HG
Tel: 01697 321207
e-mail: info@brandrawhouse.com
website: www.brandrawhouse.com

In the heart of Cumbria on the A596 Carlisle to Maryport Road is **Brandraw House**. This late Victorian bed and breakfast offers unrivalled hospitality from its friendly hosts; Robert and Jean Ahrens who are fluent in Dutch and German as well as English. Their continental roots do not affect the building however, as they have carefully retained its many original features. Guests can relax in the living room or breakfast room, each of which is filled with memorabilia from a bygone era. Each bedroom has full en suite facilities with wireless broadband.

85 THE NEW INN COUNTRY PUB

Brampton, Appleby-in-Westmorland, Cumbria CA16 6JS
Tel: 01767 351231

The New Inn Country Pub dates back to 1730 and is absolutely wonderful, exuding its history and classic features. There are open fires in the bar and restaurant, flagstone floors, beamed ceilings and old artefacts adorning the walls. There is also a huge beer garden at the rear of the property providing visitors with an enjoyable experience both inside and out. Licensees Lydia and Gregory recently took over here and Gregory has been a professional chef for 15 years. The hosts prepare exceptional food, which is served every day, and the bar is well stocked with a good selection of beverages and real ales.

83 PONDEROSA GUEST HOUSE

Uldale, Wigton, Cumbria CA7 1HA
Tel: 01697 371805
website: www.ponderosakeswick.co.uk

Nestled among the fells and valleys of the northern part of the Lake District National Park is a truly remarkable guest house. **Ponderosa Guest House** sits in its own peaceful grounds on a working sheep and dairy farm, and provides a perfect retreat from the hustle and bustle of everyday life. With over 25 years experience in welcoming guests, Margaret Wilson is a doting host, and is always on hand to make sure your say is a memorable one. Ugdale has been Margaret's home for over 40 years, and for those wishing to explore the local area Ponderosa offers the perfect base.

Guests can choose between two luxuriously furnished en suite bedrooms with fantastic views across the countryside. A superb full English breakfast starts the day and guests can enjoy a traditional home-cooked dinner if pre-arranged with Margaret. Children over the age of 12 are more than welcome but the house cannot accept dogs.

The self-catering accommodation, for up to five guests, is in an adjacent cottage equipped with all the mod cons. Both the B&B and the self-catering facilities are perfect for touring or walking holidays, and an ideal stopover between England and Scotland.

84 SCOTT'S FISH BAR AND STEAKHOUSE GRILL

34 Burrowgate, Penrith, Cumbria CA11 7TA
Tel: 01768 890838
e-mail: dharding66@btinternet.com

Scott's Fish Bar and Steakhouse Grill is located centrally in popular Penrith, in Burrowgate. Offering an array of chip shop classics, wonderful steaks and a few other mouth-watering dishes, this business is well known in the area as one of the best places to dine for fast food, with a difference. A planned refurbishment will see the establishment transformed into a restaurant, wine bar and accommodation as well as the current fish and chip takeaway.

Dave Harding is the owner of Scott's Fish Bar and Steakhouse Grill and his son Dan has just been awarded the title of 2010 UK Young Fryer of the Year. All the food served is homemade daily, using only the finest and freshest local produce. There is a large range of fantastic fish dishes available as well as award winning Lakeland steaks, which are cooked to your liking. All the meats used in the dishes are sourced from within Cumbria and the fish is brought daily from North East Ports. The father and son duo also run a chip shop in the town, linking the two businesses nicely.

This very popular place to dine is open seven days a week between 11.30am-2pm and 4.30pm-8pm, with extended hours on Thursdays, Fridays and Saturdays until 10pm.

86 CROWN AND CUSHION INN

2 Boroughgate, Appleby-in-Westmorland,
Cumbria CA16 6XB
Tel: 01768 351595

The Crown and Cushion Inn stands centrally in the historic town of Appleby-in-Westmorland next to the parish church. It is a beautiful listed building and has featured in many films and advertisements. Behind the typical Westmorland frontage, the inn offers superb facilities in all departments. Its interior is classy and has been recently refurbished. The inn has three en-suite rooms available, which are all located upstairs and available all year round. The reasonable tariff includes a hearty breakfast. You are unlikely to be disappointed because tenants and hosts Sandra and Ian focus their daily pub menu, available each lunchtime and evening, on traditional homemade food.

The pub is child friendly and such is the popularity of the food served it is advisable to book for Sunday lunch. Three real ales are served all day with Hartleys XB and Double Hop the regulars and a rotating guest ale from Robinsons Brewery. Sandra has been in the catering business for many years and took over the Crown and Cushion Inn with Ian in November 2009. They really have put the inn back on the map and many locals and visitors enjoy relaxing here during the day and evening. Disabled access is not a problem.

87 THE THREE GREYHOUNDS INN

Great Asby, Appleby-in-Westmorland,
Cumbria CA16 6EX
Tel: 017683 51428

The Three Greyhounds Inn can be found in the picturesque and hidden village of Great Asby. Situated close to the village stream, this picture postcard inn is located just a short drive from Appleby-in-Westmorland and offers the very best hospitality and traditional pub grub. Kirsty and Mark Shuttleworth are your hosts here, having taken over the leasehold in December 2009. Although it is their first venture with their own premise, Kirsty has experience in the trade. Two rotating guest ales are served at The Three Greyhounds Inn, which has a well stocked bar and is open all day on Saturday and Sunday. It is also open every session during the week, a part from Monday when it is closed (except bank holidays). Food is served between 12pm-2.30pm and 6pm – 8.30pm Tuesday – Sunday. Local produce is used wherever possible and most of the dishes are

home cooked. Roast dinners are served on a Sunday and children are always welcome at the inn, which has a superb beer garden out the back that is a real sun trap in warmer weather. Disabled access is not a problem. All major credit cards are taken.

88 SANDFORD ARMS

Sandford, Appleby-in-Westmorland,
Cumbria CA16 6NR
Tel: 017683 51121
e-mail: sandfordarms@live.co.uk
website: www.sandfordarmscumbria.co.uk

The Sandford Arms is a superb conversion of 18th century farm buildings into a beautiful residential inn, lounge and restaurant. Located in a picturesque and pleasant location, just a mile or so off the A66 in a charming village by the River Eden, this country inn provides splendid food, drink and guest accommodation. A newly constructed self-catering cottage has just been built adjacent to the main property which has three en-rooms available for B&B.

Owned and run by hosts Stephen and Nicola Porter for the last three years, the couple have a combined experience in the trade of 18 years and their hospitality and knowledge of what visitors want is 100%. The Sandford Arms has a warm and friendly atmosphere, heightened by the endless rapport that the hosts build with their visitors and the relaxing and traditional décor of the building. The property, which is enjoyed by both locals and visitors alike often enjoy one of the three real ales on offer. Food can be enjoyed daily from between 11.30am-2.30pm and 6pm-8.45pm. All the produce used is from local suppliers, wherever possible and the ingredients are used to produce many dishes, including the Chef's specials of minted lamb henry, Sandford chicken and homemade lasagne.

89 CHOFH'S TEAROOM & TAKEAWAY

New Road, Brough, Cumbria CA17 4AS
Tel: 017683 42800

Hidden away, although just yards from the busy A66, Chofh's Tearoom and Takeaway is a hotspot for hungry cyclists, walkers and tourists, and has been a well established tearoom in Brough for many years now. Current owner Jennie Dawson had worked here for 3 years, fell in love with the place and bought it together with her husband John.

Its clean and friendly country décor feel very traditional and lives up to standards serving a quality range of homemade cakes. There is room for 22 people to dine inside and room for 8 more outside, with a choice from a delicious locally produced menu and a daily specials board, though the specialties are Jennie's famous bacon sandwiches and filling all day breakfasts.

Chofh's is open Monday-Friday 7.30am to 4pm, and Saturday 8.30am to 3pm, but in the summer months on Thursdays doors are open right through until 8.30pm. Closed on Sundays. Booking is advised for larger parties. Cash only please.

And if you're after more than just tea and a scrumptious Cumbrian snack, you might be interested in John's other talents which include being local toastmaster and master of ceremonies, available to book for weddings, private parties, corporate functions, charity auctions or commentating!

90 THE GREYHOUND HOTEL

Main Street, Shap, Cumbria CA10 3PW
Tel: 01931 716474
e-mail: info@greyhoundshap.co.uk
website: www.greyhoundshap.co.uk

The Greyhound Hotel in Shap is a famous Westmorland hostelry dating back to 1680. It is recorded that Bonnie Prince Charlie stayed here overnight on the march south with his Highlanders in 1745. Just a 5 minute drive from junction 39 of the M6, the hotel enjoys panoramic views of the Lake District fells.

The Greyhound has an excellent reputation for food and drink. All dishes are freshly prepared to your order, with all of the meat coming from local farms. There is also a chef's specials board for evening meals which changes on a daily basis, with fish as the chef's speciality. The pub also has 8 traditional hand-pulled ales, a selection of lagers and spirits and a wide range of carefully chosen wines to complement your meal.

The hotel has 11 en suite rooms (6 standard, 5 deluxe), all with tea & coffee making facilities. The five new deluxe bedrooms, upgraded in March 2009, boast fell views, flat screen televisions and new en-suite bathrooms or shower rooms. The tariff includes a superb Cumbrian breakfast (which features Bella's world championship Cumberland sausage) as well as Westmorland black pudding and free range local eggs served in the Whinfell breakfast room.

91 THE GEORGE HOTEL

Front Street, Orton, Penrith,
Cumbria CA10 3RJ
Tel: 01539 624229
e-mail: thegeorgehotel-orton@hotmail.co.uk
website: www.thegeorgehotelorton.co.uk

Located in the picturesque village of Orton, just 3 minutes from junction 38 of the M6, **The George Hotel** is a traditional inn with a spacious beer garden. Your hosts, April and Marc, offer a relaxed atmosphere with a friendly personal service. Good food is one of their priorities and the varied menu caters for all tastes and appetites. You'll find a home-made soup of the day and Thai chilli prawns amongst the starters, while the main dishes range from hearty steaks through that old favourite fish & chips, to a tasty mushroom Stroganoff. You can choose to eat in the bar or go through to the dining room. There's a good variety of wines to accompany your meal, along with a choice of 3 rotating locally brewed real ales. Food is served from noon until 3pm, and from 6pm to 9pm, every day during the season and from 6pm to 9pm, Monday to Friday in winter. At weekends, booking is strongly advised.

The accommodation at The George comprises eight well appointed letting rooms with bed and breakfast available at very reasonable prices. All rooms have tea and coffee making facilities; hair dryers and ironing boards are available on request.

92 SHAKESPEARE INN AND RESTAURANT

117 London Road, Shardlow, Derby, Derbyshire DE72 2GP
Tel: 01332 792728
e-mail: shakespeareinn@live.co.uk

The Shakespeare Inn and Restaurant lies in the heart of the village of Shardlow, which is just 6 miles from Derby's city centre. The Shakespeare Inn is one of many popular pubs and restaurants in Shardlow, as the area receives most of its trade from hungry canal goers. Shardlow itself gained much of its popularity from the opening of the Mersey canal in the late 18th century, and was once the main canal hub for the midlands. Today the inn is as busy as ever, with a fine reputation for serving quality English food, day inn day out.

Located nearby the main marina in Shardlow, the Shakespeare sports pleasant views across the town, which are complimented by the inn's own green beer garden. It has been owned and run by Kevin and Sue Johnson for the past 5 years, and they have created a popular following with both locals and visitors to the area alike. Opening all day every day the pair keep their bar well stocked with up to four real ales at any one time, which usually includes Marstons Pedigree and a selection of ever changing guest ales. A fine choice of wines, lagers and spirits is also available. Bar food is available Monday to Saturday 12-2:30pm and 6-8:30pm and can be enjoyed throughout the main bar area with a range of light bites, filled rolls, sandwiches and jacket potatoes.

The inn also has a separate restaurant which is stylishly decorated whilst retaining its olde worlde feel. The restaurant is open from 12-4pm on Sunday and from 6-9:30pm on Tuesday to Saturday evenings. The menu comprises a wonderful selection of traditional English dishes, cooked fresh to order using only the best local produce. Kevin and Sue see many return customers, who enjoy the laid back, family atmosphere that the restaurant affords, with friendly and efficient service at all times. Children welcome, all major credit cards accepted.

93 THE OLD CROWN

Cavendish Bridge, Shardlow, Derbyshire DE72 2HL
Tel: 01332 792392
e-mail: the.oldcrowninn@btconnect.com

Hidden away off the B5010 in Cavendish Bridge, close to the Marina and the popular village of Shardlow is **The Old Crown**. It stands on the on one of the older roads where it was once a former coaching and posting inn for the area, dating back to the late 17th century. Today the inn retains much of its olde worlde charm and is decorated with a whole host of memorabilia from a bygone era.

It has been owned and run by Monique, James and their family for the last few years, which has given the inn the homely feel that its locals so love. The inn is renowned throughout Derbyshire and nearby areas of Leicestershire and Nottinghamshire for its astounding collection of well kept real ales. The family ensure that up to 9 real ales are available at any given time with a range of regular and guest ales to include Marstons Old Empire, Marstons Pedigree, Jennings Cumberland Ale and Cock a Hoop. To celebrate this fine selection, the inn holds beer festivals over the weekends in March and September every year when over 20 real ales are brought in to sample.

Guests also come to the Crown for its delicious home cooked menu. Food is served 12-2pm and 5-8pm Monday to Thursday, 12-2pm on Fridays, 12-8pm on Saturdays and 12-4pm on Sundays. Guests can choose from either the specials board or the main menu which encompasses a choice of filled sandwiched, baguettes and jacket potatoes, main meals, grills and vegetarian options. Popular dishes include steak and ale pie, chicken pasta Leonardo, smoked haddock fishcakes, rump steak, spicy veggie burger, and mushroom and red pepper stroganoff. Dining here is very popular, with fast and friendly service, so booking is recommended on weekends.

Guests can also enjoy a range of great family entertainment throughout the week, with Quiz night on Mondays and a popular Folk night on Tuesdays. Children welcome.

Monique and James also offer two tastefully decorated upstairs bedrooms, both of which have en suite bathrooms. Rooms are available all year round and come on a tasty bed and breakfast tariff, ideal for guests who want to take a short break away in this particularly pretty area of Derbyshire.

94 HILTON HOUSE HOTEL

1 Mill Lane, Hilton, Derbyshire DE65 5GP
Tel: 01283 732304 Fax: 01283 732799
e-mail: enquiries@hiltonhousehotel.co.uk
website: www.hiltonhousehotel.co.uk

The elegant **Hilton House Hotel** stands in the village of Hilton just 10 miles from Derby. Its handsome Georgian design creates a period feel that gives any stay here one of coziness.

Owners Zoe and Colin Clark run this hotel to the highest standards, offering guests ten superb rooms, nine of which are en suite. Six rooms are located within the main house, with a further four in the adjacent annex. All rooms are tastefully decorated and incorporate all essential commodities including colour TV, wireless internet connection, and refreshment tray plus hairdryer, iron & ironing board upon request. A range of double, king size and family rooms are available which can come on a room only, or bed and breakfast basis.

Zoe and Colin also serve up a selection of lunch and evening meals in their bar and lounge, which is open to non-residents also. Food is available from 12-2pm and 6-8:30pm Monday to Friday and from 12-2pm on Saturdays & Sundays. The menu changes regularly and includes a range of traditional dishes prepared by professional chefs. Dishes include lamb and mint pudding, pan seared salmon and roasted pork with all the trimmings.

The hotel makes an ideal base for those looking to explore this picturesque part of Derbyshire on a short break, or for a peaceful afternoon drink in the hotels impressive wood panelled bar.

96 THE MOULDERS ARMS

53 Church Street, Riddings, Derbyshire DE55 4BX
Tel: 01773 602445
e-mail: craig.hawksworth@virginmedia.com
website: www.themouldersarms.com

Although the inn is really called **The Moulders Arms**, it is affectionately known to the locals of Riddings as the Thack; perhaps owing to its status as the only thatched pub in Derbyshire. The premises dates back to the 17th century and still retains much of that olde worlde charm, with large fireplaces and low beamed ceilings. Local couple Craig and Jo have been running the inn since January 2009 and have given the Thack back its status as the hub of its community. Open all day every day, the inn is popular with ale lovers as it provides up to four real ales at any one time, one of which is the inn's own special brew; Thack IPA.

The inn also prides itself on offering great pub grub at great pub prices. Its traditional English menu has recently been enhanced by the culinary skills of new head Chef Cliff, who puts much emphasis on using fresh, local produce in all his dishes. Specialties now include a selection of homemade pies, and a classic roast dinner with proper homemade Yorkshire puddings. Food is available from 12-2pm and 5-8pm Tuesday to Saturday and 12-3pm on Sundays, with a snack menu operating between these times.

Craig and Jo are also keen to support local talent and host a number of live events, from acoustic performances, bands and DJs. A very entertaining quiz is run each Thursday from 9:30pm that includes a cryptic beer round! Please visit our facebook page 'The Moulders Arms aka The Thack in Riddings' to find out about upcoming events.

95 THREE HORSESHOES

The Green, Wessington, Derbyshire DE55 6DQ
Tel: 01773 834 854
e-mail: andrea@bottompub.eclipse.co.uk

The Three Horseshoes stands proudly in the village of Wessington which lies in the heart of the Derbyshire Dales between Matlock and the M1. The property dates back in part to the early 18th century and retains much of that olde worlde feel throughout. Although the pub was once a former coaching inn, posting inn and family home – it now stands a lively hub for its community who rave about the traditional food and drink on offer.

Owners Stephen and Andrea have been here for the past 2½ years, in which time they have cultivated a wonderful environment in which to relax or dine. They open all day every day, serving a fine choice of real ales which includes a rotating guest ale and the popular Abbot Ale and Olde Trip. A good selection of other drinks is also available including an array of fine wines and spirits. Drinks can be enjoyed throughout the pub, but can also be enjoyed on the pub's outdoor seating area which is a pleasant sun spot in the summer months.

Andrea also serves up a small, but carefully chosen menu, created with fresh local produce. In the summer months, food is available from 12-2:30pm and 5-8pm, and in the winter months from 12-2pm and 5:30-8pm. Guests can chose from a choice of traditional pub meals like homemade meat and potato pie, cod and chips, and a delicious lamb hotpot with vegetables, or try something more exotic like Andrea's specialty meat and potato pie. A range of meat and vegetarian curries are also available which all come served with wild rice, naan bread and mango chutney. Guests with a smaller appetite can also chose from a range of sandwiches and light bites, some of which are also suitable for children. On Sundays a traditional roast is added to the menu, when owing to popularity, it its best to book.

On Friday nights, a popular quiz night is run for all the family from 9:30pm, so why not come a long and get involved. In the lifetime of this edition, Stephen and Andrea are also hoping to add some guest accommodation to the pub, so please ring for details.

97 THE SPOTTED COW INN

12 Town Street, Holbrook, Derbyshire DE56 0TA
Tel: 01332 881200
e-mail: info@thespottedcow.co.uk
website: www.thespottedcow.co.uk

Situated just five minutes from Derby city centre in the village of Holbrook is the Spotted Cow Inn. This popular village inn regularly draws in the crowds to experience affordable, fine dining at its best. The inn dates back to 1820 when it was originally an Alehouse, acquiring its liquor license in 1840. Today, its owners Andrew and Fiona West-Hunt still ensure that a healthy selection of real ales, lagers and spirits are available alongside a handsome wine list which can be enjoyed all day every day.

The inn is full of character and retains some beautiful old features such as oak beams, wooden floors and brick walling. These features are complimented by an interesting selection of memorabilia and traditional farm house décor, which creates a warm and friendly feel. Although popular for drinks, the inn is best known for its food. Head Chef Robert Baker has been here for almost three years and has dedicated himself to providing guests with a their perfect meal. Robert's menus are classically English, but have a modern twist to excite the palette. He places much emphasis on using only the best in fresh local produce, and is always happy to cater for any special dietary requirements such as gluten or dairy free diets. All dishes and sauces are cooked fresh to order on the premises so most dislikes can also be catered for with the omission or replacement of various ingredients where possible. Guests can choose from a variety of delicious choices from rump steak with peppercorn sauce, salmon fillet in a pool of plum jus, spicy chicken wraps and homemade pie of the day. A wide range of hot baguettes, jackets and salads are also available, with plenty of children's and vegetarian options too. Throughout the week the team offer a variety of offers such as complementary supper at the Tuesday night quiz, free soup or coffee with every meal, children eat free on Thursdays, and a free bottle of wine with steaks on Wednesday's Steak night. Robert also caters for a variety of special occasions, please ring for details.

Andrew and Fiona also offer two luxury bedrooms and one suite, all of which are lavishly styled with sumptuous linens, scatter cushions and modern art. Conveniently located to many of Derby's best attractions, the Spotted Cow is ideal for a fantastic weekend away.

98 THE RISING SUN

26 Rise End, Middleton, Matlock,
Derbyshire DE4 4LS
Tel: 01629 822420
e-mail: davemountford@sky.com
website: www.therisingsuninn.biz

Located at the heart of Derbyshire, **The Rising Sun** is a popular inn with visitors to the Peak District. Combining relaxation with great food and live entertainment, the child friendly inn offers two superb en-suite rooms. Breathtaking views surround The Rising Sun, which is within walking distance of the High Peak Trail and Black Rocks.

Open all day every day the inn has a fantastic menu with main meals including all the traditional favourites, such as lasagne and sausage and mash. The dining area seats 20 and another 20 can dine in the bar area. Light lunches are also served with a good selection of sandwiches, paninis, jacket potatoes, baguettes and wraps. Vegetarian options are available as well as additional choices from the specials board. Food is served 12pm-9pm seven days a week and local produce is used where possible. Sunday lunches are served and it is advisable to book.

Tenants Dave and Lorraine Mountford have run the inn for the last three years and offer a warm welcome to locals and visitors. The couple hold special events several times a year (check website for details). Up to five real ales are served, with Marstons Pedigree, Bass and Speckled Hen the regulars. All major credit cards taken.

100 THE BLACK HORSE INN

Hulland Ward, Derbyshire DE6 3EE
Tel: 01335 370206 Fax: 01335 370206

The Black Horse Inn dates back to the 1690's and is located in the Derbyshire Dales on the edge of the Peak District. It is owned and run by Muriel Edwin who offers the very best in hospitality and advice for what to see and do in the area.

The inn's olde worlde interior sports many original features and has a traditional country pub feel, with beamed ceilings and original stone walling. The bar area is host to an ever changing range of beers and ales from across the country and contains plenty of classic pub games such as dominoes and darts to amuse you. The restaurant serves up a fine selection of home cooked dishes created with locally reared meats and fresh local produce. Guests are presented with an impressive choice which includes 45 main dishes, 13 vegetarian choices and 15 desserts. Popular choices include the succulent game like rabbit, pigeon, pheasant, grouse and goose. Guests can dine throughout the inn, or take a shady picnic spot in the inn's pleasant garden.

Four en suite bedrooms are also available, all of which have colour TV and tea and coffee facilities, not to mention an elegant four poster bed. Rooms come on a hearty bed and breakfast tariff, guaranteed to fill guests up for a whole days exploring.

99 THE MALT SHOVEL

Wirksworth Moor, Wirksworth, Derbyshire DE4 4GS
Tel: 01629 822427
e-mail: the.maltshovel@live.co.uk

Popular with walkers and cyclists, **The Malt Shovel** is surrounded by beautiful countryside. Dating back to the mid 18th century, the former coaching inn offers a high standard of cuisine, hospitality and accommodation and has a good reputation in the area. Tenants and business partners, Linda Spencer and Christopher Taylor have run the establishment for the past two years and its good reputation is growing.

Accommodation is available all year round. There are three comfortable rooms (two doubles and one single), which all share a bathroom. The tariff is very reasonable and includes a hearty breakfast. The rooms are all located upstairs and are extremely popular, especially with walkers, because of the facilities the inn offers and its location.

The inn is popular with locals and visitors for the food it serves, much of which is sourced locally. The extensive menu is fairly traditional with dishes including steak and ale pie, homemade lasagne, corned beef hash; and homemade chilli. Vegetarian and children's options are available. For those with a lighter appetite there is a delicious selection of light snacks. Filled sandwiches, baguettes, toasties and jacket potatoes are all very popular and the special 'puddings' board is extremely tempting. Food is served Monday – Saturday 12pm – 8pm and on a Sunday from 12pm – 6pm. It is advisable to book for Sunday lunch; such is its popularity at The Malt Shovel. From the outside the inn is an impressive establishment with beautiful windows and an inviting look about it. Inside, there is a relaxed and friendly atmosphere and many visitors return time and time again.

Four real ales can be enjoyed, with Marstons Pedigree the regular and three rotating guest ales. There is a pleasant beer garden to the rear of the child friendly inn, which is popular with punters and diners on sunnier days. There is also a play area to keep younger guests entertained. Dogs are welcome.

The inn can be found a short drive from the centre of the small town of Wirksworth on the B5035 past the railway on the left, or off the main A6 via the B5035. Many visitors to the Peak District will get chance to explore the winding streets, old buildings and beautiful views the town has to offer. The Malt Shovel is an ideal place to stay for those wanting to explore the Peak District and has plenty to offer the hungry traveller.

101 GALLERY CAFÉ

50 St. John Street, Ashbourne, Derbyshire DE6 1GH
Tel: 01335 347425
e-mail: info@sjsg.co.uk website: www.sjsg.co.uk

The St. John Street Gallery and Gallery Café is spread over four floors of a spacious grade II listed Victorian building that was once the town's magistrate court. The Gallery is now the regions premiere venue for contemporary fine arts and crafts, which include pieces in various media including ceramics, glass and jewellery. The popular café provides a steady thoroughfare for the gallery as patrons come not only for the art, but for the food.

Glen Bentley and Rob Watkin, owners and business partners, take pride in both the gallery and café, and have won themselves a variety of prestigious awards. Open from 10am-4pm in winter and until 5pm in the summer, they are known for supporting local suppliers and fair trade products, creating a menu that always ensures tasty, simple food. Guests can chose from a wide selection of cakes, breakfasts and salads, alongside dishes like stilton and walnut pate or homemade soup. A wide variety of specialty teas and coffees make for the perfect afternoon tea when paired with a gluten free chocolate brownie or slice of moist carrot cake. The café has a restaurant license, so a small selection of wines and bottled beers are also available to enjoy with your meal.

The café also now serves up a delicious range of tapas with bread and olives on selected evenings from 7-8:30pm, but these evenings are very popular so booking ahead is essential. Children and dogs welcome.

102 THE BLUEBELL INN AND RESTAURANT

Buxton Road, Tissington, Derbyshire DE6 1NH
Tel: 01335 350317 Fax: 01335 350103
e-mail: bluebell350317@aol.com
website: www.bluebelltissington.co.uk

The Bluebell Inn is situated outside the lovely village of Tissington on the A515, just three miles north of Ashbourne. It's within easy reach of the well known Tissington Trail and other attractions like trekking and gardening centres, a candle workshop and Alton Towers. The inn itself provides a beautiful setting for all occasions, whether you are having a conference, wedding, christening, funeral or birthday party. Its' glorious function room has seating for up to 100 guests, with its own private bar, dance floor and toilets. The inn has achieved a fine reputation for serving delicious cuisine, not only catering for functions, but as part of the menu for the inns restaurant.

All meals are homemade cooked fresh to order from local ingredients, many of which come from the Peak District itself. Food is served up daily from 10:30am-9pm and ranges from starters, light bites and snacks, to filling main dishes which include sage Derby chicken, wild mushroom lasagne, haddock fillet with prawn and parsley sauce, and roast pork with sage and onion stuffing. Friday nights are curry night with a spicy range of curries from Malayan chicken to a Tissington lamb balti. Whereas on Sundays its steak night; with a hearty selection of grills to choose from. Guests can dine throughout, or enjoy a relaxing drink in the inn's pretty stone walled gardens. All special diets are catered for especially gluten free and dairy free.

103 THE SARACENS HEAD

Shirley, nr Ashbourne, Derbyshire DE6 3AS
Tel: 01335 360330
e-mail: saracensheadshirley@yahoo.co.uk
website: www.saracens-head-shirley.co.uk

The Saracens Head dates back to 1791
when it was once run as a farm and
hostelry. It's found nestled in the heart
of the historic village of Shirley which
itself, dates back to the 1100s.

The inn is now run by award winning
Chef Robin Hunter and partner Terri,
who have made themselves quite a
reputation in the area for serving up
quality food. They describe the inn as a
country gastro pub where traditional
meets contemporary, effortlessly
creating the perfect night out. The
interior of the inn is stylish yet earthy;
with a mix of striking designs and
colours amongst original fireplaces and
farm house furniture. Its gentle class does not impose and allows
guests to unwind in the presence of simple good food and friends.

Food is served Monday to Saturday from 12-2pm and 6-9pm and on
Sundays from 12-2:30pm and 6-9pm. The chefs here believe that they
are only as good as the last meal they cooked, which is the reason
why people come back again and again - making booking essential.
Popular dishes include local leek and pork sausages in onion gravy
with creamy mash, pan fried cod fillet with parmesan mash and crab
butter, sea bass in garlic and prawn butter, and Moroccan style lamb
shank with figs, prunes and pistachios. A mouth-watering selection of
other mains, starters and desserts are also available, all of which are
cooked fresh to order, using only the best in local produce. The menus
change regularly to reflect the best seasonal ingredients
available, but the theme is always the same; beautifully
home cooked, modern English food.

The inn is open for drinks throughout the week, from
12-3pm and 6-11pm Monday to Saturday, and from 12-
10:30pm on Sundays. The bar stocks a good variety of
drinks, which includes a selection of real ales, lagers,
bottled beers, wines, spirits, soft drinks, and speciality
teas and coffees. Guests can enjoy drinks inside, although
the flowered beer garden outside also makes a popular
resting place in the summer months.

Robin and Terri also offer a cottage for hire, with
double and single rooms available within, complete with
shower room, toilet, comfortable modern lounge and
fully fitted kitchen. The cottage has wifi access and can
come on a full English breakfast rate, but the fridge is
kept stocked with a fine selection of honeys, jams, juices
and croissants so you may well be contented with that.

104 THE SNAKE PASS INN

Snake Road, Bamford, Hope Valley, Derbyshire S33 0BJ
Tel: 01433 651480
e-mail: info@snakepassinn.co.uk
website: www.snakepassinn.co.uk

The famous **Snake Pass Inn** is located halfway between the towns of Glossop and Bamford on the A57 road. The inn was originally built to serve as the halfway staging post between the towns in the early 19th century to support weary travellers on the last turnpike road built of its kind. It stands today as one of the area's most popular watering holes, with an unrivalled location in the heart of the Peak District.

Owners Sandra and John Atkin guarantee that guests staying there will have their batteries truly re-charged, with an abundance of rolling hills, meandering streams and wild moor all around to explore. They offer a range of accommodation from twin rooms, family rooms and single rooms, not to mention the impressive four poster bed suites. Each room is classically decorated and has full en suite facilities, TV and tea and coffee refreshment tray. En suite apartments are also available for hire which sleep up to 6 people, ideal for walking or fishing parties.

The inn is perhaps best known for its pub and restaurant, which opens all day every day to the public. The inn has a cosy, country feel with a selection of squashy arm chairs, toasty fireplaces and wooden furniture to relax in, with plenty of room to unwind outdoors too on summer days when the terrace becomes quite the sun-trap. The bar stocks a healthy selection of real ales, traditional beers and fine wines, which make the perfect accompaniment to any meal here.

Food is served from 12-9pm Wednesday to Saturday and from 12-5pm Tuesdays and Sundays. Guests can choose from a variety of light bites which include hot sandwiches, sides and salads and starters from the bar menu which include tempting treats like mushroom pepper pot, and garlic fried crevettes on a bed of salad. Main meals include rich homemade rabbit stew, chicken Diane, minted lamb shank, sirloin steak and fresh fish of the day with chips. Vegetarian options include vegetable chilli, stilton and vegetable crumble, and creamy wild mushroom and asparagus risotto. Local produce is used in dishes wherever possible, which are always cooked fresh to order each day. All major credit cards accepted, children and dogs welcome.

105 NAVIGATION INN

Brookside, Buxworth, High Peak,
Derbyshire SK23 7NE
Tel: 01663 732072
website: www.navigationinn.co.uk

Situated next to the ancient monument of Bugsworth Basin, **The Navigation Inn** became a hostelry more than two hundred years ago, and still retains its original character and atmosphere. The bar is very much the centre of the establishment, a place where local villagers and visitors alike can enjoy the warm friendly atmosphere, fine ales, good food, wood fires and friendly banter.

The pub features a pool room, snug, coffee lounge, bar area and a restaurant that can accommodate functions of various sizes.

The food is mainly traditional, home-cooked and is served daily in the bar, restaurant or outside on the large patio. The menu offers many vegetarian and healthy dishes to choose from. In addition to the main menu, there is a comprehensive specials board which changes daily. If you want something special or if you want to make sure your favourite dish is on the menu when you plan to arrive, book in advance and mine hosts Roger and Janet will do their very best to help. To accompany your meal, there's a good choice of wines , ciders and real ales. Children are welcome in all areas except the main bar and there is a children's playground for them to enjoy. Dogs are also welcome in all areas except the restaurant.

Roger and Janet, who took over here in December 2009, are sensitively refurbishing both the interior and exterior, and have also upgraded the entertainment system. With regular Barbecues, live music, karaoke, quiz nights, regular meal deals, beautiful scenery and plenty of history there is always something of interest for everyone.

If you are planning to stay in this beautiful area, the Navigation also offers comfortable accommodation in en-suite rooms that are equipped with flat screen digital TV and hospitality tray. As a special treat, why not stay in the romantic 4-poster room? Get to see where Pat Phoenix (AKA Corrie's Elsie Tanner) once lived when she and her partner and co-star Alan Brown owned The Navigation Inn.

106 CAUSEWAY HOUSE

Back Street, Castleton, Hope Valley,
Derbyshire S33 8WE
Tel: 01433 623291
e-mail: info@causewayhouse.co.uk
website: www.causewayhouse.co.uk

Located in the vibrant village of Castleton, **Causeway House** is a beautiful bed & breakfast dating back to the 14th century. Owned by Nick and Janet Steynbere, the couple offer a warm welcome to guests to their delightful cottage.

There are five bedrooms (three with luxurious en-suites) and one is located on the ground floor (ring for details on disabled access). The rooms are brimming with character, especially the four-postered room, which is popular with returning guests. The rooms have been individually decorated and boast all the usual facilities including a colour TV and hair dryer. Having been awarded the ETB breakfast award there is little chance of you being disappointed with the breakfast menu. There is something for all tastes and appetites, including a full English breakfast as well as lighter alternatives.

Causeway House is situated in the stunning village of Castleton, which lies at the heart of the Peak District. It is the ideal base for exploring the surrounding area. Nick and Janet are happy to accommodate dogs and their owners, and there are many places to go walking and cycling in the area (There is secure storage for bikes available). There is limited onsite car parking.

107 ROUND MEADOW BARN

Parsons Lane, Hope, Hope Valley, Derbyshire S33 6RB
Tel: 01433 621347
e-mail: rmbarn@bigfoot.com
website: www./http:/mysite.freeserve.com/rmbarn

The **Round Meadow Barn** is an outstanding bed & breakfast located in five acres of land and surrounded by beautiful countryside. Owned by Gill and Geoff Harris it is in an isolated location, making it an ideal place to unwind. Having been there for more than 30 years the Harris family has sensitively rebuilt the former barn stone by stone. The bed & breakfast offers four guest rooms (one en-suite), which are all individually decorated. It is open all year round and has been awarded a three diamond 'yellow' grading. Guests can look forward to a superb breakfast cooked by Gill.

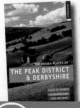

108 SCOTSMAN'S PACK COUNTRY INN

School Lane, Hathersage, Sheffield S32 1BZ
Tel: 01433 650253
e-mail: scotsmans.pack@btinternet.com
website: www.scotmanspack.com

The **Scotsman's Pack Country Inn** is well known for its traditional feel and friendly atmosphere. Located on the edge of the picturesque village of Hathersage it has five en-suite bedrooms for guests to choose from (three doubles, one twin and one single all located upstairs). Its homely accommodation has been awarded four stars by the AA's independent assessors for 2002, 2003 and 2004.

The inn is full of character and visitors and locals can sit in the welcoming bar area or either of the two seated dining areas. Scotsman's Pack Country Inn is well known in the area for the high quality of food it serves. There is a good range of dishes on the menu that will satisfy those with large and light appetites. It includes a variety of filled baguettes and sandwiches and a creative choice of vegetarian meals. On sunnier days many people like to make the most of the outside patio area, which overlooks a beautiful trout stream.

The inn provides an ideal place to stay for those wanting to explore what the Peak District National Park has to offer. There is a private function room – ring for details. Pets are not allowed in the rooms.

findSOMEWHERE.co.uk

For people who want to explore Britain and Ireland

Our easy-to use website contains details and locations of places to stay, places to eat and drink, specialist shops and places of interest throughout England, Wales, Scotland and Ireland.

Places to Stay:	Places to Eat and Drink:	Places of Interest:	Specialist Shops:	Gardens:
Hotels, guest accommodation, bed & breakfast, inns, self-catering accommodation	Restaurants, pubs, inns, cafes, tea rooms	Historic buildings, gardens, art galleries, museums, nature parks, wildlife parks, indoor and outdoor activities	Fashion shops, art and craft shops, gift shops, food and drink shops, antique shops, jewellery shops	Garden centres and retail nurseries

109 THE WHITE LION

Great Longstone, Derbyshire DE45 1TA
Tel: 01629 640252
e-mail: info@whiteliongreatlongstone.co.uk
Website: www.whiteliongreatlongstone.co.uk

Well known for the quality of food it serves, **The White Lion** is a popular place to eat out and has an ever growing reputation. Tenants, Greg and Libby Robinson took over the running of The White Lion in August 2009 and although fairly young have brought a wealth of experience with them. Downstairs, the establishment has been totally refurbished to a high standard, bringing decor and furnishings into the 21st century, but without losing the old charm and character.

Chef, Greg, has ten years experience and his dishes are extremely popular with locals and visitors. The frequently changing menu has a strong focus on local produce and the dishes served are of a high quality. Pub classics such as Beer Battered Haddock, Hand Cut Chips and Mushy Peas appear alongside dishes such as Oven Baked Salmon, Herb & Nut Crust, Basil & Coriander Linguine, Red Onion & Chilli Salsa and Critchlows Pork Cutlet, Savoury Bread & Butter Pudding, Courgette Fritter, Mini Roast Potatoes & Forestiere Sauce. For a lighter bite at lunchtime this menu is run alongside a sandwich menu including Crispy Shredded Pork Ciabatta, Apple & Sage Compote and a White Lion ploughmans. The dining area seats 60 people and it is advisable for diners to book at weekends because of the popularity of the place. Food is available Monday – Friday between 12pm-3pm and 6pm-9pm and on Saturdays 12pm-9pm and Sundays 12pm-8pm.

The hospitality is of an extremely high standard and many customers return time and time again to soak up everything the place has to offer. Situated in the village of Great Longstone, it is not far from the historic Chatsworth House and Estate, which many visitors to the area like to have a look at. The White Lion is open every session and all day on Saturday and Sunday and can be found via the A6, A6020 or A619.

Two rotating real ales are served from the Robinsons Brewery Range and the bar is well stocked with plenty of other alcoholic and non alcoholic beverages. Greg and Libby welcome children to The White Lion and disabled access is not a problem. There is a large rear car park for those visiting the establishment. The couple have aspirations to develop letting rooms in the not to distant future.

Major credit cards taken. The White Lion is highly recommended to those visiting Great Longstone and the surrounding area.

110 BAKEWELL TART SHOP, COFFEE HOUSE AND BLOOMFIELD HOUSE

Matlock Street, Bakewell,
Derbyshire DE45 1EE
Tel: *01629 814692*
e-mail: *orders@bakewelltartshop.co.uk*
website: *www.bakewelltartshop.co.uk*

In the heart of the Peak District in the charming town of Bakewell, is the **Bakewell Tart Shop and Coffee House**. On the main A6 Matlock Street, this popular shop has a little something for everyone with an impressive range of gifts and treats to suit every budget, appetite and taste.

The shop has been run by Zoe and David McBurnie since 2001, and they have created quite a following, not just locally, but globally with their online services. Most popular of course are the variety of Bakewell tarts on offer, from traditional to lemon flavoured, but the 'post-a-tart' scheme is fast becoming a popular gift idea. Customers can order a Bakewell tart, have their own message iced onto it and have it sent virtually anywhere in the world! Perfect for a variety of occasions like mother's day, valentines and much more. The shop is open daily from 8:30am-5:30pm (closing a little earlier between October and March), and also sells a variety of other homemade cakes, pies and preserves.

To the rear of the shop is the Coffee House. Its classic coffee shop décor makes for a laid back and friendly atmosphere and is open to all throughout the day. Serving much more than just coffee, Zoe and David stock a wide range of speciality teas, coffees and hot chocolates, alongside a great menu which includes delicious homemade dishes such as cottage pie, fresh soup, and roast dinner, not to mention the award winning traditional pies. A good selection of breakfasts and sandwiches are also available, not forgetting the gluttonous selection of tarts, puddings and cakes.

Bakewell itself is a lovely place to stroll around, and is ideal for a relaxed weekend away with easy access to acres of beautiful Derbyshire countryside.

Located above the shop, is Bloomfield House; a luxury conversion sleeping up to seven adults and one child. A variety of double and family rooms are available with options of either en suite facilities or the use of a large family sized bathroom. Each room is

fresh and comfortable, with neutral colours and contemporary design. The accommodation is self catering and has the use of a modern, fully fitted kitchen. Time can be spent relaxing in the spacious lounge with TV and DVD player, and of course – all guests receive a Bakewell Tart welcome pack for good measure what more could you want?

111 BIGGIN HALL COUNTRY HOUSE HOTEL

Biggin-by-Hartington, nr Buxton, Derbyshire SK17 0DH
Tel: 01298 84451
e-mail: enquiries@bigginhall.co.uk
website: www.bigginhall.co.uk

Biggin Hall Country House Hotel is a grand 17th century manor house located in the peaceful open countryside in the middle of the Peak District National park. The building itself if grade II listed and lies within eight acres of beautifully landscaped gardens. Although the inn retains its olde worlde character with open log fires, mullioned lead windows and an oak panelled lobby, it was completely renovated by its owners a few years ago.

The hotel sports six double and twin bedrooms in the main house in addition to a four poster bedded master suite. All rooms have either their own en suite or an adjoining bathroom. A further twelve rooms are available in converted outbuildings, each of which is individually decorated with a colour TV, wifi and tea and coffee facilities.

Guests at Biggin Hall also enjoy the peaceful ambience of the hotel's historic lounge, which is filled with plush, comfortable sofas and an impressive stone hewn fireplace. Also popular for an evening's entertainment is the hotels oak beamed dining room which sports stunning views across the lawns. Throughout the day, a dedicated team of experienced chefs cook up a delicious array of fine English cuisine, with a big emphasis on using fresh local produce. The straightforward approach to cooking here allows the quality of the ingredients to shine through, ensuring that diners return time and time again. Dishes on offer include creamy mixed seafood chowder, braised Derbyshire beef in Leatherbriches ale, black pudding with spiced apple chutney, and fillet of salmon in a fresh mango sauce. Desserts in the restaurant are equally decadent with choices like Peach Melba in a brandy snap basket, panna cotta with raspberry coulis and warm chocolate fudge cake.

During the day guests and non-residents are invited to the hotel for afternoon tea, where a sumptuous selection of freshly cut sandwiches, homemade cakes and scones, teas and coffees are served in the lounge or on the lawns.

The hotel also offers a range of refined meeting rooms that are ideal for small conferences, workshops and seminars. Located within an hour's drive of major business centres such as Birmingham, Manchester, Sheffield and Derby – the hotel is ideally situated to offer delegates a peaceful working environment away from the hectic demands of daily business life. Please ring for details.

112 BERESFORD TEA ROOMS

Market Place, Hartington, Buxton, Derbyshire SK17 0AL
Tel: 01298 84418
website: www.hartingtonanddistrict.com

Located in the heart of the picturesque village of Hartington is the **Beresford Tea Rooms**. Central to both local and tourist life in Hartington, it provides a great place for respite after exploring the surrounding walking and cycle paths; believed to be some of the best in the country. Hartington is right in the middle of the 'White Peak' limestone region that forms the southern part of the Peak District National Park. The village itself is centred around the pretty market square which is home to not only the tea rooms, but a duck filled pond and beautiful views across the rolling, open countryside.

The tea room started life hundreds of years ago as a butchers shop, but has since been home to the village gift shop and a jewellery shop. Sue Bruce took over in 1987 and converted the shop into a warm and welcoming tea room. Today, Sue and her hard working team open each day from 10am-4pm in winter and 9:30am-5pm in the summer months. The tea rooms might be small, but what they lack in size they make up for in character; with charming red brick alcoves and a variety of arts and crafts displayed on the walls that are also available to purchase.

Guests can choose from a large range of specialty teas, coffees and soft drinks with a tempting selection of homemade cakes and tasty treats to snack on too – just perfect for afternoon tea. Options include jam roly poly, treacle tart, spotted dick and gingerbread pudding. Guests with a slightly larger appetite are also well catered for with a range of Paninis, omelettes, breakfasts and 'something-on-toast' meals. Popular options include roasted pepper and goat's cheese Panini and the homemade hot pot.

The tea room also doubles as the local post office and ATM, but its bustling atmosphere is undoubtedly part of its charm. The service is faultless and good humoured so guests always leave with a smile on their faces. The team are all local too, so are well placed to advise guests on what to see and do in the area. Children welcome.

113 TROUT INN

Bickleigh, Tiverton, Devon EX16 8RJ
Tel: 01884 855596
e-mail: troutinn@fastnet.co.uk
website: www.troutinn-bickleigh.co.uk

The Trout Inn can be found located in the picturesque and unspoilt Exe Valley. Close to the river, it has been owned and family run by Tracy and Phil Grant for over eight years. The child friendly inn attracts a lot of walkers and overseas travellers as well as locals and families. There is plenty to do in the rural, but central, area and there is easy access to both Exmoor and Dartmoor. Inside, the Trout Inn has a lot of olde worlde charm, with exposed beams, but has all the modern comforts, including comfortable sofas.

The food menu lists plenty of fresh dishes made with some of the finest locally sourced fresh produce. All of the meat is sourced from a nearby farm on Exmoor and the inn buys in fresh fish daily. The food

is all reasonably priced and starters include, oriental crispy duck spring rolls; chef's pate of the day; chef's homemade soup of the day; and Icelandic prawn platter. The main menu is fairly traditional. Among the favourites listed are pot roasted pork with apples & cider; homemade spaghetti bolognaise; home cooked ham, egg & chips; homemade lasagne; and a range of steaks cooked in the grill. The menu has several seafood options too, including beer battered local fresh fillet of cod and homemade fish pie. Vegetarians are well catered for with some of the most popular dishes including homemade vegetable lasagne and homemade vegetable chilli. For younger guests there is a separate menu for them to choose from. For those with a lighter appetite there is a good range of filled sandwiches, baguettes and jacket potatoes to choose from as well as ploughmans. Food is served Monday – Friday between 12noon and 2.30pm and 5.30pm – 9pm Saturday 12 noon - 9.30pm and Sunday 12 noon-8.30pm. There are plenty of refreshments to be ordered from the fully stocked bar, with plenty of local ale and cider and an extensive wine menu.

There are four comfortable rooms available at the Trout Inn. Three of them have en-suite facilities and the fourth has its own private bathroom. All of the rooms have hairdryers, clock, radio, TV, hospitality tray and central heating.

The pub has a pool team, skittles team and an antique football machine. Outside, there is a large garden with a children's play area. Disabled access is not a problem. Dogs are welcome at the inn. All cards are accepted apart from American Express.

114 STAFFORD BARTON FARM

Broadhembury, Honiton, Devon EX14 3LU
Tel: 01404 841403
e-mail: jean.walters1@talktalk.net

Stafford Barton Farmhouse bed and breakfast is run by David and Jean Walters, who also maintain the farm with a pedigree South Devon beef herd. The farmhouse is a lovely modern timber built building witth glorious views towards the Blackdown Hills and the Devonshire countryside.

The accommodation at Stafford Barton is on the ground floor. Guests can choose from a choice of a twin bedroom or a double bedroom, both of which are finely appointed and traditionally decorated with en suite facilities. Guests also have the benefit of using the farmhouse's cosy lounge area which sports a traditional wood burning stove. Each morning a fine farmhouse breakfast is served up for guests using only the best in locally sourced produce.

It makes the perfect base for a tranquil Devonshire holiday with acres of countryside to explore and plenty of good shops in the towns of Exeter and Honiton. It is also easily accessible to the Jurassic coast.

115 AWLISCOMBE INN

Awliscombe, nr Honiton, Devon EX14 3PJ
Tel: 01404 42554
e-mail: roland.pearce@virgin.net

Cosily located in the heart of the farming community of Awliscombe, just two miles from the town of Honiton, is the **Awliscombe Inn**. The inn dates back in parts to the 17th century, standing in a prominent position in the village overlooking the Otter River and the gothic 19th century church. Its owner, Roland Pearce has run the inn for a number of years, priding himself on maintaining the inn's quiet character and charm. He welcomes all, from locals, to walkers and their dogs, families, and even huntsmen.

Guests can choose from a range of real ales, lagers, wines and spirits throughout the day which are best enjoyed in the rear beer garden in the summer months or before the inn's original wood burning stove in winter. The cosy atmosphere is complimented by an array of old church pews, brushed farmhouse furniture, and exposed stone walling; giving a traditional feel that is brought to life by the range of activities on offer. Guests are welcomed to get involved with a variety of events including games of skittles, darts and pool, along with regular live music sessions every few weeks. Please ring for details. Open from 12 noon each day, all major credit cards accepted.

116 THE KINGFISHER INN

Dolphin Street, Colyton, Devon EX24 6NA
Tel: 01297 552476
e-mail: nickandsally@kingfisherinn.co.uk
website: www.kingfisherinn.co.uk

Just a ten minute walk from the pretty tram station in Colyton on Dolphin Street is the **Kingfisher Inn**. This vibrant inn is run by Nick and Sally Bunkall, who are known for their endless hospitality and good sense of humour. They play a central part in their community, with a rolling programme of events held at the Kingsfisher including food theme nights, charity quizzes, live music events, sporting Everyone welcome, includingtheir dogs.

The inn dates back to the 16th century, and still sports fine oak beamed ceilings and original flint walls. The dining area has been given a more contemporary feel, to accompany its impressive and ever-changing menu which offers a range of exotic tastes alongside the usual traditional pub fayre. All meals are created using locally sourced produce, fresh to order. Dishes include home made National Trust pie and medallions of pork tenderloin in mustard, cream sauce.

At least four real cask ales are available at any one time, with a handsome range of fine wines and spirits also available. Nick and Sally are always happy to cater for special occasions whether it's a birthday party, or the monthly walking group, so please ring for details.

118 THE ROYAL OAK

Main Road, Exminster, nr Exeter,
Devon EX6 8DX
Tel: 01392 832332

Located close to the Rive Exe this Devon pub, although contemporary, is full of charm. **The Royal Oak** is run by Lawrence and Helen Martinez who are extremely friendly and welcoming. The good size pub has a warm atmosphere and is popular with families. Inside it is spacious, with wooden floors, and can seat around 70 people. The interior is modern and the leather chairs add to the comfortable nature of the establishment.

The child friendly pub has a traditional, but extensive, menu. Carvery, Steak, pasta and vegetarian options are all popular with diners, many who return again to sample the dishes on offer. In warmer months customers often like to socialise and enjoy refreshments in the garden area.

Situated in the historic village of Exminster, visitors to the area often note the former mental health asylum, situated on a hill overlooking the Exe estuary, which is now home to luxury town houses. The Exe Estuary nature reserve is also popular with tourists. The Royal Oak is open seven days a week, Monday – Saturday 11am – 11pm, Sunday 12pm – 10.30pm. There is disabled access, with a disabled ramp and disabled toilet. There is plenty of off-street parking. Credit cards are accepted.

117 SIR WALTER RALEIGH

22 High Street, East Budleigh, Devon EX9 7ED
Tel: 01395 442510

A warm welcome will greet you at **Sir Walter Raleigh**, a village pub named after the renaissance explorer. Run by Sally and Chris Miller, who grew up in the village, it is popular with locals and visitors, many who are walkers. The thatched pub is full of character. It has low, beamed ceilings and its walls are decorated in old photographs, memorabilia and even a framed signature of Sir Walter Raleigh. Born in 1552 at Hayes Barton in East Budleigh, Sir Walter Raleigh is well known for becoming a favourite of Queen Elizabeth I and for arranging the construction of one of the ships involved in fighting the Armada. Formerly a market town and a port, East Budleigh is extremely picturesque with several thatched properties and plenty of farm houses. A bronze statue of Raleigh is located in the village close to the church of All Saints, which dates back to the 15th century, at the head of the village.

The pub is child friendly and all of the food is home cooked by Sally and her daughter Kristy. The meals are hearty and there is a good range of snacks and lite bites for those with a lighter appetite. Food is served every day from 12pm – 2.30pm and 6pm – 11pm. Real ales are served and there is a good selection of spirits and mixes. Nothing seems to be too much trouble for the Millers – they are welcoming hosts and this is perhaps what makes Sir Walter Raleigh popular among locals and visitors. The pub is close to the neighbouring villages of Yettington, Colaton Raleigh and Otterton.

The historic traditional seaside town of Budleigh Salterton is only about two miles south of East Budleigh and is very popular with visitors to the area. Situated at the mouth of the River Otter, it has a pebble beach and red cliffs. East Devon has a lot to offer including spectacular views from the South West Coastal Path and numerous beaches. It is surrounded by countryside and many areas are designated as Areas of Outstanding Natural Beauty.

After a busy day exploring the east of the county Sir Walter Raleigh is an ideal drinking hole in which to relax and enjoy good quality, traditional pub grub. It is popular with locals as well as visitors and the friendly ambience of the place makes it naturally inviting. Dogs are welcome.

119 CHI RESTAURANT AND BAR

Fore Street, Kenton, Devon EX6 8LD
Tel: 01626 890213
e-mail: enquiries@chi-restaurant.co.uk
website: www.chi-restaurant.co.uk

If you would like to experience the authentic taste of the orient, make your way to Stephen and Sui Choy's outstanding **Chi Restaurant and Bar** in Kenton, just south of Exeter. The restaurant occupies a substantial former country pub which has been dazzlingly converted into a stylish restaurant with an understated oriental theme.

Diners approach the restaurant by way of a peaceful garden with lily ponds and a fountain. Inside, the eye is immediately caught by the open kitchen which, as well as the popular favourites of Chinese cuisine, also provides the dishes you want but can never find in the South West – a delicious combination of classic and modern Chinese cuisine in a delightful contemporary setting.

Stephen is the chef and has more than twenty years experience in preparing oriental dishes using the finest fresh ingredients from scallops to local oysters. Where possible, he sources fresh local ingredients such as wild sea bass for his popular dish of Thai style sea bass. Stephen refuses to use the colouring or that staple of some Chinese restaurants, MSG. Without compromising on quality, he does not need the use of flavour enhancers.

Each dish is beautifully presented and accompanied by exquisite flowers and small animals expertly carved from different fruits – look out for the swan carved from apples. Stephen specialises in fish dishes based on the 'catch of the day' – his lemon sole in Thai chilli sauce is particularly spectacular.

The restaurant's beautifully landscaped enclosed garden is lit in the evening and creates an unforgettable atmosphere. It also provides the perfect location for special events such as parties, weddings or even business events.

Chi Restaurants also offers B&B accommodation in five comfortable en-suite bedrooms all with colour TV, tea/coffee making facilities with complimentary biscuits and mineral water, hair dryer, in-room safe, telephone, alarm clock/radio and free broadband internet access. A photo copying and fax service is available at a small charge. At breakfast, guests are offered the choice of a full English breakfast, or if you prefer something different, a Chinese breakfast of freshly steamed dim sum and Jasmine tea.

The restaurant is located just six miles south of Exeter and five miles from Dawlish on the edge of the Powderham Estate. Powderham Castle, the historic home of the Earl of Devon, built more than 600 years ago is just a few minutes walk away.

120 THE ANCHOR INN

Cockwood, nr Starcross, Devon EX6 8RA
Tel: 01626 890203
e-mail: blackandwhiteinn@btconnect.com
website: www.anchorinncockwood.com

Famous for its wide range of
seafood dishes, **The Anchor Inn** is
around 450 years old and was
originally opened as a Seamen's
Mission. The Anchor Inn is just a
few steps away from the quaint
little harbour of Cockwood, and is
edged by a low cobbled stone wall
and surrounded by baskets of
flowers in summer and fairy lights in winter. Many
customers embrace the opportunity to sit in the
outside eating area and enjoy refreshments while
watching the Cockwood swans and soaking up the last
of the setting sun in the evening.

Although popular for its seafood cuisine, the inn
offers a menu to suit all tastes. There is an extensive
a la carte menu, bar snack menu and choice of daily
specials. Among the most popular seafood dishes are
king prawns in garlic butter served on a bed of rice;
snapper steak with creamed leeks with garlic; and
lobster and prawn thermidor. Slow roast duck with
Cumberland sauce; pork escallops stuffed with brie, mushrooms, sherry, cream and peppers; and
lamb cutlets with pork and redcurrant sauce are among other options on the extensive menu. The
charming inn is full of character, with low beamed ceilings, atmospheric lighting and plenty of
sea-faring paraphernalia. In 2007 the establishment opened The Wheel House, giving the owners
space to have a dedicated stage and entertainments area, where live entertainment can be seen
twice a week. (For more details see the website).The new extension means the establishment is
now suitable to hold private functions, including weddings and parties (ring for details).

The picturesque village of Cockwood has a large village green and wildlife enthusiasts will be in
their element as it is home to Canadian geese, ducks and other wild birds. Some people say The
Anchor Inn was a haven for seamen and smugglers and is still haunted by a friendly ghost and his
dog. The snack menu is available
in all areas before 6pm, but after
6 pm is only available in the bar
area and in the new Wheel House
areas. Choices include Gurt big
steak pier with ale pastry, chips
and peas; local honey roast pork
sausages, mash potato and onion
gravy; and spicy tomato
vegetable pasta with warm
bread. It is wise to make a dining
reservation, such is the inn's
popularity and if you require
assistance with the contents of
any of the food served the staff
will be happy to assist.

121 LE BISTRO

7 Watersmeet Road, Lynmouth, Devon EX35 6EP
Tel: 01598 753302 e-mail: info@lebistrolynmouth.co.uk
website: www.lebistrolynmouth.co.uk

At **Le Bistro** our concept is simple, food cooked as it should be, served in an inviting atmosphere. Based on English and French cuisine, our menu includes traditional home cooked classics', a daily fish special's board (only locally caught fish) and freshly prepared vegetarian dishes. We pride ourselves on using the best local produce from Exmoor and North Devon and as such our food is always cooked to order, so all dietary requirements and allergies (including wheat, dairy and gluten free) can be catered for. There is a separate dining area available for private parties and special occasions, and we have a fine selection of wines from around the world.

122 SYDNEY HOUSE

Highdown Hill,
Chulmleigh,
Devon EX18 7AB
Tel: 01769 580372

Dating back to the early 1900s, the **Sydney House**, is a beautiful and comfortable guest house, which has been lovingly furnished. Located in rural Devon it is owned by former farmers Rosemary and Richard Wedlake, who were both born and bred in the county. The Sydney House welcomes customers from all walks of life and it is often popular with walkers and cyclists.

There are three bedrooms (two doubles and one single) at the Sydney House, all which have their own private bathroom. There is also a self-catering cottage, which sleeps 5/6 people. It has all the modern necessities and as well as gas central heating has Egyptian cotton sheets and electric blankets.

For those wanting to visit the Sydney House for something to eat you are unlikely to be disappointed. The menu is varied and the ingredients for all of the dishes served are sourced locally creating quality, fresh dishes. Starters include pork and duck liver pate; prawn and cress mayonnaise; egg mayonnaise and apricots; garlic mushrooms; and potato and leek soup. All of the starters are served with white or brown bread and butter. Among the most popular dishes on the main menu are fresh rolled sliced ham or beef filled with fruit; cutlet of fresh salmon; poached haddock; leek and cream pie

(with a pastry top); and vegetable flan (mushrooms, peppers, cheese and egg). It is definitely advisable for diners to leave room for one of Rosie's tempting desserts. Chocolate sponge gateaux filled with pears and cream; sponge gateaux filled with strawberry or raspberry; blackberry and apple pie with cream; and sherry and fruit sponge trifle are among the favourites. Coffee or tea, and cheese and biscuits can be ordered to complete the meal and there is a good range of alcoholic and non-alcoholic beverages to wash it down.

The B&B and self catering cottage are open all year round and there is plenty to entertain visitors to Devon. There are plenty of activities to take part in, including riding, fly fishing and golf. The scenery is absolutely superb and there are some wonderful rural views to be enjoyed. The area is fantastic for walking with the moor on one side and the coastline on the other. The cottage is suitable for disabled visitors and there is a ground floor ensuite B&B room available. Ring for further details.

123 HAM FARM

Dolton, Winkleigh, Devon EX19 8QT
Tel: 01805 624000
e-mail: info@hamfarm.co.uk
website: www.hamfarm.co.uk

Surrounded by five acres of landscaped gardens and grounds, with a further 100 acres of glorious pasture and woodland to enjoy – it is an island of undisturbed peace, rich in wildlife and offering a variety of interesting walks; space to breathe, relax and forget the rush of modern living. The perfect base for exploring Dartmoor and Exmoor, and just a short drive from North Devon's spectacular coastline.

The accommodation at **Ham Farm** combines everyone's dream of country living with all the modern comforts – all properties are furnished and equipped to a very high standard throughout. Ham Farm is an excellent base for a relaxing holiday any time of the year and all cottages are available for easy breaks in the off-season.

All properties have WiFi Broadband internet access, flat screen TV and DVD players, private patios and garden furniture with access to a shared barbeque area. Cottage kitchens are fully equipped with fridge/freezer, oven, hob and microwave ovens. The Farmhouse has a fully-equipped kitchen with a gas hob, electric and microwave ovens, dishwasher, fridge/freezer, washing machine and tumble drier.

Whether guests are looking for a large family holiday, or a romantic break away for two, they are guaranteed to find what they want amongst the properties on offer, all of which have been awarded Gold Awards by Enjoy England, and either 4 or 5 stars by the Tourist Board. There is one cottage sleeping just two guests, three cottages sleeping four guests, one three bedroom cottage sleeping five guests, one four bedroom cottage sleeping eight guests, and the spectacular Ham Farmhouse itself; with six bedrooms sleeping up to 11 guests.

Aside from this array of luxurious accommodation, Ham Farm also has its own indoor heated swimming pool, sauna and showers, fitness suite, games room with toddler's area, babysitting service, cots and highchairs, library, tennis courts, and laundry room for guests' use. Within just a short drive there are also a range of activities for all ages and abilities including coarse and sea fishing, walking and cycling trails, horse riding and charming local pubs serving up fine food and drink in truly idyllic settings. Please visit website for more pictures and details.

124 WILLOWFIELD LAKE COTTAGES

Velator, Braunton, Devon EX33 2NX
Tel: 01271 814346
e-Mail : info@willowfieldlakecottages.co.uk
website: www.willowfieldlakecottages.co.uk

Nestled in the beautiful naturally tranquil surrounds of Braunton Burrows Nature Reserve, a UNESCO Biosphere, you can find **Willowfield Lake Cottages** . The self catering cottages are managed by Wendy and Terry Keavey and located just a 5 minute drive from the stunning golden sands and surf of Saunton and Croyde. This beautiful stretch of coastline is wonderful and attracts many visitors throughout the year.

The Cottages are in a perfect location for those wanting to explore the glorious country side which surrounds the area. Willowfield Lake Cottages offers secure grounds with picnic tables and benches, set amongst mature trees and shrubs surrounded by 12 acres of pastureland, where mown paths meander through wildflower meadows to encircle a tranquil and picturesque 1 acre lake,stocked to challenge the most ambitious coarse fisherman and provide entertainment for the novice. It is an ideal location for a safe and relaxing family holiday. There is a superb indoor heated swimming pool and a well equipped games room, complete with enclosed toddlers play area. The grounds have outdoor play areas to suit children of all ages, and offer ample space for football .cricket and other ball games, kite flying or perhaps an evening stroll with the family.

Away from the grounds many people like to cycle along the famous Tarka trail or enjoy endless walks across the unspoilt Burrows and dunes that lead down to the sea at Saunton Sands. Other activities in the area include golf, surfing, birdwatching , cycling and walking.

There are 12 Cottages to choose from, all furnished and equipped to the highest standard.

All cottages have a dishwasher, washer/drier, fridge, oven with grill, ceramic hob, microwave as well as digital TV with freeview and a DVD player. Linen, duvets, towels, heating and electric are all included in the price with cots, high chairs and bed guards all available, free of charge, on request. Some of the cottages have small private gardens and 3 offer private hot tubs.

Wendy and Terry are extremely welcoming and only too happy to help those staying in their cottages and those thinking of staying. The cottages are all on one level, but it is best to ring for further details regarding disabled access. NO Pets are allowed. The cottages are available from March to October and anyone wishing to book a stay can obtain further details from the informative website or by phoning Wendy or Terry

125 BAY HORSE INN

8 Cistern Street, Totnes, Devon TQ9 5SP
Tel: 01803 862088
e-mail: thebayhorse@btinternet.com
website: www.bayhorsetotnes.com

Located at the top end of the historic market town of Totnes, the Bay Horse is a traditional yet cosy establishment offering beautifully conditioned ales, excellent cider, lager and wine, as well as a good quality, locally-sourced bar menu. With a stone floor, fireplace and low beamed ceiling, the main bar brims with character. The adjoining piano lounge is a comfy welcoming area, leading through to a cosy snug bar with its own fireplace and leather sofas perfect for enjoying the ample supply of games and books. The real hidden gem is the huge outdoor space were a paved patio leads through to a lovely walled garden.

Hosts Rob & Kathy maintain a relaxed, happy atmosphere ensuring a welcoming pub for all, including being both family & dog friendly. In keeping with Totnes' artistic sensibilities, the pub transforms into the 'After Eight' Jazz Club every Sunday evening and is a great supporter of the local folk and arts scene. Another highlight is the pub's annual beer festivals, with a full Ale & Cider event held in conjunction with the Totnes Festival each September (2nd weekend) and a mini-fest every Easter.

The inn offers fine B&B accommodation with a single and two double en-suite rooms, the pick being the spacious coach house suite with its garden outlook and luxurious bathroom. It is an excellent base for exploring the area and Kathy (a qualified tour guide running heritage walks of the town each Thursday morning) can offer plenty of handy information and is available for private bookings.

126 BISTRO 67

67 Fore Street, Totnes, Devon TQ9 5NJ
Tel: 01803 862604
e-mail: gareth.bistro67@yahoo.co.uk
website: www.bistro67.co.uk

Adhering to the local style nicely, the impressive **Bistro 67** epitomises the cosmopolitan and yet relaxed feel around Totnes, with contemporary decor combined with great food and friendly service. Gareth Jones replaced the previous owners in 2008 and rather than ring the changes, he has imposed his unflappable and efficient style on the place, all the time keeping the excellent food and service for which Bistro 67 was already known. Inside the rustic wooden floor and sturdy furniture create a cosy feel while the walls are adorned with an eclectic mix of pictures and paintings by a local artist, which provide talking points as you wait for your meals.

Head chef Andy has created an extensive menu, with particular emphasis on classic home cooked fare using only the finest available ingredients; the meat is farm assured and any fish is caught daily and brought in from Plymouth. Just minutes from Brutus Stone, the restaurant is halfway up the hill before the clock tower and is the perfect place for families to eat; indeed it is one of the few places that welcome dogs!

127 EXETER INN

Church Street, Modbury, Ivybridge PL21 0QR
Tel: 01548 831225

Locally born and raised, Nicola and Phil are keen to welcome you to the **Exeter Inn**, a 14th century coaching inn that is both family run and family friendly. Nicola's family have lived in Modbury for several generations and Phil ran the inn for the previous owner and leapt at the opportunity to own it for himself. Extremely warm and welcoming, Nicola and Phil embrace all sorts, tourists, locals, walkers, ramblers and cyclists alike, during the summer you might even come across a horse moored up out the front!

The pretty building is adorned with hanging baskets that provide pleasant smells and colours during the spring and summer months, equally fragrant is the lovely walled garden to the rear of the premises. Inside there are the usual low ceilings, but unusually there is a magnificent Adam ceiling in the living room, perfect for sitting under whilst enjoying a pint after a hard days exploring. The stone floor runs throughout to the huge open fire in the bar, which roars away merrily during the cold winters. Traditionally decorated without being too pretentious, the Exeter Inn is a great place to go and relax with a nice pint, dine with the family or even spend the night.

There are four bedrooms available, all with en suite and all superbly appointed with everything one could expect in a modern hotel room. Very reasonably priced, the tariff includes a breakfast, cooked on site to the guests' specifications using locally sourced ingredients. Being surrounded by rolling hills, wooded glades and winding country lanes that lead to lovely sandy beaches, the Exeter Inn makes the perfect base of operations for those looking to explore this wonderful part of the country.

The bar is open throughout the day and boasts a wide range of beverages, which include five well-kept real ales; Bass, Sharps Doom Bar, Tetley Dark, Greene King Abbot Ale and a rotating guest - and Addlestones and Thatchers ciders. Food is available 12.00 to 3.00pm and 6.00pm to 9.00pm and a blackboard lists the day's dishes, based whenever possible on local, seasonal ingredients. A typical selection might include sandwiches with assorted fillings; whitebait with tartare sauce; filo-wrapped tiger prawns with a sweet chilli sauce; turkey, ham & leek pie; gammon; lasagne and sausages & mash with onion gravy.

128 WEEKE VIEW

Weeke View, Weeke Farm, Modbury,
Ivybridge, Devon PL21 0TT
Tel: 01548 830219
website: www.weekefarm.co.uk

Located in a beautiful rural area of the
South Hams, **Weeke View** is an ideal place
to stay for those wanting to explore the area
or simply relax. Situated on a working farm,
the bed and breakfast offers three
comfortable rooms (one double en-suite,
one family en-suite and one single room
with a private bathroom), all with stunning
countryside views. Guests to Weeke View are
welcome to relax in the large lounge area
and have use of TV, DVD and video.

Weeke Farm is a fourth generation
traditional dairy and beef farm, owned by
Ann Rogers. Ann is a friendly and welcoming host and cooks a tasty breakfast (using local
produce), which is served between 7.30am and 9am. The picturesque location attracts many
people to Weeke View, which is well maintained and contemporary. The farm is just over a mile
from the delightful village of Modbury and not too far from the stunning south Devon coast.

There are plenty of beaches to visit in the area, all of which are less than a 20 minute drive
away. A brook runs through the farm, attracting wild duck and heron, and wildlife enthusiasts will
be in their element.

129 SAMPFORD MANOR

Sampford Spiney, Yelverton, nr Tavistock,
Devon PL20 6LH
Tel: 01822 853442
e-mail: manor@sampford-spiney.fsnet.co.uk
website: www.sampford-spiney.fsnet.co.uk

Sampford Manor was well established at the time of the
Domesday Book and throughout its colourful history has
passed through the ownership of several historical figures,
including well known West Country seaman, Sir Francis Drake!
Allowed to fall into disrepair at times in the past, the present
owners have carried out extensive renovations since taking
over in 1987 and it is now back to its former glory.

Located in the lovely Dartmoor village of Sampford-Spiney,
the manor is the perfect place to stay and recharge the
batteries after exploring some of the most beautiful
countryside in the south-west. The manor is certainly unique,
featuring stone floors, thick granite walls and exposed beam
ceilings creating a warm and cosy feel to this traditional

building. The three rooms available are all well appointed and of a good size, individually
decorated, they offer views out onto Dartmoor and really are a great place to wake up. Provisions
can be made to stable your horse and dogs are very welcome.

Owner Rosalind is a very friendly and personable lady who has lived in the village for over 30
years now; she spends her time looking after her vast menagerie of animals, including 40 alpaca,
horses, ducks, chickens, dogs and a cat!

130 WHITE HART INN

Fore Street, Bridestowe, Okehampton,
Devon EX20 4EL
Tel: 01837 861318
e-mail: dave.horgans@hotmail.com

This rural village inn is full of character with its low beams and low ceilings. Dating back to the 17th century, its olde world charm adds to the atmosphere and warmth of the place. **The White Hart Inn** is popular with locals, visitors and plenty of walking and cycling enthusiasts. Owned by Dave and Annie Morgans, the couple are extremely friendly and accommodating. The menu is very traditional and the majority is locally sourced and freshly prepared. The homemade meat pies are extremely popular with diners and there is a wide range of soft and alcoholic beverages to choose from.

Located in the village of Bridestowe, it lies at the junction of two small streams, The Lew and Cranford Brook. It is situated six miles south west of the town of Okehampton and there are disused lead and copper mines nearby. The area is surrounded by moorland, being on the border of Dartmoor National Park, and this is why the area is so popular with tourists. The inn is open seven days a week from 12pm – 3pm and 6pm – 11pm. In the summer months it stays open all day. There are two comfortable guest rooms (one en suite) – ring for details. Disabled access is limited.

find**SOMEWHERE.CO.uk**

For people who want to explore Britain and Ireland

Garden Centres and Nurseries

Our easy-to use website contains details and locations of places to stay, places to eat and drink, specialist shops and places of interest throughout England, Wales, Scotland and Ireland.

Places to Stay:	**Places to Eat and Drink:**	**Places of Interest:**	**Specialist Shops:**	**Gardens:**
Hotels, guest accommodation, bed & breakfast, inns, self-catering accommodation	Restaurants, pubs, inns, cafes, tea rooms	Historic buildings, gardens, art galleries, museums, nature parks, wildlife parks, indoor and outdoor activities	Fashion shops, art and craft shops, gift shops, food and drink shops, antique shops, jewellery shops	Garden centres and retail nurseries

131 THE VANILLA POD @ THE CRIDFORD INN

Trusham, Newton Abbot, Devon TQ13 0NR
Tel: 01626 853694
e-mail: reservations@vanillapod.cridfordinn.com
website: www.vanillapod.cridfordinn.com

Nestled in the idyllic village of Trusham in the Teign Valley, **The Vanilla Pod at the Cridford Inn** is the perfect place to come and indulge in some beautifully crafted food. The main site dates back to 1086, and was probably one of the small holdings mentioned in the *Domesday Book*. The age of the inn is evident in the medieval window frame seen in the current bar area; probably the oldest example of such in the country.

Before the husband and wife team Ian and Tracey realised their dream of running a bar/restaurant in the country, they ran the widely renowned and acclaimed Vanilla Pod Restaurant in Torquay since September 2003. Ian is also the Head Chef with an absolute passion for fine food; he has won many accolades as well as collecting his top award for deserts at the Hilton London Metropole. Tracey runs the management side of the business, ensuring that excellent, friendly service (the last ingredient needed to make a night at the Vanilla Pod unforgettable) is always at the highest standard.

When you come to the Vanilla Pod, it really must be for the excellent food which is already synonymous with quality in the area. Dishes such as pan-fried sirloin steak on a potato rosti with carrot puree, wild summer mushrooms, and roasted globe artichoke, or seared fillet of seabass with wilted baby spinach, slow roasted cherry tomatoes and dauphinois potatoes, are served from their monthly renewed menu. Just be sure to save enough room for one of Ian's award winning desserts! His signature vanilla pod chocolate cup with hand crafted Tuille biscuit cup and saucer (complete with teaspoon) filled with a dark chocolate mousse, topped with vanilla cream is not to be missed, and neither are his hand-made chocolates. All the dishes can be accompanied with wine if you so wish, and you can consult the knowledgeable staff for their recommendation. In addition there is an extensive bar menu that changes seasonally and daily changing specials boards. Their opening times are; Monday - Friday open 11-3pm, 6-11pm, (food served 12-2.30pm, 6.30-9.30pm) Saturday open 11am-11pm (food served 11am-2.30pm, 6.30pm-9.30pm) Sunday 12-10.30pm (food served 12-3pm, 6.30-9.00pm)

There are four cosy and elegantly decorated suites available at the Cridford Inn, all of which have en-suite bathrooms. They also cater for wedding functions of up to 40 people and can provide flowers, cars and cakes for the big day. They are within 2 miles distance from Haldon Belvedere castle.

132 THE DROVERS

Gussage, All Saints, Dorset BH21 5ET
Tel: 01258 840084
e-mail: info@thedroversgussage.co.uk
website: www.thedroversgussage.co.uk

Voted Dorset's country pub of the year, **The Drovers**, is well known for its homemade food and friendly welcome in the countryside village of Gussage. Local seasonal produce is used wherever possible and the chefs prefer to use pans and ovens rather than microwaves. Last year the owners, Jason Anthony and Jo Gale, planted a kitchen garden and orchard so they could use the freshest of ingredients. As well as the extensive menu there is a good selection of

additional dishes listed on the daily specials blackboard. All of the dishes are reasonably priced and starters include garlic mushrooms served on toast with baby leaves and balsamic reduction; and ham hock terrine served with piccalilli, homemade bread and a hazelnut. Steak and kidney pie and home cooked ham served with free range eggs and hand cut chips are among the more traditional dishes on the main menu. There is also a wide range of steaks that come served 'on the hot rock' and chorizo & mushroom tagliatelle topped with dolcelatte & hazelnut oil served with garlic bread and salad is a popular choice.

Inside, the pub, which dates back to the 17th century, has plenty of character with English oak floors, beamed ceiling and a large inglenook fireplace. The Drovers is open between 12pm-3pm and 6pm-12am Monday – Thursday and between 12pm-3pm and 4.30pm-12am on Fridays. On Saturday, Sundays and bank holidays the opening hours is 12am-12am. Food is served between 12pm-2pm and 6pm-9pm.

132 THE CROWN

North Street,Winterborne Stickland, nr Blandford, Dorset DT11 0NJ
Tel: 01258 880838
e-mail: info@thecrownstickland.co.uk
website: www.thecrownstickland.co.uk

For those of you finding yourself closer to Winterborne Stickland, **The Crown** is highly recommended. Owned by Jason and Jo and operated by chef/manager Jack Davey, it is located close to the market town of Blandford. The thatched pub is a traditional Dorset Inn and is well liked for the award winning real ales it served and the quality food made from fresh local ingredients. Starters include breaded whitebait served with mustard mayo, bread and salad garnish; and baked box Camembert served

with homemade toast. The main menu is fairly traditional and homemade lamb's liver & bacon casserole served with mashed potato & seasonal vegetables is one of the favourites with diners.

In the garden, as well as finding additional seating you will discover a delightful well. The Crown is open Monday – Thursday 12pm-3pm and 6pm-9pm and on Fridays between 12pm-3pm and 4.30pm-12am. On Saturday, Sundays and bank holidays it is open between 12pm and 12am. Food is served between 12pm-2pm and 6pm-9pm.

133 THE SAXON INN

Gold Hill, Child Okeford, nr Blandford Forum, Dorset DT11 8HD
Tel: 01258 860310
e-mail: peterturner@saxoninn.co.uk
website: www.saxoninn.co.uk

The premises that now comprise the **Saxon Inn** were originally three farm cottages believed to date back some 300 years. There was a small shop in the middle cottage, selling groceries, general supplies and drinks. The Jug & Bottle did not become a hostelry until the early 1950s, when it was known as the New Inn. In 1965 it became the Saxon Inn, one of the most delightful and picturesque country inns you could ever encounter. It nestles under Hambledon Hill at Gold Hill, by Child Okeford, signposted off the A350 or A357 northwest of Blandford Forum.

The white-painted exterior is adorned with a colourful array of tubs and hanging baskets, and at the back is a lovely garden with trees, shrubs and plants and a Wendy house that will keep the little ones busy and happy. The interior is equally delightful, with horse brasses on old beams, log fires and a warm, welcoming ambience created by hosts Peter and Helen Turner. The drinks served in the bar include cask-conditioned ales from local breweries and a small, select range of wines from Old and New Worlds. The beers are kept in A1 condition, earning CAMRA approval and quenching the thirsts of walkers, cyclists, motorists and tourists as well as the local community.

The food is another excellent reason for seeking out this marvellous place. A wide choice of traditional pub dishes makes up the à la carte menu, which is supplemented by a daily specials board reflecting the best and freshest of what's in season at the time. Favourite dishes cooked by Helen and the talented kitchen team include cottage pie, steak & ale pie, chicken provençale, cod in batter, salmon with parsley butter and rump, fillet and gammon steaks. Sandwiches and jacket potatoes provide lighter/quicker options. Food is served lunchtime seven days a week and in the evening Monday to Saturday. The Saxon Inn has now been in its present form for two years and has now built up an excellent and well established reputation that has guests flocking from all over the country to sample.

The owners have also created four superbly appointed upstairs guest rooms with state-of-the-art en suite facilities: the inn is now not just a place to find outstanding food and drink but a comfortable, civilised base for touring a part of the world that's rich in scenic and historic interest.

134 THE DRAX ARMS

Bere Regis, nr Wareham,
Dorset BH20 7HH
Tel: 01939 271386
e-mail: jtaponder@hotmail.co.uk

Now 400 years old, this charming traditional Dorset inn has seen its fair share of landlords and ladies, the current owner is a very friendly lady who has, in just two years, ensured the reputation of **The Drax Arms** will last another 400. Filled with ancient features such as the low ceilings and log burning stove in the inglenook fireplace, the Drax Arms is the perfect place to sit awhile and unwind with a pint of excellent real ale.

The pub sits in the heart of the Dorset village of Bere Regis, which gained its royal suffix when it was a favourite stopping place for monarchs on their way to the west country. All of the delicious food is cooked fresh to order and utilises the best of local produce, in particular, the steak in Tanglefoot ale pie has to be sampled, as well as the Dorset apple cake for desert. Live music is a popular draw to the Drax Arms, with free guitar and banjo tuition on a regular basis as well as visiting bands.

135 THE BRASSERIE

9 West Street, Wareham, Dorset BH20 4JS
Tel: 01929 556061 e-mail: info@antonsbrasserie.co.uk
website: www.antonsbrasserie.co.uk

Owner Anton has previously worked in country restaurants, including a year in a French bakery. A background ideal for running **The Brasserie**, a small family run eatery set within the ancient walls of Wareham. The light and contemporary surroundings create a relaxed eating atmosphere and from 9 am to late, delicious food is served from the excellent menu.

Catering for breakfast, lunch and dinner, the Brasserie is the place to go for a light snack or one of their famous eight course themed dinners.

www.findSOMEWHERE.co.uk
For people who want to explore the United Kingdom

Places to Eat and Drink

136 MANOR HOUSE HOTEL

Manor Road, Studland, Swanage,
Dorset BH19 3AU
Tel: 01929 450288 Fax: 01929 452255
e-mail: info@themanorhousehotel.com
website: www.themanorhousehotel.com

Situated on Studland Bay in Dorset, the 21 bedroom
Manor House Hotel has some of the best views in
England to accompany its opulent luxuriousness.
Professionally trained and with over 36 years experience
in the hospitality trade, Andrew Purkis has owned the
Manor House Hotel for the past 10 years. With appeal to
all ages, the hotel is brilliant for walkers, ramblers,
tennis and golf enthusiasts, cyclists, ornithologists and
beach lovers.

The rural setting in a quiet country village, right on
the coastline, ensures peace and tranquillity, and with
three miles of beach on your doorstep, a private spot to
sunbathe is never far away. Local attractions include
Corfe Castle, just five miles, and the popular Dorset
town of Swanage is just three miles.

A traditional old fashioned manor house, the hotel
boasts unique wood carvings that date back to the
1600s, as well as antique and period furniture that
adorn each and every room. Built as a folly in the 1820s
out of Purbeck stone and featuring a wonderfully
convoluted stone and slate roof, the building was
constructed to look like a fairy tale castle. In such
spectacular surroundings, comfort is assured with the
superb bedrooms; all 21 rooms have en suite facilities
and some have four poster beds and sea views. Each
room has been individually decorated and to a very high
standard, those without a sea view have pleasing
landscape views over the extensive
gardens and countryside.

The onsite restaurant is truly
excellent; the dinner menu is a four
course extravaganza and changes daily to
reflect the day's fresh catch. All of the
ingredients are locally sourced from
reputable suppliers; a popular favourite
is the local Portland crab and Kimmerage
Bay lobster. For those wishing to stock up
on energy before and after a day's
activities, the bar menu features an
excellent choice, with traditional cream
teas a highlight.

The hotel has a great deal of facilities,
including being able to accommodate well behaved pets, even horses can be catered for. In
addition to stables, Studland Riding stables offers a unique beach riding experience on the three
miles of golden sands of Studland beach. There is a huge range of horses and ponies available for
all levels, from ex-racers and hunters through to the quietest cobs and hack ponies.

137 THE GREEN YARD CAFE

4 - 6 Barrack Street, Bridport, Dorset DT6 3LY
Tel: 01308 459466
e-mail: info@thegreenyardcafe.co.uk
website: www.thegreenyardcafe.co.uk

Taste
of the
West
Awards
2009
GOLD

The philosophy at **The Green Yard Cafe** is simple; 'we buy local produce and create delicious seasonal meals, healthy soups, hearty breakfasts, divine deserts and fabulous cakes.' Pretty much all of the food on offer is created on site, from the biscotti treats served with the coffee to the vegetarian specials and the cafe has several awards for their culinary perfection. Situated just off Bridport's main street, the cafe is a pretty stone building with a bright and airy interior, designed to offer peace and tranquillity after a day's exploring.

The cafe also serves as a kind of gallery; there are paintings on the walls and various products by local artists available for purchase, perfect for examining whilst waiting for your delicious meal. As an active member of the Slow Food Movement, an organization that tries to counter-act the deterioration into fast food chains, the Green Yard Cafe offers ethically sourced ingredients from local producers.

Also fully licensed, the cafe offers a wide range of locally brewed alcohol, including Tanglefoot beer, Sheppy's cider and Lyme Bay wines. The wide range of options makes the Green Yard Cafe perfect for all occasions, even the dog is welcome; there is a small courtyard garden.

138 TRAVELLERS REST

Dorchester Road, Bridport, Dorset DT6 4PJ
Tel: 01308 459503
e-mail: david.prickett@btconnect.com
website: www.travellers-rest.co.uk

The Travellers Rest was formerly a farm and then a pub set in the rolling hills of Dorset, nowadays it is comprised of four holiday cottages that have been refitted to a very high standard. Recently taken over by Stephanie and David, who have many years experience in the hospitality industry, the cottages sleep between two and six people in sumptuous comfort and are renovated barns, originally constructed in the 1700's. Situated on five acres of private land, the cottages also have their own secluded area in which guests are encouraged to sit and enjoy summer sunsets whilst using the barbeques, perfect after a long day at the beach.

There are also B & B rooms available at the main farmhouse; spacious and comfortable; a good nights' sleep is essentially guaranteed! With easy access to the historic Jurassic coast, guests are able to pursue all manner of outdoor activities, as well as visiting the many tourist attractions in this part of the country. All of the cottages are equipped for self catering, however there are many fine village inns in the surrounding area, as well as restaurants and hotels in local Bridport.

140 WESTWOOD GUEST HOUSE

1 Woodmead Road, Lyme Regis,
Dorset DT7 3LJ
Tel: 01297 442376
e-mail: relax@westwoodguesthouse.co.uk
website: www.westwoodguesthouse.co.uk

Westwood Guest House, located at the heart of the beautiful Jurassic Coast, is what can only be described as a 'Luxury Bed & Breakfast Retreat, refurbished throughout to the very highest standard. The guest house boasts some stunning views of the Dorset coast.

Westwood has a warm and friendly ambience and each of its 7 en-suite rooms have been elegantly designed and decorated, all offering the same superior features. The rooms at the front of Westwood Guest House enjoy spectacular views over Lyme Bay, right across to Golden Cap and Portland Bill and from the rear of the house there are amazing views of wonderful woodland scenery. All of the rooms have super king, king or twin beds and feature large en-suite shower rooms with and contemporary furnishings. Each room has a WI-if access, a flat screen TV, hairdryer, iron & ironing boards and a safe for guests to keep their valuables. On arrival you will find fresh milk in your own fridge (useful for chilling a nice bottle of wine!), and a welcome tea tray.

The sumptuous English breakfasts served at Westwood are made with locally sourced ingredients (the large pork sausages and thick cut dry cured back bacon come from the local award winning Complete Meats of Axminster) and the free range eggs are sourced locally too. There is an excellent selection of alternative breakfast choices and special diets can be catered for.

The surrounding area is extremely picturesque and many holiday makers return again and again to enjoy the charming

coastal resort of Lyme Regis and its neighbouring resorts. Westwood Guest House is very popular with enthusiastic walkers as there is plenty to explore in the area. Other local activities include fishing, sailing, golf and there are several wild life centres and gardens to visit. Friendly hospitality is of the upmost importance to the owner Lavinia and she is happy to suggest places of interest to visit and recommend quality restaurants in the area – of which their are many! Westwood is easily accessible by road and rail and the town of Lyme Regis is around 3½ hours drive from London. This charming and truly deluxe guest house is highly recommended and many visitors return again and again to make the most of this beautiful part of the country. Although suitable for couples and singles, due to the high standards of furnishing throughout, Westwood unfortunately does not cater for children under the age of 12.

139 BEACH & BARNICOTT

6 South Street, Bridport, Dorset DT6 3NQ
Tel: 01308 455688
e-mail: office@beachandbarnicott.co.uk
website: www.beachandbarnicott.co.uk

Dating back to the 1700s, Beach & Barnicott is a stunning Grade II listed bar and restaurant located in the centre of the charming Dorset town of Bridport. Owned by Mervyn Ashford, The Georgian house is extremely welcoming and has many historical features. The house is spread over three floors, with four dining areas, and has an 18th century feel with original antique furnishings. Atmospheric lighting really adds to the place making it extremely inviting and perfect for a relaxing time away from a busy life.

Beach and Barnicott is open all day from 10am and serves freshly made Beliniano coffee, excellent teas and hot chocolate. Draught lagers and ales, bottled beers, wines and spirits are also available from the well stocked bar. Nominated as the 'Best Restaurant in Dorset' at the 2006 Dorset Magazine Awards, the restaurant is extremely popular with locals and visitors. The menu boasts a mouth watering selection of fine modern British cuisine.

The area is extremely popular with holiday makers because of its rolling hills, beaches and historical sites. Many come to explore the stunning Jurassic Coast and surrounding villages and a visit to Beach and Barnicott is highly recommended.

142 66 CLAYPATH

66 Claypath, Durham City, County Durham DH1 1QT
Tel: 0191 384 3193 mobile: 07974 352372
website: www.66claypath.co.uk

66 Claypath is a grade II listed Georgian town house, with a delightful secluded garden, in the heart of Durham City. Comfortable, well-furnished rooms are beautifully decorated and quality breakfasts are prepared fresh to order.

A short walk from the Market Place, Castle, Cathedral and riverside paths, some of Durham's best restaurants and pubs are within walking distance. Ideally located for exploring not just the City of Durham but all that the North East has to offer, you can definitely be assured of a warm and friendly welcome.

141 BEREHAYES FARM COTTAGES

Berehayes Farm, Whitchurch Canonicorum, Dorset DT6 6RQ
Tel: 01297 489093
e-mail: alan@berehayes.com
website: www.berehayes.com

Set around a delightful, enclosed courtyard, **Berehayes Farm Cottages** retain the character of the old 16th century, listed, stone farm buildings whilst offering a high standard of comfort throughout. The cottages are within easy reach of Dorset's World Heritage Coastline and many visitors to the area are keen walkers. The cottages are full of character and vary in size. Original features such as beamed ceilings and arrow-slit windows give each cottage a unique atmosphere. They all have open plan living areas with remote control colour televisions and DVD players. The fully fitted kitchens are extremely well equipped and have modern split level electric cookers and hobs, microwave ovens and larder fridges with freezer compartments. The larger cottages (sleeping four or more) have a

dishwasher. The beds are very comfortable and are made up on arrival and owners, Sue and Alan, provide towels, heated towel rails and shaving points in the luxury bathrooms. The cottages are all English Tourism Council four star rated and it is easy to see why.

There is a fantastic indoor heated swimming pool, sauna and Jacuzzi, as well as a well equipped games room and wiFi Broadband access available throughout. The cottages were converted from farm buildings, which date back to the 16th century and such is their popularity with visitors many return again and again.

The cottages are near to the famous Jurassic Coast and the coast resort of Lyme Regis as well as the towns of Bridport and Charmouth. There are plenty of activities to get involved in including golf, fishing, sailing and horse-riding. Sue and Alan are lovely hosts and are warm and welcoming. The cottages provide a home from home and the idyllic peaceful location allows visitors to have the relaxing break they desire. There is a well stocked library of books and DVDs for guests to borrow and a welcome pack includes a selection of beverages, biscuits and milk.

Stays at Berehayes normally run from Saturday afternoon to the following Saturday morning, but outside the school holiday peak periods Sue and Alan are happy to accommodate short breaks of three days or more. Ratty's Cottage (sleeps two), Brook Cottage (sleeps two), Mole's Cottage (sleeps 3), Badger's Den (sleeps 4), Otter's Abode (sleeps 5), Owl's Hoot (sleeps 5) and Toad's Hall (sleeps 7) make up the cottages. Ring Sue or Alan for details on availability.

144 CLOVE LODGE

Baldersdale, Barnard Castle, County Durham DL12 9UP
Tel: 01833 650030
e-mail: carolinecarter69@aol.com
website: www.clovelodge.co.uk

Caroline Carter had always had a yen to own a farm, and she chose a wonderful part of the world when she acquired a twenty-acre livestock farm on the edge of the fells in the North Pennines Area of Outstanding Natural Beauty.

Clove Lodge, which stands next to the farmhouse, is a Victorian stone-built, slate-roofed cottage with accommodation on two floors. On the ground floor are an en suite double/twin bedroom, with disabled access, a large, comfortable sitting room, a well-equipped kitchen and a cosy dining room. Upstairs is a double bedroom with its own bath/shower room.

The cottage has an attractive south-facing area with tables, chairs and a small barbecue overlooking a wooded bank, waterfall and stream.

The two rooms at Clove Lodge can be let separately or the cottage let as a whole, for either bed & breakfast (with evening meals by arrangement) or self-catering; for the latter, fresh eggs and lamb from the farm can be supplied. Please note that payment is by cash or cheque only. Well-behaved dogs are accepted by arrangement. Caroline also offers basic, rustic accommodation for guests in a converted barn - ideal for a group of walkers or cyclists.

Peace, solitude and the dramatic scenery of the North Pennines attract a wide cross-section of visitors, including tourists, walkers, cyclists, anglers (there's excellent fishing on nearby reservoirs) and wedding guests at the wonderful Bowes Museum.

The surrounding countryside is a haven for wildlife and was once described by a RSPB officer as "amongst the best bird watching areas in the country". Wildlife common to the area include badgers, deer, hares, black grouse, owls, curlew, lapwing, plover and several birds of prey such as the red kite and peregrine falcon.

Barnard Castle is a short drive away, and other places of interest in the vicinity include High and Low Force waterfalls, magnificent Raby Castle and the picturesque villages of Romaldkirk and Cotherstone. A little further afield are the great cathedrals of Durham and York, and the city of Newcastle with its multifarious attractions.

143 THE ANCIENT UNICORN

Main Street, Bowes, nr Barnard Castle,
County Durham DL12 9HL
Tel: 01833 628321
e-mail: ancient.unicorn@virgin.net
website: www.ancient-unicorn.com

The Ancient Unicorn is a real pub-lover's pub, a 16th century stone building with enormous character and everything a proper pub should be. When Joanne Foster took over in the summer of 2006 she brought a wealth of experience in the licensed trade, adding the finishing touches of knowledge and outstanding hospitality to the pub's other assets. The three-storey building is impressive in its own right, and the expectations created by the exterior are fully realised in the public rooms, where 2ft-thick walls, beams and a huge fire create an irresistible ambience for locals, walkers, hikers, families and tourists.

Black Bull and Shepherd Neame Spitfire are the resident cask ales, but before the urge to sample the beer the pub serves morning coffee from 10 o'clock in the morning. The main menu, served lunchtime and evening, highlights prime local produce in dishes such as deep-fried Cotherstone cheese fritters; warm salad of black pudding with mushrooms and a poached egg; Cumberland sausage; and slow-roasted Teesdale lamb shank.

This is wonderful walking country, and the Ancient Unicorn offers a very comfortable, civilised base with four immaculate en suite bedrooms – including a family room – in a courtyard-style annexe.

146 THE WILLIAM BOOSEY

The Street, Hatfield Peverel,
nr Chelmsford, Essex CM3 2ET
Tel: 01245 380205
e-mail: penneeley@aol.com

With its half-timbered exterior, **The William Boosey** has for a very long time been a familiar landmark in the village of Hatfield Peverel, located on the B1137 northeast of Chelmsford just a few short moments from junction 20 of the A12. The inn is named after its first landlord who was at the helm more than 300 years ago.

A Shepherd Neame establishment, the inn has recently been thoroughly refurbished by the new landlords, Pennee and Kevin, who arrived here in the autumn of 2009. They took care to retain original features such as the gnarled old black beams in the convivial bar and they have also made good food a priority, offering the very best of English and Thai cuisine every lunchtime and evening. Such is the restaurant's popularity, it is advisable to book on Friday and Saturday evenings, and for Sunday lunchtime. To accompany your meal there's a choice of 3 real ales, with Bishop's Finger as the regular brew.

Once a month the inn hosts a disco with live bands and there are occasional events such as race nights. Children are welcome here; there's good disabled access, and all major credit cards are accepted.

145 THE BROWN HORSE

High Stoop, Tow Law, Bishop Auckland, County Durham DL13 4HJ
Tel: 01388 730498

The Brown Horse Hotel extends a warm welcome to all guests. Set in the beautiful countryside of the Wear Valley with spectacular views of the North Pennines.

The Hotel is conveniently situated on the A68 within 30 minutes of Hexham, Newcastle, Durham and Stanhope with lots of local tourist attractions such as the angel of the North, Durham Cathedral, and The Dales within the local area for you to make the most of on your stay at the Brown Horse Hotel. The hotel is also located on the main route to Scotland with picturesque views to be seen throughout the journey on this route, only approximately 100 miles from the Scottish Border.

The rural location of the Brown Horse Hotel makes it a perfect place to stay if you enjoy the countryside with many places to go walking or cycling close by. The hotel was fully refurbished in 2009 with 7 en-suite bedrooms boasting top quality beds and large screen TV's in all rooms along with tea and coffee making facilities.

The hotel restaurant offers home cooked meals and snacks throughout the day and a fully functioning bar that is open late 7 days a week. The restaurant also offers a traditional Sunday carvery and other specialties such as Indian Curry night and Steak nights on various evenings.

147 WATERSIDE TEA ROOMS AND B&B

106 High Street, Maldon, Essex CM9 5ET
Tel: 01621 859545
e-mail: watersidetearoom@aol.com
website: www.watersidetearooms.co.uk

The Waterside Tea Rooms stands proudly on the high street at the centre of Maldon. This 16th century property now operates as one of the area's best bed and breakfasts with a popular tea room running throughout the daytime. Owners Terry and Sue created the tea rooms over four years ago, and are known locally for their unrivalled hospitality.

Open seven days a week from 10am-4pm, but closed on Sundays in winter, the tea room specialises in home cooking. Each day a variety of homemade breakfasts, light bites, main meals and cakes are served for all in a charming olde worlde styling. Popular desserts include Eve's Apple pudding, Jam pudding, spotted dick and chocolate pudding. A range of teas, coffees and hot chocolates accompany the menu, alongside a good selection of soft drinks. Children and families are welcome throughout, where blue china, gingham table cloths and scrubbed wooden floors create a homely atmosphere for all.

Terry and Sue also offer a beautifully appointed family room on a bed and breakfast rate. The room has a private bathroom and private toilet facilities, and both a double and sofa bed for convenience. In keeping with the tea room's traditional styling, the bedroom maintains a true home from home feel without neglecting any of the modern comforts. All major credit cards accepted.

149 THE RED LION

47 The Street, Latchingdon, Essex CM3 6JR
Tel: 01621 740298
e-mail: aprilcaten@btconnect.com

Jim and April Caten welcome you to their home, **The Red Lion Inn**; adjacent to the A1018 just south of Malden. With over 40 years of experience together in the trade, Jim and April make for fantastic hosts, offering the warmest of welcomes whilst serving up delicious food and drink throughout the day.

Food is served from 9am-9pm seven days a week, cooked fresh to order by talented Head Chef Rod McGregor. He offers up a variety of breakfast, snack and main menus encompassing all your favourites including a generous Sunday roast, with a few special creations of his own too. Popular dishes include Catalonian Monkfish, pan fried with anchovies and capers; Somerset pork chop, Ankra chicken bake, Pan fried duck breast, Dover sole, and a mighty T-bone steak. Dishes are created using as much locally sourced produce from Essex as possible. Guests can dine within the homely restaurant atmosphere, or outside in the sunny beer garden.

Though guests mainly come for the food, the Red Lion is also a popular place to stay. With four en suite bedrooms to choose from all year round, guests can enjoy a convenient base for exploring all that Essex has to offer. Families and children are welcome, with three twin bedrooms and one family sized room. The tariff includes a delicious continental breakfast, although full English breakfasts are available on request. All major credit cards accepted.

148 THE HOT PLATE CAFÉ

10 High Street, Maldon, Essex CM9 5PJ
Tel: 01621 850524
e-mail: thehotplatecafe@aol.co.uk

Located centrally in Maldon on the main high street is the **Hot Plate Café**. Its attractive yellow façade and modern interior conceal grade II listed status, one which it's owners Chris Pye and Wendy Wade are very proud of. Chris and Wendy have been running the café for a number of years, establishing a great rapport with their guests who not only enjoy their company, but their food.

Open seven days a week from 9am-4pm, the café seats twenty downstairs and a further twelve upstairs. Light wood furniture and floorings, combined with chrome fixtures and a wall to wall window onto the street create the perfect contemporary environment for people watching. Whether you are just popping in for a quick coffee and a slice of cake, or if you and the family are settling down for a hearty meal, the café is the perfect location.

There is a good selection of speciality teas and coffees, and plenty of soft drinks too from milkshakes, to squash and sodas. The real treat here though is the food. Guests can choose from the printed menu which encompasses a range of breakfasts, snacks and main meals; or choose from the weekly blackboard which changes to reflect the best seasonal produce around at the time. Local produce is used to create dishes whenever possible, giving guests that truly authentic taste of Maldon.

At the head of the kitchen is Chris, whose dishes have given her a popular place in the local's hearts. For breakfast she offers both vegetarian and carnivorous options with lighter options for those with a smaller appetite. Main meals include all your favourites including sausage and chips, ham, egg and chips, a quarter pounder, sausage and mash, scampi and chips, and a selection of spicier dishes from homemade chicken curry, to chilli con carne and sweet and sour chicken; all of which come with a vegetarian option also. For lighter bites, guests can choose from a selection of freshly made filled sandwiches, rolls and jacket potatoes, not to mention Chris's popular homemade soup of the day. If you just fancy a slice of toast, then you can have that too with a choice of peanut butter, marmite or fruit preserves. Chris also makes a mouth-watering selection of homemade cakes and pastries which are displayed daily on the counter for those with a sweeter tooth. Under 5's also have a small choice and are welcome at all times; high chairs are available on request.

150 THE ARDLEIGH LION

The Street, Ardleigh, Colchester, Essex CO7 7LD
Tel: 01206 280083

Situated in the heart of Ardleigh near Colchester is **The Ardleigh Lion**. This historic inn dates back over 250 years and has operated under a number of different names and guises. Today the inn stands at its peak, having gone from strength to strength over the past six months since new owner Stephen Culham took over in October 2009. Stephen has been in the trade for over ten years, but has never had the pleasure of being the boss. Now holding the reins, he has turned the Lion right around, giving the village its local pub back with gusto.

Open all day every day, the inn sees a steady throng of both locals and visitors alike who often stop off on a pleasant amble through the idyllic countryside that surrounds Colchester. The inn retains a sense of history by displaying a range of interesting memorabilia on its walls, but the styling is generally modern. Cool blues and warm yellows are complimented by the dark wood furniture and contemporary place settings; making an attractive setting for drinks or dinner.

A fine collection of wines, spirits and real ales are available daily; with Green King IPA being the usual ale alongside a rotating ale from variety of local micro-breweries. Keen to support local trade, Stephen gathers not only ale from the area, but any of the ingredients for his food, sourcing as much as possible locally.

The menu changes regularly to reflect the seasonal goods available, but always has something for everyone. With a large and varied range of light bites, starters, mains and desserts, choosing will be difficult. All the usual pub classics are included cooked to a high standard, along with a select choice of special dishes, displayed daily on the blackboard. On Sundays a spectacular roast is added to the menu, served with all the trimmings; families welcome. Throughout the week, a number of themed food evenings are run with specialties from across the country and the globe, with a special drinks menu to match, please call for details. Food is available Tuesday to Saturday from 12-9pm and on Sundays from 12-6pm.

On regular evenings, there is also plenty to see and do, with a selection of live entertainment on offer, including karaoke and live music. Guests are also welcomed to get involved in games of darts and crib held at the inn, play pool, or support their favourite football team, as matches are shown with a full Sky sports package.

151 THE TREBLE TILE

Colchester Road, West Bergholt, Essex CO6 3JQ
Tel: 01206 241712
e-mail: jhjinns@hotmail.com
website: www.thetrebletile.co.uk

Located in the picturesque village of West Bergholt, **The Treble Tile** is a welcoming old hostelry which aims to offer great food at reasonable prices in a convivial atmosphere.

From Monday to Saturday there is a full menu offering both classic and seasonal dishes, along with additional 'lighter choices' available at lunch time. The menu changes monthly, but typically you will find chicken liver pate with a bitter chocolate and olive oil crust, smoked salmon, and a chickpea and halloumi salad amongst the starters and calves liver and bacon, battered haddock and chips and chicken and mushroom rough puff pie amongst the main courses, with a goats cheese and beetroot tart tatin vegetarian option. To follow, you can indulge yourself with a hot chocolate fondant, homemade ice cream or a choice of mostly British cheeses. On Sunday there is a slightly different menu including a choice of brunch dishes plus two roasts and a vegetarian option. All dishes are cooked to order and based on local produce wherever possible. You can eat either in the eye catching dining area, in the bar, or in the enclosed garden during the summer. Food is served from noon until 2.30pm and from 6pm until 9.30pm Monday to Saturday, and from 11am to 3.30pm on Sunday.

To accompany your meal there is an extensive choice of wines from around the world, several available by the glass, or if you prefer beer the wide selection includes real ale – Adnams Best and Woodfordes Wherry. Children are very welcome and all credit cards accepted apart from American Express.

152 THE STINGRAY AND THE CROWN POST RESTAURANT

56 Church Street, Harwich, Essex CO12 3DS
Tel: 01255 503507
e-mail: enquiries@thestingray.co.uk
website: www.thestingray.co.uk

Located in the heart of olde Harwich, **The Stingray** offers excellent bed and breakfast facilities. Dating back more than 600 years, the free house has been family owned and run for the past 15 years and is today run by Jamie and Laetitia Shrive, who have had a lot of support from Jamie's parents. The building once housed the English Meat Company before becoming a pub/inn around 70 years ago.

There are five en-suite bedrooms available and the quite location allows for a peaceful night. It is arguable some of the best accommodation in the area and guests will have the added convenience of numerous restaurants, bars and takeaways within walking distance. All rooms have satellite television, DVD player and tea and coffee making facilities and a fantastic home cooked breakfast is available. (Dinner rates can be arranged too).

The pub itself is open all day and two real ales are served. Plenty of locals frequent the bar area and many visitors to the area are drawn in to The Stingray, which has a friendly and warm atmosphere, and the added bonus of a restaurant next door. Attached to The Stingray is a building of the same age, which was once a tobacconist. Jamie and Laetitia purchased it a few years ago and have sympathetically refurbished it in accordance with its age. It is full of period charm and has plenty of exposed beams as well as a superb Crown Post that holds most of the building together. The Crown Post restaurant was officially opened early this year (2010) and provides an intimate and atmospheric place to dine. Seating around 60 diners, the restaurant will be open every lunchtime between 11am and 3pm and each evening between 6pm and 9.30pm. (The restaurant will be open for longer hours in the summer months). The extensive menu boasts traditional English cuisine of the finest quality. The prices are affordable to all and the dishes are freshly cooked to order using quality local produce wherever possible. There is seating upstairs as well as on the ground floor and with good disabled facilities access is not a problem (the guest rooms however are all located upstairs).

The Stingray sometimes hosts live entertainment (see website) and has discos Friday/Saturday from 9pm all year round. Major credit cards are taken.

154 THE THREE BOTTLES

Leather Lane, Great Yeldham, Essex CO9 4HY
Tel: 01787 237122

In an area well-served by country pubs, **The Three Bottles** is one of the very best. It stands in the village of Great Yeldham, south of Sible Hedingham on the A1017 Halstead to Haverhill road. Tenants Jim and Elaine Foster bring a wealth of experience to this fine old inn, parts of which date back to the late 18th century. The carpeted bar with a handsome feature fireplace, shining brass and sparkling glass gives the interior a traditional feel, creating warmth and an ambience for good conversation over a quiet drink. Outside, a recently erected gazebo on the patio provides shade as you look out onto a well-kept garden area which is a veritable sun trap. There are picnic tables in this secluded garden, a real boon on sunny days or a balmy evening.

Courage Best heads the list of traditional ales, complemented by Ringwood Best and two other guest ales which are changed regularly. The bar also stocks a fine selection of lagers, spirits, wines, soft drinks and bottled drinks.

Food is limited to nibbles and Elaine's famous Sunday lunch (between noon and 4pm) which offers a choice of roasts plus a vegetarian option. They do not take bookings so the advice is to come early to be sure of a Sunday dinner "just like Mum used to make!"

The Three Bottles is open from 6pm on a Monday; lunchtime (noon until 2.30pm) and evening (6pm to 11.30pm), and all day opening on Saturday and Sunday. Children are welcome until 8.30pm; dogs are welcome and there is good disabled access throughout. Please note that payment here is by cash only.

153 THE GREYHOUND

62 High Street, Wivenhoe, Essex, CO7 9AZ
Tel: 01206 825573
e-mail: jayne.vince@btconnect.com

Dating back to the 17th century, **The Greyhound** is a superb pub, which stands on the edge of the centre of Wivenhoe. It offers an extremely high standard of food, ale and hospitality and is popular with locals and visitors to the area. Leaseholder, Jane Vince, has been here for more than six years and has just opened a new restaurant area on the premises, which seats 24 (meals can also be eaten in the bar areas).

Home cooking is the order of the day at The Greyhound, and as well as a traditional menu diners can choose from the daily specials board too. A lot of the produce is locally sourced and the home cooked food served is popular with diners, many who return again. Such is its popularity it is advisable to book at weekends. There is an upstairs function room available for private hire, which seats 60 (ring for details).

Live music can be heard on Fridays from 9pm and every Tuesday evening from 9pm a jamming session is had. In May/June The Greyhound hosts beer festivals and additional real ales can be sampled as well as the three regular real ales. Disabled access is not a problem.

156 THE CROSS KEYS

The Street, White Notley, nr Witham,
Essex CM8 1RQ
Tel: 01376 583297

The Cross Keys is a quaint little inn dating from the 1730s and now a Grade II listed building. The pink-washed exterior makes it look very inviting and the interior is charmingly traditional with chunky black beams in the lounge and public bars.

Your young and energetic host is Carly Baker who took over here in November 2009 and quickly established a reputation for serving good quality wholesome "pub grub", cooked freshly to order and based on fresh local produce wherever possible. Breakfasts are served from 9am to noon; lunches from noon until 2.30pm; and evening meals from 6pm. To accompany your meal there's a good range of real ales from the Greene King brewery. On Thursday evenings it's "Pie and a Pint" with a choice of two different home-made pies; and on Fridays there are international food themed evenings.

Children are welcome here; there's good disabled access and all major credit cards are accepted. The inn is just a short distance from the recently opened Great Leighs race-course so it's a good place for race-goers to celebrate or drown their sorrows!

155 THE MAYPOLE

31 Mill End, Thaxted, Dunmow, Essex CM6 2LT
Tel: 01371 831152
e-mail: Frankie.miller@live.co.uk

The Maypole is located in what many consider as the jewel of Essex's crown; the picturesque village of Thaxted. An attractive backdrop of medieval houses provides the setting for a variety of other architectural gems such as the old windmill and the church. With records dating back to the doomsday book, the village has plenty of history including a strong Morris dancing community with a festival in the summertime.

The Maypole was taken over five months ago by mother and daughter team Jude and Frankie, who have worked tirelessly to turn this place around. Their down to earth attitude and hard grafting has helped to transform the Maypole into a truly fantastic establishment. Full of zest with a new lease of life, the ladies have revamped both the interior and exterior of the property, maintaining some of its timeless original features whilst updating both the facilities and the décor.

The ladies have quickly built up a following from both locals and visitors who have been impressed by the change they have seen in the pub, and the friendly, warm atmosphere that has been created within. Open all day every day for drinks, the inn is popular with ale lovers, with four on offer at any one time including Green King IPA and Abbot Ale. A good selection of wine, spirits, soft drinks and lagers are also available.

From 12 midday until 7-8pm each evening guests can enjoy a delicious selection of good old home made pub grub. Jude and Frankie employ a professional chef who has put together a handsome across the board menu which is created using as much fresh locally sourced produce as possible. Guests can dine throughout the inn, in a relaxed informal setting, or go for a more al fresco approach in the sunny terrace, full of blooming flowers in season, with a sheltered area for smokers. Children can choose from their own menu, and are welcome at all times.

Jude and Frankie also provide guests with a wealth of light hearted entertainment throughout the week, from karaoke, quizzes, live music and local acts, please call or see facebook page for details.

157 THE GEORGE

The Street, Shalford, nr Braintree, Essex CM7 5HH
Tel: 01371 850207
e-mail: the.george.inn@btconnect.com
website: www.thegeorgeshalford.co.uk

Set it the rural countryside alongside the B1053 within easy reach of Great Dunmow, Braintree and Stanstead Airport is **The George**. Dating back to the 14th century in parts, the inn has a certain charm to it, having retained many of its original features such as a brick hearth, wood panelled bar, timber beams and a walk in inglenook fireplace. This traditional feel is complimented by a selection of warm colours and handsome wooden furniture, making guests feel right at home.

Licensees Steve and Jenny took over the inn in December 2009, embracing the inn's character and taking it from strength to strength in all departments. They open from 12-3pm and 6-11pm Monday to Friday and from 12-2pm on Saturday and 12-6pm on Sundays. Popular with ale lovers, the inn serves up to six real ales at any one time with London Pride, Young's Bitter and Woodforde's Wherry being the regulars alongside a selection of rotating ales and brews from the local village. A good selection of other alcoholic beverages are also available with wine by the glass, and a range of spirits and lagers.

The inn is perhaps most popular for its food which is served daily at lunchtimes and evenings. Steve and Jenny pride themselves on being able to offer something for everyone, whether you are looking for a romantic meal for two or a full family feast. The menu is created using only locally sourced produce, each dish cooked fresh to order. The focus is on serving traditional English pub food, cooked to the highest standards. Dishes include homemade speciality steak and ale pie, Prior Hall 'off the bone' ham and eggs, smoked salmon and prawn salad, 10 oz sirloin steak, and homemade beef lasagne. For those in a hurry, a bar menu operates throughout the day offering a small selection of soups, filled sandwiches and jacket potatoes alongside other light bites like pate and toast, or pan-fried garlic mushrooms. Some dishes can be ordered on a takeaway basis, although many prefer to stay in and dine on one of the inn's popular curry nights. Owing to popularity, booking is recommended on Friday and Saturday nights and Sunday lunchtimes.

Children welcome, all credit cards accepted apart from American Express and Diners.

158 THE RED LION INN

Market Place, Northleach, Gloucestershire GL54 3EJ
Tel: 01451 860251

'Real Old-Fashioned Hospitality in the Heart of Historic Northleach'

Locals and visitors to the town are agreed that the hospitality extended by hosts Carol and Kevin at the **Red Lion Inn** is second to none. They took over here in 2006, since when they have made many friends at this lively, sociable spot.

Open all day, seven days a week, the bar serves four Cask marque accredited real ales that rotate on a regular basis, so real ale fans will find something different to sample on every visit. And when the weather is kind the courtyard and burgage garden really come into their own. Or you may prefer to take tea or coffee with a slice of homemade cake in the newly opened tea room, entered through the courtyard, quite an unexpected find at the back of the pub. Local produce, and Kevin's homegrown vegetables provide Carol with the best seasonal ingredients for cookin g healthy and hearty dishes. A typical days choice could include fourteen inches of Northleach sausauge with leek and onion gravy and thick cut honey roasted ham with organic free range eggs and proper real chips - no frozen chips allowed! Food is served every day from midday until 8 o'clock in the evening.

Northleach is an ideal base for touring the Cotswolds and the Red Lion is a very pleasant, civilised base to choose. The guest accommodation comprises three cosy rooms – two doubles and a twin. Bikers are always welcome and the inn provides secure parking for cycles and motorcycles. Northleach itself is well worth taking time to explore. Why not treat yourself to a mid-week Dinner Bed and Breakfast Break. The grandest building in town is the splendid Parish Church of St Peter & St Paul, often known as the Cathedral of the Cotswolds. It was rebuilt in the 15th century with money from the wool trade, and the brass memorials are testimony to the wealth of the wool merchants. Keith Harding's World of Mechanical Music is another attraction, and within a short drive from the town are the Cotswold Wildlife Park & Gardens and several National Trust properties.

159 THE SHERBORNE ARMS

Aldsworth, Gloucestershire GL54 3RB
Tel: 01451 844346
e-mail: thesherbornearms@btinternet.com
website: www.thesherbornearms.com

The **Sherborne Arms** is a delightful family-run country pub nestling in a dip set back from the B4425 at Aldsworth, between Bibury and Burford. It has been in the excellent care of the O'Keeffe & Jenvey families since 1984, and from the start their aim has been to provide a traditional English pub atmosphere along with honest, wholesome cooking. David and Joanne, Joanne's mum Pam, son Daniel and daughter-in-law Diana run a truly professional outfit, combining the very best in hospitality for young and old alike with the skills and experience that turn a very good inn into an outstanding one.

The interior of the inn is warm and welcoming, with plenty of space to meet friends over a glass or two of beer, and when the sun shines the pretty garden overlooking open countryside is the perfect spot for an alfresco drink or meal. Greene King IPA and Abbot Ale are the regular real ales and for the third they like to support smaller local breweries. The bar is closed Monday lunchtime but is otherwise open every lunchtime and evening. Visitors come from many miles around to enjoy Joanne and Pam's cooking. Food is available from 12 to 2 Tuesday to Sunday and from 6 to 9 Tuesday to Saturday. Food is not served on Sunday evenings but a takeaway curry service is available. Smoked salmon, spicy chicken pakora and baked camembert are great for starters or snacks, and the deli platters provide interesting combinations of smoked fish or charcuterie. Fresh fish is delivered daily to be grilled or fried, and from the grill come sirloin, pork and gammon steaks and Aberdeen Angus burgers. Listed under 'Favourites' are steak & kidney pie, ham with eggs and chips, lamb & apricot casserole and Thai red vegetable curry. Children can choose from their own special menu, or smaller portions of some 'grown-up' dishes are available. Desserts include treacle tart and speciality ices.

The inn is a popular meeting place and rally stop for groups, and morning coffee and afternoon tea can be provided by the always helpful hosts. They are also happy to cater for weddings and other parties, and a function room can be booked, with seats for up to 30. This doubles as a games room with darts, skittles and a league pool table.

160 THE EDGEMOOR INN

Edge, Painswick, Gloucestershire GL6 6ND
Tel: 01452 813576
e-mail: info@edgemoor-inn.com
website: www.edgemoor-inn.com

The **Edgemoor Inn** stands in the village of Edge, midway along the Cotswold Way that runs from Chipping Norton in the north to Bath in the south, most of the route following the Cotswold escarpment. Cheltenham is just 6 miles to the north. Resident owners of the inn, Chris and Jill Bayes, have a genuinely warm welcome for all who visit their 250-year-old stone inn, whether they be first-timers or familiar faces.

Real ale connoisseurs are in for a treat with some interesting local brews, typically including Old Spot from the Ulley Brewery, Budding Ale from Stroud Brewery, and Bob from Wickwar. The food at the Edgemoor Inn is also well worth more than a little detour, and at peak times it's best to book to be sure of a table at the time you want.

Contemplating the menu poses a problem, but a pleasant one, as everything on the daily changing menu is worth trying. Each day proposes an excellent choice of dishes that cater for a wide variety of tastes and appetites. The menu changes 3 times a year and it's all good, fresh and wholesome, with local produce used as much as possible. This splendid fare is served every lunchtime (from noon until 2pm) and every evening(6.30pm to 9pm) except Sunday evening in winter, when the inn is closed. The continuing success of this outstanding place was demonstrated with the creation in May 2008 of a large dining room extension with 70 additional covers and lovely Cotswold views.

There are equally delightful views of the Painswick Valley and the surrounding countryside from the paved terrace - an asset that's in great demand when the sun shines or on warm summer evenings. Families with children are very welcome, and the inn accepts the major credit cards. Edge has two picturesque village greens and a mid-Victorian church with an ornate spire. To the west of the village lies Scottsquarr Common, a Site of Special Scientific Interest that is home to an abundance of wild flowers and butterflies.

161 THE FOX & HOUNDS

116 Prestbury Road, Cheltenham, Gloucestershire GL52 2DP
Tel: 01242 523095

The **Fox & Hounds** is located on the B4632 Prestbury Road, not far from the town's sights and shops and very convenient for the racecourse at Prestbury Park, home of jump racing – just half a mile away. The welcoming hosts are Nigel Thatcher and Tammy Lee, who carried out a comprehensive refurbishment programme when they arrived here to take over at the end of 2009. Behind the handsome Georgian frontage it's a comfortable, stylish place with two bars, a wood-panelled lounge and a restaurant at the rear. There's good parking to the front and back and a lawned garden with tables and chairs set out on decking for taking the sun while enjoying a drink or a meal.

Nigel is a very accomplished chef, so visitors who know what good food is all about are on a winner – choosing between light bites and succulent steaks, seafood specials and seasonal game. Food is served from 12 to 2 and 6.30 to 9.30 Tuesday, Wednesday, Thursday, Saturday and Sunday; no food Friday and the pub is closed on Monday. Cheltenham, once one of Europe's leading Regency spa towns, is now best known for its racecourse, which hosts an annual meeting (and many others) that attracts the very best hurdlers and steeplechasers to its four-day meeting.

163 THE OLD CORNER CUPBOARD

83 Gloucester Street, Winchcombe, nr Cheltenham, Gloucestershire GL54 5LX
Tel: 01242 602303
e-mail: jason@tcciw.com
website: www.cornercupboardwinchcombe.com

The **Old Corner Cupboard** is a fine old hostelry in mellow Cotswold stone, with small-paned windows and tall chimneys. It's one of the town's most interesting buildings, starting life in the 16th century as a farmhouse, and it acquired its odd name after a customer pointed out that almost every angle had a cupboard! Visitors to the inn are greeted and well looked after by experienced landlord Jason Hobbs and his mother Julie. The bar is open all day, seven days a week, for drinks, which include three or four real ales, with Timothy Taylor Landlord and London Pride the regulars.

The inn is open for a Big Budget Breakfast at 10am, with the menu available from 11.30 to 3.30 and 6 to 9.30. The inn is deservedly a very popular place, so booking is recommended at all times to be sure of a table. Freshly baked baguettes and crispy baked jacket potatoes with a variety of tempting fillings are favourite lunchtime choices, while the main menu includes both pub classics (beer-battered cod, burgers, prawn cocktail with prawns *and* crayfish) and authentic Indian dishes based on chicken, prawns or vegetables. All the curries can be ordered to take away. Sunday lunch brings traditional roasts with many other options. The excellent food is complemented by a well-annotated list of mainly New World wines.

162 THE PLOUGH

Mill Street, Prestbury, nr Cheltenham,
Gloucestershire GL52 3BG
Tel: 01242 228704
e-mail: infoattheplough@googlemail.com

The **Plough** is a fine olde-worlde thatched public
house in the best tradition of English country inns.
The building, which dates back to the middle of the
17th century, is full of character, with superb,
picturesque gardens to match. It stands off the
B4632 a short drive from Cheltenham and it's a
great place to plan a trip to the races and to
celebrate a win at the end of the day – or to
exchange hard-luck stories. The young licensees
Stacey and Paul, who took over here in February
2009, have lost no time in establishing themselves,
stamping their warm personalities on the place and
making many friends among the local community
and the succession of visitors who flock here
throughout the year.

In the cheerful bar there are usually four real
ales to enjoy, typically Charles Wells Bombardier,
Adnams Broadside and Wickwar Bob brewed in a
village near Chipping Norton, with a regularly
rotating guest ale, along with a fine selection of
other beers, cider, wines, spirits and soft drinks.
Food is also a major contributor to the Plough's
success. Stacy cooks on five days a week and chef
James on the other days, both of them preparing
tasty, satisfying snacks and dishes based as far as
possible on the best seasonal local produce.
Sandwiches on granary or white bread with
interesting, generous fillings make excellent quick
snacks, while other popular choices include salmon
fishcakes and a very heart ploughman's platter with
cheddar, stilton, pickles, pickled onions, beetroot,
sliced apple, a side salad and granary bread. Other
options range from burgers – beef, chicken or bean
– to scampi, ham with eggs & chips and chicken
with chips and salad. It's best to book at peak times
and for the Sunday roast, which is always a popular
occasion. The inn can cater for special events 'at
your place or ours' and can organise marquee and
barbecue hire.

Prestbury has a reputation as one of the
country's most haunted villages. They used to say
that you could sometimes hear horses' hooves at
the plough – very appropriate in view of the racing
connection. Cheltenham is the headquarters of
jump racing but Prestbury's most famous son was one of the greatest flat jockeys of all time –
Fred Archer, born in the village in 1857.

164 THE BAKERS ARMS

Broad Campden, Chipping Campden,
Gloucestershire GL55 6UR
Tel: 01386 840375

The unspoilt village of Broad Campden, just a mile from famous Chipping Campden, lies in the heart of the Cotswolds and its pub, **The Bakers Arms**, is a classic, traditional stone-built Cotswold hostelry. Outside, there's a delightful garden and inside, snug log fires create a welcoming atmosphere. Real ale lovers will be pleased to find that the bar offers a choice of up to five genuine brews. Mine hosts, Sally and Roy Mayo, who have been here since 1997, also make good food a priority. Served in the new restaurant at the rear of the inn, the choice of wholesome and appetising food includes all the old favourites such as cottage pie, steak & kidney suet pie and chicken curry, along with fish dishes and vegetarian options such as a tasty Stilton & vegetable crumble, or a cheese, leek and potato bake. Booking ahead is strongly recommended at weekends - the Sunday roasts are particularly popular.

At lunchtimes only, a good choice of lighter meals is available - ploughman's, baguettes, filled giant Yorkshire puddings and sandwiches. Children have their own menu. Food is served from noon until 2pm; and from 6pm to 8pm.

166 THE TEDDINGTON HANDS INN

Evesham Road, Teddington, nr Tewkesbury, Gloucestershire GL20 8NE
Tel: 01386 725276 Fax: 01386 725623
e-mail: info@teddingtonhands.com
website: www.teddingtonhands.com

Licensees Peter and Heather and Heather's son Ben make a fine family team at the **Teddington Hands Inn**, which stands where the A46 meets the A435 and the B4077. The spacious interior provides plenty of room to enjoy well-kept ales, excellent food and unbeatable hospitality, and the family-friendly garden is a big bonus when the weather's kind.

Four real ales, with Flowers IPA and Timothy Taylor Landlord the regulars, are always on tap, and a splendid selection of Ben's home-cooked dishes is served from noon to 9pm (Sunday to 8pm). Among the many superb choices on the menu are chicken liver, smoked bacon and brandy pâté, chilli & ginger crab cakes, steak & kidney and steak, Guinness & mushroom pies, slow-roast lamb shank and Friday's gourmet fish & chips, the fish grilled with oil and herbs, freshly breaded or beer-battered.

The inn is a popular meeting place before or after Cheltenham races: on major race days it's open from 9 o'clock for a wide-ranging breakfast menu. Cheltenham is a 20-minute drive away, or racegoers can take the train on the nearby Gloucestershire Warwickshire steam-hauled railway.

165 THE HALFWAY HOUSE

Kineton, Guiting Power, nr Cheltenham, Gloucestershire GL54 5UG
Tel: 01451 850344
website: www.thehalfwayhousekineton.co.uk

The **Halfway House** is a fine old country inn situated in the peaceful hamlet of Kineton, halfway between temple Guiting and Guiting Power, close to the A436 and the B4077. Behind the mellow Cotswold stone frontage the inn has been carefully modernised while retaining a traditional feel assisted by oak beams and cosy winter fires. Outside is a pretty lawned garden fringed by flowers, trees and shrubs. Until 1975 the inn was owned by Corpus Christi College, Oxford, and since July 2009 it has been in the care of tenants John and Anna Maher. They have quickly established a reputation for fine food and generous hospitality, and as the word spreads they are attracting a growing clientele among both the local community and the many visitors who come to this region every year.

John, with 15 years' experience in the licensed and catering trades, is a fine chef who puts the pick of the local produce to excellent use on his wide and varied menu. Fish and seafood are always popular choices – salmon & dill fishcakes, battered king prawns, the catch of the day – and other favourites from chicken liver parfait to a trio of sausages, duck breast with red cabbage, and liver & bacon with bubble & squeak. Sandwiches and filled baguettes and panini cater for smaller appetites or those who have less time to spare. Booking is recommended at peak times and for the ever-popular Sunday lunch featuring two roasts with other options. Food is served from 12.30 to 2 and 6.30 to 9 Monday to Saturday and from 12 to 3 on Sunday.

For visitors looking for break or touring the region the Halfway House has four well-appointed double rooms that area available all year round. The tariff includes a hearty English breakfast. One of the many attractions in the vicinity of the inn is the Cotswold Farm Park, home to some 50 herds and flocks of rare-breed British farm animals.

As well as being a destination restaurant and a comfortable base for exploring a very attractive part of the world the Halfway House is very much at the social heart of the community. The locals gather to put the world to rights over a glass of Donnington's ale and a game of pool or darts.

167 THE RIVERSIDE INN

Hawbridge, Tirley, nr Tewkesbury,
Gloucestershire GL19 4HJ
Tel: 01452 780225
e-mail: ajr.talbot@hotmail.co.uk

The **Riverside Inn** is set in five acres of land, which
provides plenty of room for those who enjoy
camping. Caravans and tents are both allowed to
pitch up and there is always a hot meal to be had at
the inn. The menu is very traditional with a good
selection of homemade pies among the fine dishes
available. A lot of the produce is sourced locally and many
of the dishes are home cooked on the premises. The bar is
well stocked and there are two real ales including London
Pride and Local Guest. Bar food is served Tuesday – Saturday
between 12pm and 2pm and in the evening between 6.30pm
and 9pm. A traditional carvery is available every Sunday
between 12pm and 3pm. The outside decking area provides
a delightful setting on warmer days as it overlooks the River
Severn. The Riverside Inn is a delightful establishment with

restaurant and bar areas overlooking the River Severn. Downstairs there is a games room, where
customers can play social games of pool and darts.

There is a self catering apartment overlooking fields and it has two bedrooms and a bathroom.
Ring for details. A bus service is available to Gloucester via Tewkesbury.

168 THE RISING SUN

Iping Road, Milland, nr Liphook,
Hampshire GU30 7NA
Tel: 01428 741347 Fax: 01428 741704
e-mail: mail@risingsunmilland.com
website: www.risingsunmilland.com

The **Rising Sun** at Milland is one of the very best village inns in
the whole region, a wonderful place to relax, have fun and
enjoy a drink and a meal. It stands in a village signposted off
the A3 near Liphook in the heart of the lovely South Downs
National Park, a magnet for walkers, cyclists, tourists and lovers
of the fresh, clean country air. Ben and Frankie are the most
welcoming of hosts and the bar and lounge areas offer abundant
space and comfort for meeting friends and having a chat over a
glass of well-kept Fullers ale.

The beers and the extensive wine list complement daily
changing menus that feature the best and freshest local ingredients in the dishes served in the 40-
cover restaurant. Some dishes are all-time classics, while others come from the modern British
repertoire, such as scallops with chorizo and pea shoots and purée, or braised belly pork with
black pudding, mustard mash and leeks. Bar snacks cater for lighter appetites, children can
choose from their own menu and the chefs produce some really lip-smacking desserts. The inn
also offers pizzas and fish & chips to take away.

The Rising Sun is a popular venue for private parties and all sorts of celebrations and offers an
outside catering service for hog roasts, barbecues, buffets and lunches for groups of 12 to 200.

169 THE BLUE BELL INN

South Street, Emsworth, Hampshire PO10 7EG
Tel: 01243 373394
e-mail: info@bluebellinnemsworth.co.uk
website: www.bluebellinnemsworth.co.uk

Tucked away in the south east corner of Hampshire on the shore of Chichester Harbour, Emsworth is a quiet and attractive town which also boasts an outstanding old hostelry. **The Blue Bell Inn** occupies a superb position just yards from the Quay and is the former favourite haunt of the local fishermen. It is still the perfect spot for a drink or bite to eat after a walk around the Harbour or watching the fishing boats unload their catch.

A family owned pub, The Blue Bell is run by Thomas Babb and is a popular venue for people who wish to enjoy great home cooked food prepared by chef Thomas Giles Babb (Gilo) son of the owner. "Cooking is an art, masterpieces take time!" he says. His menu offers a huge choice of wholesome and appetising dishes. Amongst the starters you'll find Gilo's soup of the day and his chicken liver parfait. For the main course, there's a selection of Aberdeen Angus steaks supplied by the local butcher, old favourites such as beef and ale pie, and ham, egg and chips. But the speciality of the house is fresh fish - just try the oven-baked whole sea bream, for example. The regular menu is supplemented by a monthly special dish - local Funtington pork, perhaps, served on a bed of colcannon with a wild mushroom, wholegrain mustard and cider sauce.

For lighter appetites, the choice includes a tasty range of filled baguettes (Brie & tomato, for example, or chicken lettuce mayo) or jacket potatoes. To accompany your food, there's a choice of cask ales, with Old Speckled Hen as the permanent brew on tap

The Blue Bell inn is open from 11am to 11pm, every day.

170 STAG HOTEL

69 High Street, Lyndhurst, Hampshire SO43 7BE
Tel: 02380 282999
e-mail: info@stag-hotel.co.uk
website: www.stag-hotel.co.uk

Built in 1836, the **Stag Hotel** sits proudly in Lyndhurst high street - the heart of the New Forest, now a national park. Having recently been refurbished to a very high standard, the hotel offers 10 ensuite bedrooms, furnished with much needed necessities such as large comfortable beds, telephone, hair dryer, T.V. and tea and coffee making facilities. The stylish bar, with luxurious leather seating, offers a great place to catch up with friends. There is a wide selection of beverages to be sampled including fine wines, well kept real ale, draught and bottled larger, spirits and liquers and ofcourse plenty of soft drinks. Bar snacks are available at lunchtimes.

Italian restaurant, Il Cervo, provides guests and non residents with a mouth-watering menu, and a relaxed atmosphere in which to dine. Dishes include; Filetto Alla Griglia - grilled fillet steak served with chips, mushrooms & tomatoes, Pappardelle Funghi- pasta with wild mushrooms, shallots, garlic & herbs and Pollo Tarragon - chicken breast with a cream & tarragon sauce served with wild mushrooms & beans. There is also a wide selection of freshly made pizzas. In the summer months, diners can enjoy their meals outside under the marquee, and watch the sun go down. Large parties can be catered for, please ring for further details.

171 THE ANCHOR INN

Eling Lane, Totton, Southampton,
Hampshire SO40 9GD
Tel/Fax: 02380 428206
e-mail: mariedonohue@hotmail.co.uk

Since taking over **The Anchor Inn**, Marie Donoghue has given the old place a new lease of life, with a fresh family appeal. The setting is quiet and picturesque, with a nice view of the quayside and the river running close by. With the New Forest on one side and Southampton Water on the other, the Anchor attracts a wide and varied clientele. It provides a very pleasant break in a relaxing day out, and when the sun shines the beer garden – with an enclosed area where children can play – is a delightful spot for enjoying a drink and something to eat.

Inside, there's a spacious bar with some sofas and easy chairs, and a separate restaurant where the choice runs from snacks and jacket potatoes to a carvery that operates every day. It's a popular place with tourists, sailors and fishermen as well as the locals, and they all come here to enjoy a chat and a glass of Ringwood ale or Theakston's cider. The Anchor stands next to Eling Sailing Club and Eling Tide Mill, the only mill of its kind still producing flour on a regular basis. Next to the Mill is the Totton & Eling Heritage Centre telling the story of the area.

172 THE JOLLY SAILOR

Ashlett Creek, Fawley, Southampton, Hampshire SO45 1DT
Tel: 02380 891305
e-mail: jayr1200@aol.com

The **Jolly Sailor** is the social hub of the small community of Ashlett Creek, which lies off the B3053 east of Fawley overlooking busy Southampton Water. The proprietor and host is Jason Plank, who bought the pub in 2008, having been a regular customer for many years. After carrying out a major refurbishment programme at this one-time beer house, Jason re-opened the pub in April 2009 to the great delight of the locals and members of the neighbouring sailing club. A bar runs the length of the pub, with large sitting areas on either side, and there are plenty of benches outside for enjoying the sun and watching the comings and goings of vessels large and small.

It's a fine place to meet for a drink, with a wide choice of beers, wines, spirits and soft drinks, and fresh-air hungers are satisfied with a selection of classic pub dishes, from home-made soups, garlic mushrooms and whitebait to moules marinière, rump, sirloin, ribeye, fillet and gammon steaks and surf 'n' turf. Sandwiched between the refinery at Fawley and the power station at Calshot, Ashlett Creek is an oasis of calm, a conservation area with creeks, mud flats and marshland that's home to a variety of birdlife. A local attraction is Calshot Castle, restored as pre-WWI garrison.

173 LOUNGES OF LYMINGTON

122 High Street, Lymington, Hampshire SO41 9AQ
Tel: 01590 671122
e-mail: enquiries@loungesoflymington.co.uk
website: www.loungesoflymington.co.uk

Welcomes don't come friendlier than the one that awaits visitors to **Lounges of Lymington**, which since 2003 has been owned and run by Mark and Alison Chandler.

Mark, who has lived in Lymington for more than 25 years, knows many of his customers personally, and Alison has made just as many friends with her sweet and savoury delights. Everything is fresh and wholesome, from panini and baguettes with generous fillings like mozzarella with roasted peppers, soups, jacket potatoes, breakfasts and salads to the cakes and pastries and the delicious cream teas. The interior is roomy, comfortable and inviting, with oak beams and solid wood or flagged floors, and the ambience generated by Mark and Alison adds to the pleasure of a visit. To accompany the food there's a good choice of teas, coffees, cold drinks and milk shakes.

Lounges of Lymington is open from 9 to 5 Monday to Saturday and from 10 to 4 on Sunday. In addition to the inside area there is also an outside seating area in the courtyard for up to 20 people. Everything on the menu can be ordered to take away, and people in a hurry can call ahead with their order. Lounges also offers an outside catering service and a range of buffets to suit a variety of occasions.

174 THE RED LION, BOLDRE

Rope Hill, Boldre, nr Lymington, Hampshire SO41 8NE
Tel: 01590 673177
e-mail: alanpountney@aol.com
website: www.theredlionboldre.co.uk

Dating back to around the 15th century, **The Red Lion, Boldre** is a quintessential New Forest pub, an amalgamation of an old forest pub, two old cottages and a stables. With its log fires, cosy beamed rooms, well kept cask ales and most importantly a genuinely warm welcome, this is a classic forest pub not to be missed. Outside there are gardens and a heated patio where in warm weather you can eat at your own barbecue table, cooking on the central hotplate at your own pace.

The food here is outstanding. The Red Lion Chefs delight in creating traditional, homemade meals incorporating both local and seasonal produce at it's best. Associate members of the New Forest Marque for their use of New Forest produce, wherever possible they insist on buying from the New Forest area. From fresh, flavoursome ingredients come delicious dishes and here at the Red Lion they love good wholesome food. The butchers they use supply meat from Hampshire, Dorset and the renowned Sway Butchers created the Red Lion sausage especially for them, a traditional pork sausage with venison and wild boar, reflecting the flavours of the New Forest. Being so close to the sea fresh fish and seafood make regular appearances on the lively Chef's Specials board and fresh dressed Lymington Crabs are available daily in season. Traditional Sunday roasts always feature roast beef, with at least one other roast offered. Do look out for the pudding boards where a tempting selection of homemade puddings 'just like mother used to make' are always available. A popular event is the monthly 'Pie and Pudding' evening, a choice of homemade pies plus a homemade pudding for £10 per person. Booking is always advisable at the Red Lion.

175 THE POTTING SHED TEAROOM

Redcliffe Garden Centre, Bashley, Hampshire BH25 5RY
Tel: 01425 638926

Within the inspiring and contemporary Redcliffe Garden Centre (one of the finest in England - on the cutting edge of garden design), **The Potting Shed Tearoom** is a real delight. Owners Jayne and Chris Warman are possibly the hardest working and most dedicated proprietors to be found anywhere - keeping their cafe and tearoom open, along with the garden centre itself, all year round! So there is no excuse to not stop off and savour the many treats they have on offer. Situated in the heart of the Newforest, it has proven amazingly popular with locals and visitors alike, and there is always a warm friendly welcome awaiting every customer.

Within the peaceful environment, right in the heart of the garden centre, you can relax and enjoy some refreshments, while pondering your gardening or travel needs. Naturally everything is freshly made, by Chris and his enthusiastic team, and the fresh cake selection (a must for a truly authentic tearoom!) presents a magnificent, if very indulgent, sight. For something a touch more savoury there is a great range of daily specials, a fully comprehensive menu and wide selection of sandwiches.

176 THE TROUT INN

Itchen Abbas, Winchester,
Hampshire SO21 1BQ
Tel: 01962 779537 Fax: 01962 791046
e-mail: troutinn@hotmail.co.uk
website: www.thetroutitchenabbas.co.uk

The Trout Inn at Itchen Abbas has become one of the most talked about country inns in Hampshire. Situated in the picturesque valley of the River Itchen - an area popular for walking and fishing - it is winning an enviable reputation for the quality of its beer, good wines and excellent food. Landlords Max and Norma Iri have developed a successful rapport with the local regulars, and ensure the many visitors to the area receive a warm welcome and satisfying experience.

The Trout is a comfortably large inn with a fine dining restaurant, which can seat up to 40 people, yet still retaining an intimate traditional country pub atmosphere. Your food is prepared by the landlord and chef, Max who has a long experience in the catering industry, with a style regarded as classic with a twist. All dishes are prepared on site using only the best quality local products.

Aside from the restaurant and bar, the Trout has three comfortable rooms - two doubles and one twin with en-suite facilities and views across the valley. Ideal for business or pleasure, and only minutes away from Junction 9 of the M3 motorway, the Trout boasts ample parking, has an outside play area for children, and is at the heart of delightful walking country.

177 THE HURSTBOURNE INN

Hurstbourne Priors, nr Whitchurch,
Hampshire RG28 7SE
Tel: 01256 892000
e-mail: enquiries@thehurstbourne.com
website: www.thehurstbourne.com

This traditional English Inn has become very popular with ramblers, cyclists, anglers and regular visitors to this stunning area, right in the middle of the rolling Hampshire countryside. **The Hurstbourne Inn**, at feet of the Southern Downs, midway along the Test Valley, is perfectly located for visitors, and the excellent cuisine and homely rooms are always welcome after an exhausting day exploring!

As a traditional Inn should be, the locally sourced and freshly cooked-to-order cuisine is suitably hearty and filling; dishes such as *stuffed fillet of pork, dauphinoise potatoes, and an apple & cider jus* and *roast rump of lamb, rosemary polenta, and oyster mushrooms* are always popular. The specials board is also always filled with a seasonal, ever changing range of dishes to suit all tastes, created by the superb AA accredited chef and dedicated close-knit team. The Inn is open for morning coffee, light snacks, lunch and a la carte dinner.

There are three cosy large rooms available, which come with TV, hospitality tray and an affordable price, including a traditional English breakfast. They also all come with lovely views of the surrounding Hampshire countryside – a breathtaking sight to wake up to. The Inn's WiFi connection is available to those staying and patrons of the bar and restaurant.

179 THE OLD HOUSE AT HOME

Station Rd, Overton, Basingstoke, RG25 3DU
Tel: 01256 770335
e-mail: williams902@btinternet.com
website: www.theoldhouseathome.com

The Old House at Home, which has been very successfully run by proprietor Ian Williams, is a home-away-from-home for a huge variety of people; from locals, to walkers and cyclists, to visitors and families. Situated right at the heart of the village of Overton, in picturesque Basingstoke, it has all the atmosphere of a traditional English pub – including its classic exterior; red-brick and whitewashed walls, with strong black wooden beams.

The Inn serves a delicious range of home cooked food, freshly prepared on the property, and caters for adults and children. A particular favourite is the traditional Sunday roast; an impressive serving of roasted meat and all the trimmings. Lunch is served everyday through the week, and dinner is served on Tuesdays to Saturdays. In addition to the dining area, the pub has a great lounge/bar area with darts board and pool table, which is brilliant after dinner or lunch for some healthy competition with your friends or family. The bar is stocked with a large selection of wines and real ales; best enjoyed in the summer out in the large beer garden and decked area running around the pub's side.

178 WATERSHIP DOWN INN

Freefolk Priors, Freefolk, nr Whitchurch, Hampshire RG28 7NJ
Tel: 01256 892254
e-mail: watershipdowninn@live.co.uk
website: www.watershipdowninn.info

Built in 1840, the **Watership Down Inn** was previously called the Freefolk Arms but was renamed in honour of local author Richard Adams and his book *Watership Down*. Mr Adams recently received an award from Whitchurch Arts and celebrated by sampling the inn's famous rabbit pie which is available every day.

Owners Peter and Michelle Cozen arrived here in November 2009 and have preserved the inn's traditional character and have quickly established a reputation for serving excellent home-made food. At lunchtimes, they offer menus that include both traditional, home-cooked meals and light snacks - anything from a hearty rump steak to a ploughman's lunch. All the main dishes are available in smaller portions for children or those with lighter appetites. The bar offers a selection of 4 - 5 rotating real ales, lagers, fine wines and non-alcoholic drinks, as well as teas and fresh coffee. Food is available throughout the day and on Sundays, a full roast dinner is served complete with home-made Yorkshire pudding and real roast potatoes. Booking is strongly advised. Refreshments can be enjoyed in the conservatory or, in good weather, outside in the family-friendly beer garden. When it's cold outside, customers can keep warm by the real fire. While in summer everyone can enjoy the large garden with outdoor family seating area, children's play area, the two resident pigs, Minty and Cheery, and Gaspode the dog.

Peter and Michelle are accomplished crafts people and always have glass art, sculptures, jewellery and pictures for sale, all made by them. Each piece is unique in its own way, ideal for that special present. The inn is also a member of "Off The Wall" and will be showing local artists work very soon.

180 THE CLATFORD ARMS

Goodworth Clatford, nr Andover, Hampshire SP11 7RN
Tel: 01264 363298

The **Clatford Arms** is run by Tim and Jane Battey, who moved south to Hampshire in 2008 when they took over this, their first pub. This friendly Wadworth's pub, which lies off the A3057 a couple of miles south of Andover, is very much at the heart of the local community, a meeting place for enjoying a glass or two of beer and a game of pool or darts. There's usually a choice of three or four real ales, mainly from Wadsworth's. Jane is a talented interior designer, and her designer's eye is evident in the changes she has made to the décor. The Clatford Arms is gaining quite a reputation for its food, with local produce cooked to order with no compromise on quality and freshness. This is a traditional inn, so

its menu is also traditional, with favourites like ham, egg & chips and Friday's fish & chips, with sandwiches and salads for lighter options. Families are always welcome, and at the back of the pub is a two-acre garden with picnic benches, an eye-catching gazebo and a play area.

The bar is open Monday evening, lunchtime and evening Tuesday to Friday and all day Saturday and Sunday. Food is served lunchtime and evening Tuesday to Friday and 12 to 3 Saturday and Sunday.

181 HAWK CONSERVANCY TRUST

Sarson Lane, Weyhill, Andover, Hampshire SP11 8DY
Tel: 01264 773850
e-mail: info@hawkconservancy.org
website: www.hawkconservancy.org

The **Hawk Conservancy Trust** is well known for tis flying displays. There are three flying displays each day at 11:45am, 2:00pm and 3:30pm. Each display is different and is well worth a watch!

In our experience most visitors stay for between four and five hours. Many are surprised at how much there is to occupy their time at the Trust. Our activities start at 11.00am with our Wild Red Kite and Heron Feed, three displays at 11:45am, 2.00pm and 3.30pm, each in a different location and featuring a different team of birds, and the day

ends with our second Red Kite and Heron feed at 4.30pm, and often lots more in between.

Duffy's Coffee Shop is open all season and offers a range of hot and cold drinks, sandwiches and filled baguettes, snacks, and ice creams. Lunches are available, with homemade soup and a hot meal of the day. Don't forget to join us for a Sunday roast lunch throughout the winter!

The Reception/Trust Shop sells a wide variety of quality gifts and souvenirs, including hand engraved crystal from a local artist, and the world famous Swarovski binoculars, as well as Trust branded clothing. There is something to suit all budgets. We also stock films, batteries, and disposable cameras. The Trust shop stocks a wide range of gifts for Christmas and other occasions.

182 POTS AND PIECES TEASHOP & GALLERY

40 High Street, Ross-on-Wye, Herefordshire HR9 5HD
Tel: 01989 566123
e-mail: sara@potsandpieces.com
website: www.potsandpieces.com

Located on the High Street in the centre of Ross-on-Wye, just
behind the famous Market House, **Pots and Pieces Teashop and
Gallery** is a great place to enjoy quality refreshments and to
browse through a fascinating array of striking gifts. Awarded a 5-
star rating, the teashop sources as many as possible of the
ingredients it uses from Herefordshire. The popular cream teas, for
example, comprise home-made scones, Herefordshire clotted cream
and locally made jams. Savouries, cakes and tray bakes are either
made on the premises or come from the neighbouring Truffles
Delicatessen. You will find a good range of teas including Assam,
Darjeeling and Earl Grey. Freshly ground Italian coffee and
Honduras rain forest filter coffee are available as well as
'Babycinnos' for the very young, and there's a delicious creamy hot
chocolate for those who fancy a real treat.

    Pots and Pieces also boasts a gallery filled with all kinds of
beautiful, eye-catching gifts. There's some stunning jewellery (some locally made) on display,
beautiful glassware, silk scarves, ironwork, ceramics, including animals, vases and bowls as well as
picture frames, candle holders, lights and many other fascinating and unusual items within a
range of affordable prices.

183 MRS MUFFINS

1 Church Lane, Ledbury, Herefordshire HR8 1DL
Tel: 01531 633579
e-mail: leanne@mrsmuffins.co.uk
website: www.mrsmuffins.co.uk

Mrs Muffins is an Award Winning Teashop situated in the heart
of Ledbury - one of England's finest Market towns. Ideally sited
on the historic cobbled Church Lane, Mrs Muffins is set in a
beautiful 17th Century black and white oak beamed building, with a
pretty Courtyard garden ideal for al fresco dining.

    It is an ideal place to relax and sample the best the Region can
offer in traditional Teashop fayre. We specialise in using quality and
local produce to create scrumptious meals.

    We serve food all day, starting with our Herefordshire breakfast,
morning coffee and Lunches, through to Afternoon Tea and High Tea.
Our menu is complemented by a wide range of Teas, Coffees and a
range of local wines, Herefordshire cider and beer. Our homemade
cakes and clotted cream teas with homemade scones are a real treat
not to be missed. Children are most welcome and we offer special
meals for little people.

    You can find Mrs Muffins on the cobbled lane behind the black and
white Market House.

Open from 9.30am - 4.30pm Monday to Friday, 9.30am - 5pm
Saturday, and from 11am - 5pm Sunday (sometimes seasonal).

184 THE PRINCE OF WALES

Church Lane, Ledbury, Herefordshire HR8 1DL
Tel: 01531 632250
website: www.powledbury.com

In a quaint cobbled alley by the parish church, the
Prince of Wales, much of which dates from the 1570s,
is the very essence of an English tavern, with customers
treated like old friends. The Smith family have been
here for over seven years and they continue to enhance the
inn's reputation for hospitality; welcoming locals and visitors
into the warm, convivial surroundings. Behind the much-
photographed black-and-white exterior, made colourful in
spring and summer by baskets of flowers, the look in the
public rooms is charmingly traditional, with low beams, red-
tiled floors and lots of dark oak.

The Prince of Wales certainly knows its beers, and
connoisseurs will appreciate not just the variety on offer but
the information about each. Regular varieties include Hobsons
Bitter and Mild, Sharps Doom Bar from Rock in Cornwall and Wye Valley HPA. There's also a choice
of ciders. Russell also keeps a selection of a dozen or more imported bottled beers and lagers,
including Samichlaus, as strong as a full-bodied wine. Their expertise has been acknowledged as
they were the runner up in the *Herefordshire Camra Pub of the Year 2009*.

Lunchtime brings a choice of well-priced pub fare, including sandwiches, ploughman's platters,
homemade shortcrust pies, scampi, faggots, lasagne, chilli con carne and giant Yorkshire pudding
filled with roast beef. In the evenings traditional English Fayre is available from 18.00pm - 20.30pm.
Wednesday is folk music night at this splendid inn, with local and guest musicians getting together
to make music. The Prince of Wales is open from 11.00am - 23.00pm seven days days a week.

186 THE CROWN

Longtown, Herefordshire HR2 0LT
Tel: 01873 860217
e-mail: info@crowninnlongtown.co.uk
website: www.crowninnlongtown.co.uk

When Sheila and Phil Watkins took over the **Crown Inn** in Longtown in the summer of 2006, the inn had become somewhat run down. Sheila and Phil carried out a total refurbishment and today this fine old hostelry, which dates back to 1751, is once again the central meeting place of the village and a thriving business. Both Sheila and Phil were born and raised in the local area, in fact Phil has lived all his life only half a mile away from the pub. Married for over 25 years they have three children, Danny, Joe and Megan who help serve behind the bar and in the restaurant. The main bar has pleasant areas for sitting and a welcoming fire in the winter months. It stocks an

extensive range of traditional beers and local ciders. There's always two real ales on tap with Butty Back from the Wye Valley Brewery as the regular brew. The bar has a dartboard and quoits board while in the adjacent games room there's a pool table, traditional fruit machine and jukebox. From the games room there's access to the enclosed garden area with picnic tables.

Good food is a major priority here. A wide range of bar snacks and meals cater for all tests. The chef uses local produce and meats, vegetables from the pub's own garden, and produce supplied by the local community. The Walkers also have their own lambs. Customers can eat at one of the tables in the bar or dine in the restaurant. On Sundays there is a choice of traditional Sunday roasts as well as the regular menu. Food is served all day on both Saturday and Sunday, and during any of the opening times during the week. And if you want to eat or have a party of people outside opening hours, then just contact the inn. The Watkins specialise in, and are licensed to, do outside bars and catering for all your needs.

If you are planning to stay in this scenic area, the Crown offers bed & breakfast accommodation in three smartly furnished new bedrooms, all with en suite facilities and television. A further three bunkrooms are available accommodating up to 20 people, all with en suite bathroom and TV.

Set in the Olchon valley, just off Offa's Dyke Pathway and in the middle of the Golden Valley, the Crown is the ideal place to stay and explore both England and Wales whilst getting a true feel for typical village life.

185 THE BRIDGE INN

Kentchurch, Herefordshire HR2 0BY
Tel: 01981 240408
e-mail: bridgeinnkentchurch@hotmail.co.uk

Nick and Andi are the welcoming hosts at the **Bridge Inn**, which enjoys a picturesque setting in grounds running down to the River Monnow close to the Welsh border. It lies on the B4347 a mile or so off the main A465. Their hospitality and the excellent facilities have brought the inn to an ever-growing clientele since they took over here at the end of 2007. in the convivial bar a choice of four real ales is always on tap, with Otter Bitter and the locally brewed Hay Bluff the usual regulars, with two rotating guest ales.

Food is an important part of the Bridge's success, with local produce featuring strongly on the main menu and the two-course lunchtime menu. Typical choices run from garlic mushrooms and warm chorizo salad for starters to lasagne, scampi, honey and cider-baked ham, rump and sirloin steaks and super homemade pies : salmon, cod & prawn; chicken, bacon & mushroom; steak & Otter ale. Room should definitely be left for a delicious homemade dessert – perhaps lemon drizzle pudding or bread & butter pudding with ginger and orange. Food times are Monday and Tuesday evenings, lunch and dinner Wednesday to Saturday and lunchtime Sunday (also some Sunday evenings in peak season).

The Bridge has a small caravan and camping park – phone for details.

188 THE CARPENTERS ARMS

Walterstone, Herefordshire HR2 0DX
Tel: 01873 890353

Tucked away in the village of Walterstone, close to the church, **The Carpenters Arms** is the kind of traditional inn you always hope to come across but rarely do. It has been owned and run by the same family for 85 years. Vera Watkins, who was actually born at the inn, is in charge, assisted by her daughter Pauline and sons William and Alex. They create a genuinely friendly atmosphere, and the old oak beams and cosy fire in winter all add to the charm. Our cook Sharon, who has been here for more than 19 years, produces delicious home-style cooking. Her steaks are superb, and she also cooks a wonderful traditional Sunday roast (booking essential), and some scrumptious desserts. Food is served every day from noon until 3pm, and from 7pm to 9pm. The well-stocked bar offers a wide range of quality ales, lagers and wines, including two real ales - Wadsworth 6X and Golden Valley. In good weather, customers can enjoy their refreshments in the peaceful beer garden.

Despite being rather off the beaten track, the inn is well-placed for exploring the delights of the Brecon Beacons National Park and the hills of the Welsh border country.

187 ALLT YR YNYS COUNTRY HOUSE

Walterstone, nr Abergavenny, South Herefordshire HR2 0DU
Tel: 01873 890307 Fax: 01873 890579
e-mail: reception@allthotel.co.uk
website: www.allthotel.co.uk

Set in the foothills of the Black Mountains on the fringes of the magnificent Brecon Beacons, **Allt Yr Ynys Country House** has at its heart a beautifully preserved 16th century manor house. For many centuries, Allt Yr Ynys (pronounced alt-ur-inis) was the home of the Cecil family whose ancestry can be traced back to Rhodri Mawr, King of Wales in the 8th century. A more recent, and perhaps the most notable Cecil, was William, Lord Burghley, Secretary of State to Queen Elizabeth I for much of her reign.

The amenities at Allt Yr Ynys are really outstanding. After a day enjoying the many activities in the area, what better than a gentle swim in the indoor pool, a dip in the spa bath and a relaxing sauna. Then take your table in the award-winning restaurant where you can sample the very best of British cooking. The menu changes according to the season but amongst the starters you would typically find oak-smoked Scottish salmon or the hotel's very own vegetarian Glamorgan sausage. As a main course, how about pan-fried Welsh Black fillet steak, or Allt Yr Ynys's version of 'fish & chips' - beer-battered Cornish pollock fillet with chunky chips and 'Yorkshire caviar' (mushy peas!). Vegetarian's are well catered for with dishes such as roast beetroot and thyme risotto, or roasted vegetable and Shropshire blue crumble with an aged balsamic vinegar glaze. The desserts are very enticing with offerings such as Penderyn Welsh whisky crème brulee with sugar thins, a classic apple strudel with Cornish clotted cream or, if you prefer a savoury, the chef's selection of fine British cheeses.

The accommodation at Allt Yr Ynys comprises 20 beautifully appointed rooms, all with en suite facilities. Two of them are in the main building, the rest, all on the ground floor, are in imaginatively converted former farm buildings situated throughout the hotel's delightful 16 acres of grounds. Most have views over the rivers, mountains and woodlands surrounding the hotel, and one of them, an oak-panelled Jacobean suite, features an original 16th century 4-poster bed.

The hotel's setting and amenities make it ideal for a wide range of meetings and corporate events. Its conference and meeting facilities mirror the overall high standards of the hotel.

189 HAYNALL VILLA

Little Hereford, Ludlow, Shropshire SY8 4BA
Tel: 01584 711589
Fax: 01584 711589
e-mail: rachelmedwards@hotmail.com
website: www.haynallvilla.co.uk

In the heart of the tranquil Herefordshire and Shropshire countryside in Teme Valley is the **Haynall Villa**. This beautiful Georgian farmhouse is home to one of the area's finest bed and breakfasts, complete with large and spacious guest bedrooms which all have central heating, TVs and tea and coffee facilities. Guests can choose from a twin room, a double room, or a family room. Two of the rooms have en suite facilities, whilst the other has its own private bathroom.

Owner Rachel Edwards has been running the bed and breakfast for over 25 years, which means that not only do guests have unrivalled access their very own font of local knowledge, but they have a perfect breakfast each morning. Rachel is a trained cook and specialises in farmhouse cookery, winning many awards for her food. Breakfast is cooked using fresh local produce and homemade preserves. Dinner can also be arranged by request with fresh fruit and vegetables from the farm which is run by Rachel's husband David and son Michael.

Perfect for a weekend retreat, Haynall is just a short drive away from the historic town of Ludlow where the pretty architecture combines beautifully with wonderful rural landscapes.

191 THE CHOCOLATE BOX

36 High Street, Kington, Herefordshire HR5 3BJ
Tel: 01544 230737
e-mail: tina.lewis@talktalk.net
website: www.chocolateboxkington.co.uk

Located in the heart of the small market town of Kington, **The Chocolate Box** is every chocoholic's idea of heaven. The mouth-watering display offers some of the finest confectionery, including wonderful Belgian chocolates and loose sweets sold from jars. You can be sure of finding some of your most beloved childhood treats. The shop also sells a wide range of sugar-free sweets and chocolate. Customers have told owners Tina and Gary that the range here is better than at 'Boots' or 'Thorntons'.

Downstairs and upstairs are the tea room and bistro. The tea room serves freshly baked scones, cakes, breakfast, light lunches and afternoon teas, and there's also a daily specials board. A children's menu is available. All the ingredients are locally sourced wherever possible and freshly prepared. When the weather allows, customers can enjoy their refreshments in the pretty courtyard. The tea room is open from 9am to 5pm (2pm on Wednesday, and 4pm on Saturday).

Once a month - usually on the second Tuesday - The Chocolate Box hosts special themed evenings. The Best of British evening, for example, offered such indigenous favourites as steak & kidney pie and bread & butter pudding. Booking for these evenings is essential as space is limited.

190 LOWE FARM

Pembridge, nr Leominster, Herefordshire HR6 9JD
Tel: 01544 388395
e-mail: Juliet@lowe-farm.co.uk
website: www.lowe-farm.co.uk

Juliet and Clive Williams own and run **Lowe Farm**, a very special, stress-free rural retreat set in 200 acres of rolling countryside just outside Pembridge. The farm has been in the family since it was acquired by Clive's grandfather in 1939, and since 1998 they have been offering exceptional Bed & Breakfast accommodation throughout the year.

The Grade II listed farmhouse has five first-floor en suite bedrooms – a single, two twins and two doubles with TV, silent mini-fridge with fresh milk, bathrobes, toiletries and hairdryer. The stylishly appointed rooms provide an ideal base for tourists, walkers, cyclists and lovers the great outdoors. Guests have the use of a beautifully furnished lounge, a garden room and a lovely peaceful garden, and the hot tub is a marvellous place to unwind after walking or cycling.

The day starts with a superb breakfast (served from 8am to 10am) featuring fresh eggs from the farm's rescue hens and meat from local farms. The same top-quality produce is the basis of a terrific evening meal cooked by Juliet that guests can book with a day's notice (not Wednesday, Saturday or summer Mondays). Lowe Farm is recommended by all who stay here for its high standards of service and accommodation that caters for their individual needs.

The guest list is truly international, with many repeat visits, and the Farm has won numerous prestigious awards. These include the Gold Award for Best B&B at the Heart of England Excellence in Tourism Awards, a Green Business Tourism Award, National Finalist in the Enjoy England Excellence Awards, Visit Britain's Gold Award and a Breakfast Award at the Birmingham Oscars. With its farm machinery and unguarded pond, Lowe Farm is not really suitable for children or pets – but adults are guaranteed to have the time of their lives!

The recommended approach to Lowe Farm is from the A44: turn right at Marston (1.8 miles west of Pembridge) and follow the signs to the farm. Pembridge itself has many attractions for the visitor, including the 16th century Market Hall and the 14th century church with its magnificent timber belfry.

192 THE WATERING HOLE CAFÉ & MIDWAY CARAVAN AND CAMPING PARK

Hill Barn Bungalow, Aymestrey,
Herefordshire HR6 9SR
Tel: 01568 708236
website: www.midwayholidaypark.co.uk

Located in the heart of north Herefordshire's scenic Mortimer Country, **The Watering Hole Café & Midway Caravan and Camping Park** is very much a family business with Wendy and Mark and their son Garath all involved in the enterprise. The menu offers an extensive selection that includes burgers, snacks and main courses such as steak & kidney pudding, and breaded or battered cod and chips. Children have their own mini-menu of treats. On the first and third Sunday of each month there's a Carvery from 12.30pm until they run out. Meals are served in the conservatory and, in good weather, on the terrace looking out over peaceful countryside. The café is open from 8am to 8pm, (6pm out of season); payment is by cash only. The café also stocks some food items and camping necessities, along with a selection of gifts, some of them locally made.

The Camping & Caravan Park is open all year round and has space for up to 5 caravans and for numerous campers. There's hard and soft standing, electric hook-ups, showers and toilets (including a disabled toilet) all on site. Other amenities include a drive-by stand pipe for water, laundry facilities, and a pet's corner.

193 YE OLDE OAK INN

Wigmore, Herefordshire HR6 9UJ
Tel: 01568 770247

Ye Olde Oak Inn occupies a prominent corner site at the top of the village of Wigmore, just off the A411o Hereford to Leintwardine road. Visitors to this excellent 300-year-old free house can expect a friendly greeting from hosts Penny and Geoff, and savour the convivial surroundings of the cosy little bar, enjoy a chat and savour a glass or two of real ale from various micro breweries.

Penny is an accomplished cook and her home-made meat and fish pies are popular choices from a menu of classic pub dishes served in the country style conservatory restaurant. Sunday lunch brings a choice of roasts - it's guaranteed to bring in a good crowd, so booking is recommended to be sure of a table.

The inn is open lunchtime (noon until 2.30pm) and evening (6pm to 9pm), and all day Saturday with food available every session except Sunday evening. Children are welcome; dogs are welcome in the public bar, and there's a pleasant beer garden for fair-weather days. Please note that payment is by cash or cheque only.

194 THE WYNDHAM HOTEL

1 Church Road Marina, Douglas, Isle of Man IM1 2HQ
Tel: 01624 676913
e-mail: calvertronnie@manx.net
website: www.alphamanagementservices.co.uk

The **Wyndham Hotel** offers practical, comfortable accommodation just a few yards from the promenade and an easy walk from Douglas town centre. Owned and run by Ronnie and Tony Calvert (Ronnie is also a tax consultant), it has 17 bedrooms, six with en suite facilities, that are available for short or long stay letting at all times of the year. Dating from 1846, the hotel occupies one of a large number of terraced houses that were built at a time when the Isle of Man was becoming a popular place to reside or to visit. The tariff is on a Bed & Breakfast basis, but an evening meal is available with a little notice. There's a full on-licence for residents, and the hotel has plenty of off-road parking.

The Wyndham is a very pleasant and convenient base for a business visit or for discovering all that Douglas has to offer – a favourite introduction for the tourist is a leisurely ride along the promenade on the Douglas Bay Horse Tramway. It's also an ideal start point for a tour of the Island, which has a wealth of scenic, historic and sporting attractions to enjoy. Cash and cheque only.

196 THE WELBECK HOTEL

Mona Drive, off Central Promenade, Douglas,
Isle of Man IM2 4LF
Tel: 01624 675663 Fax: 01624 661545
e-mail: mail@welbeckhotel.com
website: www.welbeckhotel.com

Michael and Irene are at the head of the family who have owned and run **The Welbeck Hotel** for well over 30 years and the reputation for hospitality they have built over the years is second to none. Up the hill just off the main promenade, the location is fairly quiet but at the same time convenient for all that Douglas has to offer. The main accommodation comprises 27 en suite rooms, some with sea views, all with central heating, safe, fridge, digital TV, free Wi-Fi, direct dial telephone, iron, trouser press and hot beverage tray. The Welbeck also has seven excellent self-catering apartments - six one-bedroom, one with 2 bedrooms and all with bathroom, lounge/diner and partitioned kitchen area. Guests in these apartments have full use of the hotel's amenities.

In the conservatory Restaurant, open to residents and non-residents, the chefs prepare a fine selection of dishes of world-wide inspiration, all based on quality local ingredients. The hotel also boasts a wonderful bar where guests can relax and enjoy a refreshment or two. The owners and staff are ready with advice on all the island's places of interest and can arrange booking for golf and riding.

195 JAK'S BAR & STEAKHOUSE

43 Loch Promenade, Douglas,
Isle of Man IM1 2LZ
Tel: 01624 663786
Fax: 01624 677859
e-mail: darren@jakspub.com
website: www.jakspub.com

Jaks Bar & Steakhouse is one of the busiest pubs and restaurants on the Isle of Man and has just re-opened after extensive refurbishment. It is located right at the heart of Douglas night life and the friendly, relaxed atmosphere is popular with customers of all ages. Jaks was established in 1990 and still under the same owners

Jaks has an extensive, award-winning food menu at competitive prices. Customers can eat in the spacious bar area or can dine downstairs where there is a separate family restaurant with a private bar. At lunchtime 12 - 5pm the menu offers a good selection of old favourites such as a traditional roast, along with a range of other main meals, baguettes and Jak's jacket potatoes. In the evening, Jak's lives up to its name, adding an excellent choice of steaks and char-grilled selection to the menu. Food is served from 5pm to 10pm, Monday to Saturday, and all day on Sunday from 12noon to 10pm; booking is strongly advised. To accompany your meal, there's a well-chosen wine list featuring wines from around the world or, if you prefer beer, choose from one of the largest selections of draught beers on the island. The restaurant is also available for private parties and functions.

Jak's is very popular with sports fans and all live sports are shown on a number of TV screens, one of which, a 10ft Full HD Wide Screen, is the largest on the island! Jak's proudly boasts that they can show up to 7 different football matches at the same time! There are also three 20" LCD Screens providing live football results. Jak's is also Wi-Fi enabled free of charge for all customers and more high technology is evident in the MP3 Music System with the best of classic dance/R&B at weekends and classic music during the week with live bands every Friday and Saturday.

Jaks is open seven days a week: from 11am to midnight, Monday to Thursday; 11am to 1am, Friday and Saturday; and from 12 noon until midnight on Sunday. All major credit/debit cards and luncheon vouchers are accepted and the main bar has a cash machine. There is ample parking available on the main promenade and there are stops directly outside the door for bus and horse tram services, as well as a taxi rank.

197 CHAPTERS

14 Victoria Street, Douglas,
Isle of Man IM1 2LH
Tel: 01624 663662
e-mail: info@chaptersdouglas.com
website: www.chaptersdouglas.com

Located in the heart of Douglas, **Chapters** offers not just one but a choice of 3 dining experiences. The basement lounge is your retro retreat from everything and anything you want. Featuring a fully-equipped bar for after-dinner drinks (Chapters only have a restaurant licence) with a wide selection of hot and cold beverages, this is a place to relax and unwind. Or, you might fancy hooking up to the complimentary wi-fi while the staff take care of your every need.

On the ground floor is a Coffee Shop & Bistro, the island's newest all-day dining destination. The menu is designed for those with time to spare as much as for those where time is of the essence. Serving freshly-ground Segafredo coffees, a wide range of alcohol is also available to our diners and the coffee shop is open from early until late. Good food is what Chapters is all about, and there's nowhere better to enjoy the finest the island has to offer than in the first floor restaurant. Discreet, yet attentive, 5-star service, a menu featuring a wide selection of both contemporary and classical dishes with a twist, coupled with a comprehensive wine list is sure to have your taste-buds dancing.

199 MANX SEA QUEST

5 Ballaterson Crex, Peel, Isle of Man 1M5 1BL
Tel: 07624 450688 e-mail: info@manxseaquest.com
website: www.manxseaquest.com

Operating out of Peel Harbour, the **Manx Sea Quest** is a powerful pleasure craft manned by a highly experienced crew, all of whom possess all the relevant safety qualifications. A variety of sea-trips are available and they usually last for around an hour, taking in some truly breath-taking scenery that can only be appreciated from the sea. When the conditions are right, you will see a wide variety of marine life, including the island's famous basking sharks which are impressive in size but completely harmless. Peel itself is a particularly attractive location with an impressive cathedral, a spectacular castle, and a host of visitor attractions.

200 BALLAJORA ARTISTS

Cheu Grianagh, Ballajora Hill, Ramsey, Isle of Man IM7 1AZ
Tel: 01624 812006 Fax: 01624 813941
e-mail: daphne@iom.com
website: www.ballajoraartists.co.uk

Daphne MacOwan has a love for arts and crafts, and she has created an informal art gallery, **Ballajora Artists**, at her home in Ballajora. The gallery offers a beautiful range of different art and crafts, all created locally on the island. You will find original paintings, framed prints, greetings cards and notelets, and craftwork including miniature wooden jigsaw puzzles, coasters, mouse mats and much more. The gallery is open Wed - Sun between 2pm and 5pm, (although occasionally closed at weekends) and Daphne will happily open out of normal hours by request.

198 THE MARINE HOTEL

Peel Promenade, Peel IM5 1AH
Tel: 01624 842337
e-mail: themarinehotel@manx.net

The Marine Hotel, located on Peel Promenade, is now under the watchful eye of new Licensee Mick Hewer who took over in August 2009. This exceptional Freehouse has a long and outstanding reputation for serving fresh home cooked food using local Manx produce. Specialising in traditional favourites such as Roast dinners or Fish and Chips the Marine also offers an extensive day time menu suplemented by an ever changing specials board featuring delights such as home cooked pies and a variety of fresh locally caught fish. The food is of excellent quality and is prepared on the premises by friendly staff. Food is served daily from noon until 9.00pm in a spacious restraunt or, should you wish, in one of the two bars. The Marine has a warm comfortable atmosphere with TVs, a Juke box and excellent views over Peel Bay, Beach and Castle. The Marine is a Free House and Mick uses this freedom to ensure that the well stocked bars offer a range of localy brewed Manx beers for the 'Real Ale' lover.

201 THE ROADSIDE INN

Nettlestone Green, Seaview, Isle of Wight PO34 5DX
Tel: 01983 616969
e-mail: suzanne.mackay@hotmail.co.uk
website: www.kinglud.co.uk

The beautifully presented **Roadside Inn**, located on the Isle of Wight's dramatic coastline, provides a picturesque place to eat, relax and stay. Recently taken on by the owners of the King Lud in Ryde, where they have made a name for themselves for authentic and delicious food in a relaxed environment, encapsulating the flavour of the island; they have now brought their magic touch to the Roadside Inn. From the main bar and spacious dining area, or the more formal spacious dining room, the Inn serves a delightful variety of traditional cuisine, to suit all tastes. There is even room to cater for 60 people, should you be having a big event! When the sun is shining, a drink in the large beer garden is a must; for less favourable weather the Inn's games room with pool and darts, is bound to be popular with young and old alike.

The accommodation is just as delightful; the four light and spacious en-suit rooms, comfortably furnished, make you feel right at home. The perfect base from which to explore the island, the price also includes a hearty breakfast to set you up for the day.

202 THE FOUR SEASONS INN

2 Clarence Rd, Wroxall, Isle of Wight PO38 3BY
Tel: 01983 854701
e-mail: info@the-fourseasons-inn.co.uk
website: www.the-fourseasons-inn.co.uk

The secret of the **Four Seasons Inn**'s success is (other than the breathtakingly scenic backdrop), quite aptly, the fresh seasonal produce they use to create their many beautiful dishes. To the owners of this gorgeous white-washed traditional pub, who once worked on the QE2, there is no secret to quality and taste; and the food really speaks for itself! The fresh and vibrant menu, which adapts constantly with the seasons, attracts locals and visitors to the Inn's doors time after time.

Add to this their friendly, knowledgeable staff, along with the relaxed homely setting, and you have all the elements for a perfect visit; be it a family lunch sat out in the sun, a cosy romantic dinner for two, or a haven to warm and relax if the weather turns bitter. The food is all cooked to order, so they are only too happy to make any changes for taste and dietary requirements; children are also well catered for.

In addition to the lovely dinning area, with a la carte menu, is the large bar (very popular with the locals) which serves a traditional pub menu; a take-away service is also available. The spacious car park provides ample parking. Food is served 12noon-9pm daily.

203 THE WHITE HORSE

High Street, Whitwell,
Isle of Wight PO38 2PY
Tel: 01983 730375
website: www.whitehorsewhitwell.com

Where better to enjoy the sight and sounds of the Isle of Wight than from one of the island's oldest buildings? **The White Horse**, located in the heart of the pretty village of Whitwell, is a grand stone building, amazingly built around 1454; a real piece of the island's history. Today it is as renowned for its award-winning food, as it is for its age, and is very popular with locals and visitors alike. The chefs have been given the freedom to create an extensive menu, using the highest quality fresh produce available; the pride in the quality of the food is apparent, from the pub's atmosphere to the friendly, knowledgeable staff. The bar serves a great selection of larger, beer, wine and spirits, but the main attraction here is the quality and selection of real ales.

A recent extension has been added to the pub, creating an ideal space for functions, celebrations, and more formal dining. The large beer garden is beautiful on long summer days, preferably with a cool glass of ale in hand! And the generous car park means finding parking will never be a worry. The pub is also child and pet friendly.

204 HERMITAGE COUNTRY HOUSE

St Catherines Down, Whitwell, Ventor,
Isle of Wight PO38 2PD
Tel: 01983 730010
e-mail: enquiries@hermitage-iow.co.uk
website: www.hermitage-iow.co.uk

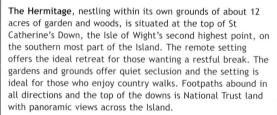

The Hermitage, nestling within its own grounds of about 12 acres of garden and woods, is situated at the top of St Catherine's Down, the Isle of Wight's second highest point, on the southern most part of the Island. The remote setting offers the ideal retreat for those wanting a restful break. The gardens and grounds offer quiet seclusion and the setting is ideal for those who enjoy country walks. Footpaths abound in all directions and the top of the downs is National Trust land with panoramic views across the Island.

A study on the first floor overlooking the gardens offers guests a selection of books and magazines as well as being an excellent vantage point to admire the flora and fauna.

All bedrooms are non-smoking, but ashtrays are provided on the patio. We regret we cannot accommodate children or pets.

Several public houses serving food are a short drive away and several island restaurants are highly recommended.

205 THE WHEATSHEAF

8 High Cross Road, Westwood, Southfleet, Gravesend, Kent DA13 9PH
Tel: 01474 833210
e-mail: morris679623@aol.com

The Wheatsheaf is owned by Chris Morris who is dedicated to serving home cooked food. The extensive menu has something to suit all tastes and appetites and there is a good choice of snacks too. The thatched building dates back to the 15th century and has plenty of character and charm about it. Inside, the ceilings are beamed and there is a traditional Tudor fireplace. The regulars of The Wheatsheaf are warm and welcoming and there is always a friendly atmosphere and good conversation to be had. Designated drivers are offered free soft drinks and there are good deals to be had on evening meals.

The bar is well-stocked with plenty of beers, ales, wines, spirits and soft drinks to choose from. On warmer days there is a large garden, where customers often like to enjoy a meal and refreshments. The Wheatsheaf is open between 12pm – 11.30pm Sunday – Wednesday and between 12pm and 12.30am Thursday – Saturday. Every second Wednesday from 7pm til late customers are entertained by a group of traditional morris men. Off-street parking is not a problem with a large car park for customers.

206 THE PLOUGH INN

Lewson Street, Norton, Sittingbourne, Kent ME9 9JJ
Tel: 01795 521348
e-mail: david.george@talktalk.net
website: www.theploughatlewsonst.com

If it's quality food, fine ale and good conversation you are after then **The Plough Inn** might be an ideal place to start. The doors to the pub are always open to those looking for a home cooked meal. Dating back to the 13th century the ale house can be found in the heart of the Kent countryside between the towns of Sittingbourne and Faversham.

The historic pub provides the ideal place for people wanting to relax in the afternoon or evening. Inside, the decor is traditional with original oak beams and an inglenook fireplace adding to its character. It is very cosy making it a perfect get-away on a winter's night and it is very comfortable, warm and welcoming. The main area of the pub was built as a cow byre around 1260 AD and it was later converted into a blacksmith's shop. The Plough Inn caters for families as well as to the older generation.

Traditional home cooked food is the main focus of the menu which has something for all appetites and diets. There is a bar snack menu as well as an a la carte menu, which has plenty of choice for vegetarians. Such is the popularity of the food served it is advisable to book for Friday, Saturday and Sunday. Starters include deep fried brie served with a warm cranberry dressing, breaded Japanese style prawns with a sweet & sour dip, and wild mushrooms cooked in garlic and tarragon. On the main menu diners are tempted with, among others, sirloin steak with homemade chips, grilled tomato, mushrooms, onion rings and a side salad, lamb rump on a bed of sweet potato crisps in a red wine and rosemary jus and pan-fried fillet of salmon with roasted vegetables and hasselback potatoes with a provencal sauce. Vegetarian options include wild mushroom and goats cheese risotto with parsnip crisps, and nut wellington.

Your landlord at The Plough Inn is David George and has more than 40 years of experience running a successful pub and inn. Children are welcomed and there is a large garden with a play area for younger guests. Live bands perform on Wednesday nights. This traditional village pub has it all - traditional home cooked food of the highest quality and a selection of ales and beers with many seasonal specials, including four real ales.

207 CHEQUERS AT LAMBERHURST

The Broadway, Lamberhurst, Kent TN3 8DB
Tel: 01892 890260
e-mail: nigelhilton@mac.com
website: www.thechequersinnlamberhurst.com

Lamberhusrt village is found in the regal and historic castle district of Kent, with many nearby castles including Scotney, Leeds, and Bedge Burry just a short drive away. Formerly known as the garden of England, this area of Kent is popular with young families as its wealth of green picnic and national trust areas make easy getaways from the busy London lifestyle, under an hour away. For the shopaholics amongst you, Lamberhurst is also only a short drive from the impressive Blue Water Mall, complete with a mind boggling array of shops, cafes, restaurants and play areas; a full family day out in itself.

Residing peacefully within Lamberhurst is the **Chequers at Lamberhurst**. Built in the early 12th century, the inn befits its historic surroundings well. Its warmth of character is maintained through its architecture, with large bright windows, exposed oak beams and brushed wooden floors all complimenting the olde worlde charm. Despite its age, the inn remains light and airy, the clever use of modern spotlights illuminating the cosy corners well.

Open from 11am to 11pm Monday to Saturday and from 12-5pm on Sundays, the inn sees a steady thoroughfare of visitors from the local area and from further afield, being comfortably halfway between London and Hastings. Popular with young families and couples undertaking summer bike rides in the area, the inn can always be relied on to provide respite and a cool drink to refresh. Three well kept real ales are always on offer on a rotational basis, accompanied by an extensive and thoughtfully chosen wine list. Other draught options include cider, Guinness and lagers, two of which are Dutch brews. In the summer months drinks are often taken in the inns sunny garden, with pretty views across the village.

For food, guests can choose from a full a la carte menu or the garden menu, comprising a range of lighter bites and bar snacks. All dishes are made using the very best in local produce, homemade on the premises each day from the inn's own tried and tested country cooking recipes. On Sundays a hearty roast is added to the menu with a choice of meats and trimmings.

208 THE DERING ARMS

Station Road, Pluckley, Kent TN27 0RR
Tel: 01233 840371
e-mail: jim@deringarms.com
website: www.deringarms.com

Dating back to the 1840s, **The Dering Arms** is a former hunting lodge, which is now a fantastic seafood restaurant. Located in Pluckley, it serves up the finest seafood dishes in Kent and has been awarded the Egon Ronay Seafood Restaurant of the year three times since 1997.

It is well known in the area for its high quality fresh food and friendly atmosphere and it is popular with locals and visitors. Ingredients are sourced locally and every dish is prepared to order. The restaurant seats approximately 25 people and can be altered to offer both intimate dining areas or to cater for a larger group or a party. Owner, James runs the kitchen himself in order to maintain the high standards customers have come to expect. The daily evening menu is predominantly fish due to James' love of seafood however there are other dishes available too. Everything is home-made on the premises, even down to the marmalade that is served at breakfast. Starters include provencale fish soup served with cheese, rouille and croutons; soft herring roes pan fried with crispy smoked bacon and served on a bed of shredded lettuce; and sardines grilled with rosemary butter. Main courses include tuna steak pan fried with garlic and lemon butter and confit

of duck served with bubble and squeak potato cake and wild mushroom sauce. There are additional choices on the daily specials board and a great value three course lunch is served Tuesday - Friday. The inn has two traditional bar area and has a fine selection of ale and cider from the local area, and some of the best vintage wines from around the world.

In addition to all the eating and drinking that goes on it also operates as a guest house. There are three tastefully decorated bedrooms available (two en-suite and one with a shared bathroom). The guest house is ideally located for those travelling down to the continent and can be found just ten minutes away from J9 of the M20. Rates include a tasty breakfast and with a tasty seafood restaurant on the premises, finding somewhere to eat in the evening isn't too much of a challenge.

The restaurant is open between 11am and 3.30pm and 6pm – 11pm every Tuesday – Saturday and between 12pm and 3.30pm on a Sunday.

209 THE GEORGE HOTEL

11 High Street, Lydd, Kent TN29 9AJ
Tel: 01797 321710
e-mail: info@thegeorgelydd.com
website: www.thegeorgelydd.com

Located in the heart of the beautiful country town of Lydd, **The George Hotel** has been host to many different activities since it was built in 1620. It has been used as a meeting point for famous smuggling gangs, as a place to keep prisoners before trial, as a staging post for London coaches and, of course as an inn and hotel.

Today, it continues its long history of offering hospitality with the additional benefit of a high quality restaurant "The Green Room" which serves a great English menu based on local fresh food and chef's specials from around the world. The wide and varied menu includes a well-thought out and interesting vegetarian choice. A popular amenity here is the Patio Deck with its comfortable "bistro type" chairs and furnishings, heaters, gazebos and parasols, an attraction to all customers no matter what the weather. Eating and drinking al fresco can happen on all but the coldest days in complete comfort: if the sun is to strong there is plenty of shade, or if rain threatens you do not have to run inside. The restaurant's full menu is offered on the deck area and waitress service is provided for both food and drinks at busy times, so that customers can relax and enjoy themselves without having to keep going into the bars. This area is also a great solution to the Government smoking ban, the gazebos having halogen heaters to keep customers comfortable. Inside, there's an open log fire for the colder days, and two bars with a good range of five real ales, lagers and a fine wine cellar. The modern sports bar is equipped with a pool table, fruit machines, dart boards and television. It also hosts live music and is available for parties and functions.

The hotel also offers comfortable accommodation in its nine English inn type character rooms.

Lydd lies in the southern part of Romney Marsh which is traversed by the Romney Hythe & Dymchurch Railway whose steam trains at one third scale were designed and built in 1923 are still running today. Why not try a weekend of water sports fun at Lydd's famous Action Water Sports centre? Or take up the hotel's Fly-&-Stay deals - eat & sleep at The George then fly to Le Touquet for the day with Lydd Air.

210 HOPE INN

144 Canterbury Road, Lydden, Dover,
Kent CT15 7ET
Tel: 01304 830392
e-mail: esmetham@googlemail.com
website: www.hopeinnlydden.co.uk

The Hope Inn is found nearby the Dover port to France on
the Kentish coastline in Lydden and is popular with overnight
visitors looking for a convenient place to stay or bite to eat en route.
The inn dates back in parts to the 1830s when it was believed to
have been built. Although the inn has naturally has undergone much
modernization, it retains its original charm, sporting exposed brick
fireplaces, original oak beams, and character black sash windows.

The inn's menu is entirely homemade and aims to use as much
fresh local produce within its dishes as possible. Guests will find all
their pub favourites on the menu from pies to roasts, salads and
sandwiches, and lighter bites. Those with special dietary requirements are also well catered for,
as are families and children who are welcome to dine at any time. Special old age pensioners'
lunches are offered throughout the week from Tues-Fri 12-3pm, with deals for all available on
weekends when two people can get two courses and a bottle of house wine for a special price.
Guests can choose from a wide selection of drinks including wine, real ales, lagers and spirits,
which can be enjoyed within, either before a fire in the winter or over the glorious views across
the countryside in the summer months. The inn also caters for weddings and other functions by
arrangement, please call for details.

211 THE BOAT YARD

Bolton Road, Riley Green, Preston,
Lancashire PR5 0SP
Tel: 01254 209841
e-mail: info@boatyardhoghton.co.uk
website: www.boatyardhoghton.co.uk

It is **The Boat Yards'** canal side location that makes it
that extra bit special. The quality establishment has
everything the local, visitor or businessman could need. The
food is exceptional and the high standard luxury
accommodation is ideal for those visiting the area. There are
six tastefully decorated en suite rooms (doubles and twins
available) and one has been adapted for disabled guests, with
its very own wet room and shower. All of the rooms have
contemporary furnishings and a private balcony overlooking the
picturesque canal. Full English breakfasts can be ordered.

Located close to the Lancashire towns of Blackburn and
Chorley, The Boat Yard offers a contemporary blend of bar,
restaurant, coffee shop and accommodation. It provides the ideal venue for a business meeting
being less than a minute drive from Junction 3 of the M65 and close to the M6 and M61. The onsite coffee shop, Braca, opens from 9am on Sat and Sun, offering delicious coffees and snacks. It
also has free Wi-Fi. The modern restaurant and bar area has a wide selection of lite bites and
main meals all carefully prepared and cooked by head chef. Smaller portions are available for
younger guests. There is plenty of free parking.

212 THE WHITE LION

117 Mossy Lea Road, Wrightington, Wigan, Lancashire WN6 9RE
Tel: 01257 425977
e-mail: mattandelliefurzeman@hotmail.co.uk
website: www.thewhitelionlancs.co.uk

The White Lion Inn has an interesting history dating back to the early 20th century when it was owned and run by a local couple, and then the famous 'Owd Bob' whose real name was Robert Mawdesley. He proudly ran the inn with his wife for over 45 years as an alehouse, and the inn is still known affectionately to some as 'Owd Bob's.' The inn has since been taken over by Matt and Ellie Furzeman who keep the inn's more recent additions running smoothly, including the popular restaurant.

The restaurant is manned by four professional chefs, who ensure that the menu is kept fresh and exciting, without excluding all the old favourites. Breakfast is served from 10am-12pm, with main meals available from 12-9pm. Guests are never short of choice here with a fabulous selection that includes puff pastry steak and ale pie, braised lamb shank, mushroom stroganoff, vegetable tortellini, goat's cheese, olive and sun-dried tomato salad, and a spicy chilli. Guests can also choose from a hearty selection of grills such as lamb rump steak, and pork and black pudding stack. Fish dishes include tuna nicoise, traditional fish pie, fish cakes and a spicy Cajun salmon stir fry. Amazingly, that's not all that's on offer; an early bird menu offers a tasty choice of specialty dishes alongside a range of lighter bites, Sunday roasts and children's choices. Owing to popularity it's best to book Fridays and weekends.

Matt and Ellie also offer up a great range of drinks, and pride themselves on offering up to eight real ales at any one time, often including Banks Bitter and Jennings Cumberland Ale. Drinks can be enjoyed within the pub's atmospheric bar or on sunnier days can be taken in the inns spacious beer garden. The friendly family environment is complimented by the refreshing range of events that are on at the inn throughout the year including scavenger hunts, beer festivals, pancake day, themed food nights for St Patrick's and St George's Day and special deals like a free cocktail for all dining mums on Mothering Sunday. Whether local or visiting the area, the White Lion really has it all. All major credit cards accepted, apart from American Express and Diners.

213 BRANDRETH BARN

Tarlscough Lane, Burscough, nr Ormskirk, Lancashire L40 0RJ
Tel: 01704 893510
e-mail: enquiries@brandreth-barn.co.uk
website: www.brandreth-barn.co.uk

Located just a few miles from Burscough near the town of Ormskirk in Lancashire is **Brandreth Barn**. This charming family run bed and breakfast is rurally situated in the midst of a working arable farm. Located just minutes from the Wildfowl Trust, Martin Mere and a host of championship golf courses, Brandreth is ideally placed to offer guests easy access to a range of great activities.

Margaret and William Wilson have been opening their home to the public since 1990 and have many repeat visitors. Their bed and breakfast offers just eight en suite rooms all of which are centrally heated and have flat screen TV, refreshment trays and wifi access. Rooms come in a range of sizes from twins to doubles, with the ground floor rooms being adapted with disabled guests in mind. All rooms come on a bed and breakfast tariff, apart from the Christmas and New Year period, when rooms come on a room only basis. Rooms here not only offer guests a handy base for exploring this pretty area of Lancashire, but a tranquil setting in which to relax and re-charge their batteries. All rooms have glorious views of the surrounding countryside and pretty red brick farmhouse buildings.

Guests here can also benefit from the farms own tea rooms, which are popular with both locals and visitors to the area alike. Open all year round Tuesday - Sunday. The tea rooms offer a fantastic selection of light bites and specialty teas and coffees throughout the day from mid-morning until around 5pm.

Margaret does all the cooking at the tea rooms and prides herself on using only the best local produce in her dishes, some of which is grown on her own farm, and some of which comes from neighbouring farms which are run by Margaret's extended family. Guests can choose from a wide selection of freshly made filled sandwiches, salads and jacket potatoes, or one of the speciality Welsh rarebits. A good selection of other dishes is also on offer on the daily specials board where homemade soup of the day is often a feature. A delicious range of homemade cakes and scones are also available including a traditional farmhouse cream tea, ladled with local cream and jam. Also why not consider the tearoom for your intimate daytime family celebrations? The tearoom can cater for up to 50 people, please ring for further details.

The tea rooms are also home to a range of locally made arts and crafts made which can be purchased or simply admired in the ambience of this fine traditional English tea room.

214 THE DOG INN

King Street, Whalley, nr Clitheroe, Lancashire BB7 9SP
Tel: 01254 823009
e-mail: attydoghouse@tesco.net

The Dog Inn has been run by Rev Canon Norman Atty and his wife Christine for the past 18 years. It is a sturdy corner-site building of local stone, with tall, white painted chimneys and white painted door and window surrounds. The couple have built up a large and loyal following with their special brand of hospitality, the genuine smile, the ales and the wholesome lunchtime food.

There is always a fine array of real ales to enjoy and up to six to sample. They rotate regularly, but there's always one brew available from the local Moorhouses Brewery. The pub has a warm and inviting ambience and excellent food is available every lunch time between 12pm – 2.30pm. No evening meals, unless pre-arranged – ring for details. Such is the popularity of Sunday lunch at The Dog Inn, it is advisable to book. The chef, Manuel, freshly prepares and cooks food using the finest of ingredients, sourced locally (whenever possible) and cooked to order. The extensive menu is very traditional offering a wide selection of starters and old favourites including homemade steak & kidney (made with Guinness and served with a Yorkshire pudding); Cumberland Sausage (made locally to a traditional Lakeland recipe, served with a fried egg); and grilled gammon (served with a choice of egg, pineapple, or both). Famous for its omelettes, there is also a range of lite bites on offer for those with a lighter appetite. There is a good range of filled jacket potatoes, sandwiches, tortilla wraps, and salads as well as a Ploughman's lunch. A selection of tempting desserts can be ordered at the bar from the daily specials board. In addition to the main menu, there is also a specials board where diners can choose from additional dishes changed on a daily basis. Vegetarians are well catered for and the licensees will do their best to cater for those with any special dietary requirements.

The child (and dog) friendly inn is open every session and longer hours at the discretion of the licensees. Disabled access is not a problem and there is ample space to park. Major credit cards taken. Whalley is well worth taking time to explore, with a 14th century abbey, the ancient parish church of St Mary and the famous 48-arched Whalley viaduct, built in 1850 to carry the Blackburn to Clitheroe railway line across the broad valley of the River Calder.

215 CORNER CAFE

582 Burnley Road, Crawshawbooth, Rossendale, Lancashire BB4 8AJ
Tel: 01706 217721

Owned by business partners Jane Morgan and Julie Ferenczi the **Corner Cafe** is a quality establishment to dine out at in the Rossendale Valley. Jane and Julie have owned the cafe since June 2008 with Jane taking care of front of house and Julie looking after the kitchen.

Julie's cooking is very much homemade. The food portions are generous and there is a wide range of options on the varied menu. All of the dishes are cooked fresh to order and a lot of the produce is sourced locally. The All Day Breakfast menu is extremely popular with visitors and there are plenty of returning customers. The breakfast menu is extensive offering everything from your traditional Full English breakfast to scrambled or poached egg, and a range of filled sandwiches.

Whether it is a good lunch, snack or drink you are after, this delightful little cafe offers it all. There is a good selection of filled sandwiches, jacket potatoes, toasted sandwiches and salads to choose from and most of these are also offered as a takeaway. Homemade soup is another popular option as is homemade shepherd's pie. In addition to the standard menu diners are also offered a different 'hot special' every day. Homemade cakes are extremely popular at The Corner Cafe. There is always a delicious choice of homemade cakes, scones, cookies and muffins, which are made fresh on a daily basis.

The cafe is child friendly and smaller portions can be ordered for younger diners. The Corner Cafe is open seven days a week and seats 22 diners. The cafe is open Monday 8am – 3pm, Tuesday 8am – 1.30pm, Wednesday – Friday 8am – 3pm, Saturday 9am – 3pm and Sunday 10am - 2pm. The cafe offers food to eat in or takeaway and is licensed for diners. Telephone orders are welcome.

Situated in the beautiful hamlet of Crawshawbooth the Corner Cafe can be found just a short drive out of the marker town of Rawtenstall, Lancashire, north along the A682 towards Burnley. The hamlet is surrounded by farm and moor land and the area is extremely popular with walkers, many who like to stop for a rest at the corner cafe, where hospitality and homemade food is the order of the day. Cash only. Disabled access is not a problem.

216 THE BUCK INN

9 Aston Buildings, Cowpe Road, Cowpe, Rossendale, Lancashire BB4 7DS
Tel: 01706 213612
website: www.thebuck-inn.com

Tucked away in the tiny hamlet of Cowpe, **The Buck Inn** is growing in quality since Nick and Michelle took over the running of the establishment in October 2009. They have put an awful lot of effort into the inn and are still working to get it just how they would like it. The couple want to make it the home for mountain bikers and walkers, where they can enjoy quality hospitality, food and drink. It was formerly a row of cottages and the building dates back to the early 19th century.

At the moment food is available Tuesday – Thursday between 6pm and 9pm and on the weekend between 12pm and 9pm. On a Sunday there is a limited menu as roast dinners become an additional option to diners. Home cooking is the order of the day at The Buck Inn and steaks and gammon are firm favourites with customers. The menu may not be too extensive at present, but Nick and Michelle have big plans for The Buck Inn and are looking to introduce a wide selection of hearty dishes and additional tasty favourites to the specials board. The kitchen has just undergone a major refurbishment and this will pave the way for a good range of quality dishes.

To the rear of the inn there is a decked area and beer garden, allowing customers to dine outside and enjoy refreshments on warmer days. Well known for the beautiful scenery surrounding the village, Cowpe is home to some of the best farms in the area as well as a Christmas tree farm. The local council is pumping a large amount of money into the area and it's hoped there will soon be new mountain bike trails in the area as well as walkways. Situated in the borough of Rossendale, which has the River Irwell flowing through it, there are plenty of small former mill towns in easy reaching distance of the village.

The inn holds a quiz on a Thursday from 8.30pm and everyone is welcome to get involved. Disabled access is not a problem. The inn can be found by turning into Cowpe Road, from the centre of Waterfoot off the A681. It leads motorists along a windy road and the inn is located on the right with a car park.

217 FISHERMAN'S RETREAT

Riding Head Lane, Shuttleworth, Ramsbottom,
Lancashire BL0 0HH
Tel: 01706 825314 e-mail: info@fishermansretreat.com
website: www.fishermansretreat.com

Nestled in beautiful countryside on the edge of the Pennines, **The Fisherman's Retreat** is in an idyllic location just outside the town of Ramsbottom. This hidden gem is found within 80 acres and has been family owned and run since the early 1990s. The Fisherman's Retreat is a very popular restaurant serving a wide variety of freshly prepared, home-reared and quality local produce, which includes some of the finest dry aged steak from its own herd of prize winning Charolais cattle. There is a fantastic range of over 500 single malt Scottish whiskies and a Whisky Shop on site. Try a dram or take home a bottle!

There are also award winning real ales and lagers on tap and a new world wine list to rival any fine dining restaurant.

Situated on the site of an old mill, The Fisherman's Retreat was built by Hervey and his family, who run their own farm alongside the restaurant, rearing beef, pork, venison and trout, which all feature on the menu.

The Fisherman's Retreat is closed on Mondays (excluding Bank Holidays), but is open from 12pm - late every other day. Food is available from 12pm-9pm every day and from 12pm-9.30pm on Saturdays. The establishment does not take bookings, except for the Sucking Pig feast which is available for parties of 10 or more.

219 THE SWAN AT KIBWORTH

High Street, Kibworth Beauchamp,
Leicestershire LE8 0LR
Tel: 01162 796540

Mark Lloyd, Head Chef at **The Swan in Kibworth** Beauchamp, has an enviable reputation. Former Head Chef at Hugh Fearnley-Whittingstall's "River Cottage", he has a passion for fresh, locally produced ingredients. The lunch menu offers a range of bar snacks, open sandwiches, devilled kidneys on toast, pie of the day, pigeon & hedgerow salad & slow- cooked wild rabbit to name a few.

Wednesday is their legendary "steak night" which starts from as little as 2 steaks for 12.00 up to pre-ordered chateaubriand. Thursday hosts "Fish night" including beer-battered fish with chips & homemade mushy peas, seared scallops & "Poxon's" black pudding, grilled Cornish sardines, posh fish pie & Hebridean mussels with the menu changing weekly.

Lunch on Sunday can be a traditional affair with a full roast or a simple light lunch. Kids roasts are free!

The central courtyard is heated at night and, in Summer, the canopy is retracted and is a great sun trap for barbecues. The pub itself is bright, airy and utterly unpretentious. This is not a "fine dining" restaurant but a wonderful example of a proper village pub and when it comes to quality of food & drink, a true benchmark.

218 THE SHIP INN

23 Lancaster Road, Caton, Lancaster LA2 9QJ
Tel: 01524 770265
e-mail: mark.marrifield@btconnect.com
website: www.theshipinn-caton.co.uk

This well run and popular establishment is the ideal place to visit for those who appreciate good food and drink. Mark Merrifield has been at **The Ship Inn** for 12 years and took over the ownership of the establishment two years ago. Established in 1610 the premise has become well known throughout the county for its selection of fine beverages, home cooked food created using the finest local produce and its friendly atmosphere.

The menu has a strong focus on local produce and a lot of the dishes are homemade, with pies, steaks, haddock and gammon among the favourites. The dishes are all reasonably priced and starters include soup of the day; smoked salmon and prawns; and chicken liver pate. The main courses are fairly traditional with choices including homemade steak, ale & mushroom pie; homemade beef lasagne; and homemade stroganoff. There is a specially designed menu for younger guests as well as a specials board full of tempting desserts. For those with a lighter appetite there is a delicious range of filled sandwiches, ciabattas and salads. Vegetarians are well catered for and there is a choice of side dishes that diners can have with their meals. Following a good hearty meal customers can enjoy a tea, coffee or other hot beverage at their leisure. Of course there is also a good selection of spirits, wines, lagers and soft drinks. Food is served Monday – Friday between 12pm - 2pm and 5pm – 9pm, Saturday 12pm – 9pm and Sunday 12pm – 9pm along with a special Sunday breakfast service between 8am and 10am. There is a choice of three real ales to enjoy including Thwaites Cask Original, Thwaites Wainwrights and rotating guest ale from the Thwaites Brewery.

With a large open fire for those chilly winter months and a traditional beer garden for those long summer evenings, The Ship Inn is a popular choice among locals and visitors to the area. The inn, which is one of the longest established Lancaster pubs, is open every session and all day on Saturday, Sundays and Bank Holidays. It is located a short drive from Lancaster on the A683 towards Kirkby Lonsdale. If its crisp ales, traditional beers, home cooked food and a warm and welcoming atmosphere you are after then The Ship Inn is a must. Ring for details about accommodation availability.

220 THE OLD BARN INN

Andrews Lane, Glooston,
Leicestershire LE16 7ST
Tel: 01858 545215
e-mail: mail@oldbarninn.co.uk
website: www.oldbarninn.co.uk

Dating back 500 years, **The Old Barn Inn** was a thriving coaching inn situated on the busy country route heading into the Leicestershire uplands and Rutland and is now a popular village pub and restaurant. Glooston is a charming little village in the heart of rural Leicestershire, yet only five miles from Kibworth and seven from Market Harborough. Retaining much of its old charm, the building has been well maintained through the years and inside is no different; exposed beams and a magnificent old bar enhance the ambience.

Three lovely en suite bedrooms form the accommodation and a comfortable night's sleep is guaranteed, the Foxton room is a triple bed room that also can be used as a family room. The reasonable rates include a full English breakfast in the mornings, cooked in the excellent kitchens.

A thriving restaurant, the Old Barn Inn has an extensive menu that follows the seasons; utilising the fine suppliers in the area to produce fresh, delicious meals such as liver & bacon, and scallops with black pudding. Surrounded by rolling countryside, the Old Barn Inn is the perfect place to escape the hustle and bustle of everyday life.

221 THE WINDMILL INN AND BRASCOTE RESTAURANT

Brascote, Newbold Verdon, Leicestershire LE9 9LE
Tel: 01455 824433
e-mail: chris@thewindmillinn.net
website: www.thewindmillinn.net

Ivy clad and recently refurbished, **The Windmill Inn and Brascote Restaurant** manages to retain its rustic charm with original features such as cobbled floors and exposed beams. Chris and janet are warm and friendly hosts who will strive to ensure your visit is a memorable one. Having become a freehouse in 1992, the the inn boasts a superb collection of cask conditioned real ales, including a few from the local Battlefield Brewery. Charmingly named after the combatants of the nearby Battle of Bosworth, for example Henry Tudor, a dark ale and Richard Plantagenet, a pale ale brewed to 4.9%. It is because of the inn's great name in the ale world that CAMRA has recognised it.

Using locally sourced produce and fresh ingredients, the chefs have created an extensive menu that caters for everyone.

222 THE ODD HOUSE COUNTRY INN

Bosworth Road, Snarestone, Leicestershire DE12 7DQ
Tel: 01530 270223
e-mail: theoddhouse@btconnect.co.uk
website: www.theoddhouse.co.uk

High quality freshly prepared food is what **The Odd House Country Inn** prides itself on. The family owned free house and restaurant is situated at the heart of the national forest and is mid-way between Ashby-De-La-Zouch and Coalville. Originally a 17th century coaching Inn, the building has retained several character features with timber beams and an open fire in the lounge bar enhances the warm and friendly atmosphere. The bar stocks a selection of real ales, lagers, wines, spirits and soft drinks. All dishes are reasonably priced and bar meals are served seven nights a week plus Saturday and Sunday lunch times. The ever changing dishes on the restaurant menu are made with the finest locally sourced ingredients and special themed nights are sometimes held. Outside, there is a large garden with a children's play area and plenty of outside seating for those who want to dine in the sunshine. There are seven bedrooms

available (double and single rooms) and all have en-suite facilities. Breakfasts can be arranged at an extra cost. For those who prefer the outdoors, camping pitches are available and there is a function room suitable for small meetings and private parties.

223 THE MARQUIS OF GRANBY

High Street, Waltham on the Wolds,
Leicestershire LE14 4AH
Tel: 01664 464212

A lovely 17th century building with bay windows and a warm and welcoming exterior, **The Marquis of Granby** has a great deal of charm and character that enhances any visit. Situated on the route of several popular walks in the area, the pub is a great place to pause and replenish your energy stores, with a wide and varied menu.

The spectacular home cooked food is complemented by the well stocked bar; four real ales including a guest ale as well as a great selection of fine wines. Just five miles north of Melton Mowbray, the pub is the ideal place to dine for any occasion.

www.findSOMEWHERE.co.uk
For people who want to explore the United Kingdom

Specialist Shops

224 THE WISHING WELL INN

Main Street, Dyke, nr Bourne, Lincolnshire PE10 0AF
Tel: 01778 422970 Fax: 01778 394508
e-mail: wishingwellinn@hotmail.com
website: www.kellytaverns.co.uk

Just a few miles North of Bourne off the A15 is the Wishing Well Inn. It has been privately owned for the past ten years, with experienced licensee Paul Woodcock at the helm for the last six. Paul opens every session and all day on Fridays, Saturdays and Sundays, with food served daily from 12-2pm and 5:30-9pm Monday to Thursday, and 12-9pm the rest of the time. Unusually there are two dining rooms at the wishing well, although guests are welcomed to dine in the bar or in the garden on warmer days. The menu focuses on serving high class English cuisine with dishes like braised lamb shank, roasted duck, and beef medallions in a creamy peppercorn sauce, not to mention fish dishes like sea bass, or yellow fin sole fillets stuffed with smoke haddock and spinach. Sunday lunchtime is roast time, children and families welcome.

The inn serves up a good selection of drinks, with wines, spirits, lagers and at least three real ales at any one time.

Paul also offers a choice of twelve guest bedrooms for those who want to take a little longer to explore Dyke. All rooms have great facilities, nine having en suite bathrooms. Those who prefer the outdoors can take advantage of the inns caravan/camping area complete with electric hook ups, running water and toilet disposals; open all year round.

225 THE JOLLY BREWER

Foundry Road, Stamford,
Lincolnshire PE9 2PP
Tel: 01780 755141
e-mail: thejollybrewer@aol.com
website: www.jollybrewer.com

Dean and Jill are the welcoming hosts at the Jolly Brewer, a substantial town pub dating back to the early 18th century. Its lively and inviting atmosphere is created not only by its hosts, but its warm red walls, blazing fireplace and traditional wood panelled bar. Open all day every day there are five real ales to enjoy from across the country, rotating every 2/3 days.

Food is available from 12-3pm seven days a week and from 6-9pm Fridays and Saturday nights. Dean and Jill employ a professional chef to help them, who has created an enticing across the board menu from light bites and sandwiches to more substantial mains. Popular dishes include the 10oz rib eye steak, piri piri chicken, the fish platter comprising filo pastry prawns, scampi, whitebait and squid with chips, and carbonara pasta served with garlic toast. On Sundays the menu reverts to a succulent roast dinner, when booking is heavily recommended. All dishes are cooked fresh to order and are created using local produce from local suppliers.

Guests are welcomed to enjoy a game of pool or take a turn on the old pushpenny board, though many are contented with a glass of ale and the good old art of conversation.

227 THE BLUE COW INN

High Street, South Witham, Lincolnshire NG33 5QB
Tel: 01572 768432
e-mail: enquiries@bluecowinn.co.uk
website: www.bluecowinn.co.uk

Dating back to the late 13th century, the Blue Cow Inn began life as a small cottage. Since then the inn has seen various other additions, from extra bedrooms, to full blown conversions into a functioning post office. The inn later took on the name of the Royal Oak inn before changing hands to the Duke of Buckminster who decided that all his properties including pubs, farms and other outlets should have blue gates and affixed with the word 'blue' to signify his political allegiance. Today the inn retains its blue gates and its blue name; ever proud of its heritage.

Owner Simon Crathorn opens the inn for business 365 days a year for food ale and accommodation. Through maintaining the inn's olde world décor, Simon has created a traditional feel to the place that is brought to life by his and his staff's light hearted and friendly attitude. The team are always more than happy to relay one of the inn's many ghost stories to interested children who are welcome throughout.

The inn has brewed its own real ales for over ten years and is proud to serve Blue Cow Best Bitter; well respected by CAMRA. A good selection of wines, lagers and spirits are also available to make the perfect accompaniment to your meal.

Guests can enjoy a full a la carte menu at the inn from 6-9:30pm Tuesday to Saturday sampling a range of gourmet food such as smoked haddock and leek fishcakes, fillet of pork with mash, savoy cabbage and a rich mustard gravy, and succulent strips of beef served in a sweet chilli and tomato sauce with egg noodles. A bar menu operates each day from 12-9:30pm serving a wide range of more traditional pub food with a selection of filled sandwiches, baps and basket meals alongside a wide range of classic main meals. Popular dishes include home cooked gammon, egg and chips, 8oz sirloin steak, steak and mushroom pie, tender lamb shank in a mint gravy, lasagne, or Mediterranean vegetable risotto. On Sundays a carvery is served from 12-2:30pm, reverting to the main menu from 6-9:30pm. Booking is recommended on weekends.

Guests looking to stay at the Blue Cow can choose from six comfortable en suite bedrooms in a variety of sizes and tariffs, but each guest will receive a freshly cooked breakfast each morning to start their day. All major credit cards taken except American Express.

226 WHITE LION

High Street, Colsterworth, Grantham,
Lincolnshire NG33 5NE
Tel: 01476 861466
e-mail: info@whitelioncolsterworth.co.uk
website: www.whitelioncolsterworth.co.uk

Dave and Madeleine Smith's down to earth attitude
combined with their desire to deliver top quality food and
drink to their customers ensures that their pub, **White Lion**,
is fast becoming a destination inn. Open all day every day,
they serve up a minimum of three real ales which have
achieved a casque marque grading for their quality,
alongside a good selection of wines, lagers and spirits. In
the kitchen department, Dave and Madeleine are assisted by
Head Chef Gary who serves up fine English cuisine from 12-
9pm seven days a week.

Gary ensures that all the ingredients used to create the
food here are locally sourced or sourced from within the surrounding counties. A bar and
restaurant menu operates throughout the day offering a wide range of main meals, light bites and
snacks from homemade soup of the day, cheesy nachos and a range of filled sandwiches,
baguettes, jacket potatoes and salads and more substantial meals including steaks, guinea fowl,
stuffed pork fillet, king prawn linguine and lamb with a roasted garlic and rosemary sauce, or why
not try the renowned homemade steak, ale and mushroom pie. During the summer months, why
not enjoy your meal outside in the beer garden. Thursdays at 8.30pm is quiz night with cash
prizes.Children are welcome at all times, major credit cards accepted.

229 THE COFFEE POT

19 High Street, Ruskington,
Sleaford, Lincolnshire NG34 9DY
Tel: 01526 833013

The Coffee Pot is situated on the high street in Ruskington,
luring customers in with the wonderfully tempting aroma of
home baking that wafts through its doors. Owner Carol Tokley
and her dedicated team of staff have been running the Coffee
Pot for the past nine years opening from 9am-3:30pm Monday
to Friday and from 9am-12:30pm on Saturdays.

The team moved from across the road three years ago into
the current premises, which has allowed the team to offer
the customers better facilities, whilst retaining the old
fashioned charm of the business. There is now room for
twenty guests indoors, with a further eight seats outdoors
with ramped access for disabled customers.

Ninety percent of the dishes here are homemade and are
created with as much locally sourced produce as possible. The
menu may be small in size, but offers plenty of choice from salads, filled sandwiches, rolls and
jacket potatoes to homemade soup of the day and good old beans on toast. A daily special main
dish is always served with dishes like chilli con carne or chicken and leek pasta bake as popular
choices. For those who are just stopping by for a cup of tea and a slice of cake, there is also
plenty of choice with everything from cream teas, chocolate sponge cakes or coffee and walnut
cake to lemon drizzle and carrot cake. Children welcome, cash and cheque only please.

228 THE RED LION

62 High Street, Caythorpe, nr Grantham, Lincolnshire NG32 3DN
Tel: 01400 272632
e-mail: john@redlioncaythorpe.org.uk
website: www.redlioncaythorpe.org.uk

The Red Lion stands on the main street in Caythorpe, just off the A607. Over the years it has developed a fine reputation both locally and further afield for not only serving fine food and drink, but for offering one of the warmest welcomes the area has known. Its owner John Cork has been running the inn for over four years now, using his experience in the Everards brewery to his advantage. He knows the trade and his customers well, and has enjoyed providing them with the classic qualities of the quintessential English pub since his arrival. The inn itself dates back from the 1650s and retains many original features including open log fireplaces and beamed ceilings, which have been sympathetically updated with first class facilities and comfortable furnishings. Guests can relax in the main bar filled with squashy arm chairs, one of the two main dining rooms, elegantly laid for a refined dinner, or the recently added patio area, a welcome haven for casual dining in the sunnier weather.

Regardless of where you dine though, you will not be disappointed. Food is served from Monday to Saturday 12-2pm, Sundays 12-3pm, Mondays to Thursdays 6-9pm and Fridays and Saturdays 6-9:30pm. Guests can choose from the lunch menu, the grill menu, the full a la carte menu in the evenings, or try something off the ever-changing specials board. Each menu is bursting with locally sourced ingredients with dishes cooked fresh to order each day by head Chef Mark. The lunch menu samples a range of light bites from pressed ham hock terrine, mussels in garlic, white wine and cream, or sun blush tomatoes, goats cheese and olive brushettas, whilst main meals include

Rumpole steak and ale pudding, crayfish and lemon risotto, confit of belly pork, and a selection of dressed ciabattas, omelettes, jackets and salads. The a la carte menu offers a range of tempting creations from slowly braised lamb shank, stilton stuffed fillet steak and oven baked red snapper fillet with tomato fondue and fresh egg fettuccini. Described as restaurant food in a warm pub atmosphere, it's not surprising that booking is recommended, especially at weekends. Each Tuesday night guests come in droves to sample the steak and wine night where two prime steaks are available at a reduced price together with your choice of house wine.

The bar is always well stocked to offer the perfect accompaniment to your meal, with a John's personally selected wine list, a range of top quality spirits and a fine selection of traditional real ales. Open every session apart from Sunday evenings, all major credit cards accepted, children welcome.

230 THE BLACK SWAN GUEST HOUSE

21 High Street, Marton, nr Gainsborough, Lincolnshire DN21 5AH
Tel: 01427 718878
e-mail: info@blackswanguesthouse.co.uk
website: www.blackswanguesthouse.co.uk

A former coaching inn, **The Black Swan Guest House**, dates back to the 18th century. The beautiful Grade II listed building and the converted stable block adjacent to it, offer nine en-suite bed and breakfast rooms, which differ in size. John and Judy Patrick and their son Graham are welcoming hosts and the guest house is well known for the breakfasts they rustle up. Top quality produce is used and the family has had plenty of comments full of praise in its visitor's book.

The main house and cottage provide very comfortable guest accommodation that attracts business travellers and tourists from near and far. All of the rooms have en-suite facilities as well as TV, tea and coffee tray, and wireless broadband is available. Top of the range is the spacious premier room with a four-poster bed and sofa. Guests have the use of a comfortable lounge where they can enjoy a drink, and the house has plenty of safe off-road parking. It is said that the existing cellar in the house is where Oliver Cromwell rested during the Battle of Gainsborough in 1643. The guest house can be found in the main street of Marton, five miles south of Gainsborough.

231 THE NAGS HEAD

Gainsborough Road, Middle Rasen, Market Rasen, Lincolnshire LN8 3JU
Tel: 01673 843163

Having realised its true potential, Heather Appleyard took it upon herself to give **The Nags Head** a complete refurbishment. She has painstakingly updated both the décor and facilities to offer her clients a light hearted and welcoming community pub.

Heather has had over three years experience in the trade, but has never had the opportunity to run her own place before and has taken like a fish to water. Opening all day every day, she offers her guests a wide variety of wines, lagers and spirits, including a cask ale with many more to follow. Food is served daily each lunchtime and evening from an across the board menu that offers a range of tasty meals at excellent value for money. All dishes are prepared fresh on the

premises daily, cooked to order by a professional chef. Where possible as much locally sourced produce is used in order to support the local community.

Heather also offers a good selection on entertainment, from quizzes, charity nights, bike nights, discos and karaoke and much more; but guests are also welcomed just to sit back and relax either before a roaring fire in winter, or in the pleasant beer garden in the summer months where a children's play area is currently being installed. All major credit cards accepted.

232 THE BULL INN

Caistor Road, South Kelsey,
North Lincolnshire LN7 6PR
Tel: 01652 678417

In the heart of the Lincolnshire countryside in the idyllic
village of South Kelsey lies **The Bull Inn**. This olde worlde
premises dates back to 1794 and holds a list of licensees that
can be traced to the 1840's. Current owners Ken and Judy
Campbell have been running the inn for over seven years now,
establishing an excellent rapport with their customers who come
from both near and far to sample the award winning ales and fine
food available.

The inn has gained the prestigious cask marque award for the
quality of the ales they keep and always have two real ales on
offer; Bombardier and Black Sheep. Food is available each day
from 12-2pm on Sundays, and from 6-9pm Tuesday to Saturday
however booking is recommended at all times. The reason for the
popularity here is the sheer quality of the food; home cooked
fresh to order each day by Judy. Her menu is simple and traditional, offering guests tried and tested
home recipes that are guaranteed to please. Popular dishes include fresh salmon with hollandaise
sauce, gammon and egg, and large fresh Grimsby Haddock. All dishes come with a choice of five
different sides, including the succulent selection of prime beef steaks from the grill. Guests love the
menu so much that Ken and Judy have only changed the menu four times since their arrival. The inn
also occasionally offers themed food evenings and has a room available to hire for small parties,
please ring for details. Children welcome, all credit cards except American Express and Diners.

233 MY FATHERS MOUSTACHE

North Holme Road, Louth, Lincolnshire LN11 0HQ
Tel: 01507 607796

The rather unusually named pub and restaurant **My Fathers
Moustache** is found conveniently in the centre of Louth and is
now a popular venue for families, couples, locals and visitors
to Louth who come to enjoy the great entertainment and
fantastic food.

The premises had previously been run as a grain store and
a private club before becoming a public house in the 1980's
and hasn't looked back since. Jos and Sue Joslin are the
current landlords offering up a selection of real ales all day
every day. The pair are best known however for their
entertainment. Throughout the week a selection of events are
held at the inn with Bingo on Tuesdays from 7pm and Jazz
nights every other Sunday from 1:30-3:30pm; a Weight
Watchers meeting is even held on Thursdays from 6:30pm for
those days when you're over indulgent in the restaurant!

Food is available from Monday to Saturday 12-2:30pm and 5-8pm and on Sundays from 12-6pm
when the daily carvery is served all day long. Other popular dishes include the homemade steak
and ale pie, homemade lasagne and the daily fish specials. Vegetarians also have plenty of choice
with a selection of omelettes, pasta bakes and vegetable curries and chillies. Children are
welcome and they can dine from their own separate menu. All dishes are created using locally
sourced produce and locally reared meat for that authentic Lincolnshire taste. Jos and Sue also
offer a 150 seater function room for hire, please call for details.

234 THE CASTLE INN

50 High Street, Coningsby, Lincolnshire LN4 4RF
Tel: 01526 342336

The Castle Inn is found on the main high street in Coningsby; well known for its RAF depot. The inn has been run by the charming Cooper family for the past three years, made up of Sam and Darren and Darren's mum Kath. The family have built up a steady following from both their local community and from those further afield who rave about the food and the lively atmosphere.

In the summer months the inn serves food from 4-9pm from Thursday to Saturday, with a hearty Sunday lunch also served between 12-2:30pm all year round. Kath heads up the kitchen here offering everyone a handsome range of wholesome homemade pub food, ranging from pies and homemade soups, to sausage and mash and homemade battered fish and chips. In the summer months a popular steak night packs out the inn when booking is recommended.

Sam and Darren keep the bar side of things busy with two real ales and a full selection of draught keg ales, lagers, wine and soft drinks served throughout the day. On weekends they put on a show with karaoke sessions from 8:30pm on Saturdays and live music from local bands; please call for details. Cash only please.

235 POPPY'S RESTAURANT

Burgh Road, Skegness,
Lincolnshire PE24 4UF
Tel: 01754 898111

Carol and Helen have been running **Poppy's Restaurant** since 1998, building up a timeless reputation for serving delicious home cooked food in a family orientated environment. Open daily from 9am until 3-4pm in January and February, and until 7:30-8pm in the height of the summer, the restaurant offers a pleasant environment bedecked with an array of pine furniture, booths and warm colours.

Just two minutes from Skegness, the restaurant is popular with families, locals and tourers who can make use of the free parking. The licensed bar offers a wide range of wines, spirits, draught beers and bottled lagers, whilst a good range of soft drinks are also available. The highlight of any visit here however is the food. Breakfasts and snacks are served throughout the day from omelettes, buttered toast to full farmer's breakfasts, jacket potatoes and filled Paninis and baguettes. Main dishes includes burgers, battered haddock and chips, fresh salmon fillets, Ploughman's, hot roasted chicken salad, rump steak, steak and ale pie, liver and onions, pork steak with apples and apricots, sausages and Yorkshire puddings and lamb shank. If you fancy something a little different, a good selection of speciality curries, Chinese, Italian and Mexican dishes are also available. Children and vegetarians also have plenty of choice, as do those with special dietary requirements who have their own special menu. Sunday lunches are exceedingly popular at Poppy's too as the ladies offer four different meats all day long. All major credit cards taken, please call to book a table – though all food is also available as a takeaway.

236 THE BLACK BULL

3 Wrawby Street, Brigg,
North Lincolnshire DN20 8JH
Tel: 01652 652153
e-mail: theblackbullbrigg@hotmail.com

The Black Bull can be found on the main high street in Brigg just a short walk from the town's popular market square. It has been run by Tony and Carolyn for the past thirty years with the help of their family. Their daughter Amber and her husband Richard have been helping to run the place for the last two years with Richard taking up the helm as the chef in the kitchen.

The family serves food from 11:30am -2pm Mondays and Tuesdays, from 11:30am-7pm Wednesdays to Saturdays and from 12-7pm on Sundays when booking is recommended. The menu is based on using great locally sourced produce to create traditional and tasty food. Children and families are welcome to dine at all times, finding the Bull a particularly popular family haunt on Sundays when a hearty roast is added to the menu.

The inn is also popular with those just coming for a drink with three real ales on offer. Guests can choose from John Smith's Cask, and a couple of brews from the nearby Bateman's brewery. Although many guests choose to take their drinks or dinner in one of the many comfortable seating areas within, the inn's rear courtyard is also a popular choice; when blooming hanging baskets please the eye in the summer time. All major credit cards taken.

237 THE BLACK HORSE INN

Melton Road, Wrawby, nr Brigg,
North Lincolnshire DN20 8SL
Tel: 01652 652382

The running of The Black Horse Inn was taken over by Simon Raby in February 2010. Having been in the trade for almost five years he has big plans for this place, to give it a fresh and stylish feel. All of the dishes served are made with local produce and the professional chef has created a tasty menu of dishes. Roast dinners are available on Sunday. Two real ales are among the wide selection of alcoholic and non alcoholic beverages available from the well stocked bar. There is a delightful beer garden and quiz nights are held every Thursday from 9.30pm.

www.findSOMEWHERE.co.uk
For people who want to explore the United Kingdom

Places to Stay

238 THE KINGS HEAD

18 Victoria Road, Keelby, North East
Lincolnshire, DN41 8EH
Tel: 01469 560224
website: www.keelbykings.co.uk

Located in the picturesque village of Keelby, **The Kings Head** is a quality establishment run by Gloria and Peter Berry. The Berry's have been here for more than two years and give a warm welcome to locals and visitors alike. The Brocklesby Hunt (the oldest hunt in the country) meets at the pub, which is open all day every day. One real ale is available along with a wide selection of other refreshments from the well stocked bar. Old fashioned style basket meals are available between 6pm and 11pm Monday – Friday and 12 - 6pm on Saturday. After a complete refurbishment in October 2010 meals will be available all day between Wednesday and Sunday. Gloria does all of the cooking at The Kings Head and her meals are delicious. Basket meals will be available following the refurbishment as well as a choice of new dishes

from a full printed menu. There is one upstairs guest room available, which has a double bed, but no en-suite. It is available all year around a part from the Christmas and Easter periods. There is a good sized outside patio area and plenty of off road parking.

239 THE WEST END

43 Long Lane, Feltwell, Thetford,
Norfolk IP26 4BJ
Tel: 01842 827711

Just 10 miles west of Thetford in Norfolk, lies the pretty village of Feltwell, a thriving community that boasts a great place to stop and eat or just sit awhile and enjoy a pint. **The West End** is situated on the edge of the village and is run by Paula and her family, who have been here for the last two years. The attractive building appears well kept and welcoming, an impression that is enhanced on entering, the interior is bright and airy with a warm and lively ambience.

Well known for its superb food, the West End serves food between 12 and 2pm and 6 to 9pm Monday to Saturday and between 12 and 3pm on Sundays. The extensive menu features classic pub favourites cooked using locally sourced fresh ingredients and the chefs are keen to cater for any dietary requirements. Scrumptious examples of the fine menu include minted lamb shank and a mushroom, brie and cranberry Wellington. Assisting the kitchen is the well stocked bar, both real ales; Greene King IPA and a rotating guest ale, are cask conditioned to perfection by this cask marquee graded bar.

240 COLVESTON MANOR

Mundford, nr Thetford,
Norfolk IP26 5HU
Tel: 01842878218
e-mail: mail@colveston-manor.co.uk
website: www.colveston-manor.co.uk

Colveston Manor sits at the heart of the farm, a charming Georgian house that boasts its own extensive grounds and gardens where guests can get away from the hustle and bustle of everyday life.So quiet and peaceful. Colveston itself used to be a hamlet part of Lord Amhursts Didlington Estate that is mentioned in the Domesday book, nowadays though it is the hub of an arable and livestock farm in the heart of Breckland.

Inside the handsome chalk and redbrick manor are four spacious rooms, which provide warm and comfortable accommodation for up to seven guests. All the rooms have been individually furnished to a very high standard and manage to marry modern comfort with antique style. There is also an antique furnished lounge and dining room for the sole use of guests; log fires warm the cockles in the winter whilst during the summer an outside seating area provides an excellent spot to enjoy warm summer evenings and possibly a barbeque with exceptional bird and wildlife all around.

Edwin and Wendy are very proud of their reputation in the kitchen, all the meals are freshly prepared on the Aga and cooked using home grown or at least locally grown produce.

242 SAFFRON TEA ROOMS

Alby Crafts & Gardens, Cromer Road, Eppingham, Norwich, Norfolk NR11 7QE
Tel: 01236 768719
e-mail: saffrontearooms@yahoo.co.uk
website: www.albycrafts.co.uk

The Saffron Tea Rooms can be found located within the popular Alby Crafts and Gardens. Run by Emma Wright this delightful Tea Room has plenty of homemade lite bites and cakes to offer using locally sourced ingredients. Filled sandwiches and jacket potatoes are ideal for those wanting a light lunch and there are also breakfasts, salads, quiches and soups waiting to be sampled. Sunday lunch is popular and it is always best to book for parties of more than six. Local produce, preserves and ice-creams are also available to buy.

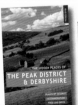

241 THE CROWN INN

Harleston Road, Pulham Market, Norfolk IP21 4TA
Tel: 01397 676652
website: www.thepulhamcrown.co.uk

Located at the heart of the quiet village of Pulham Market, **The Crown Inn** is surrounded by countryside. The village has plenty of thatched cottages and the pub is in a beautiful position opposite the village green. Dating back to 1610, it is a typical country inn with a lot of olde worlde charm. Approaching the building from the outside it is an attractive and inviting establishment and the inside does not disappoint. Landlord, Stephen Girdler has run The Crown Inn for nearly three years and has added to the good reputation of the place. Renowned for its hospitality and the quality of its ale as well as the fine food served, The Crown Inn is highly recommended to those visiting the area. The Crown Inn is popular with locals and it attracts plenty of walkers, holiday makers and day trippers.

Three real ales are available normally consisting of Woodfordes Wherry, Abbot Ale and a rotating guest ale. All of the food is freshly prepared and cooked by head chef Jerry Copeman. It is served seven days a week between 12pm-3pm and 6pm-9pm and it is best to book to avoid disappointment. The dishes are all reasonably priced with starters including game terrine with plum and apple chutney; crispy leek, pecan and stilton filo parcel; and moules marinieres. A lot of the food is sourced locally and there is a good selection of main dishes as well as plenty of traditional meals listed on the bar menu. Favourites from the bar menu include pork and apple burger and relish served with chunky chips and salad; and swordfish served with wilted spinach chorizo and peppers with new potatoes. Dishes on the main menu include oven baked trout with tarragon hollandaise sauce; pan fried lamb's liver with crispy bacon and caramelised onions; and blackened chicken with roasted fennel,

cherry tomatoes, black olives and olive oil. International food themed evenings are held on Monday nights and there are usually nine differing dishes to choose from. For more information visit the website. Although closed between 3pm and 5pm on Monday and Tuesdays the pub is otherwise open every session. The Crown Inn has set a really high standard for pubs in the area and it is the high quality service and idyllic location that makes it so popular.

Disabled access is not a problem. Credit cards except American Express and Diners are taken.

243 NEW INN AND SEREMBAN RESTAURANT

Norwich Road, Roughton, Norwich, Norfolk NR11 8SJ
Tel: 01263 761389
e-mail: newinnroughton@aol.com
website: www.thenewinnroughton.com

Located in the countryside village of Roughton the **New Inn and Seremban Restaurant** really does have something for everyone. Whether it is a simple drink, snack or three course meal you are looking for, owners Sean and Tina, with their son Ingo, welcome you whole heartedly.

The extensive and imaginative oriental and English menus have a lot to offer and all of the dishes are freshly prepared and cooked to order. On the oriental (Malaysian and Chinese) menu the mouth-watering dishes offered are everything you would expect from a good quality oriental restaurant and choices include shredded char sui chow mein and malaka style chicken with mango.

Alternatively if it is good British cooking you are after then the British menu is sure to have something to suit your taste. Steaks, burgers, chicken and fish dishes are all available as well as some traditional homemade pies. There is separate lunch and evening menus, set or a la carte. If it is more of a bar meal or snack you are after The New Inn has a fine selection of filled baguettes, jacket potatoes, omelettes, salads and burgers that can be consumed in the bar area and there is a delightful beer garden for people to enjoy on sunnier days, with a small play area where younger guests will be aptly occupied.

Just three miles from the seaside town of Cromer the restaurant and inn are located in the ideal location for visitors to the area. The small village of Roughton, steeped in history, is a few miles inland on the main road to Norwich and has a church with a 1000 year old tower. In September 1933 Albert Einstein famously stopped off in a hut on Roughton Heath en route to America, while fleeing Nazi persecution.

The New Inn is an impressive building and well presented. Outside, the entrance is extremely inviting, with plenty of floral pots and hanging baskets and the interior of the building is clean and tastefully decorated throughout. Built in 1878 the impressive establishment retains original features, including fireplaces and is traditionally furnished throughout, giving it a wonderful and warm atmosphere. One event that is definitely not to be missed is the annual beer festival, held at the end of March, this event grows in stature every year!

The premise is open Monday to Friday between 12-3pm and 5pm-12am. On Saturdays and Sundays opening hours are between 12pm-12am. Reservations on Friday and Saturday evenings are recommended to avoid disappointment. Traditional roast dinners are served and there is also an extensive choice on the daily specials board.

244 THE HILL HOUSE INN

The Hill, Happisburgh, Norfolk NR12 OPW
Tel: 01692 650004
e-mail: clive.stockton@hillhouseinn.plus.com

The Hill House Inn has a past stepped in history, originally comprising three Tudor cottages circa 1540. At some point in the 17th century they were knocked through to form its first days as an alehouse. It became a coaching house in the early 18th century as the main point between Kings Lynn and Great Yarmouth, and gained some notoriety being frequented by beach men and smugglers. Later renamed the Hill House to regain some decorum, the inn then became the haunt of novelist Sir Arthur Conan-Doyle whose silhouette now graces the front of the menu. Other famous guests include Henry Moore and Barbara Hepworth, however today the inn offers a warm welcome to all, children and dogs included.

The inn is run by Clive and Sue Stockton and their son Sam, who pride themselves on operating a cheerful and quality establishment, complete with its own bar and restaurant. The bars unique atmosphere is kept alive by its original features and wood burning stove for the colder months. Known for serving a fine selection of well kept ales, there are usually up to six on offer at any one time, with

over 100 beers and ciders available during the annual June beer festival, held over 5 days at the inn.

The inn also serves up a delicious array of culinary treats for lunch and dinner, with a menu that comprises everything from sandwiches and snacks through to hearty homemade mains. Guests can choose from burgers, to Thai curries, pub favourites like lasagne and bangers and mash, rump steak, salmon and prawn tagliatelle, chicken and leek suet pudding or a range of vegetarian dishes to include stroganoff and nut roast. Whether dining in the restaurant or the more intimate garden bar, you are sure to find something you like. Food served from 12-2:30pm and 7-9:30pm Monday to Saturday and 12-2:30pm and 7-9pm on Sundays.

The family also provide a small selection of luxury guest accommodation that comes on a bed and breakfast tariff. Rooms vary from doubles decorated in sumptuous silks, to family rooms and economy rooms for convenience stays. One room is fully converted for disabled customers. Camping is also available during the beer festival, please call for details.

245 BURE RIVER COTTAGE RESTAURANT

27 Lower Street, Horning, Norfolk NR12 8AA
Tel: 01692 631421

Located centrally in the picturesque village of Horning is the
Bure River Cottage. Truly atmospheric, the restaurant was
lovingly created by its proprietors Abbie and Nigel to cater for
the needs of the areas food lovers. It is a seafood restaurant
through and through, serving up the best fresh fish from the
nearby fishing ports in Norfolk and Suffolk.

Popular with locals and visitors alike, the restaurant has
struck up an impressive following who rave about not only the
quality of the food, but the service. The chilled out vibe and
contemporary design of the restaurant mixes well with the
friendly and efficient service received at all times.

Abbie has been a professional chef for over 15 years, and her
experience really shows. Her innovative cooking style is based
on using only fresh local produce and the menu changes daily to
reflect this. A typical menu includes a variety of seafood from
slices of oak smoked salmon, to pan fried tiger prawns in garlic
butter and chargrilled fresh scallops with chilli and ginger. Other
favourites include fresh line caught tuna steak, whole grilled Dover sole and Morston mussels
steamed in wine, shallots and garlic. A twenty strong wine list ensures the perfect accompaniment
to your meal, though other soft and alcoholic beverages are available. All major credit cards
accepted. Booking necessary at all times. Open Tuesday - Saturday evenings only.

246 THE KINGS HEAD

Main Road, Filby, Great Yarmouth, NR29 3HY
Tel: 01493 730992
e-mail: kingshead@gmx.com

Just a short drive North West of Great Yarmouth is the Kings
Head in Filby. Run by Laura and Chris for the past two years,
the inn has a traditional feel with a fine brick fireplace and
wood burning stove to offer all its guests the warmest of
welcomes. With up to three ales on offer at any one time,
the inn is a popular watering hole. Chris takes great pride in
running the kitchen here, serving food from 12-3pm and 6-
9pm Tuesday to Saturday, and from 12-4pm on Sundays.
Guests can make their selection from the daily specials
board, or from the main menu which encompasses a range
of light bites, generous mains and tempting desserts.
Popular mains include roast pork and beef, creamy
tagliatelle pasta, vegetarian goulash and steak and ale pie.
Throughout the week a range of special food evenings are
run, with steak night on Tuesdays, Fishy Friday, and a two or

three course meal for a special price on Sundays from 12-4pm, owing to its popularity, booking is
recommended.

The inn welcomes children and dogs at all times, and also allows camper vans to stay in the car
park. All credit cards accepted apart from Diners.

247 THE LORD NELSON

38 Riverside Road, Reedham, Norwich, Norfolk NR13 3TE
Tel: 01493 701548
website: www.lordnelsonpub.com

The magnificent **Lord Nelson** inn sits in an unrivalled location on the banks of the River Yare in Reedham. The village itself has one of the only two ferry and railway swing bridges in the country and sees a steady thoroughfare in the summer months from tourists and boaters who come to enjoy the eclectic mix of tranquil summer views and vibrant village life on offer.

The Lord Nelson is at the heart of that village life, having been brought back to life by its current owners Bill and Ros who took over in April 2008. The pair re-opened the inn in May that year after an extensive refurbishment. They have maintained the inn's old worlde alehouse feel, offering anything between 6 and 10 real ales at any one time. The regular brews include Green King IPA and the village brew Humpty Dumpty Ale, whilst others rotate.

Food is available at the inn each day from 12-2:30pm and 6:30-9pm, courtesy of Ros who acts as chef. She serves up a large and varied selection of filled sandwiches and jackets, salads, burgers, meat and fish dishes; all cooked fresh to order. Curries, burgers and the steak sandwiches are particularly popular with tourists; however other favourites include plaice and chips, the might mixed grill, and the quarter chicken. Guests can dine within the main dining room, or more casually in the bar area, or perhaps al fresco in the summer months in the beer garden which overs the river where boating customers have access to free moorings.

Aside from the excellent food and drink, the Neslon is also known for its entertainment schedule. Bill and Ros are dedicated to supporting local music and put on a variety of live events including folk nights, jazz evenings, rock 'n' roll nights and blues sessions. Please see website for details. Each summer in August, the Nelson is also home to the village's annual beer festival on the bank holiday weekend when over eighty real ales are brought in to sample. All major credit cards accepted, children and dogs welcome at all times.

248 THE COACH AND HORSES INN

Lynn Road, Tilney St Lawrence, Kings Lynn, Norfolk PE34 4RU
Tel: 01945 880 266
e-mail: Gillian_sheppard@yahoo.co.uk

Just a short drive from Kings Lynn in Tilney St Lawrence is the **Coach and Horses Inn**. This modest public house was once a coaching inn, dating back over 400 years. Its owners Gill and Eddie Sheppard took over the inn in August 2009, with over 45 years of experience behind them in the licensing and hospitality trade to help them. Their experience really shows, as in this short period they have put the Coach and Horses back on the map as one of the area's destination pubs.

Open every session except Monday lunchtimes, the inn is popular with ale lovers who always have two rotating brews to sample. A good range of wines, beers and soft drinks are also available. One of the main reasons to visit here though, is the cooking. With Gill at the stove, the inn sees many repeat visitors who claim her food is unrivalled in the area. Gill describes her food as basic English traditional pub food, which simply does not do it justice. Though guests are sure to find all their favourite pub classics on the menu, they are expertly cooked and full of fantastic locally sourced produce. Guests are welcome to dine throughout the inn, where classic décor adds a traditional feel. Dark wooden furniture is brought to life by the flashes of brass memorabilia that lines the walls, focusing proudly on the inn's feature fireplace.

Guests are also welcomed to take their drinks or dinner outside to the pretty beer garden, which overlooks the inn's campsite. There is room for up to five caravans, with plenty of room for tents too, and can be used all year round. Although the site has limited water facilities, campers are more than welcome to use the pubs facilities during opening hours. The area itself has plenty to explore throughout the day with acres of rolling countryside and a variety of village museums and national gardens to enjoy. What better way to relax after a pleasant afternoon out, than taking a cold glass of ale with a handsome pub meal. Children welcome, all major credit cards accepted.

249 FISHERS OF HUNSTANTON

2-4 Greevegate, Hunstanton, Norfolk PE36 6BJ
Tel: 01485 532487

The popular seaside resort of Hunstanton is equally as popular today as it was when in the 1860s when it first became known as one of Norfolks best holiday destinations. The town has a pleasant mix of traditional Victorian architecture and more modern tourist attractions; all housed within easy reach of each other. Known for its stunning sunsets across the water, Hunstanton is sometimes known as 'Sunny Hunny' or the 'highway to the heavens' and has been known to reach record highs for sun time in the UK.

Fishers of Hunstanton is located centrally, just 100 metres from the town's Princess Theatre, with a variety of shows throughout the year. The restaurant was established in 1998 and has grown to be a very popular place with both locals and visitors alike who proudly claim it as the best fish and chip shop around. A reward card is available for regular customers, of whom there are many. Though Fishers does offer a takeaway service it is essentially a restaurant, serving quality freshly prepared food all day every day. The restaurant has recently been refurbished to bring the décor into the 21st century with style. The contemporary, yet comfortable new interior has good

disabled access, and provides a relaxed environment in which to enjoy a meal or drink. The restaurant also has its own roof garden, which affords stunning views across the bay; which is understandably a particularly popular place to be at sunset.

The restaurant itself serves up a very traditional menu of pies and burgers amongst other things, with popular choices of beef and onion pie, chicken and mushroom pie, chicken nuggets, spam fritters, vegetable burgers, fried chicken and a food long battered sausage with chips if you are up to the task! The restaurant is best known for its fish menu, which includes prime deep fried cod, haddock and plaice all with a generous serving of chips, salad and a choice of beans or peas. Other fish dishes include whole tail scampi, rock eel, jumbo fishcakes, lobster tails in breadcrumbs or the mouth watering seafood platter which comprises pieces of plaice, haddock, cod, scallops and scampi. Children can choose from their own menu, and a dessert menu is also available. Those who want a lighter bite also have plenty of options with a small selection of jacket potatoes and side orders available.

Restaurant is fully licensed, all major credit cards taken; open every day from Easter to the end of October, closing on Thursdays in winter months.

250 WHITEHALL FARM

Burnham Thorpe, Norfolk PE31 8HN
Tel: 01328 738416
e-mail: barrysoutherland@aol.com
website: www.whitehallfarm-accommodation.com

Valerie and Barry Southerland have been providing B & B accommodation for visitors to this pretty part of Norfolk for 13 years now and **Whitehall Farm** has built up a great reputation in that time. Set in the heart of a working farm, the accommodation takes the form of three lovely rooms in the main house and a self catering bungalow. The farm sits on 560 acres of arable land, overseen by the pretty white farmhouse, which boast a visit Britian 4 star silver award plus a farm house breakfast award.

All three rooms have been decorated and furnished to a very high standard and have their own en suite bathrooms. With large king size beds and lovely views, relaxation and comfort are provided as standard along with the full range of amenities expected of a modern B & B. The self catering 15 year old bungalow is situated across the valley from the farmhouse and features four bedrooms with a large kitchen and living area.

Being a working farm, facilities are varied and extensive; for those with equine interests there are stables available, there is also a caravan site with electric hook-ups and a camp site.

252 BOXWOOD GUEST HOUSE

Northfield Lane, Wells-next-the-Sea, Norfolk NR23 1JZ
Tel: 01328 711493 Mobile: 07884233369
e-mail: info@boxwood-guesthouse.co.uk or paula.ayres@btinternet.com
website: www.boxwood-guesthouse.co.uk

Perfect for exploring the beautiful North Norfolk Heritage Coast, Boxwood Guest House provides a peaceful holiday base all year round. Run by Paula and Richard Ayres since the spring of 2005, the guesthouse is a popular place for both couples and families alike who want to take a break from the buzz of city life and recharge their batteries; and what better place than the picturesque village of Wells-Next-The-Sea.

The guesthouse is very much a family home, creating a warm and friendly environment. It has been awarded a four star silver award for its facilities which are second to none; each room having full en suite facilities, TV, hair dryer, CD player and tea/coffee tray. There are three rooms located upstairs in the main house, offering contemporary styling in sumptuous creams and chocolates; with a separate annexe towards the rear of the property, where families with children are welcome. The annexe has its own spacious bathroom with super king or twin beds available, and access to a private sunny courtyard.

Each morning Paula serves up a delicious breakfast with both continental or cooked options including a fish dish. Dinners are available by request in the stylish conservatory, and can be included in the tariff with breakfast.

251 THE HERO

Bar and Restaurant, Wells Road, Burnham Overy Staithe, Norfolk PE31 8JE
Tel: 01328 738334
e-mail: info@theheroburnhamovery.co.uk
website: www.theheroburnhamovery.co.uk

Located in the village of Burnham Overy Straithe stands the village's **Hero**; the local pub. Adjacent to the A149, the Hero is ideally placed for a stop off when visiting any of the area's attractions which include the birthplace of Horatio Nelson and the Scolt Head Island National Nature Reserve. The town itself is now a major recreational sailing centre, its creek spreading to a birding heaven with a wealth of salt marshes and embankments.

The Hero has been run by Ali and Robin for the past five years who have truly brought it to life. The warmest of welcomes awaits all guests as they enter, with the tempting aroma of traditional home cooking. Ali is the self taught chef here, and her passion for food really shows in her menus, carefully created using the best local produce from local suppliers to create that authentic English taste. All dishes are freshly prepared on the premises each day, served daily between 12-2:30pm and 6-9pm.

The lunch menu offers a selection of light bites including a creative range of filled doorstep sandwiches, toasties and baguettes such as chicken and chorizo with red pepper mayonnaise or falafel, hummus, olive and lemon yoghurt dressing. Guests can also sample small meals like soup of the day, Welsh rarebit, or country pate with caperberries and cornichons and toast. The evening menu also serves up a delightful range of dishes with starters like Indian spiced Marlin with mango chutney, twice baked goat's cheese soufflé, or slow roasted pork belly with Agrodolce peppers. For mains, why not try one of the a la carte dishes which include slow braised venison shank, chestnut and Portabello mushroom risotto, steamed fillet of grey mullet with Caponata, and butternut squash, leek, pecan nut and cream cheese strudel. Those who fancy a more traditional main will not be disappointed with a small selection of classic dishes from succulent steak, to fish pie, beer battered fish and chips, burgers and homemade steak and kidney pudding also on offer. Unsurprisingly, Ali's food is exceptionally popular, so it's essential to book at all times in the summer, and at weekends in winter.

The inn also prides itself on serving up a fine wine list with a range of reds, whites, roses, sparkling, champagnes and vintage wines to sample. A good range of real ales are also available, with Woodforde's Wherry being the regular brew. Closed Mondays, except bank holidays. All major credit cards taken except Diners.

253 THE VICTORIA AT HOLKHAM

Park Road, Holkham, Norfolk NR23 1RG
Tel: 01328 711008 Fax: 01328 711009
e-mail: victoria@holkham.co.uk
website: www.adnams.co.uk

Just a few minutes walk from the beautiful sands of Holkham beach and at the gates of the magnificent Holkham Hall, you'll find The Victoria. This unique hotel is perfectly placed for discovering miles of stunning coastline, pretty seaside towns and abundant natural life including excellent birdwatching opportunities.

The ten highly individual rooms at The Victoria each have a distinct personality. Some reflect an opulent colonial style with exotic fabrics and rich colours, and those with double ended roll top baths make for an even more luxurious stay. The top floor has been transformed in to a contemporary coastal retreat with interconnecting rooms and spacious bathrooms which make ideal family accommodation.

The menu at The Victoria uses the freshest, seasonal ingredients all carefully sourced from the surrounding areas such as crab from Cromer, mussels from Brancaster or venison, beef and game from the Holkham Estate itself. You can enjoy dining in the large garden and courtyard, the relaxed lounge or the more formal conservatory. The wine list reflects Adnams passion for small, independent winemakers and includes a wide selection of organic and biodynamic wines from around the world.

255 MANOR HOUSE FARM

Wellingham, nr Fakenham, Kings Lynn,
Norfolk PE32 2TH
Tel: 01328 838227
Fax: 01328 838348
e-mail: libby.ellis@btconnect.com
website: www.manor-house-farm.co.uk

Tucked away in the heart of rural Norfolk, this conservation award winning farm offers you bed and breakfast and an enchanting country escape. Just seven miles from Fakenham in Wellingham, **Manor House Farm** is within easy reach of many amenities, but provides a luxurious and tranquil retreat away from the rest of the world.

Though the farm is still a working one, it is also well-known for its bed and breakfast. The converted stable wing offers two large and airy bedrooms, both of which have en suite facilities with bath and shower. Bedrooms are well furnished with antiques and collectables, kelim rugs and blissfully comfortable beds made up with linen dried in the pure Norfolk air and pretty, fresh flowers on the dressing tables; bringing that splash of colour throughout the year. The stables have an adjoining sitting room with a wood burning stove and a small kitchen where tea and coffee is always available. Guests benefit from a delicious farmhouse breakfast each morning served in the elegant dining room of the main house using mostly produce sourced on the farm and the garden; including bacon and sausages from their pigs, fresh brown eggs from the chickens wandering around and ripe fruit from the gardens. This area is fully wheelchair accessible and has central heating.

Guests wanting to stay longer can choose to stay in the self catering barn which has been sympathetically and beautifully converted to sleep just two guests in spacious accommodation. The bedroom has a decadent four poster bed, with en suite shower and bathroom attached. The barn also sports a spacious open plan living room and kitchen, which houses a large hob, oven, microwave, washing machine and fridge. Large patio doors open out onto the barns own sun terrace, perfect for a lazy breakfast or sunset drink.

Manor House Farm is also part of the National Garden Scheme and is a garden lover's heaven. Guests are more than welcome to spend their afternoons wandering through the landscaped gardens, immaculate lawns and rows upon rows of old fashioned roses and herbaceous borders. Bursting with rich colour throughout the year, this country haven is England at its absolute best.

254 THE LAWNS WINE BAR AND HOTEL

26 Station Road, Holt, Norfolk NR25 6BS
Tel: 01263 713390
e-mail: mail@lawnsatholt.co.uk
website: www.lawnsatholt.co.uk

Sue and Daniel Rees have run the Lawns Wine Bar and Hotel for the past three years, after they spent the previous 14 years running the local pub in nearby Blakeney. The Lawns is a spacious Georgian house in the centre of Holt and has recently undergone a stunning renovation to turn it into a top quality luxury hotel with a fully licensed wine bar and dining room.

There are eight beautifully appointed rooms to choose from, all of which have full bath en suite facilities and king size beds. Rooms come in a range of styles and sizes with handsome views across the hotel's gardens or nearby playing fields. Each guest receives a generous full English breakfast each morning, served downstairs in the dining room which is also open to non-residents for meals throughout the day.

The restaurant serves up a large and varied menu that focuses on quality seasonal food. Experienced chefs Leon Brookes and Jenner Hilton offer up a large range of light bites, filled sandwiches and salads, alongside sumptuous mains that include pan fried sea bass, lamb chump chop hotpot style, rich local game pie, and slow roasted belly pork. A handsome wine list accompanies the menu, served in the hotel's contemporary dining room or al fresco style in the gardens.

257 CORFIELD HOUSE

Sporle, nr Swaffham, Norfolk PE32 2EA
Tel: 01760 723636
e-mail: info@corfieldhouse.co.uk
website: www.corfieldhouse.co.uk

Pauline and John Shead offer you the warmest of welcomes to **Corfield House**, their period bed and breakfast. Corfield House dates back in parts to 1810, and has at one stage been a Doctor's House. Today guests come from near and far to enjoy the spotless and cosy accommodation that the couple provide.

There are four en suite rooms to choose from, with either double or twin beds. Rooms come with colour television, clock radio, hairdryer, tea/coffee making tray and unrivalled views across the Norfolk countryside. Guests also have the added benefit of the comfortable guest lounge and half an acre of beautifully kept garden to relax in. Guests are served a full English or continental breakfast each morning, made with only the very best in local produce. Packed lunches are also available on request, perfect for a day touring Norfolk. Just a short drive or walk away there are many National trust properties, Sandringham, Thetford Forest, the popular towns of Kings Lynn and Norwich and the stunning coastline.

The village of Sporle itself also has a few pleasant attractions, including the local pub, where the Shead's will happily arrange dinner for you.

256 THE DABBLING DUCK

11 Abbey Road, Great Massingham, Norfolk PE32 2HN
Tel: 01485 520827 Fax: 01485 520879
e-mail: info@thedabblingduck.co.uk
website: www.thedabblingduck.co.uk

The Dabbling Duck is located in the centre of the picturesque village of Great Massingham. It was formerly known as the Rose and Crown, and has been closed for the past five years. Its fate was turned around by the lively and enthusiastic team that now own it; Steve Kilham, Dominic Symington and Jess Lapping. The owners are ably assisted by the talents of managers Matt Bickerton and Kerri Whitmore, and head Chef Mark Johnson. Together the team aimed to give the village its pub back, creating a friendly and light hearted atmosphere where both locals and visitors alike can enjoy fine food and quality drink throughout the day.

Open all day every day, the inn caters well for ale lovers with five real ales on offer each day. Brews are on offer from both local and national breweries, including Adams Broadside, Green King IPA, Woodforde's Wherry and Worth the Wait. A well chosen selection of wines are also available, which make for the perfect accompaniment to one of the simply delicious meals made here.

Food is available from 12-2:30pm ad 6:30-9pm Monday to Saturday, and 12-3pm on Sundays when a succulent roast dinner is served up for all the family. The main menu is creative and exciting, changing regularly to offer a wide range of seasonal food. Guests can choose from light bites like home smoked cod croquet, duck and spring onion rillette and crispy pork belly with lemon butter king prawns. Those wanting a larger meal also have plenty of exquisite choices; popular mains include pan roasted red snapper, supreme guinea fowl with wild mushrooms and chestnuts, pan roasted lab rump with mussel gratin. The chefs pride themselves on sourcing their ingredients locally wherever possible, and are more than happy to cater for any allergies or special diets. Although there are seats for up to ninety diners, owing to the popularity of the place, it is best to book to avoid disappointment.

The team also offer just three finely appointed bedrooms, all of which has been individually decorated to the highest standards. There are two double rooms and one twin room, but all have en suite facilities. Guest can enjoy a handsome cooked breakfast at the inn, which also holds much information on what there is to see and do in the area. The town's local walking group 'The Great Massingham Strollers,' have created a number of walks that start and end at the inn, just ask for details.

258 THE RED LION & TRUCK STOP

Weedon Road (A45), M1 Junction 16, Upper Heyford, Northampton, NN7 4DE
Tel: 01604 831914
e-mail: ali@redliontruckstop.com
website: www.redliontruckstop.com

Built as a coaching inn in the 1700's, and located at Junction 16 of the M1 motorway, signposted on both sides of the A45 dual carriageway, and also close to the A5, The Red Lion & Truck Stop is a very busy and popular stopping place for truck drivers and anyone alike wanting a refreshment break from a long hard journey on the motorway or the trunkroad network. There are great facilities on offer, such as overnight secuirty patrols and cctv cameras that monitor the site 24 hours a day, male and female shower facilities and great customer service to name a few.

Simple dishes, hearty and filling, are listed on chalkboard menus. The long choice includes just about anything you would expect to find on a classic pub menu: bangers & mash, Cornish pasty, liver and sausages with onion gravy, steak & kidney pudding, steak & stout pie, mixed grill, pork chops, lamb steaks, roast chicken, spaghetti bolognese, chilli con carne, battered cod, burgers, scampi, 10oz rump steak....all guaranteed to provide fuel for the next journey - the chefs guarantee that nobody leaves here hungry. The Pub, quite quaint and traditional stocks a wide and varied menu of drinks from draught beers, house wines to a good selection of Real Ales.

260 THE CHEQUERS

Ravensthorpe, Northamptonshire NN6 8ER
Tel: 01604 770379
e-mail: chequers@ravensthorpe.net

Freshly prepared food is the order of the day at **The Chequers** in Northamptonshire. Sea Bream, Salmon, Sea Bass and Plaice all feature on the extensive menu. There is a good selection of dishes including steak and kidney pie, which is a favourite of visitors and locals to the pub. Sunday Roasts and a Full range of Lunches and Hot & Cold Filled Rolls, Various Salads etc. Homemade Puddings are extremely popular and the additional specials boards give daily options to diners. The dining area seats 50 people and food is served Monday – Sunday:- Lunches 12pm till 2pm. Evenings 6pm till 9pm.

Inside, The Chequers is full of character with memorabilia and pictures covering the walls. The ceiling is beamed and there is a real traditional country feel to it. Dating back to the 1800s the exterior of the pub is clad in ivy. There is a nice garden with Kiddies Play Area at the side of the pub and many punters and diners like to make the most of this area, Barbecues etc on warmer days.

There are three stately homes all within a few minutes' drive and each have gardens open to the public. The village of Ravensthorpe is popular with walkers and the local reservoir is open for Trout Fishing as an additional attraction to visitors to the area.

259 THE OLDE SUN INN

Nether Heyford, Northamptonshire NN7 3LL
Tel: 01327 340164

Although it is sandwiched between the A5, A45 and the M1, the village of Nether Heyford is a pleasant, peaceful place. It has one of the biggest village greens in the country, but what brings many visitors is one of the most delightful pubs anywhere, the sort of pub for which the words, eclectic, eccentric and quirky might have been invented and one that restores faith in the time-honoured but increasingly threatened ideal of the quintessentially English country pub.

When Peter Yates and Alan Ford took over in the summer of 2006 they inherited a pub that was, and is, very, very different. **The Olde Sun Inn** is an 18th century golden-stone pub with a steeply-tiled roof and small-paned windows. But it's what's behind the porticoed entrance and heavy wooden door that makes this place one in a million. A merry jumble of bric-a-brac, bygones and memorabilia fills just about every spare inch of the little linked rooms: one fireplace flanked by a grotto of brass animals, old advertising signs, horse tackle and farm implements, cigarette cards, colourful relief plates, railway memorabilia. Even without the fascinating curiosities this would be a very inviting place with its friendly hosts and staff and the traditional look of beams and low ceilings, wooden dividing panels, rugs on parquet floors, tiles or flagstones, a log fire and properly pubby furniture. On the left is a games room with skittles, darts, cribbage, dominoes and sports TV, while outside, the pub has a pleasant lawned garden with a children's play area and a front terrace with picnic sets and old farm machines.

The Olde Sun is, of course, essentially a much-loved local, serving the local community and the surrounding area with an excellent selection of food and drink. Four cask ales are on tap, typically Ruddles Best, Marston's Pedigree, a Banks's brew and a guest. The philosophy behind the food is to keep it simple and good, and the bar snack menu spans hot bites (jacket potatoes, panini, ham, egg & chips), soup, sandwiches, home-made steak pie and lemon peppered haddock. This remarkable pub is open lunchtime and evening Monday to Thursday and all day Friday, Saturday and Sunday.

261 OVERSTONE MANOR

Ecton Lane, Sywell,
Northamptonshire NN6 0BB
Tel: 01604 7904447
website: www.mypubheaven.co.uk

Nestled in an idyllic countryside location, **The Overstone Manor**, is a delightful family food house. It was refurbished to a high standard in May 2008 and now boasts an open plan design. It has maintained many of its original manor house features, which add to the character and charm of the place. Fire places, beamed ceilings and wood panelling help create a fantastic atmosphere and with room to seat a total of 400 diners in the inside and outside areas there is always a good afternoon or evening to be had. The Overstone Manor is open between 12pm and 11pm every day, shutting half an hour earlier on a Sunday.

Quality food is served all day and as well as an extensive main menu there is a daily carvery to choose from. The bar area used to be a ballroom and the high ceilings add to the impressive nature of the establishment. It provides an ideal location for an array of functions, including wedding receptions and is easily accessible from the M1. With so much space, diners can enjoy meals in private annexes and families are well catered for. The garden area is just splendid and there is a children's play area to keep younger guests entertained.

www.findSOMEWHERE.co.uk
For people who want to explore the United Kingdom

Places to Visit

262 THE RED LION

High Street, Yardley Hastings, nr Northampton,
Northamptonshire NN7 1ER
Tel: 01604 696210
website: www.redlionatyardleyhastings.co.uk

Nestled in the picturesque village of Yardley Hastings, The Red Lion is a traditional country pub waiting to take your order. Owned by Diane and Mark the pub is picture perfect and can be found just off the main A428 Bedford Road. Home cooked food is the focus of the extensive menu and delicious dishes can be enjoyed in a friendly family environment. Friendly service is important to Diane and Mark and along with their staff they execute it very well. There is an outside seating area as well as well as a skittles tables in the games room.

263 THE BUTCHERS ARMS

10 High Street, Greens Norton, Towcester, Northamptonshire NN12 8BA
Tel: 01327 350488
website: www.thebutchersarmsgreennorton.co.uk

Located centrally in the pleasant village of Greens Norton is **The Butchers Arms**. This handsome village inn is now home to Sarah and Roland Jones who offer the warmest of welcomes to all. The couple have a wealth of experience in the trade, having run six other pubs in the past – and have put that experience to good use here. They have truly revitalized the inn and its village by introducing a number of community evenings and updating the interior to emphasis its traditional standing.

With original wooden beams, large brick fireplaces and a host of solid wood furniture, the inn has a true country pub atmosphere; supplemented by a range of fine wines and real ales. With up to four cask marquee ales on offer at any one time, and with more guest ales rotating – ale lovers will not be disappointed. London Pride, Hook Norton, Hooky Ale and Timothy Taylor Landlord always make regular appearances. The inn has won accreditation for the quality of its ales, along with a Great British Pub Award.

The inn is also popular with food lovers, serving a range of delicious themed food each session. The menu here specialises in Thai, Italian and French cuisine, drawing on a fantastic selection of locally sourced produce to create its dishes. Cooked fresh to order, dishes include Thai chilli beef with jasmine rice, piri piri chicken with chips and salad, or mussels in a tomato and fresh herb sauce with garlic bread. The inn also runs a popular steak night on a Thursday and an even more popular curry night on Mondays. Guests can even swing by for the inn's 'School Dinner night' where all your old favourites are served up canteen style.

Sarah and Roland are keen to entertain their guests with not just great food and drink, but with the range of 'Old School' games available. In the summer months, the inn's spacious beer garden truly comes to life with games like Aunt Sally and famous Northamptonshire skittles. Inside guests can choose from a few rounds of pool, darts or dominoes, or get a team together of family or friends to enter for the fortnightly Sunday evening quiz. Please see website for details.

264 THE STAR INN

Bridge Street, Geddington, nr Corby, Northamptonshire NN14 1AD
Tel: 01536 742 386
website: www.star-inn-geddington.com

In the centre of Geddington, just moments from the main A43, **The Star** is an inn of very wide appeal. It is an ideal resting spot for locals enjoying a trip to their favourite pub, for workers, shoppers and business people dropping in for lunch, and for visitors to Geddington. The historic town is home of the best-preserved of the Eleanor Crosses and the Star Inn, which was known firstly as The Swan, then as the Black Swan, is a popular refreshment stop.

The handsome stone built, slate-roofed inn is a formidable sight in the town and is a favourite with locals and visitors. Ali and Angela have a genuinely warm welcome for all of their patrons, who since taking over the reins in 2002 have made this a real pub-lover's pub. It has become a convivial place where locals and visitors meet and chat in the cosy ambience of the traditionally appointed public and lounge bars. The Star is truly a happy hunting ground for those who like their real ale. The bar keeps a superb selection of brews from small local breweries, which are all kept in tip-top condition, earning the pub the accolade of CAMRA's Northamptonshire Summer Pub of the Year for 2006.

Food lovers are equally well catered for at the Star. Ali has been a chef for more than 25 years, and his printed menus and specials board satisfy a wide range of tastes and appetites. Local produce is a strong focus of the extensive menu as is classic home cooked food. There is plenty of choice for vegetarians, who always have at least four main course options to choose from. Paintings in a variety of media by professional artists are displayed in the pub's gallery area, with exhibitions changing every two months, an annual grand review at the turn of the year and all the artwork for sale. A charity quiz, with bargain food specials, is held every other Tuesday, and the pub holds a popular themed food night on the last Thursday of every month.

The inn is popular with walkers who come to see Eleanor's Cross in the village square, just opposite the pub, and there are two new en-suite rooms available as of 2010. Ring for details.

265 BOUCHON BISTROT

4-6 Gilesgate, Hexham, Northumberland NE46 3NJ
Tel: 01434 609 943
e-mail: info@bouchonbistrot.co.uk
website: www.bouchonbistrot.co.uk

Situated in a beautiful grade II listed building, **Bouchon Bistrot** in Hexham offers a touch of classic French cuisine in elegance, professional and relaxing surroundings. Award winning restaurateur Gregory Bureau and his head chef Nicolas Duhil manage to provide a traditional French menu at attractive prices.

Greg, who learnt his trade in several Michelin-starred restaurant in France, creates simple, traditional recipes with good quality produce. The restaurant itself is decorated with a French Bistrot feel in mind with its original Oak beams and open fires on each of the restaurant's three levels. The French bistrot feel is continued with french music playing and the menu is in French and English.

The rustic menu created by chef Nicolas contains mouth watering dishes such as "Assiette de Charcuterie, Monkfish Loin with Sauce Gascogne, French Onion Soup and Crispy Duck Confit. The food has been critically acclaimed, with the restaurant being reviewed in The Good Food Guide, The Michelin Guide & more lately won the title of "UK best local French Restaurant" on Gordon Ramsay's F word!

With Bouchon Bistrot growing in popularity all the time, reservations are recommended, children are welcome and there is full disabled access.

267 THE ANGLERS ARMS

Kielder Village,
Northumberland NE48 1ER
Tel: 01434 250072

Hosts Dave and Christine, who took over **The Anglers Arms** at the beginning of 2010, welcome visitors young and old to their cheerful pub in Kielder Village. The village was built in the 1950s to house workers employed in the man-made Kielder Forest, and the pub building used to be a workmen's club, on land where the village tennis courts once stood.

In the bar, a choice of real ales is always on tap, including the award-winning Anglers Ale, and in the separate restaurant area fresh, wholesome home cooking includes a good selection for vegetarians. Favourites include home-baked ham, curries and the super Kielder Cobbler with steak, mushrooms and a rich brown ale gravy.

The Forest, which covers 200 square miles to the west of the Northumberland National Park, attracts walkers, cyclists and lovers of nature and the great outdoors with its red squirrels, otters, deer and rare birds and plants. Kielder also its own Castle and an Observatory where stargazers gather at key times in the year to scan the skies. Within the Forest is Kielder Water, where the many activities include sailing, riding and fishing.

266 THE BLACK BULL

Market Square, Haltwhistle,
Northumberland NE49 0BL
Tel: 01434 320463
e-mail: kev.ellis@btinternet.com

As facilities and transport improve year by year, an ever-growing number of visitors come from near and far to explore the World Heritage site of Hadrian's Wall. The little town of Haltwhistle is close to one of the best-preserved stretches of the Wall, and at the heart of the community, down a cobbled street off the Market Square, stands the **Black Bull**, the town's oldest cask ale pub. Visitors to this small delightful hostelry are ensured of a warm welcome from Kevin Ellis, who with his wife Barbara, chef Amie and his team, has restored and enhanced the traditional pub ambience. The bar is cosy, warm and inviting, with plenty of chairs and tables, an open fire, beams, brasses and old photographs and local memorabilia.

The pub is a magnet for lovers of cask ales, with six regularly changing brews kept in tip-top condition. A typical selection might include Wychwood's Hobgoblin, Marston's Sweet Chariot, Deuchars IPA, Theakston Old Peculier and always a beer from one of the big southern breweries – perhaps London Pride, Courage directors or Old Speckled Hen. The Black Bull is also a place to seek out for its food, satisfying the appetites of the regulars and of visitors from afar who discover just how good traditional home cooking can be. Among the popular dishes on the wide-ranging menu are starters like deep fried goats cheese, the infamous Black Bull's Stack and home-made chicken liver pâté, and mains dishes such as Cumberland sausage with onion gravy, homemade chilli con carne, fish & chips, the famous Black Bull burger, succulent steaks and and the renowned Black Bull savoury bread and butter pudding. The choice is supplemented by daily specials, some of which feature produce from the local fish and game merchant. Sweets are equally traditional and equally hard to resist. For lighter appetites, a selection of made-to-order sandwiches with hot and cold fillings is available. Attractions in and around Haltwhistle include the 13th century Holy Cross Church – literally right behind the pub, which also has 13th century foundations, suggesting that it might have been built to house the servants of the church or its builders; and Walltown Quarry, a recreation site with laid-out trails and a wealth of birdlife.

The name of Haltwhistle literally means 'a meeting of streams by the hill' but suggests an old-time railway station. Haltwhistle does indeed have a station serving the east-west Newcastle-Carlisle line.It also used to serve Alston, and this ex-line is now a very popular and easy walk over the Alston arches and to the Lambley viaduct.

268 THE SUN INN

Main Street, Acomb,
Northumberland NE46 4PW
Tel: 01434 602934
e-mail: info@thesuninnacomb.co.uk
website: www.thesuninn-acomb.co.uk

Brian Dodd, a member of the British Institute of
Innkeepers, puts his experience to excellent use at
The Sun Inn, where a cheerful, relaxed ambience
and fine home cooking attract a loyal clientele from
Acomb and the nearby towns and villages (Acomb is
situated just off the A6079 a couple of miles from Hexham). Having
come most recently from the successful Boatside Inn at High
Warden, he knows exactly how to keep his customers happy.

It's much more than a popular local, with a good choice of beers
served in the cosy bar and a games room with pool and satellite TV
for the big sporting events. It's also a great choice for a meal, with
a menu of traditional Britsh comfort food that keeps all his patrons
content and well fed. The Sun is located in an area that's rich in
history and scenic splendour, and for visitors touring this lovely part
of Northumberland the Sun has comfortable, well-priced guest accommodation – two en suite
rooms and two with shared facilities. Nearby Hexham is a town with plenty to see and do – and
the picturesque Hexham racecourse is actually in Acomb itself. Hadrian's Wall, the best known
Roman monument in Britain, is very close by.

269 THE HADRIAN HOTEL

Wall, nr Hexham, Northumberland NE46 4EE
Tel: 01434 681232
e-mail: david.lindsay13@btinternet.com
website: www.hadrianhotel.com

Tourists, walkers and lovers of the countryside will find an excellent refreshment stop or holiday
base at the **Hadrian Hotel**, which stands off the A69, four miles from Hexham at the gateway to
the Northumberland National Park and Hadrian's Wall country. Behind the substantial, part
creeper-covered stone façade, the public bar, lounge and restaurant are appealingly traditional,
with open fires and period-style pictures and ornaments. Jennings Cumberland Ale is the resident
cask ale, and a fine choice of food is served all day in the main bar and lunchtime and evening in
the restaurant. When the sun shines, the large
garden is a popular alternative.

The six guest bedrooms – four en suite, some
with four-posters – provide ample space and
comfort, offering an ideal base for discovering
the many attractions and activities that are
almost on the doorstep.

Notable among the sights is Hadrian's Wall:
some of the best sections of this World Heritage
Site are close to the hotel. The hotel is also a
popular place for locals to meet and socialise,
with a pool table, dominoes, gaming machines
and a big-screen TV for top sporting events.

270 GREENCARTS

Greencarts Farm, Neal, Humshaugh, nr Hexham,
Northumberland NE46 4BW
Tel: 01434 681320 e-mail: Sandra@greencarts.co.uk
website: www.greencarts.co.uk

A variety of accommodation caters for all at **Greencarts**, which lies in stunning countryside right by Hadrian's Wall. The Maughan family's 14th century farmhouse has two double and one twin bedroom, all en suite, for B&B guests, whose day starts with a hearty Northumbrian breakfast (evening meals with notice). The bunk barn provides excellent bunkhouse accommodation for up to 8 guests, with good kitchen and washroom facilities and a drying/boot room. A camping barn offers more basic dormitory-style sleeping in four bunk beds, and the campsite has space for 30 pitches, with washrooms and toilets that can also be used by camping barn guests.

271 THE BAY HORSE INN

West Woodburn, Kielder,
Northumberland NE48 2RX
Tel: 01434 270218
website: www.bayhorseinn.org

The **Bay Horse Inn** is a late-18th century mellow sandstone hostelry standing in the heart of the Cheviot Hills, by a stone bridge on the main A68. Hilda Wright, who was first associated with the inn 20 years ago, is an admirable host and her immaculate inn is a delightful place to pause for a drink, to relax over a leisurely meal or to enjoy a break in a picturesque setting. Food is very much the star here, with prime local produce taking centre stage for the home-cooked dishes on the wide-ranging menus. Among the perennial favourites are beer-battered haddock, lasagne, chilli con carne, mince with dumplings, lamb chops, chicken tikka masala and specials featuring seafood caught off the nearby Northumberland coast.

The seven cottage-style guest bedrooms, each with its own individual character, have en suite facilities, TV and hot drinks tray; they provide an ideal base for tourists, cyclists and walkers – the Pennine Way passes close by. The Bay Horse hosts occasional live music nights and a quiz every other Thursday.

www.findSOMEWHERE.co.uk
For people who want to explore the United Kingdom

Places to Eat and Drink

272 TATE HOUSE

11 Bondgate Without, Alnwick,
Northumberland NE66 1PR
Tel: 01665 604661
e-mail: info@stayinalnwick.co.uk
website: www.tatehouse.info

Tate House Bed and Breakfast is a three-story late
Victorian town house beautifully restored and
opposite the Alnwick Gardens.

Our accommodation has been lovingly refurbished
and upgraded, bringing this town house back to life.
All rooms are comfortable, spacious and are full of
character. With a meticulous attention to cleanliness
and flawless decoration throughout you can be sure
of a relaxing stay.

Tate House is a great base in which to explore all
the attractions, heritage and culture within North
Northumberland. Alnwick town is filled with history
with its Alnwick Castle dominating the landscape. It
has been the home of the Dukes of Northumberland
since 1309 and more recently shot to fame as a
result of the Harry Potter films. Close to the Alnwick
Castle are the magnificent Alnwick Gardens which
are a 'must' see when visiting Alnwick.

274 THE BLACK BULL HOTEL

2 High Street, Wooler, Northumberland NE71 6BY
Tel: 01668 281309
e-mail: theblackbullhotel@hotmail.com
website: www.theblackbullhotel.co.uk

Dating back to the 17th century, **The Black Bull Hotel** is a
former coaching inn located at the heart of Wooler. It
maintains a lot of its original character and is popular with
walkers, golfers and fishermen visiting the area. The area is
extremely picturesque and the popular towns of Berwick
upon Tweed and Alnwick are all within easy reach. The
hotel has 13 rooms, all with en-suite facilities. All prices
are inclusive of a full english breakfast. All of the rooms
have hairdryers, tea and coffee making facilities, Freeview
TV and wireless internet access.

Guests can now enjoy the hotel's very own gym and
facilities, ideal for those wanting a relaxing break away in
Northumberland. The hotel is fully licensed and good
homemade food is served every evening and lunch time in
the restaurant or bar areas.

The Milan Restaurant serves the very best in Italian and contemporary cuisine and caters for all
occasions from romantic dinners to family get-togethers. The menu focuses on freshly prepared
classic and modern Italian dishes with plenty of pizza, pasta, seafood and meats to enjoy. Room
prices are from £50 based on 2 people sharing.

273 THE ELM TREE COFFEE SHOP

High Street, Rothbury, Northumberland NE65 7TE
Tel: 01669 621337

Helen Renton and her family continue to win friends at the **Elm Tree Coffee Shop**. Since arriving here they have built up a fine reputation for quality and value for money in their handsome former Victorian town house, which looks down Rothbury's High Street from its elevated position.

The two rooms offer a delightfully unfussy and relaxed ambience in which to enjoy good honest home cooking. Counter service provides excellent teas and coffees and hot and cold drinks to accompany scones, cakes, filled rolls, toasties, jacket potatoes with interesting toppings, savoury pies and daily specials. Everything is fresh and wholesome, freshly made each day on the premises and pleasantly light on the pocket. Helen, her family and their staff are always friendly, willing and ready to help, making it a pleasure to return time and again to the Elm Tree, which is open from 10 to 5 (till 4 off season) seven days a week.

It's fully accessible (including the toilets) to wheel chairs. Some free parking is usually available directly outside the coffee shop, and the large village car park by the river is just two minutes' walk away.

The Elm Tree would make a lovely place for a small party or get together: groups are welcome – phone to arrange – and a private room is available. Rothbury is a pleasant little town and a perfect base for exploring the lovely valley of the River Coquet. Once the setting of an important livestock market, it's now an attractive resort for walkers and fisherman. The former Saxon parish church is well worth a visit, and just outside town is the National Trust's Cragside, the first house in the world to be lit by hydroelectricity. After a shopping expedition, a walk round the town or a breath of fresh air in the

surrounding countryside there are few more agreeable places to take a break than the Elm Tree Coffee Shop.

275 SINNERS CAFE

1 Sidey Court, Berwick Upon Tweed,
Northumberland TD15 1DR
Tel: 01289 302621

Quality home cooked food cooked to order is the main aim of the **Sinners Cafe**. The cafe has a relaxing and friendly atmosphere and has seating inside and outside. There are plenty of homemade dishes on offer including filled jacket potatoes, sandwiches and paninis and meals available for vegeterians, vegans & gluten free. The homemade Sinners Burgers and homemade macaroni cheese are among the favourites with customers, many who return time and time again. The cafe is known to serve the best coffee in the town. It is open 10am – 4pm in the summer and between 10am and 3pm in the winter.

276 THE RED LION

Main Road, Milfield, Wooler,
Northumberland NE71 6JD
Tel: 01668 216224
e-mail: iaindburn@fsmail.net
website: www.redlion-milfield.co.uk

The Red Lion in Milfield village, Northumberland is a classic wind stone building dating back to the mid 1700s. Originally the inn was frequented by the sheep drovers of the northern counties. Between 1785 and 1835 the Red Lion Inn became a major resting point for the mail stage coach which carried passengers and mail between Edinburgh and London via Oldster and Newcastle.

Iain Burn and Claire, his wife, know the value of tradition and welcome all travellers to the area offering them outstanding cuisine, great beer and a relaxing atmosphere. The Red Lion inn boasts several bedrooms, all with shower en suite, available on a B & B basis.

Booking in advance is recommended as availability can be limited. All the food served at the Red Lion Inn is prepared on the premises using ingredients produced locally. Fish from Newcastle and Eyemouth, Northumberland cheese and the seasonal vegetables are grown locally by the farmers in the surrounding area. Even the dreamy ice cream comes from just up the road.

Alongside the finest Scottish and Newcastle ales, over the last three years the Red Lion Inn has played host to over 130 guest beers. You can be sure of a decent pint without any loud jukebox or large screen TV to disturb you, just gentle background music and great conversation.

277 THE BLACK LION

Main Road, Radcliffe-on-Trent,
Nottinghamshire NG12 2FD
Tel: 01159 332138
e-mail: deborah.badcock1@unicombox.com

This big, bold landmark pub is easy to spot in the busy village of Radcliffe-on-Trent, just off the A52 east of Nottingham. It has been run by former coach driver Deborah Badcock for the past two years and is a busy meeting place for locals and visitors.

Behind its stone and brick frontage, with a black-and-white upper storey, there's plenty of elbow and sitting room in the public bar and traditional lounge/dining area, where six cask ales, including Greene King IPA and Charles Wells Bombardier, provide a fine choice for real ale fans. Up to 50 can be sampled in the marquees during the late-May beer festival.

Hungry patrons are also well catered for, with a wide range of snacks and meals that run from filled cobs and baguettes, burgers, jacket potatoes and salads to omelettes, chilli, lasagne, beer battered cod and steak and ale pie. (Additional choices on daily specials board). The Sunday roasts come in three sizes – child, small and large – and a fine meal ends with a great selection of naughty desserts. As well as the annual beer festival, the pub, which is open from 11.30am every day, hosts many events throughout the year. Ring for details.

278 THE GRIFFIN AT PLUMTREE

1 Main Road, Plumtree, Nottinghamshire NG12 5EZ
Tel: 01159 376742
e-mail: info@thegriffinplumtree.co.uk
website: www.thegriffinplumtree.co.uk

At the heart of the village of Plumtree, stands The Griffin at Plumtree, which has transformed into a stylish, yet relaxed venue. The gastro-pub has a modern twist and having been awarded 5 Stars for excellence in Food Health and Hygiene Control by Rushcliffe Borough Council on November 10th 2009, the Griffin offers peace of mind as well as quality of service.

The talented chef Luke and his dedicated team use fresh local ingredients, and produce excellent traditional British and contemporary European cuisine in a comfortable, relaxed and customer friendly environment. Managed by Paul Cummings and run by Danny Prince, it has become a destination pub for lovers of quality cuisine, fine ales and good hospitality. It has a warm and inviting ambience and offers an ideal setting for all occasions. With a choice of light lunches, bar meals and a la carte, in the warmer evenings al fresco dining will be available on the tastefully landscaped terrace. Among the starters on the a la carte evening menu is smoked salmon, with a roquette salad and a caper and lemon dressing; and chicken liver parfait with homemade chutney and toast. Main course include 10oz sirloin of Blackberry Farm reared beef, hand cut chips & roast tomato; fresh salmon tagliatelle, parmesan cream and homedried tomatoes; and whole roast quail with braised red cabbage and pomme rosti. If diners have room for dessert, temptations include coffee cremé brulee with a palmier biscuit; and chocolate tart with vanilla mascarpone. There is also a lunch and bar menu, great British classics menu, Sunday lunch menu and event menus. The pub is child friendly and has seating for up to 120 people (including 45 seats in the upstairs dining area). The bar serves a great selection of continental beers, cask marque ales, wines, spirits, champagnes and cocktails, and boasts a luxurious lounge area to relax with coffee and newspapers at any time of the day or night. There are three real ales to enjoy, with Greene King IPA the regular and two rotating guest ales.

Private dining and function rooms are available for intimate dinner parties, family celebrations and corporate functions, with capacity for anything from eight-50 people depending on the occasion. Ring for details.

The impressive establishment can be found in the village of Plumtree, which is a short drive from the centre of Nottingham.

279 THE OLD BAKERY

4 Queens Head Court, Newark,
Nottinghamshire NG24 1EL
Tel: 01636 611501
e-mail: iorioroberto@hotmail.com
website: www.theoldbakerytearooms.co.uk

In the heart of Newark, the olde worlde charms of **The Old Bakery** draws in many customers from near and far to sample the mouth-watering array of homemade treats on offer. Its Italian owners Roberto and Ellie Iorio and Roberto's brother Luigi have been running the tea rooms for many years, delivering a wide variety of food and drink in a jovial atmosphere.

Open six days a week from 9am-5pm (closed on Sundays), the Iorio's serve up a wide array of home cooking that is created using locally sourced produce. The menu changes regularly to reflect the seasonal nature of their goods, but each menu always features a selection of light bites and snacks, desserts, puddings and homemade scones. Popular dishes include smoked bacon muffin, the Mediterranean platter and the croque monsieur. Other lunch dishes include the brunch grill, smoked salmon brioche and old fashioned sardines on toast. Up at the counter, guests will find some true eye candy with a shameless display of cream cakes, cheesecakes, fruit crumbles, pavlovas and truffles guaranteed to topple the will of even the most pious dieter.

Some might say that certain guests have become delirious over the richness of the food here; as many have joined the owners in spotting the ghost of a little girl who has even been investigated by parapsychologists! Just ask for details. Cash only please.

280 LA PARISIENNE CAFÉ BISTRO

12 King Street, Southwell,
Nottinghamshire NG25 0EN
Tel: 01636 816513
e-mail: boothyworld@yahoo.co.uk
website: www.laparisienne.co.uk

Stephen and Noelle Booth welcome all to **La Parisienne Café Bistro** in the centre of busting Southwell. For the last year the couple have been offering up delicious homemade French and Moroccan themed food five days a week.

Virtually all of the produce used in dishes here is locally sourced and is skilfully given its exotic taste by Noelle who acts as chef here. Dishes include light bites like croque monsieur, Moroccan omelette and grilled rump steak baguette, with mains like rich beef bourguignon, cassoulet de Toulouse, fish tagine with monk fish, sea bass, mussels and prawns. Moroccan options include Marrakech tagine with roasted vegetables, dried fruit and herbs served with flat bread or sweet potato and spinach cooked in coriander with free range eggs.

Open from 9:30am-6pm Tuesdays, 9:30am-7pm Wednesday and Thursdays and from 9:30am-12am Fridays and Saturdays when booking is essential.

281 THE PLOUGH

Main Street, Farnsfield, Nottinghamshire NG22 8EA
Tel: 01623 882265
e-mail: bubblybob@tiscali.co.uk

Located in the village of Farnsfield, The Plough is a popular village pub run by Bob and June. Dating back to 1724, the pub serves traditional home cooked food. The menu is extensive and there is a specials board with plenty of additional dishes, all freshly cooked to order. Inside, The Plough has an olde worlde feel to it and the beamed ceilings add to its character and charm. There are three rotating real ales to enjoy and the well stocked bar has plenty of other beverages. The Plough is open all day every day, but no food is served on Saturday or Sunday evenings.

282 THE CROWN INN

South Street, Normanton-on-Trent,
Nottinghamshire NG23 6RQ
Tel: 01636 821973

Located in the picturesque and secluded village of Normanton-on-Trent, just off the A1, the recently refurbished **Crown Inn** is particularly noted for its excellent cuisine and its choice of real ales.

Owners Ken and Fran Munro have their own brewery located in the nearby village of Cromwell. Known as the Milestone Brewery, it produces up to 8 brews ranging from 3.6% strength up to 6.5% strength. At any one time, up to 4 of these brews are on tap at The Crown.

The inn is also renowned for its quality cuisine which is based on local produce wherever possible. Typical dishes include a starter of crayfish cocktail with fresh mango salsa; and main dishes such as pork loin steak with an apple and cognac sauce. Children are welcome and have their own menu. Food is served from noon until 2.30pm; and from 5pm to 9pm, Monday to Saturday; and from noon until 8pm on Sunday. Booking is essential at weekends. The inn hosts food-themed evenings every Monday and on weekdays there's a special "Early Bird" menu. Diners can eat either in the 54-seat dining room, in the bar areas or, weather permitting, outside.

www.findSOMEWHERE.co.uk
For people who want to explore the United Kingdom

Specialist Shops

510

283 THE QUEENS HOTEL

High Street, East Markham, Nottinghamshire NG22 0RE
Tel: 01777 870288
e-mail: bluenose16@live.co.uk
website: www.queenshoteleastmarkham.co.uk

One of the many fine assets of the Queen's Hotel is its long-serving landlord and land-lady Chris and Barbara Russon. They took over here in 1990, ever since when they have been welcoming locals and seasonal visitors with their excellent brand of hospitality. Behind its white-painted exterior with huge name boards and summer hanging baskets, the hotel (not a hotel in spite of its name) is spotless and very comfortable with plenty of inviting seats in which to enjoy a chat and a glass of real ale.

Open all day every day the Russon's pride themselves on offering up to five real ales at any one time. Regular brews include Tiger, Beacon and Adnams alongside two rotating ales from local breweries. Chris also dabbles in brewing himself and occasionally offers guests his own ale called 'Copperknob.' The inn has won many awards from the Real Ale Campaign, but sees a steady clientele throughout the year, not just to sample the fine ale, but to sample the food.

Served daily between 12-9:30pm on Tuesdays to Saturdays and from 12-6pm on Sundays, the food here is generous, very reasonably priced and utterly delicious. Barbara heads up the kitchen, using her skills to create an across the board traditional menu of wholesome homemade food.

To start guests can choose from garlic prawns and mushrooms served in potato skins, homemade soup of the day, and mini duck spring rolls. Main courses include a meaty braised pork shank in a rich cider gravy, grilled lamb chump chops coated in an orange marmalade, sherry and garlic sauce and chicken supreme with wild mushrooms in a creamy brandy sauce. Dishes from around the world include homemade chilli, lasagne, aromatic ribs, sweet and sour chicken and a selection of speciality curries. Those with a love for the traditional will not be disappointed either with plenty of favourite pub dishes like lamb hot pot, steak and ale pie, cottage pie and Cumberland sausage. Fish dishes include fillet of salmon in a cream and chive sauce, scampi, battered cod, fish pie, and salmon and broccoli pasta. Both carnivores and vegetarians are also well catered for with a both vegetarian and grill sections to the menu also. Guests are also welcome to take a simple snack or just a dessert with a ten strong homemade pudding selection. Dishes are created using as much locally sourced produce as possible.

On Sundays why not round up the family for the hotel's traditional Sunday roast dinner and stay for the popular evening quiz from 8pm. Children and families welcome. All major credit cards taken.

511

284 THE BAY TREE CAFE BAR

The Courtyard, Thoresby Park, nr Ollerton, Nottinghamshire NG22 9EP
Tel: 01623 825225
website: www.thoresby.com

With a strong reputation for fine food and good hospitality, **The Bay Tree Cafe Bar** can be found in the Victorian Courtyard at Thoresby Park. Located in the heart of Nottinghamshire and with plenty of attractions to suit the whole family, many visitors to the county pay a visit to Thoresby Park.

The fully licensed cafe, which has been owned by Adam Valintine for the past five years, offers a wide range of delicacies, from continental dishes to cream teas. Local produce is used wherever possible and the menu changes with the season. The home made cakes served are particularly popular with visitors to the child friendly cafe and many people make regular visits. There is seating for 44 people inside and a further 44 outside and the cafe is popular with those wanting a pre-theatre dinner and intermission drinks (Theatre at Thoresby Riding Hall). Such is its popularity it is advisable to book on weekends and Bank Holidays to avoid disappointment. Owner Adam doubles as chef and he is very experienced and talented at what he does. As well as freshly baked cakes, the menu boasts a selection of delicious snacks and lunches. Filled sandwiches, baguettes, soups, quiches, toasted

paninis, salad bowls and platters can all be enjoyed at the cafe in its picturesque and historic location. Toasted bagels, croissants, scones, Danish pastries and fruit salads are served all day and there is a range of additional choices on the daily specials board. Refreshments include alcoholic beverages, cold drinks and a range of hot drinks, including speciality teas.

The cafe is an ideal resting place for those visiting the Art and Crafts Gallery, visiting exhibitions, going to the theatre, or attending a wedding at Thoresby Park. Thoresby Park covers more than 1000 acres of unspoilt English countryside and has a fantastic range of facilities and attractions open to the public all year round. The grand mansion at Thoresby Park (the largest park in the country) is a Victorian mansion designed by Anthony Salvin and now is a private hotel. In the winter months the cafe is open seven days a week. It is open between 10am – 4pm Monday – Friday and between 10am – 5pm on Saturday and Sunday. In summer it remains open seven days a week, but extends its opening hours to 10am – 5pm every day. There is good access for disabled diners as well as disabled toilets. All major credit cards taken.

285 THE CROWN & THISTLE

18 Bridge Street, Abingdon, Oxfordshire OX14 3HS
Tel: 01235 522556 Fax: 01235 553281
e-mail: reception@crownandthistle.com
website: www.crownandthistle.com

Situated at the heart of the market town of Abingon, the
traditional 17th century coaching inn of **The Crown & Thistle**
still offers accommodation to weary travellers and tourists.
Surrounding a lovely cobbled courtyard, the Crown & Thistle has
19 en suite rooms available as well as a restaurant, bar and
function room. Most of the building has been recently
refurbished, whilst being sympathetic to the establishment's
heritage; the refurbishment has married modern amenities with
traditional features.

The 19 rooms are comprised of a mix of single, double and
twin bedded rooms, as well as two four poster bedrooms for
maximum luxury. Reasonably priced, the tariff includes a full
English or continental breakfast. The Gallery restaurant offers a
range of British and continental dishes, all created fresh to
order using locally sourced produce. Stylishly decorated, the
restaurant is ideal for catering for large parties and private
events. Set alongside the Gallery restaurant is the Stocks bar; a
traditional pub with a strong local population that boasts a wide
selection of beers and a simple bar menu. There is also a pool
table and a darts board, frequented by the pub's pool and darts teams.

286 THE PLOUGH

Rectory Road, Great Haseley,
Oxford, Oxfordshire OX44 7JQ
Tel: 01844 279283

Alison had been working in Oxford city centre
before taking over at **The Plough** in Great
Haseley, having lived in the village for 8 years, it
has been a dream come true for Alison. Spurred
on by the other villagers, Alison has made a
great job of enhancing the pub's reputation and
as head chef, the food has improved
tremendously. The pretty thatched roof inn
entices guests in and inside they are greeted
with a warm and friendly atmosphere created by
an inglenook fireplace that crackles away as the
locals chatter at the bar.

Recently the subject of a review in the Oxford
Times, the Plough received a very good write up,
the food singled out for high praise, as well as
tasty, the cost wasn't prohibitive and the wine
list offered very good support. Alison ensures that
all of the food is cooked fresh to order using only
the best of locally sourced ingredients from
excellent suppliers.

287 THE GOOSE

Britwell Salome, Oxfordshire OX49 5LG
Tel: 01491 612 304
e-mail: info@thegoosebritwellsalome.com
website: www.thegoosebritwellsalome.com

Situated in the heart of Oxfordshire, near Watlington and the M40, Britwell Salome is a hamlet with some residential housing, farms and **The Goose** public house. Awarded a Michelin Star on three occasions by various Chefs over the past 5 years, The Goose has its own local Chef John Footman at the helm having worked in various Michelin Star restaurants over his 17 year career.

The grade 2 listed, and handsome, red brick building has some parts dating back to 1728. Beautifully decorated, that home-away-from-home feeling brings comfort in a relaxing environment. With food that speaks for itself, John sources local and seasonal produce to compliment the English countryside served, not only in the restaurant, but in the bar and garden as well.

Lunch food service is from 12-2:30pm Tuesday to Friday and until 3:30pm Saturdays, Sundays and Bank Holiday Mondays. Dinner is served from 7pm until 9:30pm Tuesday to Saturday where you are also welcome to come for a drink and socialise.

The Goose team look forward to welcoming you, whether you want to come for lunch, dinner, a drink or a coffee.

288 THE BEETLE & WEDGE BOATHOUSE

Ferry Lane, Moulsford-on-Thames,
Oxfordshire OX10 9JF
Tel: 01491 651381 Fax: 01491 651376
e-mail: boathouse@beetleandwedge.co.uk
website: www.beetleandwedge.co.uk

Set on the banks of the River Thames, **The Beetle &**
Wedge is a unique, buzzy, informal riverside restaurant
with rooms. In the Restaurant the emphasis is on quality of
food and head chef Georges Delorme manages an ever-
changing menu that may include sparkling fresh fish, game
in season, soups, salads and shellfish. The older part of the
Boathouse offers the famous open charcoal grill where
delicacies are created before your very eyes. In fine
weather the Boathouse goes alfresco onto the terrace just
a few feet from the river, beautifully set and lit in the
evening. No wonder the restaurant was accorder the
honour of being listed amongst Harper's Bazaar 2009 Going
Out Guide 'Britain's 250 Best Restaurants' and also number
24 in the Times's 2010 'Best Places to eat Al Fresco'.

The Beetle & Wedge has also achieved a 'Four Star Restaurant with rooms rating' under the
British Common Standard for Guest Accommodation. There are three beautiful rooms overlooking
the River Thames, with king-size beds and lovely roll-top baths; one of the ground floor rooms
offers a spacious en suite shower room. Breakfast is served in The Boathouse and on fine weather
mornings can also be served outside on the jetty.

289 THE FLEUR DE LYS

9 High Street, Dorchester-on-Thames, Wallingford,
Oxfordshire OX10 7HH
Tel: 01865 340502
e-mail: info@fleurdorchester.co.uk
website: www.fleurdelys-dorchester.co.uk

The 16th century **Fleur de Lys** provides the perfect place to
get away from the hustle and bustle of city life for a
weekend or mid-week break. Set in the medieval village of
Dorchester-on-Thames which is full of historic English charm
and includes a magnificent Augustinian Abbey to admire. All
five rooms have en suite facilities and have been decorated
to an extremely high standard; featuring king sized beds with
Egyptian cotton linen, guests are assured of a comfortable
night's sleep.

Very much family orientated inside, the bright and airy
restaurant seats between 20 and 30 people in comfort as they
choose from the sumptuous menu. Owner Will has trained at
a very high standard and prepares all of the food fresh to order; Will also ensures that the menu
changes with respect to the in season ingredients.

Keen to entice more and more custom, the Fleur de Lys hosts several events throughout the
year, including themed £5 supper nights, a mini beer fest with a bbq and spit roast and regular
quiz evenings. The pub also boasts an enormous beer garden which makes the Fleur de Lys the
perfect place to relax with a pint during the summer sunshine.

290 THE RAILWAY INN

Station Road, Culham, Oxfordshire OX14 3BT
Tel: 01235 528046
Fax: 01235 525183
e-mail: info@railwayinnculham.co.uk
website: www.railwayinnculham.co.uk

Located adjacent to Culham railway station, **The Railway Inn** is a fine old traditional pub and inn offering delicious home-cooked food and comfortable Bed and Breakfast accommodation at affordable rates.

Spacious and attractively decorated throughout, with a bar area, games room and restaurant, the inn also has a beautiful rear garden where children are most welcome. Inside, the bar serves real ales and the large flat screen TV provides great coverage of all your favourite sports including football, rugby, Formula 1 and more. There's also a dedicated games room with pool, darts, fruit machines and a jukebox. This lively inn also hosts regular quiz nights, karaoke, pool competitions and more!

The main restaurant serves traditional home-cooked food and seats 50 people. It is open for breakfasts at 6.30am to 9am, lunchtime from 12 noon to 3pm, and for evening meals from 6pm to 9.30pm. On Saturday and Sunday, the restaurant is open all day for food until 9.30pm.

The accommodation at the Railway Inn comprises 11 en suite rooms, all equipped with colour TV with freeview, 24 hour wireless Internet access, and tea/coffee making facilities. A full English breakfast, cooked to order, is included in the tariff.

291 THE CROWN

1 Packhorse Lane, Marcham, Abingdon,
Oxfordshire OX13 6NT
Tel: 01865 391522
e-mail: caspar46@talktalkbusiness.net
website: www.thecrownmarcham.com

The Crown pub is a traditional country pub serving good home cooked food and exceptionally well kept real ales. Situated in the quiet and tranquil village of Marcham, Keith and Tricia ensure that any visitors are warmly received and welcomed just as a local is. A traditional 16th century inn with a great deal of the antique features remaining, the Crown is a nice place to be, whether for a good pint or a game of Aunt Sally, the pub hosting two teams.

Keith takes great pride in the ale served at the Crown, normally serving five at any one time, he rotates guest ales every couple of days, keeping the locals guessing as to what will be on the pumps from one day to the next. As well as the exceptional ale on offer, the kitchens utilise fresh and local produce to create a fine menu that is packed full of classic favourites.

Inside there is lovely dark oak furniture and a roaring log fire to create a real feeling of cosyness during the winter months, in the summer, the beer garden offers a great spot to sit and enjoy the sun.

292 THE BLACK HORSE

Main Street, East Hanney, Wantage,
Oxfordshire OX12 0JE
Tel: 01235 868212
e-mail: wikidmum@hotmail.co.uk
website: www.theblackhorseineasthanney.co.uk

The **Black Horse** in East Hanney has been owned and run by
Claire Walters and her family for over two years now and the
pub has built up an enviable reputation for fine food, excellent
service and a warm welcome. With a bright and airy interior,
enhanced by the open plan layout that accommodates up to 30
covers, the Black Horse has plenty of room for everybody; from
ramblers and walkers with their dogs to families on a day out.

During the summer months, the Black Horse holds games in its
lovely garden, Auntie Sally being a particular favourite (rules on
the excellent website) as well as Hanneyfest, a charity music and
ale festival. A popular venue, there are regular appearances by
local bands, as well as quiz evenings, murder mystery nights and
you can even cheer on Oxford in the local boat race.

Claire sources all of the ingredients for the menu from local,
reputable suppliers and prepares the food fresh to order. The
extensive menu ranges from small snacks to large meals for the
hungry, ever popular are Claire's homemade pies, which are
made on a daily basis.

293 THE TALBOT HOTEL

Bridge Street, Bampton,
Oxfordshire OX18 2HA
Tel: 01993 850326
e-mail: ajr.talbot@hotmail.co.uk

The **Talbot Hotel** is a very popular 'pub' located in
the pleasant village of Bampton. Its owner Adam
Russell has been here for 17 years and offers six
comfortable bedrooms – all which boast en-suite
facilities (one of the bedrooms has a bath). The hotel
is located just two miles from the River Thames and
is ideal for visitors planning on visiting Oxford and
the Cotswolds. It is also close to the Thames Path, so
there are many walkers that like to stay at the hotel.
A good hearty breakfast can be arranged although no
food is served at lunchtimes or of an evening. The
rooms are all tastefully decorated and there is a good
variety, including twins, doubles and a family room.

The Talbot Hotel dates back to the 16th century
and is a former coaching inn. It has a lot of character
and in the summer months there is a pleasant outside
courtyard which is popular amongst guests. Adam is
also the owner of The Riverside Inn near Tewkesbury which serves home cooked food and real
ales. The Riverside Inn also has camping pitches and a self catering apartment available.

294 ROCKE COTTAGE TEA ROOMS

Clungunford, nr Craven Arms, Shropshire SY7 OPX
Tel: 01588 660631
e-mail: kr.clarke@btinternet.com
website: www.rockecottagetearoom.co.uk

Visitors to **Rocke Cottage Tea Rooms** enjoy stepping back in time and soaking up the quintessential experience of taking tea within the old-world charm of an English setting. Soft music from the 1920s and 1930s creates just the right note in this delightful tea room, which seats up to 28 people inside as well as 12 in the garden area.

Home cooking is extremely important to owner, Karin Clarke, as is buying fresh local produce. Breakfast, lunches, refreshments and teas are all available along with a superb range of homemade cakes and chef's specials. Among the most popular of the dishes served is ploughman's with Shropshire blue, the day's homemade quiche, specials such as creamy trout and lime pate, Shropshire figet pie and fresh homemade scones served with clotted cream, preserve and strawberries. Food is served between 10am and 5pm Wednesday to Sunday (and Bank Holidays).

On brighter days customers often like to enjoy refreshments in the outside garden area and many take the opportunity for a stroll in the pretty gardens, which has a stream and a tree house. A cosy self-catering cottage is also available all year round and sleeps up to three people. Ring for further details.

296 BARLEY MOW HOUSE

Aston Rogers, nr Shrewsbury,
Shropshire SY5 9HQ
Tel: 01743 891234 Mobile: 07890215412
e-mail: colinrigby@astonrogers.fsnet.co.uk
website: www.stmem.com/barleymowhouse

Dating back to the 18th century in parts, this former farmhouse now stands as a fine bed and breakfast, perfect for peaceful weekends away, or longer breaks in the countryside. Owners Colin and Linda Rigby fell in love with the place in 2000, and have run it as a successful bed and breakfast since.

They provide three beautiful en suite rooms, each of which is individually styled and spacious with luxurious king size beds. One room is located on the ground floor, whilst another is family sized, welcoming children. Guests can wake each morning to Linda's spectacular full English breakfast, which she creates using as much local produce as possible. Guests say they fill you up for the whole day, which can easily be spent exploring the two acres of idyllic grounds in which the bed and breakfast is set.

The medieval market town of Shrewsbury is also just a short drive away, providing plenty of pleasant days exploring the range of castles and museums on offer. But guests can also use this 4 gold diamond graded haven for a base for exploring the nearby areas of Telford, Shropshire, mid-Wales and the Welsh Marches.

295 THE BARON AT BUCKNELL

Bucknell, nr Knighton, Shropshire SY7 0AH
Tel: 01547 530549
e-mail: info@baronatbucknell.co.uk
website: www.baronatbucknell.co.uk

The Baron at Bucknell is one of Shropshire's finest Country inns in the heart of beautiful countryside. Situated 5 miles east of Knighton and 12 miles west of Ludlow, patrons come from many miles to savour the welcome, the hospitality and the excellent food. With a crackling log fire in the lounge and a wonderful old apple press dated 1770 in the Restaurant, this country inn is full of charm and character. The menu will excite your taste buds with traditional honest food, inspired by the countryside and cooked from the heart. In addition to the restaurant menu, diners can also choose from a daily specials board, sandwiches, paninis or the authentic stone baked pizza menu. A well chosen wine list and Cask Marquee accredited real ales compliment the food, as does a good selection of soft drinks, freshly ground coffees and teas.

Children have their own menu and are welcome to dine throughout. The current menu is available on the website. With a large car park, a pretty beer garden, and choice of rooms to suit any party size, the Baron is the perfect location to celebrate any occasion, from a small surprise birthday party to a large wedding reception. The owners, Debra & Phil Wright plan to add 5 luxury bedrooms in 2010. Please ring for details.

The pubs stands in an area of Outstanding Natural Beauty which is wonderful walking country. The owners have compiled a book of walks that all start at the pub and vary in length and difficulty. Opportunities for cycling and horse riding are also plenty, with many woodland tracks and a new down hill mountain biking course in Bucknell Wood. Opening hours are 12-3pm and 6:30-11pm Monday to Friday. Open all day Saturday, Sunday and bank holidays.

Food is served 12-2:30pm and 6:30-9pm seven days a week.

297 THE BOTTLE AND GLASS INN

Picklescott, Church Stretton, Shropshire SY6 6NR
Tel: 01694 751345 Fax: 01694 751361
website: www.picklescott.org.uk

Situated in the pretty village of Picklescott village, just a short drive from the main A458 is **The Bottle and Glass Inn**. The exact date of the inn's beginnings varies depending on who you talk to but the owners believe that it dates back as far as the 15th century. In its lifetime it has had a number of personas, including a coaching inn, a farmhouse, and a postal inn and was even used as mortuary at one point. It's somewhat macabre past does not extent to the current day however, as the inn is as lively as ever, offering unbeatable cuisine, a fine selection of well kept ales and great guest accommodation all year round.

Owner Paula Gurney has been running the inn for the past 18 months, giving herself quite the reputation for being the 'Queen' of Picklescott's cooking. She serves up food from 12-2:30pm and 6:30-9pm seven days a week. The menu changes daily to reflect the seasonal local produce used to create all the dishes, but guests are guaranteed to find something they like. There are a range of light bites and starters which include soup of the day, king prawns in tempura batter and homemade chicken liver pate. Mains include a handsome array of meat and game dishes such as Welsh lamb cutlets, sirloin steaks cooked to your liking, horseshoe gammon and game pie filled with venison, pigeon and pheasant cooked in red wine and herbs with a short crust pastry. Fish lovers and vegetarians also have a good choice with dishes like lime and honey salmon fillet and goat's cheese, mushroom and spinach pancake on offer. The relaxed home cooking style of the food here ensures that the restaurant is usually busy, particularly from Thursday to Sunday; when it is best to book.

Paula also offers two double guest bedrooms, both of which have en suite facilities and the option of adding a cot. These light and airy rooms make an ideal base for guests wanting to explore Shropshire, with a wealth of classic English villages just a short drive away, and plenty of rolling open countryside to ramble through. All guests come on a bed and breakfast rate, which is sure to set you up for the day, cooked with fresh local produce.

298 THE GEORGE AND DRAGON INN

2 High Street, Much Wenlock, Shropshire TF13 6AA
Tel: 01952 727312
e-mail: thegeorge.dragon@btinternet.com

Beverley and James have been running the **George and Dragon Inn** since January 2009, though they have been in business together since 2002. Beverley was born and bred in Much Wenlock so brings much local charm into the inn, which dates back to the 17th century in parts. The inn's traditional décor is complimented by a collection of memorabilia, low beamed ceiling and a beautiful brick fireplace.

Guests here can enjoy a minimum of four real ales at any one time from both local and national breweries alongside a good selection of fine wines and spirits. The inn is particularly popular for its food, which is served daily from 12-2.30pm ad 6-9pm throughout the week apart from Wednesday and Sundays night. The menu focuses on homemade traditional food, and is created by long serving Chef Marg. Some of her speciality dishes include homemade cottage pie, chicken breast stuffed with ham and cheese and wrapped in bacon and poached salmon in white wine and rosemary. On Sunday lunchtime a fine roast is added to the menu, when booking is heavily recommended.

Guests are welcome to join James and Beverley on the second Wednesday of every month for an amusing quiz night, with plenty of other community events also on regularly such as Morris dancing. The inn is a friendly and fun place to be that is truly at the heart of the Much Wenlock Community. Children and dogs welcome.

299 THE RED LION

Holyhead Road, Wellington, Telford,
Shropshire TF1 2EW
Tel: 01952 223937 Fax: 01952 223937

After 25 years in the computer science industry Julian Goode changed careers and acquired **The Red Lion**. That was in 2003, and since then he has built up a strong following among local residents with the help of his wife Sarah. Their pretty late 19th century roadside inn is just a mile outside Wellington. It's in immaculate condition both outside and inside, where the neat, compact bar and stylish lounge provide the perfect setting for enjoying a glass of cask ale from local breweries. All are welcome to dine or drink, or join in with the Tuesday night quiz.

Food is available from 12-2:30pm Monday to Saturday and from 5:30-8:30pm Tuesday to Saturday. Julian and Sarah put a lot of effort into creating a wholesome and varied menu created with great local produce. Dishes include classics like homemade curry, steak and kidney pudding, Shropshire ham and eggs, and specials like fisherman's medley or oyster mushroom, champagne and rocket risotto.

Located beside the Wrekin, the area's best landmark reaching up 1,300 feet criss-crossed with plenty of charming and challenging foot paths, it's an ideal place to build up a thirst and appetite that Julian and Sarah are ready and waiting to satisfy from noon, all day every day.

300 THE COALBROOKDALE INN AND FOUNDRY MASTERS HOUSE

Wellington Road, Coalbrookdale, Ironbridge, Shropshire TF8 7DX
Tel: Coalbrookdale - 01952 433953 Foundry - 01952 433658
Fax: 01952 458514
e-mail: tudorhotels@aol.com
website: www.coalbrookdaleinn.co.uk

Danny and Dawn Wood make a great team at the **Coalbrookdale Inn**, which stands opposite the museum of Iron and the historic Darby Furnace. A flight of stone steps leads into this handsome dark brick hostelry, where the bar features heavy oak, tiled floors and a log fire. It began life in the 1830s, when it provided rest and refreshment for hundreds of iron workers; it now attracts patrons from all walks of life, who come here to enjoy the unrivalled hospitality, the wonderful friendly atmosphere, the food and the outstanding collection of real ales and other draught and bottled beers.

The ever-changing variety of real ales includes brews from both local and national breweries with over 40 different ales available during each month. Regular ales include Ironbridge Gold, Hobsons Town Crier and Wye Valley Butty Bach.

Food is available each evening from 6-8:30pm and for Sunday lunch between 12-3pm in the inn's award winning restaurant. Prizes for healthy eating prove to guests they are dining well at this place, as sumptuous flavours are combined with good old home cooking. An impressive range of food is served up to suit every palette and budget from light bites to gourmet game dishes. Choose from starters like smoked tuna and sweet chilli sauce, sautéed mushrooms or battered brie, and a selection of mains that encompasses a range of fish, meat and game dishes. Popular choices include sizzling fajitas, pan fried halibut finished with Anchovy Butter, sautéed Gressingham duck with fresh peppercorn jus, a mature Shropshire fillet steak, and spiced sea bass served with creamy gorgonzola mash. Vegetarians are also well catered for with options like red Thai curry satay, and feta cheese and oven roasted vegetables over chilli and tomato penne pasta. Owing to popularity its best to book, particularly on weekends.

The inn also offers three luxury en suite bedrooms, refurbished to the highest standards whilst still preserving the best period elements. Guests also have the options of staying in the Foundry Masters House, just a short walk down the road where modern comforts like satellite TV and DVD players are seamlessly merged with heritage Georgian furniture and design. This decadent period accommodation is perfect for business or pleasure, just minutes from many scenic and historic attractions.

301 MAWS CAFÉ AND CHOCOLATE SHACK

Ferry Road, Jackfield, nr Ironbridge, Shropshire TF8 7LS
Tel: 01952 883843
e-mail: chocolateshack@hotmail.co.uk
website: www.chocolateshack.co.uk

Hidden away in Jackfield near Ironbridge is **Maws Café and Chocolate Shack**. Owned by Marsha and her mum Jacky they run the café with the help of their friend Sarah. Catering for visitors to the Jackfield Tile Museum and nearby craft shops it offers a range of breakfasts, snacks and main meals. All meals are made with fresh produce supplied from the local butchers and bakers. Guests will be hard pushed to refuse one of Jacky's ornate homemade chocolates which create a wonderfully chocolately aroma throughout the café.

302 THE BELL INN

Old Wenlock Road, Cross Houses, Shrewsbury,
Shropshire SY5 6JJ
Tel: 01743 761264 e-mail: Darren.lewis@sky.com

The Bell Inn at Cross Houses in Shrewsbury was built in the 18th century, but stands today as a fine family run country inn. Annie and Darren open all day every day apart from Tuesdays when they don't open until 5pm. They pride themselves on offering a true country inn experience serving Shropshire Gold ale and fine country cooking throughout the week. There are three upstairs en suite bedrooms with a hearty breakfast, ideal for a short break away. To the rear is a spacious caravan and camping park with electric hook ups and bathroom facilities. Families are welcome and children have plenty to see and do with the inn's own pigs, pygmy goats, duck and rabbits to pet.

304 COURTYARD CAFÉ

Griffin Courtyard, Leg Street, Oswestry, Shropshire SY11 2NN
Tel: 01691 679805

The irresistible aroma of premium home cooking greets you as you enter the **Courtyard Café**, located in the town of Oswestry. Hidden in Griffin Courtyard in the centre of town the café conveniently caters for young and old, Monday to Saturday 9am-4pm. Owner Mrs Kettle serves up a handsome menu of cakes, treats, light bites and main meals. All dishes are prepared fresh to order on the premises each day, using the best in locally sourced produce, including Mrs Kettle's special homemade soup. The specials board changes daily, so there is always something for everyone. Whether for a full meal, or a quaint afternoon tea, this cosy café provides the perfect spot. Cash and cheque only please.

www.findSOMEWHERE.co.uk
For people who want to explore the United Kingdom

Places to Stay

303 THE WINGFIELD ARMS

Montford Bridge, nr Shrewsbury, Shropshire SY4 1EB
Tel: 01743 850750
e-mail: mail@thewingfieldarms.com
website: www.thewingfieldarms.com

Homemade food is the main focus of the extensive menu on offer at **The Wingfield Arms**, which was known for a while as the Old Swan. This outstanding pub of great appeal to the whole family stands in the picturesque village of Montford Bridge, on the B4380 just off the main A5 three mile from Shrewsbury. Business partners and good friends Frank and Denise; and Stephen and Julie continue to add to the pub's growing reputation. Parts of the building date back some 400 years and behind the mellow yellow-painted, part creeper-clad exterior the public areas feature beams and some interesting exposed brickwork, setting a welcoming, traditional note.

Three real ales are always available and the various menus and daily specials tempt with a wide ranging selection of home cooked food. Chef, Tim Southern, is helped by Denise and Julie in the kitchen and together they are putting this place on the map as a dining destination. In the recently refurbished Riverside Restaurant booking is recommended at peak times, particularly for the very popular Sunday carvery, available from 12pm – 2pm. Everything on its menus is worth trying, and room should definitely be left for one of the super sweets. Lunch and evening menus are available along with a special menu designed for younger customers. The menus are fairly traditional and favourites on the main menu include homemade cottage pie, lasagne; and fish pie. There is a wide selection of homemade desserts and many people return again and again to the pub to sample the delights on offer. On brighter days, the terrace and beer garden are extremely popular, as is the children's play area, which occupy younger guests while they wait for their delicious meal. Food is served Thursday – Saturday between 12pm – 2.30pm and 6pm -9pm. (Available on more days during the summer months). The pub can cater for all special occasions, from business lunches to birthdays, weddings and funerals (Marquees can be erected for functions).

The Wingfield Arms has an extensive site for caravans and motor homes (23 pitches), tents and trailer tents, with showers, toilets and hook ups. This provides a super base for a walking holiday, or for exploring the local villages and the historic town of Shrewsbury (the bus for Shrewsbury stops outside the pub). It also has fishing rights along a three quarter-mile stretch of the River Severn, with salmon, roach and barbell among the expected catch.

305 THE WALLS

Welsh Walls, Oswestry, Shropshire SY11 1AW
Tel: 01691 670970
e-mail: info@the-walls.co.uk
website: www.the-walls.co.uk

If you've become a little jaded with your dining out experiences lately, then perhaps its time you made your way to **The Walls**. Started in 1992 following an inspired conversion, this Oswestry restaurant is an institution. It is now safely back in the hands of its creators, Geoff & Kate Hughes. Capable of comfortably seating over 200 guests, The Walls successfully manages to marry the scale of a big building with a really personal way of looking after its customers.

Rachael, the manger, has worked here for over 7 years, Simon, the head chef, even longer (in two spells) and lots of other staff are very familiar faces to the many regulars that frequent the Walls. This gives The Walls a very family feel; the customers really feel they matter. With over 100 years of combined kitchen experience in the highly skilled kitchen team, the ridiculously varied, wide ranging and bewildering array of menus, all sourced from local suppliers, is enough to satisfy even the handful of clients who eat there almost everyday of the week.

When generally restaurant food seems to still be getting a lot more elaborate than is good for anybody, The Walls is continuing in its tried and tested formula of providing food with integrity, prepared in the correct manner, with the minimum amount of "Ego" ending up on the plate. Sunday lunch is a carnivorous feast, the carvery format is executed with juicy ribs of Welsh beef, legs of lamb, shoulders of pork, turkey crowns and roast ham and an array of roasted vegetables. Vegetarians & fish eaters are also provided for and there is a really wonderful atmosphere throughout the afternoon: it's usual that the last lunch guests are still with us when the first of Sunday evening diners arrive.

A fixed price menu is available, currently £13.50 for 2 courses at lunchtime and before 7.30 p.m. every day, a third course is always available at an extra charge. Alongside this menu is the seasonal a la Carte menu and the daily & market specials dishes, complete the smorgasbord. Puddings are taken seriously and Richie, the pastry chef, is another of the die-hards who

has worked for us on more than one occasion. The wine list is also pretty extraordinary with a global selection of affordable house wines, particularly strong on Italian offerings and a further more serious list (Humpty's Hiccups – The Off Piste selection), which contains some real gems.

Our web site is usually up to date particularly after the early monthly menu change and is a great source of information about all we are up to. Regular electronic mailings of the cleverly named "Walls Street Journal" will keep you up to date with events at this dynamic restaurant. The Walls is open 7 days a week, lunch & dinner and for morning coffee and teas in the afternoon.

306 THE PEN MILL HOTEL

Sherbourne Road, Yeovil,
Somerset BA21 5DB
Tel: 01935 423081
e-mail: penmillhotel07@btconnect.com
website: www.penmillhotel.co.uk

The Pen Mill Hotel is located on the edge of the Yeovil countryside. Jon and Sarah Palmer bought the hotel from Sarah's parents in 2003 and were devastated when a fire destroyed it in 2006. Since then the hotel has been totally refurbished and it is extremely popular with walkers and cyclists.

There are eight rooms available to guests. Four of these boast en-suite facilities. Ring for details. The hotel dates back to 1837 when it was originally a Coaching Inn built using local Ham Stone under a Welsh slate roof. The interior is modern and there is a warm and welcoming atmosphere.

Most of the bar and restaurant areas enjoy views of the Somerset and Dorset countryside. Where possible all suppliers are local and the specials board changes continuously to make the most of the seasonal local produce available. Most of the dishes are made fresh on the premises by the dedicated team of chefs, headed by Sarah. Food is served between 12pm to 8.30pm every day and booking is advised because the restaurant is extremely popular with locals and visitors. Disabled access is not a problem. All major credit cards taken.

308 THE SQUARE AND COMPASS INN

Windmill Hill, Ashill, nr Ilminster, Somerset TA19 9NX
Tel: 01823 480467
e-mail: squareandcompass@tiscali.co.uk
website: www.squareandcompasspub.com

Surrounded by fields and with large gardens enjoying views of the Blackdown Hills, **The Square and Compass Inn** is a fine old traditional hostelry that looks very inviting with its hanging baskets and tubs of flowers. The interior features wooden ceiling beams and heavy hand-made wooden furniture. In winter, there is always a roaring log fire.

There has been a pub at Windmill Hill for around 200 years. The present owners, Chris and Janet Slow, are celebrating their 12th year here and in that time have built up a reputation for very good food and drink served in a warm and friendly atmosphere. Janet is an excellent chef and leads a team of qualified chefs. Their job was made easier in 2008 when a new kitchen, as large as the pub itself, was added.

Behind the pub is The Barn, which provides a purpose built venue for weddings, conferences, music and parties. The Barn has a civil licence for weddings and a fully licensed bar, modern toilets and large dance area.

From June 2010, the Inn will also be offering quality accommodation in 8 large double en suite bedrooms that have been created in an imaginatively purpose designed stable block.

307 FROG STREET FARMHOUSE

Hatch Beauchamp, Taunton, Somerset TA3 6AF
Tel: 01823 481883
e-mail: frogstreet@hotmail.com
website: www.frogstreet.co.uk

Frog Street Farmhouse provides a haven of tranquillity for those wanting to escape the noise and stress of the modern world. Awaiting you at this delightful listed Somerset Longhouse is relaxing accommodation surrounded by open countryside. Dating back the 15th century this Somerset longhouse is situated at the end of a 'no through road' and is just over five miles from the M5 motorway and approximately 20 miles from both the north and south coast, making it the perfect base for either business or pleasure.

The house has been tastefully restored to a high standard, retaining the character of the house with its beamed ceilings, fine Jacobean panelling and open fireplaces. During winter guests can curl up and relax by the log fire or in the summer enjoy the beautiful secluded gardens.

The bedrooms are beautifully appointed and comfortable, having the benefit of en-suite facilities. All are equipped with internet access, hair dryer and tea/coffee making facilities and several boast the luxury of Super King beds. In the morning guests can wake up to a full English Breakfast made from the very best local produce, including the farm's own free range eggs, local butcher's sausages and homemade preserves. An evening meal can be provided if pre-booked and dietary requirements can be accommodated for.

There is plenty to do for visitors to the area and something to suit most tastes. Glastonbury Tor, Wells and Dunster Castle, several Manor Houses, Hestercombe Gardens, Fleet Air Arm Museum, Cricket St Thomas and Haynes Motor Museum are all within easy reaching distance. For those after a different experience there is plenty to explore at Cheddar Caves and Wookey Hole or why not catch a show at the Brewhouse Theatre. There are also plenty of National Trust and English Heritage properties waiting to be discovered as well as the Quantock Hills and Exmoor National Park.

Frog Street Farmhouse is not just a place to stay but a place to enjoy.

309 ASH HOUSE HOTEL

41 Main Street, Ash, Martock,
Somerset TA12 6PB
Tel: 01935 822036
e-mail: reception@ashhousehotel.co.uk
website: www.ashhousehotel.co.uk

Ash House Hotel provides top quality accommodation set in 1.5 acres of beautiful gardens. The Ham stone building dates back to the early 18th century and inside the hotel has been restored to its former glory. The Georgian building, which has a flagstone floor dating back 300 years, contains nine en-suite rooms, which are all full of character and charm. The rooms are comfortable and the beds have Italian cotton sheets and fluffy towels. All of the beds have mattress toppers and the bathrooms are equipped with power showers. Most of the rooms boast spectacular views over the hotel's gardens, which are floodlit at night and each have a hospitality tray of local treats. Produce is sourced locally and lunches and dinners are available in the hotel's Orangery, with daily changing menus, which are imaginative and finely executed.

The owner of Ash House Hotel, Gordon Doodson, has 25 years of experience in the hospitality trade, and he and his staff offer a warm and friendly welcome to all guests. For those on business trips the hotel has meeting rooms, business facilities and wireless internet connection. Well behaved dogs are also welcome. Ring for details.

There are plenty of things to do in the area with clay pigeon shooting, fishing, golf and bird watching among the most popular. For those seeking a cultural experience, there are plenty of museums and galleries in the vicinity as well as cider tasting. Walkers, cyclists and horse riders will be in their element with plenty of nature trails to explore. Passing through Martock, is the 50 mile long Parrett Trail. And for shopaholics there are plenty of shopping outlets nearby.

The hotel is located close to the village of Martock which is a mile from the A303 London to Exeter road. Yeovil is six miles away and the hotel is also within easy reach of the Blackdown Hills, the Mendips, the Quantocks, Exmoor and the Dorset coast. There are plenty of historical sites in the area including Montacute House, Barrington Court, Muchelney Abbey, East Lambrook Manor and Cadbury Castle.

310 MANOR FARM B&B

Dulcote, Wells, Somerset BA5 3PZ
Tel/Fax: 01749 672125
e-mail: rosalind.bufton@talktalk.net
website: www.wells-accommodation.co.uk

Imagine gazing across a mile of unspoiled English countryside to the magnificent Cathedral of Wells which has presided over these ancient lands since the 12th century...Imagine the afternoon sun warming the creamy limestone walls while you sip Earl Grey tea in an English country garden... Such is life at **Manor Farm Bed & Breakfast.** This delightful 17th century farmhouse, its frontage covered with old roses and clematis, is the home of Rosalind Bufton, a geologist and keen walker who enjoys talking to guests about the local area.

Guests at Manor Farm eat well. Rosalind has her own smallholding with chickens, ducks, geese and sheep. "They are all friends!" she says. "We only eat the eggs from the birds and never the animals". She also has two friendly cats. Breakfast with a variety of choices is served in the oak-beamed dining room. After a day of exploring, relax in the comfortable sitting room and look out over the garden to the fields and Wells Cathedral in the distance.

The accommodation at Manor Farm comprises 4 charming rooms, 3 of them with en suite facilities, the fourth with its own bathroom. One of them is a disabled access ground floor suite that opens onto the peaceful, spacious gardens.

311 THE GEORGE AT NUNNEY

Church Street, Nunney, Somerset BA11 4LW
Tel: 01373 836458 Fax: 01373 836565
e-mail: info@thegeorgeatnunney.co.uk
website: www.thegeorgeatnunney.co.uk

You have to envy the inhabitants of the Somerset village of Nunney, with breathtaking views of their own moated castle built in 1373 and their effortlessly comfortable 14th century coaching inn **The George at Nunney** serving fantastic food seven days a week; this is utopia.

Owners Fraser Carruth and Wayne Carnegie have been running The George for almost two years and business has never been better. The coaching inn boasts nine en-suite bedrooms, two of which have elegant four-poster beds.

At the heart of the inn is the restaurant which is open for breakfast, lunch and dinner, serving delicious food made from produce, locally sourced and delivered daily.

The George at Nunney embraces locals and visitors who all come together to enjoy the warm atmosphere of this delightful establishment.

House rules: Children over 14 welcome. Dogs welcome.

312 THE BELL INN

High Street, Buckland Dinham,
nr Frome, Somerset BA11 2QT
Tel: 01373 462956
e-mail: jerwestcott@aol.com
website: www.bellatbuckland.co.uk

The Bell Inn is a truly fine historic village inn located at
Buckland Dinham, Somerset. Dating back to the 16th century,
The Bell Inn is very traditional and has a popular restaurant
serving traditional British food. The well stocked bar has a
wide range of real ciders, beers and fine wines. Log fires
keep diners warm in colder months and create a cosy and
friendly atmosphere.

Food is served lunch times and evenings and choices
include premium sausages served with mash, red onion gravy
and fresh vegetables; beer battered fish and chips served with
peas, lemon and tartare sauce; and locally reared ham with
an egg laid by the pub's own free range chickens. Desserts
like jam roly poly and custard; mixed fruit compote served in a brandy snap basket; and warm
chocolate fudge cake are among the most popular of dishes to finish an evening.

The child friendly Bell Inn is owned by Jeremy Westcott and Lucy Davis-Coward and is popular
among walkers, cyclists and horse riders. Disabled access is not a problem and there is plenty of
disabled parking too. Although there is no accommodation offered at The Bell Inn there are
camping options available. Ring for details. All credit cards accepted.

313 LOWER WITHIAL FARM COTTAGES

East Pennard, Somerset BA4 6UE
Tel: 01749 860719 Fax: 01749 860719
e-mail: enquiries@lowerwithialfarmcottages.co.uk
website: www.lowerwithialfarmcottages.co.uk

Lower Withial Farm lies in a quiet rural spot within the picturesque village
of East Pennard, just six miles east of Glastonbury and within easy reach of
the Castle Cary train station. Owners Robin and Bridget Lawford took over
the farm in 2007 and have spent the past few years re-
developing the farm to create four beautiful holiday cottages.

Perfect for those who are seeking a quiet rural retreat in
the beautiful area of Somerset, the farm is surrounded by
acres of countryside, ideal for hours of exploring or tranquil
walks and wildlife spotting. All the cottages, Bradely Barn ,
Parbrook Cottage, Lottisham Barn and the Pennard Barn, can
accommodate up to six people with one double room and one
twin room and a sofa bed in the lounge. All cottages also are
elegantly styled and equipped to luxury standards with
handsome wooden floors, large floor to ceiling windows, beamed ceilings and decadently
comfortable beds. Guests can enjoy unspoilt views across the countryside from every room, or
relax in one of the sheltered courtyards, complete with their own hot tubs and barbeque
facilities. Just a few yards from the cottages themselves there is a convenient shower and laundry
room and a games room which comes equipped with pool and tennis tables, large flat screen TV
with Freeview, Playstation, Wii, dartboard and board game facilities for entertainment.

314 COBBLESTONES

71 Eastover, Bridgwater, Somerset TA6 5AP
Tel: 01278 452628

Bree Dransfield and Jackie Gill are the successful and well loved owners of **Cobblestones**; a popular inn in the heart of Bridgwater. In idyllic surroundings on the outskirts of the town, the inn is found on the banks of the river Parrett at the lowest bridging point. With glorious views to the front and a tranquil beer garden to the rear, it is a popular haven for both locals and visitors alike. Inside, guests can enjoy a homely atmosphere, with an inviting collection of books, comfy leather chairs and cosy corners, looking out through quaint shuttered windows. Guests can also take their chances on the pool table, the skittle alley, or on the darts board, or perhaps relax to the sound of some live music, usually held on weekends.

Bree and Jackie keep the ale lovers happy by offering a range of real ales on a rotational basis, along with a wide selection of other beers, lagers, wines and spirits. Those who fancy something a little sweeter will also like the drinks menu as it includes most well loved cocktails, including its signature cosmopolitan. Open all day every day, the inn also takes small bookings for its function room at the back of the inn; please call for details.

315 ADMIRAL BLAKE LTD

4-6 St Mary Street, Bridgewater,
Somerset TA6 3LT
Tel: 01278 423798

Admiral Blake takes its name from Bridgwater's most famous son Robert Blake. Born in 1599, his birthplace nearby in now a museum and well worth a visit.

The Admiral Blake is a family owned business, producing fish and chips at this address since 1960 over (fifty years).

The impressive brand of family style hospitality sees many repeat visitors who are always made to feel welcome. The bright and airy interior of the restaurant can be seen through the large shop, windows across the front that detail the restaurant's original status as a local shop. The Admiral Blake is open all day six days a week from 11:30am -10:30pm.

What guests really come for though is the food. The wide ranging menu naturally covers all the fish and chip options you could hope for with over six different varieties of fish available all served in a clean and homely restaurant . Other dishes include burgers, jacket potatoes, pies, pasties, vegetarian options and spit roasted chicken. The restaurant is licensed. The same extensive menu is available as a takeaway.

316 THE BOAT AND ANCHOR

Huntworth, nr Bridgwater,
Somerset TA7 0AQ
Tel: 01278 662473
website: www.theboatandanchor.co.uk

Nestled alongside the pretty Taunton- Bridgwater canal, with a picturesque view of the Somerset Levels, **The Boat and Anchor** is an ideal location for any location. The traditional Westcountry hostelry is in a beautiful location and is at the social heart of the little village of Huntworth, which can be found a short distance from J24 of the M5. The setting and the views are a real delight, and the inn, which has been refurbished and extended in recent years, is an ideal spot to pause for refreshment on a journey to or from Devon and Cornwall. Many people like to stop off here for a relaxing drink or lunch and many return again to sample what is on offer.

The welcome from owner Michael Rodosthenous and his staff is invariably warm and friendly, and the bar is a convivial spot for enjoying a chat and a drink. Real ales (Butcombe bitter is the regular) are among a fine range of draught and bottle beers, lagers, wines, spirits and soft drinks served lunchtime and evening and all day in the summer months. The dishes listed on the big chalkboard offer an excellent choice for all, with baguettes, ploughman's platters and jacket potatoes for light lunchtime choices and steaks, seafood specials and sizzling dishes among the favourites on the main list.

The Boat and Anchor also provides a very pleasant base for discovering all the scenic, historic and sporting attractions that Somerset has to offer. There are seven en-suite rooms available and there are exceptional views from the olive mill. Its location close to the M5 is a perfect spot for conferences and business meetings and there is plenty of overnight accommodation. The rooms are comfortable and available throughout the year. The inn has a self contained function suite with a private bar and the staff can cater for a wide variety of special occasions. The versatile space is excellent for all celebrations and caters for 90 seated guests of 150 guests if there are no tables. Wedding reception menus are available to cater for all requirements. Ring for details.

The Olive Mill (formerly the Toby) at nearby Chilton Polden is in the same ownership. A warm welcome always greets visitors to The Boat and Anchor and in summer months the canal-side garden is popular with locals and visitors to the area.

317 TYNTE ARMS

Enmore, nr Bridgwater, Somerset TA5 2DP
Tel: 01278 671351 Fax: 01278 671611

The small village of Enmore sits at the foot of the Quantock Hills in an area of outstanding natural beauty. Small though it is, this unspoilt village boasts a thriving traditional inn, the **Tynte Arms,** which has been owned and run for the past 25 years by Peter Genrey, a welcoming and hospitable host has also had extensive experience as a hotel owner. Dating back to 1848 and originally 3 farmer's cottages, the pub has an adjoining restaurant which offers an excellent menu of home-cooked food based on locally sourced ingredients and freshly prepared to order. Fresh fish dishes are something of a speciality and on Sundays there's a Carvery. To accompany your meal there's an extensive wine list, a choice of 3 real ales along with a very wide range of spirits. In good weather, customers can enjoy their refreshments in the spacious beer garden.

If you are planning to stay in this scenic corner of the county, the Tynte Arms offers quality accommodation in 4 guest bedrooms which are full of character and charm. There are beamed ceilings, very comfortable leather chairs and lots of interesting brass items and ornaments. All the rooms are on the ground floor and all have en suite facilities as well as colour TV and a hospitality tray. Each room also has its own wet room.

Visitors to the Tynte Arms will find plenty to see and do in the area. Golf is just a quarter of a mile away; sailing only one mile distant, and good fishing about 2 miles away. Other activities within easy reach include horse riding, cycling and walking. Busy Bridgwater is a 10-minute drive away and the county town, Taunton, only 20 minutes in the opposite direction.

The pub is open all year round from 10am to 3pm, and from 6pm to 11pm, daily; all major credit cards are accepted and there's a private car park. Sorry, no animals.

318 PITFOUR HOUSE

High Street, Timsbury,
Bath BA2 0HT
Tel: 01761 479554
e-mail: pitfourhouse@btinternet.com

Pitfour House is a beautiful Georgian house that offers luxury bed and breakfast accomodation. The five star silver awarded property is located in the village of Timsbury, with easy access to Bath, Wells and Bristol. For the more energetic walking in the Somerset countryside.

The house is tastefully decorated and furnished. There are two elegant bedrooms with six foot double beds and top quality duvets, linen and towels. One bedroom has ensuite shower and the other has a private bathroom. There is a formal sitting room with an open fire and a second for the use of guests.

The house is owned by Martin and Frances HARDMAN and has a half acre walled garden with interesting trees and shrubs, as well as a thriving vegetable garden.

Tea and homemade cakes are served on arrival and dinner is provided on request using seasonal produce from the garden when available.

Payment by cash or cheque only.

320 LAKESIDE TAVERN

Meaford Road, Meaford, Barlaston,
Staffordshire ST15 8UX
Tel: 01782 373242
e-mail: traceyg2@virginmedia.com

The Lakeside Tavern is a hidden gem, located just a short drive north of Stone from the main A34. This substantial white building houses within it a vibrant and lively tavern, run by a friendly local family. With a warm and inviting atmosphere, guests return time and time again to enjoy the fantastic range of food and drink on offer.

The bar is always kept well stocked with a range of fine wines and real ales which include Bass and the inn's own special brew; Lakeside Lancaster. Food is served daily from 12-2:30pm and 6-9:30pm with a choice of excellent cooked traditional pub fayre. All dishes are prepared fresh to order by a professional chef, whose specialities are homemade pies and lamb shanks. Children are welcome, and it is best to book to avoid disappointment.

Although the tavern has no indoor accommodation, it runs a caravan park to its rear which is open all year round. The site features running water, with space for up to 50 caravans in a pretty, rural setting. It makes an ideal base for touring the area which sports acres of rugged moorland, but when the open road loses its appeal, caravaners are more than welcome within the Tavern to

319 THE SWAN AT FRADLEY

Fradley Junction, nr Alrewas, Staffordshire DE13 7DN
Tel: 01283 790330

The Swan at Fradley is perhaps one of the most photographed pubs in the country. It is a charming grade II listed building of beautiful whitewashed brick, located within a local conservation area. It has looked out over the junction of the Trent, Mersey and Coventry Canals for over two centuries. It has played a crucial part in the everyday life of the canals for years, originally being constructed to serve the workmen that dug the canals and later used as a stabling point for boat horses. Nowadays, the inn is still popular with day trippers, walkers and canal lovers, not to mention locals who live right alongside it in their narrow boats.

It is owned and run by Rick and Tracey who met when working for the previous owners some years ago. They fell in love with both the inn and each other and have since taken the inn from strength to strength, making it a popular resting point for passersby. The tranquil view outside is matched by a cosy interior full of character with many original features and roaring real fires.

Ale lovers will be contented with a choice of up to five real ales always on offer. Abbot Ale, Black Sheep and Marstons Pedigree are the regulars, with plenty of rotating guests ales also making appearances. To accompany the ale, guests are invited to sample some of the culinary delights on offer, courtesy of the Swan's in house chef Neil. Specialising in wholesome home cooked food, Neil serves up dishes fresh to order Monday to Saturday from 12-2:30pm and 5:30-9pm. On Sundays a handsome carvery is on offer between 12-3pm, reverting to the main menu again between 6-9pm. The menu comprises a good range of chicken, grills, fish and vegetarian meals with a separate children's menu also available. Dishes on the main menu include sirloin steak, chicken kiev, Whitby breaded scampi and a broccoli and cream cheese bake. A selection of light bites are also available with various filled sandwiches, rolls, baguettes and jacket potatoes to choose from. Booking is not usually necessary but is essential for parties of 10 or more.

Rick and Tracey also put on a good show, with live entertainment every Saturday night from 9-12pm, just ask at the bar for who's playing. Children and dogs welcome, all major credit cards accepted.

321 THE GREYHOUND INN

Burston, nr Sandon, Stafford, Staffordshire ST18 0DR
Tel: 01889 508263

This wonderful traditional country inn can be found in the delightful rural village of Burston. Owned by Alan, son Peter and their wives Joyce and Zoe Jordan, **The Greyhound Inn** has been owned and personally run by the family since 1963. This family run pub welcomes children and as well as a spacious beer garden to make the most of in sunnier weather there are also animals outside the back of the pub, including Highland cattle, donkeys, goats, sheep and horses.

There is an extensive menu to choose from as well as an additional specials board, which changes daily. The Jordan's source some of their produce from local suppliers. The food choice is impressive from English favourites (chicken liver pate, prawn cocktail, beer-battered haddock, salads, roasts, steak & ale pie, and char grilled steaks) to chicken tikka masala, mousakka and broccoli & brie rosti. The desserts are extremely tempting. Sherry trifle, treacle sponge and apple pie are among the favourites. Food is served Monday-Saturday between 12pm - 2.30pm and 6pm - 9pm. On a Sunday food is served 12pm - 9pm (roast dinners are added to the main menu) and such is its popularity on weekends it is advisable to book to avoid disappointment. Lunch time special offers are available Monday - Saturday.

Three real ales can be enjoyed at The Greyhound Inn with Burton Ale the regular and the other two rotating guest ales, using local Micro Breweries if possible. There is also a good selection of beers, wines, spirits, lagers and liqueurs served every session.

This wonderful inn stands in the beautiful village of Burston, just yards off the A51 south east of Stone and its reputation brings patrons from all over Staffordshire, Cheshire and beyond. The Greyhound Inn is close to the neighbouring village of Sandon, which is home to the historic Sandon Hall, a fascinating little museum and 400 acres of lovely parkland. There is a caravan site at the back of the pub, which has space for up to five vans. It is ideal for those touring the area – ring for further details.

The Greyhound Inn also has facilities to cater for a wide range of functions, including birthday celebrations – ring for further details. All major credit cards accepted. Disabled access is not a problem. If it is a friendly welcome, good hospitality and a wide choice of dishes to choose from then The Greyhound Inn is highly recommended.

322 THE GRANGE

Lower Loxley, Uttoxeter, Staffordshire ST14 8RZ
Tel: 01889 502021
e-mail: mary.grange@hotmail.co.uk
website: www.bandbthegrangestaffs.co.uk

The Grange is a lovingly-converted 17th century barn located on a family farm. Owners Mary and Mike are delightful hosts and the traditional farm house food, hospitality and accommodation is of a very high standard. On your arrival Mary and Mike will give you a warm welcome, offering you freshly made complimentary homemade cakes and tea.

There are four luxury en-suite guest rooms, which are all comfortable and newly decorated and overlook 200 acres of pastureland and woodlands alongside the River Blythe. Breakfast and other meals (home-cooked dinners and packed lunches by prior arrangement) are served in the bright, attractive dining room, and the lounge area is an ideal place to relax after a busy day. Breakfast options include cereals, fruit, juices, full English, traditional potteries oatcakes with different fillings, continental options, vegetarian or eggs on toast.

Its countryside location is fantastic, with plenty of beautiful views to be enjoyed. It has a beautiful and spacious garden and there are plenty of walks along the River Blythe and a woodland trail. Originally built in the 1600s to store hay and grain, it was used as a milking parlour in the 1970s and 1980s before it was converted in 2002. The old stone was refurbished and it has wood floors, oak beams and pine woodwork. The Grange's peaceful rural location makes it the ideal get-away. It is a good base for family holidays, relaxing or romantic breaks.

There are plenty of attractions within easy reaching distance should you want to visit a theme park, historic estates, museums or market town. There are a good range of activities to try your hand at in the surrounding area, including fishing at Blithfield and on the River Dove. Many guests also choose to play golf at The Manor at Kingston and Uttoxeter Golf Clubs and there is horse racing at Uttoxeter if that is more your scene.

If you fancy time just soaking up the peaceful surroundings of The Grange, there is a good selection of board games, books and magazines to help you while away the time, or guidebooks and information on local attractions so you can plan another day out. Wireless Broadband is available on site. In each room there are extra blankets and a hair dryer, and an ironing board can be provided. There is ample car parking. No pets or smoking. All of the rooms are upstairs – ring for details on disabled access.

323 THE HARTLEY ARMS

56 Long Street, Wheaton Aston, Stafford, Staffordshire ST19 9NF
Tel: 01785 840232 Fax: 01785 840930

The Hartley Arms sits peacefully in a glorious location alongside the Shropshire Union Canal, next to Bridge 19 in the heart of Wheaton Aston. Wheaton Aston is a small and quiet old farming community that benefits from being away from the main roads, with more horse and bike riders than cars on its roads. The Hartley therefore embodies this community, offering a pleasant and pretty respite to walkers and canal goers alike.

Its owners, Donna and Andy have built up an outstanding reputation amongst both locals and visitors with the help of their hardworking team Jenny, Phil, Tracey, Kath and Chris. Their hospitality is second to none and complimented by the excellent food served up each day. Guests can choose from the specials board or the main menu which specialises in traditional, wholesome English food. All dishes are created using as many local suppliers as possible, which includes free-rage eggs from the village Dairy, meat from local butchers, and vegetables from the local market. There is something for everyone on the menu, the main problem is having decide between delicious dishes like peppered diced pork in poivre sauce, sirloin steak, steak and kidney pie, shoulder of lamb on a bed of carrot and Swede mash and red currant sauce, and chicken and leek suet pudding. A good choice of curries and pasta dishes are also available, alongside a small selection of vegetarian dishes. The inn is also known for its vast range of puddings which include a rich chocolate pudding, blackberry and apple crumble, lemon sponge and a Banoffee sundae. Food is served Monday to Friday 12-2:30pm and 6-9pm, and weekends and bank holidays between 12-9pm.

Guests can dine or drink throughout the inn, or take a laid back seat in the inn's gardens which overlook both the canal and the surrounding countryside. The bar is always well stocked, and opens all day every day. There are always up to 6 real ales on offer, with more ales appearing in the summer months. Guests are always welcome to join in some of the events that the Hartley has to offer which includes a quiz for charity on the first Tuesday of every month and occasional live acts on weekends. Twice a year, the inn opens up for popular beer festivals, held in March and October, please ring for details.

324 THE HORNS INN

High Street, Gnosall, Staffordshire ST20 0EX
Tel: 0785 822441
website: www.thehornsgnosall.co.uk

In the heart of Staffordshire you will find **The Horns Inn**, located in the picturesque village of Gnosall. Kevin Clague has run the pub since June 2009 and his friendly and welcoming manner is well known in the area. The restaurant area, which has recently been refurbished, seats 30 and such is its popularity it is advisable to book on a weekend to avoid disappointment. The extensive menu is fairly traditional and there are additional daily choices listed on the specials board.

Among the main meals on offer is battered fish of the day served with chunky homemade chips & mushy peas; 'Spanish Chicken' - chicken breast served in a choirizo sausage, mushroom & sherry sauce; and braised beef served with butter mash & seasonal vegetables. The bar and lunch time menu has plenty of options for those with a lighter appetite, with a range of jacket potatoes and baguettes.

Open all day every day, three real ales are served, including two regular and one guest ale. Special events can be catered for in a separate function room and the courtyard on sunnier days. Ring for more details. A quiz night is held from 8.30pm on a Sunday and there is sometimes live entertainment.

325 LABOUR IN VAIN

Yarnfield, nr Stone, Staffordshire ST15 0NJ
Tel: 01785 761401
e-mail: vince@thelabourinvain.co.uk
website: www.thelabourinvain.co.uk

The Labour in Vain is a traditional English village pub set in the heart of the community. The quality establishment is located in the village of Yarnfield and is popular with locals and visitors. Fresh produce, which is locally sourced, is at the heart of the reasonably priced menus. On the extensive evening menu popular choices include, duck fillet with black cherry sauce; herb crusted salmon fillet; and pork medallions with creamy mushroom sauce. The lunch time menu has a range of filled jacket potatoes, sandwiches and baguettes as well as traditional favourites including ham, egg and chips.

Whether you want to socialise and enjoy a drink from the selection of beer and ales, play a game of darts or pool, or dine in the restaurant you are made to feel welcome by tenants Debbie and Vince. They are happy to cater for coach trips and special evening events in their 60 seat restaurant and will tailor your visit to your needs. Four real ales are served including regulars Marstons Pedigree, Flowers IPA and two rotating guest ales. The Labour In Vain is closed Monday lunchtimes (except Bank Holidays), but is open every other session and all day Saturday and Sunday.

326 THE BUTTERCROSS CAFÉ

1 Stanley Street, Leek, Staffordshire ST13 5HG
Tel: 01538 373200
e-mail: angie.artus@unicornbox.co.uk

The Buttercross Café is located in the bustling market town of Leek, which lies in the heart of the glorious Staffordshire Moorlands. Leek is known for once being the home of the country's silk and textile industry, but is also host to a whole variety of interesting and historical buildings which include water mills, steam railways, potteries and National Trust gardens.

The café, previously known as 'Blueberrys,' changed its name to Buttercross in June 2009, but it is still run by the same friendly team that it always has been. Owner Angie Artus opens on Monday to Saturday from 9:30am-3 or 4pm depending on how busy it is that day. She specialises in serving up a tempting array of carefully home cooked dishes for people with every kind of appetite and taste.

Each day breakfasts are served until 11am with a choice of a full English breakfast, warm croissants and preserves or good old toast and marmalade. A fantastic selection of light meals are served throughout the day which include a range of bacon, egg and sausage baps, scrambled or poached eggs on toast, Cornish pasties, sausage rolls, Mediterranean and cheese parcels and a variety of tasty omelettes. Guests can also choose from an impressive selection of sandwiches, baguettes, jackets and toasted sandwiches with fillings from roasted gammon ham, to coronation chicken, or BLT.

Most popular at Buttercross however, are the handmade cakes. Guests can chose from a traditional afternoon cream tea, or take a wander over to the display cabinet and let their temptations run wild with a vast array of delicious treats such as cherry and coconut cake, chocolate orange cake, Edwardian fruit cake, and toffee and butterscotch cake. Many guests end up returning time and time again in a bid to work their way through the entire cake selection, but with new recipes always appearing amongst the tried and tested, you'll never be short for choice here.

Choose from a wide selection of speciality teas and coffees, hot chocolates and soft drinks, with plenty of children's drinks and meals also available on a separate menu. All major credit cards accepted.

328 PLOUGH INN

Ravens Lane, Bignall End,
Stoke on Trent, Staffordshire ST7 8PS
Tel: 01782 720469
e-mail: ploughbignallend@googlemail.com
website: www.ThePlough-BignallEnd.com

This delightful inn is a superb find in the village of
Bignall End. Tenants, Julie and Phil, have run the
Plough Inn for more than two years and are ably
assisted by Kitchen Manager and cook Steph and chef
Jeremy. Dating back to the mid 19th century the
premises has always had the same name and began
life as an alehouse, it was used a temporary mortuary
probably around the time of the famous Diglake Pit
disaster.

Inside there is seating for up to 35 people in the
lounge areas, but people are welcome to eat at the bar
and of course in the outside beer garden on warmer
days. The inn is child friendly and there is a specially
designed menu for younger customers.

Dogs are also welcome A lot of the food is homemade
and the homemade

pies and curries are extremely popular. The food is
all reasonably priced. For those with a lighter appetite
there is a good range of filled sandwiches, jacket
potatoes and salads. The main menu has a strong focus
on hearty homemade traditional dishes including
cottage pie, liver and onions and chilli con carne. There
are plenty of fish and meat options and vegetarians are
well catered for too. The inn offers a tea time special,
allowing customers to have two meals from a select
menu for £9.95. In addition to the main menu diners
can choose additional dishes

from the daily specials board. The food served at the
Plough Inn is delicious and extremely popular with
visitors. Such is the popularity with diners; it is
advisable to book on weekends. Food is available
Monday 5pm - 9pm, Tuesday - Saturday 12pm - 9pm and
Sunday 12pm - 4pm.

Up to seven real ales can be enjoyed by customers
and regulars include Hydes Original, their own T'Rayte
(the Staffordshire term for 'Are you alright?'), Black
Sheep, Timothy Taylor Landlord and plenty of rotating
guest ales. The inn holds occasional food themed
evenings - ring for details. Bignall End can be found
signposted off the main A34 via the B5500, north of
Newcastle under Lyme.

The Plough Inn is open from 5pm on Mondays
(excluding Bank Holidays, when it is open all day) and
on all other days is open throughout the day. Credit and
debit cards accepted.

327 THE HOLLYBUSH INN

Denford Road, Denford, Leek,
Staffordshire ST13 7JT
Tel: 01538 371819
e-mail: hollybushdenford@btconnect.com
website: www.hollybushdenford.co.uk

It is the olde worlde atmosphere of **The Hollybush Inn** that gives it its charm as well as its canal-side location. It was family run and owned by the Prime family for many years, and having had a break from the trade Steve and Linda returned in November 2008 as leaseholders, employing Richard and Eve as general managers.

Up to six real ales can be enjoyed at The Hollybush Inn. Food is available every evening and lunchtime and there is a separate dining area for those wanting to enjoy one of the many fine dishes on offer. The menu is extremely traditional with choices including homemade steak & ale pie, beef in beer casserole; and large gammon steak with egg or pineapple, onion rings & mushrooms. There is also a selection of starters, vegetarian dishes and salads. For those with a lighter appetite, there are plenty of filled baguettes and sandwiches to choose from the bar menu. There is a special menu for younger guests and a weekly Sunday lunch is popular amongst customers.

Major credit cards taken. Disabled access not a problem. The restaurant area seats 35 and it is advisable to book at weekends to avoid disappointment.

330 THE CABIN

Riverside, Mildenhall Road, Bury St Edmunds,
Suffolk IP32 6EN
Tel: 01284 764958

A warm welcome and delicious food awaits visitors, both young and old alike, to **The Cabin**, which is a real hidden gem located on the outskirts of Bury St Edmunds. The establishment provides all weather facilities and is a real oasis in a built up area and has a strong focus on a variety of homemade dishes cooked to order (bread pudding is a favourite). It has been owned by John and Maureen for the past three years and they like to use local produce wherever possible. There is seating for 40 guests inside and a further 30 outside in the wonderful garden area. It is open 10am-2pm on Mondays and 8.30am-3.30pm Tues-Sat.

331 THE WEEPING WILLOW

39 Bury Road, Barrow, Suffolk IP29 5AB
Tel: 01284 810492

The sleepy Suffolk village of Barrow is home to the grade II listed **Weeping Willow**, run by born and bred Barrow couple Mandy and Alan. Open lunchtimes and evenings and all day from Friday-Sunday, they serve up a range of quality real ales and home cooked food for all. Mandy serves up dishes from 12-2pm and 6-9pm daily, with a selection of sandwiches, baguettes, salads, steaks, starters and mains. Dishes are created using locally sourced produce where possible, including favourites like peppered salmon steak, mixed grill, and bangers and mash. There is always a roast of the day, but on Sundays there is a choice of two meats.

329 CHESHIRE VIEW

Top Station Road, Mow Cop, Staffordshire ST7 3NP
Tel: 01782 514211
e-mail: josiereign@hotmail.co.uk

Cheshire View is a spectacular public house known best for its unrivalled views across the Cheshire Plains as far as the eye can see to Liverpool and Wales. The inn has stood in its lofty position for over 300 years, when it was originally built as a summer house for Lords and Ladies to view the nine surrounding counties.

For the past 4 ½ years, owner Josie Bedson has welcomed guests into her pub to enjoy not only the glorious views, but the fine selection of food and drink she has to offer. Open all day every day, she is proud to stock two fine real ales in the summer time which usually includes Burton Ale and an ever changing guest ale. There is also a good choice of wine, spirits and soft drinks if ale isn't your thing.

Most popular here though, is the food. Josie serves up a delicious menu every day from 12-3pm and 6-9pm which includes handsome dishes like the mixed grill, sirloin steak and a range of speciality curries. All the food here is cooked fresh to order, and is very reasonably priced. Everyone will be able to find something they like as the menu is large, covering those with lighter appetites too, including choices like homemade soup of the day, a selection of hot and cold baguettes and sandwiches, chef's special pasta and traditional Staffordshire oatcakes. Josie also puts on a range of special food themed nights which include steak night on Wednesday when speciality steaks even include bison, venison, kangaroo and ostrich! These evenings are very popular, so it's best to book; please ring for details. At certain times, guests on a budget can benefit from a very generous '2 courses and coffee for £5' deal – who could ask for more?

The inn also finds itself in a perfect location for short breaks away as not only do all its bedrooms have simply stunning views, but they are ideally situated for exploring the areas rich history with Mow Cop Castle just minutes away. Josie offers a choice of two upstairs bedrooms, which share a private bathroom. Rooms can come on either a room only basis or enjoy a hearty breakfast too for just a little more.

332 THE FIVE BELLS

Rattlesden, Suffolk IP30 0RA
Tel: 01449 731373

Dating back to the 1700s, The Five Bells can be found in the picturesque village of Rattlesden. Close to the village church, this oustanding property is owned and personally run by Debbie Oliver who has been in charge since 1996. Inside, the pub is full of character, with black beams running along the ceiling in the extended games area.

The Five Bells is open all day every day and is extremely popular with the locals. Visitors are always welcomed and many like to sample the three real ales available (there is always a new brew to try). Although no meals are served here, sandwiches can be ordered. The pub is child friendly and youngsters are welcomed during the day time, but in the evenings it is a child free zone.

Once a month the pub hosts live entertainment on a Friday evening from 8.45pm (ring for details). Parts of the pub overlook the beautiful garden area which is popular with punters in the summer months. The garden houses an aviary, which is home to a pair of barn owls and a Turkemanian eagle that answers to the name of 'Maud'. Disabled access is not a problem.

333 THE METCALFE ARMS

Lawshall Road, Hawstead, Suffolk IP29 5NR
Tel: 01284 386321
website: www.redratcraftbrewery.co.uk

Situated at the edge of the picturesque village of Hawstead, just a short drive south of Bury St. Edmunds is **The Metcalfe Arms**. Its new owners Samantha Lamb and Kevin McHenry have much experience in the trade, Kevin being a partner in the Red Rat Craft brewery in Denham. With this in mind, the inn serves up a selection of three real ales; two rotating and one from the Red Rat itself. Food is available at the Metcalfe from 12-9:30pm each day, prepared fresh on the premises by Head Chef Ben. Favourite dishes include chicken wrapped in bacon in a sage, lemon and garlic butter; salmon and prawn Tian, game and pork sausages with mash, and a vegetable risotto. All dishes are created using locally sourced produce.

www.findSOMEWHERE.co.uk
For people who want to explore the United Kingdom

Places to Visit

334 WAGGON AND HORSES

Church Walk, Sudbury, Suffolk CO10 1HJ
Tel: 01787 312147

Situated just yards from the centre of Sudbury in Church Walk is the **Waggon and Horses**. This historic inn found its original fame as the brewery for Grimways in the 1890s, but has operated under a number of other guises too. Its owners George and Fiona say they still have much to do in terms of renovation, however they have already given the place back its buzz. The couple took over the Waggon in January this year after running a successful restaurant in France for many years.

Open every session, the pair are true to the inn's routes and serve up three real ales. Food is served daily from 12-2pm and from 7pm onwards from Thursday to Saturday only. Dishes are created using as much locally sourced produce as possible, and range from traditional Sunday lunches to a la carte specialities in which a good portion of French influence can be seen. A variety of special themed meals are available, alongside a selection of weekly offers including pensioners specials, two steaks for £15 or three course meals for £14. Meals can be enjoyed within the cosy indoor atmosphere or outdoors on the hidden rear courtyard; which is bursting with blooming flowers and hanging baskets in season.

George and Fiona also offer three guest bedrooms in a mix of sizes that can come on a room only or generous bed and breakfast tariff.

335 THE BLACK LION

Lion Road, Glemsford, Sudbury, Suffolk CO10 7RF
Tel: 01787 280684
e-mail: theblacklion@hotmail.co.uk

The Black Lion is situated in the village of Glemsford, opposite the primary school. Its owners Sarah and Steve have only just moved in, bringing over twenty years of experience in the trade with them. They intend to completely refurbish the inn, restoring it to its former glory days. They put great weight on the importance of local community and want to ensure that the inn is an active part of that, acting as a great place to be for both locals and visitors from further afield.

The inn will open from 5pm only on Mondays and Tuesdays, all day on Fridays, Saturdays and Sundays, and every session on Wednesday and Thursdays. Guests will be able to choose from a variety of real ales and fine wines, and order food from Wednesday to Sunday lunch times and evenings. Out of dining times, the dining area will function as a pleasant coffee shop with a range of speciality teas, coffees, hot chocolates and tasty homemade treats. On Saturday mornings breakfast will be served from 9am and during the rest of the week a selection of tried and tested menus will run; aiming to deliver top quality food at affordable family prices.

Children are welcomed at all times, and can enjoy their own menu. Outdoors in the gated beer garden there is a safe children's play area too. The beer garden also provides the home for inn's future annual beer festival, please see call for details.

336 THE PINKUAH ARMS

Pinkauh Lane, Pinkuah, Sudbury CO10 7JW
Tel: 01787 280857
e-mail: mike_gale@live.co.uk
website: www.pinkuaharms.co.uk

Just five miles from Sudbury, **The Pinkuah Arms** is tucked away on Essex/Suffolk border, perfect for a quick pint, a get together with pals or dinner out with that someone special. Hard to miss, the Pinkuah Arms has an attractive pink exterior, which is in contrast to its rather traditional interior. Original beams and feature fireplaces compliment a range of Pinkuah memorabilia, adding to the nostalgic feel of the place. Popular with both visitors to the area and the locals, the inn has a certain buzz about it, sustained by the great personalities of its hosts Mike and Laura. The couple have been running the inn for a number of years, combining traditional English pub values with a more rustic feel that stems from Laura's Italian roots.

She is the queen of the kitchen at Pinkuah, and uses her heritage to her advantage. Born in Rome, a number of her dishes have inspiration from the Lazio region and feature not only on the main menu, but on the frequent themed food evenings held at the inn. Other themed evenings include St George's, Pie and pint night, and the breakfast club; where a variety of traditional and unusual breakfasts are laid out to sample. The main menu runs from Tuesday to Sunday from 12-3pm and 7-9pm,

when booking is considered a necessity. There is truly something for everyone with a selection of classic pub meals, Italian favourites, light bites and luxurious mains to try. Favourites include Laura's legendary short crust steak and kidney pie with a rich gravy, chunky smoked fish pie with salmon and prawns, roast beef, seared steaks, and the anti pasti sharer.

The inn is also known for serving up a magnificent array of beverages, specialising particularly in quality real ales. A good selection are always available from both local and national breweries including Spitfire from the Shepherd Neames Brewery, and Woodfordes Wherry from Youngs Best brewery, amongst other from local brewery Nethergate. Laura and Mike also stock a good range of white and red wines, which are affordably priced, particularly if you download one of the vouchers from their website which entitle the holder to a free house bottle per couple when ordering two course meals, please see website for conditions. Children and dogs welcome, all major credit cards accepted.

337 THE WHEATSHEAF INN

45 Chapel Street, Exning, Newmarket,
Suffolk CB8 7HA
Tel: 01638 577237
e-mail: wheatsheaf.exning@btconnect.com
website: www.wheatsheaf.exning.co.uk

Located in the heart of Exning village, just a 5-minute drive
from Newmarket town centre, **The Wheatsheaf Inn** is a
charming 17th century coaching inn which is family-run by
Sharon and Kevin and their family.

The inn is particularly noted for its excellent home-cooked
food, prepared by a full time chef using fresh, locally grown
produce wherever possible. At lunchtime (noon until 2pm) the
menu features old favourites such as sausage & mash, ham, egg
& chips, and steak & ale pie. In the evening, from 7pm to
10pm, the extensive menu ranges from grills and chicken dishes
to fish and pasta offerings, as well as vegetarian options such as
Cajun mushrooms, spinach and ricotta cannelloni, or omelettes.
On Sundays, roast dinners are served from 12.30pm until 3pm
(booking advisable), and on Wednesdays there's a special meal
deal for the over-55s, as well as roasts. In the bar you'll find 3
real ales on tap - Greene King IPA, Abbot Ale and a guest ale.

The inn has recently added bed & breakfast facilities to its amenities and now offers 4
attractively furnished and decorated guest rooms, all en suite and all equipped with television
and hospitality tray.

338 FOUNTAIN HOUSE TEA ROOM

The Street, East Bergholt, Suffolk CO7 6TB
Tel: 01206 299955
e-mail: fhtearoom@btconnect.com

The Fountain House Tea Room is a delightful little
establishment owned and run by Mary and her daughter
Dawn. The pair arrived here 18 months ago and
completely refurbished what was a hardware store into
what is now a traditional tea room. Homemade food is
the order of the day and there are plenty of delicious
cakes, pastries and filled sandwiches on offer. Daily
specials, including lasagne, chilli and fishcakes are also
available. All of the dishes are reasonably priced and
customers return again and again to sample the quality
food and delicious refreshments on offer. The Fountain
House Tea Room has a warm and friendly atmosphere
and seats 20 people with room for a further 12 in the
pretty courtyard area. Since opening it has built up a
fantastic reputation and it can be an advantage to book
as it is often full with happy diners. Both Mary and Dawn
cook and they like to use local produce when possible.

The child friendly tea room is open seven days a week
(Monday - Friday 9.30am - 4pm and Saturday - Sunday
10am - 4pm). Disabled access is not a problem.

339 THE ORANGERIE

Victoria House, Market Place, Hadleigh,
Suffolk IP7 5DL
Tel: 01473 823600

Home cooking is at the heart of **The Orangerie**, which is located in the popular market town of Hadleigh. The Orangerie has been family run by Mariesa and her daughter Toyah for the past couple of years and it is well known for its delicious food. Local produce is used wherever possible and everything is home cooked to a high standard. The home made cakes on offer are a favourite with visitors and locals.

Breakfast is served until 11.30am and all of the dishes on the menu are reasonably priced. There is a good selection of lite bites as well as a range of freshly prepared sandwiches, toasted sandwiches and jacket potatoes. Additional home cooked dishes are available from the daily lunchtime specials board along with some tempting desserts. The warm hospitality extends to younger guests too and there is a special children's menu.

The Orangerie is open Tuesday – Saturday between 9am and 4.30pm and seats around 30 people inside and a further 20 outside if the weather is brighter. Booking is advisable between 12pm – 2pm because of the popularity of the place. Disabled access is not a problem. Cash and credit cards taken.

340 THE FOX AND HOUNDS

Church Street, Groton, Sudbury, Suffolk CO10 5ED
Tel: 01787 210474
e-mail: stevenmayo@hotmail.com
website: www.foxandhounds.webeden.co.uk

The Fox and Hounds is found in a scenic location on the edge of the village of Groton. Steven and Kerry and their family, including Steven's brothers Philip and George who are qualified chefs have been running the establishment for the past year, bringing a vibrant and fun family feel to the place. Its traditional structure is complimented by contemporary décor, original oak beams and two open fires with the building dating back to the 16th century.

Open all day every day, families most welcome, the inn serves food daily all day from 12pm. Phil and George take responsibility for the cooking and offer a handsome collection of traditional English cuisine throughout the day. The lunch menu offers all the pub classics at their best with homemade beef burgers, beer battered fish and chips and vegetable lasagne, whilst the evening menu samples a range of speciality dishes like pork chop with apple sauce, lamb shank in a rich mint sauce, sirloin steak in a mushroom and pepper sauce, and poached salmon with dill sauce. On Wednesday nights its curry night with three homemade varieties, whereas on Sundays it is roast dinner time, and during the week from 12-3pm guests can get two main meals for a special price.

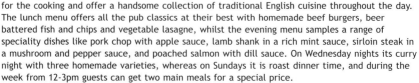

Guests can choose from a wide selection of spirits and wines, not to mention the range of well kept ales which include Woodfordes Wherry, Green King IPA and London Pride.

341 EDWARDSTONE WHITE HORSE

Mill Green, Edwardstone, Sudbury, Suffolk CO10 5PX
Tel: 01787 211211
e-mail: drinking@theedwardstonewhitehorse.co.uk
website: www.edwardstonewhitehorse.co.uk

In the heart of Edwardstone lies the **Edwardstone White Horse** inn. Its scenic location in the midst of the idyllic Suffolk countryside means that it sees many ramblers and families in the summer months alongside its usual clientele. Known across the county and further afield for having its own brewery, it will not come as a surprise that the inn is popular with ale lovers.

The Mill Green brewery started brewing in August 2008 and has built up a fine name for itself, producing both traditional and artisan beers in an eco-friendly manner. Boasting solar power and wood boilers, the beers made here are hand-crafted with the finest malt, hops and (according to the owners) – plenty of passion! Tours of the brewery are possible, given 48 hours notice.

John Norton has owned the inn for the past five years, ably assisted by his managers Gavin and Amy. The team offer up a choice of eight real ales at any one time alongside a good selection of wines, spirits and soft drinks. The inn isn't just known for its drink selection though; it sees many repeat visitors in demand of the delicious food served daily. Food is available 7 lunchtimes a week (in the summer months) and tues - sat evenings (and fri, sat and sun lunches in the winter months). Professional chef Johnny Wilsher creates a brilliant across the board menu bursting with local produce and organic goods. Popular dishes include a succulent Rib-eye steak, homemade steak and kidney pie, scampi with homemade chips, beef burger, organic spicy bean burger and the wild bunny burger. On Sundays a traditional roast lunch is added to the menu. Children and families are welcome, and can dine throughout the inn, or play outside in the spacious beer garden; always a popular choice in the summer months.

Guests are also welcomed to stay at the inn, either in one of the self catering cottages or in the inn's own campsite. There are two cottages to choose from, each having their own kitchen/living room, bedroom and bathroom, all fully decorated in a warm log cabin style. Spruce cottage sleeps up to three guests, whilst Larch cottage sleeps up to four guests. The campsite is particularly popular during festival season, with a brand new solar powered shower and toilet block for convenience; so booking ahead is recommended to avoid disappointment.

342 THE RED LION

High Street, Bildeston, Ipswich, Suffolk IP7 7EX
Tel: 01449 740476
e-mail: mandy.wayne2@googlemail.com
website: www.theredlionbildeston.com

Dating back to the 16th century, **The Red Lion** is a former Smithy, which is now a lively village pub. The traditional country pub has been at the heart of the community since Mandy and Wayne Hillhouse took over as leaseholders in 2007. There is a separate dining area and diners have a good choice of dishes to choose from. Home cooking is at the heart of the menu and all of the dishes are reasonably priced. Starters include tomato or vegetable soup served with French bread; and whitebait served with bread and butter and a salad garnish. The main courses are fairly traditional and favourites include bacon, egg chips and beans; all day breakfast; and chilli con carne served with Basmati rice. A wide range of steaks, fish dishes and vegetarian dishes are also served.

There are three real ales to be enjoyed at The Red Lion, with Greene King IPA and Woodfordes Wherry the regulars. In the bar area there is Sky TV, ESPN TV, a pool table, darts board and live bands play once a month. The Red Lion is closed on Mondays (except bank holidays), but is open every other session and all day on Saturday and Sundays. Ring for details on accommodation.

findSOMEWHERE.co.uk
For people who want to explore Britain and Ireland

Places to Stay

Our easy-to use website contains details and locations of places to stay, places to eat and drink, specialist shops and places of interest throughout England, Wales, Scotland and Ireland.

Places to Stay:	**Places to Eat and Drink:**	**Places of Interest:**	**Specialist Shops:**	**Gardens:**
Hotels, guest accommodation, bed & breakfast, inns, self-catering accommodation	Restaurants, pubs, inns, cafes, tea rooms	Historic buildings, gardens, art galleries, museums, nature parks, wildlife parks, indoor and outdoor activities	Fashion shops, art and craft shops, gift shops, food and drink shops, antique shops, jewellery shops	Garden centres and retail nurseries

343 THE SHIP INN AT BLAXHALL

Blaxhall, nr Snape, Suffolk IP12 2DY
Tel: 01728 688316

Just two miles from Snape, and six
miles from the Suffolk Heritage coast is
The Ship Inn at Blaxhall. It is a
traditional pub offering a real taste of
the country through unrivalled
atmosphere and delicious food and
drink. David and Sharon, long time
Blaxhall residents themselves, are very
proud of their inn which they believe is
truly at the heart of village life. They
are dedicated to serving their guests
the absolute best food and drink
available, drawing many visitors from
near and far.

The most popular feature of the inn is its fine
restaurant. Only the highest quality home
cooked food is served here, with a focus on using
the best in locally sourced produce and locally
reared meats. The menu changes regularly to
keep up with the seasonal goods available, and is
displayed daily on the blackboards. Guests will
be pleased to see all their country favourites up
there, alongside a number of globally inspired
specials and a good range of seafood dishes,
bought freshly from the fishing boats at nearby
Lowestoft. Popular dishes include farm sausages
and mash with a rich gravy and seasonal
vegetables, homemade parfait with brown bread
and salad, and goats cheese with caramelised
onion relish on a bed of leaves. Favourite fish
dishes include tempting tempura king prawns
with a sweet 'n' sour dip, seared scallops with
chilli jam and crème fraiche, crayfish tails in a
Thai mayo poppadum basket, and smoked trout
salad with horseradish and new potatoes, not
forgetting the speciality fisherman's pie with a
chunky selection of cod, prawns, salmon and
haddock. Food is served between 12-2:30pm and
6-9:30pm seven days a week, but owing to
popularity booking is heavily recommended at all times.

To accompany the fine food, is an equally fine selection of drink, including a carefully chosen
wine list and range of real ales. Up to six real ales are available at any one time, with regular ales
including Timothy Taylor Landlord and Woodfordes Wherry.

Detached from the inn itself are eight chalets available for hire throughout the year. Guests
can chose from two double bedrooms and six twin rooms, four of which have luxury status. Each
chalet boasts en suite facilities, small catering area and one of Sharon's generous cooked
breakfasts each morning. One chalet has been built with disabled customers in mind, whilst others
can be rearranged for family use.

344 THE RED HERRING BAR & RESTAURANT

152 Bridge Road, Oulton Broad, Lowestoft,
Suffolk NR33 9JT
Tel: 01502 566499
website: www.redherringrestaurant.co.uk

Situated in Oulton Broad **The Red Herring Bar and Restaurant** is renowned far and wide for its fine cuisine. The restaurant has a predominantly Meditteranean style and offers a good selection of tapas, fish and steak dishes. It is well known in the area for its fresh cuisine and has been run by Jeff Snr and Jackie for the past 18 months. The restaurant is located in a beautiful area

often referred to as the 'southern gateway to the Broads'. The area attracts a lot of people because of its beautiful rivers, lakes, locks, nature reserves and the plenty of water sports activities and facilities available. The standard of food at the restaurant is of the highest quality and freshly prepared and cooked by professional chefs and this is perhaps why it attracts

plenty of diners from further afield. The restaurant is open seven days a week between 10am and 12pm, 12pm – 2.30pm and 6.30pm-9.30pm. There is no evening service on a Sunday. The bar and restaurant is extremely popular and bookings are advisable for Friday, Saturday and Sunday.

344 THE THIRD CROSSING SEAFOOD & STEAK RESTAURANT

Haven Marina, School Road, Oulton Broad, Lowestoft, Suffolk NR33 9NB
Tel: 01502 583596
website: www.thethirdcrossing.co.uk

If it is a quality seafood restaurant you are looking for then look no further than The Third Crossing, which overlooks Haven Marina and only opened this year. It is run by Jeff Snr and his son Jeff jnr.

It is open daily from 9.30am until 9.30pm and has seating for around 36 people. There is additional seating outside which diners can make the most of on brighter days. The seafood restaurant serves a fantastic array of locally caught fish and the menu is varied and extensive. It has only recently opened, but is already attracting many diners and has a growing reputation for fine cuisine. It also has a good selection of beverages for diners to choose from, alcoholic and non alcoholic. Disabled access is not a problem. Major credit cards taken.

345 THE WHITE HORSE

The Street, Corton, Suffolk NR32 5HP
Tel: 01502 730294
e-mail: info@whitehorsecorton.co.uk
website: www.whitehorsecorton.co.uk

The White Horse has long been at the centre of village life in Corton and is extremely popular with locals and visitors to the area. The pub and restaurant is arguably the best premises of its kind in the area and has a fine reputation for fine food and excellent ales.

Leaseholder, Bryan Rawstron, took over the running of The White Horse in August 2009 and has continued to add to its good reputation. The White Horse offers all that is needed for an excellent evening out and stocks an excellent range of beers, wines, spirits and non alcoholic drinks. Two well known real ales are served, Greene King IPA and Abbot Ale and an occasional guest ale is added to the list. Located in a beautiful seaside village, The White Horse has something for everyone.

The food is excellent and diners are advised to book at all times to avoid disappointment. Sunday lunchtime is roast only, but at all other times there is an extensive traditional menu for people to choose from, with the dishes made from the finest locally sourced produce. The White Horse menu is an excellent blend of freshly prepared family favourites, pub classics and elegant restaurant style dishes. The restaurant is open daily from 12 noon to 2.30pm and evenings from 6pm. With a menu containing all the best local ingredients and traditional dishes cooked to order there is something for everyone at the White Horse. Starters include crispy coated mushrooms deep fried and served with a garlic or blue cheese dip; and whitebait served with fresh sliced bread. Traditional steak and kidney pudding with fresh vegetables and fries or mashed potatoes is among one of the favourite dishes on the main menu along with beef stew served with fresh vegetables and herb dumpling. As well as traditional favourites there are plenty of grills, fish dishes, salads and vegetarian options. The pub's daily lunchtime specials have become renowned in the area for providing great food at a great value price.

The White Horse provides plenty of space to relax. The restaurant area seats 30 diners and an additional 16 people can be seated in the conservatory area, as well as more in the bar areas and separate family room. Children are very welcome at The White Horse and there is a special children's menu for younger guests, including a range of tempting desserts.

346 THE VILLAGE MAID

71 The Street, Lound, Lowestoft, Suffolk NR32 5LP
Tel: 01502 730441

The Village Maid is a picturesque village pub serving quality cuisine. Located in Loud, the tenant, Daniel Ecclestone, is also the chef of the pub. He has been a qualified chef for many years and locals and visitors are extremely complimentary about the food he serves. A lot of the produce used is locally sourced and there is an extensive menu of reasonably priced traditional dishes. Vegetarians are well catered for and there is a special children's menu for younger diners. The pub can be found across the road from the village pond and is found east off the A12 and west off the A143.

Food is available Monday – Saturday between 12pm – 2pm and 6.45pm – 9pm and on Sundays between 12pm-3.30pm and 6.30pm – 9pm. The Village Maid is very popular and although seating a generous 60 diners inside it is highly recommended to book at weekends. Starters are priced between £4 and £5 and include salmon and dill fishcake sat on a mixed salad and served with a sweet chilli dip; chicken liver and mushroom pate served with salad and melba toast; and breaded brie wedges sat on a bed of salad with a cranberry dip. There are plenty of fish dishes and grills on the main menu as well as traditional favourites including steak and kidney pie; spicy chilli con carne served with rice and a salad garnish; and beef lasagne served with salad and garlic bread. For those wanting something a little lighter there is a fantastic fresh selection of salads

including prawns and ham. Vegetarian diners have a range of dishes to choose from. Spinach and ricotta cannelloni served with salad and garlic bread; and three cheese and broccoli bake combined in a white sauce with sliced potatoes, crisp broccoli and topped with cheese (served with salad and French bread). In addition to the printed menu there is also a daily specials board. On Fridays takeaway fish and chips from the pub are a must for a lot of villagers and there is entertainment once a month on the same day. In the summer months entertainment is hosted every other Sunday.

The olde world pub, which is bursting with charm, has plenty of countryside surrounding it, and serves three real ales. Bombadier and Adnams Bitter are among the most popular. There is a large rear car park. Disabled access isn't a problem. All major credit cards accepted.

347 THE WATERFRONT

310 Church Road, Kessingland, Suffolk NR33 7RW
Tel: 01502 741525

Overlooking the seashore at Kingsland, **The Waterfront** boasts stunning views of an award winning rural beach. The restaurant is ideally situated on the Suffolk heritage coast and has a popular and extensive menu of continental and modern English cuisine.

The Waterfront has been owned by David and Tina Wall for more than ten years along with their daughter Bridie. Diners can relax in comfortable surroundings in the intimate Mediterranean style restaurant and enjoy food made with the finest produce. Inside, the child friendly restaurant seats 36 people and an additional 30 people can be seated outside. All of the dishes are freshly prepared and the menus change regularly. David has been a chef for 38 years and is extremely passionate about what he does.

Starters include grilled kipper served with poached egg; crayfish and mango cocktail; and goats cheese tart. The main menu has a good variety and all of the dishes are reasonably priced. Grilled bass fillets with fine beans asparagus, tomatoes, crispy bacon and new potatoes; langoustine tails sautéed in lemon oil with basil and sun dried tomatoes tossed in tagliatelle pasta; and brisket of beef slow roasted with seasonal vegetables and creamed potatoes in red wine are among the dishes on offer. A traditional roast is served on Sunday as well as the full a la carte menu. To go alongside the fine food there is a wide selection of quality wines

from around the world to choose from. There is also a good range of spirits, lagers and soft drinks. Every Thursday a special paella evening is held and such is its popularity it is advisable to book (there will be a choice of 2 or 3 paellas). On sunnier days there is a large patio area for alfresco dining surrounded by beautiful scenery.

The Waterfront is open from 12pm-2.30pm and 5pm-9pm every day except from Sunday evenings (but not in the summer school holidays) and bookings are required all year around. The restaurant is also closed every Monday except bank holidays. Lunchtime diners can choose from the main menu as well as a large selection of baguettes and ciabattas. Whether it is for a quick cappuccino and cake, baguette and a glass of wine, or a three course meal, David and Tina offer a friendly and warm welcome to all of their customers.

Credit cards except diners taken. Disabled access is not a problem.

348 THE HALF WAY CAFÉ

At the level crossing, Main Road,
Darsham, Suffolk IP17 3PL
Tel: 07972 398934
e-mail: halfwaycafe@fsmail.net

This light and airy café is found adjacent to the level crossing
to the rear of Darsham railway station. Mark and Lynne took
over the **Half Way Café** in December 2006 and they haven't
looked back. The homely atmosphere they have created
within the café is enhanced further by the personably and
efficient service offered.

Open seven days a week from 8am-3pm Monday to Friday,
8:30am-3pm on Saturdays and 9am-2pm on Sundays, the café
sees a solid thoroughfare of guests from near and far. The focus
here is on serving a wide and varying menu created with only
the best locally sourced produce, including locally made
sausages, free range eggs, locally reared pigs for the bacon, and even the ketchup and preserves are
made in the area! The menu itself encompasses a range of light bites and mains from homemade
Cornish pasties, fish specials like Tuna steak, chicken tikka massala, lasagne and homemade filled
Yorkshire puddings. The most popular dishes are undoubtedly the breakfast range. Locals give rave
reviews about the full English, though a variety of other options are served; and guests are always
welcome to help themselves to toast. A small selection of tempting homemade treats and sweets are
also available from the counter. Both food and drink can be enjoyed inside or out, where there is a
pleasant rear garden. Children welcome, cash only please.

350 THE RINGSFIELD HORSESHOES

Cromwell Road, Ringsfield, Beccles, Suffolk NR34 8LR
Tel: 01502 713114
e-mail: danielwong_68@live.co.uk

The **Ringsfield Horseshoes** is a picturesque village
inn named after the village it is located in. Having
swopped the hustle and bustle of running a night
club, Daniel and Benita Wong have run the pub for
the past three years and it is open all day every day.
Surrounded by the Suffolk countryside the pub is in
an idyllic peaceful location and offers locals and
visitors fine food and well kept ales. The three
rotating real ales are brewed either in Suffolk or
Norfolk and are popular with punters.

Food is available all day and nothing is too much trouble
for Daniel or Benita. There is a wide selection of dishes
with something to suit all tastes. Seafood platters and
Sunday Roasts are among the most favoured dishes, which
are all made using fresh and locally sourced produce. The
pub is child friendly and there are dishes to suit younger
diners. Themed food evenings are held occasionally (it is
best to ring for details) and poker nights are held every
Monday evening. Cash and cheque only. The Ringsfield
Horseshoes can be found west off the A144, east off the A145 and south off the B1062.

349 THE KINGS HEAD (THE LOW HOUSE)

Gorams Mill Lane, Laxfield, Suffolk IP13 8DW
Tel: 01986 798395
e-mail: lowhouse@keme.co.uk
website: www.laxfield-kingshead.co.uk

Noted as one of the most attractive places in Suffolk, the village of Laxfield lies amid a variety of historic attractions such as Framlingham Castle and the church of All Saints, making an interesting stop off point on a day exploring the surrounding seaside towns of Aldeburgh and Southwold. **The Kings Head**, also known as the Low House, is the main attraction in Laxfield, providing an unusual thatched watering hole for its guests.

The inn's owners Bob and Linda have an impressive background working in pub architecture. Bob and Linda are proud to have one of the country's few remaining pubs without a bar; guests cueing for drinks at the tap room door. The inn dates back to the 16th century in parts and has operated under many guises, but has changed little since its days as a Victorian ale house. Bob believes that true pubs are places for socialising, and as such the inn has few separate tables and chairs, and is instead filled with a range of high backed wooden pews and benches that have been worn with many a bottom from yesteryear. This social environment operates on the quality of food, drink and conversation with no irritants like TV, duke boxes, or pool tables.

At any one time there are usually around five real ales to sample, all of which are drawn straight from the barrel upon request. A good range of other lagers, wines and spirits are also available. The food here is also something of a speciality. Linda is the chef, and focuses delivering a simple but interesting menu. She notes that mains can be light or hearty, meaty or vegetarian, with plenty of option for fresh fish as they are just half an hour from the coast. Food is available from 12-2pm and 7-9pm, and booking is recommended on weekends. Popular dishes include homemade steak and ale pie, cod and salmon loins in lemon butter, lamb shank in rich garden mint gravy, and sausage and mash from the local farm.

Guests who want to stay at the Low House are always welcomed, with a choice between a ground floor self catering flat, or two double bedrooms; both of which have en suite facilities. These rooms remain steeped in the inn's olde worlde cottage theme without forgoing comfort. Guests can enjoy a full English breakfast each day in the pub. Perfect for exploring the heritage coast, the inn makes a handsome base with its own beautiful gardens. Horse and carriage rides available on request.

351 TWO SAWYERS

Pett Road, Pett Village, Hastings, Sussex TN35 4HB
Tel: 01424 812255
website: www.twosawyers.co.uk

Located in the tranquil rural village of Pett, just beyond the outskirts of Hastings and Rye is the **Two Sawyers**. This popular village inn dates back to the 16th century, proudly displaying its heritage with beautiful exposed oak beams and original red brick work throughout. Despite its age the inn is well lit, having recently been refurbished, and has a fresh and airy feel that remains full of the charm from years gone by.

The well stocked bar offers an excellent selection of real ales, fine wines and spirits, not to mention the vast collection of single malt whiskeys on offer. The inn is popular with walkers, cyclists and tourists to the area, who mix freely with the inn's locals which include the village's own cricket club. Drinks are best enjoyed before a crackling open fire housed in the inn's impressive inglenook fireplaces, although the inn also has a pretty rear courtyard which is popular in the summer months when its cherry blossom is at its best.

The Two Sawyers also serves up a fine menu each day that focuses on using only the best in local produce to create a variety of wholesome, traditional dishes. Guests can choose from a selection of contemporary and traditional dishes, or opt for a lighter bite from the range of bar meals and filled baguettes. A daily specials board is also available and offers up an ever changing choice of fresh seasonal dishes. Favourites include pot roasted lamb shank, steak and kidney pudding, pan-friend liver and bacon, and a char-grilled rump steak with chunky chips. The inn is open from 12-11pm Monday to Saturday, and from 12-10:30pm on Sundays when up to several roast are added to the menu. Food is served from 12 noon to 2.30pm and from 6-9pm Monday to Saturday and from 12 noon - 8pm on Sundays and Bank Holidays

Guests who enjoy the quieter pace of village life have the option of taking a room at the Two Sawyers, with a choice of three guest bedrooms, all of which have en suite facilities. Rooms are all spacious and stylish decorated with plenty of storage space, affording picturesque views across the surrounding countryside. The inn is perfect for that weekend away, as it's within a short drive of plenty of shopping spots, and the popular coastal town of Hastings.

352 THE SEVEN STARS

High Street, Robertsbridge, East Sussex TN32 5AJ
Tel: 01580 880333
e-mail: cjboyde@gmail.com
website: www.seven7stars.co.uk

Robertsbridge is a popular starting place for walkers, with Bodiam Castle, the South Downs and Hastings all within a walking distance. Its resident pub, **The Seven Stars** is almost as old as the castle, built in the 13th century but remains prosperous and popular whilst the castle, though seeing many visitors is now in ruins. Noted as one of the top ten haunted pubs in England, it sees a steady trickle of spirit seekers, although the landlady Caroline Boyde notes that most settle for a Scotch. Aside from spirit seekers, the inn is also frequented by sports fans as it has a full sky and ESPN packages. Live music is also hosted every third Sunday between 6-8pm.

Open all day everyday, and late on Fridays and Saturdays, the inn offers a great selection of local Sussex ales and good home cooked food year round. Guests can choose from a selection of light bites to include paninis, toasties, salads and sandwiches, though a handsome array of mains are also available. Popular choices are the all day breakfasts, gourmet ploughman's and the Sussex burger, made with locally reared beef. On Sundays guests can sample the inn's signature Sunday roast with three succulent options including pressed belly pork with shallot puree, cider and wholegrain mustard sauce, topside of Sussex beef with Yorkshire puddings and red wine gravy, or a pan fried fillet of salmon with a prawn, lemon and caper butter sauce.

353 THE QUEENS HEAD

The Green, Sedlescombe, Hastings, East Sussex TN33 0QA
Tel/Fax: 01424 870228
e-mail: book@queensheadsedlescombe.co.uk
website: www.queensheadsedlescombe.co.uk

The Queens Head, as it stands today, is an Ancient Pub that was built in the 14th century. Its location however, on the side of a Roman road, suggests that the pub might have a much longer history. It was also used by the notorious Hawkhurst Gang, and the Smuggler's Tunnel can still be seen from the cellar. Elizabeth I was once stayed at the Queens Head and in celebration, the villagers planted an oak tree on The Green that is still there today.

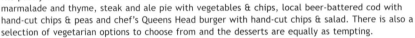

The pub is now managed by Mel, who is chef trained and has been in the catering industry for over twenty years. She has also lived in the area for 25 years and so knows the village well. The pub overlooks the Green at Sedlescombe, which is a pretty village just 5 miles away from Hastings.

The food here is outstanding and diners can expect to see dishes such as warm goat's cheese in filo pastry on a bed of leaf saled with red onion marmalade and thyme, steak and ale pie with vegetables & chips, local beer-battered cod with hand-cut chips & peas and chef's Queens Head burger with hand-cut chips & salad. There is also a selection of vegetarian options to choose from and the desserts are equally as tempting.

From May, there will be an alternating Roast Dinner and Meditteranean Barbecue each Sunday. All main course food will be barbecued, from rib-eye steaks, ribs and other meats, burgers and sausages through to lobster and the fresh fish catch of the day.

Every other weekend, diners can enjoy the Sunday Roast Dinner which is £10.95 for best quality roast beef, £9.95 for roast pork and £6.95 for children. The gravy is real and entirely homemade and there are seconds on Yorkshire Puddings.

If you book a table using the Open Table system on the website, you will be automatically included in the Queens Head Prize Draw. This is held monthly, and the prize is a free meal for two.

354 THE BULL INN

27 High Street, Battle, East Sussex TN33 0EA
Tel: 01424 775171
e-mail: kerideeprose@yahoo.co.uk
website: www.bullinnbattle.eu

The handsome **Bull Inn** is located in the historic town of Battle, just a stone's throw from Battle Abbey and many other local attractions. The inn itself is one of the town's many attractions and it features in the town's guided tour, being not only one of the prettiest buildings in town, but one with an interesting history. Dating back to 1688 when it was built, the inn is made from beautiful Abbey stone and today retains much of that bygone charm with exposed stone walling, and original oak beamed ceilings within.

The Bull's owner Keri has been here a number of years and has built up quite the following with members of her local community and also sees many repeat visitors from further afield. The inn is particularly popular with walkers and families who can enjoy the benefit of their own family dining room. She opens her doors from 11am-11:30pm Monday to Thursday and Sundays, and from 11am-12pm on Fridays and Saturdays. Guests are assured that they will find something they like behind the bar, as it is always well stocked with a good selection of real ales from the local brewery, lagers and fine wines which appear on the inn's extensive wine list. Although the inn has plenty of character within, guests are welcome to take a seat outdoors in the Bull's own private courtyard throughout the year.

The inn is also known for its great tasting food. A fine traditional menu is served up each day that encompasses a variety of homemade dishes, all of which are freshly prepared on the premises each day. Local produce is used as much as possible to create that authentic English taste. Guests can choose from the main menu or the daily specials board which changes regularly to reflect the best seasonal produce available. A handsome roast is also added to the menu on Sunday's when the Bull's specialty homemade Yorkshire puddings are in popular demand.

Each weekend, guests can enjoy some quality entertainment at the Bull, provided by up and coming local bands. Please ring for details. A pool table is also available for quieter evenings, or guests can simple relax in front of the fire. Children and dogs welcome.

355 THE NETHERFIELD ARMS

Netherfield, Battle, East Sussex TN33 9QD
Tel: 01424 838282
e-mail: info@netherfieldarms.co.uk
website: www.netherfieldarms.co.uk

Set on the Weald Ridge amongst the rolling countryside of East Sussex, **The Netherfield Arms** overlooks the picturesque town of Battle and boasts panoramic views of the English Channel. Mentioned in the Domesday Book, Netherfield stands just off the B2096 and is named from the Anglo Saxon words for 'field of adders'. Five time winners of the Flowers in Bloom competition, the exterior of this popular pub is stunning. Built in 1725, the Netherfield Arms stands proud in the quaint village of Netherfield and oozes charm and character, creating a welcoming atmosphere as you approach. The interior has been decorated to a high standard; a superb inglenook fireplace crackles away, exposed brickwork and oak beams producing a traditional English pub look that entices you in. 13 year owners Mike and Caroline are keen to preserve the history of the building and ensure the decor fits in with the antique feel of the building.

By far the biggest draw to the Netherfield Arms is the splendid a la carte menu; the excellent chefs source ingredients from local suppliers to ensure quality and freshness in every dish they produce. Changing the specials daily to reflect the in season ingredients, the chefs also create sumptuous fish dishes, caught locally, the fish has to be sampled to be believed. The extensive a la carte menu is available all week long and the Sunday roasts are local favourites; additionally, the chefs are really good with guests who have dietary requirements, happily rearranging dishes to provide an alternative. For those

who are just peckish, the bar snacks menu provides the perfect accompaniment to the well kept real ales to be enjoyed in the lovely beer garden.

The beer garden is simply beautiful during the summer months and the Aston Martin owners club regularly use the pub and its grounds to meet. Open between 11 am and 3 pm and from 6.30 in the evenings all week long and between 12 and 3.30 pm on Sundays, the smiling staff are always on hand to ensure you have a fantastic visit.

356 STAR INN

Church Street, Old Heathfield, East Sussex TN21 9AH
Tel: 01435 863570 Fax: 01435 862020
e-mail: heathfieldstar@aol.com
website: www.starinnheathfield.co.uk

Originally a two room medieval house dating back to the middle of the 15th century, the **Star Inn** is now an amalgam of century's worth of building work resulting in the stunning property that stands today. The Star Inn is set in the centre of Old Heathfield, next to the parish church of All Saints amongst the attractive buildings that make up this quaint village. Old Heathfield sits on High Weald, in the middle of an area of outstanding beauty; designated as such for its rolling hills, irregular fields and pretty woods. The great location of the pub means that it is a honey trap for walkers, ramblers, cyclists and tourists from all over the country as well as being the popular local.

Inside the atmosphere is always warm and welcoming, the smiling staff on hand to ensure a great visit, whether just sampling the excellent real ales or a full dining experience in the magnificent restaurant. On the first floor, the restaurant features a 'barrel' ceiling, constructed by masons early in the building's history, and the shape of the room is truly unique. With seven tables and space for around 45 covers, the restaurant is often used for private functions and special occasions, such as small weddings, christenings and corporate events. With the chefs ensuring the ingredients are always fresh, the extensive menu is excellent, featuring hearty classic pub fare as well as smaller snacks for the peckish.

The saloon bar and tap room offer relaxed areas in which to enjoy a pint, sample the impressive cuisine or dine in the seclusion of the snug. Exposed beams and wooden floors throughout and a lovely inglenook fireplace enhance the charm and character of this unique pub and add to the experience. Chalk boards display the daily specials which range from locally caught fresh fish dishes to vegetarian options, there truly is something for everyone here. During the summer, the garden is the place to go, the views of the south coast are simply stunning as depicted in Turner's paintings and the garden itself has won awards. Open from 11.30 am through to 11 pm Monday to Saturday and between 12 pm and 11 pm on Sundays, the pub is especially busy for Sunday lunches, the roast dinners are spectacular!

357 SPRINGFIELDS

Springfield Park Road, Horsham,
West Sussex RH12 2PW
Tel: 01403 246770
Fax: 01403 265091
e-mail: lyn-williams@springfieldshotel.co.uk
website: www.springfieldshotel.co.uk

Springfields hotel as it stands today was built over two different periods. The original, lower, part of the building dates from 1939, and was built using the reclaimed bricks from the old 'Michelle Arms' (built in 1901). This pub, which stood immediately in front of where the Malt Shovel is today, was demolished in 1938 when Springfield Road was widened.

The older part of the hotel was originally used as a furniture store for an antiques business, but has recently been extended to form an 11 double bedroom hotel with en suite facilities. Now guests can stay in an award winning, stylish, modern, well appointed, clean, comfortable, cosy and convenient guest accommodation and be looked after by Lyn Williams and her friendly team.

Each room has been individually decorated. All rooms are en suite and equipped with a flat screen television and a broadband internet connection. All of the rooms are either Super King, King Sized, Doubles or Twins and every room has tea and coffee making facilities, irons, ironing board and hair dryer.

Breakfast at Springfields is definitely something to look forward to. Lyn offers a delicious and hearty breakfast, freshly cooked to order from the varied menu and served in the dining room between 7am and 9am. Earlier breakfasts are available by special arrangement. The kitchen can cater for most dietary requirements but if you need anything in particular please advise when booking so that Lyn and her staff can ensure they can provide you with what you need.

Breakfasts start with fresh fruit juices, a selection of cereals and yoghurts before getting down to the cooked selection of sausages, bacon, eggs (however you like them), tomatoes, mushrooms and beans in any combination you choose. They are accompanied by brown or white toast and a freshly brewed cup of tea or fresh ground coffee.

The hotel, which has its own on site parking, is conveniently situated within walking distance of the Horsham town centre and is next door to the popular Malt Shovel pub which boasts the largest selection of real ales for miles. The numerous attractions within easy reach include historic Arundel Castle, Nymans Gardens at Handcross and the Royal Botanic Gardens at Wakehurst Place, theatres at Horsham and Chichester, golf courses at Mannings Heath, Rookwood and Slinfold, and horse racing at Goodwood.

358 CAMELIA BOTNAR HOMES AND GARDENS

01403 864773

Littleworth Lane (Off A272) Cowfold, Sussex RH13 8NA

Open Mon - Sat 9-5, Sunday 10-4

Just outside of Cowfold in the heart of West Sussex lies Camelia Botnar Homes & Gardens. A large nursery with superb displays of high quality plants, shrubs, bedding and trees. We also have showroom displays of our award-winning ironwork, tradiditional handcrafted furniture in oak, beech and pine, hand thrown terracotta and studio ceramics. All our products are made at the Camelia Botnar Foundation by our skilled craftsmen and finished to a high standard. We are happy to quote on bespoke orders to give your home or garden that unique experience. Our gift shop has an exceptional range of quality, unusual and good value gifts and cards.

Our licensed restaurant, Camelia Botnar Bistro, is open daily for breakfasts, lunches, snacks, teas and delicious Sunday roasts. Our creative chefs produce seasonal menus with locally sourced, freshly prepared food. (see website for menus) . We are well worth a visit

Camelia Botnar Bistro - tel 01403 864588

Email sales@ cameliabotnar.com website www.cameliabotnar.com

360 HOLLY HOUSE B&B

Beaconsfield Road, Chelwood Gate,
East Sussex RH17 7LF
Tel: 01825 740484
e-mail: db@hollyhousebnb.demon.co.uk
website: www.hollyhousebnb.co.uk

Holly House B&B stands on the edge of Ashdown Forest in a rural village setting. A one hundred and forty year old forest farmhouse, it has been converted to create a comfortable family home. During its long existence it has seen Chelwood Gate change from a hamlet to a parish, two churches and two pubs. It provides the ideal location from which to explore Sussex and its many attractions.

Owners Mr and Mrs Birchell offer a warm welcome to their guests and are noted for their memorable breakfasts which are served in the conservatory overlooking the interesting one-acre garden. The menu offers the choice of a full English breakfast, or smoked salmon and scrambled eggs, or kippers and there's home-made marmalade or jam to go with your toast. Guests have the use of an inviting lounge and the accommodation offers a choice of single, twin or double rooms, with or without en suite facilities. The beds are especially comfortable and the rooms are equipped with digital flat screen TVs with integral DVD players. Holly House is open 7 days a week, 365 days a year, and dogs are welcome by prior arrangement.

359 THE SELSEY ARMS

Coolham, nr Horsham, West Sussex RH13 8QJ
Tel: 01403 741537
e-mail: theselseyarms@btconnect.com

Coolham is a small hamlet deep in the Sussex Weald set around a crossroads with, at its heart, an appealing old hostelry, **The Selsey Arms** which dates back to the 15th century. It has a pleasant garden at the front and another, more secluded, to the rear. Inside, exposed oak beams, an inglenook fireplace, wood and stone floors, and two log fires all help create a cosy atmosphere and add to the charm and character of the inn. At the bar you'll find 3 real ales on tap - Harveys Sussex Bitter, Doombar and Flowers IPA - along with a good selection of fine wines. A blackboard lists the fare on offer, all of it home-cooked and, on Sundays, there's also a choice of 2 traditional roasts. Specialities here are dishes featuring crab and lobster from Selsey, a few miles to the south.

The pub also has comfortable accommodation in four en suite rooms, two of them in what used to be a forge. All rooms are provided with a hospitality tray. The Selsey Arms is open from 11am to 11pm, Monday to Saturday; and from noon until 10.30pm on Sunday.

Coolham hamlet has strong connections with the Quaker movement. William Penn, founder of the state of Pennsylvania, established a meeting house in the hamlet in 1691 which is still in use. The local primary school is named after him. And if you go to Shipley, a few miles east of the pub, you can see the restored windmill which used to be the home of the poet Hilaire Belloc and was also featured in the TV series *Jonathan Creek* as the home of the lead actor, Alan Davies.

361 THE BRICKLAYERS ARMS

Whitehill Road, Crowborough, East Sussex TN6 1JT
Tel: 01892 668786
e-mail: b_stephen@hotmail.co.uk
website: www.bricklayersarmscrowborough.co.uk

Located right in the heart of the Crowborough community is the Bricklayers Arms, previously known as the Whitehill Tavern. Its owners Bill and Dawn previously helped to run the White Hart in Lower Horsebridge, but decided it was time to take over their own place a few years ago. They changed the inn back to its former name and restored it to the vibrant and friendly hot spot it once was. Bill and Dawn are well experienced in the trade and offer a warm and relaxing environment in which to enjoy a bite to eat or drink whilst exploring Crowborough.

The inn itself if beautifully traditional with a Tudor like exterior and many original features within such as exposed bricks, oak beamed ceilings and oak floors. There is plenty of entertainment available with a pool table, juke box and darts board all for guests to use, not to mention a selection of other indoor table games. Guests can also enjoy a quiet drink on the other side of the inn in the cosy snug area.

The bar is kept well stocked with an exclusive selection of wines that cannot be shop bought, and a fine selection of lagers, ciders and spirits too. Bill and Dawn also stock two casque marquee real ales, so ale lovers will be contented. There is a spacious beer garden to the rear which is perfect for all the family on sunny days; children are most welcome until 6pm.

A hearty selection of traditional pub dishes are also offered up throughout the day, all of which are cooked fresh to order. Guests can chose from the set menu, or the specials board, which is made up of dishes like homemade faggots and mash with onion gravy, a delicious swordfish steak, BBQ spare ribs, and homemade steak and kidney pie. A good choice of light bites are also available which includes a range of filled jacket potatoes, sandwiches, baguettes, salads and omelettes. The team are keen to please and invite guests to ask for what they fancy if they cannot see anything they like on the menu.

Guests are welcomed to stay and enjoy a variety of entertainment events which include regular beer festivals, bi-monthly open mike nights, all the best sports TV, and live entertainment from a variety of local bands. Please see website for details. Open 12-11pm Monday-Thursday, 12pm-12am Fridays and Saturdays and 12-10:30pm on Sundays.

362 THE BULL ON THE GREEN

The Green, Newick, East Sussex BN8 4CA
Tel: 01825 722055
e-mail: bullnewick@hotmail.co.uk
website: www.thebullonthegreen.co.uk

As its name suggests, **The Bull on the Green** is situated on the village green of the sizeable village of Newick in the heart of the Sussex countryside. As well as being a fine old traditional inn complete with ancient beams, it also has an excellent restaurant and offers comfortable B&B accommodation. Its history goes back a long way - the pub was the stopping place for pilgrims in 1510 travelling between Winchester and Canterbury.

Today, the pub has a welcoming atmosphere, enhanced during the winter months by blazing log fires. Settle down in the snug bar or, in good weather, in the secluded courtyard at the rear of the pub, a great place to enjoy your refreshments on lovely summer evenings. Customers can enjoy a light snack or a tasty dinner in the restaurant where dishes range from old favourites such as the Bull Inn steak and ale pie or beer-battered fish and chips, to wild boar sausages, home-made lasagne or a vegetarian button mushroom and courgette tagliatelli. The restaurant is available for private functions and special occasions such as weddings, meetings or any other gatherings.

You could even make a weekend of it by staying in the lovely bed and breakfast accommodation. There are eight B&B rooms, all with private en suite bathrooms, and coffee and tea making facilities. The tariff includes a fantastic home-cooked breakfast to set you up for the day.

Throughout the year The Bull caters for various special events. At present, every Tuesday is open mic night when customers get the opportunity to perform live and show off their talents! Throughout February, the inn offers a special menu for St Valentine's night.

But the biggest night by far is in November when Newick village attracts the largest number of visitors to watch the spectacle of Guy Fawkes night. A giant procession goes all the way through the village, a sight not to be missed.

Newick village is close to the South Downs, 20 minutes from Brighton and 10 minutes from Lewes. It is also a short distance from Plumpton Racecourse and Glyndebourne Opera House is only 15 minutes away. And for golfers, East Sussex National is a 10 minute drive and Piltdown is just 5 minutes away.

364 THE DINING ROOM

31 North Street, Chichester,
West Sussex PO19 1LY
Tel: 01243 537352
Fax: 01243 780773
e-mail: info@thediningroom.biz
website: www.thediningroom.biz

Occupying a gracious Georgian mansion that dates back to 1790 and still retains a host of original features, **The Dining Room** offers an outstanding dining experience in elegant surroundings. For restaurant patrons, there is a conservatory and an enchanting courtyard garden, complete with wrought-iron pavilions and parasols to deter the rain to complete what is a really delightful restaurant.

The Dining Room is run under the watchful eye of the chef and patron, Neil Rusbridger. Neil trained at such eminent places as the Chewton Glen Hotel and for Michel Roux at the Waterside Inn making him suitably qualified to utilise the local produce and marry them with some more exotic flavours and ideas, creating a really great place to dine.

The restaurant is very careful in selecting its suppliers and produce to ensure traceability and sustainability; they do not use imported goods unless absolutely necessary.

The menu offers a delicious range of foods, from mouth watering Danish open sandwiches to more elaborate dishes such as homemade foie gras terrine, lovely plump Irish oysters, superb local fish, game and of course delectable homemade sorbets, ice creams and desserts. During the season for game, you'll find a wealth of it on offer: Yorkshire grouse, local partridge and venison along with wild duck and pigeon. There are also superb cockles from Chichester harbour and golden trout from Hampshire making guest appearances! A range of fine cheeses – mainly English or British – is also offered to tempt you if you prefer a savoury finish to your meal. It is the restaurant's policy to offer the best ingredients by using local, free-range or organic foods wherever possible. It is also working with the Chichester City Council to serve more Fairtrade products - as the city has been elected as a 'Fairtrade City'.

To accompany your meal, select from the very comprehensive list of wines from all over the world together with more than 20 wines and Champagnes available by the glass.

Alternatively, if you just want a drink, you can soak up the atmosphere in the Champagne, wine and cocktail bar (separately branded as 31 North), which is a great place to meet friends and sample one of the many Champagnes by the glass in stylish surroundings.

The Dining Room is open for lunch from noon until 2.45pm, Monday to Saturday; and from 5.30pm (7pm out of season) with last orders at 8.45pm.

363 BLACKBERRY FARM

Whitesmith near Lewes, East Sussex, BN8 6JD
Tel: 01825 872912
e-mail: info@blackberry-farm.co.uk
website: www.blackberry-farm.co.uk

Located in the heart of the beautiful Sussex countryside in the village of Whitesmith, is Blackberry Farm. The farm is run by Karen Harris and her family, who open seven days a week from 9:30am-6pm in the summer and from 10am-5pm in the winter months.

The farm is home to over 180 animals so children can enjoy their days meeting and greeting all kinds of wonderful farm yard and exotic animals, including pigs, sheep, goats, ponies, cattle, donkeys, guinea pigs, llamas and alpacas. For lunch, guests can make a visit to the onsite café which sells a great range of homemade treats, sweets and ice-creams. Guests can rest assured that all the dishes are cooked fresh to order from locally sourced produce, using ingredients that are GM, additive and hydrogenated fat free. Most dietary requirements and allergies can also be catered for. The café is also licensed for alcoholic beverages.

For the afternoon, kids (and grownups!) can take to one of the many play areas to tire themselves out with a range of swings, roundabouts, miniature tractors and diggers, zip rides, fortresses and even space boppers! When the rain sets in, there is also a large indoor play barn, with a special baby and toddler area too for more gentle play. For special occasions or birthday parties, why not give the kids a chance to be a farmer for the day and get involved with feeding all the animals, tractor rides and collecting chicken eggs.

366 AMBERLEY MUSEUM & HERITAGE CENTRE

Amberley, nr Arundel, West Sussex BN18 9LT
Tel: 01798 831370 Fax: 01798 831831
e-mail: office@amberleymuseum.co.uk
website: www.amberleymuseum.co.uk

So much to offer in a beautiful location - Set within an area of outstanding natural beauty against the South Downs, Amberley Museum & Heritage Centre has something for everyone to enjoy. Over 30 special events are held throughout the year. A free vintage bus service and recently extended narrow gauge railway enables visitors to savour the nostalgia of historic transport. Both services take visitors around the site to see traditional resident craftspeople such as a potter, broom-maker, blacksmith and wood-turner, and other areas of interest.

Something for everyone - This fabulous 36 acre open air site is dedicated to the industrial heritage of the South East and boasts some truly remarkable static and live exhibits:- Blacksmith's Forge, Brickyard Drying Shed, Cycle Exhibition, Engineering Machine Shop, Foundry, Lime Kilns, Print Workshop, Roadmakers' Exhibition, Stationary Engines, Telecommunications Exhibition, Timber Yard, Woodturners, Vintage Wireless Exhibition, Electricity Hall, Estate Pump House, Lime Grinding Mill, Narrow Gauge Railway, Railway Exhibition Hall, Southdown Bus Garage, Steam Road Vehicles, Telephone Exchange, Tool & Trades History Exhibition. The site also offers a range of picturesque nature trails, hillside walks and picnic areas where a variety of wildlife can be enjoyed. There is a gift shop that sells a range of souvenirs, novelty items and toys.

Refreshingly Good - The Limeburners Restaurant provides an excellent choice of food and refreshments for all the family – from light snacks to more formal meals.

365 MOUNT PLEASANT HOUSE

Level Mare Lane, Eastergate, nr Chichester, West Sussex PO20 3SB
Tel: 01243 545368
e-mail: gforsyth1@btinternet.com
website: www.mountpleasant-bedandbreakfast.co.uk

Whether you are looking for a short overnight day or a longer stay, you will instantly feel at home at **Mount Pleasant House** which boasts a 4-star rating from Quality in Tourism. This gracious Georgian house of character, dating back to 1750, stands in three acres of tranquil and pleasant gardens with an outdoor heated swimming pool and a vinery.

On arrival guests are greeted with welcome refreshment with a choice of wines and soft drinks. The interior is beautifully furnished and decorated to a very high standard, including the guest bedrooms. There are four of them, two with en suite facilities, one with a 4-poster bed and another decorated in French style. All rooms are provided with a colour TV and a hospitality tray. Breakfast is definitely something to look forward to at Mount Pleasant. It is served in the conservatory and vinery and the choice includes smoked salmon and scrambled eggs, kedgeree, smoked haddock with a poached egg, and, of course, a full English breakfast. Vegetarian options are also available.

Mount Pleasant House's location makes it very convenient for horse racing at Fontwell and Goodwood, historic Chichester's many attractions; Arundel Castle; the South Downs; and the coast which is just six miles away.

Mount Pleasant is open all year round; children are welcome by arrangement and some dogs are accepted. Please note that payment is by cash or cheque only.

367 ELMER HOTEL

89 Elmer Road, Middleton on Sea, Bognor Regis, West Sussex PO22 6HD
Tel: 01243 855580
e-mail: theelmer@elmer hotel.co.uk
website: www.elmerhotel.co.uk

Two miles from Bognor Regis in West Sussex, **The Elmer Hotel** provides the best of both worlds; a stone's throw from the seaside and from stunning scenery. It's just a five minute walk to an unspoiled sandy patch of the south coast, and only a 20-mile drive to the beautiful South Downs, an Area of Outstanding Natural Beauty.

The Elmer is perfect for families, couples, friends and business folk who want to walk, cycle, sightsee or simply unwind by the seaside and then relax in the evening in the comfort of a friendly traditional pub.

In the restaurant you'll find a satisfying selection of traditional dishes. Whether it's a light lunch you're after, or a full evening meal, a healthy chicken Caesar salad or a hearty peppered beef and rice, they are all on the menu along with much more. The Elmer's chef prepares every meal using the freshest ingredients. Sunday is roast day! Come along for a full roast lunch served with all the trimmings. But if you fancy a hand-pulled pint and a panini, the pub with its full snack menu could be the place for you. There's a good selection of basket meals, sandwiches and paninis available from the bar. Or try the Elmer cooked English breakfast, served with tea or coffee and toast (from 12 noon - 3pm). Have a game of darts or pool. Enjoy a choice of Fuller's cask ales, draught lagers, or choose from the selection of wines and spirits in an atmosphere of lively banter in the public bar or the relaxed calm of the lounge.

The Elmer offers a choice of three light and airy rooms and two smaller rooms, all capable of sleeping two. Each has an en suite bathroom or shower, coffee making facility and a television/DVD player. Wi-fi is available. Room rates include a full English or Continental breakfast.

If you would like to bring your pet dog, please advise the hotel in advance. They love dogs but "Please, no cats, gerbils, crocs or other animals!"

You'll find plenty to see and do in the area. The South Downs provides beautiful surrounding, ideal for horse riding, ballooning, cycling, paragliding, golf and, for walkers, the South Downs Way. For sophisticated shoppers and history buffs alike, Chichester, a Roman walled town, is a 15-minute drive away, and historic Arundel Castle, Petworth and Uppark are all within easy reach.

368 MALTHOUSE RESTAURANT

Waterloo Road, Felpham, Bognor Regis, PO22 7EH
Tel: 01243 864609
e-mail: enquiries@yeoldemalthouse.co.uk
website: www.yeoldemalthouse.co.uk

Located just a stone's throw away from the beach, **Malthouse Restaurant** serves a full range of traditional a la carte dishes, succulent roasts and fresh seafood specialities. The family run business aims to give diners a superb dining experience in a relaxed atmosphere. Local produce is a strong focus of the varied menu and the restaurant can cater for up to 30 people. The restaurant has introduced new styles to compliment its traditional offerings harvesting the bounty of local produce from its seaside location. All of the dishes are reasonably priced and starters include garlic mussels with white wine & cream, sauté mushrooms in stilton sauce, and roasted goats cheese with sweet peppers, onions & cherry tomatoes. As well as a daily specials board listing fresh seafood dishes daily, the main menu includes other tasty option such as pan roasted fillet of lamb on curly kale with Cumberland sauce, and sauté Gressingham duck breast on braised red cabbage with orange & ginger

sauce. It is advisable to leave room for one of the restaurant's delicious homemade desserts. A lunch menu is available between Tuesday – Sunday, with roast dinners on Sunday too.

370 THE RISING SUN

Iping Road, Milland, nr Liphook, Sussex GU30 7NA
Tel: 01428 741347 Fax: 01428 741704
e-mail: mail@risingsunmilland.com
website: www.risingsunmilland.com

The **Rising Sun** at Milland is one of the very best village inns in the whole region, a wonderful place to relax, have fun and enjoy a drink and a meal. It stands in a village signposted off the A3 near Liphook in the heart of the lovely South Downs National Park, a magnet for walkers, cyclists, tourists and lovers of the fresh, clean country air. Ben and Frankie are the most welcoming of hosts and the bar and lounge areas offer abundant space and comfort for meeting friends and having a chat over a glass of well-kept Fullers ale.

The beers and the extensive wine list complement daily changing menus that feature the best and freshest local ingredients in the dishes served in the 40-cover restaurant. Some dishes are all-time classics, while others come from the modern British repertoire, such as scallops with chorizo and pea shoots and purée, or braised belly pork with black pudding, mustard mash and leeks. Bar snacks cater for lighter appetites, children can choose from their own menu and the chefs produce some really lip-smacking desserts. The inn also offers pizzas and fish & chips to take away.

The Rising Sun is a popular venue for private parties and all sorts of celebrations and offers an outside catering service for hog roasts, barbecues, buffets and lunches for groups of 12 to 200.

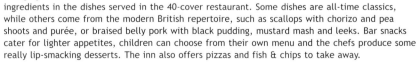

369 THE BARLEY CORN

Main Road, Nutbourne, Chichester, Sussex PO18 8RS
Tel: 01243 573172
e-mail: hamishandnatalie@hotmail.co.uk

The Barley Corn attracts a wide range of clientele from families to groups of young and old who meet there. The pub provides an ideal space for people to meet on the outskirts of Chichester, including locals and visitors. There is a restaurant area, traditional bar area, games room and an outside beer garden, which is popular on warmer days. Large sash windows make the pub a light and welcoming place to spend lunch times or evenings. It dates back to the 17th century and has been dispensing beer since the 1800s as it was previously a beer shop. This establishment has plenty of charm to offer and wooden floors throughout add to the olde worlde atmosphere of the place.

Four real ales are served from the well-stocked bar, which has plenty of fine wines to choose from as well as beers, lagers, spirits and soft drinks. The food served at The Barley Corn is popular with those who frequent the establishment. The menu has a strong focus on traditional a la carte home cooked food and there are always fresh daily specials to choose from too. Access for disabled customers is not a problem and there are disabled toilet facilities too. The Barley Corn is open every day between 12pm and 11pm and food is served between 12pm and 3pm and 6pm and 9pm Monday - Saturday. On a Sunday a traditional carvery can be enjoyed between 12pm and 6pm.

This friendly pub offers a warm welcome to everyone and is an ideal drinking spot for locals and those visiting the area who want home cooked food and good conversation.

371 THE FOX & GOOSE COUNTRY INN

Armscote, nr Stratford-upon-Avon, Warwickshire CV37 8DD
Tel: 01608 682293
e-mail: mail@foxandgoose.co.uk
website: www.foxandgoosearmscote.co.uk

The Fox and Goose Country Inn is located eight miles south of Startford-upon-Avon in the hamlet of Armscote. This popular country inn is run and owned by Colin Royal, who has built up a sturdy reputation amongst his guests for offering truly delicious food and drink at great value prices.

Like all good country inns the Fox and Goose offers a traditional theme with beamed ceilings, bare floorboards and an assortment of brushed wooden furniture, but is complimented by a selection of contemporary and unusual items from plush upholstered handmade chairs and stuffed animals. The pearlescent walls and cream tones create a calming environment, readily filled by the inn's crackling fire and warm hospitality.

Guests most often come to the inn for its food. Colin offers a delicious selection of restaurant styled food, bursting with local flavours and produce. A real specialty are the pies which come in many varieties including pork and leek, chicken and ham, beef and Guinness, creamy fish, duck and cherry, and Hunter's game to name a few. Other favourite dishes include smoked salmon with a dill tagliatelle, rib eye steak with hand cut chips, and Lightmorne Lamb with minted gravy.

372 LARKRISE COTTAGE

Upper Billesley, Wilmcote, Stratford Upon Avon,
Warwickshire CV37 9RA   Tel: 01789 268618
e-mail: alanbailey17@googlemail.com
website: www.larkrisecottage.co.uk

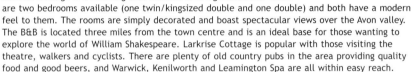

Nestled in the beautiful countryside surrounding Stratford-upon-Avon, Larkrise Cottage is a stunning B&B finished to a high standard. There are two bedrooms available (one twin/kingsized double and one double) and both have a modern feel to them. The rooms are simply decorated and boast spectacular views over the Avon valley. The B&B is located three miles from the town centre and is an ideal base for those wanting to explore the world of William Shakespeare. Larkrise Cottage is popular with those visiting the theatre, walkers and cyclists. There are plenty of old country pubs in the area providing quality food and good beers, and Warwick, Kenilworth and Leamington Spa are all within easy reach.

373 THE LORD NELSON

Priory Rd, Alcester, Warwickshire B49 5EA
Tel: 01789 762632
e-mail: chrisatthenelson@hotmail.co.uk

The Lord Nelson is a beautiful historic pub, around 200 years old, located in the Roman market town of Alcester. Recently taken over by a delightful local family, the pub is attracting a range of customers through the variety of events being held; from senior lunches to music and quiz nights. From the beamed ceilings to roaring open fireplaces in winter, this is every bit a traditional local pub. The food is traditional English fayre, but with a unique modern twist, and is excellent value for such superb quality. The Sunday lunch is a particular favourite with their local patrons, who visit here every week for the delicious roast, sourced from the local butcher. Children, vegetarians, and seniors are also catered for. Outside is an excellent garden, with play area for children, and a spacious car park.

Staying at the Lord Nelson can also be quite a treat, with three bedrooms to choose from; two en-suite, and one with a private bathroom. Recently modernised and refurbished, these cosy rooms are perfect for a night to relax while travelling through this beautiful region. All the rooms include flat-screen TV, DVD and WiFi internet access.

374 ROBBIE'S OF WARWICK

74 Smith Street, Warwick, Warwickshire CV34 4HU
Tel: 01926 400470
website: www.robbiesrestaurant.com

Located on Smith Street; one of Warwick's oldest roads is **Robbie's of Warwick**. Its status as a grade two listed early 15th century building sets it apart from other eateries in the area, with stylish décor complimented beautifully by original Tudor features. Specialising in high class international cuisine, Robbie's have created a fine reputation for delicious dishes, all of which are created by their very own master chef.

Guests can choose from the daily specials board, or the main menu which truly has something for every palette. Starters include pan seared wood pigeon on peach and ginger compote, honey roasted pork hock and apricot terrine, and roasted butternut squash. Popular main dishes range from Gressingham Duck, rack of lamb and venison steak to wild mushroom and broad bean stroganoff. A separate seafood menu also runs with a selection of mouth-watering treats like butterflied Creole prawns; pan seared scallops; whole grilled lobster; and rainbow trout.

A phenomenal wine list compliments the menu, with a carefully chosen selection of 50 wines from around the world. A range of themed evenings and music nights are also held at Robbie's, please ring for details.

375 THE BULL AT WITHERLEY

Watlins Street, Witherley, Atherstone,
Warwickshire CV9 1RD
Tel: 01847 712323
e-mail: fuhard.saunders2@tesco.net
website: www.thebullinnwitherley.co.uk

The owners of **The Bull at Witherley** took over in 2009 and have made many changes to it since then. They have retained many of the inn's original 18th century coaching inn features, whilst converting its restaurant and bar into a modern and stylish place to dine.

Open Monday to Saturday from 12-3pm and 5-9pm and from 12-8:30pm on Sundays, the inn is popular with both young and old who can enjoy the inn's pleasant location by the River Amber in the spacious beer garden. Inside there is plenty of room too, with an open bar area and lots of cosy snugs for food. A selection of bar meals are available at lunchtime ranging from filled sandwiches, soups and mains to include beer battered haddock and chips, BBQ chicken and ribs, and rigatoni pasta with a kids menu and pudding selection attached. Each evening an a la carte menu is offered with something for everyone from steamed mussels or homemade ham hock to start and grilled mackerel, Herefordshire beef steak and pan seared duck breast and much, much more for mains. Popular desserts include vanilla panacotta with roasted rhubarb, hot chocolate fondant and espresso crème Brulee. On Sundays a five choice Sunday roast is added to the menu.

The Bull also has five en suite guest bedrooms on offer, perfect for couples or families who want to explore this tranquil area further.

376 THE RED LION

Wall Hill Road, Corley Moor, Coventry CV7 8AP
Tel: 01676 542345
website: www.redlioncorley.co.uk

Attractively positioned on Corley Moor in Coventry, **The Red Lion** has a fine reputation for excellent hospitality and fine food. Popular with families, this 16th century inn is surrounded by spacious gardens, perfect for enjoying a cool glass of real ale whilst the children play in the summer time. Three ales are always on offer alongside a range of fine wines. The inn is also known for its delicious cuisine, showcased on an ever changing menu, dedicated to serving locally sourced produce.

www.findSOMEWHERE.co.uk
For people who want to explore the United Kingdom

Places to Eat and Drink

377 PATRIOTS ARMS

6 New Road, Chiseldon, Swindon,
Wiltshire SN4 0LU
Tel: 01793 740331
e-mail: lenamariesands@hotmail.com

A sizeable village set in the Marlborough Downs, Chiseldon is fortunate in having a fine old hostelry in the form of the recently refurbished **Patriots Arms**. It has a spacious beer garden with a play area for children and a front garden where dogs are welcome. Mine hosts are Lena and Mervyn Sands, a friendly and welcoming couple who took over here in the autumn of 2008. Good food is a priority here with an extensive menu offering a good choice of dishes that ranges from traditional favourites to some exotic offerings. The regular menu is supplemented by daily specials listed on the blackboard. Vegetarians are particularly well catered for, as are lovers of real ales. Food is served from noon until 2pm and 6pm - 9pm, Monday to Friday; from noon until 3pm and 6pm - 9pm on Saturday; and from noon until 9pm on Sundays when a traditional roast with all the trimmings is served throughout the day.

The inn hosts live music evenings from time to time, as well as Jam Nights and Quiz Nights.

378 MAGGIE VIGAR-SMITH

Wernham Farm, Clench Common, Marlborough,
Wiltshire SN8 4DR
Tel: 01672 512236
e-mail: margglvsg@aol.com

Offering bed & breakfast accommodation with a difference, **Maggie Vigar-Smith** is based at Wernham Farm which itself is located in a beautiful rural location close to Avebury and its famous stone circle, the White Horses and Stonehenge. Maggie has a wide spectrum of interests ranging from animal healing to the paranormal. She teaches reiki for dogs, arranges bird watching and star watching - the area is free from light pollution - and is also an accomplished artist whose watercolours adorn the walls of the farmhouse. You'll also find crafts, pottery, jewellery and knitted items available to buy.

The house itself dates back to the 16th century but was largely restored in the Georgian style following a fire. There are wonderful views from every window and the farm is home to sheep, cows, chickens, ducks - and a dog.

The house has just 2 rooms, each with a private bath room, and a full breakfast based on locally sourced ingredients is included in the menu. Maggie is also happy to provide an evening meal by previous arrangement, and during the day guests can also enjoy a cream tea. Guests are welcome to bring their own horses and enjoy riding over the Downs and along the Ridgeway.

379 THE SWAN INN

Wilton, Marlborough, Wiltshire SN8 3SS
Tel: 01672 870274
e-mail: info@theswanwilton.co.uk
website: www.theswanwilton.co.uk

Set in the heart of the picturesque village of Wilton with its roadside duck pond and quaint old cottages, **The Swan Inn** is noted for its excellent food, service and a warm, relaxed and friendly atmosphere.

Inside, the décor is unfussy, with wooden floors, dried hops around the walls, and chunky scrubbed pine farmhouse style furniture. The inn prides itself on its fantastic home-cooked food. The experienced chef produces a well-balanced menu, with a mix of haute cuisine and popular traditional pub meals. The ingredients are sourced locally wherever possible and the daily changing menus feature delights such as hand-made terrines, pies and chutneys. There's also fresh fish delivered daily from Looe in Cornwall and good local game in season. Food is served from noon until 2pm, and from 6pm to 9pm, Monday to Friday; noon until 2.30pm, and from 6pm to 9pm on Saturday; and from noon until 3pm on Sundays when a fine roast heads the menu. To complement your meal, the inn offers an outstanding selection of wines.

The inn is just 10 minutes walk from the Kennet & Avon Canal and the Crofton Beam Engines. Even closer is the Wilton Windmill, the only working windmill in southwest England.

380 THE FRENCH HORN

Marlborough Road, Pewsey,
Wiltshire SN9 5NT
Tel: 01672 562443
e-mail: frenchhornpewsey@yahoo.co.uk
website: www.frenchhornpewsey.co.uk

Once owned by King Alfred, the attractive village of Pewsey boasts a fine statue of the king, some beautiful thatched cottages, a 700-year-old church, access to the Kennet and Avon Canal and, nearby, an excellent hostelry, **The French Horn**. Outside, hanging baskets make it look very inviting and, inside, Australian memorabilia provide an unusual motif. They are there because Chef Greg Toogood is himself Australian, a welcoming character who flies microlights in his spare time and enjoys listening to rock music while cooking. It certainly seems to have a good effect. His extensive menu ranges from traditional pub favourites and fresh seafood to dishes based on kangaroo and wild boar meat.

Food is served in the bright and airy dining area, and in good weather customers can enjoy their refreshments in the pleasant beer garden. Opening hours - 12pm - 3pm and 6pm to 11pm (Closed tuesdays). Food is served 12pm - 2.30pm and 6pm - 9pm - booking is essential. Dogs are welcome in the bar area; all major credit cards are accepted.

381 THE DUKE AT BRATTON

Melbourne Street, Bratton, Westbury BA13 4RW
Tel: 01380 830242
e-mail: lynettemhobbs@live.co.uk
website: www.thedukeatbratton.co.uk

The Duke at Bratton is a traditional country pub that dates back to the 18th century. Formerly three cottages, it was at some unknown date converted into a public house with outside tea rooms and was named The Duke William. One of the many features of this quaint pub is a pair of whale jaw bones which were present at the time of the old tea rooms. These were misplaced for many years but were rediscovered and erected over the garden gate in April 1995.

The Duke is situated just outside Westbury in the beautiful countryside village of Bratton. It is a Moles pub and can therefore offer their real ales that are brewed in Melksham. The menu offers traditional homemade food with an extensive gluten free range of dishes and an exciting new children's menu. All food is freshly cooked to order, using locally sourced produce where possible. The menu offers la carte, hearty bar meals and traditional Sunday lunches. The restaurant seats 38 and provides a delightful setting for any wedding, anniversary or birthday celebration. Families are always welcome, with high chairs provided along with a small children's play area situated outside in the attractive beer garden. The Duke at Bratton is open every day from 12pm until 11pm.

382 THE NEW INN

Lower Westwood, nr Bradford-on-Avon,
Wiltshire BA15 2AE
Tel: 01225 863123

Lined with pretty hanging baskets of flowers, the building of **The New Inn,** dating 1810, is the epitome of a traditional countryside Inn, brimming with character. Inside you can find a real treat in quality local food. Well known locally, the owners Mike and his daughter Hannah are passionate about fresh food, and in fact both shoot and fly fish; the spoils of which are served at the restaurant. You can't get much fresher than that! Mike's twenty five years experience in the restaurant business is evident through the organisation and brilliant service from the dedicated staff, as well as the food. Home-cooked dishes include such in season delicacies as muscles, crab, lobster, game, local beef and venison, and delightful home-made sausages - not to mention a hearty roast lunch on a Sunday.

The brilliant reputation, and relaxed, sporting-influenced atmosphere, has made The New Inn very popular with visitors and locals. The beautiful rustic decor, including slate floors, wooden country-style furniture, and bunches of fresh flowers, lend itself to such a traditional country inn, and make it a cosy place to visit whatever the weather. The two grand houses Westwood Manor and Ilford Manor are conveniently located nearby. The Inn is open seven days a week, lunch is served from 12 -3pm and dinner is 6-11pm, except on Sundays when the Inn is open 12-4pm with food being served until 3pm.

383 ENFORD HOUSE

Enford, nr Pewsey, Wiltshire SN9 6DJ
Tel: 01980 671206
e-mail: marycampbell@ukonline.co.uk
website: www.enfordhouse.co.uk

Situated in the charming Wiltshire village of Enford, in the
heart of Salisbury Plain, Enford House is a charming 18th
Century Grade 2 listed rectory surrounded by a
picturesque thatched wall and garden. Enford House
provides either self catering weekend and holiday lets, or bed &
breakfast, in a self contained wing of the house. With 3 fully
furnished and contemporarily decorated en-suite bedrooms,
sitting room, kitchen/dining room and south facing patio it
offers guests flexibility and plenty of space for a stress-free
family holiday. The patio is the perfect place to enjoy your
breakfast before a busy day begins. WiFi is available throughout.

The house is family owned, now in its second generation
within the same family, and has a beautifully relaxed and unique
flair, very in-keeping with the beautiful countryside surrounding it. The village church and River
Avon are next to the property and there are lots of local walks or bike rides to discover while
exploring Salisbury Plain. Over the river is the local pub, which has a lovely ambience and serves
delicious food. For a small charge guests can privately fish here during their stay. The property
is 8 miles from Stonehenge and 15 miles from Longleat as well as the historic cities of Salisbury
and Marlborough.

384 THE PORTON HOTEL

Porton, nr Salisbury, Wiltshire, SP4 0LA
Tel: 01980 610203 Fax: 01980 619398
e-mail: laura.jones@theportonhotel.com
website: www.theportonhotel.com

Settled within the sleepy village of Porton, and only a
stone's throw (4 to 5 miles) from bustling Salisbury, is the
gorgeous red-brick building of **The Porton Hotel**. An old
railway hotel dating from around 1900, it is now a
contemporary Hotel and Restaurant which has made quite
a name for itself in the area for outstanding quality and service.
The interior is just as elegant; guests are welcomed by plush
carpets, traditional wooden furniture and glorious roaring open
fires in the colder months.

The food is simple but spectacular, all locally sourced (including
delicious smoked salmon from the nearby Fjordling Smokehouse)
and lovingly prepared on the premises - you will find yourself
reluctant to leave! Convenient, then, that the Porton Hotel
provides wonderful accommodation, with beautiful views over the rural setting and cosy furnishings
to ensure you will feel right at home. All of the rooms also come with en-suite bathrooms.

The hotel can accommodate parties and events, often being the location for wedding
receptions, and also contains a games room, projection screen, and large garden with play area.
Food is served Monday to Saturday 12noon to 2.30pm and 6pm to 9pm, on Sundays the kitchen is
closed for dinner, but lunch is served between 12noon and 4pm. Children and dogs welcome.

385 THE KINGS HEAD

The Street, Whiteparish, Wiltshire SP5 2SG
Tel: 01794 884287
e-mail: thekingshead99@googlemail.com

Nestled in the heart of unspoilt and picturesque Whiteparish, just outside of Salisbury, is **The Kings Head**; a unique village pub with a focus on tradition. The owners, who have just celebrated three happy and successful years at the Kings Head, have infused the building and its beautiful garden with their own unusual style. Throughout you will find handmade sculpture (including a rather adorable mini-Stonehenge in the garden) and art, as well as peacocks proudly strutting through the grass. The traditional influence of the building spills out into the garden, which has been kept as natural as possible, and is beautiful and fragrant with wild English flowers and grasses – a relaxing treat away from the crowds and noise!

This friendly and welcoming pub is popular with the locals, and often attracts visitors – especially as everyone through the village recommends the food and service here. The food, which is all sourced within a 10 mile radius and is wonderfully fresh, is bursting with colours and flavours. All homemade, the menu constantly changes, to remain fresh and tasty, and also to change with the seasons, with the best quality ingredients. Classic traditional dishes are always available also. Food is served from 6pm on Monday, 12noon until 3pm and 6pm until late Tuesday to Thursday, and from 12noon Friday until Sunday.

386 THE LORD NELSON

Middleton, Middle Winterslow, Salisbury, Wiltshire SP5 1QS
Tel: 01980 862218
e-mail: rogerstanwell@btinternet.com

This historic pub is conveniently located in the small village of Winterslow, approximately 7 miles east of Salisbury on the Clarendon Way, a popular walking route through this tranquil part of Wiltshire. The pub is close to Roche Court Sculpture Garden and Bentley Wood which is home to several rare butterfly species. Stonehenge is about 25mins drive away.

The driving force behind The Lord Nelson is the owner and enthusiastic cook, who after many years in international business has used his experience and passion to re invigorate this quintessentially English pub. Real ales, excellent food and a first class wine list reflect his interest in wines from around the world.

The building, which is roughly 200 years old, was originally described as a 'Beer House' on old maps and continues to retain to its traditional roots with a traditional wood burner, pub games and pleasant garden. The food here is all cooked to order and served in satisfyingly hearty portions, as real pub food should be! If you seek a lighter meal, they also serve a delightful choice of tapas to pick at with a partner or family – very sociable food, which perfectly complements the cosy and friendly

387 ANGEL CORNER TEA ROOMS

The Square, Mere, Wiltshire BA12 6DH
Tel: 01747 860187
e-mail: immie.r@btinternet.com

The lovely **Angel Corner Tea Rooms** appears every bit the traditional tea-room, in a beautiful building, dating around 1756, bursting with character. It has been successfully owned by Imogen for six years. Kenyan born, she has infused the classic tea-room with her own unique flair, and selectionof delightful handmade crafts and gifts bought directly from Kenya, South Africa and Zimbabwe. Examples include beadwork, jewellery and basket work.

All food is homemade with cooked breakfasts and lunches, cream teas and wide selection of fresh cakes. Special dietary requirements are catered for and there are local ice-creams available.

Visitors to the area are close to many walks and cycle trails, including the mid-Wiltshire Way, and also many top attractions such as Stonehenge, Longleat House & Safari Park, King Alfred's Tower and Stourhead gardens. Mere is just off the A303 from London to the West Country, an ideal stopover for refreshments at Angel Corner.

It is open from 9.30am to 5pm everyday, apart from Tuesdays, Sundays and Bank Holidays.

388 BLUEBIRD TEAROOMS

9 Church Street, Malvern, Worcestershire WR14 2AA
Tel: 01684 561166

The home cooked cakes and scones at **Bluebird Tearooms** are one of the great attractions to visitors to this delightful little place. Caroline & Barry took over here in September 2009 and the tearooms have gone from strength to strength. They offer a wide selection of home cooked fayre including gluten free, vegan and dairy free options. Fresh sandwiches and meals are available throughout the day along with a good range of refreshments and excellent cream teas. Open Tues to Sat 10am - 5pm and many Sundays (please phone for details). The tearooms are located 2 doors up from the Tourist Information Centre, above Elts shoes.

www.findSOMEWHERE.co.uk
For people who want to explore the United Kingdom

Specialist Shops

389 THE DELL HOUSE

Green Lane, Little Malvern,
Worcestershire WR14 4HU
Tel: 01684 564448
e-mail: helen@dellhouse.co.uk
website: www.dellhouse.co.uk

This award winning B&B can be found nestled in two acres of woodland on the sheltered eastern slopes of The Malvern Hills. Owned by Helen and Ian Burrage, the grand house offers three en-suite period bedrooms, which are comfortable and elegantly proportioned. Superb home cooked breakfasts are served in the morning and guests can enjoy wonderful views and make the most of WiFi internet. **The Dell House**, a former rectory, is listed in the AA's 'Britain's Best B&B Collection – 500 perfect places for bed & breakfast' since 2004. From the grounds there are spectacular views to take in across the Severn Valley to the Cotswold Hills.

As well as B&B there is also the option to stay in one of three self catering homes. Each has been beautifully converted from the Victorian former servants' quarters which surround the cobbled courtyard at the rear of this unusual and historic Regency house. The holiday homes sleep from two to six persons and broadband internet access is available through the WiFi network of the main house. Self-catering guests return regularly to enjoy the peace and quiet and four star comforts of The Dell House Holiday Homes.

390 THE THREE KINGS

Church End, Hanley Castle,
Worcestershire WR8 0BL
Tel: 01684 592686

Local lady Sue Roberts – she was born here and the family will have been here 100 years in 2011 – welcomes visitors of all ages to the **Three Kings**, which has the timeless charm and traditional appeal of a much-loved country inn. The building dates back to the early 16th century, and some original beams can still be seen in one of three public rooms, the homely, cosy and down-to-earth Nell's Lounge Bar. It's a great place for connoisseurs of real ales, with varieties from the Hobson and Butcombe Breweries supplemented by three ever-changing guests (upwards of 400 different brews in a year!). For those with a taste for whisky the inn keeps an impressive selection of malts. Food is limited to a choice of hot and cold snacks, including popular toasties. The pub fields a quiz team and hosts live music sessions on Sunday nights. Opening hours are 12 to 3 and 7 to 11 seven days a week.

The Three Kings stands just off the B4211 Upton-Malvern road at Hanley Castle. The village takes its name from the castle, which was originally a hunting lodge for King John. Except for the moat, the castle is long gone, but the village still has number of attractions for the visitor, including picturesque cottages, a 16th century school and the brick-and-stone Church of St Mary. In addition there are lovely walks along the River Severn.

391 THE ROYAL OAK

Broadwas-on-Teme, nr Worcester WR6 5NE
Tel: 01836 821353 Fax: 01836 821954
website: www.oakatbroadwas.co.uk

Located in the village of Broadwas in the scenic Teme Valley, **The Royal Oak** is a 19th century red brick road house with a spacious converted barn. Good quality local food is one of the main attractions. At lunchtimes there's a choice of sandwiches, light lunches and main courses, while in the evening diners can select from the extensive menu and special boards. And on Sunday, the all day Carvery of roast beef, pork and turkey with seasonal vegetables is not to be missed! Food is served from noon until 2.30pm, and from 6pm to 9pm, Monday to Friday; from noon until 10pm on Saturday; and from noon until 9pm on Sunday.

The pub is suited for intimate diners, fun family meals and large parties. Other events such as funerals and other occasions can be catered for in the large medieval style barn. For those who just want to call in for a drink and chat, the choice is between the large cosy contemporary barn area or the smaller bar with a juke box, fruit machine and pool table. Both bars serve a good selection of real ales, lagers, wines and spirits. There's also a very large beer garden with a terrace and covered seating.

393 THE FOX & HOUNDS INN

Church Street, Bredon, nr Tewkesbury,
Gloucestershire GL20 7LA
Tel: 01684 772377
website: www.thefoxandhounds.biz

There are many reasons why visitors to the area should make tracks for the **Fox & Hounds Inn**. The first is the setting, in a pleasant village close to the Gloucestershire/Worcestershire border. The second is the inn itself, a wonderful 16th century thatched and timbered country hostelry with hanging baskets contributing to the picturesque exterior and hunting memorabilia enhancing the traditional scene in the bars and dining areas. The third reason is the warm welcome provided by hosts Chris and Cilla Lambe and their friendly staff. The fourth reason is the fine food and drink that brings both a loyal local clientele and visitors from further afield to this splendid place.

An excellent choice of drinks, including three real ales, is served in the cosy bar, and food is available in the lovely restaurant and dining areas every lunchtime and evening. Extensive menus offer a wide choice, from sandwiches and salads to scallops, sea bass and other fish specials, Mediterranean and Eastern dishes, steaks, seasonal game and always dishes for vegetarians. Traditional roasts are the centrepiece of the popular Sunday lunch, with fish and vegetarian alternatives. The many attractions of Bredon include the National Trust's medieval barn and the Norman church of St Giles, whose bells are celebrated in a poem by A E Housman.

392 EVESHAM COUNTRY PARK

Evesham, Worcestershire WR11 4TP
Tel: 01386 41661
website: www.eveshamcountrypark.co.uk

Enjoy a perfect day out at **Evesham Country Park** in a relaxed countryside setting where you'll discover a farm shop, extensive garden centre, wide range of courtyard shops, restaurant, miniature railway and animal sanctuary - all within a five minute drive from Evesham town centre. There is plenty of free parking and is open seven days a week*.

Millets Farm Shop makes entertaining easier. It provides a taste of the countryside with a quality range of fresh and local produce. Their priority is to grow or make their own products; or to source from local and British producers wherever possible. The fresh fruit and vegetable department is at the heart of the shop, which is complemented perfectly by the sumptuously stocked bakery, extensive delicatessen and butchery. A few extras are thrown in to guarantee that they can meet your every need, whether that is completing your weekly shop, helping you cater the perfect dinner party or finding that perfect gift.

Evesham Garden Centre has everything to transform your home and garden plus a superb selection of gifts. You are guaranteed to find something for everyone! Once you have finished browsing pop in to the Applebarn Restaurant where delicious meals and snacks are served all day.

In the courtyard shops you will find everything from needlecraft and clothes to nibbles and fudge, as well as active leisure clothes and equipment. The little ones definitely haven't got time to get bored, as there is a miniature steam railway, which travels for over a mile through the old apple orchards and around Evesham Country Park, stopping briefly at Evesham Vale Station. Where you could take a break from your journey to have a picnic, walk to the River Avon or just enjoy the views overlooking some of the most picturesque scenery the Vale of Evesham has to offer.

Millets
Farm Shop

All ages are catered for at the Ark Animal Sanctuary, where over 300 rescued and tame animals live including deer, foxes, meerkats, reptiles, otters and owls! As well as meeting the animals you can also paint your own pottery.

Located in over 130 acres of beautiful Worcestershire countryside, Evesham Country Park is at the northern end of the Evesham bypass (A46) at its junction with the Stratford Road. Once on the Evesham bypass simply follow the brown tourist signs.

*Please note that Evesham Vale Light Railway is open every weekend and during school holidays throughout the year.

Other useful website links: Millets Farm Shop: www.milletsfarmcentre.com
Evesham Garden Centre: www.eveshamgardencentre.co.uk
Evesham Vale Light Railway: www.evlr.co.uk
Animal Sanctuary: www.thearkanimalsanctuary.co.uk

394 HADLEY BOWLING GREEN INN

Hadley Heath, nr Droitwich, Worcestershire WR9 0AR
Tel: 01905 620294 Fax: 01905 620771
e-mail: Malcolm@hadleybowlinggreen.com
website: www.hadleybowlinggreen.com

The original **Hadley Bowling Green Inn** dates back to 1575, since when many generations have relished the hospitality, the fine food and the excellent wines and ales. Log fires, hop-hung beams and darkwood furniture paint a traditional picture in the bars, and in the summer months tables and chairs are set outside overlooking the bowling green. Bar and restaurant menus offer 'fine dining without the formality', with an excellent choice of classic British and European dishes using the best local produce.

The guest accommodation, some in cottages, numbers 9 well-equipped en suite rooms, from cosy doubles/twins to family rooms and two Executive suites with four-posters. The Bowling Green on site is one of the oldest in the British Isles, and is available for guests to use. Families are always welcome at the inn, which is also well geared up for functions, wedding parties and other celebrations.

395 THE FOUNTAIN INN

Oldwood Road, Tenbury Wells,
Worcestershire WR15 8TB
Tel: 01584 810701
e-mail: fountain.tenbury@ymail.com
website: www.fountaintenbury.co.uk

Mark Griffiths and his family are the affable hosts at the **Fountain Inn**, which sprang back to life in August 2009 after they restored this lovely 17th century black-and-white property to its former glory. The inn, which enjoys a delightful setting above the Teme Valley, is a great favourite with the locals, who come here to enjoy a glass of locally brewed ale over a chat or a game of darts or pool.

It also attracts a strong following, both local and from further afield, with Mark's excellent cooking. Seeking out the pick of the local produce, he prepares dishes that cater for appetites large and small with classic snacks, starters, main courses and sweets. Typical choices run from garlic mushrooms and prawns with a sweet chilli dipping sauce to fish & chips, pork & leek faggots, chicken curry and sirloin, rump and gammon steaks. Sandwiches are prepared to order on white or brown bread or baguettes, and other popular orders include basket meals, salads and omelettes. The centrepiece of Sunday lunch is a traditional roast with all the trimmings.

The Fountain is a perfect choice for parties (there's a lovely garden) and for guests staying in this pleasant part of the world there are ten comfortably appointed bedrooms with bath en suite (one with a Jacuzzi).

396 THE WHARFEDALE INN & RESTAURANT

Arthington Lane, Arthington, nr Otley, Leeds LS21 1NL
Tel: 0113 284 2921 Fax: 0113 284 1204

David and Maria Gregory extend a warm Yorkshire welcome at the **Wharfedale Inn**, which lies east of Otley in the heart of the lovely Lower Wharfedale Valley. The inn offers something for everyone – a place for locals to meet over a glass of real ale, an outstanding restaurant serving meals based on fresh local produce, heart home-cooked bar meals and comfortable guest accommodation. The accommodation comprises three individually styled en suite bedrooms with TV, DVD/CD player, mini-fridge and free Wi-Fi interconnect connection.

398 MOONRAKER FLOATING TEA ROOM

Huddersfield Narrow Canal, Slaithwaite, Huddersfield HD7 5HB
Tel: 01484 846370

This quaint, unusual tearoom is housed on a narrow boat on the Huddersfield canal where host Valerie Todd serves up a range of delicious home cooking throughout the day. The narrow boat was originally built in 1992 especially for Valerie, and was launched into the canal the summer of that year.

Valerie receives many repeat visitors throughout the year who enjoy not only the quirky atmosphere in which they can relax, but the tasty range of treats on offer. Guests can choose from a fine selection of salads, sandwiches, toasties and hot snacks, with a choice of homemade cakes and biscuits also available, all of which are created using as much fresh local produce as possible. Popular choices are crumpets and honey, the chilli con carne toastie, and the chocolate chip, walnut and orange cake. A large range of specialty teas and coffees are also available, which can be enjoyed within the boat, or on the adjacent canal towpath.

Valerie also caters for private parties or dinners for 10 or more in the evenings by arrangement. Please ring for details.

397 GOLCAR LILY

99-101 Slades Road, Bolster Road, Golcar,
Huddersfield HD7 4JR
Tel: 01484 659277
e-mail: info@golcarlily.co.uk
website: www.golcarlily.co.uk

Daryl and his team welcome you to the Golcar Lily
public house and restaurant, nestling high on the
Pennines above Huddersfield with commanding
views over the Colne Valley and beyond. Whether
you are visiting simply to enjoy a drink from the
well stocked bar, sample one of the many
homemade bar snacks, celebrate a special
occasions in the restaurant or party the night away
in the function room; the Golcar Lily has
something for everyone.

The Lily dates back to 1873 when it was first
built. It has had a wealth of different occupations
under various owners which have lodged it firmly
in the local community, who remain very proud of
their pub. Most notably the inn was the first
supermarket on Bolster Moor, springing up to
provide the areas inhabitants their weekly goods
necessitated by the booming Mill industry which
took over the area in the mid 19th century.

The warm, country pub feel of the bar extends
throughout to the restaurant which is open Monday
to Friday 12-2pm and 6-9:30pm, Saturday 12-
9:30pm and Sunday 12-8pm. The restaurant has a
fine reputation for serving quality food, all of
which is created using the best in local produce,
crafted by Darryl himself who is a professional
chef by trade. The restaurant welcomes families
and larger parties, but booking ahead is necessary
to avoid disappointment. Starters range from
chicken liver parfait, baked goats cheese and red
onion tartlet to hummus, black olive and leaf
salad. Main dishes, cooked fresh to order, include
duck breast with a blueberry port sauce, Guinness
braised beef topped with melted Gorgonzola and
crispy fried leeks, and seared salmon teriyaki and
spring onion sauce. A daily specials board is also available, changing to
reflect the best seasonal produce around.

Alongside the utterly delicious cuisine, Darryl serves up a fine
collection of wines and real ales including Tetley Bitter and two
rotating guest ales from both local and national breweries. Drinks can
be enjoyed throughout where the inn's large windows provide a glorious
gateway to the stunning views beyond.

The function room can be hired for evening events, parties and
larger dinners, but also has facilities for intimate conferences with TV/
DVD and flipchart available with a choice of a la carte or buffet dining. Please ring or see website
for details.

399 THE WHITE SWAN INN

Low Street, Thornton le Clay, York YO60 7TG
Tel: 01653 618286
e-mail: whiteswantlc@btconnect.com
website: www.tlcwhiteswan.co.uk

Situated in the picturesque village of Thornton-Le-Clay,
The White Swan Inn is an outstanding premise with
magnificent gardens to the rear. The inn is owned by
Susan and John Pilgrim and their daughter Lucy. The
family has been here for 28 years and provide a friendly
and warm welcome to locals and visitors.

Food is available between 11.45pm and 2pm every day
(except Mondays). On Sundays and Thursdays food is also
served between 6pm and 9pm and all other evenings
between 6.45pm and 9pm. Rich venison casserole served
with a selection of vegetables and potatoes; halibut
goujons in homemade batter with a choice of
accompaniments and homemade cottage pie are just
some of the dishes that feature on the extensive menu.
All of the dishes are created using fresh local ingredients
and such is the popularity of the food served it is
advisable to book on weekends. Vegetarians and children are catered for and Susan, who takes
charge of the kitchen, cooks superb food.

The well stocked bar has plenty of beers, lagers and fine wines as well as rotating real ales,
which are brewed locally. Major credit cards taken. Disabled access is not a problem.

400 THE NEW GLOBE INN

Yorkersgate, Malton, Yorkshire YO17 7AA
Tel: 01653 692395

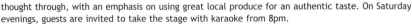

Rob and Shelley have been warmly welcoming guests to
The New Globe Inn for the past four years, earning them
an excellent reputation for their fine hospitality. You'll
find the inn at the heart of the popular Yorkshire town of
Malton, adjacent to the river Derwent. Although Malton's
history dictates that it was originally a Roman settlement
for battle, it now enjoys a vibrant café/restaurant
culture, bursting with plenty of quirky shops and boutiques.
Rob and Shelley are proud to be a part of that culture,
offering their guests a traditional Yorkshire experience in
their charming inn.

Open all day every day, they serve a variety of real ales
including Camerons Strongarm and two rotating guest ales from
local and national brewers. From Tuesday to Friday 12-7pm and
on Saturdays from 12-3pm the pair also serve up a delicious
selection of homemade food. The menu is small but carefully
thought through, with an emphasis on using great local produce for an authentic taste. On Saturday
evenings, guests are invited to take the stage with karaoke from 8pm.

Three guest bedrooms are also available throughout the year for those wanting to explore
Malton a little longer, all of which have full en suite facilities. All major credit cards accepted
apart from American Express and Diners.

401 HYDE PARK

29 Mill Street, Norton, Malton,
Yorkshire YO17 9JH
Tel: 01653 690274
e-mail: susan@rice6.orangehome.co.uk
website: www.hydepark.co.uk

A short five minute walk away from the centre of bustling
Malton will find you in the equally popular village of Norton.
This idyllic village is visually typical of rural Yorkshire, but
embodies a thriving community spirit, bringing culture to the dales. At the heart of Norton is the
Hyde Park; a family run inn that prides itself on offering its local and guests from further afield
an exceptionally warm welcome all day every day.

The family could be described as more of a clan, with Sue and Steve at the helm with their
children and family friends all helping out. The friendly environment and family banter keeps the
atmosphere light and fresh, ensuring a visit here is one full of laughs.

Guests can enjoy a regular rotation of guest ales at the inn, along with two other real ales;
Tetley's and John Smiths as the regulars. The family take great care over their ales and have been
awarded the prestigious 'cask marque' accreditation for the quality of their brews. Guests can
also enjoy a good selection of fine wines, spirits and lagers.

Throughout the day guests can choose from a choice of bar snacks from salads, sandwiches and
jacket potatoes to traditional dishes and all the good old pub favourites. All dishes are cooked
fresh to order by the family each day, who strive to use as much locally sourced produce as
possible. Families are of course most welcome, with good options for children.

Each Friday evening the locals gather to enjoy entertainment at the inn to enjoy the best in
live music, often coming from local bands. Make sure to arrive around 8:30pm when the music
starts as these nights are always well attended. On Sundays all are welcome to join in the weekly
quiz, and on bank holidays special children's parties are held. Guests can also hire out the
premises for a range of other functions like birthday or anniversary parties, wakes and business
events for which catering is available by arrangement, please call for details.

402 THE GRAPES INN

Railway Street, Slingsby, York YO62 4AL
Tel: 01653 628229
e-mail: andy@grapesinn.co.uk
website: www.grapesinn.co.uk

The picturesque village of Slingsby is found at the heart of the rugged North Yorkshire Moors, just a short drive from this historic Castle Howard. Slingsby is home to **The Grapes Inn** and its owners Andy and Cheri. The pair have only been running the inn since January 2010 but have already won the hearts of the locals with their vibrant yet laid-back characters and dedication to the village.

Apart from Monday and Tuesday lunchtimes, the inn is open every session and all day on weekends. Guests have a choice of rotating real ales with the regulars being Black Sheep and Camerons Strongarm. Food is served daily from Wed-Sat 12-2pm, Mon-Sat 6-9pm and Sundays 12-9pm. Andy offers up a delicious menu bursting with local produce and Yorkshire favourites. Popular dishes include roasts, Whitby scampi and chips, homemade pie of the day, filled Yorkshire pudding and a tender rump steak. Guests can also choose from a range of light bites, salads and desserts. Children and vegetarians are well catered for and can enjoy the family orientated feel. Guests can enjoy occasional live music at the Grapes, please call for details.

The other main attraction at the Grapes is Cheri's art. She specialises in drawing and painting animals, many of which can be seen displayed in the inn's own dining room. All major credit cards accepted.

404 THE SHIP INN

Scarborough Road, Langtoft,
East Yorkshire YO25 3TH
Tel: 01377 267243 / 07795412466
website: www.theshipinnlangtoft.co.uk

This famous historic inn dates back to the 17th century and is located at the heart of the Yorkshire Wolds. Richard and Judy have owned The Ship Inn for the past seven years and they offer a fine selection of home cooked food served from local produce and a selection of quality ales.

Judy takes charge of the kitchen and her delicious dishes include; Chef's Homemade Steak & Ale Pie, Whitby Scampi and Beer Battered Fish & Chips. The desserts are very tempting with choices including 'Ship Inn Sundaes' and Hanky Panky Chocolate Pie. Food is served Monday – Thursday between 12pm and 2pm and between 6pm and 8.30pm. On Friday and Saturdays food is served between 12pm and 8.30pm and on Sunday between 12pm and 6pm. Such is its popularity it is advisable for larger parties to book.

On brighter days there is a beer garden for customers to make the most of and on colder evenings a log fire provides a relaxing and cosy atmosphere. Four child friendly en-suite guest rooms are available and each have a colour television, hairdryer and tea and coffee making facilities. Ring for details.

403 THE THREE TUNS INN

West Lutton, Malton, North Yorkshire YO17 8TA
Tel: 01944 738200

The idyllic Yorkshire village of West Lutton is home to scenic views across rolling hills of the Great Wolds Valley and the popular **The Three Tuns Inn**. The village captures rural Yorkshire life at its best, homely and tranquil, paying tribute to its inhabitants' traditional values. In the surrounding area visitors can enjoy a range of pleasant walks through the countryside, or visit some of the traditional parish churches that still stand. The Three Tuns is also a popular haunt with visitors, who come to experience a taste of local life.

The inn was taken over two years ago by Jacqui Vickers, a hardworking and vibrant woman who has delighted in giving the inn the new lease of life it had been calling for. Locals say that she has given them back the heart of their community, offering unbeatable hospitality in a down to earth and friendly way. She has worked tirelessly to improve the inns facilities whilst preserving its heritage, creating a traditional and comfortable haven. Opening hours are Monday to Thursday 7-11pm, Fridays 7pm-12am, Saturdays 12-3pm and 7pm-12am, and Sundays 12-3pm and 7-11pm.

Guests can choose from a wide variety of beverages, with real ales, lagers, wines and spirits readily available. The favourite ale here is Tetleys, although a guest ale rotates throughout the summer. Guests are also welcomed to dine at the Three Tuns. Why not stop at the Three Tuns for a bite to eat whilst challenging yourself on one of the popular footpaths within the area? Usually a favourite with ramblers and cyclists, guests can take also take their snacks on one of the outdoor tables, sporting glorious views of the village.

On Sunday evenings, Jacqui hosts a quiz from 9pm onwards, welcoming families, children, guests and locals together. Other events held at the inn can be seen on the village's website www.luttonsandweaverthorpe.ryedaleconnect.org.uk and include YCA meetings, charity events and much, much more. Cash only please.

405 NORTHCOTE HOTEL

8-10 Trinity Road, Bridlington, East Yorkshire YO15 2EY
Tel: 01262 675764 Guests: 01262 678888
e-mail: northcote.hotel@yahoo.co.uk
website: www.northcote-hotel.co.uk

Located in the heart of Bridlington, just a short walk from the sea front, the **Northcote Hotel** was founded and has been owned and run by the same family for the past 35 years. There is a comfortable, relaxing guests' lounge with a pool table and a bar which is open to residents and non-residents from 11am, and is stocked with a wide range of lagers, beers, spirits and fine wines. John Smith's Smooth is a popular tipple here. Children are welcome in the lounge until 6pm, and all major credit cards are accepted.

The accommodation at The Northcote comprises 6 attractively furnished and decorated suites, each with its own sitting room and some with 4-poster beds. All rooms are equipped with en suite facilities, colour television, hospitality tray and central heating. The tariff includes a truly hearty breakfast, generous enough to sustain you throughout the day.

The hotel's location provides an excellent base for exploring the fine Yorkshire countryside that surrounds Bridlington and contains attractions such as Sewerby Hall, Burton Agnes Hall, Flamborough Head and Sledmere House.

406 THE SHIP INN

Cliff Road, Sewerby, Bridlington,
East Yorkshire YO15 1EW
Tel: 01262 672374
e-mail: shipinnsewerby@aol.com
website: www.shipinnsewerby.co.uk

The Ship Inn is a terrific find located in the tiny village of Sewerby, 500 yards from the coastline. The inn is just a short drive from the popular town of Bridlington and has been run by Charlie and Louise Kilburn and Graham Murphy since October 2006. Charlie has more than 20 years experience in catering and the inn offers the very best in hospitality, cuisine and ales. Open all day every day two real ales are served with the regular being Banks Bitter.

Charlie describes his dishes as 'English Fayre with a twist'. They are all reasonably priced and starters include haggis, neeps and tatty cakes; potted crab; and cherry tomato, basil and garlic foccacia. Braised belly pork with a cider and apple gravy; chicken 'reggae reggae' melt; and braised steak with colcannon mash are among the most popular dishes on the extensive menu. There is a good range of dishes on the menu, with plenty of vegetarian options, fish dishes and healthy options. The inn is child friendly and there is a specially adapted menu for younger diners. The desserts menu is extremely tempting with a fine selection of mouth watering dishes perfect for finishing off a meal out. Apple and blackberry flapjack crumble; Italian tiramisu gateau; and four layer chocolate fudge cake are among the dishes listed. For those with a lighter appetite there is a good range of filled sandwiches, salads and lite bites to choose from. In the winter food is served between 12pm and 2pm and 5.30pm and 8.30pm Monday – Saturday and between 12pm and 3pm on Sundays. During summer months food is served between 12pm and 3pm and 5.30pm and 8.30pm Monday – Saturday and 12pm and 7pm on Sundays.

The Ship Inn is very popular with locals and visitors and such is its popularity it is advisable to book at all times. Although there is no accommodation available here camper vans are allowed to stay within the grounds. Ring for details. Two beer festivals are held at The Ship Inn with music held over the May day weekend and another held over the August bank holiday. Ring for details. The picturesque village boasts some fantastic views

from the cliff tops overlooking the bay between the seaside tow of Bridlington and the fishing village of Flamborough and in the summer the beer garden at The Ship Inn is very popular with customers.

407 THE NORTH STAR HOTEL

North Marine Road, Flamborough, East Yorkshire YO15 IBL
Tel: 01262 850379
e-mail: info@thenorthstarhotel.co.uk
website: www.thenorthstarhotel.co.uk

Located on the beautiful and dramatic cliffs of East Yorkshire, **The North Star Hotel** has an award winning restaurant famous for fresh Flamborough seafood and wild game caught on the Yorkshire Wolds. Local produce is prepared and presented by classically trained Chef Michael Johnston, his wife Karen, and their team of loyal staff, to bring French cuisine and traditional Yorkshire fare to this exceptional, historical location. Be assured of the warm welcome and personal attention that only a small family owned hotel can offer. The Johnston family has owned the hotel for almost 20 years and during their time here has carried out extensive refurbishments. The hotel's traditional decor and comfort are just two of its many attractions adding to its warm ambience. It has traded as a traditional hostelry since 1840 and the restaurant and olde worlde bar has area has plenty of charm.

The elegant restaurant, with its crisp linen cloths and intimate atmosphere is stylish and comfortable and the perfect setting for all occasions. It can seat around 50 people and there is space for a further 90 in the lounge areas. There is a wide range of game, fish, steaks and vegetarian options on the menu, with seafood the speciality. Favourites include grilled yellow catfish with lemon & anchovy butte, poached fresh Scotch salmon fillet coasted in a prawn & brandy sauce, and venison steak with a full red wine, mushroom & onion sauce. The majority of produce used here is sourced locally. Food is served between 11.30am-2pm and from 6.15pm and 9pm. (No food is served Monday lunch times).

The hotel offers seven en-suite comfortable bedrooms. It is an ideal place to stay for visitors to the area wanting to explore the Yorkshire Wolds and The North Star Hotel is a regular destination for parties who visit Flamborough to explore the cliffs, caves and coves of this unique coastline. Most of the guest bedrooms, including the master with its four-poster bed, enjoy sea views and all have the essential ingredients for a relaxing, peaceful break. Hotel residents have complimentary tea & coffee in their rooms and unlimited use of the residents' lounge. The tariff includes a full Flamborough farmhouse home-cooked breakfast.

The child-friendly hotel caters for a full range of functions with capacity for weddings, birthday parties, anniversaries, christenings, visiting coach parties, dinner dances, funerals and afternoon tea parties.

408 THE GAIT INN

Millington, York, East Yorkshire YO42 1TX
Tel: 01759 302045
website: www.gaitinn.co.uk

Occupying a picturesque location on the edge of the Yorkshire Wolds, **The Gait Inn** is as authentic a village hostelry as you could hope to find. Outside, picnic tables set on a grassy bank overlook the quiet main street; to the rear is a superb beer garden which really is a garden with well-tended flower beds and a pond.

Inside, the décor of the 16th century building is traditional, full of character and charm with horse brasses and other decorations adorning the old beams. Owners Stuart and Helen Stephenson, both former farmers, took over here in summer of 2005. Since then they've established a glowing reputation for providing excellent, food, drink and hospitality.

Helen is in charge of the kitchen and bases all her dishes on locally sourced produce: the meat, for example, comes from the local butcher who only buys from nearby farms. The extensive menu, which has recently been revised, offers a wide choice of wholesome and appetising food. Amongst the starters are some wonderful crispy and soft Yorkshire Puddings with onion gravy, or you could settle for the soup of the day or breaded garlic mushrooms. For the main course, choose between a selection of steaks, a honey roast half duckling, or home-made offerings such as the steak pie or lasagne. There are also fish dishes, vegetarian options such as broccoli and cream cheese bake or veggie burger. For lighter appetites, there are salads, omelettes, salads, ploughman's, jacket potatoes and a selection of sandwiches. Children have their own choice of dishes. The inn is closed on Mondays, except for Bank Holidays, on other days food is served from noon until 2pm, Friday to Sunday; and from 6.30pm to 9pm, Tuesday to Sunday. On Sundays, a Roast of the Day is added to the menu. Booking is strongly recommended for Friday and Saturday evenings, and for Sunday lunch.

To accompany your meal, the well-stocked bar offers a comprehensive range of beverages, including 5 real ales - John Smiths, Tetleys, Theakston's Best, Black Sheep and a rotating brew.

The inn accepts all major credit cards; there's off-road parking; and good disabled access throughout.

409 THE OLD STAR INN

Church Street, Kilham, nr Driffield, East Yorkshire YO25 4RG
Tel: 01262 420619
e-mail: oldstarkilham@hotmail.com

The Old Star Inn is a super country inn and restaurant located in the quiet, picturesque village of Kilham, which lies northeast of Driffield off the A614 or B1249. Rightly describing itself as 'the Wold famous' Old Star, this outstanding inn has excellent, friendly and highly professional leaseholders in Lauren and Helen, who brought many years' experience in the catering trade when they took over the reins at the beginning of 2007. In the short time since then they have delighted the local community and made many new friends with their own special brand of hospitality, allied to the very highest standards of food, drink and service. Behind the whitewashed exterior, with tiled roof and shuttered windows, the public areas are immaculate, with beams, open fires, half-panelling and paintings by a local artist.

There are always four real ales available and the choice increases to more than a dozen during the beer festival held over a weekend in Autumn – ring for exact times and details. The bar is open from 6pm to 11.30pm on Monday, 5pm to 11.30pm on Tuesday, 12pm to 2.30pm and 5pm to 11.30pm Wednesday to Saturday and 12pm to 10.30pm on Sunday.

The hosts believe in 'proper' home cooked food, never sacrificing quality for profit. They pride themselves on using only the best seasonal ingredients from local suppliers, and everything is freshly prepared and cooked to order. Lauren produces a mouth watering selection of dishes that really do provide something for everyone. Starters range from mini croissants stuffed with creamy garlic mushrooms to fish goujons and chicken liver, garlic and tomato pate with balsamic onion relish. From the list of main courses come rack of burdass lamb with parsnip mash and minted jus, haddock on a bed of parsley with wholegrain mustard sauce, the Sunday roasts and vegetarian options decided on the day. The menu changes regularly so there's always something different to try and the early bird menu (available at lunch times and tea times) changes quarterly. Even the sandwiches are several cuts above the average: roast beef dipped in gravy, tuna with lemon and black pepper mayonnaise. Desserts like bread and butter pudding, crème brulee, apple crumble or chocolate brownie make the perfect finale to a memorable meal. Such is its popularity it is advisable to book at weekends. Ring for accommodation details.

Conference facilities are available. Ring for details.

410 THE TROUT INN

Wansford, nr Driffield, East Yorkshire YO25 8NX
Tel: 01377 254204

Keith and Marie Robinson are the long established tenants at **The Trout Inn**. The former farmhouse is very comfortable and has roomy public areas ideal for enjoying a relaxing evening or lunch time meal. The inn is full of character and atmosphere and it has many attractive Victorian features.

The bar stocks a good selection of keg beers, with the most popular being John Smiths Smooth ale. The bar and restaurant menus offer an excellent choice of good wholesome home cooking, from classics like their tasty game soup, lasagne, steak and kidney pie, scampi, goujons of plaice to evening specialities such as steaks, roast duckling and fresh fish. All of the dishes are freshly prepared and cooked to order. Food is served Tuesday to Sunday lunchtime between 12pm and 1.30pm and Wednesday to Saturday evenings between 7pm and 8.30pm.

Children are more than welcome at The Trout Inn, which has extremely loyal clients. The Trout Inn is closed on Mondays. Wansford lies on the B1249 three miles south east of Driffield. Major credit cards are taken.

411 THE POPPY SEED

13 North Bar Within, Beverley,
East Yorkshire HU17 8AP
Tel: 01482 871598

Located just down the road from Beverley's medieval gateway, **The Poppy Seed** is an outstanding delicatessen and coffee shop serving quality home-cooked food prepared to the highest standards. It is owned and run by the mother and daughter team of Rita Jones and Kate Johnson who came here in 2001 after some years cooking for weddings at a stately home.

In their ground floor delicatessen you'll find an extensive choice of quiches, patisseries, traditional puddings and picnic 'kits'. The deli items are also served in the two restaurant areas, along with a variety of other dishes. These include a choice of breakfasts, served daily until 11am, an extensive selection of sandwiches and paninis with fillings ranging from rare roast beef to goat's cheese & beetroot; salads and daily specials such as aromatic lamb meatballs. The huge choice of

drinks includes a dozen different teas, coffees and iced coffees; pure fruit juices, home-made lemonade, and fresh fruit smoothies and milk shakes.

The Poppy Seed is open from 9am to 5pm, Monday to Saturday, plus Sundays during the season, and is licensed. Rita and Kate are also happy to provide outside catering. "We can cater for any size - from whole quiches to whole parties!"

412 THE WOOLPACK INN

37 Westwood Road, Beverley, East Yorkshire HU17 8EN
Tel: 01482 867095
e-mail: woolpack@woolpack.karoo.co.uk
website: www.woolpackbeverley.co.uk

Located just a short walk from Beverley's elegant town centre, **The Woolpack Inn** is a fine old traditional public house with a truly welcoming atmosphere. It was originally built in 1826 as two cottages but became a public house just a few years later. Today, it retains its early 19th century charm and character, complete with an open log fire, settle window seats and gleaming copper ornaments. Mine hosts are Kim and Tony who arrived here in the winter of 2009 and already have a thriving success on their hands. They employ a professional chef whose menu offers an appetising choice of old favourites and some newer creations. Amongst the starters you'll find a home-made soup of the day, a goat's cheese fritter, and a dish called Pancake Finistere - mixed shellfish in a white wine sauce, served wrapped in a pancake and topped with gratinated cheese and garnish.

Topping the list of main courses is The Woolpack Pie - succulent pieces of beef steak, slow braised in Hobgoblin Ale, then encased in short crust pastry. Also on offer are a variety of steaks, traditional dishes such as gammon and eggs, or fish and chips, along with a home-made curry and a vegetarian mushroom and red pepper Stroganoff. The regular menu is supplemented by daily specials. Children are very welcome at The Woolpack and they have their own 'Little Lambs' menu. Food is served from noon until 2pm, Tuesday to Saturday; and from 5pm to 8.30pm, Monday to Saturday. On Sundays, food is available from 10am (for breakfast) right through until 5pm. Booking ahead is strongly recommended from Thursday through Sunday.

The well-stocked bar has a comprehensive range of beverages, including at least six different real ales with Snecklifter, Lakeland, Cock-a-Hoop and Hobgoblin as the regulars. In good weather drinkers can enjoy their refreshments either in the smoking area at the rear, or at benches to the front.

Monday evening is a particularly good time to visit if you enjoy live music. It's a free and easy event at which all are welcome to join in with their own instruments.

The inn has good disabled access throughout; dogs are welcome in the Snug, and all major credit cards apart from American Express are accepted.

413 THE CHEQUERS INN

Bilton-in-Ainsty, nr Wetherby,
North Yorkshire YO26 7NN
Tel: 01423 359637
e-mail: info@thechequersbilton.co.uk
website: www.thechequersbilton.co.uk

The **Chequers** is a 19th century coaching inn of real character in a pretty village, the picturesque setting enhanced by lovely gardens. The inn is run in fine style by the mother-and-son team of Heather and Alex Main, who arrived here in early 2006 and oversaw a top-to-toe refurbishment of the premises before opening the doors once more to the public in May of that year. They brightened up the place with flowers and plants and added a heated sheltered terrace to the beautifully kept gardens.

This much-loved local is at the very heart of the community, with villagers coming to enjoy a chat and a drink. There's always a good selection of Cask Marque approved beers, typically including some or all of Black Sheep, Young's Bitter and Special, Marston's Pedigree, Wychwood Hobgoblin, Bateman's XXXB, Charles Wells Bombardier and JW Lees John Willies. But the Chequers is much more than a friendly, traditional local, it's also an increasingly popular destination restaurant and a comfortable base for Bed & Breakfast guests. Alex is a very talented, professionally trained chef whose aim here is to provide traditional food with a few twists, sourcing the very best local produce, freshly cooked and served. His menus combine classics with interesting contemporary dishes and snacks, from quick bites to a leisurely meal, business lunches, dinner for two and family get-togethers. Club sandwiches, ploughman's platters and croquet monsieur provide tasty, satisfying quick meals and a lunchtime value menu tempts with classics such as liver & onions, fish pie and the day's roast. From the main menu come terrine of Yorkshire game, smoked haddock & parsley fishcakes, spinach-stuffed chicken breast, braised lamb shank and 28-day aged Givendale sirloin and rump steaks. Daily specials add further to the excellent choice, and the fine food is complemented by well-chosen wines.

The Chequers is well placed for enjoying the delights of the region and the three guest bedrooms are particularly well equipped, with fully tiled shower rooms, adjustable heating, TV with DVD player, radio alarm clock and free Wi-Fi internet access. The interest in food extends to breakfast, which offers classic English options and lighter dishes and Continental meat and cheese platters.

To find the inn leave the A1(M) north of Wetherby at J48 on to the B1224 towards York. Turn right after about 5 miles on to a minor road signposted to the village and the inn.

414 THE CROWN INN

Main Street, Great Ouseburn,
York, Yorkshire YO26 9RF
Tel: 01423 330430/01423 330013
e-mail: paul@thecrown-inn.com
website: www.thecrown-inn.com

The impressive **Crown Inn** lies within the heart of the picturesque village of Great Ouseburn near York. Dating back in parts to the 18th century, it retains its heritage proudly giving it a real sense of character.

For many years the Crown had been one of the most popular inns in the area to visit, however due to a variety of circumstances numbers dwindled and sadly experienced a number of closures. The Crown's saving grace was the arrival of its current owners Paul and Liz Jackson in December 2009 who vowed to take the Crown by the horns and restore it to its former glory. Paul and Liz have over 25 years combined experience in the catering trade. They met in the trade 11 years ago, finally marrying 5 years ago and recently fulfilling their dream of running their own pub.

The couple are now dedicated to not only serving the many guests and tourists they see walk through their doors, but to serving their local community. They regularly open the Crown's doors to community events including wine tasting, cooking demonstrations, quizzes and charity evenings as well as offering quality food and drink day in day out.

They offer three excellent quality real ales; Tasty Black Sheep and Timothy Taylors along with a guest ale from local brewers. A good selection of fine wines and spirits are also available. The inn is really a destination now for its cuisine. Served Mondays 5-9:30pm, Wed-Sat from 12-2:30pm and 5-9:30pm, and on Sundays and bank holidays from 12-8.30pm, all of the food is cooked fresh to order by Paul who endeavours to ensure that 99% of the ingredients are locally sourced. The menu changes monthly to reflect the best seasonal produce, but typically include a range of starters, a la carte mains, grills and traditional dishes, not to mention a range of mouth-watering desserts. Popular dishes include wild venison, lamb rump, seafood quartet, pan seared duck breast and wild mushroom and asparagus risotto. Owing to popularity, booking is essential on weekends.

Although there is currently no guest accommodation at the Crown, it is hoped to be completed within the lifetime of this edition so please call for details.

415 THE BLACK BULL INN

6 St James Square, Boroughbridge, North Yorkshire YO51 9AR
Tel: 01423 322413 Fax: 01423 323915

Yorkshire abounds in ancient hostelries but **The Black Bull Inn** in the heart of Boroughbridge is one of the most venerable with a history going back to 1262. For many years it provided hospitality for travellers on the stage coaches running between Thirsk and Harrogate. Lots of traditional features remain inside, complemented by up-to-the-minute décor and furnishings.

The inn is notable for the quality of the food it serves. There's an extensive bar snacks menu with a choice of dishes ranging through char grilled dishes to traditional favourites such as haddock & chips, curry and a home-made pie of the day. The regular choice is supplemented by seasonal specials and fresh seafood dishes. If you choose from the à la carte menu, you'll find a tasty dish of king prawn tails and queen scallops amongst the starters; for the main course there are steaks, char-grilled dishes, a selection of 'Sizzlers', and dishes such as tenderloin of pork with a pink peppercorn and Calvados sauce. Round off your meal with one of the wonderful desserts, - Lemon Heaven, perhaps, or baked jam sponge, dark chocolate truffle torte, or a banoffee meringue roulade. If you prefer a savoury,, a selection of English and continental cheeses is available. Food is served every day from noon until 2pm (2.30pm on Sunday); and from 6pm to 9pm. Booking a table at weekends is strongly recommended. The inn itself is open from 11am to 11pm daily. To accompany your meal, the bar offers an extensive choice of beverages, including 3 real ales - John Smiths, Timothy Taylor Bitter and a rotating ale.

The Black Bull also offers comfortable accommodation in 6 well-appointed bedrooms, (4 doubles and 2 singles), all with en suite facilities. The very reasonable tariff includes a hearty English breakfast.

Children and dogs are welcome at the Black Bull; all major credit cards are accepted, and the inn has good disabled access to the bar and restaurant, but the bedrooms are upstairs.

Within easy reach of the inn are some of Yorkshire's major visitor attractions. The World Heritage Site of Fountains Abbey; the magnificent Studley Royal Gardens; Ripon with its great cathedral; and the spa town of Harrogate are all just a short drive away.

416 THE BLACK HORSE

Newton Road, Tollerton, York YO61 1QT
Tel: 01347 838280
e-mail: info@blackhorse-tollerton.co.uk
website: www.blackhorse-tollerton.co.uk

The only pub in the village of Tollerton, **The Black Horse** is one of the few remaining pubs with a traditional 'Tap Room' as well as a Lounge Bar, Pool Room and an intimate Dining Room. The pub dates back to the mid-18th century when it was a coaching inn on the main toll road from York to the north.

Judi and Dave Duff took over as leaseholders here in April 2006 as their first venture into this type of business. Since then, their reputation for hospitality, quality food and well-kept ales has steadily grown and the inn is now very popular. A professional chef is employed and brings with him his well-known menu and cooking style which offers a range of 'Platter' dishes. On Sundays, Judi takes over for her popular Traditional Carvery. It's an advantage for parties of more than 6 to book ahead. Food is served from noon until 2pm, Tuesday to Monday; and from 5.30pm to 8.30pm, Wednesday to Monday. To accompany your meal, there's a choice of 3 real ales - John Smith's Cask, Timothy Taylor Landlord and Hambleton Bitter. Other amenities at the inn include a children's playground, a rear patio and a courtyard beer garden.

417 THE GOLDEN LION

Main Street, Helperby, York, Yorkshire YO61 2NT
Tel/Fax: 01423 360870

Tucked away in scenic countryside northeast of Boroughbridge, the picturesque village of Helperby is fortunate in having a quality traditional pub complete with inglenook fireplace, lots of horse brasses and gleaming copper. Mine hosts at **The Golden Lion,** Paul and Denise, took over here early in 2006 and have built up a loyal local following with visitors also being drawn in to enjoy good company, well-kept ales and appetising food based on fresh local produce as far as possible. The regular menu is supplemented by daily specials. Food is served from noon until 9pm, Monday to Saturday. On Sundays, roasts replace the usual menu and are served from noon until they run out. Three real ales are on tap to complement your meal which, in good weather, can also be enjoyed at picnic tables at the front of the inn.

The Golden Lion is a lively place with something going on most nights, whether it's pool, ladies and men's darts, a quiz, open mic evenings or live bands. Children are welcome; there is good disabled access throughout, and the inn accepts all major credit cards aparts from American Express and Diners.

418 THE ASHFIELD COUNTRY MANOR HOTEL

Kirby Misperton, nr Malton, North Yorkshire YO17 6UU
Tel: 01653 668221

The Ashfield Country Manor Hotel has recently been
taken over by Chris and Linda Brooker who run the hotel
with their daughter Rosi and her partner Mark – who is the
head chef. The hotel, which can be found a short drive
from Pickering and Malton off he A169, recently reopened
after a full refurbishment of the restaurant. Located in the
picturesque village of Kirby Misperton the hotel has five
comfortable en-suite rooms available all year round. There
is one twin room, two doubles and two family rooms
available and the tariff includes a hearty breakfast.

Mark Davis is the head chef and he produces quality
dishes. There is a regular change of menu which includes
ever popular dishes such as slow roast shoulder of lamb;
wild bass fillet; grilled whole plaice and pan fried lamb's
liver. There is a bar menu and for those with a lighter
appetite there are a good choice of filled sandwiches like
honey roast ham and mustard mayonnaise, and mature
cheddar and chutney. It is an advantage to book at
weekends.

The hotel is in a beautiful area and is ideally situated
for guests who want to visit local attractions, including Flamingo Land.

419 BLACK BULL INN

Malton Road, Pickering, Yorkshire YO18 8EA
Tel: 01751 471590
e-mail: theblackbullpickering@googlemail.com

The Black Bull in is found just a mile south of Pickering on
the road to Malton. It dates back in parts to the late 17th
century and has a traditional styling with handsome wood
panelled bar and a huge stone hearth that sports an
inviting fire most days.

Tina and her nephew Andrew took over the Bull in
November 2009 and have dedicated themselves to giving
their customers first class hospitality in a relaxed,
traditional country inn environment. Open every session
and all day weekends and during the summer, the inn is
known for its selection of quality cuisine. Food is served
daily from 12-2:30pm and 6-9pm in the winter and 5-9pm
in the summer, serving until 9:30pm on weekends. Andrew
offers classy yet wholesome menus with a selection of fine
home cooked treats. Dishes include homemade salmon and

smoked haddock fishcakes, chicken liver pate with homemade tomato chutney, speciality steak
and mushroom pie, rump steak, and local sausages with wholegrain mustard mash. Children's
meals, vegetarians and light bites are also readily available.

Guests also have the option to stay at the Bull, with a choice of five ground floor en suite guest
bedrooms, all of which are decorated in a contemporary style and have their own entrances.

421 THE MIDDLE EARTH TAVERN

25/26 Church Street, Whitby, North Yorkshire YO22 4AE
Tel: 01947 606014
e-mail: jill.blackburn@hotmail.com

Occupying a superb position overlooking Whitby's harbour, **The Middle Earth Tavern** is one of the town's finest hostelries. A Free House, the inn is owned and personally run by Jill Blackburn with the help of a dedicated team that includes Kelly who has worked here for many years. The pub is open every day of the year and during the summer months offers a choice of two real ales, both kept in tip-top condition. During the winter months, there's a fine selection of keg beers, lagers, stouts and so on. Throughout opening hours, a variety of sandwiches and soups are available. The inn is well-known for its entertainment. On Friday evenings there's either karaoke or a DJ from 8.30pm, and on Saturday evenings, also from 8.30pm, live entertainment is laid on.

The inn also offers quality accommodation in 5 upstairs rooms, all of which have en suite facilities. One of the rooms is family sized and can accommodate up to 6 people. The reasonable tariff includes a hearty English breakfast.

Children and dogs are welcome here; and there's good wheelchair access to the ground floor. Please note that payment at The Middle Earth is by either cash or cheque.

420 THE GROVE

36 Bagdale, Whitby, North Yorkshire YO21 1QL
Tel: 01947 603551 e-mail: angela@thegrovewhitby.co.uk
website: www.thegrovewhitby.co.uk

Just a 2-minute walk from the harbour, The Grove is a handsome Edwardian building which has been providing accommodation for more than 50 years. A quality establishment with a 4-star grading, it is one of the most stylish places in Whitby to stay. It has 7 guest bedrooms, all spacious, with quality décor and furnishings, and all with en suite facilities. A hearty breakfast is included in the tariff and, very important in Whitby, there is a secure parking space for each room. Children are welcome and all major credit cards are accepted.

422 TIFFIN CAFÉ

56 Baxtergate, Whitby,
North Yorkshire YO21 1BL
Tel: 01947 604275

Located in the heart of historic Whitby, the **Tiffin Café** is a family-owned business run by the mother and daughter team of Kay and Rebecca. This very popular establishment owes its glowing reputation to the quality of the food on offer. Rebecca is the cook and her menu is based on fresh, locally sourced ingredients, including locally reared meat, locally caught fish and locally grown vegetables wherever possible.

The day starts with a selection of breakfasts with the Tiffin Breakfast catering for those with hearty appetites. Throughout the day, there's an extensive choice of main meals with fresh Whitby cod, haddock or scampi taking pride of place. Amongst other home-made dishes are steak pie, quiche, pasta carbonara, chilli con carne and, for vegetarians, a tasty roasted vegetable lasagne. There's also a range of light meals and snacks, and children have their own menu. For those with a sweet tooth, the choice includes a variety of cakes and puddings.

The café is open from 9am to 5pm, Monday to Saturday; and from 10am to 4pm on Sunday. There's good wheelchair access. Please note that payment is by cash only.

423 JAVA

20 Flowergate, Whitby, North Yorkshire YO21 3BA
Tel: 01947 821975

Located just a 2-minute walk from Whitby's picturesque harbour, **Java** is a welcoming café offering an appetising selection of wholesome food based on locally sourced ingredients. Personally owned and run by Ben Laws since 2003, this popular eating-place has seating for up to 50 people on two floors. In addition to its tasty food, the café offers Internet access and free Wi-Fi. Open all year round from 8am to 6pm, Java welcomes children and accepts cash or cheques only.

424 ESTBEK HOUSE

East Row, Sandsend, Whitby, North Yorkshire YO21 3SU
Tel: 01947 893424 Fax: 01947 893625
e-mail: info@estbekhouse.co.uk
website: www.estbekhouse.co.uk or www.cellarcollection.co.uk

The magnificent **Estbek House** is found nestled within the picturesque coastal village of Sandsend. Some describe the village itself as hidden away from the hustle and bustle of normal life, in a place where time has stood still. Estbek follows suit in this respect; a glorious Georgian property built in the mid 17th century and was once the Alum mines office. It now operated as a successful, award winning restaurant that highly values using fresh local produce in its dishes.

Estbek has been owned and run by Tim and David for many years now, building up a grand reputation for delivering excellence. They tell all their customers that even if they arrive as strangers, they will leave as friends. The team receive compliment after compliment from their diners who comment on the faultless service that is both down to earth and friendly, but never intrusive. The restaurant has attained two AA rosettes for the quality of the food, with a daily changing menu drawing in fresh ideas and fresh produce. With both the rugged north Yorkshire moors and the sea at its doorstep, it is easy to see why the fish are so fresh and the locally reared meats so succulent.

To start why not try the highly recommended garlic crevettes, or the pan seared Shetland King scallops, or perhaps wild mushrooms in a bubble and squeak basket, or the seductive stilton and port homemade pate. Main dishes include a selection of wild fresh fish served on the bone, pan seared to perfection with a dash of black pepper and lemon juice, all served with a delicious twice baked chive potato and vegetable wrap. Other popular choices include lobster thermador, smoked duck with figs and a balsamic reduction and a creamed spring onion mash and a fillet of the finest local steak cooked in Estbek's signature Shiraz glaze. The dessert menu, aptly titled 'the temptation list' plays host to a mouth-watering selection of tarts, trifles, soufflés and sorbets, also changing daily. Guests can choose from a gargantuan but intelligent wine list that boasts over 200 wines, each chosen to compliment the menu that day.

For those wanting to extend the luxury beyond an evening meal, guests are welcomed to stay at Estbek with a choice of four handsomely appointed bedrooms that offer a taste of Georgian charm with real attention to detail. Each room has full en suite facilities and glorious views across the village, recently being awarded the prestigious 4 star rating.

425 BAGBY INN

Bagby, Thirsk, Yorkshire YO7 2PF
Tel: 01845 597315
e-mail: thebagbyinn@hotmail.com

Previously called the Roebuck, **The Bagby Inn** was renamed as such in September 2009 when its present owners took over. Victoria and Patrick Brizio have over fifty years of experience in the trade and have used it well to form a popular alliance with its locals who are now proud to call the Bagby the heart of their village once again.

Open every session and all day on weekends, the inn is popular with food and ale lovers alike who can choose from a fine home cooked menu, or sample one of the three ales on offer. Victoria is the cook her, preparing each dish fresh to order on the premises using local produce where possible. She describes her food as 'good pub grub,' but the menu is varied and much more elegant than that description allows. Dishes include lamb Henry, roasted duck with a homemade apple sauce and stuffing, grilled goats cheese petit salad with a balsamic and honey dressing, mushrooms in a creamy garlic and brie sauce, and Cumberland sausage with wholegrain mustard mash. The most popular dishes though are the Bagby Belly Buster mixed grill which comes with a challenge and Mrs B's famous Bagby burger. Food is served Tues-Sat 12-2pm and 5-9pm and on Sundays from 12-3:30pm when a Sunday lunch menu is offered. Children can dine from their own menu, and guests can use the takeaway service Tues-Sat 5-9pm, or perhaps sample the inn's sweet shops selection. Each month a themed food night is held, check facebook for details. Dogs welcome.

426 THE BLACKWELL OX INN

Carlton-in-Cleveland, nr Stokesley, Cleveland TS9 7DJ
Tel: 01642 712287
website: www.theblackwellox.co.uk

East meets West in the kitchens of the **Blackwell Ox Inn**, which lies just off the A172 between Stokesley and Northallerton on the northern fringe of the North York Moors. Thai chefs prepare a mouthwatering variety of authentic Thai dishes, running from the wonderful Tom Yum soups to a splendid selection of dishes based on chicken (20 varieties!), duck, beef, lamb, pork, seafood and vegetables. Those who prefer more familiar British and European favourites have an equally wide choice, including cod, scampi and salmon, steaks, lamb chops, roast or sauced chicken, surf 'n' turf, lasagne, mixed grill and hearty steak & mushroom pie. It's also a great place to meet friends or join the locals in a glass or two or well-kept real ale.

The atmosphere throughout is cosy and relaxed, with open log fires in winter and picnic tables set outside for when the sun shines. There's plenty to do in the area and superb scenery to enjoy, and the Blackwell Ox has a caravan park licensed for both visitors' touring caravans and static vans that can be bought or rented. Amenities include washing and laundry facilities, electric hook-ups and a children's adventure play area. The park is open all year except for the month of February.

427 WOODY'S AT THE BLACK SWAN

Thornton-Le-Moor, nr Northrallerton, North Yorkshire DL7 9DN
Tel: 01609 774117
e-mail: woodys@thornton-le-moor.co.uk
website: www.thorntonlemoor.co.uk

Having found considerable acclaim and success in a restaurant in Northallerton, Peter and Angela Wood transferred their skills in 2004 to nearby Thornton-le-Moor, located just off the A168 Northallerton to Thirsk road. Taking as their start point a popular, traditional village local, they oversaw a top-notch, toe-to-toe refurbishment

programme, adding a fine destination restaurant and creating **Woody's at the Black Swan**. With John Smith's Cask and two other real ales on tap and a full range of other drinks, this remains a super place to meet for a drink and a chat, but those in the know take time to relax and enjoy a leisurely lunch or dinner.

Peter, a chef for more than 30 years, is renowned near and far for his cooking skills, and many of his customers regularly drive many miles for a meal. Peter and his team set great store by the freshest ingredients, locally sourced as far as possible, and everything is prepared and cooked on the premises. Lunchtime specials, served from 12pm-2pm Tuesday to Saturday, offer tried-and-tested favourites like soup, scampi, battered haddock, steak & ale pie, gammon, steaks and jacket potatoes. Three roasts are the centrepiece of the Sunday lunch. Classics also feature strongly on the main menu, along with dishes given the distinctive Peter twist: grilled tuna steak served on noodles with a lemon & tarragon sauce; warm salad of black pudding and pigeon breast topped with a poached egg and béarnaise sauce; grilled lamb cutlets with a piquant redcurrant & cracked black pepper sauce. There's always a good choice for vegetarians (roasted Mediterranean vegetables; wild mushroom risotto), and a memorable meal ends in fine style with desserts like lemon and ginger mousse cake or sticky toffee pudding. Dinner is served from 6.30pm to 9pm, and although the dining area has 80 covers, booking is definitely advisable to be sure of a table on Friday and Saturday evenings as well as Sunday lunch.

Children are welcome, and they can even choose from their own menu. Picnic table on a paved outside area are popular in the summer months, and the inn has plenty of off-road parking.

Woody's at the Black Swan has recently added yet another string to its bow with the creation of four quality guest bedrooms with superb decor and finishings, outstanding bathrooms and modern amenities like flat-screen TV. At the rear of the pub is a certified caravan site with some electric hook-ups.

428 THE OLD ROYAL GEORGE

Morton-upon-Swale, nr Northallerton, North Yorkshire DL7 9QS
Tel: 01609 780254
e-mail: theoldroyalgeorge@hotmail.co.uk

On the A684 Bedale-Northallerton road and just five miles from the A1(M), the **Old Royal George** is an ideal refreshment stop for motorists and tourists. In the comfortably traditional bar and lounge (beams, brasses, banquettes, a ship's wheel) - Neil, Shirley and son Jamie - dispense amiable hospitality and a good choice of drinks, including 4 real ales - Jennings Bitter, Cumberland Ale and two rotating guest ales.

For lunches (noon to 2pm, not Monday) and dinners (5pm to 9pm) Jamie makes fine use of local produce for his home-cooked dishes. There's always a home-made soup amongst the starters and old favourites such as steak, ale and mushroom pie; liver, sausage and onions; and fish and chips. The home-made cheesy chicken Kiev is excellent, and if you are vegetarian, the options include roast vegetable and goat's cheese pie, and a pepper and tomato risotto. For those with lighter appetites, there's a good choice of sandwiches and light bites. On Sundays, a traditional roast dinner with all the trimmings is served with large, small or children's portions available.

Food is served from 5.30pm to 8.30pm on Monday; from noon until 2.30pm and 5.30-9pm, Tuesday to Friday (Friday & Saturday, until 9.30pm); Saturday noon until 3pm and from noon until 8pm on Sunday. Booking is strongly at weekends. Functions can cater for up to 40 people. Children are welcome; all major credit cards are accepted, and there's good disabled access throughout.

429 THE BLACK BULL INN

Great Smeaton, North Allerton,
North Yorkshire DL6 2EH
Tel: 01609 881219
e-mail: PGMACS@hotmail.com
website: www.bandbnthyorkspub.com

The Black Bull Inn is a traditional 18th century coaching inn,
now operating as a successful bed and breakfast in the heart
of Great Smeaton, historically known as the village of the
blacksmith. On the banks of the river Wiske, Great Smeaton is
nearby the historic market towns of Yarm and Northallerton,
making it an ideal base for a country break away. There is always
plenty to amuse with an abundance of quaint shopping and
restaurants not to mention hours of rural walks in the idyllic
Yorkshire countryside.

Guests can choose from a selection of four rooms; two twin
rooms and two double rooms, all of which are classically decorated and have convenient tea and
coffee making facilities and a colour TV. Some rooms come with memory foam mattresses for truly
divine sleep, and soft fluffy towels for use in the inns shared bathroom facilities. Guests can also
benefit from the inn's downstairs bar and restaurant, befitting its historical status with dark
wooden furniture, beamed ceilings and memorabilia from years gone by. Legend has it that Dick
Turpin himself stayed in the basement whilst awaiting the gallows in York for horse-rustling. Today
though, guests can choose from a range of light bites and hearty mains, or perhaps a cold glass of
ale taken in the Bull's pretty courtyard.

430 THE WHITE SWAN

Danby Lane, Danby Wiske, Northallerton,
North Yorkshire DL7 ONQ
Tel: 01609 775131 Mobile: 07708862466
e-mail: thewhiteswandanbywiske@googlemail.com

Gill, Steve and Andrew welcome you to The White Swan at
Danby Wiske. The White Swan was built originally around the
17th Century and is in the centre of the pretty village of
Danby Wiske overlooking the village green and the setting sun
to the West. The name Danby means village of the Danes and
Wiske refers to the nearby river.

We moved into the pub as new owners in September 2009
and have renovated the bar area and updated the B&B
accommodation. The pub is now traditional in character with
log fires, local real ale, good food and a cosy, friendly
atmosphere

The pub is directly on Wainwright's Coast to Coast walk leaving 66 miles walk to Robin Hood's
Bay. We are situated in the beautiful county of North Yorkshire, nestled between the Yorkshire
Dales and the stunning wilderness of the North York Moors. Danby Wiske is also just 4 miles from
the county town of Northallerton and just 12 miles from Thirsk where you can visit the James
Herriot Museum, which is situated in the original house where he practiced as a vet in the 1940s
and the area where he later wrote his famous stories.

Camping is available in our sheltered, enclosed, flat quarter of an acre camping field (below).
There is tap water in the field and hot showers available at the pub.

431 THE SANDPIPER INN

Market Place, Leyburn, North Yorkshire DL8 5AT
Tel: 01969 622206
e-mail: hsandpiper99@aol.com
website: www.sandpiperinn.co.uk

Located at the heart of the market town of Leyburn, **The Sandpiper Inn** is a popular destination for locals and visitors. Dating back to the 17th century, this ivy clad inn offers an ideal place to meet with friends over a bite to eat or refreshing ale.

Modern British food is the focus here, and the menu is created using the finest ingredients with each dish being freshly prepared. The traditional bar has a selection of real ales, fine wines and a superb selection of quality malt whiskies, which are well known amongst regular customers and visitors. The Sandpiper inn is an award winning pub and the Harrison family has taken every care to establish a friendly and effective business with the main emphasis on serving quality food using the finest local ingredients wherever possible. The three real ales served are from Yorkshire breweries including Black Sheep. Jonathan and Janine have owned The Sandpiper Inn for 11 years and Andrew, the sous chef, looks after the kitchen along with Jonathan as head chef, a former roux scholar.

The restaurant can seat 40 people, but customers are also welcome to dine in the bar area as well as the outside courtyard and patio area. A lot of the produce used is sourced locally and homemade bread and ice cream is served. The main menu offers plenty of choice for diners and all of the dishes are reasonably priced. Ham hock & rabbit terrine with piccalilli; warm goats cheese with tomato, basil & rocket; and haddock & spring onion fishcakes with a parsley & chive sauce are among the dishes on the menu. Lunch specials include plenty of filled sandwiches and traditional favourites like fish & chips in real ale batter; Sandpiper pie of the day; and sausage & mash with onion gravy. On Sundays roast dinners are served. Food is available Tuesday – Sunday between 12pm – 2.30pm and 6.30pm – 9.30pm. Such is the popularity of the inn it is advisable to book on Saturdays.

The Sandpiper Inn has two pleasant, double, ensuite berooms which are comfortably furnished and provide tea and coffee making facilities. They are available all year round, and the tariff includes a hearty breakfast. The inn is closed on Mondays except bank holidays. Major credit cards taken. Disabled access is not a problem, although the rooms are located upstairs.

432 THE BULL INN

Church Street, West Tanfield,
nr Ripon, North Yorkshire HG4 5JQ
Tel: 01677 470678
e-mail: info@thebullinwesttanfield.com
website: www.thebullinnwesttanfield.com

Since arriving here in the spring of 2008, affable landlady Jules van Veen has helped to make **The Bull Inn** one of the finest and best loved pubs in this part of Yorkshire. The inn was built in the 17th century on the ruins of a ferryman's cottage, and Jules oversaw a complete refurbishment that retained all its best features. With her hardworking bar staff and a team of professional chefs she has built up a wide and expanding clientele attracted by the warm, genuine welcome, the food, the drink, the accommodation and the lovely riverside gardens.

In its original role as a country inn serving the neighbourhood the Bull is still very much at the heart of village life, a popular meeting place where locals gather to put the world to rights over pint of well-kept Theakston's, Black Sheep or Guest ale. But the Bull's appeal is much wider, bringing visitors from near and far as a destination restaurant and a s a comfortable, civilised base for exploring the scenic and historic sights of the area. Jules and her talented team in the kitchen cater for a wide range of tastes and appetites. Lunchtime offerings include rolls, paninis, omelettes and bar favourites like ham, egg & chips, while choices on the main menu run from smooth duck liver pâté and crab linguini with a chilli kick to traditional fish and chips in Theakston's batter, sausages with cider and a red onion gravy, venison & mushroom shortcrust pie and succulent sirloin steak with all the trimmings. From Easter to September a garden menu is available to enjoy in the garden by the ancient bridge over the River Ure.

For guests staying awhile in this pleasant part of the world the Bull has five recently refurbished en suite rooms – four doubles and a single – that provide an excellent base for tourists, walkers and lovers of outdoor activities – fishing, golf and shooting are available nearby. The bar is open from 12 to 3 and 5 to 11 Monday, Wednesday, Thursday and Friday, with food served lunchtime and evening; from 12 to 11 Saturday, food to 9.30; and

from 12 to 10.30 on Sunday, food, including traditional roasts, until 4. The Bull is closed on Tuesdays except in high season. Families with children are always welcome here, and dogs are allowed in the garden. West Tanfield stands on the A6108 some six miles northwest of Ripon.

433 MASONS ARMS

St Johns Road, Bishop Monkton, Harrogate, North Yorkshire HG3 3QU
Tel: 01765 676631
e-mail: masonsarmsbishopmonkton@btconnect.com
website: www.masonsarmsbishopmonkton.org.uk

Nestled in the picturesque village of Bishop Monkton, Masons Arms is a popular restaurant offering a warm welcome, good food and real ales. Leaseholder Niki Skaife has run Masons Arms for two years and has implemented a French themed restaurant with French decor and new French chef.

All of the food served at Masons Arms is homemade and freshly prepared to order. The menu changes regularly to make the most of seasonal produce. Typical of the evening dishes served are steak and ale pie, fish pie, gammon and eggs, chicken breast in pepper sauce, sea bass with sautéed red peppers, and lamb stew with celeriac. There is a good range of starters and tempting desserts including sticky toffee pudding, crème brulee and lemon tart. There is a good range of real ales and for those with a lighter appetite there is a good range of hot and cold sandwiches.

The bar is open all day on Saturday and Sundays between 12pm and 11pm and on Wednesday to Friday it is open between 11.30pm and 3pm and 6.30pm to 11pm. On Monday and Tuesday evenings the bar is open between 6.30pm and 11pm. Quiz nights are held every Tuesday, a music quiz every Friday, poker every Monday, and bingo and sing along on Sundays.

434 THE CROWN INN

Roecliffe, North Yorkshire YO51 9LY
Tel: 01423 322300 Fax: 01423 322033
e-mail: info@crowninnroecliffe.com
website: www.crowninnroecliffe.com

Owner-chef Karl Mainey and head chef Stephen Ardern make an excellent team at **The Crown**, a lovely old coaching inn in the picturesque conservation village of Roecliffe, near Boroughbridge. Karl came here in 2007 and carried out a major refurbishment programme that enhanced the facilities while retaining historic features like the stone flag floors and the ancient oak beams.

Karl and Stephen have made The Crown one of the most highly regarded eating places in the region, with bar and restaurant menus, a children's menu, early evening meals and traditional Sunday lunches. Chalk boards in the three rooms list the day's dishes, which feature the finest Yorkshire produce, mainly from small local growers/suppliers. A meal might start with organic white onion & cider soup, home-smoked salmon or belly pork with a ginger, lime and soy dipping sauce and move on to East Coast fish, steak & kidney pie or Gloucester Old Spot hotpot, ribeye steak or organic vegetable pie. The children's menu treats the little ones a grown-ups with classic dishes like bangers & mash, fish pie and cottage pie. All the breads, jams, chutneys and pastries are made on the premises. Diners should make sure to leave room for a dessert, for in Annette the pub has a pastry chef of rare talent who holds the honour of being National Pub Pastry Chef 2008. Her treacle tart, Irish whiskey bread-and-butter pudding and doughnut with organic apples and Calvados crème brûlée will prove irresistible to most, but those with a preference for something savoury could indulge in a platter of hand-made Yorkshire cheeses with Anette's home-made biscuits. To accompany this outstanding food is an extensive wine list with copious tasting notes – some 20 wines are available by the glass. Food is served from 12 to 2.15 and 6 to 9.15, Sunday 12 to 7.

For guests staying awhile The Crown has four really splendid bedrooms in Continental style, Farrow & Ball paints and papers, French and antique mahogany furniture, rattan or sleigh beds, oak floors and freestanding baths. Rooms can be booked on a B&B or Dinner, B&B basis. The Crown has an excellent amenity in a handsome function suite in a converted barn, with truss beams, stone flags and exposed stone – an ideal setting for functions, parties and celebrations for up to 80. The place is licensed for Civil Wedding ceremonies.

435 THE ROYAL OAK

Main Street, Staveley, nr Knaresborough,
North Yorkshire HG5 9LD
Tel: 01423 340267
e-mail: info@royaloakstaveley.co.uk
website: www.royaloakstaveley.co.uk

'A Wonderful Place to Hide'

King Charles II took refuge from Cromwell's army in an oak tree, and visitors will find sanctuary and much greater comfort in the **Royal Oak** on the main street of Staveley. The oak that gave the pub its name is a huge old tree standing proudly at the front, perfectly complementing the traditional frontage with its welcoming red door. Behind that door the look continues to be inviting and traditional, with a central brick fireplace, exposed beams, rich wood panelling, china ornaments and two large bay window seating areas. Beer gardens to the front and rear add to the appeal, and the surrounding scenery is also a magnet to the area, attracting motorists, cyclists and walkers – the old railway line and a nearby nature reserve provide ample opportunities for enjoying the fresh Yorkshire air.

The Royal Oak has been given a new lease of life by hosts Daniel and Cheryl, who took over in November 2009. Daniel, who had been chef and manager since March of that year, has been in the catering business for more than 15 years. The locals are returning, and visitors from further afield are discovering the inn's attractions and passing on the good news. It's a great place for lovers of real ale, with four well-kept brews on tap to quench discerning thirsts. Daniel offers an across-the-board menu that satisfies all tastes and appetites, with everything from the bread to the ice cream made on the premises and raw materials garnered from the very best local, producers/ suppliers, who are given a name check on the printed menu. Popular dishes run from the pie or stew of the day to rump of Killinghall lamb, Hutchinson's game pie, smoked haddock risotto and superb steaks from beef hung for 28 days. The Royal Oak is closed Monday lunchtimes

except on Bank Holidays, otherwise open all sessions and all day Sunday. Food is served lunchtime and evening Tuesday to Saturday and from 12 to 6 on Sunday. Booking is advisable at the weekend.

Behind the inn is a caravan/camping site with electric hook-ups and beyond that the village allotments that produce some of the fruit, vegetables and herbs for the Royal Oak's kitchen.

Staveley is reached off the A6055 4 miles north of Knaresborough or off the A168 or A1(M) J48.

436 BLEIKERS AT THE MALT SHOVEL

Brearton, nr Harrogate, North Yorkshire HG3 3BX
Tel/Fax: 01423 862939
e-mail: bleikers@themaltshovelbrearton.co.uk
website: www.themaltshovelbrearton.co.uk

Located off the B6165 midway between
Knaresborough and Ripley, **Bleikers at the Malt
Shovel** is a destination restaurant renowned
throughout Yorkshire and far beyond. Since 2006 the
Malt Shovel has been in the capable hands of Swiss-
born Jürg Bleiker, his wife Jane, their son D'Arcy and
daughter-in-law Anna. Classically trained head chef
Jürg, with more than 50 years in the business, ran a
restaurant in Ripon with Jane between 1967 and
1988, bringing up six children at the same time.
When the children grew up, the couple moved on to
create the very successful Bleikers Smokehouse,
which has gained numerous awards for quality and
which still operates with great success.

They still had a hankering after running a
restaurant and D'Arcy was keen to follow in their
footsteps, and in the Malt Shovel they found the
perfect solution: Jürg and Jane were back in the
business they loved and D'Arcy and Anna would be
able to spend more time with their children. Dating
from the 16th century, the Malt Shovel retains many
original features, including exposed beams and a
splendid oak partition wall. Open fires, brasses,
tankards, pictures and prints complete the
traditional scene in the three main rooms, and when
the sun shines the tables out outside come into their
own. The food brings the crowds to this marvellous
place: it's all locally sourced (some from D'Arcy and
Anna's new farm), cooked to order and served by
staff who are outstandingly friendly and efficient.
Typical items on the main menu include Jürg's
wonderful smoked dishes (he uses his original kiln),
East Coast sole meunière, wiener schnitzel and slow-
cooked belly pork with bubble & squeak. Authentic
Thai cooking features strongly with superb dishes like
salt and chilli squid, monkfish red curry and the
amazing 'Weeping Tiger' – sizzling fillet steak with
oyster, mint and chilli sauce served with jasmine
rice. Lunchtimes and early evening bring lighter
options including sandwiches, French onion soup,
fishcakes and moules frites. The fine food is
accompanied by an extensive wine list, and the bar
always has a choice of real ales.

D'Arcy and Anna are fine opera singers and they
hold 'Opera with Dinner' evenings here one Monday a
month. A jazz trio accompanies lunch on the first
Sunday of the month, with a jazz pianist on other
Sundays.

437 REGENT COTTAGE

13a Regent Parade, High Harrogate,
North Yorkshire HG1 5AW
Tel: 01394 382565
e-mail: robert@blake4110.fsbusiness.co.uk
website: www.robertblakeholidays.co.uk

Regent Cottage is a lovely early 19th century town house set in a private courtyard in the heart of High Harrogate, ideally situated as a holiday base just 5 - 10 minutes from the town centure. Within just a 25 mile radius is York, Leeds, Bradford, Skipton, Ripon, Fountains Abbey and Brimham Rocks meaning Regent Cottage is the perfect base from which to explore these attractions. The cottage is also within a short drive of the Yorkshire Dales, James Herriot and Catherine Cookson country, the Lake District and both the east and west coasts.

Comfortably sleeping six in resplendent luxury, the cottage has been recently refurbished to a very high standard and has retained a lot of the original features from the 19th century, including high ceilings and fireplaces. Decorated in an appropriate style for the property, even the furnishings are period pieces and add to the authenticity of this delightful holiday cottage.

Harrogate itself offers a wide range of attractions and High Harrogate is virtually self sufficient with its own butcher, grocer, newsagents, hairdressers, garage, antique and picture galleries.

Postal address for correspondence: Robert Blake, 1a Moorfield Road, Woodbridge, Suffolk IP12 4JN

438 YE OLDE CHYMIST SHOPPE AND THE LAVENDER ROOMS

16 Market Place, Knaresborough,
North Yorkshire HG5 8AG
Tel: 01423 860555 / 01423 863153
e-mail: maurice_bardon@yahoo.co.uk
website: www.lavenderrooms.co.uk or
www.yeoldechymistshoppe.co.uk

Located at the heart of Knaresborough two superb premises can be found within one olde worlde property. Brothers Maurice and Peter Bardon have owned **Ye Olde Chymist Shoppe** and **The Lavender Rooms** since 2001. Downstairs, Ye Olde Chymist Shoppe draws in locals and visitors with a sweet tooth. There are a variety of products on sale including fine Belgian Chocolates, a range of jams and preserves and fine array of lavender based products from Yorkshire and Norfolk.

Upstairs, the quality, busy and bustling Lavender Rooms seats 38 diners and there are plenty of dishes to choose from including a good range of filled sandwiches, wraps and melts. There are also several hot dishes on the menu as well as soups and cream teas available. The Lavender Rooms is open between 9.30am and 5pm and many people pay a visit to sample the speciality lemon and lavender scones. Home cooking is the main focus here and all dishes are freshly prepares and cooked to order. The tea rooms are child friendly and customers can eat in or take away. There are plenty of tempting homemade cakes by the till – you might find it difficult to decide which one to have. All major credit cards taken.

439 THE SUN INN

Brame Lane, Norwood, Harrogate,
North Yorkshire HG3 1SZ
Tel: 01943 880220
e-mail: thebar@thesun-inn.co.uk
website: www.thesun-inn.co.uk

Established over 200 years ago as a coaching inn, **The Sun Inn** is situated within the picturesque Washburn Valley close to the Lindley, Fewston and Swinsty reservoirs. Its scenic location makes it a popular spot for visitors to the area, and a favourite with its locals.

Owners Neil and Fiona who took over in 2008 are proud to call the Sun a traditional country inn with stone walling, open fires and low beamed ceilings that give it that olde worlde charm. It's very much a family friendly pub, welcoming children and dogs throughout the day with the best of Yorkshire hospitality.

Open all day every day, guests can enjoy a minimum of three real ales with Theakstons Best, Old Peculiar and Speckled Hen being the usual culprits. The inn is also popular for its food; served Mon-Fri 12-2:30pm and 6-8pm, Sat 12-8pm and Sun 12-6pm in the summer, and Mon-Fri 12-2:30pm, Wed-Fri 6-8pm, Sat 12-7pm and Sun 12-5pm in the winter. The specialty here are Fiona's delicious homemade pies, but the menus cover starters, salads, jackets, sandwiches, burgers, Paninis, basket meals, grills and mains. Favourites include Giant filled Yorkshire puddings, sirloin steak, the seafood platter and the vegetarian lasagne. All dishes are created using fresh locally sourced produce. Owing to popularity, it's best to book on weekends.

441 COLD COTES GUEST ACCOMMODATION

Cold Cotes Road, nr Harrogate, North Yorkshire HG3 2LW
Tel: 01423 770937
e-mail: info@coldcotes.com website: www.coldcotes.com

Offering the very best in accommodation, this quality premises has six delightful en-suite bedrooms. Set in five acres of land, the rooms are spread across a Yorkshire stone-built house and renovated barn and are very popular with visitors. The accommodation has been graded five stars and gold award with some located upstairs and some on the ground floor. The main house and barn is nestled in superb gardens and many of the rooms boast beautiful views. It really is an ideal place to stay for visitors looking for a relaxing and tranquil break.

440 THE BLACK BULL

Skipton Road, Kettlesing, Harrogate, North Yorkshire HG3 2LP
Tel: 01423 770233

Conveniently located close to the A59 just west of Harrogate, **The Black Bull** is a traditional country inn that is both family run and family friendly. Parts of the premises date back to the mid-17th century and during its long lifetime the building has served as a farmhouse, a toll house and a post house before becoming a coaching inn. Since the autumn of 2009, the hosts at the Black Bull have been Kate and Pete Parker who have established a glowing reputation for serving appetising food and real ales at value for money prices.

Kate is a superb cook and her extensive menu, based on fresh local produce, offers something for everyone. Amongst the starters you'll find a Vegetarian Soup of the Day, Garlic Mushrooms and 'Mozza Melts' - coated mozzarella cheese straws served with a sweet chilli sauce. The extensive choice of main courses includes traditional favourites such as various Steaks (very popular here), Fish & Chips, Steak & Kidney Pie, Gammon and Eggs and Chilli Con Carne, along with pasta dishes and vegetarian options such as Stilton & Vegetable Crumble, Vegetable Balti and Spinach and Ricotta Cannelloni. The regular menu is supplemented by daily specials listed on the board above the bar. Those with hearty appetites might like to face the challenge of the monster 'Black Bull Mixed Grill' which contains a Black Bull burger, beef steak, gammon steak, pork sausage, black pudding, two fried eggs, hash browns, mushrooms, onion rings and chips! For lighter appetites, jacket potatoes, ploughman's and sandwiches are available until 6pm, Monday to Saturday. The sandwiches are made freshly to order using locally baked fresh bread. Food is served from noon until 8.45pm, Monday to Saturday; and from noon until 8pm on Sundays when a choice of roasts is added to the menu. Booking ahead at weekends is strongly recommended.

The well-stocked bar offers a comprehensive range of beverages including two real ales, Tetley's and Black Sheep. The inn welcomes children - high chairs are available; there's good disabled access throughout and all major credit cards are accepted.

442 NEWTON GRANGE B&B AND SELF-CATERING

Bank Newton, Gargrave, Skipton, North Yorkshire BD23 3NT
Tel: 01756 748140 / 796016
e-mail: bookings@newton-grange.co.uk
website: www.newton-grange.co.uk

Occupying a secluded rural location adjacent to the
Leeds-Liverpool Canal, **Newton Grange** is a charming
Grade II listed Georgian house offering both bed &
breakfast and self-catering accommodation. Bed &
breakfast guests stay in the main house which has a
choice of double, twin and single rooms, all with en suite
facilities, colour TV and hospitality tray. An excellent
farmhouse breakfast is included in the tariff. For those
preferring self-catering, a former barn and byres have
been sympathetically restored to provide comfortable
accommodation. There are 6 properties in all, sleeping from 2 to

6 people, and they all enjoy lovely open views. The cottages are
available for weekly lets or short term breaks. Guests are
welcome to bring a pony with them as the surrounding
countryside is ideal for pony-trekking. It is also perfect for
cycling and walking - the Pennine Way actually runs through the
farm where in late March and April guests can see the lambing.
The village of Gargrave with its several shops is just two miles
away, and the historic market town of Skipton just four miles. A variety of eating places are to be
found within a short drive.

443 NEW BUTTS FARM

High Bentham, nr Ingleton,
Yorkshire Dales LA2 7AN
Tel: 015242 41238
e-mail: jeanandterry@googlemail.com
website: www.newbutts.co.uk

Originally built in 1865, this attractive farmhouse B&B
not only provides quality accommodation to suit all, but
it also boasts magnificent views over Ingleborough and
the south west fringe of the Yorkshire Dales National
Park. The small holding is set within six hectares and is
surrounded by hundreds of acres of beautiful countryside.

Owners Jean and Terry Newhouse provide an extremely
warm welcome to guests and New Butts Farm has a lot of
returning visitors. Jean is a superb cook and the tariff
includes a wonderful and hearty breakfast. Guests can
visit the B&B on a dinner, bed and breakfast rate or just
B&B. Open all year around and given a three star rating

by Visit England, the B&B has seven upstairs bedrooms available (five en-suite). The rooms vary in
size and are all comfortable.

The B&B is located just four miles from Clapham and many walkers are attracted to the B&B
because of the opportunity to walk around the lakes and Dales. Pets can stay if pre-arranged. The
premise is licensed and there is good off road parking. A small function room, which can cater for
up to 30 people, is available for hire. Ring for details. Cash and cheque only.

444 BECKINDALES LICENSED CAFÉ

Burtersett Road, Hawes, North Yorkshire DL8 3NP
Tel: 01969 667784
e-mail: kerrysleightholm274@btinternet.com

The popular little town of Hawes, in the heart of scenic Wensleydale, is lucky in having the excellent **Beckindales Licensed Café,** located on the eastern side of the town. It's a family-run enterprise with local girl Liz Sleightholm looking after the front of house, and daughters Lindsey and Kerry taking care of the kitchen. They offer an extensive menu that includes a truly hearty full English breakfast and other breakfast options. Other home-made dishes include a quiche of the day; soup; a chicken, ham & leek pie, and a steak pie. Whitby's famous scampi is featured and, of course, a giant Yorkshire pudding served with either local Cumberland sausage or home-cooked roast beef. Vegetarians are well-catered for with dishes such as a mushroom, Stilton & broccoli pasta bake; spinach & ricotta cannelloni or a platter of tasty locally made Wensleydale cheeses. The regular menu is supplemented by daily specials. Children have their own menu and several of the dishes on the main menu are available in half portions. This is a child-friendly place with a baby changing room and the staff will warm baby food if you wish.

The café has a table licence and offers red, white and rose wines either by the glass or bottle. Also available are various beers and Fosters, John Smith's and Strongbow on draft. In good weather customers can enjoy their refreshments in the front courtyard which has seating for 30 people. Four times a year, usually on a Friday, the café hosts a Steak Night for which booking is essential, as it is also for Sunday lunchtimes. The café is open every day from 9am onwards, Easter to October. During the winter months, opening hours are from 10am to 3pm with the café closed on Fridays. And in January it is only open on Tuesday, Saturday and Sunday.

Beckindales is close to most of the town's attractions. The Wensleydale Gallery is just across the road; almost next door is Hawes Ropeworks which still maintains the ancient craft of ropemaking; and just around the corner is the Dales Countryside Museum which covers many aspects of life in the Dales over the past 10,000 years.

445 SWALEDALE WOOLLENS

Strawbeck, Muker in Swaledale, Richmond,
North Yorkshire DL11 6QG
Tel: 01748 886251
e-mail: mail@swaledalewoollens.co.uk
website: www.swaledalewoollens.co.uk

Swaledale Woollens was founded in Muker in Swaledale more than 30 years ago by villagers reviving the old cottage industry of knitting. Here in one of the most beautiful areas of Northern England the tradition of hand knitting in local wool goes back more than 400 years to the days of Queen Elizabeth I. It was Elizabeth who set a new fashion by wearing hand knitted stockings and, with demand increasing, every family in the Dale - men, women and children - became involved in knitting woollen stockings. By the end of the 19th century however, changes in fashions together with the arrival of knitting machines ended most of the Dales hand knitting trade.

Swaledale Woollens is now owned and run by Kathleen Hird who carries on using local Swaledale and Wensleydale wool for the knitwear. There are more than 30 people knitting from their homes and producing a unique range of quality woollen knitwear. The wool provided for the knitters is mainly from Swaledale sheep, but use is also made of the different shades and textures provided by the nearby Wensleydale breed and Welsh hill sheep. The Swaledale, Wensleydale and Welsh wools are spun at the only remaining traditional worsted Woollen Mill in Bradford. Then it is dyed in to soft country colours and delivered to Muker. Real horn buttons are used on many of the garments. Kathleen takes it to her team of conscientious knitters then collects it when the ladies and gentlemen have knitted or crocheted it into garments.

The shop stocks a wide range of high quality knitwear, including sweaters, cardigans, hats, gloves, rugs, hangings, shawls, scarves, slippers and socks. It also stocks sheepskin slippers, gloves and rugs. What better choice could there be for a quality and unique, hand-crafted gift for yourself, friends and family? And you can also place your order online from the comfort of home!

Swaledale Woollens is open from 10am to 5pm every day except Christmas Day and Boxing Day. The shop closes at 4pm during November, December, January and February.

IMAGE COPYRIGHT HOLDERS

COPYRIGHT HOLDERS ARE AS FOLLOWS:

Bedford Suspension Bridge © Robin Drayton	pg 2
Old Warden Village © Richard Thomas	pg 2
Whipsnade Tree Cathedral © Sheila Russell	pg 3
Woburn Abbey © Kenneth Allen	pg 3
Kennet & Avon Canal, Newbury © Graham Horn	pg 5
Abbey Gateway, Reading © Graham Horn	pg 6
Windsor Castle © Colin Smith	pg 8
Hellfire Caves, West Wycombe © Mark Percy	pg 10
Chenies Manor House © Nigel Cox	pg 11
Milton's Cottage, Chalfont St Giles © Chris Gunns	pg 11
River Thames, Marlow © Rob Farrow	pg 12
Stowe House, Buckingham © Kevin Gordon	pg 13
Mathematical Bridge, Cambridge © Keith Evans	pg 15
The Orchard, Grantchester © M J Richardson	pg 15
Wimpole Hall, Arrington © Chris Cole	pg 16
Ely Cathedral © Evelyn Simak	pg 17
Haddenham Great Mill © Rodney Burton	pg 17
Ramsey Abbey School © Chris Stafford	pg 18
Kimbolton Castle, Grafham © Graham Taylor	pg 20
The Rows, Chester © Dennis Turner	pg 22
Beeston Castle Gateway © Eirian Evans	pg 24
Port Sunlight © Ian Petticrew	pg 25
St Mary's Church, Nantwich © Margaret Sutton	pg 26
Tatton Park, nr Mere © Tom Pennington	pg 27
White Nancy, Bollington © Andrew Huggett	pg 28
Mount Edgcumbe Country Park, Cremyll © Anthony Volante	pg 34
Looe River © dinglefoot	pg 35
Lanhydrock House © JThomas	pg 36
Bude Haven © Steve Daniels	pg 36
Padstow Harbour © Trevor Rickard	pg 38
Charlestown Docks © Pam Brophy	pg 39
Rocks at Polstreath, nr Mevagissey © Derek Harper	pg 39
Pendennis Point © Chris Downer	pg 40
Wheal Coates Mine, nr St Agnes © Richard Rogerson	pg 42
Barbara Hepworth Sculpture Garden, St Ives © Sarah Charlesworth	pg 43
St Michaels Mount © Sheila Russell	pg 44

Cautley Crag, Sedburgh © Rudi Winter	pg 47
Furness Abbey, nr Dalton in Furness © Ian Taylor	pg 49
Muncaster Castle, Ravenglass © Alexander P Kapp	pg 50
Lake Windermere © Paul Shreeve	pg 50
Dove Cottage, Grasmere © Brian Clift	pg 52
Buttermere with Fleetwith Pike © Rebecca Beeston	pg 53
Penrith Castle © Alexander P Kapp	pg 55
Derby Guildhall © Sam Styles	pg 60
Melbourne Hall © David Lally	pg 61
Cromford Mill, Cromford © Angela Streluk	pg 62
Buxton Opera House © Janine Forbes	pg 65
Kinder Scout, Hayfield © Stephen Burton	pg 66
Snake Pass © Tom Courtney	pg 66
Peveril Castle, Castleton © Tom Courtney	pg 68
Chatsworth House Gardens © Lambert	pg 69
Rougemont Castle, Exeter © Derek Harper	pg 71
Knighthayes Court, Tiverton © John Spivey	pg 72
Hartland Point, Clovelly © Ernie Camacho	pg 76
Gatehouse of Compton Castle, Torquay © Mike Searle	pg 77
Oldway Mansion, Paignton © Lewis Clarke	pg 78
Smeaton's Tower, Plymouth © Sheila Tarlton	pg 81
Russell-Cotes Museum, Bournemouth © Simon Palmer	pg 83
West Lake, Brownsea Island © Pierre Terre	pg 84
Shaftesbury Abbey Ruins © Chris Downer	pg 85
Wolfeton House, Dorchester © Mike Searle	pg 86
Corfe Castle © Chris Downer	pg 87
Lulworth Cove © Christine Matthews	pg 87
Portland Castle © Eugene Birchall	pg 88
The Cobb, Lyme Regis © Dave Skinner	pg 89
Durham Cathedral © Richard Howell	pg 91
Beamish Open Air Museum © Kevin Rushton	pg 92
Bishop Auckland Castle © John Phillips	pg 94
Killhope Mine © Elliott Simpson	pg 94
Maldon © Gill Edwards	pg 97
Coalhouse Fort, Tilbury © John Winfield	pg 98
Epping Forest, Harlow © Stephen Craven	pg 99

Hidden Places of England

Image Copyright Holders

IMAGE COPYRIGHT HOLDERS

IMAGE COPYRIGHT HOLDERS

ORDER FORM

To order any of our publications just fill in the payment details below and complete the order form. For orders of less than 4 copies please add £1 per book for postage and packing. Orders over 4 copies are P & P free.

Please Complete Either:
I enclose a cheque for £ [ ]   made payable to Travel Publishing Ltd
Or:

CARD NO: [ ]   EXPIRY DATE: [ ]

SIGNATURE: [ ]

NAME: [ ]

ADDRESS: [ ]

TEL NO: [ ]

Please either send, telephone, fax or e-mail your order to:
Travel Publishing Ltd, Airport Business Centre, 10 Thornbury Road, Estover, Plymouth PL6 7PP
Tel: 01752 697280   Fax: 01752 697299 e-mail: info@travelpublishing.co.uk

	PRICE	QUANTITY		PRICE	QUANTITY
HIDDEN PLACES REGIONAL TITLES			**COUNTRY LIVING RURAL GUIDES**		
Cornwall	£8.99	....	East Anglia	£10.99	....
Devon	£8.99	....	Heart of England	£10.99	....
Dorset, Hants & Isle of Wight	£8.99	....	Ireland	£11.99	....
East Anglia	£8.99	....	North East of England	£10.99	....
Lake District & Cumbria	£8.99	....	North West of England	£10.99	....
Lancashire & Cheshire	£8.99	....	Scotland	£11.99	....
Northumberland & Durham	£8.99	....	South of England	£10.99	....
Peak District and Derbyshire	£8.99	....	South East of England	£10.99	....
Yorkshire	£8.99	....	Wales	£11.99	....
HIDDEN PLACES NATIONAL TITLES			West Country	£10.99	....
England	£11.99	....			
Ireland	£11.99	....			
Scotland	£11.99	....			
Wales	£11.99	....	**TOTAL QUANTITY**	[ ]	
OTHER TITLES			**TOTAL VALUE**	[ ]	
Off The Motorway	£11.99	....			
Garden Centres and Nurseries of Britain	£11.99	....			

READER REACTION FORM

The *Travel Publishing* research team would like to receive readers' comments on any visitor attractions or places reviewed in the book and also recommendations for suitable entries to be included in the next edition. This will help ensure that the *Country Living series of Rural Guides* continues to provide its readers with useful information on the more interesting, unusual or unique features of each attraction or place ensuring that their visit to the local area is an enjoyable and stimulating experience. To provide your comments or recommendations would you please complete the forms below and overleaf as indicated and send to:

The Research Department, Travel Publishing Ltd, Airport Business Centre,
10 Thornbury Road, Estover, Plymouth PL6 7PP

YOUR NAME:

YOUR ADDRESS:

YOUR TEL NO:

Please tick as appropriate: COMMENTS ☐   RECOMMENDATION ☐

ESTABLISHMENT:

ADDRESS:

TEL NO:

CONTACT NAME:

PLEASE COMPLETE FORM OVERLEAF

629

READER REACTION FORM

COMMENT OR REASON FOR RECOMMENDATION:

....

....

....

....

....

....

....

....

....

....

....

....

....

....

....

READER REACTION FORM

The *Travel Publishing* research team would like to receive readers' comments on any visitor attractions or places reviewed in the book and also recommendations for suitable entries to be included in the next edition. This will help ensure that the *Country Living series of Rural Guides* continues to provide its readers with useful information on the more interesting, unusual or unique features of each attraction or place ensuring that their visit to the local area is an enjoyable and stimulating experience. To provide your comments or recommendations would you please complete the forms below and overleaf as indicated and send to:

The Research Department, Travel Publishing Ltd, Airport Business Centre,
10 Thornbury Road, Estover, Plymouth PL6 7PP

YOUR NAME:

YOUR ADDRESS:

YOUR TEL NO:

Please tick as appropriate: COMMENTS   RECOMMENDATION

ESTABLISHMENT:

ADDRESS:

TEL NO:

CONTACT NAME:

PLEASE COMPLETE FORM OVERLEAF

READER REACTION FORM

COMMENT OR REASON FOR RECOMMENDATION:

....

....

....

....

....

....

....

....

....

....

....

....

....

....

....

READER REACTION FORM

The **Travel Publishing** research team would like to receive readers' comments on any visitor attractions or places reviewed in the book and also recommendations for suitable entries to be included in the next edition. This will help ensure that the **Country Living series of Rural Guides** continues to provide its readers with useful information on the more interesting, unusual or unique features of each attraction or place ensuring that their visit to the local area is an enjoyable and stimulating experience. To provide your comments or recommendations would you please complete the forms below and overleaf as indicated and send to:

The Research Department, Travel Publishing Ltd, Airport Business Centre, 10 Thornbury Road, Estover, Plymouth PL6 7PP

YOUR NAME:

YOUR ADDRESS:

YOUR TEL NO:

Please tick as appropriate: COMMENTS   RECOMMENDATION

ESTABLISHMENT:

ADDRESS:

TEL NO:

CONTACT NAME:

PLEASE COMPLETE FORM OVERLEAF

READER REACTION FORM

COMMENT OR REASON FOR RECOMMENDATION:

....

....

....

....

....

....

....

....

....

....

....

....

....

....

....

INDEX OF TOWNS, VILLAGES AND PLACES OF INTEREST

INDEX OF TOWNS, VILLAGES AND PLACES OF INTEREST

INDEX OF TOWNS, VILLAGES AND PLACES OF INTEREST

INDEX OF TOWNS, VILLAGES AND PLACES OF INTEREST

INDEX OF TOWNS, VILLAGES AND PLACES OF INTEREST

INDEX OF TOWNS, VILLAGES AND PLACES OF INTEREST

INDEX OF TOWNS, VILLAGES AND PLACES OF INTEREST

INDEX OF TOWNS, VILLAGES AND PLACES OF INTEREST

INDEX OF TOWNS, VILLAGES AND PLACES OF INTEREST

INDEX OF TOWNS, VILLAGES AND PLACES OF INTEREST

INDEX OF TOWNS, VILLAGES AND PLACES OF INTEREST

INDEX OF TOWNS, VILLAGES AND PLACES OF INTEREST

ADVERTISERS

ADVERTISERS

661

ADVERTISERS

Hidden Places of England — Advertisers

ADVERTISERS

ADVERTISERS

ADVERTISERS

ADVERTISERS

PLACES OF INTEREST